A Hard Rain

Also by Frye Gaillard

Nonfiction

Watermelon Wine (1978)

Race, Rock & Religion (1982)

The Catawba River (1983)

The Dream Long Deferred (1988)

Southern Voices: Profiles and Other Stories (1991)

Kyle at 200 M.P.H. (1993)

Lessons from the Big House (1994)

The Way We See It (with Rachel Gaillard, 1995)

If I Were a Carpenter (1996)

The Heart of Dixie: Southern Rebels, Renegades and Heroes (1996)

Voices from the Attic (1997)

Mobile and the Eastern Shore (with Nancy and Tracy Gaillard, 1997)

As Long As the Waters Flow (with photos by Carolyn DeMeritt, 1998)

The 521 All-Stars (with photos by Byron Baldwin, 1999)

The Greensboro Four: Civil Rights Pioneers (2001)

Cradle of Freedom (2004)

Prophet from Plains: Jimmy Carter and His Legacy (2007)

In the Path of the Storms (with Sheila Hagler, Peggy Denniston, 2008)

With Music and Justice for All (2008)

Alabama's Civil Rights Trail (2010)

The Books That Mattered (2013)

Journey to the Wilderness (2015)

Fiction

The Secret Diary of Mikhail Gorbachev (1990)

Children's

Spacechimp: NASA's Ape in Space (with Melinda Farbman, 2000)

Go South to Freedom (2016)

A HARD RAIN

America in the 1960s, Our Decade of Hope, Possibility, and Innocence Lost

FRYE GAILLARD

NEWSOUTH BOOKS
An imprint of
The University of Georgia Press
Athens

NSB

Published by NewSouth Books,
an imprint of the University of Georgia Press
Athens, Georgia 30602
https://ugapress.org/imprints/newsouth-books/

Paperback edition, 2023

Edited and designed by Randall Williams
Printed and bound by SheridanBooks, Inc.

The paper in this book meets the guidelines for permanence and durability of the Committee on Production Guidelines for Book Longevity of the Council on Library Resources.

Most NewSouth/University of Georgia Press titles are available from popular e-book vendors.

Printed in the United States of America
23 24 25 26 27 P 5 4 3 2 1

Library of Congress Cataloging-in-Publication Data

Names: Gaillard, Frye, 1946– author.
Title: A hard rain : America in the 1960s, our decade of hope, possibility, and innocence lost / by Frye Gaillard.
Other titles: America in the 1960s, our decade of hope, possibility, and innocence lost
Description: Montgomery, AL : NewSouth Books, [2018]
Identifiers: LCCN 2018003191| ISBN 9781588383440 (trade cloth : alk. paper) | ISBN 9781603064545 (ebook)
Subjects: LCSH: United States—History—1961–1969. | Social change—United States—History—20th century. | Popular culture—United States—20th century. | United States—Politics and government—1945–1989. | United States—Social conditions—1945– | Civil rights movements—United States—History—20th century. | Race relations—United States—History—20th century. | National characteristics, American—History—20th century. | Nineteen sixties.
Classification: LCC E839 .G35 2018 | DDC 973.9—dc23
LC record available at https://lccn.loc.gov/2018003191

ISBN 978-1-58838-515-4

For Nancy with love . . .

for sharing this journey and all the others

And in memory of Tom Peacock

I heard the sound of a thunder that roared out a warning...
It's a hard rain's a-gonna fall

Bob Dylan

The arc of the moral universe is long
but it bends toward justice

Martin Luther King, Jr.

In our sleep, pain which cannot forget
falls drop by drop upon the heart
until in our own despair, against our will
comes wisdom through the awful grace of God

Aeschylus (as quoted by Robert Kennedy)

Contents

Preface

There are many different ways to remember the 1960s, and this is mine. I have used interviews, journalistic accounts, and the work of other scholars and memoirists to add flesh to the bones of personal recollection. I have set out to capture in these pages—for those who lived it and wish to remember, and for those who didn't but still want to know—the competing story arcs of tragedy and hope. There was in these years the sense of a steady unfolding of time, as if history were on a forced march, and the changes spread to every corner of our lives. As future generations debate the meaning (I also seek to do some of that here), I hope to offer a sense of how it *felt*. For me this is history of a personal kind, the story of a decade in which I came of age, and in which my professional aspirations took shape. I graduated from college in the terrible year of 1968, a year in which two assassinations altered the psyche and spirit of the country in ways from which we have not yet recovered. I knew as a journalist beginning my career in that year that I wanted to write about these things, and that the line between history and journalism was thin. In many ways, I think, everything I have written is rooted in that time.

Thus I offer within these pages one writer's reconstruction and remembrance of a transcendent era—one that, for better or worse, lives with us still.

As OUR THOUGHTS RETURN to those turbulent times, which they do so often, many of us remember in fragments—in bits and pieces of cherished recollection in which the world seems brimming over with hope. There is the face of JFK, confident and smiling, frozen in memory on the television screen, delivering the words now chiseled on his grave:

> Now the trumpet summons us again—not as a call to bear arms, though arms we need, not as a call to battle, though embattled we are—but a call to bear the burden of a long twilight struggle, year in and year out, "rejoicing in

> hope, patient in tribulation"—a struggle against the common enemies of man: tyranny, poverty, disease and war itself.

And there is the image, too, of Dr. Martin Luther King Jr. speaking on a temperate summer afternoon, a crowd of 250,000 stretching out before him as far as the eye could see. He has not strayed far from the words on his written draft when Mahalia Jackson, standing nearby, urges him gently: "Tell them about the dream, Martin." And we remember how his words then took flight, how the poetry and the cadence blended, as he left his printed text behind.

> I say to you today, my friends, even though we face the difficulties of today and tomorrow, I still have a dream. It is a dream deeply rooted in the American dream. I have a dream that one day this nation will rise up and live out the true meaning of its creed—we hold these truths to be self-evident, that all men are created equal.

Those were defining moments of a decade, the 1960s, when we seemed on the brink of a different kind of greatness, rooted not only in our national might, but in our capacity for introspection. In America, there were men stepping forward to lead us—and women too, whose passionate voices grew stronger with time—and they seemed to be unafraid of our flaws. For most of our troubled history as a nation, we had seemed not to mean some of what the Founding Fathers had said. Certainly, it was clear that not all men were created equal, nor women either, but now as the sixties came into focus, we were swept along, many of us, by the frightening power of a patriotic notion. Maybe we could, as Dr. King said, "live out the true meaning of our creed."

But there were also darker forces among us. For one thing, we were living in fear, which was at the start—and at its heart—a rational response to our moment in history. On May 1, 1960, thirty-year-old pilot Francis Gary Powers was shot down over the Soviet Union. He was on an espionage mission for the CIA, flying his U-2 aircraft at high altitude, gathering intelligence about Soviet weapons. The diplomatic furor that followed his capture was a stark reminder that we were living in a Cold War, a competition between two countries armed to the teeth with nuclear weapons—each bomb capable of inconceivable devastation, far beyond even Hiroshima or Nagasaki.

In addition to the constant undertow of dread there was also the political mind-game of global competition. Soviet Premier Nikita Khrushchev, an erratic, balding man of great menace, given to sudden fits of temper, had promised to "bury" the American way of life, spreading the doctrine of Soviet Communism to every corner of the world. This threat, and the fear of lost freedom it induced, sent shock waves through the American psyche, pushing us toward a faraway war. All of this, too, was a part of the sixties. Our escalating war in Vietnam—and after a while the protests against it—became enmeshed with the turbulent demand for racial justice. For some Americans it was simply too much, and the specter of war and backlash and violence cast its shadow of desperation over those times.

I remember a rainy and cold night in 1968 when Robert F. Kennedy came to Vanderbilt, the university where I was then a senior contemplating a career as a writer. Kennedy was running for President of the United States, lifting again the torch of his brother who was murdered five years earlier in Dallas. You could hear the echoes of JFK, the same affront to smugness, the call to something better, but perhaps with another dimension as well, for there was in the message of the younger Kennedy a passionate identification with people who hurt:

> There are millions of Americans, living in hidden places, whose faces and names we will never know. But I have seen children starving in Mississippi, idling their lives away in the ghetto, living without hope or future amid the despair on Indian reservations, with no jobs and little hope. I have seen proud men in the hills of Appalachia, who wish only to work in dignity—but the mines are closed, and the jobs are gone and no one, neither industry or labor or government, has cared enough to help. Those conditions will change, those children will live, only if we dissent. So I dissent, and I know you do too.

I remember as clearly as if it were yesterday his Massachusetts twang, the jab of his forefinger and the tousle of his hair, the enigmatic intensity of his icy blue stare. But there is something I remember even more. When Kennedy arrived in Nashville that night, a massive crowd was waiting at the airport. I never heard an official estimate of numbers, but it took him nearly half an hour to walk from the gate set aside for his plane to the car that was waiting for him outside. It was a journey accomplished a short step at a time through a crowd of people screaming out his name, many of them desperate to shake his hand, or merely to touch him as he inched slowly past.

It was hard in the delirium of that scene not to think of the afternoon in Dallas, November 22, 1963, when Robert Kennedy lost a brother, and the rest of us lost a president, and shared in the shattered grief and disbelief. Everybody I know who was alive that day can recall exactly where they were and what they were doing when Walter Cronkite delivered the news: "President Kennedy died at 1 p.m. Central Standard Time."

I marveled in 1968 that another Kennedy would move so willingly through the throng, even if the hysteria on this occasion was friendly. On the same night, one of his friends in Nashville, a former Justice Department attorney named John Jay Hooker, asked him whether the risk was worth it. Kennedy brushed the question aside.

"I can't think about it," he said. "What happens, happens."

And then it did. In June in the middle of a similar crowd, a young Arab with a gun pushed his way toward Kennedy and opened fire. Only two months earlier, Martin Luther King had been murdered in Memphis, and now the death of Kennedy in California became, in a sense, the end of the story.

But now as we let our minds drift back, we remember a rich and complicated time, not fully defined by tragedy, nor by the eloquence of our leaders. Politics and social movements were only the most obvious piece of that history. There were also artists and entertainers, as well as scientists and engineers, whose creativity in the 1960s helped change our understanding of ourselves—and of the country in which we lived. As the decade progressed, there were the discernible straight-line themes, war and resistance, the quest for social justice and a powerful resistance against rapid change. But there were also the other scattered moments, seemingly disconnected, that added their own enrichment to the times, and I have written about those things as well.

In the beginning, and above all else, there was a widespread feeling of extraordinary promise, some of which had begun to take shape in the 1950s. Rosa Parks and Martin Luther King had emerged by then as iconic figures in a civil rights uprising trying to find its way. The nuclear arms race, terrifying as it was, was already tied to the development of powerful rockets making possible the exploration of space. Researchers were working on the birth control pill. And Elvis Presley and other young artists had ushered in the era of rock 'n' roll by blending the black and white music of the South—their exuberant rebellion suddenly offering a voice and a new identity for the young.

And yet, paradoxically, for many of those same young people, the '50s represented not so much a foreshadowing of change, as a somnolent time of complacency and quiet that gave them a reason to rebel. Their parents' generation was in need of rest. Its members had survived the Great Depression, some losing fortunes, many more losing jobs, stalked by desperation and hunger as the country threatened to come unglued. Then came a World War in which their strength was put to a different kind of test.

On December 7, 1941, more than 350 Japanese airplanes had attacked the U.S. Naval base at Pearl Harbor, sinking half its battleship fleet and killing 2,400 Americans. In retrospect, it was little more than a despicable skirmish in a war where sixty million people would die, a grisly testament to the technology of combat. Of that total, 400,000 were U.S. soldiers, but despite those numbers we would defeat not only the Japanese, but the evil empire of Adolph Hitler. That was how most Americans saw it, and in the following flush of righteousness and power, the U.S. economy—so recently ravaged by the Great Depression—entered into a period of boom.

There was also, beginning in 1952, the steadying presence of Dwight Eisenhower, the first Republican president in twenty years, calm, battle-tested and wise; a military hero who seemed, earnestly, to be seeking peace. Early in his term, he ended the Korean War, which had raged for three years, and later he warned of a "military-industrial complex"—a defense industry that might, he thought, seduce the nation into needless war. Most Americans found reassurance in Eisenhower's message, combined, as it was, with a surging economy and a growing middle class. But after a while, a kind of monotony seemed to settle in, "normalcy on steroids," as one member of my generation put it.

"In the years following the traumatic experiences of the Depression and World War II," wrote journalist-historian David Halberstam, "the American Dream . . . meant finding a good, white-collar job with a large, benevolent company, getting married, having children, and buying a house in the suburbs."

Jack Newfield, a young writer whose book, *A Prophetic Minority*, would chronicle the rebellions of the 1960s, mocked the sterility of those suburban aspirations when he wrote of his own generation in the '50s: "Marry well and early, don't be a troublemaker, start a career in daddy's business or in a large corporation, and save up for a split-level home in the lily-white suburbs."

Newfield was not alone in his irony and scorn. It was clear as the '50s drew to a close that a restlessness simmered just beneath the surface—a contagious yearning for deeper meaning and purpose—and with the coming of the '60s, it was astonishing how quickly everything would change.

Thus, as I began to seek to untangle the interweaving strands of history and memory that together make up the story of that time, I began with a moment in 1960—quite specifically, a mid-winter afternoon in the city of Greensboro, North Carolina . . .

PART I

Possibilities

1960—"We Shall Overcome": *The Sit-ins, the subversive joy of rock 'n' roll, Harper Lee and Black Like Me, Inspiration from JFK, the Pill, a conservative manifesto, A ten-dollar fine*

1961—"Ask Not": *Eisenhower farewell, the JFK inaugural, The New Frontier and the race for space, The Bay of Pigs and the Freedom Rides, The Berlin Wall, Roger Maris and Babe Ruth, A song in Alabama*

1962—"If I Had a Hammer": *The novelists, Silent Spring, The Other America, A crime to be gay, orbiting the earth, Marilyn Monroe, Johnny Carson, James Baldwin, Pete Seeger, Joan Baez, Ole Miss and the Cuban Missile Crisis, George Wallace wins, a farewell to Eleanor Roosevelt*

1963—"I Have a Dream": *George Wallace, Birmingham, the Schoolhouse Door, Medgar Evers, Eudora Welty, the President speaks, Betty Friedan, Gloria Steinem and Patsy Cline, Dr. King and the March on Washington, The bombing of a church, the assassination of JFK*

1

The Movement

For Franklin McCain, there are moments when the memory of it comes rushing back—the feeling he had when he took his place at the counter, on the padded swivel stool beneath the laminated signs promoting lemon pie. He and his friends had given little thought to the history they would be making. They were barely eighteen, and only much later did they marvel at the mystery of what they achieved. All they knew on this particular day, February 1, 1960, was that the world was not what they thought it should be. Everywhere they turned there were whites-only signs and a way of life in the South and beyond that was rooted in the common affront of segregation.

As a young black man, McCain got the message—the insult was never very far from his mind. With Joe McNeill, David Richmond and Ezell Blair, his three closest friends at North Carolina A&T University, he made a decision so basic and clear that he couldn't believe they hadn't thought of it before. For the sake of their dignity and pride, they simply would not take it anymore. As far as McCain and the others were concerned, the laws of segregation no longer applied.

Thus did they make their way on this cold afternoon to the Woolworth's lunch counter, a popular gathering place in downtown Greensboro, and took seats on the white people's stools. It was the first sit-in of the 1960s, the day the sputtering civil rights movement finally came alive. There had been a victory here and there—the 1955–56 Montgomery bus boycott, for example, which introduced the nation to Martin Luther King—but in the intervening years, King had struggled over what to do next. He had preached in pulpits across the South, and delivered his speeches all over the world, winning acclaim for his eloquence and passion. But the civil rights movement he was seeking to build was so far a series of disconnected events, a caricature of his dreams.

Then came Greensboro, where history began in a college bull session. On the night of January 31, 1960, it was too cold outside, they decided, to go anywhere, so they gathered as they had many times in a dorm room shared by McNeill and Blair. McCain and Richmond were there as well. They were just four college freshmen talking about the world. Their conversation soon turned to the issue of race, and they began to rail against their parents, who had struggled so bravely to make it in America and urged their sons to do the same. But parents and sons, for no reason other than the color of their skin, were demeaned every day by segregated buses, restaurants, and schools. Why, these young men wanted to know, had the older generations allowed it to happen? Why hadn't they fought back?

But then a more disturbing question arose. What had *they* done, the four of them right there in the room? They talked about the dignity of Rosa Parks and Dr. Martin Luther King, and the heroism of the Little Rock Nine, those remarkable Arkansas high school students who, in 1957, had braved white mobs—eventually with the help of federal troops—to batter the walls of segregation there. But in Greensboro, they themselves had done absolutely nothing. The more they talked, the worse they felt, and their mood sank lower by the hour.

"I felt dirty," remembered McCain. "I felt ashamed."

Finally, in the early morning quiet of February 1, just an hour or two before dawn, Joe McNeill looked at the others and demanded simply: "Let's do something."

From there the ideas came in a torrent. They would go that day—no need to put it off—to confront the reality of Southern segregation. Specifically, as soon as their classes were over, they would march to the Woolworth's store downtown. That particular establishment was especially galling. The clerks were happy to take the black students' money for school supplies or anything else, except for food. The Woolworth's lunch counter served only whites.

McNeill and his friends, who would soon become known as the Greensboro Four, decided to confront that policy directly. They would take seats and demand to be served.

Many years later, Ezell Blair remembered the surge of terror when it occurred to him that they were really serious. Like most young blacks of his generation, he knew about Emmett Till, a fourteen-year-old boy from Chicago who in 1955 visited relatives in Mississippi. Showing off for his country cousins, Till had said something fresh to a white woman, and for that breach of Southern etiquette he was murdered—his mutilated body dumped from a bridge into the murky Tallahatchie River. Two white men were arrested but soon acquitted by an all-white jury, despite eyewitness testimony against them. Black parents all across the South warned their sons to be more cautious, or they could become the next Emmett Till.

As he tossed and turned in his bed in Greensboro, Blair felt mounting dread. Till, after all, had been murdered for a trivial act—a harmless aside to a white woman—while Blair and his friends were planning nothing less than a frontal assault on segregation. Later, he remembered how he woke up early and called his parents. His mother, Corene, was a member of the NAACP, and when he asked her opinion, she told him simply to do what he must and to carry himself with dignity and grace. There was nothing more to say.

Joe McNeill, who would later become a general in the U.S. Air Force, pointed out that they were all afraid. Under the circumstances it was normal. The question was how they would manage the fear.

For McCain, especially, the answer was easy. They might go to jail, or maybe they would even be killed. But in a segregated world, they had to be willing to pay such a price. "We had nothing to lose," he later explained. His anger, quite simply, was stronger than his fear, and he could see that the others felt the same. Their moment of personal liberation was at hand.

The following morning, they all went to class. McCain remembered how he fretted through chemistry and English composition, until finally it was time to meet his friends. They didn't talk much on the thirty-minute walk from campus to town, and when they reached Woolworth's they split into pairs—McCain and McNeill, Richmond and Blair. They bought school supplies and kept the receipts, then McCain and McNeill, who happened to be closest, decided to move toward the counter. McCain said they hesitated for a minute, maybe even five, before they took their seats, to the general astonishment of people all around. For McCain it was a moment unique in his life, a sense of exhilaration and relief.

"I can't even describe it," he said. "Never have I experienced such an incredible emotion, such an uplift. As a journalist friend of mine once put it, 'My soul was rested.'"

But the moment soon became more tense. McNeill remembered that a

Greensboro policeman quickly arrived and began pacing back and forth behind the stools, tapping his nightstick in the palm of his hand.

"Joe," said McCain, "I think this is it."

"Yeah," said McNeill, "I think so." The gesture, however, was merely a bluff, and when the two young men didn't flinch, the policeman seemed confused. So was everybody else in authority, and as Richmond and Blair made their way toward the stools, the waitress tried once again to explain: "We don't serve Negroes here."

But McCain replied with manicured politeness, pointing to the school supplies they had bought, "I beg to disagree. You do serve us and you have."

"We have the receipts to prove it," McNeill added stubbornly.

The standoff continued until almost five p.m., when the Woolworth's manager closed the counter. As stiffly polite as they had been from the start, McCain and his friends got up and left. They reveled in their moment of deliverance, but they knew already that this was something much bigger than themselves.

Two things happened that same night, as word of their action began to ripple outward and to capture the attention of the young. On the campus of North Carolina A&T, the Greensboro Four called a meeting of student leaders. They talked about their afternoon adventure and the shimmering possibilities that lay just ahead, and they were startled when at first nobody believed them. Nobody could imagine that four college freshmen, acting on their own, had defied white supremacy and lived to tell it. The lone exception was Albert Rozier, the student newspaper editor. The following morning he published an extra edition of the *A&T Register*—the first in its history—and suddenly it seemed as if the whole world knew. The sit-ins continued that week in Greensboro, and with mounting publicity the protesters numbered well into the hundreds—with black students joined by a sprinkling of whites.

Several hundred miles away, meanwhile, a young black man was driving alone through the hills of Virginia, the radio crackling through the cold morning air. Charles Jones, a theology student at Johnson C. Smith University in Charlotte, was on his way to North Carolina when he heard the astonishing story on the news. Four college freshmen—teenagers!—had taken a stand against segregation and called on others to do the same. As an African American, the grandson of slaves, Jones was proud of his ancestors' perseverance and believed that every generation must build on the past. But how? What could he and others like him do to push the cause of freedom even further?

At the age of twenty-three, Jones was wrestling with that very question when he heard the news on his car radio, and there in the loneliness of rural Virginia, he found himself shouting to the great, empty sky: "Thank you, God! This is how we can do it." As soon as he made it back to Charlotte, he, too, called a meeting of the campus leadership, telling his friends, "I don't know about y'all, but tomorrow morning I'm going downtown, and I'm gon' do what the students in Greensboro did."

And so the sit-ins continued to spread. Jones and his friends began sitting in at a half-dozen restaurants, coming back day after day. There were racial insults and scattered acts of violence as young white toughs came to heckle and threaten, and on the first day a policeman struck a student squarely in her face. But the police mostly were professional, and, perhaps more importantly, so were the reporters who covered the story. The local morning newspaper, the *Charlotte Observer*, recounted not only what the demonstrators did but their explanations about why. The journalists seemed drawn to Jones's eloquence as he quoted the Constitution and the Old Testament prophets and talked about brotherhood and justice.

The stories went out on the national wires, and Jones was sure the Charlotte demonstrations inspired supporters all over the country. Whatever the reason, by the end of February the sit-ins had spread beyond the South and to more than fifty towns. About a thousand people, many of them white, formed a picket line around a Woolworth's store in Harlem, and students from Rutgers, Antioch, and Yale rushed to join the demonstrations. But it was in the South, the most conservative part of the country, where the roots of social change reached deepest, nourished by leaders whose names are largely forgotten.

In Nashville, Tennessee, a city that would soon emerge as the new epicenter of the sit-in movement, three ministers—two black, one white, two of them Southern, one of them not—became the unofficial advisers to a remarkable group of activist students.

Kelly Miller Smith was one of those mentors—a Baptist minister whose church was a staging ground for the movement. Three years earlier, he had volunteered his six-year-old daughter, Joy, to be a civil rights pioneer. The city of Nashville, like a handful of other Southern towns, including Charlotte, Winston-Salem, and Greensboro, decided to begin incremental desegregation of public schools. But instead of starting with high school, as the other cities had, Nashville chose to take its first steps at the elementary level, where prejudice might not be as ingrained. That was the hope. And so on the morning of September 9, 1957, Kelly Miller Smith held tight to Joy's hand as he enrolled her in a previously all-white school.

The day went smoothly enough for Joy, but at other Nashville schools the story was different. Nineteen African American children broke the color barrier that morning at a total of eight different schools, and many were greeted by angry mobs. That night a bomb exploded at Hattie Cotton Elementary, where a lone black child had enrolled, and a wave of fear swept through the city. But on the morning of September 10, Kelly Miller Smith once again led his daughter by the hand to the doorway of her first grade class.

Death threats followed against Kelly and Joy, and a white minister, Will Campbell, came to Smith's house to help keep watch. As they peered from a window, searching for danger in the shadows outside, Campbell asked a question he couldn't quite suppress.

"Kelly, what if something happens to little Joy?"

As Campbell would remember it later, Smith opened his Bible and began to read the story of Abraham and Isaac—how God demanded the sacrifice of a son, and Abraham had been prepared to obey. But there in the thicket, a ram was caught by the horns, and God relented, allowing instead the sacrifice of the ram. "Lord," said Smith, quietly closing his Bible, "make the thicket tight and the ram's horns long. Amen."

Such was the understanding of faith that Smith brought to the dangers of the civil rights movement. The Bible, he thought, was full of "hard sayings," and it was a point on which Will Campbell agreed. Campbell was a Mississippi Baptist, thirty-six years old, who had earned a divinity degree from Yale, and he had simply never believed, even as a boy growing up in the South, that the Brotherhood of Man should include only whites. By 1960, he was deeply committed to the cause of civil rights, and he joined Kelly Smith in supporting the sit-ins.

For many of the young Nashville activists it was heartening indeed when a white man decided to share in the risks. But their most important mentor by far, the man who taught them nonviolence as a way of life, was Methodist minister James Lawson.

Lawson was black, a thirty-one-year-old activist from Ohio who had served a year in prison for refusing to fight in the Korean War. Upon his release, he became a missionary to India, where he immersed himself in Mohandas Gandhi's theories of nonviolence. In 1957, after returning to the United States, he met and befriended Dr. Martin Luther King, a man he already admired from a distance. He remembered Gandhi's prophecy that perhaps one day a black man from America would take up the cause of nonviolence and push it to heights more impressive than the Mahatma himself had achieved.

Lawson thought King might be that man. The admiration between them was mutual. King had never met anybody like Lawson, with such a tightly woven understanding of the philosophy of Gandhi and the gospel of Jesus. King immediately urged his Methodist friend to move to the South and impart his knowledge to the civil rights movement. Lawson agreed. He moved to Nashville and in the fall of 1958 began holding workshops at Kelly Miller Smith's First Baptist Church. It was a venerated institution, the oldest black church in Nashville, with roots going back to the 1830s. Frederick Douglass had spoken there, and later Martin Luther King, but no one had the impact that James Lawson did as the 1950s drew to a close. He was teaching, in effect, a Christian adaptation of Gandhi, the radical pursuit of brotherhood and justice that would soon become the animating force of the sit-ins.

In Lawson's understanding, this was not a tactic, but a way of living rooted in the notion of redemptive suffering. For some it was counterintuitive, this idea that pain can open the heart to compassion, and that a heart without malice can transform other hearts, turning enemies into friends. In Lawson's hands, the sheer magnitude of the idealism was mesmerizing for many of the students, tied as it was to the notion of freedom, and they left the meetings with their heads in a spin.

"There was something of a mystic about him," remembered John Lewis, a farm boy from south Alabama who had come to Nashville to study theology, "something holy about his manner. . . ."

Lawson told them they were about to start a war. But only one side would fight with violence. Theirs would not. They would accept the blows that might rain down when they challenged the laws of racial segregation. But self-discipline and tolerance would not be enough—they must also *love* the people who abused them, must see and respect the humanity of their attackers, who were also victims, in their own ways, of the hate-filled system in which they lived. If that system were ever to change, Lawson declared, the means employed to bring about that change must be consistent with the ends they were seeking to attain. And so it was not enough simply to resist the urge to hit back. "The urge can't *be* there," Lawson said. "You have to have no *desire* to hit back."

Slowly but surely, the lessons took hold, buttressed by readings from Gandhi, Thoreau, and Reinhold Niebuhr. And there were the practical workshops as well, classes on how to protect their bodies from attack. By the early weeks of 1960 Lawson thought they were ready—fully prepared to descend on the restaurants and stores downtown and demand to be served the same as anybody else. They were startled to learn in early February that they had been upstaged, that four young men in Greensboro, with no training at all, had launched the movement they had been planning with such care. But they took their places in the wave of dissent, and the Nashville sit-ins became the strongest in the South. Week after week, as winter drifted into spring, the students kept coming, kept sitting in, always polite, but always persistent, dressed as if they were going to church.

By the end of March, hundreds had been arrested, and the city gradually became more tense. Roving bands of white teenagers began showing up at the sit-ins, pushing, taunting, stubbing lit cigarettes onto the demonstrators' skins. The violent climax came on the morning of April 19, when a bomb exploded at the home of Z. Alexander Looby, a veteran Nashville attorney, born in 1899 in the Caribbean nation of Dominica. As a young black man, Looby came to America on a whaling ship, determined to pursue an education, which he did at Howard University and later the Columbia University School of Law. In Nashville, he became the lead attorney for the sit-in students, a man of legendary physical courage who had spent decades battling for the rights of African Americans. So powerful was the bomb hurled through the front window of his home that the house was nearly destroyed in the blast. Down the street, more than 140 windows were shattered at Meharry Medical College, and dozens of people were cut by the glass.

Miraculously, neither Looby nor his wife were hurt, but outrage at the attempt on their lives swept through the black community. The sit-in leaders decided at once to march in protest, and they demanded that Nashville Mayor Ben West meet them on the steps of city hall.

In many ways it was as if the 1960s came alive that day, for such processions became a defining image of the decade. In Nashville on April 19, some three thousand people shuffled silently three abreast through the streets of downtown, their numbers swelling for blocks through the city. As they began to mass outside city hall, a young white man at the top of the steps pulled out his guitar and began to sing. Guy Carawan was a folk singer in the tradition of Pete Seeger and Woody Guthrie, an activist born in California now living in the mountains of Tennessee. On this particular day, he chose as his anthem a traditional African American hymn, reshaping the lyrics to fit the occasion. With his friends Zilphia Horton and Seeger, he changed the pronoun from "I" to "We." The echoes of faith were unmistakable, and though the chord progressions were somber, his message rang with redemption and the hope of social change—"We shall overcome someday."

As a part of his job at the Highlander Folk School in Monteagle, Tennessee, Carawan had taught the song to a few of the leaders of the civil rights movement. But this was the moment of public unveiling when its powers of inspiration were fully on display.

It was not, however, the most remarkable moment of the march. That would come a few minutes later in a face-off between the demonstrators and the mayor. It was not going well at first. C. T. Vivian, a fiery leader of the sit-ins, read a statement, accusing Mayor West of a failure to lead.

West responded with anger: "I deny the statement and resent to the bottom of my soul the implications of what you have just read."

Standing nearby, a young woman named Diane Nash, also a stalwart in the Nashville movement, listened to the confrontation with dismay. She remembered the lessons of Lawson's workshops: *Love your enemies. Respect their humanity. Turn them into friends*. It seemed clear enough that Vivian, whatever his fearlessness in the moment, was not doing that, so Nash stepped forward. In a voice that was soft and sure and strong, she asked Mayor West if he would use the prestige of his office to end discrimination.

"I appeal to all citizens to end discrimination," West replied, "to have no bigotry, no bias, no hatred."

"Then, Mayor," insisted Diane, continuing to push, firmly, gently, not backing down, "do you recommend that the lunch counters be desegregated?"

"Yes," said West.

Suddenly it was as if the whole city knew that a corner was turned. The following morning, the *Nashville Tennessean* trumpeted the news in a banner headline: INTEGRATE COUNTERS—MAYOR.

From that moment on, Diane Nash assumed a position of leadership in the civil rights movement that she had neither sought nor expected. She was, after all, a woman, and leadership was the province of men. That was simply the way of the world. But suddenly, in more ways than one, she found herself on the cutting edge. As African Americans, they were all on a quest for equal rights, but she knew already that she was part of another upheaval as well, a redefinition of the role of women.

She discovered that she was not alone. Other women in the sit-in movement were caught up in the same unsettling sense of possibility. They set out now to knit the pieces together.

ON EASTER WEEKEND IN 1960, just a few days before Nash's triumph, more than two hundred student activists from forty communities in ten states gathered in Raleigh, North Carolina. The call for the meeting came from Ella Baker, regarded by many as one of the most important leaders in the civil rights movement. In 1960, she was certainly the most outspoken woman, serving as interim director of Dr. Martin Luther King's fledgling Southern Christian Leadership Conference until King could find a man to replace her. Growing up in rural North Carolina, Baker was raised on stories of slave revolts, told by a grandmother who had been a slave and, among other horrors, was beaten by her owner when she refused to marry a man he selected.

At the age of fifty-seven, Baker was a committed apostle of grassroots democracy, the idea that charismatic leadership was not enough. She admired King's eloquence, his ability to frame the public debate, but she also thought this movement of students, erupting so powerfully across the South, held a promise unmatched since Rosa Parks had refused to give up her seat on a bus. The boycott in Montgomery was itself a movement of the masses—thousands of African American citizens who simply refused, day after day, to ride in the rear of segregated buses.

Eventually, the boycotters won, but their triumph had not led to other victories over segregation, and Baker wanted to be sure that the same thing didn't happen with the sit-ins. She wanted to create—or more precisely, help the students *themselves* create—an organization to build systematically on their momentum. She arranged for the Easter meeting at Shaw University, her alma mater where she had graduated as valedictorian. Though Dr. King attended the conference and delivered a moving and powerful address, it remained for James Lawson to define the movement's philosophy:

> Love is the central motif of nonviolence. Love is the force by which God binds man to himself and man to man. Such love goes to the extreme; it remains loving and forgiving even in the midst of hostility. It matches the capacity of evil to inflict suffering with an even more enduring capacity to absorb evil . . . Nonviolence nurtures an atmosphere in which reconciliation and justice become actual possibilities.

It was idealism in its purest form, and the students were moved. But there was also a fierce, revolutionary edge in their public announcement of a new organization, the Student Nonviolent Coordinating Committee (SNCC). They called themselves "freedom fighters" and compared their struggle to the revolts against colonialism in Africa. And though their own revolt would be nonviolent, they vowed that they would carry the struggle to "every nook and cranny" in the South.

In the weeks that followed SNCC's public announcement, the sit-ins began to produce results—victories in cities like Nashville, Greensboro, and Charlotte, as downtown merchants took their measure of the demonstrators' resolve and agreed to integrate lunch counters. As the students' visibility increased, even opponents were grudgingly impressed.

James J. Kilpatrick was the conservative editor of the *Richmond News-Leader*, a segregationist who stated as late as 1963 that "the Negro race, as a race, is in fact an inferior race." Later, he would renounce those views and decry "the absolute evil of segregation." But in 1960, even before his change of heart, he took note of the dignity of the sit-ins:

> Here were the colored students, in coats, white shirts, ties, and one of them was reading Goethe and one was taking notes from a biology text. And here, on the sidewalk outside, was a gang of white boys come to heckle, a rattail rabble, slack-jawed, black-jacketed, grinning fit to kill. . . . It gives one pause.

What Kilpatrick seemed to understand, at least superficially, was that something powerful was taking shape in the South. Soon enough the whole nation would notice.

2

The Voices

Living in Mobile, Alabama, I didn't know much about the sit-ins. Not at first. There were newspaper stories here and there and scattered grumblings among friends of my parents. But my contemporaries and I, all of us white and barely in our teens, had other things on our minds. First of all, there was rock 'n' roll. In the summer of 1960, I remember hearing a song on the radio; the singer sounded black and the subject matter was something I had never even thought about, and certainly never expected to experience. Nevertheless, I was transfixed when Sam Cooke sang about a Southern chain gang.

All day long they work so hard
Till the sun is going' down
Workin' on the highways and byways
And wearing, wearing a frown
You hear them moanin' their lives away
Then you hear somebody say
That's the sound of the men
Workin' on the chain gang

I had heard Sam Cooke's music before. In 1957, he had "crossed over," as people in the music business liked to say, with "You Send Me," a number one ballad on the Billboard charts, and again in April 1960, he had a major hit with "Wonderful World." The latter was aimed squarely at the teen market, being about a boy who is not very good in school, who doesn't know much about history, biology, or any of his other classroom subjects, but is very sure that he is in love. The message is delivered with an innocent sweetness and a lilting rhythm that was hard for listeners to put out of their minds. "Chain Gang" sounded similar, with a chorus that was easy to sing along with every time it came on the radio. But the images were downright astonishing, as my friends and I listened to the song and tried to figure out why it made us care.

We didn't know the backstory, of course—how Cooke was born in Clarksdale, Mississippi, the home of the blues, but grew up in Chicago where his family moved when he was only three. Sam was raised on the music of the Southern church, really, for most of his neighbors were refugees from the South. He began his career in a family singing group, traveling the church circuit with his preacher-father, and later with the Soul Stirrers, a gospel group that more than lived up to its name. "Shouting, straining, sweat-soaked catharsis" was the way Cooke biographer Peter Guralnick described the group's singing style. But even at the peak of this gospel success, Cooke dreamed of something more. In the mid-1950s, after extended soul-searching, he decided finally to cast his lot with secular music.

By 1960, he was a twenty-nine-year-old star, with immense vocal talent and an air of likability and charm. He seemed to love every kind of music. In 1958, he was the headliner on a national tour that included white artists—the Everly Brothers, Paul Anka, George Hamilton IV—and between shows he could often be found in the back of the bus, sitting with Hamilton or the Everlys, playing Hank Williams songs on one of their guitars. Later, he would have his own country hit with the classic "Tennessee Waltz," and even in 1958 he and the others on the tour sensed that they were part of something bigger—not so much a battering as simply a dissolving of the artificial walls of racial segregation.

Even those of us who merely listened on the radio felt a vague, intoxicating sense of subversion. Nor was it only the black singers who made us feel that way. In all our pretensions to adolescent cool—our three-minute transports to a whole different world as Sam Cooke sang about chain gang workers (men he had befriended, we would later learn, on one of his tours through North Carolina)—there was another singer who made us feel it even more.

Elvis Presley, of course, was white. But his background and musical tastes bore an astonishing similarity to Cooke's. Presley was also born in Mississippi—in the town of Tupelo roughly a hundred miles from Cooke's birthplace. A difference was that Presley's family did not escape. They moved to Memphis, but that was still the hot and steamy South. Before that, in the latter half of the Great Depression, their lives were constricted by small-town poverty—and by a sense of shame when Elvis's father, Vernon Presley, was sent away to prison for passing a $4 bad check. But the family was close. Elvis grew up as an only child after his twin brother, Jesse, was stillborn, and one of the things that bonded the Presleys was a deep love of music.

As with Sam Cooke, the love affair began in the church, a Pentecostal congregation not altogether different in worship style from the ones where Cooke's father preached. The Presleys also had a family singing group, and Elvis was forever stamped by his love of old hymns. But music of any kind became a source of meaning in his life—country music, the blues, it didn't really matter; he was surrounded by it in north Mississippi, and even more when they moved to Memphis, where Beale Street throbbed with the music of African Americans: people much like his Tupelo neighbors when his family lived on the black side of town.

During his teenage years in Memphis, Elvis played and sang wherever he could. On one fine day in 1953, he wandered down to 706 Union Avenue. There he met a man who would change his life and, in a sense, the course of American music. Sam Phillips was an Alabamian by birth. In 1950, he opened a recording studio in Memphis. He was driven by a mix of art and commerce, a desire to make and sell good records by the African American artists in the area. Soon enough, they came in a steady stream to his door—Rufus Thomas, Howlin' Wolf, Little Junior Parker, even a group called the Prisonaires, inmates who with Phillips's help and the backing of Tennessee Governor Frank Clement secured a day pass from the penitentiary to cut a record at Phillips's studio.

In all this, Phillips was partly driven by a leap of moral imagination that was quite remarkable at the time. "I saw—I don't remember when, but I saw as a child—I thought to myself: suppose that I would have been born black," he told Peter Guralnick. "I think I felt from the beginning the total inequity of man's inhumanity to his brother. And it didn't take its place with me of getting up in the pulpit and preaching. It took on the aspect with me that someday I would act on my feelings. I would show them on an individual, one-to-one basis."

His Sun Records studio became the place to fulfill that promise, and as the records he produced started hitting the charts, Phillips began to receive publicity. It may have been, in fact, an article in the *Memphis Commercial Appeal* that led Elvis Presley to his studio. Elvis was eighteen on his first visit, not given to the reflectiveness of Phillips when it came to the social order of the South. But in the memory of those who knew him then, there was always a certain kindness about him—even a sweetness, some people said—and nothing of cultural condescension toward African Americans or anyone else. When it came to his personal ambitions as an artist, Presley was happy to follow in the footsteps of blacks.

It took a few months before he and Phillips finally made a record. But in the summer of 1954 they went into the Sun Records studio with guitarist Scotty Moore and bass player Bill Black and cut a truly remarkable version of "That's All Right, Mama," a song originally done by blues artist Arthur "Big Boy" Crudup. At first they were just kind of clowning around, Elvis "jumping around and acting the fool," as Moore remembered it, but Phillips, a producer with an ear for originality, was certain they were onto something important. Elvis sang with such exuberance, and you could hear in his voice the black influence as well as the white, yet he sounded so utterly himself. The same was true for the B-side of the record, "Blue Moon of Kentucky," a song that began in 1946 as a hillbilly waltz by Bill Monroe. The Elvis version was certainly not that, but what was it exactly?

All over Memphis and soon the South, disc jockeys were intrigued but puzzled. Was it country? Was it rhythm and blues? Or both? And if the latter, then it was something new, like the fusing of atoms, with all the implied explosive potential. Certainly, the racists saw that potential. The White Citizens Council labeled "rock 'n' roll," as the new music came to be called, "a communist plot using the music of the American Negro to undermine American youth." An Alabama WCC member put it even more crudely: "We've set up a twenty-man committee," he said, "to do away with this vulgar, animalistic, nigger rock and roll bop."

The racists didn't stand a chance. Their objections were swept aside by the power of music. In the summer of 1960, the only remaining controversy came in the grumbling by our parents—a stubborn insistence that Elvis and the other young rock 'n' rollers couldn't "really sing." But Elvis again proved them wrong. In July, he released "It's Now or Never," which quickly became the biggest hit of his career. There was nothing raw or gritty about it, no echo of country or the blues, the starting point for his earlier music. This was an ode to Mario Lanza, the great American tenor whose records Elvis had listened to as a boy—and perhaps more directly to Enrico Caruso, whose "O Sole Mio" the Elvis hit copied note for note. Only the lyrics were different.

The thing that made us proud, my friends and I at age thirteen, was that Elvis pulled it off. The spine-tingling vocal crescendo—*it's now or never, my love won't wait*—demonstrated beyond doubt that Elvis was a vocal talent to be reckoned with. That same summer, Roy Orbison showed similar range and prowess with "Only the Lonely," and this music we called rock 'n' roll sprawled into every corner of our lives. Some of it crossed old barriers of race and class; the rest of it just made us feel good. But we knew it *mattered* in a way we were trying to understand.

ABOUT THAT SAME TIME, another singer with a bell-like voice unlike any we had heard stepped gently onto the public stage. Joan Baez released her first album in 1960, but she was already a fixture on the folk music circuit. She was born with what she knew was a gift, a singing voice bestowed upon her, she said, "by forces which confound genetics, environment, race, or ambition." Perhaps because she did not create it, she knew by her teenage years that she wanted to use it for some larger purpose.

As a high school junior in Palo Alto, California, she attended a conference sponsored by the American Friends Service Committee, the social action arm of the Quakers, and listened in rapt amazement to the keynote address by Dr. Martin Luther King. "Everyone in the room was mesmerized," she remembered. "He talked about injustice and suffering, and about fighting with the weapons of love. . . . When he finished his speech, I was on my feet, cheering and crying."

After high school she moved with her family to Boston, where she entered Boston University, but quickly dropped out. She began to sing in clubs and coffeehouses all over town, and the crowds most often were awed by her voice, so high and pure, so delicate and strong, whatever the music seemed to require. She performed barefooted, even when the weather was cold, and with her long, dark hair and Mexican skin she possessed a kind of virginal yet vaguely flirtatious beauty. When people saw her they seldom forgot her.

In 1958 Baez met Odetta Holmes, a native of Birmingham, Alabama, who performed simply under the name Odetta. She was already one of Baez's heroes. Odetta's songs were an artful exploration of the human heart, though much of her music was also political. Growing up in the South during the Great Depression, she had fallen in love with protest music, which was a way for desperate people to cope. "They were liberation songs," Odetta remembered. "You're walking down life's road, society's foot is on your throat, every which way you turn you can't get from under that foot. And you reach a fork in the road and you can either lie down and die or insist upon your life . . . those people who made up the songs were the ones who insisted upon life."

For Baez, Odetta embodied a sense of possibility. Then in 1959 she met Pete Seeger, whom she had seen in a concert when she was still living in Palo Alto. It had been one of the turning points of her life, and as she listened to his songs it occurred to her that this was something she could do with her life, singing to people about things that mattered. That's what Seeger had done, going back to the 1930s and '40s when he and Woody Guthrie rambled around, sometimes together, sometimes not, singing the songs of America's dispossessed.

As a teenager in the 1930s, Seeger had joined the Young Communist League when he saw the magnitude of suffering in the land; compassion seemed to require something radical. But soon enough he also saw Stalin's atrocities in the Soviet Union and Hitler's crimes in Europe. To make his own position clear he sang a song that was, in effect, a patriotic anthem on the eve of war:

> Now, as I think of our great land . . . I know it ain't perfect, but it will be someday, just give us a little time. This is the reason that I want to fight, not 'cause everything's perfect, or everything's right. No, it's just the opposite: I'm fightin' because I want a better America, and better laws, and better homes, and jobs, and schools, and no more Jim Crow, and no more rules like . . . "You can't ride on this train 'cause you're a Negro," "You can't live here 'cause you're a Jew," "You can't work here 'cause you're a union man."

That mantra of patriotic dissent defined Pete Seeger as the 1950s came to an end and the '60s began and he wrote his unforgettable anthems: "If I Had a Hammer," "Turn, Turn, Turn," and "Where Have All the Flowers Gone?" Baez soon would follow in his path, her music becoming more political. But when they met at the Newport Folk Festival on a rainy summer day in 1959, she still preferred old ballads about tragedy and death, or gospel laments about the peace found only in the world yet to come. Her listeners had no way of knowing—for she seemed so sure of herself when she sang—that the passionate sadness throbbing in her songs reflected demons of insecurity and doubt.

But her empathy, her identification with people who hurt, was palpable, and in the summer of 1960, when she was nineteen, she cut her first album for Vanguard Records. It was entitled simply *Joan Baez*, and it was filled with grief and lament, songs of heartache, infidelity, and even murder, some going back to the sixteenth century. For many of us, one song stood out from the rest. Some music historians say "All My Trials" began its life as a Bahamian lullaby; others say it was a slave song about death, the only relief that those in bondage could really imagine. Whatever the origins, as Baez sang it, it held the gentle promise of more pointed commentary yet to come.

If living were a thing that money could buy
The rich would live and the poor would die
All my trials, Lord, soon be over

I remember, sometime after the release of her album, when I first saw Baez perform in person. She entered the small auditorium from the rear, walking barefoot down the aisle—wearing, as I recall, a long peasant dress, strumming her guitar and singing "Kumbaya." By the cynical end of the 1960s, that sweet and haunting Negro spiritual would be a cliché, a parody of the search for community and peace, but I remember thinking on that particular night that I had never heard anything so lovely.

Musicians, it should be said, were not the only artists whose work foreshadowed a decade of change. There were also the authors, moved by the admonition of William Faulkner that the only thing worth writing about was the human heart in conflict with itself. They saw in the collective heart of the nation, and especially the South, an urgent state of distress that cried out powerfully for their attention. In the spring and summer of 1960, journalist John Howard Griffin would hit a raw nerve.

In April, Griffin began an astonishing six-part series in the African American magazine, *Sepia*. Griffin, who was white, decided to darken his skin and pass for black, testing the segregationist assumption that discrimination was based not on color, but rather on larger, deeper flaws in the collective character of African Americans. In retrospect, the arrogance of that racist belief is shocking. But in 1960, it was the majority opinion among white Southerners. As a boy growing up in Alabama, I had never met anybody who doubted it.

In his series, "Journey Into Shame," which soon became an iconic book called *Black Like Me*, Griffin set out to shatter that assumption. "I tried to establish one simple fact," he explained, "which was to reveal the insanity of a situation where a man is judged by his skin color, by his philosophical 'accident'—rather than by who he is in his humanity."

Griffin was uniquely positioned to prove that point. Born in 1920, he grew up in Dallas, sharing the "genteel" racism of his family. His conversion came in stages, beginning in 1935 when he journeyed to France and became a student at the prestigious Lycee Descartes in Tours. In 1939, during the Nazi occupation, he joined the French underground and helped smuggle Jewish families to safety. He learned that the Gestapo had marked him for death, and he returned to America, where in 1941 he joined the Army Air Force.

Over the next four years in the Solomon Islands, he came to admire the courage of the islanders as they fought against the Japanese. And then one night in 1945 he was blinded by the explosion of a bomb. Suddenly he could not see, and just as suddenly, he said, he knew what it was like to be "the Other," to have people assume because he was blind that he was inferior in other ways as well. "A man loses his sight," Griffin wrote, "but let it be understood that he loses nothing else. He does not lose his intelligence, his taste, his sensitivity, his ideals, his right to respect."

Remarkably, on January 9, 1957, Griffin's sight returned, gradually at first, but steadily, miraculously, and inexplicably. He could only understand it as God's will, which left him with a powerful sense of obligation. In his twelve years of blindness, he had come to see the similarity between the anti-Semitism of the Nazis and the casual racism on which he was raised. Both were rooted in vanity and arrogance, and both carried a cruelty that could be deadly for people who were different from the dominant group. Most fundamentally, during this time when he could not see, the Southern obsession with skin color struck him as even more absurd.

Griffin set out boldly to expose the lie. He met with a dermatologist in New Orleans, and they agreed on a protocol of oral medication and sunlamp treatments. Five days later, on November 7, 1959, Griffin stepped into a darkened bathroom and hesitated before he turned on the lights. He had shaved his head so that his straight, Caucasian hair wouldn't give him away, regardless of the color of his skin. But now he froze, suddenly afraid of what he would see.

"I stood in the darkness before the mirror," he wrote, "my hand on the light switch. I forced myself to flick it on. In the flood of light against the white tile, the face and shoulders of a stranger—a fierce, bald, very dark Negro—glared at me from the glass. He in no way resembled me."

Was the flicker of distaste on Griffin's face as he saw his own black visage in the mirror a reflection of his own unconscious racism? Or was it just shock, the sudden uncertainty anyone might feel upon glancing at a mirror and seeing someone else looking back? Critics have debated those questions through the years, but few have questioned the searing honesty of Griffin's account, or the depth of his passion and empathy and hurt. In the first installment of his *Sepia* series, he ends with a passage about the n-word. In retrospect, he had heard it frequently enough when he was white, but now that he wasn't—at least temporarily—he was astonished and stung by the cruel and casual frequency of its usage.

Hey, nigger, you can't go in. Hey, nigger, you can't sit there. We don't serve niggers.

Throughout his racial experiment nearly everything grew steadily worse, especially after he left New Orleans and set out for Alabama and Mississippi. He did discover moments of kindness in the company of other African Americans. Once in Mississippi, he found himself on a lonely highway and a black man stopped to give him a ride, taking him home to spend the night when he discovered that Griffin had no place to stay. Always, it seemed, there were people—almost all of them black—who were willing to give him directions or advice, offer him food, or help him find shelter. But time and time again he was startled by the gratuitous cruelty he encountered from whites—a bus driver in Mississippi who allowed his white passengers, but not the blacks, to disembark at a rest stop to use the bathroom; a white man in Alabama who gave him a ride and warned against stirring racial unrest.

> "Do you know what we do to troublemakers down here?"
> "No, sir."
> "We either ship them off to the pen or kill them."

Griffin continued:

> He spoke in a tone that sickened me, casual, merciless. I looked at him. His decent blue eyes turned yellow. I knew that nothing could touch him to have mercy once he decided a Negro should be "taught a lesson." The immensity of it terrified me. But it caught him up like a lust now. He entertained it, his voice unctuous with pleasure and cruelty. The highway stretched deserted through the swamp forests. He nodded toward the solid wall of brush flying past our windows.

"You can kill a nigger and toss him into that swamp and no one'll ever know what happened to him."

John Howard Griffin lasted exactly five weeks as a black man. He couldn't take it anymore. "My heart sickened," he wrote, "at the thought of any more hate."

Even before the *Sepia* series began in April 1960, the national media got wind of the story; everybody wanted to hear Griffin tell it—a white man turning himself black, discovering life on the other side. The sheer improbability of it, the remarkable *audacity*, prompted interview requests from *Time* and a long list of radio and television hosts, from Mike Wallace to Dave Garroway. Griffin accommodated them all. He thought the story needed to be told.

After the television shows, and even more as his series ran in *Sepia*, mail flooded his home in Texas—more than 6,000 letters between April and June. Most were favorable, including many from white Southerners praising his honesty. But on April 2, he was hanged in effigy in Mansfield, Texas, the town where he lived, and telephone calls and encounters on the streets carried threats of death, castration, or both. Most of the hatred came from the South. That was, after all, where his story was focused—both in *Sepia* and in *Black Like Me*, the book that followed to even greater acclaim.

Griffin later thought he had made a mistake, for the ugliness he found in Alabama, Mississippi, and Louisiana could just as easily have been uncovered in New York, Illinois, or California. He thought he should have written that story as well. But his was at least a start, part of a larger, more terrible truth that the country, at last, might have to face.

As THE ACCOLADES CAME and controversy swirled around Griffin, Harper Lee waited impatiently for the publication of her novel. She had no idea, of course, that *To Kill a Mockingbird* would become one of the most beloved and bestselling books of all time. But she did know that she had worked hard on it. As a writer she was sure of her voice, her ability to tell the story through the eyes of Scout Finch, an eight-year-old girl. It was a remarkable double narrator effect: the innocence of child, the whispered wisdom of a woman looking back. But the shape and structure of the novel gave her fits, and she spent more time than she cared to remember holed up by herself in a cold water flat in New York City, fighting the pages, trying desperately to make the pieces fit.

Once in a fit of frustration she threw the manuscript out the window and watched it blow through the Manhattan snow. Fortunately she was able to gather herself and hurry outside, retrieving the pages before it was too late.

The story she knew she had to tell was one that had long been swirling in her mind. It began with the image of an Alabama town—a place she thought that others might like even if they knew its dark underside. In the 1930s she had been a child in such a place, when racial injustice was a hard-edged thing, filled with lynchings and black men punished for things they never did, and only the strongest, most honorable white people were able to muster the strength to oppose it.

In the character of Atticus Finch, her iconic and archetypical protagonist, Harper Lee created for the millions who bought her book a lonely white Southerner who was worthy of respect. In this, her timing could not have been better. When her novel was published on July 11, 1960, the sit-in movement and the backlash against it were sweeping through the South, and many people feared—quite correctly—that the unleashed tension would only get worse.

On some level, the book itself may have added to that tension. It was "by its very existence an act of protest," wrote Pulitzer Prize-winning historian Diane McWhorter. An injustice against an innocent black man lay at its heart—a message many Southerners did not want to hear. But so many of us were drawn to the other side of the story, for here was Atticus Finch, a small-town lawyer willing to stand for what he knew was right. He defended Tom Robinson, a black man falsely accused of rape, and though he ultimately failed in that defense, his eloquence and calm amid all the ugly tensions of his time offered real-life hope for ours.

Atticus was not an unfamiliar character. Many of us knew somebody like him, or people at least who bore some resemblance, and as America struggled with its original sin, this figure from the pages of a splendid novel helped us believe we might make it through.

3

JFK

There was one other writer who helped put a stamp on the new decade, though not in a way that she would have dreamed. Lillian Smith was working that year on a new edition of *Killers of the Dream*, a groundbreaking book published in 1949. As a white woman living in the mountains of Georgia in the years just after World War II, Smith produced a work of nonfiction so astonishing in its bravery that it sent shock waves throughout the South. She believed—and this is not overstating the case—that the absurdities of racial segregation had crippled her region's ability to think.

In rhythmic, elegant prose, Smith wrote, "In this South I lived as a child, and it is of that my story is made . . . Out of the intricate weaving of unnumbered threads, I shall pick out a few strands that have to do with what we call color and race . . . and sex . . . and love . . . and dreams of the Good and the killers of dreams."

She began specifically with the story of a day when she was a girl and there were hushed and urgent conversations at her house. Neighbors reported that on the colored side of town (that was the term they used) a little white girl was living with Negroes. This could not be allowed. So the authorities were summoned, arrangements were made, and soon the little girl—over the desperate protests of her black foster family—was brought to live with the Smiths.

For a while the arrangement worked out well. Lillian was delighted with her new sweet-tempered younger sister as they played with dolls and roamed the fields near the family farm. But then one day there were more hushed whispers. "All afternoon," Smith wrote, "the ladies went in and out of our house talking to Mother in tones too low for children to hear. As they passed us at play, they looked at Jamie and quickly looked away, though a few stopped and stared at her as if they could not tear their eyes from her face."

What the ladies of the community had learned was that Jamie, despite her white skin, was the orphaned child of Negro parents. She was returned immediately to the foster family from which she was taken, and Lillian was sternly instructed by her mother: "Don't ever ask me about this again." Smith wrote,

> As I grew older, and more experiences collected around that faithless time, as memories of older, more profound hurts crept closer, drawn to that night as if by a magnet, I began to know that people who talked of love and children did not mean it. That is a hard thing for a child to learn. I still admired my parents, there was so much that was strong and vital and sane and good about them and I never forgot this . . . Yet in my heart they were under suspicion. . . . I was shamed by their failure and frightened, for I felt they were no longer as powerful as I had thought. There was something Out There that was stronger than they and I could not bear to believe it. . . .

The thing "out there" was segregation, a tangled knot of arrogance, insecurity, and fear that produced a society of moral cripples—people who professed to believe in democracy, while they practiced the cruelties of white supremacy. Thus were minds torn loose from their moorings and moral values severed from the truth.

This was Smith's devastating critique, and as she worked to update it in 1960, taking into account the recent surge of civil rights protests, she was also battling breast cancer. On May 4, two friends in Atlanta, Dr. Martin Luther King and his wife Coretta, were driving her to Emory University Hospital for one of her treatments when a white policeman noticed this strange racial grouping and pulled them over. He discovered that King, despite having moved from Montgomery to Atlanta, still had an Alabama driver's license. For this misdemeanor, King received a one-year suspended prison sentence, and the following fall, when he was arrested during an Atlanta sit-in, the judge revoked the suspension and ordered King to spend four months on a Georgia chain gang. He was led away from the courtroom in chains.

Senator John F. Kennedy, when he heard the news, was deep into his presidential campaign. His advisers debated how he should respond, but Kennedy simply picked up the phone, called Coretta, and asked if there was anything he could do. He had no way of knowing this simple gesture would change the course of presidential history.

Jack Kennedy did a lot of things right in 1960. The handsome young senator from Massachusetts had emerged as a post-WWII rising star in the Democratic Party, a man of energy, intelligence, and charm whose soaring ambition was set on the presidency. He came from a family of extraordinary privilege. As a young man, he had studied at the Choate School and Harvard University and vacationed in France or wherever else his family might choose. But the enjoyment of wealth was never enough, even if Kennedy had wanted it to be. Public service was next on his father's agenda, part of a demanding, unrelenting vision for the Kennedy family. Joseph Kennedy Sr., the stern patriarch, had made his money through shrewd investments ranging from the stock market to liquor imports. By some measures, he was one of the ten richest men in America, but now he thought it was time for something more. Joseph himself served for a time as U.S. ambassador to the United Kingdom, but his political ambition—his passion for attainment that went beyond wealth—was realized mostly through his sons.

In 1946, at twenty-nine, John F. Kennedy won election to Congress, and six years later he defeated Republican incumbent Henry Cabot Lodge for a seat in the Senate. Now the forty-three-year-old Kennedy was running for president, a meteoric rise fueled in part by his nearly boundless self-confidence. But it was also true that he was a magnet for gifted people—"the best and the brightest," in the words of journalist David Halberstam. In the presidential campaign of 1960, Kennedy's staff consisted of names that would soon become familiar. Kennedy's speechwriter was Ted Sorensen, a thirty-two-year-old Nebraska lawyer whose eloquence was nearly indistinguishable from the candidate's. Pierre Salinger was the press secretary, Kenneth O'Donnell and Lawrence O'Brien were the Kennedy tacticians, and Louis Harris was the campaign pollster.

In his Pulitzer Prize-winning book, *The Making of the President 1960*, journalist Theodore White argued that the mood in America that election year was more complex than it seemed on the surface. Using data from the U.S. Census, White sketched a portrait of profound change. The gathering storms of racial dissent were only the most obvious piece of the whole, for not since 1890, said White, had the country seen such a demographic shift. In that year, the population figures recorded the end of the American frontier, a pattern of settlement on the Great Plains that left no clear line of demarcation.

Seventy years later, the census made it clear that America, for the first time, was now a suburban, white-collar nation, living on credit. Fourteen of our largest cities, Los Angeles being the only exception, were losing population. So were the farms and the rural countryside, while the suburbs were exploding with growth. This new America was a melting pot. All those earlier immigrants—the Irish in the 1840s, the Germans just after the Civil War, and the southern and central Europeans who flooded our shores in the early 1900s—had begun to intermarry, blurring the edges, creating a more homogenous identity. But some of the old divisions remained. Race was one. Skin color still set the Negro apart. And there was also the invisible matter of religion, most specifically the cleavage between Protestant and Catholic. No Catholic had ever been elected president, and there were Protestants who wanted to keep it that way.

"We've never had a Catholic President and I hope we never do," one West Virginia voter told Theodore White. "Our people built this country. If they had wanted a Catholic to be President, they would have said so in the Constitution."

It was to West Virginia that Jack Kennedy traveled in April 1960 in his pursuit of the Democratic Party nomination. He had already won the Wisconsin primary, but not decisively. He had won the Catholic districts, but lost the Protestant ones, and his formidable Democratic opponents—Hubert Humphrey, Stuart Symington, and Lyndon Johnson—were ready to make the case that Kennedy, as a Catholic, simply couldn't win the general election. West Virginia was the chance to prove them wrong, and Kennedy understood that the stakes were high. The state was overwhelmingly Protestant and a place where politics had an edge of economic desperation. West Virginia was coal-mining country where the work was often dangerous and hard, but in its own way a fierce source of pride. "Like a fiend with his dope or a drunkard his wine, a man will have lust for the lure of the mine," wrote Appalachian folk singer Merle Travis. But with coal declining as a percentage of the nation's energy supply, the West Virginia mines were hemorrhaging jobs, and the state was one of three—with Mississippi and Arkansas—that had lost population between 1950 and 1960.

Entering this unpredictable fray, Kennedy decided to address the religion issue head-on. "When any man stands on the steps of the Capitol," he declared, "and takes the oath of office of President, he is swearing to support the separation of church and state; he puts one hand on the Bible and raises the other hand to God as he takes the oath. And if he breaks his oath, he is not only committing a crime against the Constitution for which the Congress can impeach him—and should impeach him—but he is committing a sin against God."

Theodore White described what happened next: "Here Kennedy raised his hand from an imaginary Bible, as if lifting it to God, and, repeating softly, said, 'A sin against God, for he has sworn on the Bible.'"

Judging from the primary results, Kennedy's palpable sincerity about religion played well with the West Virginia voters. But there was something else. As he traveled through the state, he was stunned by the poverty he saw in the West Virginia hollows, the proud men who had lost their jobs, and the children who didn't have enough to eat. His own privilege may have added to his indignation and surprise. How could such conditions exist in America? In the course of his evolving campaign speeches, Kennedy convinced West Virginians that he cared, and thus began a remarkable legacy in American politics—three office-holding brothers from one of the country's wealthiest families who were viscerally moved by problems of people very different from themselves. For Kennedy and his brothers, Robert and Edward—this engagement only grew stronger with time. In 1960, it helped JFK win the West Virginia primary.

When the ballots were counted on May 10, Kennedy had won 60 percent of the vote, and he swept from there to the Democratic nomination. In his acceptance speech at the Los Angeles Coliseum, Kennedy spoke of a New Frontier, a notion that became a central piece of his legacy, and more immediately, I always thought, an ingredient at the heart of his charisma. For although he was handsome and carried himself with confidence and grace, there was for many of us who heard him, even on TV, something magical about his words:

> The problems are not all solved and the battles are not all won, and we stand today on the edge of a New Frontier—the frontier of the 1960s—a frontier of unknown opportunities and perils—a frontier of unfulfilled hopes and threats. . . . The New Frontier of which I speak is not a set of promises—it is a set of challenges. It sums up not what I intend to offer the American people, but what I intend to ask of them. It appeals to their pride, not to their pocketbook—it holds out the promise of more sacrifice instead of more security.

It was also true that even as he stirred our imaginations and offered a shimmering sense of possibility, Kennedy ran on his reassuring record. Throughout his nearly eight years in the Senate, he had carefully positioned himself as a moderate, and that was the heart of his campaign; he was measured, cool, pragmatic, centrist, leaving as little as possible to chance. On the issue of civil rights, which was already sending shock waves of through the South, he voiced his support for the 1954 *Brown* decision, calling it simply "the law of the land," but he chose as his running mate Lyndon Johnson, a senator from Texas, who he hoped would help secure the Southern vote. On foreign affairs, he positioned himself to the right of the venerable man he hoped to replace, President Dwight D. Eisenhower. He charged that Eisenhower, the American hero of World War II, had allowed a "missile gap" to develop between the United States and the Soviet Union, putting the country's security at risk. Eisenhower was furious at what he regarded as Kennedy's demagoguery, and even more so because the issue was effective. Eisenhower knew—but couldn't say—that secret reconnaissance flights over Russia demonstrated conclusively that the Soviets owned no advantage over the United States in their ability to launch a nuclear attack. But the nation was worried. In 1957, the Soviet Union *had* launched Sputnik, the first satellite to orbit the earth, while similar rockets in the United States all too often blew up on the ground.

Even Richard Nixon, Eisenhower's vice president and in 1960 the Republican Party's nominee for president, wanted to see more spending on defense. But Nixon never voiced his disagreements in public. He was in many ways the ideal vice president, certainly a man whose time in office redefined the very nature of the job. Eisenhower knew, and thought it irresponsible, that President Roosevelt had kept Vice President Harry Truman out of the loop on the Manhattan Project, which unleashed the nuclear bomb upon the world. As president, Eisenhower not only kept Nixon informed, but sent him out to represent the Administration, both in Congress and on diplomatic trips to every continent except Antarctica.

The two disagreed occasionally. In addition to urging more spending on nuclear weapons, Nixon also favored an invasion of Cuba to overthrow its leader, Fidel Castro, who had spread communism to the Western Hemisphere. But when Eisenhower rejected that advice, Nixon was loyal in support of his president.

Still, their relationship was difficult, especially for Nixon. Despite the vice president's job performance, Eisenhower seemed uncomfortable with Nixon as a man, and in both 1952 and '56 considered dropping him from the ticket. Nixon, he thought, was more of a bare-knuckled brawler, a politician who nurtured his hurts and resentments and found it hard to stay above the fray, and Eisenhower preferred a different style. Even when he decided in 1956, to keep Nixon on as his running mate, he delivered the news in a way that only caused deeper hurt. "You're my boy," he said in a private conversation.

To Nixon the condescension was clear, and there were moments when it was also public. In 1960, after Nixon won the Republican nomination, a reporter asked Eisenhower to name a major contribution—something from the realm of public policy—that Nixon had made to the administration.

"Well," said Ike, "if you give me a week I might think of one."

The lapse of political tact was astonishing, but in his book *Ike and Dick: Portrait of a Strange Political Marriage*, journalist Jeffrey Frank maintains that throughout his presidency Eisenhower viewed Nixon with "mild disdain," despite the vice president's loyalty and effort. For Nixon it was yet another wound, the kind he had nursed since his law school days, when he graduated third in his class from Duke University and received not a single offer from a major law firm. "Richard M. Nixon," wrote Theodore White, "has brought from his impoverished middle-class youth many strange qualities—the thrust of enormous internal drives, an overwhelming desire to be liked and, where he is rebuffed, a bitter, impulsive reflex of lashbacks . . . A brooding, moody man, given to long stretches of introspection, he trusts only himself and his wife—and after that his confidence, in any situation, is yielded only to the smallest number of people."

These were qualities that served Nixon badly in the presidential election of 1960 (and later in his career as well, but that is getting ahead of the story.) Among those he mistrusted most were members of the press, and his disdain, too often, became a self-fulfilling prophecy. He expected hostility from the reporters covering his campaign, and sometimes that was what he received, while John F. Kennedy expected and often received the opposite. Kennedy liked reporters, enjoyed their company, and made himself as accessible as he could. The newsmen, by nature a wary and cynical bunch, bombarded every day by campaign phrases that once may have seemed fresh, developed over time a cult of admiration for Kennedy. As Theodore White attests, they worked to keep it out of their stories, but they were human beings, grateful for a candidate who made things as easy for them as he could.

"One of the graces of the Kennedy campaign," wrote White, "was the nearly immediate availability of a stenotype transcript of what the candidate had said, whether in mine, factory, village square or New York Coliseum . . . Thus reporters were able to relax and enjoy the oratory, knowing that in an hour they would have an accurate transcript."

The reporters also could not miss the effect of the oratory on the crowds—a fact that came most clearly into focus after the first presidential debate. Even at the time, people understood the debate was a turning point for Kennedy. He prepared for it as he did most things, leaving as little as possible to chance. On the morning of September 26, he woke up early and spent four hours meeting with his brain trust—speechwriter Sorensen, former Ivy League law professor Mike Feldman, and a twenty-eight-year-old attorney named Richard Goodwin, who had graduated first in his class at Harvard. Later, they reported how Kennedy lounged casually on his hotel bed, read through the notecards they had prepared, and after digesting the information on each, sent it spinning to the floor. To the people around him, he seemed so calm, so full of confidence and resolve.

"The man behaves in any crisis," wrote Theodore White, "as if it consisted only of a sequence of necessary things to be done that will become complicated if emotions intrude."

In that spirit, Kennedy completed his morning preparation, delivered a campaign speech to a local union group in Chicago, then returned to his hotel room for a nap. There was another prep session at 5 p.m., before he dressed and headed for the studio, while more than seventy million Americans gathered around their television sets. In the ten years between 1950 and 1960, TV ownership in the country had increased ten-fold, and the U.S. Census estimated that 88 percent of American households had at least one set.

The viewers had never seen anything like this. A half century later televised presidential debates, particularly in primaries, would become so ubiquitous as to lose any serious meaning. But in 1960 the idea was new, and Kennedy in particular understood the possibilities. His opponent was campaigning on his years of experience: as vice president, Nixon had traveled to more than fifty countries, had held his own in debate with Soviet Premier Nikita Khrushchev, while Kennedy was young—*just look at the man*—and essentially untested at a critical time in the history of the world. This was now the Republican mantra, and Kennedy saw in the TV debate a chance to lay it to rest in a single evening. Nixon's advisers saw the same possibility; many warned him against the debate. But if the candidate insisted on going ahead, which Nixon did, they pleaded with him to at least get some rest, to take a break from the campaign trail and come to Chicago a day before the broadcast.

Nixon rejected that advice. He campaigned hard the day before the debate, and the following morning, as Kennedy was huddled with his brain trust, Nixon addressed a hostile union audience in Chicago. He returned to his hotel moody and depressed and spent the rest of the day in his room, alone except for his wife. He looked tired when the evening arrived and the broadcast began, and everything went downhill from there. The Lazy Shave, applied to cover his five o'clock beard shadow, began to streak with sweat in the heat of the television lights, and the camera became a remorseless foe. In person Nixon could be an impressive man, vigorous and strong—he was only five years older than Kennedy—but during the television debate his deep-set eyes seemed both hollow and ominous.

Writing more than fifty years later in his book, *The Kennedy Half Century*, political scientist Larry Sabato assessed the significance of the moment. There were the little things, Sabato wrote, like Nixon leaning against the podium, trying to ease the pain in an injured knee, his jowly face a portrait of strain: "He came across as nervous, overly inclined to approve Kennedy's arguments, and unpresidential in appearance and approach." For the TV audience the verdict was clear, and even though radio listeners had a different response (Kennedy's mother, who preferred to listen rather than watch, thought Nixon was "smoother"), the power of television prevailed. As Kennedy returned to the campaign trail Americans turned out by the tens of thousands, and the historians' consensus in the years since is that most were dazzled by the Kennedy mystique—by the glamour of what Larry Sabato called "America's first made-for-TV politician."

All that is true as far as it goes. But I remember something else as well. I recall even now my own reaction as a boy of thirteen, which was shaped of course by the response of my father, a conservative judge in Mobile, Alabama, who was also a man of decency and principle, and who detected those qualities in John F. Kennedy. I knew we were not alone in our admiration not only of the Kennedy charisma but of the things he said, his fundamental vision for the country.

This is a great country. But I think it can be greater. I think we can do better.

It was easy to believe, with the approach of November in 1960, that Kennedy not only meant what he said but he was also a man who could make it come true.

As the days went by, the campaign press corps wrote as if a Kennedy victory were certain and a landslide likely. And of course the campaign press corps was wrong. The presidential election of 1960 was one of the closest in the history of the country. Out of the sixty-nine million votes cast, Kennedy won by 113,000, and historians and pundits have argued ever since about what, exactly, put him over the top. Was it the debate? Was it campaign strategy? The extraordinary efficiency of his staff? All were critically important, of course, along with a dozen other factors, but it's also incontrovertibly true that Kennedy would not have won if not for the least scripted moment of the whole campaign, his response to Martin Luther King's arrest in Atlanta, Georgia, as described near the beginning of this chapter.

To the horror of his pregnant wife, King was led away from the courtroom in chains to jail, and then chained again in the middle of the night, and moved to a maximum-security prison. King's family and staff were afraid for his life, and Harris Wofford, a mid-level staffer in the Kennedy campaign, was determined to see the Senator take a stand. If not a public statement, Wofford said—if the campaign strategists who outranked him were afraid of losing white Southern votes—then how about a simple call to Mrs. King? Kennedy's brother-in-law Sargent Shriver took the suggestion to the candidate, and Kennedy immediately agreed.

"What the hell," he said. "That's a decent thing to do. Why not? Get her on the phone."

Shriver did, and Kennedy's message was simple and direct: "I know this must be very hard for you. I understand you are expecting a baby, and I just wanted you to know that I was thinking about you and Dr. King. If there is anything I can do to help, please feel free to call on me."

"I certainly appreciate your concern," replied Mrs. King, deeply moved and surprised by the call. "I would appreciate anything you could do to help."

From all accounts, Robert Kennedy, who managed his brother's campaign, was furious at first with Shriver and Wofford for giving what he thought was bad advice. He was afraid they had put the Southern vote at risk. But when he heard the details of King's incarceration, so obviously outrageous on their face, he called the judge in the case and demanded that he release Dr. King.

Judge Oscar Mitchell did as he was asked, and word of the Kennedy's intervention raced through the black community of America. Martin Luther King Sr., the crusty patriarch in Atlanta, had been a Lincoln Republican all his life, but now he threw his support to Kennedy. "I had expected to vote against Senator Kennedy because of his religion," said the elder King, a fervent Baptist. "But now he can be my President, Catholic or whatever he is. It took courage to call my daughter-in-law at a time like this. He has the moral courage to stand up for what he knows is right. I've got all my votes and I've got a suitcase, and I'm going to take them up there and dump them in his lap."

In private, Kennedy reacted to Daddy King's declaration with a mixture of irony and bemusement. "That was a hell of a bigoted statement," he told Harris Wofford, regarding King Sr.'s reference to Catholicism. "Imagine Martin Luther King having a bigot for a father. Well, we all have fathers, don't we?"

In public Kennedy said as little as possible. He and his brother, both acting spontaneously, had tried to do what they thought was right, and if the black community was happy about it, they were hoping white voters in the South wouldn't notice. Thus, when a reporter asked about his call to Mrs. King, Kennedy said simply, "She is a friend of mine and I was concerned about the situation."

Richard Nixon, meanwhile, said nothing. Despite his past support for civil rights, he thought that with silence he might carry the white vote in Georgia. But he did not.

On November 8, Kennedy won 68 percent of the African American vote, seven points more than Democratic nominee Adlai Stevenson had won in 1956. Anything less and Richard Nixon would have been the thirty-fifth President of the United States.

It soon became apparent that civil rights leaders, speaking on behalf of the black community, thought John Kennedy owed them a debt. The question was how he intended to pay it.

4

The Pill and Other Changes

The glamour and promise of presidential politics momentarily overshadowed other harbingers of change. But the implications were no less profound.

On May 9, the U.S. Food and Drug Administration approved the Pill. For more than a few American women, Margaret Sanger chief among them, this had been a lifelong dream. For fifty years she had waged her personal war against the multiple pregnancies that crippled women's lives—that was how she saw it. Her own mother had died at age forty-nine after being pregnant eighteen times and giving birth eleven. Margaret knew her father, Michael Higgins, was a decent man, an Irish stonecutter with progressive political sensibilities, a supporter of women's suffrage, among other causes. Her husband, an architect named William Sanger, was also a man with leftist inclinations, and Margaret absorbed some of those politics. Ultimately, however, it was her work as a nurse in the East Side slums of New York City that radicalized her. There she encountered among poor women the devastating effects of unwanted pregnancy—the miscarriages and self-induced abortions and the sheer and sometimes deadly exhaustion of too many births.

In the early years of the twentieth century, as she launched a movement for "birth control"—a term she had coined—she would tell the story of Sadie Sachs, who may have been a composite figure, but who represented for Sanger the degradations inflicted on women in the slums. Sanger recounted how she was called to Sadie's apartment and found her gravely ill after a self-induced abortion. Sadie begged her doctor for information about how she could avoid getting pregnant again. The male physician simply suggested that she abstain from sex. But Sadie and her husband did not abstain, and a few months later, Sanger was called to her apartment again. Sadie died before the doctor could get there.

"I threw my nursing bag in the corner," wrote Sanger, "and announced . . . that I would never take another case until I had made it possible for working women in America to have the knowledge to control birth."

In 1914, she launched a newsletter called *The Woman Rebel* in which she proclaimed that every woman should be "the absolute mistress of her own body." Not only was this a radical idea, it was also, astonishingly enough, against the law. Under the 1873 federal anti-obscenity statute named for U.S. Postal Inspector Anthony Comstock, any mention of contraception was by definition obscene. The whole idea, after all, involved contemplation of the sexual apparatus of a woman's body. Thus when Sanger began to distribute birth control information, she was indicted under the Comstock law and faced a minimum six months in jail.

Sanger jumped bail and set out for Europe, where the issues she was raising in America suddenly took on an added dimension. In England she met a physician and writer named Havelock Ellis, whose field of study was human sexuality. Though both were married, they became lovers, which added immediacy to Ellis's theory, then still controversial, that sex should be as pleasurable for women as for men. For Sanger, birth control now was more than simply a matter of health, of avoiding the rigors of unwanted pregnancy every time a woman had vaginal sex with her husband. Though never an advocate of promiscuity, Sanger came to believe that sex was a part of women's humanity, as indeed it was for men.

She also discovered the diaphragm. In 1915, she visited a birth control clinic in the Netherlands and became convinced that the device was more effective than suppositories, condoms, or the hopeful reliance on a man to withdraw.

Sanger soon began smuggling diaphragms into the United States, where they were still illegal. In this pursuit, she soon found an ally in a wealthy American named Katharine McCormick, whose husband Stanley was heir to the International Harvester fortune. Stanley was also mentally ill, a schizophrenic whose incapacitation left Katharine free to pursue her feminist passions. McCormick knew this was a critical time. The beginnings of the birth control movement overlapped with the final push for the Nineteenth Amendment, which finally gave women the right to vote.

When the amendment passed Congress in 1919 and was ratified in 1920, McCormick went to work with the League of Women Voters and made common cause with Sanger. In 1922 she sailed for London to attend the

Fifth Annual International Birth Control Conference, chaired by Sanger. Before she returned to the United States, McCormick purchased hundreds of diaphragms from manufacturers in Rome and Paris, and hired a team of French seamstresses to sew them into dresses she had bought by the dozens. She carried her contraband undetected through U.S. Customs and delivered it to Sanger's New York clinic.

The following summer, she secreted a thousand diaphragms in a shipment of cosmetics bound for Canada. There she arranged for liquor smugglers to get them into the United States, once again for delivery to Sanger.

Such was their mutual devotion to the cause.

Finally, in the early 1950s, the two set their sights even higher. For decades, Sanger had hoped for a "magic pill," something more reliable than the birth control methods she had already fought so hard to make available. Now, in the shadow of her seventieth birthday, she was determined to make that dream a reality. In 1951, at a dinner party in New York, she met Massachusetts biologist Gregory Pincus and broached the idea with him. To her surprise, Pincus was intrigued. Sanger arranged a small grant from the Planned Parenthood Federation of America, which she had served as founding president. Pincus and his colleague Min Chueh Chang began testing the notion that progesterone would inhibit ovulation. Their results were compelling. The hormone stopped ovulation completely in rabbits, and the question was whether it would work on humans.

In 1952, Pincus met with Harvard-trained obstetrician John Rock, who was already testing progesterone on patients having trouble with their menstrual cycles. They agreed to expand the tests with a specific focus on controlling ovulation. Rock seemed an unlikely partner in the project. A silver-haired and handsome New England patrician, he was a devout Roman Catholic who attended mass every day and knew his church opposed birth control. But he was also a doctor, and like Margaret Sanger in her early career, he had seen the devastating effects on women—particularly poor women—of the multiple pregnancies that ravaged their bodies and crippled their lives. Rock was certain that morality was on the side of contraception.

Soon, however, the search for a pill was running out of funds. On June 7, 1953, with Planned Parenthood refusing to offer more money (its initial grant was less than $4,000), Sanger and McCormick traveled to Shrewsbury, Massachusetts, to meet with Pincus at his Worchester Foundation for

Experimental Biology. After McCormick brusquely demanded a tour of the facility, Pincus was astonished when she wrote him a check on the spot for $20,000. Another check for the same amount arrived soon after, and Pincus, Chang, and Rock expanded their trials.

By 1957, they had secured approval from the Food and Drug Administration for a version of the pill called Enovid to be used by women with severe menstrual problems. In issuing that approval, the FDA warned that a major side effect of Enovid was the interruption of ovulation—an oblique acknowledgment that this was, in fact, a birth control pill. There was a sudden spike in the number of women reporting menstrual cramps, and in the number of doctors prescribing Enovid. But official approval of the pill for contraception would not come until 1960. For the FDA, this was new and delicate ground. The agency had never sanctioned a drug for people not sick, and the drug in question was controversial.

After two years' delay, John Rock set out in 1959 for Washington to try to speed things along. On a bitterly cold December day he boarded a train in Massachusetts, accompanied by Irwin Winter, the medical director for Searle & Co., the manufacturer of Enovid. Winter would later remember with wry amusement the curious indignity of the experience. After waiting for an hour and a half, he and Rock were eventually introduced to Pasquale DeFelice, a thirty-year-old FDA hearing officer who was not yet a board-certified physician. DeFelice sought to mask his own discomfort, and that of the FDA, by lecturing his visitors—first on moral objections to the Pill, and then, erroneously, on its link to cancer.

Rock could barely contain his fury.

"He wouldn't even refer to [DeFelice] by his name," remembered Winter. "Kept calling him 'young man.' He told that kid, 'I don't know how much training you've had treating women with cancer, but I have been treating patients my entire life and you have no idea how wrong you are.'"

The meeting ended on that note, but Searle & Co., understanding the stakes, kept up its pressure on the FDA. On May 4, 1960, the agency approved the Pill for contraception, and the country would never be the same.

LILLIAN SMITH HAD WRITTEN in *Killers of the Dream* of the lonely pedestal of American women, of the denial of healthy sexual expression that was, essentially, a denial of a woman's identity as a person. But now with the Pill, personhood had a powerful ally, and for many women there was joy in the moment.

"'It was marvelous," wrote Joan Baez of her discovery of sex at the age of eighteen. "We would crawl into his tiny bed and have our dreams, both private and shared, and have each other, like two small woodland animals hidden in a dry stump, safe in the night from dangers both real and imagined."

But of course there was often more to it, and jealousy became the curse of the times, the companion stalker of the new liberation. "Michael was my God," Baez wrote of her first lover, "and I didn't question him because I didn't want to lose him. But when I was showered with compliments and praise, he became wretched, blaming me for the disintegration of our relationship. In between fights, we made love. . . ."

It was a reality we all had to face, wrestling to redefine ourselves in relationship to one another. However, there was no turning back from the Pill, and its legacy was larger than the sexual revolution of which it quickly became a part. Journalist-historian Natalie Angier, writing in *Smithsonian* magazine, argued that the Pill was not an agent of promiscuity, but rather of stability in women's lives. "The successes of the feminist movement, and the mass entry of women into the workforce, the professions and academia, might never have been possible without the Pill's power of predictability," Angier wrote. "Far from fomenting recklessness, the pill proved a source of stability, allowing women and couples to shape their narrative arcs as they never had before."

THE SAME, UNFORTUNATELY, COULD not be said for another major piece of chemical research also taking place in New England. Few would argue looking back that the work of Timothy Leary would leave a legacy of personal responsibility. But Leary himself became a true believer, as he began, under the auspices of Harvard University, to study the effect of psychedelic drugs.

In 1960, as a single father of two emerging from the grief of his wife's suicide (Marianne Leary had grown despondent over the mutual infidelities of their marriage), Leary set off on a summer vacation to Mexico. He had finished year one of a three-year contract at Harvard, where he taught psychology, a field to which he may have been drawn because of personal demons of his own. Leary was the often unhappy son of an alcoholic father, and even before the death of his wife he freely admitted that he drank too much. By August 1960, however, he was increasingly drawn to metaphysics, a deeper, more mystical understanding of reality that he thought was available to the human mind.

He had read the works of William James, one of Harvard's most legendary scholars, whose textbook *The Principles of Psychology* was a cornerstone of the field. But Leary was more interested in *The Varieties of Religious Experience*, published by James in 1902 after the great psychologist had explored for himself the mind-bending qualities of nitrous oxide. "Our normal waking consciousness," James wrote, "rational consciousness as we call it, is but one special type of consciousness, whilst all about it, parted from it by the filmiest of screens, there lie potential forms of consciousness entirely different."

On August 9, Leary tried his own experiment with the mystic sensations James had described. On his vacation trip to Mexico, he and a small group of friends collected a handful of mushrooms from a woman who was known in the area as a shaman. These were psilocybin mushrooms, known by the Aztecs as "the flesh of the gods," and Leary ate seven, washing them down with an ice-cold beer.

In his book, *The Harvard Psychedelic Club*, author Don Lattin offers this account of what happened next:

> Everything was quivering with life, even inanimate objects. Leary saw Nile palaces, Hindu temples, Babylonian boudoirs, Bedouin pleasure tents. Then came silk gowns breathing color and mosaics of flaming emeralds, followed by jeweled Moorish serpents.
>
> Three hours passed in an instant . . .
>
> That's all it took. Leary was forced to confront the fragile nature of his beliefs. The mushroom ride shattered the foundation of his philosophy of life and his view of himself. What we call "reality" was just a social fabrication. He would later call his trip "the deepest religious experience of my life."

As soon as he returned from Mexico, Leary launched the Harvard Psilocybin Project, setting out to study, under the protective umbrella of a great university, the mystical effects of this psychedelic mushroom. He was joined in the effort by Richard Alpert, a Harvard faculty colleague, and Huston Smith, a religious scholar at the Massachusetts Institute of Technology. Their plan and methodology were simple. They would invite faculty and graduate students from the great universities in the Boston area to ingest controlled doses of psilocybin, the central ingredient in the Mexican mushrooms, and record their experiences.

The Leary experiment would last three years before Harvard officials finally shut it down, but the aftereffects swept through a whole generation. Leary emerged by self-proclamation as a kind of psychedelic evangelist, touting a new and outrageous gospel: "Turn on, tune in, drop out." It was heady stuff for many young Americans. But for others, Leary was merely one more symptom—one of the most disturbing, in fact—of a world that was spinning out of control.

A conservative movement against that spin also found its spokesman in 1960. Barry Goldwater was a U.S. Senator from Arizona who published that year a personal manifesto entitled *The Conscience of a Conservative*. For many, he quickly became a blunt and reassuring bulwark against the forces of change. But those who actually read his book saw implications that went much deeper. What Goldwater extolled in these one hundred and twenty-three pages was a fundamentally different understanding of government than the one practiced by Democrats from Franklin Roosevelt to John F. Kennedy, or for that matter, by Republicans such as Dwight Eisenhower.

Goldwater was a product of the American West, born in 1909, three years before his native Arizona became the nation's forty-eighth state. Though an Episcopalian, he was the grandson of Michel Goldwasser, a Jewish immigrant and pioneer who Americanized his name. Big Mike Goldwater, as he was known, came to Arizona amid the 1860s' hostility between white settlers and indigenous Navajos and Apaches.

"The Goldwaters helped build the State of Arizona," wrote journalist Theodore White, "not only as merchants (they developed the two best department stores in the state) but as fighters, school-board members, territorial legislators, citizens involved in every public affair . . ."

In 1960, Barry himself was widely regarded as a perfect descendant of pioneer stock—a tanned and vigorous man of fifty-one, six feet tall, a hundred and eighty-five pounds, with silver hair and dark-rimmed glasses, and an unblemished reputation for candor. He was popular among his Senate colleagues, including JFK, who enjoyed his company but thought his political views were absurd.

As a rugged individualist, Goldwater hated big government and saw the New Deal, and every government program it spawned, as the socialist folly of Roosevelt and those who followed in his path. He also mistrusted the federal courts and their recent rulings on civil rights, beginning with the *Brown* decision of 1954. He wrote,

> It so happens that I am in agreement with the objectives of the Supreme Court as stated in the *Brown* decision. I believe that it *is* both wise and just for negro (sic) children to attend the same schools as whites, and that to deny them this opportunity carries with it strong implications of inferiority. I am not prepared, however, to impose that judgment of mine on the people of Mississippi or South Carolina, or to tell them what methods should be adopted and what pace should be kept in striving toward that goal. That is their business, not mine. I believe that the problem of race relations, like all social and cultural problems, is best handled by the people directly concerned. Social and cultural change, however desirable, should not be effected by the engines of national power.

Thus did Goldwater help to define the great fault lines of the coming decade. He stood as a national defender of tradition and preached a gospel of limited government. But he also gave philosophical cover to a racism he did not share, a bigotry that would soon erupt into violence and stain the heart of the political right.

Goldwater was not alone in this. Indeed in September of that same year, a group of student conservatives, roughly one hundred strong, met in Sharon, Connecticut, at the home of *National Review* publisher William F. Buckley, to form a new organization called Young Americans for Freedom. They proclaimed their commitment to individual liberty, and like Goldwater, who would soon become their political champion, they intended to make their voices heard.

And finally, on December 5, 1960, in what seemed an afterthought to a momentous year, the U.S. Supreme Court issued a ruling in the case of *Boynton v. Virginia*. Only a few people paid attention at the time, for the case involved a fine of ten dollars.

Almost exactly two years earlier, a young law school student at Howard University was feeling homesick. Bruce Boynton was barely twenty-one when he boarded a Trailways bus from Washington, D.C., to Selma, Alabama, where his parents, Sam and Amelia, were the most outspoken black leaders. The Boyntons were proud of their family heritage. Amelia's great-uncle, Robert

Smalls, had been a Civil War hero—a slave who commandeered a Confederate ship in the Charleston harbor and turned it over to the Union Navy. After the war, Smalls became a five-time member of Congress, one of those leaders in the African American community who intended to take his place as a citizen, pursuing the interests of former slaves but also reconciliation between the white and black populations of the South. And when Southern whites rejected that notion and reasserted their power, using a combination of Ku Klux Klan terror and laws that stripped black people of the vote, Smalls issued a warning that rang through the intervening decades: "We do not intend to go anywhere," he admonished his white colleagues in Congress, "but will be right here."

Bruce Boynton said later he was thinking of that family history during the confrontation that occurred just before midnight on December 18, 1958, when his Trailways bus stopped in Richmond. The passengers were urged to get something to eat in a segregated bus station. When Boynton entered the terminal he saw "a clinically clean white restaurant and an absolutely filthy black café. I was really insulted," he said, "that someone would expect me to eat in the black restaurant in that kind of condition. I went over and sat in the white restaurant. Even though I did not expect to be served, I expected something like, 'It's not me. It's the law.' But the white waitress called the manager who put his finger in my face and said, 'Nigger, move.' That crystallized what I was going to do. I did not move."

Boynton was arrested and taken to jail, where he spent the weekend studying for his law school exams. On Monday morning he appeared in court and was ordered to pay a fine of ten dollars. Boynton appealed . . . and kept on appealing all the way to the U.S. Supreme Court. On December 5, 1960, Justice Hugo Black, a native Alabamian writing for the majority, ruled in Boynton's favor, declaring that not only were segregated buses illegal—something the court had ruled on before—but so were segregated bus *terminals*.

By the following spring the ruling would trigger the first great reality check of the decade. Most Americans did not see it coming. We were blinded instead by the promise.

5

Out With the Old

In January, Dwight D. Eisenhower was preparing for his final presidential speech. In terms of popularity, he'd had a good run. His campaign slogan was "We Like Ike," and the truth of it was that most Americans did. He was a reassuring presence in the White House—balding, avuncular, with the bland accents of his native Kansas—but he was also a war hero, a five-star general capable of the cold and steely calculations that helped bring victory in World War II. Though he preferred to focus on foreign affairs, his domestic legacy was undeniable. With money allocated for defense, he started the Interstate Highway System, ostensibly to increase mobility in case the country was ever invaded. But the mobility became an end in itself, a reality that changed American lives, shrinking vehicular travel times, and once the system was fully in place it was hard to imagine the country without it. He launched NASA, the National Aeronautics and Space Administration, and in the realm of civil rights he became more of an activist president than he ever expected to be.

In 1948, his predecessor, Harry S. Truman, had ordered the desegregation of the military, but when Eisenhower took office in 1953, the job was far from complete. Some of the military brass still argued against it, imploring one of their own—for that was how they still saw Eisenhower—to understand the realities of the task. Many military bases were in the South, where racial segregation was a way of life. But Eisenhower stood firm. "We have not taken and we shall not take a single backward step," he declared. "There must be no second class citizens in this country."

In 1953, he appointed Earl Warren, the Republican governor of California, to be Chief Justice of the U.S. Supreme Court, and over the next sixteen years the Warren Court handed down a series of landmark rulings that broadened the scope of civil liberties and civil rights. Eisenhower sometimes worried that things were moving too fast (a view not shared by African Americans), particularly after the 1954 *Brown* decision ordering an end to segregated schools. Three years later, when the governor of Arkansas defied that order, and when white mobs descended on Central High School in Little Rock on the day that desegregation began, Eisenhower reluctantly but resolutely sent troops to enforce the ruling.

All of this was a part of his legacy. But matters of war and peace in the world were on Eisenhower's mind as he prepared his final address. He was a man of middle-of-the-road instincts. He had ended the Korean War and refused to send troops in support of the French for their ill-fated war in Indo-China. But he also advanced the "domino theory," the fear of a Communist advance through Asia one country at a time, and this theory would become the heart of U.S. policy in Vietnam.

As a committed Cold Warrior determined to build a nuclear deterrent, Eisenhower nevertheless sought improved relations with the Soviet Union, and he was disappointed in 1960 by a sudden increase in tensions. That was the year that Francis Gary Powers, pilot of an American spy plane, was shot down over Soviet territory, resulting in the collapse of a four-nation summit. Meanwhile, presidential candidate Senator John F. Kennedy insisted that a "missile gap" had emerged between the United States and the Soviets, putting American security at risk. Eisenhower knew the claim was false. U.S. reconnaissance had made it clear that there was no gap, and, more to the point, each nation could blow the other to pieces many times over if either was insane enough to try. As president, Eisenhower understood all this. But he saw other dangers in a world defined by nuclear standoff, and in his final days in office, those were the issues he wanted to address.

On January 17, 1961, he took his seat before the television cameras, bespectacled, hands folded before him, and began to speak in a style that at first seemed colorless and bland. But he delivered, as the *Huffington Post* would put it on the fiftieth anniversary of the speech, "some of the bravest and most prescient words and thoughts ever uttered by an American president."

The address had been through twenty-one drafts. Eisenhower offered not a single boast about his own accomplishments, but rather a warning about the dangers ahead. He extolled the need for negotiation, not only between the two superpowers but among the smaller nations of the world:

> The weakest must come to the conference table with the same confidence as do we, protected as we are by our moral, economic and military strength. That table, though scarred by many past frustrations, cannot be abandoned for the certain agony of the battlefield.

He spoke about curbing the nuclear arms race:

> Because this need is so sharp and apparent I confess that I lay down my official responsibilities in this field with a definite sense of disappointment. As one who has witnessed the horror and the lingering sadness of war—as one who knows that another war could utterly destroy this civilization which has been so slowly and painfully built over thousands of years—I wish I could say tonight that a lasting peace is in sight.

And finally and most prophetically perhaps, he defined the multiple threats he perceived from a new reality in American life:

> Until the latest of our world conflicts, the United States had no armaments industry. American makers of plowshares could, with time and as required, make swords as well. But we can no longer risk emergency improvisation of national defense. We have been compelled to create a permanent armaments industry of vast proportions . . . This conjunction of an immense military establishment and a large arms industry is new in the American experience. The total influence—economic, political, even spiritual—is felt in every city, every State house, every office of the Federal government. We recognize the imperative need for this development. Yet we must not fail to comprehend its grave implications. Our toil, resources and livelihood are all involved; so is the very structure of our society. In the councils of government, we must guard against the acquisition of unwarranted influence, whether sought or unsought, by the military-industrial complex.

In the 1960s, as peace again gave way to war, Eisenhower's words resounded. Though many had no idea whom they were quoting, young activists often repeated his cautions against the "military-industrial complex." But in January 1961, the gravity of Eisenhower's warning was overshadowed by a national mood of celebration, as John F. Kennedy prepared to take the oath of office.

The morning of January 20 dawned clear and cold in Washington, D.C. Just before daylight the snow had stopped, but the city still shimmered in a dusting of white, as Kennedy prepared to deliver an address that he seemed to know, even then, might be the cornerstone of his legacy. He had never worked so hard on a speech. Even now, nobody knows the number of drafts that Kennedy went through with speechwriter Ted Sorensen, a man he had worked with for eight years and who had come to see himself as a vessel through whom Kennedy's thoughts and feelings could pour. In his book, *Ask Not,* an extended analysis of the Kennedy inaugural, author Thurston Clarke concludes that more than any speech of his career, this one was written by Kennedy himself. The most memorable phrases in it can be traced to the evening of January 10—9:15 p.m., to be precise—when Kennedy, on a flight from Washington to Palm Beach, began dictating to his secretary, Evelyn Lincoln. Like Eisenhower's a few days earlier, JFK's message was shaped by the perils of life in a Cold War world. But as Kennedy began to speak on the eastern steps of the U.S. Capitol, the effect was wholly different:

> Let the word go forth from this time and place, to friend and foe alike, that the torch has been passed to a new generation of Americans—born in this century, tempered by war, disciplined by a hard and bitter peace, proud of our ancient heritage—and unwilling to witness or permit the slow undoing of those human rights to which this Nation has always been committed, and to which we are committed today at home and around the world.

I remember watching in my ninth-grade class, mesmerized by the language and the flickering image on the screen, Kennedy so handsome and confident and calm, his face so tan, his eyes pale blue (somehow you knew those had to be the colors, even on a black-and-white television set), and still the steady stream of the words:

> Let every nation know, whether it wishes us well or ill, that we shall pay any price, bear any burden, meet any hardship, support any friend, oppose any foe, in order to assure the survival and success of liberty.

Looking back now more than fifty years later, we can see future dangers in those words, the assumptions of power and responsibility and burden that were part of the World War II generation, those triumphant warriors against the forces of evil. Kennedy was one of them, of course—not only a veteran, but also a hero, the commander of PT-109, a small torpedo boat cut in two by a Japanese destroyer on August 2, 1943. Eleven of Kennedy's crew survived by clinging to a timber beam from the boat and swimming four hours to a tiny island. With a life jacket clenched between his teeth, Kennedy helped tow the others to shore, where they lived six days on coconuts before rescuers finally arrived.

This was Kennedy's experience with war—bravery, sacrifice, patriotic resolve, rewarded in the end by a moment of triumph. But as we listened to him in 1961, he, like his predecessor, sounded less like a warrior than a man of peace, searching for justice in a dangerous world:

> Let both sides unite to heed in all corners of the earth the command of Isaiah—to "undo the heavy burdens . . . and to let the oppressed go free." And if a beachhead of cooperation may push back the jungles of suspicion, let both sides join in creating a new endeavor, not a new balance of power, but a new world of law, where the strong are just and the weak secure and the peace preserved. All this will not be finished in the first 100 days. Nor will it be finished in the first 1,000 days, nor in the life of this Administration, nor even perhaps in our lifetime on this planet. But let us begin.

Even before the speech was finished, I remember glancing at my teacher. I no longer recall her name, but I remember that she was young and pretty, and I remember the tear that rolled down her face. "I just love things like this," she whispered, but not too loud, for there was more to come from the television screen:

> And so, my fellow Americans, ask not what your country can do for you—ask what you can do for your country . . . With good conscience our only sure reward, with history the final judge of our deeds, let us go forth to lead the land we love, asking His blessing and His help, but knowing that here on earth God's work must truly be our own.

Nancy Pelosi, future Speaker of the U.S. House of Representatives, was a girl of nineteen, a Congressman's daughter who was there in the crowd, and she never before or since heard political speech quite like it. "His words were so . . . I want to say, otherworldly," she explained. "He was so enhanced as a person. Here was this lovely, young, brilliant, talented, politically astute person who was now the president of the United States. He was speaking for the ages. It was spectacular."

Pope Paul VI, then still a cardinal, listened to the speech on radio and reread it many times through the years, and historians including Thurston Clarke have concluded that the pope drew upon it for his 1967 encyclical on the issues of poverty and social justice. Even Barry Goldwater, the cantankerous Republican who was Kennedy's opposite number in politics, was heard to declare: "God, I'd like to be able to do what that boy did there."

But there was also this. We would learn much later that even in the midst of the celebration, amid the inaugural galas and dinners and balls—after Jacqueline Kennedy, his beautiful wife, had whispered in his ear, "Oh, Jack, what a day!"—Kennedy still managed to slip away for one or more of the sexual dalliances that had come to define his private life. He may have been a good father, even a good husband in other ways, but his reckless, predatory sexuality was something he made no effort to control. In *The Kennedy Half Century,* Larry Sabato notes that one of his inaugural conquests was Angie Dickinson, an actress best known for her roles in more than fifty films, including *Ocean's Eleven* and *The Sins of Rachel Cade*. Later, Dickinson affirmed with an irony not entirely complimentary to the president that sex with Kennedy was "the most memorable fifteen seconds of my life."

All of that was a part of who he was. But if Kennedy touched the earth in private, his public ideals offered hope and purpose and began giving shape to the 1960s, as he and the bright young men around him added flesh to his words. The new president had been thinking for a while about combatting the image of "the ugly American," a national reputation for condescension and arrogance that he knew was rooted partly in the truth. The previous year Kennedy had read a novel with that title, co-written by William Lederer and Eugene Burdick, and had been so impressed that he bought copies for all ninety-nine of his Senate colleagues. Already, the impact of *The Ugly American* had been compared to *Uncle Tom's Cabin,* or perhaps *The Jungle* by Upton Sinclair, in its ability to touch the conscience of the country.

Burdick and Lederer told the story of diplomats in Southeast Asia whose persistent bungling arose ironically from their sense of American superiority.

These characters, based on people the authors had known, showed no interest in the language, culture, or even the people in the region they had been sent to serve. As a candidate in 1960, Kennedy had begun to talk about policies based on the opposite, on a generosity and cultural understanding that he thought were America at its best. To Kennedy this was simply the right thing to do, the right way to think about the rest of the world, particularly the places where people were poor and fighting for their freedom against the colonial powers of Europe. But in Kennedy's mind more was at stake than simple morality. There was the added urgency of Cold War competition—the United States with its legacy of freedom versus the remorseless march of Soviet communism.

"We will bury you!" Nikita Khrushchev had proclaimed, and his malevolent confidence haunted American dreams and fears.

Part of Kennedy's strategy, which began to take shape in the earliest days of his Administration, included his March 1961 announcement of Alliance for Progress, a $20 billion U.S. investment in Latin America, aimed at stimulating growth, eliminating adult illiteracy, supporting democracy, and working toward a redistribution of land. Over the following decade, the program drew mixed reviews, but in the beginning it was part of the surge of idealism that defined the Kennedy presidential honeymoon.

More significant still was the Peace Corps. On March 1, Kennedy issued Executive Order 10924, creating an agency to recruit young Americans for peaceful service overseas. It was an idea he had first proposed the previous October during a late-night campaign speech at the University of Michigan. Today, a bronze plaque marks the spot where Kennedy gave voice to what became a cornerstone of his legacy. Thousands of young Americans—already stirred by his inaugural address, especially the second half of its most famous line: "Ask what you can do for your country"—rushed to volunteer in the Corps' early days, which initially included pilot projects in two countries. The first was Tanganyika, the heart of what soon became the African nation of Tanzania. In 1961, when the initial Peace Corps workers arrived, it was still a territory working toward freedom from British rule. Amid the chaotic crumbling of colonialism, Kennedy wanted America to be there, winning hearts and minds, and he could think of no better representatives than young people stirred by an eagerness to serve. Not everyone shared that leap of faith. Richard Nixon, always a man of darker instincts, predicted glumly that the Peace Corps would be "a haven for draft dodgers." But Kennedy was convinced that—first in Africa, and then in Colombia, the second Peace Corps target—the volunteers were among the brightest of their generation.

His choice to lead the agency was his brother-in-law, Sargent Shriver, a man known in the family for his genuine concern for people on the margins. It was Shriver who had prevailed most directly upon Kennedy to call Coretta King when her husband was imprisoned the previous fall. So Shriver set out to lead the two pilot projects and to bring the Peace Corps idea to Congress later in the year, seeking full approval and funding.

Meanwhile, another New Frontier presided over by the brand new president was, if anything, even more gripping to those of us who were seeing science fiction come to life before our eyes. America was engaged in a two-nation space race. Already, unmanned satellites were circling the globe, some launched by the United States, some by the Soviet Union, and early in 1961 we knew that human beings were next. NASA had selected seven astronauts, and even before any had left the ground, they were heroes in a class by themselves.

We marveled at their willingness to risk their lives, perched atop a giant rocket ship that smoldered with the fury of liquid oxygen. That was the fuel with the necessary power to blast them free of gravity, which heretofore had shackled every human being to earth. And we had seen what happened when things went wrong. So often (more for us, it seemed, than the Soviets) the early rocket ships blew up during launch, and as Project Mercury proceeded we were gripped with horror that the same fate awaited an astronaut.

Writing almost two decades later in *The Right Stuff*, author Tom Wolfe told, with trademark irony, of a Congressional hearing for the astronauts during the buildup toward the first flight:

> There was something gloriously goofy about it. The congressmen in the room just wanted to see them, to use their position to arrange a personal audience, to gaze upon them with their own eyes across the committee table, no more than four feet away, to shake hands with them, occupy the same space on this earth with them for an hour or so, fawn over them, pay homage to them, bathe in their magical aura, feel the radiation of their righteous stuff, salute them, wish upon them the smile of God . . . and to do their bit in bestowing honor upon them *before the fact* . . . upon our little Davids . . . before they got up

on top of the rockets to face the Russians, death, flames, and fragmentation. *(Ours all blow up!)*

And then came a curious piece of news—NASA planned to send up a chimpanzee first to see what hazards humans might encounter. They chose a mild-mannered three-year-old named Ham, and on January 31, they put him into a capsule that was essentially identical to the one that would carry Alan Shepard, the astronaut chosen to go first. Shepard was not happy about it. As a Navy test pilot whose cool under pressure had carried him to the top of his profession, he worried that the test flight with an ape, which inevitably delayed Shepard's own mission, might well cost him a place in history as the first human being to travel into space. He knew the Soviets were working toward the same goal and he could only hope Ham's mission went well.

As for Ham, he had been well trained. First at Holloman Air Force Base in New Mexico, and then at Cape Canaveral in Florida, he spent nineteen months in 1959–60 under the tutelage of Army medic Edward Dittmer, a combat veteran of World War II, forty-two years old, with rimless glasses and a reputation for kindness toward the six little apes assigned to his care. Ham was always one of his favorites. "I know he liked me," Dittmer remembered. "I'd hold him and he was just like a little kid. He'd put his arm around me and he'd play." But all was not fun and games. First Ham had to learn to sit still, not an easy thing for a baby chimp, and he soon graduated to buttons and levers, rewarded with banana pellets when he pushed the right ones and with mild electric shocks when he didn't. Like human astronauts, he trained on a centrifuge, learning to endure the sudden G-forces that would come when his rocket blasted into space.

By January 31, 1961, he seemed ready. After his breakfast of baby cereal, condensed milk, half an egg, cooking oil, and gelatin, Ham offered no resistance when Dittmer strapped him into the capsule. For the next five hours, as mechanical problems and iffy weather delayed the launch, his vital signs stayed steady and strong.

Finally, at 11:55 a.m., the Redstone rocket roared beneath him, fire spewing from its tail, and as it began its powerful ascent, Ham, true to his training, began pushing levers, banana pellets tumbling out in reward. But the rocket was burning fuel too fast, and its retrorockets, intended to slow his descent, fired too soon, creating an extra 52,000 pounds of thrust—seventeen times the force of gravity bearing down on Ham's little body. It was hard now to push the buttons and levers, and when he didn't, his distress was compounded by the electric shocks he had learned to fear and loathe in training. He found his left hand faster than his right, and resumed his duties, pushing the buttons as banana pellets once again began to flow. There was a reprieve from gravity when he made it briefly, mercifully to space, and his capsule separated from the rocket and reached its peak 157 miles from earth. On the ground, the mission team knew he had traveled forty-two miles too high, and now he had no retrorockets to slow his descent. If he made it back at all he would miss his landing area in the ocean—the place where the Navy ships were waiting.

Ham did make it back. At ten thousand feet the parachute on his capsule deployed, and sixteen minutes, thirty-nine seconds after liftoff, Ham splashed down in the Atlantic. But he was 130 miles from the recovery ships, as Navy planes searched frantically to find him. An hour passed. Two hours. The capsule bobbed and began to leak, taking on eight hundred pounds of water and listing perilously to the side. Finally, after nearly three hours, a search plane spotted the capsule and a Navy helicopter plucked it from the sea.

On the deck of the *LSD Donner*, crewmen opened the capsule's hatch and there was the chimp, arms folded, waiting to be set free. He took the apple a crew member offered, and began to eat it, and a few minutes later he bared his teeth at the press corps waiting on the ship. The press reported that Ham had smiled, a furry little trooper to the end.

Remarkably, Ham seemed to be fine. He had a bruise on his nose, sustained apparently during reentry, but upon his return to Cape Canaveral, he rushed to Dittmer's arms, and the two played together for a while before a barrage of medical testing confirmed the obvious. Ham had emerged from space unharmed, paving the way for human primates to follow.

Ham was a media hero for a few days, his picture splashed on television screens and magazine covers and newspaper pages nationwide. But soon enough the frenzy subsided and Ham was shipped to the Washington National Zoo, where he lived for seventeen years in a cage. Solitary confinement, as it were. In 1969, Jane Goodall's book, *My Friends, the Wild Chimpanzees*, raised what was then a radical notion: "It isn't only human beings who have personality, who are capable of rational thought [and] emotions like joy and sorrow." Meanwhile, Ham the space chimp languished in boredom for another decade.

Finally, for the last three years of his life he was moved to a natural habitat zoo where at last he was permitted to live as a chimpanzee. When he died of liver failure in 1983, a female chimp named Maggie, his new best friend, was by his side, holding his hand.

But all of that was far in the future. Meanwhile, back among the humans, Alan Shepard was beside himself. He was hoping mightily that his own flight would occur in March, thus increasing the chances that as standard-bearer for the United States, he would beat the Russians into space. Shepard was a patriotic man who saw the race as kind of an Olympic competition—a peaceful metaphor for a more ominous contest, for the same rocketry that opened humanity's window into space could now deliver weapons of mass destruction that would dwarf Hiroshima. And the only way to keep the peace, so the Cold War thinking went, was never to fall behind lest the other side be tempted to strike first. In this chilling context of the world living on the edge of destruction, but trying to avoid it by building more weapons, the space race became more urgent. But now the rumors filtered down from Washington that people high in the Kennedy Administration were thinking maybe we should send another chimp. It was true that Ham had proved beyond doubt that an astronaut could survive in space, assuming everything went well. But what if it didn't? What if the glitches of January 31—the retrorockets firing too soon, a capsule lost at sea and about to sink—what if those things were worse this time and a human astronaut was killed? Beyond a concern for Shepard himself, what a terrible blow this would be for the country!

Such was the tenor of the debate until finally the word came down that Alan Shepard would fly in May—no chimp mission to slow things down, but a little more time for the NASA engineers to work out the bugs. And then it happened. On April 12, Russian cosmonaut Yuri Gagarin blasted into space and circled the earth, landing safely on solid ground. Oddly, Gagarin was chosen for his history-making flight partly because he was short—only five-foot-two—and thus fit more comfortably into the capsule. But he was also a man of extraordinary character. As one of his official evaluations put it, Gagarin "distinguishes himself from his colleagues by his sharp and far-ranging sense of attention to his surroundings; a well-developed imagination; quick reactions; persevering, prepares himself painstakingly for his activities and training exercises, handles celestial mechanics and mathematical formulae with ease as well as excels in higher mathematics; does not feel constrained when he has to defend his point of view if he considers himself right; appears that he understands life better than a lot of his friends."

I remember even now the grudging admiration many of us felt, certainly my teenaged friends and I, toward this brave young pilot who had accomplished such an extraordinary feat. But it was also a moment of gloom. Once again the Russians had won. In fact, they had circled the earth, while Shepard's flight would be, like Ham's, only a parabolic lob, a consolation prize for the American team. But at least it was something, and excitement mounted as the date grew near. On the morning of May 5, with the nation watching on live TV, a Redstone rocket roared again and Alan Shepard hurtled into space. The flight went off without a hitch, its trajectory calculated by one of the unsung heroes of the space program, Dr. Katherine Johnson, an African American mathematician who would later work on orbital missions and flights to the Moon. Now, on Shepard's historic first flight, the capsule soared, the retrorockets fired on cue, and the splashdown happened exactly as it should. Shepard emerged with a confident smile, and the parades of celebration began.

As the nation cheered for Alan Shepard—and for itself, even though we had come in second in a two-nation race—President Kennedy did a remarkable thing. He decided to raise the stakes. On May 25, speaking before a joint session of Congress, he turned our subliminal disappointment on its head, proclaiming in a clear and confident voice: "I believe that this nation should commit itself to achieving the goal, before this decade is out, of landing a man on the Moon and returning him safely to earth."

Again, it seemed, he was pushing the country, raising our sights, testing the limits of our national greatness, and we loved him for it. But Kennedy knew also that our greatness was already under siege, facing a wholly different kind of test. Presidents are the ultimate multitaskers, and even as he spoke about reaching for the Moon, Kennedy understood that his presidential honeymoon was over.

6

Reality Check

They called themselves the Freedom Riders. Initially there were thirteen of them, seven black, six white, setting out together on a perilous journey. As representatives of the Congress of Racial Equality (CORE), a civil rights group founded in 1942, their plan was to board two buses in mixed racial groups and travel through the South. CORE had co-sponsored, along with the Fellowship of Reconciliation, a similar expedition in 1947. On both occasions, the organizers knew this was not even civil disobedience. Now in 1961, they merely intended to test the Supreme Court ruling in *Boynton v. Virginia*, handed down the previous December, banning segregation in interstate travel.

"The plan was simplicity itself," recalled Stokely Carmichael, who would join a second wave of the Freedom Rides and would be so embittered by the experience that he lost faith in nonviolence as a civil rights tactic. "In any sane, even half-civilized society it would have been completely innocuous, hardly worth a second thought or meriting any comment at all. CORE would be sending an integrated team—*black and white together*—from the nation's capital to New Orleans on public transportation. That's all. Except, of course, that they would sit randomly on the buses in integrated pairs and in the stations they would use waiting room facilities casually, ignoring the white/colored signs. What could be more harmless . . . in any even marginally healthy society."

But this was America in 1961, and the riders were headed for the belly of the beast. They left Washington on May 4, intending to travel south through Virginia and the Carolinas, then into Georgia with a stop in Atlanta, and finally through Alabama, Mississippi, and Louisiana. As Carmichael said, it sounded simple enough. But the night before the odyssey began, Simeon Booker, a respected African American journalist who would ride with the group, met privately with U.S. Attorney General Robert Kennedy. Booker tried to explain to Kennedy that this indeed would be a dangerous mission, particularly when the riders came to Alabama and Mississippi. Kennedy, however, didn't seem to get it, and Booker was left to wonder, especially in the bloody days that followed, if innocence or indifference lay at the heart of the attorney general's blindness.

"I wish I could go with you," Kennedy offered pleasantly. He told Booker to "call" if there was a problem.

The truth was the Kennedy Administration had its mind on other things. Less than three weeks earlier President Kennedy had made what he thought was the worst mistake of his career on the public stage. On April 17, with Kennedy's approval, a band of 1,400 Cuban exiles, trained and funded by the CIA, landed at the Bay of Pigs in Cuba, intending to overthrow Fidel Castro. Their failure was bloody, swift, and complete, rooted in assumptions by the CIA that proved wildly off the mark. The first was that the assault by the anti-Castro brigade would trigger uprisings among Cubans dissatisfied with Fidel. It did not. The second assumption, more flawed than the first, was that once fighting began at the Bay of Pigs, President Kennedy would change his mind and authorize American air strikes and perhaps the deployment of U.S. troops. But Kennedy did not. Even as the mission began to go badly, he held fast to what he had said from the start; only Cubans would fight in Cuba. He simply was not willing this early in his term to order American troops to Cuban soil.

When the mission collapsed, the press began using the word "debacle," and Kennedy understood immediately that his own decisions contained bitter lessons in how not to exercise power. Harvard historian and Kennedy special adviser Arthur Schlesinger was deeply immersed in the Bay of Pigs planning. Later, in *A Thousand Days*, he wrote extensively about what went wrong. In the cabinet-level discussions leading up to the invasion, Schlesinger noted that the opponents, including himself, were vastly outnumbered. He praised the valiant efforts of U.S. Senator J. William Fulbright, chairman of the Senate Foreign Relations Committee, who made a powerful case against the operation. Fulbright conceded Fidel Castro's embrace of communism—would he be a Russian puppet ninety miles from America?—was a problem for U.S. diplomacy. But the invasion, he thought, was a bigger problem, a resurrection of the image of the ugly American, our reputation as a hemispheric bully, just as Kennedy was seeking to offer something new. Against such considerations,

Fulbright concluded, "the Castro regime is a thorn in the flesh; but it is not a dagger to the heart."

In the end, however, the operation had too much inertia, nearly two years of planning going back to the Eisenhower Administration at a cost of nearly $13 million. But perhaps the most important factor—the irresistible force for John F. Kennedy, who had been president for only seventy-seven days—was explained this way by Arthur Schlesinger: ". . . the advocates of the adventure had a rhetorical advantage. They could strike virile poses and talk of tangible things—firepower, air strikes, landing craft and so on. To oppose the plan, one had to invoke intangibles—the moral position of the United States, the reputation of the President, the response of the United Nations, 'world public opinion' and other such odious concepts."

Thus did Kennedy succumb in his early presidency to the bane of American foreign policy from World War II to the present—the belief that our *might* and *right* were deeply meshed and thus could be imposed at will upon the lesser nations of the world. But in this case Kennedy recognized the disaster and manfully set out to lessen the cost. He invited the political leaders of the anti-Castro resistance—those not on the beaches at the Bay of Pigs—to meet with him at the White House. He knew already that they were filled with rage and a sense of betrayal. They had been assured by the CIA that the United States would provide whatever it took—air support, troops on the ground—to make certain the invasion did not fail. American prestige demanded no less.

"But what is prestige?" Kennedy had said to his advisers. "Is it the shadow of power or the substance of power? We are going to work on the substance . . ."

Now, to the Cubans seated before him, he said he was sorry for what had happened. He explained his reasons for refusing to commit American troops ("the future of Cuba must be determined by Cubans") and his reasons for believing the mission might succeed. As he spoke he was sitting, legs crossed, in a rocking chair in his office, looking drawn and tired but, as Schlesinger wrote, persuasively in command as he continued to explain that he, too, had seen brave men die for their country—had lost a brother, in fact, in one of the battles of World War II—and thus he shared their "grief and despair."

"So many regrets," Arthur Schlesinger wrote, "must have flowed through his mind during those bitter hours—the advice so authoritatively rendered and so respectfully accepted, the unexamined assumptions and the misconceived plans, the blow to the bright hopes of the new administration, the problems at home and abroad; but most of all, I think, it was the vision of the men on the beaches, who had gone off with such splendid expectations, who had fought so bravely and who now would be shot down like dogs or carted off to Castro's prisons."

To the country Kennedy announced that responsibility for the misadventure was his alone, and added with a wry aside that was one of his trademarks, "There's an old saying that victory has a thousand fathers and defeat is an orphan."

I remember my own father's reaction as he listened to the news on the radio. "This is a *man*," he said, with a catch in his voice as he heard the president accept full blame. Such was Kennedy's grace in the moment that Americans overwhelmingly forgave him. By the end of April, his approval ratings soared to 80 percent.

BUT THEN CAME THE Freedom Rides. "Tell them to call it off," Kennedy told Harris Wofford, his special assistant for civil rights. Wofford understood that as the rides were beginning in early May, Kennedy was in the throes of repairing the Bay of Pigs damage. The president, in addition, was preparing for a June summit with Nikita Khrushchev, and the last thing he needed was another round of bad press. But Wofford was astonished. Did Kennedy really think that it was as simple as that? Did he really believe that the civil rights movement, which had gained such momentum with the recent sit-ins, would bend its agenda to presidential convenience? Wofford told Kennedy as gently as he could that the Freedom Rides could not be stopped.

Indeed, the journey had already begun. The riders had made it mostly unscathed to Atlanta (there had been a minor skirmish and two arrests in South Carolina), but when they gathered for dinner with Martin Luther King, the mood was mixed. King was gracious and full of praise, but also deeply concerned for their safety. "You'll never make it through Alabama," he told Simeon Booker, the black reporter traveling with the group. Though Booker tried to laugh it off, he thought King might be right.

The following day the Greyhound bus came to Anniston, Alabama, a hill country town a few miles west of the Georgia line. As the bus pulled into the station, a mob was waiting—Klansmen mostly, armed with metal pipes, brass knuckles, and baseball bats. There were fifteen people on the bus—the driver, seven freedom riders, two journalists, two undercover policemen sent by Alabama's director of public safety, and three petrified passengers. They saw the mob surge toward the bus, screaming threats and racial slurs, like some great howling beast, one witness thought, closing in for the kill. Undercover officer E. L. Cowling rushed to the front of the bus and somehow managed to hold the door closed, as the Klansmen tried to clamber on board. Frustrated, the attackers turned their fury on the bus itself, breaking windows, slashing tires, beating the sides with their baseball bats.

The driver tried to flee the station, but an armada of Klansmen gave chase in their cars. Six miles later the tires on the bus went flat and the Greyhound lurched to a stop. An attacker threw a firebomb through a broken window, the seats caught fire, and acrid smoke filled the bus, making it nearly impossible to breathe. As the freedom riders tried frantically to escape, the Klansmen blocked the door, some of them screaming, "burn them alive! . . . fry the goddam niggers!"

Only the cool of Officer Cowling enabled the passengers to survive. Cowling grabbed his gun and rushed to the front of the bus, where he pried open the door and held the mob at bay with his weapon. Other Highway Patrolmen soon arrived and fired warning shots into the air as the riders lay choking and gasping in the grass.

Janie Miller, a twelve-year-old white girl, lived nearby. Ignoring the taunts of the Ku Kluxers, she brought water to the wounded riders, filling and refilling her five-gallon bucket. For this simple act she and her family would be hounded out of Anniston, but on this day her kindness meant as much as the cooling water in the comfort it brought to those who were injured.

Finally an ambulance arrived and the driver was eventually persuaded to carry black riders as well as white to the Anniston hospital. But a mob soon gathered there as well, and once again these civil rights pilgrims were in fear for their lives. Sixty miles away in Birmingham, the Reverend Fred Shuttlesworth got word of their plight. Shuttlesworth, Birmingham's most fiery civil rights leader, called together some of his most fearless followers, including a union organizer named Colonel Stone Johnson, and sent them roaring down the highway in eight cars to rescue the riders. Despite Shuttlesworth's reminder that this was a nonviolent mission, the rescue team went armed that day, and upon reaching Anniston in less than an hour they marched grimly past the astonished Klansmen who still surrounded the Anniston hospital.

"We walked right through those Ku Klux," remembered Johnson. "Some of them had clubs. There were some deputies, too. You couldn't tell the deputies from the Ku Klux."

They gathered up the terrified freedom riders, and the convoy immediately rushed back to Birmingham where the activists were taken to places of safety. But the drama and the bloodshed were not over. When the Trailways bus carrying the second group of riders pulled into the Birmingham station, a different mob of Klansmen was waiting. Incredibly, the Kluxers had been informed by the Birmingham police that they would have fifteen minutes to inflict whatever harm they could, a fact that had been relayed to the FBI by Klan informant Gary Thomas Rowe. But the Trailways riders knew nothing of this. All they could do was stare with uncertain terror at the hatred they saw in the faces of the crowd, and try to brace for the coming attack.

Then it began.

"The riders were being dragged from the bus into the station," remembered journalist Howard K. Smith, who was there on assignment for CBS. "In a corridor I entered they were being beaten with bicycle chains and blackjacks and steel knucks. When they fell they were kicked mercilessly, the scrotum being the favored target, and pounded with baseball bats. One man made his way to the waiting room still vertical, but his head was a red mass of blood. Another was on all fours and could not get up."

The following morning, all across the country, newspapers carried the horrifying photos of the burning bus in Anniston and the Birmingham attacks. One of the people most disturbed by the news was Robert Kennedy. This was exactly what his brother, the President, didn't need, a self-inflicted taint on the image of America so soon after the Bay of Pigs. But more than that, the whole episode was beginning to offend his fierce and fundamental sense of justice. Such a savage attack on people who were simply riding on a bus! The Attorney General immediately sent his special assistant and close friend, John Seigenthaler, a Southerner, to Birmingham where the traumatized riders were trying to find a way out of town.

Seigenthaler discovered them huddled at the Birmingham airport. Both bus companies, Greyhound and Trailways, had refused to let them ride any further, and their plan now was to get on a plane and fly to New Orleans and put the whole adventure behind them. But Delta Airlines was refusing to fly. There had been a bomb threat, and while the airline officials were debating what to do, another crowd of Klansmen had gathered at the airport. Seigenthaler could see that time was running out.

"I went to the people at Delta," he remembered, "and told them, 'This is what we want to do. Look through the baggage, make sure there is no bomb, and then don't take any more calls until the plane is in the air.'"

The Delta representatives did as he asked, and Seigenthaler flew with the riders to New Orleans, where they were greeted by a group of supporters and friends. Shell-shocked and tired, still nursing their physical injuries, they had, nevertheless, made it out of Alabama alive.

Seigenthaler went to bed happy that night. He remembered thinking to himself, "well done, young man," for he was still in his thirties and proud to be part of the Kennedy team, proud to play a role at such an epic moment in history. But as he was thinking such thoughts and drifting slowly off to sleep, the telephone rang. It was 2 a.m. and Robert Kennedy was on the line.

"John," he said, "this isn't over. Do you know a woman named Diane Nash?"

In fact, Seigenthaler did. He had been a newspaper reporter in Nashville while Nash was a leader in the sit-in movement there. Now, Kennedy said, there were credible rumors that Nash and other sit-in veterans were planning a second round of freedom rides. This the nation could not stand. *Talk her out of it,* Kennedy demanded.

Seigenthaler tried. But Nash and the others would not be dissuaded.

"Mr. Seigenthaler," she said, "you are a good man, but we are not going to going to be moved. This has to end. We will not let violence overcome nonviolence."

For Seigenthaler, the irony of the moment came quickly into focus. People like himself and the Kennedys, who moved so comfortably in the corridors of power, were no longer in control. A new generation of civil rights leaders, some barely in their twenties, were setting the political agenda for the country.

DIANE NASH AND HER friends in Nashville felt compassion for the freedom riders. They had been traumatized, battered and bruised, and perhaps it was true that they needed a rest. But to Nash and the others, the end of the rides in Birmingham was a total disaster. The mobs had won. That was how it appeared, but Nash, John Lewis, and all the other young leaders of SNCC refused to leave it at that. The Freedom Rides would continue, they decided, for they themselves would pick up the torch.

Their audacity was difficult for even some of their allies to grasp. Fred Shuttlesworth reminded them firmly that the riders in Anniston had barely escaped being burned alive, and there was no reason whatsoever to believe that the Ku Klux Klan, having tasted blood, would not be more efficient next time. *People could die*, Shuttlesworth warned. Indeed, many of the young SNCC activists in Nashville, as they prepared to resume the Freedom Rides under the leadership of Nash and Lewis, solemnly wrote out their wills.

As they gathered in Birmingham, John Seigenthaler, knowing the perils that lay before them, rushed to Montgomery to meet with Alabama's segregationist governor, John Patterson. He had been told that on many issues Patterson was actually a moderate man. He had been the first Southern governor to endorse John Kennedy for president. But Seigenthaler was wary, for he had seen the governor in the previous days proclaiming on the television news, "We can't act as nursemaids to agitators." Patterson seemed so smug, facing the camera with a flower in his lapel and a look of menace on his face, offering a tacit approval of violence: "You can't guarantee the safety of a fool."

"You would watch him on TV," Seigenthaler remembered, "saying the things he said with that carnation in his buttonhole. You think to yourself, 'what an asshole.'"

But when the meeting began, Seigenthaler was surprised. Patterson seemed a man of substance, just as Robert Kennedy had said, not an advocate of violence but a politician resigned to its inevitability once the people of his state were provoked. "We can't protect them," he told Seigenthaler. Turning to his Director of Public Safety, Floyd Mann, he added, "Tell him, Floyd."

Abruptly, the conversation took an unexpected turn. Mann, who would soon emerge as one of the heroes in the story, was a slow-talking native of Alexander City, Alabama, a former B-17 tail-gunner who had served with distinction in World War II. In private, he was known for his sense of humor, even as a practical joker at times, but he was also a serious law enforcement professional, a man dedicated to his job.

"Governor," he said, "you tell me to protect them, and I will protect them."

Seigenthaler glanced quickly at Patterson. "What I expected to see," he remembered, "was a look that said, 'the son of a bitch has betrayed me.' I didn't get that at all. What I got was puzzlement."

Reluctantly, perhaps, the governor agreed to let Mann try, and soon the freedom riders were on a bus from Birmingham with Highway Patrol cars in front and behind and others waiting at intervals along the way. A helicopter followed overhead, and everything was quiet as the Greyhound reached the Montgomery city limits. There, the Montgomery police had promised to take over. "You can count on us," the city's police commissioner had told Floyd Mann. "We'll maintain order." As the bus approached the station, however, the city policemen melted away, leaving at first an eerie silence—to a person, that was how the freedom riders described it—followed abruptly by the roar of a mob.

Suddenly, it was Birmingham all over again—a swarm of Klansmen given carte blanche, and inflicting more serious harm. As John Lewis stepped from the bus he was knocked to the ground by a wooden crate. Jim Zwerg, who seemed to draw special wrath because he was white, knelt to pray and a Klansman broke his back with a kick. William Barbee was thrown to the pavement, and a white man stood with a boot to his throat and jammed a metal pipe in his ear. Even Seigenthaler was left unconscious with a fractured skull when he tried to rescue three of the riders.

It would have been worse if not for Floyd Mann. He didn't trust Montgomery police commissioner L. B. Sullivan and went to the station himself to check on the situation. He arrived just after the carnage began and waded immediately into the fray. "There'll be no killing here today," he declared as he fired two warning shots in the air. Nearby, a Klansman with a baseball bat kept swinging, and Mann put his pistol to the man's head. "One more swing and you're dead," he said softly. As the furor subsided, Mann called in more highway patrolmen, and soon the attack at the Montgomery Greyhound station was over.

As word quickly spread, civil rights leaders, including Dr. Martin Luther King, now living in Atlanta, rushed to Montgomery. They came together on Sunday afternoon, May 21, at Ralph Abernathy's First Baptist Church, and more than a thousand people—almost all African Americans—gathered in the pews for an anticipated few stirring hours of preaching and song. Abernathy had been a stalwart in the Montgomery bus boycott, and back in those days such mass meetings were common. But as dusk approached, as many as three thousand whites, some from the attacking mob the day before, gathered outside the church. After a while they began throwing rocks, smashing car windows, and surging periodically toward the doors of the church, where a haggard line of U.S. marshals tried to keep them at bay.

As the evening grew increasingly tense, King demonstrated a dimension of leadership that some of his followers had never witnessed.

Everybody knew his gifts as a speaker, how his words would soar and sweep you away and touch the deepest places in your heart. And it was more than mere eloquence. He had such an ability to frame the debate, to deliver a call for radical change rooted in traditional values—those Jeffersonian notions of equality that were the cornerstones of the nation's founding, and the Christian ideal of brotherhood. Even white people, whether they agreed with him in the moment or not, were often touched by his words, and more and more as the decade progressed King became a figure they could not ignore.

But in the First Baptist Church on March 21, the people in the pews saw something else. As darkness fell and the mob outside became more intense, overturning and setting a car on fire, throwing bricks through the stained-glass windows, King divided his time between phone calls from the church's basement office to Robert Kennedy in Washington, explaining urgently that the marshals outside needed reinforcement, and quiet moments in the pulpit upstairs, speaking to the people in his calm, steady, baritone: "The main thing I want to say to you is fear not. We've gone too far to turn back. Let us be calm. We are together. We are not afraid. And we shall overcome."

At one point he decided to venture outside, much to the horror of his advisers. Nobody was quite sure of his reasons. Did he simply want to see the beast for himself—this collective lunacy that could sometimes seize the people of the South, or as he would later learn, people in every part of the country? Did he want to hear the roar and rage and soak in the magnitude of the mission—this sickness that he hoped to heal? Or was he on the brink, as some people wondered, of offering himself as a sacrifice to save the others in the church?

Whatever the reason, he walked deliberately toward the crowd, braving their taunts and the rocks and other objects they began to throw, before one of his aides, Bernard Lee, managed to pull him back towards the church. Lee insisted that nothing would be gained by his death, and King slowly returned to the sanctuary inside. Bernard Lafayette, one of the freedom riders, had grown accustomed to acts of courage, but thought he had never witnessed anything braver. By any measure, Lafayette decided, this was a leader who was worthy of the moment.

As the night wore on, the danger mounted, and men in high places agonized about what to do. By 10 p.m., Robert Kennedy feared a pitched battle in the streets of Montgomery, if not the wholesale slaughter of the people in the church. There were rumors of black citizens arming to mount a rescue of those trapped in the church. Kennedy was ready to send in troops. But then came word that John Patterson had decided, finally, that enough was enough. The governor ordered in the National Guard, buttressed by state and local police, and over the next several hours law and order was restored.

Not that many of these new protectors of the church were especially happy about their assignment. Reporter Bob Ingram of the *Montgomery Advertiser* remembered a late night scene when one of the civil rights leaders asked for an urn of fresh coffee for the people in the pews. One of the state troopers tasked with delivering the coffee urinated into the urn. The commander of the National Guard refused until almost dawn to let anyone leave the sweltering church, even though the crowd outside had long since been dispersed.

Eventually, however, this night of confrontation and fear finally came to an end. After more rounds of negotiation with the bus companies, on May 24 the freedom riders resumed their journey and left Montgomery.

Wave after wave of new riders followed, their numbers slowly overwhelming the resistance. As they continued to sweep through the South—more than a thousand before they were through—Robert Kennedy petitioned the Interstate Commerce Commission to establish clear regulations ending segregation in interstate travel once and for all. On September 22 the new regulations became official, and the Justice Department began filing lawsuits against local communities that didn't comply. The rides thus accomplished their strategic objective. But perhaps more importantly they sent a message to the country that the nonviolent movement would not be cowed, no matter how violent the opposition.

But there was also this. When the riders who left Montgomery on May 24 reached Jackson, Mississippi, they were immediately arrested and taken away to Parchman Penitentiary. There, as they had on so many occasions, they sang freedom songs to buoy their spirits. Their guards were annoyed and when the freedom riders refused to stop singing, the guards took away their mattresses, leaving them to sleep on bare metal cots.

Fred Leonard, a student at Tennessee A&I College, held tight to his mattress. In an interview for the documentary, *Eyes on the Prize*, Leonard described what happened:

> I was holding my mattress. They drug me out into the cellblock. I still had my mattress. . . . They would use the black inmates to get our mattresses . . . There was this guy, Peewee, they called him, short, muscular. They said, "Pewee, get him!" Peewee came down on my head, man, whomp, whomp. He was crying. Peewee was crying . . . You remember how when your parents used to whip you they would say, "It's gon' hurt me more than it hurts you?" It hurt Peewee more than it hurt me.

Leonard's cellmate, Stokely Carmichael, could only watch with a mounting sense of frustration and rage. Five years later, he would become a prominent spokesman for the Black Power movement, a journey that gained momentum in this Parchman cell he shared with Leonard. He had to wonder about the philosophy of nonviolence. Did it stand a chance against such cruelty and hate? Or might the day soon come when they would have to fight fire with fire?

7

The Wall

Having delegated, at least for the moment, the domestic dramas in America to his brother, President Kennedy prepared for his June 3 summit in Vienna with Nikita Khrushchev. Kennedy knew the stakes were enormous. The point of greatest tension was Berlin, East Germany, which had been divided since the end of World War II. The Soviet Union controlled the eastern half of the city, while the United States and its NATO allies controlled the west.

Khrushchev had declared repeatedly that he found the situation intolerable. By the summer of 1961, more than 4.5 million East Germans—20 percent of the population—had fled the drab oppressiveness of Soviet occupation, the sluggish economy, the grim concrete buildings. Most refugees had made their escape into the western sector of Berlin. For the rulers of the Soviet Union, it was maddening disproof of their repeated claim that communism was winning the hearts and minds of the world.

Khrushchev's predecessor, Josef Stalin, had attempted soon after World War II to drive western forces out of Berlin and reunify Germany as a satellite state under Soviet control. In June 1948, Soviet troops blocked access to the city by water and land. Berlin was vulnerable to such a blockade; it lay a hundred miles inside East Germany.

In response, President Harry Truman ordered the Berlin Airlift. For the next eleven months planes from Great Britain, France, and the United States ferried in more than two million tons of food, fuel, and other supplies. As tensions grew, Stalin eventually backed down, knowing that if it came to war the U.S. had nuclear weapons and the Soviets did not.

But by 1961, both superpowers had the Bomb, and thus an extra layer of tension pervaded preparations for Vienna. At a minimum, Khrushchev wanted control of Berlin, a notion that Kennedy rejected out of hand, and in the coming test of wills, the president knew the Bay of Pigs could be a complicating factor. Khrushchev was widely regarded in diplomatic circles as a calculating bully who was given to fits of temper. Would he try to run roughshod over Kennedy, this new and untested leader who had approved the recent invasion of Cuba and then let it fail?

All of this was on Kennedy's mind when he left for Vienna. But his entourage stopped on the way for a welcome interlude in Paris. Kennedy met privately with French President Charles DeGaulle, and the two talked about Berlin. DeGaulle felt certain Khrushchev was bluffing. Nobody wanted war, the French leader observed, not even Khrushchev with all his threats and ill-tempered bluster. Kennedy must simply stand firm. The West, after all, was asking for nothing; it was the Soviet leader who was seeking to change the status quo, hoping to win by threats what he would not go to war to achieve.

For Kennedy, it was a reassuring assessment, and one he shared, though there remained a flicker of a doubt—made more urgent by the consequences of miscalculation. In a nuclear age, war was an irrational option.

Such reflections provided a sober backdrop for what was otherwise a gala occasion in Paris—state dinners and motorcades through the streets of the city, and citizens turning out by the thousands to cheer the President of the United States. But it was his beautiful wife, so impeccably gracious and fluent in French, who captured their hearts. There was always a certain mesmerizing radiance about Jackie (that was what all of us called her by then). But there was something more. She appeared to possess the perfect sensibilities, an instinct for saying just the right thing, and at a luncheon in Paris, where she was seated next to President DeGaulle, she began a conversation with him, in French, of course, about the ironic reign of Louis XVI, a king who supported the American Revolution but was deposed and executed in the French one. Jackie was full of questions about the Bourbon family and its return to power after Napoleon, and John Kennedy watched with a mixture of grand bemusement and pride. It was as if, he observed, Mrs. DeGaulle had sat next to him and wanted to know about Henry Clay.

At every ceremony, and at the motorcades that followed, the French who lined the streets of Paris marveled at the First Lady's attire—especially the pink and white dress of French design that she wore with such extraordinary grace. "Her softly glowing beauty," remembered Arthur Schlesinger, who was with the president's entourage, "her mastery of the language, her passion for the arts, her perfection of style—all were conquering the skeptical city."

At a luncheon with the French press corps, Kennedy introduced himself with an ironic smile: "I am the man who accompanied Jacqueline Kennedy to Paris, and I have enjoyed it."

HOWEVER, NIKITA KHRUSHCHEV WAS waiting in Austria. The Soviet chairman had arrived a day early to prepare for the summit at the American Embassy. When Kennedy arrived on the following morning, the weather itself seemed to carry a warning about what kind of meeting it was likely to be. A bone-chilling drizzle fell on the streets of Vienna as Kennedy's motorcade made its way from the airport. From all accounts the President's mood was both expectant and somber. He had modest aspirations for the summit. He hoped the most powerful leaders in the world could agree specifically to support a neutral government in Laos, where a civil war threatened not only that country but the stability of Southeast Asia. And indeed, that agreement was accomplished quickly, partly, it seemed, because Khrushchev did not regard the issue as important. But Kennedy's larger goals were elusive. In the global competition of a nuclear age, he wanted to avoid mistakes by either side that could escalate to nuclear war. The objective, Kennedy declared, should be to preserve the current balance of power.

Khrushchev immediately bristled. The President clearly didn't mean what he said, for had not the United States, by proxy, sought to overthrow Fidel Castro? How was that preserving the status quo? And did Kennedy really believe their current competition of ideas—communism versus the capitalist system in the United States—should stop at geographic borders? How was such a thing even possible?

With that they were off—a day of dialectic haggling, which was an art Khrushchev had long since mastered. "Is he always like this?" Kennedy asked Llewellyn Thompson, the American ambassador to the Soviet Union. "Par for the course," Thompson replied.

From all accounts, Kennedy spent that evening depressed. "He treated me like a little boy," he said in dismay. And he knew if indeed that was Khrushchev's assessment, the underestimation was dangerous. The following day they would turn to Berlin, and if Khrushchev believed in the power of his own bluff, the consequence might actually be war. Kennedy had no illusions about what that meant. He had read *Hiroshima* by John Hersey, a reporter who in

1945 had made it into Japan not long after the bombs were dropped and had seen the devastation for himself. On August 31, 1946, Hersey wrote about it in the *New Yorker*, a 31,000-word article that filled the entire magazine and suddenly gave a face to the devastation unleashed upon the world.

> Wounded people supported maimed people; disfigured families leaned together. Many people were vomiting . . . In a city of two hundred and forty-five thousand, nearly a hundred thousand people had been killed or doomed at one blow; a hundred thousand more were hurt. At least ten thousand of the wounded made their way to the best hospital in town, which was altogether unequal to such a trampling, since it only had six hundred beds and they had all been occupied . . . The hurt ones were quiet; no one wept, much less screamed in pain; no one complained; none of the many who died did so noisily; not even the children cried; very few people even spoke. And when Father Kleinsorge gave water to some whose faces had been almost blotted out by flash burns, they took their share and then raised themselves a little and bowed to him, in thanks.

According to a friend of mine who knew him, Kennedy was moved by Hersey's account, and by now the whole country had gotten the gist. Nuclear war was no longer an abstraction, no longer a testament to the genius of man. It was, within a few months of those first bombs, a reality too horrible to contemplate, and in the summer of 1961 we knew something else about it as well. It could happen to us. If these two men, these mortal human beings who were meeting in Vienna, took the wrong measure of each other's resolve, the end of civilization might be in sight.

Kennedy understood it in precisely those terms, and he also knew he was facing a Machiavellian dictator who was willing to push the world to the brink. The unanswered question was how close they would come.

Thus did the second day begin, and if anything it was harder and rougher than the first. They argued first over a nuclear test ban treaty, with Khrushchev flatly rejecting the presence of U.N. inspectors on Soviet soil. The question for discussion, he insisted, should be total nuclear disarmament, which the Soviet Union supported. Kennedy replied that disarmament was far more complicated than a test ban. Why not start with the easier step?

Unable to agree, and with acrimony rising, they turned to the dangerous matter of Berlin. U.S. troops in West Berlin were "a bone in the Soviet throat,"

Khrushchev declared, and the situation must change. He intended to sign a treaty with East Germany by the end of the year, recognizing its sovereignty and its right to absorb the whole city of Berlin. After that, American forces could remain in the city only if East Germany allowed it.

Kennedy replied that the United States would never agree to such a thing. If it did, it would be a betrayal of the people of West Berlin, and proof to the world that America's commitments were not worth the paper on which they were written. Khrushchev wondered sarcastically if Kennedy wanted U.S. troops in Moscow as well, to which Kennedy replied in a sharp exchange that American troops were not going anywhere. They were simply going to stay where they were.

It was clear to both delegations that the two heads of state were rapidly drawing a line in the sand. Once the treaty with East Germany was signed, Khrushchev vowed, U.S. troops in West Berlin would be viewed as an act of aggression—against East Germany and against the Soviet Union. "If the United States wants to start a war over Germany," the chairman proclaimed, "let it be so."

Historian Larry Sabato reported that Khrushchev "bellowed" when he said it. Arthur Schlesinger, who was in Vienna with Kennedy at the time, put it differently: "It was not quite a tirade; it was too controlled and hard and therefore the more menacing."

Whatever the case, Kennedy didn't blink.

"Then Mr. Chairman," he replied in a tone of voice that was formal and hard, "There will be war. It will be a cold winter."

Kennedy was worried as he left Vienna. At the summit table, the only two options had been American withdrawal from West Berlin or nuclear war. Neither was acceptable; the question was how to find a third alternative, and the hard truth was that nobody knew.

Back in Washington, Kennedy called his advisers together and found them divided about what to do next. Former Secretary of State Dean Acheson urged Kennedy to adopt a hard line, calling Khrushchev's bluff with a policy that was not a bluff—a willingness to fight if we had to. A little known intellectual named Henry Kissinger, later to earn his share of notoriety as a policy adviser to President Richard Nixon, offered a memo that now seems surreal—a proposal for "limited" nuclear war, something less than an all-out exchange. Others such as Adlai Stevenson, Kennedy's Ambassador to the United Nations, sought to point out the lunacy of war, as the debate raged on behind the scenes.

Kennedy bought time with a bland announcement on June 6. "Mr. Khrushchev and I had a very full and frank exchange of views on the major issues that now divide our two countries," he reported. "I will tell you now that it was a very sober two days. There was no discourtesy, no loss of temper, no threats or ultimatums by either side."

Kennedy, of course, was misstating the case. The courtesy had been strained at best, and there had, in fact, been ultimatums, even threats of war by both sides. Perhaps he simply intended to maintain calm, at least until he was ready to act. According to Schlesinger's first-hand account, Kennedy spent the next six weeks sorting through the disagreements within his own administration, trying to reconcile these opposing views with his own impressions of Nikita Khrushchev. "That son of a bitch won't pay any attention to words," Schlesinger remembered the president saying. "He has to see you move."

So Kennedy moved. On July 25, he addressed the nation in a televised speech intended as much for Khrushchev as for the American people.

"Seven weeks ago tonight," he said, "I returned from Europe to report on my meeting with Premier Khrushchev . . . In Berlin, as you recall, [Khrushchev] intends to bring to an end, through a stroke of the pen, first our legal rights to be in West Berlin—and secondly our ability to make good on our commitment to the two million free people in that city. That we cannot permit." Kennedy called for an immediate increase of $3.2 billion in military spending, a build-up of both weapons and troops, and while he held out an olive branch—"We do not intend to abandon our duty to mankind to seek a peaceful solution"—he also offered a chilling afterthought about the need for spending on civil defense: "In the event of an attack, the lives of those families which are not hit in a nuclear blast and fire can still be saved—if they can be warned to take shelter and if that shelter is available. We owe that kind of insurance to our families—and to our country."

I have a vague memory of listening to the speech on the radio. Mine was a very political family. My father was a judge, an elected official, and an uncle was an avid environmentalist, and political discussions in the family were frequent. We had developed a habit, even after the purchase of our first TV, of listening to presidential speeches on the radio. I'm not sure why. Perhaps it went back to my parents and the Great Depression and Franklin Roosevelt's Fireside Chats. Whatever the reason, in my hazy memories of Kennedy and Berlin, my mother and father and one or two others—my uncle, perhaps?—were gathered around the radio and when Kennedy had finished, one of the men in the family, deeply moved, offered with a catch of admiration in his voice: "The man's a fighter."

The other men nodded gravely, but I remember seeing that my mother was appalled, her face a mask of unmitigated terror, mixed with a flash of anger at the men who seemed so badly to miss the point. Kennedy was not our knight in shining armor heading off bravely to joust in single combat with the Russians. He and Khrushchev were about to blow us all to pieces.

Meanwhile, back on the center stage of history, Walter Ulbricht, the Communist leader of East Germany, had an idea. Instead of war, why not build a wall? After all, the most practical problem had been the flood of refugees to the West, an ideological embarrassment that had also cost his country some of its most talented professionals. Khrushchev quickly approved the plan, perhaps understanding its utility, perhaps as a face-saving act of defiance. In any case on August 13, East German troops began their work on the Berlin Wall, stretching a hundred miles through the heart of the city. They embarked on their task just after midnight as other members of their unit stood guard, and by morning they had torn up the streets leading to where the wall would be and had strung barbed wire that was soon replaced by a wall of reinforced concrete.

To much of the world it was a stark and ugly symbol of oppression, and in West Berlin especially there were calls for a strong international response. But President Kennedy seemed to take it in stride. He was photographed sailing in Nantucket Sound, looking tanned and relaxed, his hair windblown, a smile on his face. A wall, he seemed to be saying to the world, was very much better than a nuclear war.

Immediately after construction of the wall, he sent Vice President Lyndon Johnson to Berlin, along with another 1,500 U.S. soldiers, to underscore the United States' commitment to the city. He also authorized a public statement about America's nuclear superiority should a war ever come.

But the president had peace on his mind. As tensions eased in September, Kennedy turned his attention to the Peace Corps.

The Peace Corps, according to the people who knew him best, sprang from his idealism, his most cherished hopes about the role that America could play in the world. He knew very well that it was a leap of faith. In the summer of 1961, Richard Goodwin, one of Kennedy's special assistants, had attended a conference in Uruguay, where another of the delegates was Che Guevara, the Marxist revolutionary from Argentina who had played a major role in the Cuban revolution. In a conversation with Goodwin, Guevara had scoffed at the Peace Corps, as well as at Kennedy's Alliance for Progress, saying that both would raise the hopes of peasants and workers—the disenfranchised masses in Latin America—in a way that would turn them into Communists.

Oddly, the same warning had come from American conservatives, including Richard Nixon and Barry Goldwater, but Kennedy believed otherwise. On September 7, he met at the White House with Colombia One, the first group of Peace Corps volunteers to finish their training and who were about to embark for a year of service in South America. There were sixty-two of them, all men, mostly white, but with more than a dozen people of color—Latino, Asian, African American. A few were military veterans, but most were just young people ready for adventure, and only secondarily, one admitted, moved by the need to make the world better.

They were impressed, however, with John F. Kennedy, who met them in the West Wing of the White House, flashed his vintage campaign smile, then spoke with passion about the opportunity that lay before them—and about America's place in the world. Theirs was the generation, he said, that could erase the image of the ugly American. Working in the jungles and mountains of Colombia, they would help build roads, health centers, and schools, and they would know the local language and they would listen as people explained their own needs. And that, for many, was the way it worked. When their plane touched down in Bogota, they were greeted warmly as "Kennedy's children," and when the President himself came to visit in December, the people lined the streets of the city and called out his name. Colombian President Alberto Lleras, standing next to Kennedy, told him simply: "It is because they believe you are on their side."

Tragedy came a few weeks later with the first of the occasional Peace Corps fatalities. David Crozier and Larry Radley were killed when the plane on which they were passengers slammed into a mountaintop in the jungle. But even that horrifying moment, with its twisted wreckage and victims' bodies torn into pieces, was defined in the end by a spirit of sacrifice and courage. From Colombia, David Crozier had written a letter to his parents, summarizing his view of the Peace Corps: "Should it come to that, I would rather give my life trying to help someone than to have to give my life looking down the barrel of a gun at them."

The Croziers gave the letter to Peace Corps Director Sargent Shriver, who framed it and hung it on the wall of his office, for this was the spirit of the New Frontier. *We shall pay any price, bear any burden . . .* Those were the words the President had spoken, echoed now in a hand-written letter from South America.

Many Americans saw Kennedy that way, a leader with a steady hand on the wheel whose noblest intentions gave people hope.

BUT WE ALSO LIVED in the shadow of the bomb, in a Cold War-world where our nemesis, Nikita Khrushchev, having retreated from a war over West Berlin, unleashed what seemed a nuclear tantrum. On September 1, the Soviet Union, at Khrushchev's direction, detonated a sixteen-kiloton nuclear bomb in the atmosphere over Kazakhstan. Kennedy hated that. He knew such bombs spewed nuclear poison into the air, where the winds could take it who knows where, and thus since 1958 the two superpowers had observed a moratorium on testing. But now the Soviets were at it again. The explosion on September 1 was merely the first of fifty-seven tests Khrushchev would order that fall. In the gloomy estimation of Kennedy's advisers, one of the bombs about which Khrushchev boasted carried more explosive force than all the bombs previously detonated in the history of the world.

The President knew that his country had conducted similar tests in the past, particularly in the 1940s and '50s after we had persuaded the United Nations to create the Strategic Trust Territory of Micronesia, administered by the United States. That mandate became little more than a license to test our nuclear bombs, and our favorite target was Bikini Atoll, a chain of twenty-three South Pacific islands encircling an otherwise lovely lagoon.

Kennedy regarded that history of A-bomb tests with shame, knowing the shabby treatment accorded the islanders uprooted from their homes to make room for the bombs. But there was also the terrible environmental damage—to the atoll, certainly, but also to other parts of the world as the fallout drifted across the globe. Early in his presidency, Kennedy was meeting with his science adviser, Jerome Wiesner, and they began talking about such things. It was raining outside. Wiesner noted that fallout got worse in the rain, for that was when it was washed from the clouds and fell with the droplets of water to the earth.

"You mean," said Kennedy, "that stuff is in the rain out there?"

"Yes," said Wiesner.

Recording the moment in *A Thousand Days*, Arthur Schlesinger reported: "The President continued gazing out the window, deep sadness on his face, and did not say a word for several minutes."

In the coming days, Kennedy rejected, temporarily, the advice of military advisers urging him to resume atmospheric testing. The reality of fall-out weighed too heavily. But on September 5, he did order new tests underground, where the nuclear residue would be contained.

"What choice did we have?" he asked rhetorically when U.N. Ambassador Adlai Stevenson wondered about an escalation of the arms race. "They had spit in our eye . . . We couldn't possibly sit back and do nothing at all. We had to do this . . . I'm not saying it was the right decision. Who the hell knows? But it is the decision which has been taken."

If there was irritation in Kennedy's voice, the reason for it seemed simple enough. This was not how he wanted things to go.

Less than two months later, on November 1, he stared out the window of the White House at a group of demonstrators—some 1,500 women who were part of an international protest against the arms race: the threat of annihilation it posed, but also the health risks and environmental damage. Marchers with Women Strike for Peace demonstrated in more than 60 cities, 50,000 strong, carrying signs that read, "End the Arms Race, not the Human Race."

One of the organizers was Bella Abzug, a Jewish lawyer from New York who had taken on civil rights cases in the South and would later become a member of Congress, where she was an outspoken feminist and supporter of gay rights. Abzug and others saw to it that the strike was not a one-day event. They continued to push the cause of peace in a nuclear age, helping transform the traditional role of women in political movements, and demanding, among other things, an end to above-ground nuclear testing.

Gazing reflectively from the windows of the White House, Jack Kennedy knew that morally, rationally, the women in the streets were right.

8

Sixty-One Dingers

For the rest of the country, there remained a cloud of uncertainty and fear. In this nuclear jousting match between the two superpowers, how much closer to the edge would we come?

Even for those of us still in school, it was a question we confronted in the curious form of civil defense drills, which even then we regarded as absurd. We were instructed to "duck and cover," to take shelter under our wooden desks at the very first flash of a nuclear bomb. We knew this was nuts; it only instilled a vague sense of doom.

Fortunately, there were distractions, and never more so than in the glorious autumn of 1961. As the baseball season entered the home stretch, Baltimore Orioles first baseman Jim Gentile was headed toward his finest season—a batting average of .302 with forty-six home runs and 141 runs batted in; prodigious numbers that almost everybody ignored, except perhaps for the fans in Baltimore, and a few of us in Mobile, Alabama, where Gentile had played in the minor leagues. For everybody else, when it came to hero worship that fall, poor Gentile never had a chance. This was the season of Mantle and Maris—the M&M boys, the media called them—bearing down on one of the greatest records of all time.

For thirty-four years, the great Babe Ruth had held the single season home run title with the magical number of sixty. Now in the season of '61—and who could have written a better script?—not one but two Major League All-Stars, both playing for the Babe's own New York Yankees, had a genuine chance to break the record. We could barely believe it, but there they were—Roger Maris with fifty-one home runs by the end of August, and Mickey Mantle, who hit the ball farther than anybody, trailing Maris by only two or three.

Fans of all ages had been mesmerized since June, for Mantle had set a blistering pace and Maris by then was hitting his stride. The record seemed more and more within reach. Then a curious thing began to happen. A media narrative took on a life of its own, unencumbered by facts, as sports writers invented a bitter rivalry between the two superstars. Surely that had to be the way it was. The previous season Maris had been named Most Valuable Player when Mantle had hit more homers, and now here they were locked in a quest for the greatest home run feat of all time. It stood to reason that Mantle was angry. After all, he was the highest paid player in the game, making $75,000 a year, and Maris was just some guy from North Dakota stealing the glory that should have been Mantle's.

No wonder there had been that day in batting practice when Mantle yelled out, just loud enough for the writers to hear: "Maris, I hate your guts."

A few minutes later, away from the ears of the press, Mantle got a good laugh out of it, for he regarded the reporters' stories as a joke. The truth was, he and Maris were friends, and they grew even closer in 1961. In their own minds they were not rivals—they were teammates, fellow sojourners on a high-pressure quest which became, for Maris especially, more bitter and painful as the season went along. The problems began in July when Baseball Commissioner Ford Frick, a close friend of Ruth's, set out to denigrate the record chase. This was an expansion year, Frick argued, with two new teams in the American League and an additional eight games added to the schedule. Unless a new mark was set in 154 games, the number Ruth had played in when he hit his sixty home runs in 1927, the old record would stand. If Mantle or Maris reached sixty-one in the final eight games, that achievement would be noted with a metaphorical asterisk—a "distinctive mark," as the commissioner put it—but Ruth would remain the home run king.

Other commentators pointed out that expansion had led to a thinning of talent, good players spread across additional teams, and the quality of pitching especially had declined. Thus it was easier to hit home runs. Hall of Famer Rogers Hornsby noted that Ruth had hit .356 in 1927, while Maris was batting .269 in 1961. "It would be a disappointment," Hornsby declared, "if Ruth's home run record were bested by a .270 hitter."

From there the derision spread to the fans, and as Maris pulled ahead in the home run race he was booed whenever he came to the plate. Behind the scenes, his biggest cheerleader was Mantle. The two shared an apartment with steady Yankee outfielder Bob Cerv. Cerv was not a superstar like his housemates, but he and Maris kept Mantle in line. Left to himself, party boy Mantle was just an overgrown kid, some people said—hard-drinking, womanizing; he seemed to be running away from something, and even Mantle himself couldn't say what it was.

Perhaps it was rooted in part in abuse that he had endured from the press when he first put on a Yankee uniform. The year was 1951 and Mantle was heir to Joe DiMaggio, one of the greatest Yankees of all time, a Hall of Fame hitter who had roamed centerfield with extraordinary grace. Off the field he was just as smooth, and nobody was surprised in 1954 when he dated, then married, Marilyn Monroe, the most beautiful femme fatale in Hollywood. Mantle, by contrast, seemed to be a hick country boy from Oklahoma who didn't much care for the New York press and the way they seemed to make stuff up. The reporters returned the contempt in full.

Finally, Whitey Ford, the great Yankee pitcher, took Mantle aside and told him to relax, schmooze a little with the media boys, give them a taste of that Oklahoma charm, and they would come around soon enough. The 1956 season didn't hurt, when Mantle hit .353 with fifty-two home runs, remarkable numbers by anybody's standards. But he had also learned to play the media game, just a flash here and there of his aw-shucks grin and soft western drawl, and by 1961 Mickey Mantle was a baseball legend.

He wanted the same for his friend, Roger Maris, who might not hit for an eye-popping average but was blessed with power and did the little things to help his team win, like throwing base-runners out at home plate. It became clear as the pressure mounted, however, that the only game Maris knew how to play—the only one he was *willing* to play—was baseball itself. He had no idea how to create an image, to play to the crowd, to deflect the questions that shouldn't be answered.

How did he feel, one reporter asked, about the fans who had booed him that night from the bleachers?

"Terrible," Maris said. "Maybe the worst in the league."

And what about Babe Ruth? somebody else wondered. Did he really want to break such a venerable record?

"Damn right," said Maris.

And so it went.

Roger Kahn wrote in *Sports Illustrated*,

> Beyond anything else, Maris is a professional baseball player. His speech, his mannerisms, his attitudes, derive from the curious society that is a ball club. But into this society he has brought an integrity that is entirely his own, a fierce, combative kind of integrity that is unusual in baseball as it would be unusual anywhere. It is the integrity, and his desperate effort to retain it, that has made the ordeal of Roger Maris a compelling and disturbing thing to behold.

For Maris, integrity meant speaking his mind, and though he did it softly, simply, directly, almost always intending no offense, just answering reporters' questions, his unpopularity seemed to grow with every answer. So Maris simply played baseball. Once when asked about the pressure of the chase, and how he must feel it during every at bat, Maris replied with characteristic candor: "I don't feel a damn thing once the game starts. I honestly don't. But before the game, and afterward, the writers and the photographers and the questions—that's pressure. That's hard."

The crescendo came in the crucial 154th game of the season, within which, according to Commissioner Frick, Ruth's record would have to be broken. The Yankees were playing in Baltimore that night, and Maris had hit fifty-eight home runs. Mantle had only fifty-four, but he was not even playing because he was sick. So Mantle was cheering from his hospital bed as his buddy, Roger, stepped to the plate. Kahn, again:

> No one who saw game 154, who beheld Maris's response to the challenge, is likely soon to forget it. His play was as brave and as moving and as thrilling as a baseball player's can be. There were more reporters and photographers around him now than ever before. Newsmen swelled the Yankee party, which normally numbers 45, to 71. And this was the town where Babe Ruth was born, and the crowd had not come to cheer Maris.

On his first at-bat, Maris whistled a hard and low liner right to the glove of Orioles' right-fielder Earl Robinson. But when Maris stepped to the plate in the third inning, he promptly hit number fifty-nine, a blistering drive that traveled three hundred and ninety feet, and as Kahn put it, "all but broke a seat in the bleachers."

Now Maris had his chance at history. He would get at least two more at-bats, maybe three, to tie or surpass one of the greatest records in sports.

Whitey Ford, watching from the dugout, muttered to no one in particular, "You know, I'm really nervous."

A strikeout followed, and then a long fly to center field, and finally it all came down to the ninth. On the mound for the Orioles was Hoyt Wilhelm, a knuckleballer whose pitches had no spin and thus danced in the air to home plate. No one knew quite where these pitches were going, including Wilhelm, and Maris, who was badly fooled, tapped a weak ground ball back to the pitcher. Thus ended his chance at Babe Ruth's record. At least in 154 games.

"I'm just sorry I didn't go out with a real good swing," he said after the game. "But that Wilhelm—" He smiled and shook his head. He knew he had hit at least three pitches hard enough to be home runs, but only one had left the ball park. "Like they say," he added softly, "you got to be lucky."

It seemed almost an afterthought when Maris hit number sixty in the 158th game, a towering blast to the upper deck off Orioles starter Jack Fisher. A curve ball, Maris said later. He failed to homer in the next three games, as the Yankees headed home to close out the season. In the final game at Yankee Stadium, a paltry crowd of 23,154—roughly a third of capacity—turned out to see if Maris could reach sixty-one. Red Barber, the voice of the Yankees who shared the broadcast booth with Mel Allen, sounded typically low-key when Maris came up in the bottom of the third. Third innings had been good for Maris; home runs fifty-nine and sixty had both come in the third, and you could sense a restless stirring in the crowd as Tracy Stallard of the Boston Red Sox, a journeyman pitcher with a 2–6 record, started his windup.

"Fast ball wide," reported Barber. "Lays off of it. Ball one."

Then: "Low. Ball two. The crowd is reacting negatively. They want to see Maris get something he can swing on."

Finally, Stallard delivered a strike, and Maris swung, forearms extended, triceps rippling, and even the generally laconic Barber had to sound excited this time: "There it is! Sixty-one! He got his pitch . . . Well, you haven't seen anything like this, have you?"

"Nobody has, Red!" Mel Allen exclaimed. "Nobody has ever seen anything like this!"

In that moment, it seemed to many who followed baseball that despite the official denigrations of Commissioner Frick, Maris—our blue-collar hero, the crew-cut slugger from North Dakota, an anti-hero to the New York media who was genuinely admired by his Yankee teammates—had accomplished something truly unforgettable. For me and for many of my friends, it was one of sports' goose-bump moments, and we marveled at the power of the swing and the blistering speed with which the ball left the park.

In this blur of good feeling the terrors of the world were all but forgotten, and we replayed the moment again and again before our minds moved on to other things.

For me on any given day, those other things included rock 'n' roll, the music made for our generation, and '61 had been a good year with records like Del Shannon's "Runaway" and Dion's "Runaround Sue" and Gene Pitney's "Town Without Pity." But another song released in December, though not as big a hit as the other two, seemed to be grittier and more real. Arthur Alexander's "You Better Move On," later covered by the Rolling Stones, told the story of a guy who's angry with somebody trying to steal his girl.

You asked me to give up the hand
Of the girl I love
You tell me I'm not the man
She's worthy of
But who are you to tell her who to love?
That's up to her
Yes, and the Lord, above
You better move on

I didn't know when I first heard the song on the radio that I was listening to a piece of cultural history. Alexander, who was black, had a voice one critic labeled "country-soul," a high baritone with an ache of understated vulnerability. He was twenty-one years old when he cut his record, a refugee from the cotton fields of Alabama who had more recently worked as a bellhop in a small hotel. He came of age near the town of Florence, the birthplace of both W. C. Handy, the "Father of the Blues," and Sam Phillips.

The latter had left Alabama for Memphis, where he would produce such rhythm and blues artists as B. B. King and Bobby "Blue" Bland and help launch the career of Elvis Presley. There was something in the air of northern Alabama, in Florence and the nearby town of Muscle Shoals, that led young white and black men to collaborate in making music. When Arthur Alexander went into the studio, his producer, Rick Hall, was white and so were his session musicians—David Briggs, Jerry Carrigan, and Norbert Putnam.

That tradition grew stronger in the 1960s, as Hall used some of the money from "You Better Move On," which peaked at number 24 on the national charts, to launch his FAME recording studio in Muscle Shoals. The town soon became a mecca for young black artists like Wilson Pickett and Percy Sledge, who recorded major hits backed by white musicians in the studio.

There would be other times in the 1960s when the decade seemed as fully defined by cultural change as it was by politics and protest. For many of us, it was sometimes hard to tell the difference.

9

The Words of Change

In March, Walker Percy won the National Book Award for his debut novel, *The Moviegoer*. Many critics saw this as a literary upset, for when the book was published the previous year it failed to sell out its original printing. It was, in a sense, an existentialist novel of middle-class anguish, similar in that way to John Updike's *Rabbit Run* or Richard Yates's *Revolutionary Road*, both published at about the same time.

Percy built his story around the character of Binx Bolling, a well-bred Southerner who seems both adrift and embarked on a quest, committed only to his own integrity—his amiable rejection of the foolishness and pretense he sees all around him. Friends of Percy couldn't help noticing a touch of autobiography.

Percy came from a star-crossed Southern family haunted by the tragedies of time and place—first by the moral burdens of slavery, that great original sin of the South, then by the aura of defeat and ruin that came with the end of the Civil War. All weighed heavily on the hearts of the Percys, for there was in their tangled feelings of loss a sense that something *good* had been stripped away when the guns fell silent at Appomattox: some intermingled quality of civility and grace, doomed by the tragedies of history.

But the family's gloom was more personal. In 1917, for reasons that were never clear, Percy's grandfather, John Walker Percy, walked up the stairs to the attic of his house and shot himself in the head. Suicides were common in the Percy family; hardly a generation went by without one. In 1929, LeRoy Pratt Percy—Walker's father—also shot himself in the head. Walker went to live after that with his uncle, William Alexander Percy, a Mississippi Renaissance man and writer, a lover of the arts and history and the symphony, and a defender of Mississippi's black citizens against the random cruelties of segregation. His was a paternalistic defense, rooted still in a sense of privilege that carried with it the obligations of decency.

By the 1960s, Walker Percy had moved beyond his uncle's view of race. He saw white supremacy for what it was, a crippling force that dehumanized African Americans and, in a curious, self-inflicted way (as a Percy, he understood about self-inflicted wounds), damaged the psyches of their oppressors. Percy, a whole-hearted proponent of civil rights, became part of a loose confederation of left-of-center Catholic intellectuals that included Dorothy Day, founder and editor of the *Catholic Worker*; the celebrated Trappist monk and writer, Thomas Merton; Southern novelist Flannery O'Connor; and the brothers Berrigan, two Catholic priests who became increasingly radical in their opposition to the war in Vietnam. Together they embodied a powerful force in American religion, and some of their politics of faith would appear in the pages of *Love in the Ruins,* a novel Percy wrote at the end of decade.

But none of that was present in *The Moviegoer.* It was, instead, the story of a young man alone in a crowd, a book that traced its philosophical roots to the existentialist essays of Soren Kierkegaard, one of Percy's favorite writers. Kierkegaard's concern was not so much for the tides of history as the meaning of an individual life, and because we are born without knowing what that meaning is, all of us are searching.

Binx Bolling, the central character in *The Moviegoer,* narrates his own journey in present tense, giving it a sense of immediacy and drift. Bolling, so he insists, finds pleasure and purpose in only three things—going to the movies, doggedly refusing to be a phony, and in the very ordinariness of life:

> I subscribe to *Consumer Reports* and as a consequence I own a first-class television set, an all but silent air conditioner and a very long lasting deodorant. My armpits never stink. I pay attention to all spot announcements on the radio about mental health, the seven signs of cancer, and safe driving—though, as I say, I usually prefer to ride the bus. Yesterday a favorite of mine, William Holden, delivered a radio announcement on litterbugs. "Let's face it," said Holden, "Nobody can do anything about it—but you and me." This is true. I have tried to be careful ever since.

And then:

> In the evenings I usually watch television or go to the movies . . . Other people, so I have read, treasure memorable moments in their lives: the time one climbed the Parthenon at sunrise, the summer night one met a lonely girl in Central Park and achieved with her a sweet and natural relationship, as they say in books. I too once met a girl in Central Park, but it is not much to remember. What I remember is the time John Wayne killed three men with a carbine as he was falling to the dusty street in *Stagecoach* . . .

And finally, much later in the book, as he compares his detachment to the terrors of life in a nuclear age, Bolling is forced to admit:

> The malaise has settled like a fall-out and what people really fear is not that the bomb will fall but that the bomb will not fall—on this my thirtieth birthday, I know nothing and there is nothing to do but fall prey to desire.

I didn't read the novel until 1968, a date I remember because I had become a moviegoer myself. This was after the assassinations of Robert Kennedy and Martin Luther King, and I had just seen the film adaptation of *The Heart Is a Lonely Hunter*, the powerful first novel of Carson McCullers. Alan Arkin played the role of Singer, a deaf-mute who is loved by his friends, but who nevertheless feels so alone that he finally decides to take his own life. The existential despair of the movie, and of Percy's novel, fit the mood of 1968. Many young Americans were so disillusioned by national tragedy that, as with Binx Bolling, a desperate hedonistic desire became their final line of defense.

But 1968 was different from 1962, the year Percy won his acclaim, and many critics wondered at the time if another of the finalists for the National Book Award might not have been a better choice. The favorite was *Catch-22*. Joseph Heller's satirical novel was a huge success—so uproariously funny it was startling, for its purpose was deadly serious. It mocked the very fact of war and the foolishness of those who make it. Heller was a veteran of World War II, a bombardier who flew sixty missions on the Mediterranean front, and by all rights that should have been enough to kill him. In 1953 Heller set out to write about that experience, and though he shared in his country's feeling of triumph, the war had deepened his sense of the absurd.

The protagonist in his long and intricate novel is Captain John Yossarian, also a bombardier, who hates the Germans because, he says, they are trying to kill him. "They are trying to kill everybody," one of his friends replies. "Exactly," says Yossarian. But his purest hatred is reserved for his commander, Colonel Cathcart, who continues to raise the number of missions that the men serving under him must fly.

For Yossarian and others who were terrified by this prospect, there was one possible out. According to military regulations, anyone who was crazy could be excused from flying, and all that person had to do was ask. But asking to be excused from such hazardous assignments—thus demonstrating a rational concern for safety—was proof of sanity, and therefore the person could not be excused. This was a rule known as Catch-22, and Yossarian and the other members of his squadron were, as Heller wrote, "very deeply moved by the absolute simplicity of this clause . . ."

This mocking of the military and of misused authority would resonate powerfully in the years just ahead, making *Catch-22* one of the most popular books of the 1960s. Nor was it the only one of its kind. Somewhat more darkly, Ken Kesey, who had worked as an orderly in a California mental hospital, wrote *One Flew Over the Cuckoo's Nest,* a seething indictment of the mental health system. Kesey's novel gave us the character of Nurse Ratched, the villainous ruler of the psychiatric ward—an abuser of authority against whom we could muster a delicious rage, which would soon spill from literature into politics.

SOME HAVE ARGUED THAT the most important writings of 1962 were a pair of books that sprang, not from irony, but from the purest idealism—a belief that terrible and unacknowledged problems might be solved if only more people would understand. The most iconic of those books was *Silent Spring.*

Its author, Rachel Carson, had made her mark a decade earlier with *The Sea Around Us*, a bestselling blend of science and poetic prose. As critic Neil Baldwin described the sweep and the majesty of Carson's achievement, "From the beginnings of all life out of the synthesis of minerals and elements within the sea, we are taken to its wind-driven surfaces, thence to its sunless depths, where we meet its many exotic inhabitants, gigantic and microscopic. We learn how islands are born, how mountain ranges rivaling any on land parade between continental masses, how sediments of every conceivable variety coat the floor of the sea, how the shape of one continent mirrors the face of another. . . ."

Accepting the National Book Award for that earlier book, Carson, a forty-four-year-old marine biologist, deflected the acclaim from herself to her subject.

"The winds, the sea, and the moving tides are what they are," she said. "If there is wonder and beauty and majesty in them, science will discover these qualities. If they are not there, science cannot create them. If there is poetry in my book about the sea, it is not because I deliberately put it there, but because no one could write truthfully about the sea and leave out the poetry."

But now in 1962, Carson was writing with a purpose more urgent. *Silent Spring* was not poetry but a call to action against the devastations of the earth's environment, largely caused by pesticides. More than fifty years later much of what she wrote sounds so obvious and familiar that a modern reader might wonder about the reasons for its acclaim. Before *Silent Spring*, however, nobody had put the pieces together as Carson did.

Writing about the five hundred new chemicals released upon the environment every year, she sounded the alarm on a massive experiment gone awry. She wrote:

> These sprays, dusts and aerosols are now applied almost universally to farms, gardens, forests, and homes—nonselective chemicals that have the power to kill every insect, the "good" and the "bad," to still the song of birds and the leaping of fish in the streams, to coat the leaves with a deadly film, and to linger on in the soil—all this though the intended target may be only a few weeds or insects . . . Future historians may well be amazed by our distorted sense of proportion. How could intelligent beings seek to control a few unwanted species by a method that contaminated the entire environment and brought the threat of disease and death even to their own kind.

As apocalyptic as it sounded at the time, other scientists knew she was right. E. O. Wilson was an entomologist at Harvard University when he first read *Silent Spring*. He understood the bravery of Carson's writing. In the scientific community, people who aimed their message at the masses, as opposed to fellow scientists, were seldom taken seriously, particularly if their field was ecology. Biologists, Wilson noted, were fixated on the chemical workings of life, and on the notion that inventions in the laboratories of science had become a cornerstone of human progress. "Better living through chemistry," a slogan popularized by the DuPont corporation, was also the mantra of the scientific world—a belief in the ability of our scientific minds to solve any problem, from eradicating disease to building our arsenals of national defense.

"For the sake of our prosperity and security," Wilson wrote in an essay about *Silent Spring*, "we rewarded science and technology with high esteem and placed great trust in the seeming infallibility of material ingenuity. As a consequence, environmental warnings were treated with irritable impatience."

Wilson first saw the fallacy of that view in a particular fool's errand that Carson wrote about—the government's war against fire ants. Wilson, as it happened, was the person who discovered these pests on U.S. soil. He was a thirteen-year-old Boy Scout at the time, living in Mobile, Alabama, a thriving port on the Gulf of Mexico where the ants first came in as stowaways. Though his discovery occurred in 1942, the ants had been in the country for a while—since the 1930s, Wilson estimated. Carson guessed they had arrived even earlier. In any case, they were spreading rapidly.

Later, as a biologist, Wilson was hired by the state of Alabama to study the habitat of this maddening insect—named for its burning sting—which would sometimes attack seedling corn or ground-nesting bird hatchlings. Wilson discovered the fire ants had spread from Alabama to Mississippi and predicted they would soon be found all the way to Texas. A nuisance for sure, Wilson concluded, but not a health or economic threat.

Like others, he was surprised in 1958 when the U.S. Department of Agriculture decided to spray a million acres in the South with powerful toxins, aimed not at controlling the ants, but rather at total eradication. The effects were disastrous. As Rachel Carson noted in *Silent Spring*, wildlife and cattle in areas where the poisons were used developed fatal nervous disorders, birds died, and insect populations beneficial to the food chain were suddenly decimated. The ants, however, bounced back quickly.

It was Carson's gift to connect the dots of environmental damage and deliver a warning that was sweeping in its mixture of passion and science. She wrote:

> In this now universal contamination of the environment, chemicals are the sinister and little-recognized partners of radiation in changing the very nature of the world—the very nature of its life. Strontium 90, released through nuclear explosions into the air, comes to earth in rain or drifts down as fallout, lodges in soil, enters into the grass or corn or wheat grown there, and in time takes up its abode in the bones of a human being, there to remain until his death. Similarly, chemicals sprayed on croplands or forests or gardens lie long in soil, entering into living organisms, passing from one to another in a chain of

> poisoning and death. Or they pass mysteriously by underground streams until they emerge and, through the alchemy of air and sunlight, combine into new forms that kill vegetation, sicken cattle, and work unknown harm on those who drink from once pure wells. As Albert Schweitzer has said, "Man can hardly even recognize the devils of his own creation."

The outraged chemical industry responded with sputtering fury, not only against the message of *Silent Spring* but against the sheer presumption of its author. Former U.S. Secretary of Agriculture Ezra Taft Benson suggested oddly that Carson was "probably a Communist" because she was attractive but unmarried. American Cyanamid biochemist Robert White-Stevens speculated darkly, "If man were to follow the teachings of Miss Carson, we would return to the Dark Ages, and the insects and diseases and vermin would once again inherit the earth."

Seeking to explain the contemptuous edge to such attacks, Carson biographer Linda Lear noted, "In postwar America, science was god, and science was male."

As a woman in this world of men, Carson charted a deeply personal path to acclaim. She was born into poverty near Pittsburgh and raised within the sight and smell of a glue factory—its product made from the bodies of horses. In these early years of the twentieth century, all around her family's cabin she could see the dark underside of the industrial revolution—the rapid despoiling of the natural world. And yet not far away she could wander the banks of the Allegheny River, studying the flowers and the fish and the birds, and feeling even as a little girl her own connection to all living things. That sense of human beings as a part of the world—not its master—animated her work from the start, as she earned her master's degree at Johns Hopkins University and became an editor at the U.S. Fish and Wildlife Service.

The Sea Around Us was her labor of love, but *Silent Spring* she wrote with reluctance—the "poison book," she sometimes called it—a project undertaken out of duty, with an urgent sense of resolve. As Carson was rushing to finish the book, she knew she was dying. Her body was ravaged by a rapidly metastasizing breast cancer, and who knew what poisons may have been the trigger?

The chemical industry spokesmen may not have known about her health (Carson did her best to keep it a secret) when they attacked her for being a "bird and bunny lover." But a curious thing began to happen. The more they attacked, the more her visibility and accolades grew. In June 1962, her book was serialized in *The New Yorker* and then in *Audubon* magazine. Carson was invited to appear on an hour-long edition of *CBS Reports*, hosted by Eric Sevareid.

At the White House, President John Kennedy read the book excerpts. He was already an admirer and had read two of Carson's earlier books, *The Sea Around Us* and *The Edge of the Sea*; they sat on his bookshelf next to the writings of Henry David Thoreau. According to historian Douglas Brinkley, Kennedy was impressed by *Silent Spring* and immediately wanted to help protect Carson from the attacks that he knew would come. Perhaps at Kennedy's behest, U.S. Supreme Court Justice William O. Douglas, an avid conservationist and close friend of the president, called *Silent Spring* "the most revolutionary book since *Uncle Tom's Cabin*."

Kennedy himself ordered the U.S. Department of Agriculture to study the health concerns raised by "Miss Carson's book," and he convened a special panel of the President's Science Advisory Committee to study pesticides more broadly. Carson herself testified before the panel. By then her health was failing badly; she wore a wig to cover baldness caused by chemotherapy, and because her bones were riddled with tumors she struggled to walk to the witness table. But her manner was calm and measured as she spoke. She did not contend that pesticides should be abolished, or that mankind would be better off without them. She simply underscored the central contention of her book—that the overuse of chemical poisons was rapidly causing irreversible harm.

The following spring, the president's panel released its report, forty-six pages that in the estimation of Douglas Brinkley "might as well have been called 'Rachel Carson Wins.'" Brinkley overstated the case. The power and influence of the chemical industry are also reflected in the report, which strikes an even-handed tone and acknowledged the necessity of pest control. But the panel's very attempt at balance was a victory of sorts—a presidential commission that warned against "the toxicity of pesticides," and called for greater public awareness, helped alter the course of national debate. Cautiously, with a politician's shrewdness, Kennedy had given a stamp of legitimacy to the concerns that Rachel Carson was raising.

Over the next decade changing attitudes rippled through the U.S. government, leading to the creation of the Environmental Protection Agency, passage of the National Environmental Policy Act, and the domestic banning of DDT, one of the most deadly pesticides. More broadly, Rachel invigorated an environmental movement that had been defined by its past champions—by the Presidents Roosevelt, for example—as a matter of conservation, of preserving national parks and public land for the enjoyment of future generations.

Carson made it more than that. She linked the environment to the health of humanity and gave legitimacy to the notion we were never meant to be masters of the earth, just the stewards of a fragile planet against which we were inflicting great harm.

As E. O. Wilson put it, "*Silent Spring* delivered a galvanic jolt to public consciousness and, as a result, infused the environmental movement with new meaning." When Carson died in 1964, she had reason to believe that even if environmental problems were far from solved, the world, nevertheless, might be headed down a different path.

A SECOND BOOK IN 1962 soon made waves almost as large. *The Other America* by Michael Harrington was not as heralded as *Silent Spring*, but Harrington achieved with the issue of poverty what Carson had accomplished for the environment. Harrington thought of his book as a sequel of sorts to *The Affluent Society*, published in 1958 by Harvard economist John Kenneth Galbraith. Galbraith had argued that America had become the first country on earth where the majority of citizens were affluent, living in a middle-class world in which their needs for survival and comfort were met. In *The Other America,* Harrington offered a corollary view—that the American poor were increasingly invisible, out of sight, out of mind, in a nation defined by conspicuous consumption. He wrote:

> Here are the unskilled workers, the migrant farm workers, the aged, the minorities, and all the others who live in the economic underworld of American life. If these people are not starving, they are hungry, and sometimes fat with hunger, for that is what cheap foods do. They are without adequate housing and education and medical care . . . But even more basic, this poverty twists and deforms the spirit. The American poor are pessimistic and defeated . . . and the truly human reaction can only be outrage. As W. H. Auden wrote: ". . . *We must love one another or die.*"

Harrington estimated that as many as fifty million Americans were part of this underworld of poverty, and though some scholars and politicians argued that his estimate was high, *The Other America* had a powerful effect on the national conscience. In less than two years, the President of the United States would propose in his State of the Union address an unconditional "War on Poverty," and perhaps as importantly Harrington's writings helped to inspire an activist movement that would add new urgency to the times.

In June 1962, Harrington attended a meeting in Port Huron, Michigan, trying to bring the wisdom of a lifelong socialist to a gathering of young American radicals. Most had read *The Other America,* which served for them as a kind of text, not quite Biblical in its inspiration, but close. They respected the depth of Harrington's commitment going back to the 1950s and his days an editor at *The Catholic Worker*, a paper known for its commitment to the poor.

At this assembly of activists, who called themselves Students for a Democratic Society (SDS), Harrington sought to be a moderating force, a reflection perhaps of his ability to balance the multiple components of his own philosophy. The Catholic son of Irish-American parents in St. Louis, he became an atheist in the 1950s. But he remained, he said, deeply influenced by the rigors of Catholic thought, particularly by the Jesuits he knew growing up, and their Christian understanding of justice. Harrington was staunchly anti-communist, preferring the democratic socialism of Norman Thomas, the seventy-eight-year-old, six-time Socialist candidate for president. Thomas had long opposed racial segregation, anti-labor laws, environmental damage from pesticides, and Japanese internment camps during World War II. Thomas had also campaigned strongly for opening America's shores to Jewish refugees from Nazi oppression. For registered Democrat Michael Harrington, Norman Thomas's socialism—Christian at its heart, for Thomas had been a Presbyterian minister—offered the country a moral compass.

Harrington could see a kindred spirit in Tom Hayden, one of the SDS founders, who had been at work since March on something he was calling the Port Huron Statement. Hayden, too, had been raised Catholic. He was named for St. Thomas Aquinas and attended Catholic schools in Detroit, where he was banned from his high school graduation for being too disruptive as a student. Known among friends for his dark, tousled hair, easy laugh, and wicked sense of humor, Hayden was serious about his politics. In 1960, at age twenty, he had hitchhiked across the country. On that journey of discovery, he met people who helped transform him from a campus leader—the student newspaper editor at the University of Michigan—to one of the 1960s' most committed radicals.

In Delano, California, he encountered Mexican farmworkers toiling for minimal pay in conditions that reminded him of slavery. In Los Angeles, he interviewed Dr. Martin Luther King, who was walking a picket line outside the Democratic National Convention. "There I was," Hayden would remember, "with pencil in hand, trying to conduct an objective interview with Martin Luther King, whose whole implicit message was: 'Stop writing, start acting.' That was a compelling moment." He found King patient, approachable and kind—as most people did in such situations. The civil rights leader told him gently: "Ultimately, you have to take a stand with your life."

As Peter Dreier later wrote in the *Huffington Post*, "When Hayden returned to Ann Arbor that fall, he committed himself to the life of an activist."

Thus, in the lead-up to the Port Huron conference, Hayden drafted a twenty-five-thousand-word manifesto that began with the following affirmation: "We are people of this generation, bred in at least modest comfort, housed now in universities, looking uncomfortably to the world we inherit."

In this founding document for SDS, ratified on June 15, Hayden and more than fifty activists (their numbers soon swelled to the tens of thousands) pledged their support for racial equality, economic justice, the pursuit of peace in a nuclear age, and a radical if vague commitment to "participatory democracy"—a system in which citizens would have a more direct role in controlling institutions that affected their lives.

"We would replace power rooted in possession, privilege, or circumstance by power and uniqueness rooted in love, reflectiveness, reason, and creativity," the young radicals declared. If some of their language sounded naïve, and if their eagerness and hope were soon overtaken by disillusionment and rage, there seemed little doubt that Hayden and the others meant every word.

BACK IN 1962, I didn't know about the Port Huron Statement. But at the age of fifteen, I was beginning a slow infatuation with the idealism that lay at its heart. I can remember almost the moment it began. I was at a party in Mobile, Alabama, where a friend was playing a stack of 45-rpm records. There among the ballads by Gene Pitney, Elvis, and the Everly Brothers was a song I had never heard before. It was not rock 'n' roll. This was something brand new, or so it seemed to me in the moment. Here was a group called Peter, Paul &

Mary—a Biblical name, I thought, not knowing yet that these were the singers' first names—and they sounded so pure with their acoustic guitars and the blend of two tenor voices and an alto, all so strong, and their harmonies all so intricate and clean, and then the ringing affirmation of the lyrics:

It's the hammer of Justice,
It's the bell of Freedom,
It's the song about Love between my brothers and my sisters,
All over this land . . .

As I recall it, all of us at the party that night understood immediately what this meant. Although the song was composed in 1949, it was as if Pete Seeger's lyrics had been written directly for the civil rights movement. Dr. Martin Luther King, the freedom riders, the ones sitting in at Southern lunch counters—all used the same imagery and language, the same evocations of justice and love and the brotherhood of man, and these were notions deliciously forbidden to young white Southerners of our day. But here was this song, this message, wrapped in the beauty of three strong voices and two guitars. I remember how my friend Ted Fillette and I listened to the record again and again that night.

"Damn," he said, in a voice that was soft with adolescent awe. "Just listen to that!"

10

The Rainbow Sign

From the beginning of 1962 until the very end, the cultural happenings were a curious intermingling of tradition and change, sometimes one, sometimes another, and sometimes both. There was a randomness about them at first, a feeling that events unfolding around us lacked any kind of pattern or focus. But they kept coming.

On January 1, a new law in Illinois made that state the first in the union where it was no longer a crime to be gay. In the other forty-nine states, that particular accident of birth was defined as sodomy, or a crime against nature, at least at the moment the person in question ceased being celibate. Now at least that was no longer true in Illinois.

On July 28, 1961, Governor Otto Kerner had signed into law an overhaul of the state's criminal code, set to take effect on New Year's Day. Sexual relations between consenting adults represented only one part of the change, and went virtually unnoticed except for an article buried in the *Chicago Sun-Times*. On December 21, 1961, the newspaper noted on page 43: "Under the new code it will not be a criminal offense for homosexuals to engage in sexual relations in private as long as the participants are adults, neither of whom has been pressured into the acts."

That was it. No further outcry or public scrutiny except for the skeptical response of Pearl Hart, a lawyer and lesbian activist who predicted, "It's true, of course, that the new legislation is not likely to be accompanied by social approval; nor will it abate the over-activity of certain police officers whose own feeling of guilt, perhaps, results in violence towards others . . ."

The Ladder, a nationally distributed lesbian magazine—the first in the country—praised the change but warned of a long road ahead: "The legality of homosexual practices in private will not bring social acceptance."

The Illinois decriminalization was therefore merely a little-noticed foreshadowing, but for those who battled the stigma of being gay, and whose secret was often the central agony of their lives, at least it was something.

THE REST OF US simply went about our lives, happy enough with the way things were going. On February 15, Ray Charles entered a Hollywood studio and recorded "I Can't Stop Loving You," a song that had been a country hit for its composer, Don Gibson. Producer Sid Feller had been skeptical when Charles—already a star with soul music hits like "I Got a Woman," "What'd I Say," and the Grammy-winning "Georgia on My Mind"— said he wanted to cut a whole album of country songs. But ever since Charles was a little boy in Florida, slowly going blind and finding consolation in music, he was drawn to the Grand Ole Opry as surely as to the big band ballads of Nat "King" Cole or the jazz compositions of Louis Armstrong.

In 1947, at age seventeen and before he had shortened his name from Ray Charles Robinson, he landed a job in Tampa as the piano player for a country band called the Florida Playboys. "Hillbilly music is totally honest," he said later. "They don't sing, 'I sat there and dreamed of you.' They say, 'I missed you and I went out and got drunk.' There are a lot of parallels between blues and country."

And so this artist who quite literally could not see any shades of skin, and who believed in the common bond of music, infused the sadness of a country song with the edge and the anguish he heard in the blues. "I Can't Stop Loving You" soared to number one on the charts and there it remained for five straight weeks.

At about the same time, R&B singer Arthur Alexander decided to make his next record in Nashville. It was an unusual choice for a black artist then, but Alexander recorded a song called "Anna" with some of Nashville's finest session players, all of them white. The record was only a regional hit, but a new British band called The Beatles heard the song and recorded their version of it. Lead singer John Lennon had a cold when the record was cut, and he thought later that his scratchy voice made the Beatles' rendition sound bluesy and hard, while Alexander's seemed wistful and country. Not long afterward, another new band called the Rolling Stones covered Alexander's "You Better Move On," and he became—along with Ray Charles and the Beatles—a symbol of the remarkable ability of music to cross old barriers of geography and race.

There was a sense of the world getting smaller, more interconnected.

On February 20, our eyes were turned toward Cape Canaveral as astronaut John Glenn became the first American to orbit the earth. His flight of four hours, fifty-five minutes, and twenty-three seconds included three loops around the globe—a feat repeated in May by Scott Carpenter. Glenn especially became the face of the space program, a national hero and a friend of the Kennedys; his patriotism and Marine Corps toughness launched him toward a future career in the U.S. Senate.

All of us were cheered, meanwhile, by the thrilling notion that America had finally caught up with the Russians. In the spring of 1962, we were feeling very good about ourselves.

Then came summer and a moment of sadness. That was how it was in those days, random moments that stayed in our minds, stitches in the tapestry of the time. On August 5, actress Marilyn Monroe was found dead in her California home from a massive overdose of barbiturates.

"Marilyn's sad story began and ended with abandonment and exploitation by almost everyone she knew," wrote Robert Gore-Langton in the United Kingdom newspaper *Express.*

Born Norma Jean Mortenson in 1926—the daughter of a schizophrenic mother and a father she never knew—she bounced around as a ward of the state, sexually molested at age eight, and again, she said, when she was eleven. Immediately after turning sixteen, she literally married the boy next door, a WWII Merchant Marine. But their four-year marriage ended in divorce. Other marriages followed—to baseball great Joe DiMaggio, who was jealous and possessive, and to playwright Arthur Miller, who was condescending about her intelligence. There were multiple affairs, including one with President John F. Kennedy. But there was also her remarkable success on the silver screen—in comedies like *Gentlemen Prefer Blondes* and *How to Marry a Millionaire*, and her Golden Globe award for a dramatic role in *Some Like It Hot.*

She asserted control of her career, defying movie industry executives who wanted to pay her too little or force her into roles she didn't want. Through it all, she sank into loneliness, depression, and a reliance on prescription drugs, until finally at the age of thirty-six, she overdosed—once again, alone—in her own bed. Some feminists in later years would praise her as a woman who "owned" her sexuality, though others came to see her story as one of desperation and sadness. At the time, most of us were merely shocked that such a vibrant cultural presence was suddenly and tragically gone from our midst.

But the moment passed, and in the fall we greeted another icon—very different, but no less important in our lives. On October 1, Johnny Carson took over as host of NBC's *Tonight Show*, and for the next thirty years he would be a regular guest in our homes. He was middle America, born in Iowa, raised in Nebraska, a little shy it sometimes seemed, but he possessed the comedian's gift of timing and the interviewer's gift of gab. Even more, he came prepared. As Billy Wilder noted, "If he's talking to an author, he has read the book." Each of us had our favorite interviews, our favorite guests—actress Diane Keaton perhaps, or comedian Don Rickles—but Carson's was a reassuring presence, there every weeknight, no matter what else might be going on.

And of course there was always something. On October 3, two days after Carson's debut, Wally Schirra flew six orbits around the earth, traveling at a speed that boggled the mind—17,557 miles per hour—and putting us now ahead of the Russians in the number of astronauts we had launched. But the cultural tapestry of 1962 included a darker thread as well. In the November 17 issue of *The New Yorker*, and then in the December issue of *The Progressive*, African American author James Baldwin published a pair of articles that would soon become a book, *The Fire Next Time*. He was writing about the issue of race, our enduring agony as Americans, and he was making the point—in prose so beautiful and searing it seemed almost to be burned on the page—that this was not a problem confined to the South:

> My friends were now "downtown," busy, as they put it, "fighting the man." They began to care less about the way they looked, the way they dressed, the things they did; presently, one found them in twos and threes and fours, in a hallway, sharing a jug of wine or a bottle of whiskey, talking, cursing, fighting, sometimes weeping: lost, and unable to say what it was that oppressed them, except that they knew it was "the man"—the white man. And there seemed to be no way whatever to remove this cloud that stood between them and the sun, between them and love and life and power, between them and whatever it was that they wanted. One did not have to be very bright to realize how little one could do to change one's situation; one did not have to be abnormally sensitive to be worn down to a cutting edge by the incessant and gratuitous humiliation and danger one encountered every working day, all day long. The

> humiliation did not apply merely to working days, or workers; I was thirteen and was crossing Fifth Avenue on my way to the Forty-second Street library, and the cop in the middle of the street muttered as I passed him, "Why don't you niggers stay uptown where you belong?" When I was ten, and didn't look, certainly, any older, two policemen amused themselves with me by frisking me, making comic (and terrifying) speculations concerning my ancestry and probable sexual prowess, and, for good measure, leaving me flat on my back in one of Harlem's empty lots.

And there was also this in an open letter to his teenaged nephew, published in *The Progressive*:

> This innocent country set you down in a ghetto in which, in fact, it intended that you should perish. Let me spell out precisely what I mean by that for the heart of the matter is here and the crux of my dispute with my country. You were born where you were born and faced the future you faced because you were black and for no other reason. The limits to your ambition were thus expected to be settled. You were born into a society which spelled out with brutal clarity and in as many ways as possible that you were a worthless human being.

As a black man born and raised in Harlem, coming of age in an era of segregation—legal in the South, a way of life in the North—Baldwin was seeking to issue a warning to a nation he thought was running out of time. As he expanded that warning into a book, he chose a title taken from an old slave song.

> *God gave Noah the rainbow sign, no more water, but fire next time.*

Already in 1962, events outside the world of art were making James Baldwin seem like a prophet.

11

Ole Miss

The pursuit of racial justice hit a stumbling block in 1962. For much of the year Martin Luther King found himself bogged down in Albany, Georgia. King had come to this small Southern town in support of protests that seemed to be going nowhere, due primarily to the wily resistance of Police Chief Laurie Pritchett.

At first glance, Pritchett looked like a character out of central casting, a large man, slow-talking, paunchy, proud of being white; but the chief had studied the writings of Dr. King—all his theories about nonviolence—and come to a shrewd realization. The civil rights movement did best when it had a villain. During the sit-ins and freedom rides, the protesters always got good press when they were being abused, and this in turn often prompted concessions among whites who feared for their community's reputation.

Pritchett ordered his officers to refrain from violence as they politely and methodically arrested every protester in Albany. When the local jail was full, Pritchett made arrangements with other jails within a fifty-mile radius to take the overflow prisoners. Eventually, the "Albany Movement" began to run short of bail money, and when Dr. King came to town to add visibility to the demonstrations, he too was arrested and jailed. Meanwhile, Albany's white leaders stood firm, rejecting virtually all of the movement's demands, and to the extent the national press noticed, there were speculations about King being past his prime. The Southern civil rights movement was clearly on the wane.

Then suddenly it wasn't. In September it began to dominate the news again in a most spectacular and unexpected way, triggering not only a violent response, but an all-out revolt among Southern whites, an insurrection the likes of which had not been seen since Reconstruction. The figure at the heart of this development was not Dr. King or any other recognized civil rights leader, but James Meredith, a twenty-nine-year-old African American who stood five-foot-six, weighed one hundred and thirty pounds, and was described by a journalist from *Newsweek* as a man with "doe-like eyes, and a delicate little ebony face."

The drama had begun the previous year. On January 20, 1961, shortly after John Kennedy's inaugural address, Meredith wrote the registrar at the University of Mississippi, requesting an application for admission. The registrar, not knowing his race, happily sent along a form, which Meredith completed and returned with a brief cover letter:

> I am an American-Mississippi-Negro citizen. With all of the occurring events regarding changes in our educational system taking place in our country in this new age, I feel certain that this application does not come as a surprise to you. I certainly hope that this matter will be handled in a manner that will be complimentary to the University of Mississippi and to the State of Mississippi. Of course, I am the one that will, no doubt, suffer the greatest consequences of this event.

Other civil rights leaders had their doubts about Meredith. "He was a strange bird from the beginning, always . . . acting on his own . . .," confided John Lewis, a leader in SNCC. In an interview with Karl Fleming of *Newsweek*, Meredith explained—his voice disarmingly matter-of-fact—that he was on a "divine mission" to break down the walls of white supremacy. But if even his admirers had to wonder about such a claim, there was no doubt Meredith was fiercely determined and brave. He was the son of a proud and independent Mississippi farmer, Cap Meredith, who had managed to buy his own patch of ground. "Death is preferred to indignity," the elder Meredith told his children. As the seventh of fourteen brothers and sisters, James shared his father's ferocious sense of worth—even a feeling, as Karl Fleming wrote, "that he was possessed of 'superhuman powers.'"

However odd such a notion might sound, in 1962 it may have taken something like that to challenge the University of Mississippi, the South's most stubborn citadel of whiteness. Founded in 1848, Ole Miss (as almost everybody called it) briefly closed its doors in 1861 when the entire student body—131 men—joined Company A of the 11th Mississippi Regiment and went off to fight in the Civil War. They served proudly under General Robert

E. Lee in the Army of Northern Virginia, and at the Battle of Gettysburg penetrated further into the enemy position than any other unit. For this they paid a terrible price—one hundred percent casualties; every member of the unit either killed, wounded, or captured. Thus did the University Greys, as they became known, personify the courage and carnage of a terrible war in which 622,000 soldiers died on American soil.

For later generations it was too much to bear, too painful to remember as it actually happened, so they heaped it with glory, turning it into a gallant Lost Cause. The mythology, of course, served an ancillary purpose: it obscured, sometimes subconsciously, sometimes deliberately, the South's hideous racial sins. And now James Meredith, a tiny black man, was about to strip away the veneer—about to force a collision between the present and the past that drove many thousands of white Mississippians into a spasm of frenzy and rage.

This 1962 eruption of melodrama, which quickly morphed into armed insurrection, included a remarkable cast of characters, ranging from heroes to villainous buffoons. One of the latter was Mississippi's governor, Ross Barnett. An ardent opponent of civil rights, Barnett once proclaimed in his Sunday school class (he was a fervent Baptist) that "the Good Lord was the original segregationist. He put the black man in Africa . . . He made us white because he wanted us white."

Born in 1898 as the youngest son of a Confederate veteran, Barnett was a successful Mississippi lawyer before being elected governor on his third try. By the time he took office in 1960, he had earned a reputation for racial animosity that easily crossed the line into hate. "God made niggers black," he once declared, "because they are so mean and evil." And yet it was also easy to see him as a joke, a cartoonish character who once addressed B'nai B'rith members in Jackson, Mississippi, as "you fine Christian gentlemen."

In his book, *Son of the Rough South*, reporter Karl Fleming recounted the time Barnett was asked by one of his aides about a matter of international diplomacy:

> During the Kennedy-Nixon presidential debates in 1960, there was a headline-making exchange about what the U.S. posture should be over China threatening the islands of Matsui and Quemoy to intimidate Taiwan. Barnett's PR man thought the governor should weigh in.

> "What do you think we should do about Matsui and Quemoy?" he asked Barnett.
>
> "I guess we can find a place for them over in the Fish and Game Commission," the governor said.

When it came to racial segregation, however, Barnett proved that he was not a man to be taken lightly. On September 20, James Meredith arrived at the Ole Miss campus in Oxford, flanked by federal officials and armed with an order from the U.S. Fifth Circuit Court of Appeals requiring the university to admit him. Barnett was there to block his way. "No school in our state will be integrated while I am your governor," he declared.

In Washington, the brothers Kennedy watched events unfold with a mixture of astonishment and concern. In his book, *A Thousand Days*, Arthur Schlesinger wrote about the verbal sparring between Attorney General Robert Kennedy and Barnett, mostly by phone. In an early conversation between the two, the governor declared, "I consider the Mississippi courts as high as any other court and a lot more capable . . . I am going to obey the laws of Mississippi." To which the attorney general coldly replied: "My job is to enforce the laws of the United States. I intend to fulfill it."

For a while the president stayed above the fray, simply speaking in support of racial progress. On September 22, he spoke at the Lincoln Memorial on the hundredth anniversary of the Emancipation Proclamation—or more specifically of a preliminary executive order issued by President Lincoln, making the end of slavery an explicit goal of the Civil War. On the following January 1, said Lincoln, slaves in the South would be considered free.

In his centennial message, Kennedy gave Lincoln only part of the credit:

> The essential effort, the sustained struggle, was borne by the Negro alone with steadfast dignity and faith . . . It can be said, I believe, that Abraham Lincoln emancipated the slaves, but that in this century since, our Negro citizens have emancipated themselves . . . Like the proclamation we celebrate, this observance must be regarded not as an end, but a beginning.

Many African Americans were impressed by the president's tone, his obvious respect for their achievements and the promise of greater freedom he embraced. But Ross Barnett regarded the statement as further proof that the Kennedy Administration was pro-civil rights, and therefore an enemy of the South, and the governor merely became more defiant. On three separate occasions, Barnett and his lieutenant governor, Paul Johnson, refused to allow James Meredith—despite clear rulings from the federal courts—to register as a student at Ole Miss. Finally, President Kennedy himself put in a call to Barnett, hoping the power and prestige of his office might change the governor's mind.

Schlesinger, who was in the president's office at the time, along with Robert Kennedy, offered this wry description of the scene:

> Awaiting the call, the Kennedys were calm and dispassionate, talking quietly between themselves in fraternal shorthand and, as ever, lightening the tension with jokes. As the phone rang, the President, with the air of a master of ceremonies, announced, "And now—Governor Ross Barnett." Bobby, mocking a prize-fight manager, said, "Go get him, Johnny boy." As if rehearsing to himself, the President went on, "Governor, this is the President of the United States—not Bobby, not Teddy." Then he picked up the receiver. His expression serious, his voice calm, he began, "I am concerned about this matter as I know you must be. . . . Here's my problem, Governor. I don't know Mr. Meredith, and I didn't put him in there. But under the Constitution I have to carry out the law. I want your help in doing it."

Schlesinger could tell from Kennedy's response that Barnett was trying to evade the issue, but Kennedy kept pressing. "I want to work this out in an amicable way. I don't want a lot of people down there to be hurt or killed." When the conversation ended with Barnett's position still unclear, the President shook his head in astonishment. "You know what that fellow said?" he reported to the others in the room. "He said, 'I want to thank you for your help on the poultry program.'"

The Kennedys were never sure if Barnett was simply not very smart, or if his buffoonery was a cover. In any case, he was a moving target. Facing jail time for contempt of court, and fines of up to $10,000 a day, the governor agreed, finally, to let James Meredith register at the University of Mississippi. But he continued to fan the flames of defiance. On the Saturday before the final showdown, he appeared at an Ole Miss football game where 41,000 of the most rabid fans in the South were waving their Confederate flags. The Rebels (the team's official nickname) would go undefeated in 1962, and on this day they beat Kentucky 14–0. But the highlight came at halftime.

Ross Barnett ambled out to the fifty-yard line and delivered a sixteen-word address: "I love Mississippi!" he roared. "I love her people! Our customs. I love and I respect our heritage."

The next day, there was a riot. Barnett had suggested to the Kennedys that Meredith come to campus on Sunday, September 30, to register, then begin his classes on Monday. Sunday should have been a day of quiet, but word of Barnett's plan leaked, spreading rapidly among white supremacists all over Mississippi and beyond. In Texas, former Major General Edwin Walker, who had recently retired from the U.S. Army after accusing the Kennedy Administration of "collaboration and collusion with the international Communist conspiracy," went on radio to urge all-out resistance to Meredith's entry into Ole Miss:

> Now is the time to be heard! Thousands strong from every State in the Union! Rally to the cause of freedom! The Battle Cry of the Republic! Barnett yes, Castro no! Bring your flags, your tents and your skillets! It is time! Now or never!

The irony was that six years earlier Walker had commanded the troops deployed to Little Rock, Arkansas, by President Eisenhower to quell a similar mob resisting the court-ordered desegregation of Central High School. But now, in Oxford, Mississippi, he climbed to the base of a Confederate monument near the entrance to Ole Miss. "This time I am on the right side," he shouted. "You may lose this battle but you will have to be heard. You must be prepared for possible death. If you are not, go home now!"

Cheering his words and streaming onto the campus were hundreds of white people armed with squirrel guns, rifles, bricks, clubs, knives, crying for the blood of this black interloper, this five-foot-six-inch Air Force veteran who intended to defile their sacred institution; and crying also for the blood of the three hundred federal marshals who had been sent by Robert Kennedy to protect Meredith.

Remarkably, almost unbelievably in the midst of this terrifying insanity, another white man climbed to the base of the Confederate statue and also spoke to the crowd. The Reverend Duncan Gray was a native Mississippian, the rector of St. Peter's Episcopal Church in Oxford, where he had already proclaimed from the pulpit that morning:

> For these are times which not only try men's souls, but also infect and poison them. The seeds of anger and hatred, bitterness and prejudice are already widely sown, and as Christians, we need to do our utmost to uproot and cast them out.

Now at the statue, he exhorted the mob, pleading with them in the name of God to lay down their weapons, turn around, and go home. In response, the crowd began to cry for his blood as well, grabbing at him, pulling him roughly from the statue to the ground. "Kill him!" they screamed. "Kill him! Kill him!" In his biography of Gray, *And Also With You*, another Christian liberal from Mississippi, the Reverend Will Campbell, described what happened next:

> Two massive young men had maneuvered Gray to the opposite side of the monument . . . The larger one had him pinned to the ground, wrestler fashion. The other one was trying to dissuade the big one.
>
> "No, no, no," he kept saying. "Let's don't hurt the preacher."
>
> "You heard what he said on TV. Let's kill the son-of-a-bitch." Gray had addressed the admission of Meredith on radio and had been interviewed by television and newspaper journalists.
>
> "I know, I know, I know. But he's a preacher. He really believes that stuff." They argued. "Well, who the hell are you? Maybe you believe it too."
>
> Gray recalls that the one who didn't want him harmed was a deputy sheriff from a neighboring county.

Evans Harrington, one of Gray's church members and an Ole Miss English professor, now waded into the fray as well, determined to rescue his preacher, and somehow Gray made it out alive. But the violence he was trying to stop worsened. By nightfall the crowd had swelled to 2,500, inflamed in part by the presence of the U.S. marshals who gathered at the Lyceum Building, where Meredith was expected to register for class. They stood three deep in front of a row of Grecian columns—such a stately symbol of the South, for this was the oldest building on campus, the place where the University Greys had attended class before they left for the Civil War. To many in the crowd that day, this must have felt somehow like a replay, an opportunity to defend their traditions yet again, and I remember a friend from Mississippi who wondered if a desperate, antebellum pride had not been an animating factor in the rage.

Whatever its complicated motivation, the anger quickly morphed into insurrection. In *Son of the Rough South*, *Newsweek*'s Karl Fleming recalled how the crowd of white people, some of them students, most not, were screaming epithets—"Kill the nigger!" "Down with the goddamned Kennedys!"—as they surged en masse toward the Lyceum, where they had heard that Meredith would arrive any minute. But plans had changed. At 6 p.m., a small government plane with Meredith aboard touched down at the Oxford airport, and U.S. officials drove him directly to Baxter Hall, a campus dormitory, where federal marshals stood guard at his door. Meredith opened his books and began to study, his icy demeanor a disconcerting contrast to the bedlam outside.

As Fleming reported,

> The sickly sweet smell of tear gas filled the air . . . The rioters seemed immune to its effects as they rushed forward hurling rocks, bottles, pieces of concrete, and steel rods—anything that could be found or torn loose.

Soon, those with guns began to use them, firing—incredibly—round after round at the U.S. marshals, who responded with tear gas, having been forbidden by Kennedy to return fire with live ammunition. Shortly after 10 p.m., with the supply of tear gas running low, Kennedy ordered in a federalized unit of the Mississippi National Guard, but even then the battle raged on. Fleming, who had been among the journalists inside the Lyceum, stepped out on the porch to get a better look and heard the splat of two bullets in quick succession, hitting the white wood column six inches from his head.

"If I was James Meredith, I wouldn't *go* to school with these people," he muttered.

Just before midnight, Governor Barnett went on statewide radio, not to plead for calm, but to urge the resisters to keep on fighting. "I call on all Mississippians to keep the faith and courage," he declared. "We will never surrender."

For the next several hours, the rioters did as the governor demanded, setting cars on fire, throwing rocks and Molotov cocktails, until finally around 4 a.m. a convoy of regular Army units, ordered in by President Kennedy, arrived on campus. Armed with M-14 rifles, they formed a line at the Lyceum building and marched forward through the lingering drifts of tear gas, past burning cars and broken glass and all the littered aftermath of battle, and they drove the remaining rioters from campus.

Morning came and federal officials took their measure of the carnage. Two people were dead. One was Paul Guihard, a French reporter who had been shot in the back—"execution-style," one official said. The other was Ray Gunter, a local jukebox repairman who had ventured to the campus just to see what was going on and took a bullet to the head. More than two hundred soldiers and marshals were injured, including twenty-nine marshals with gunshot wounds and another half-dozen with acid burns.

It had been a terrible night. But at 7:30 a.m. James Meredith came into the Lyceum, where he signed the necessary forms for admission, and immediately reported to his first class. "Was it worth two lives, nigger?" one student shouted as Meredith passed by. "The blood is on your hands, nigger bastard," another one cried. Meredith did not flinch.

After class, still accompanied by U.S. marshals, he held a press conference. He was neatly dressed in a dark suit, and as always he carried a briefcase. His composure was impeccable, as if all of this were simply routine, but when a reporter asked if he was happy to be a student, he replied with a tight and measured irony.

"No," he said," this is not a happy occasion."

He was a lonely figure in the weeks after that. One of his only friends at Ole Miss was historian James Silver, a native of New York State, who had taught at the university for nearly thirty years. A week into Meredith's tenure as a student, Silver invited him to dinner with journalists Karl Fleming and Claude Sitton of the *New York Times*, who had also covered the insurrection. The four had a pleasant visit and later attended a play, actor Hal Holbrook's one-man show about Mark Twain. In their conversations Meredith was always stiffly polite, though not much more, and Silver and the others found it hard to blame him. His dogged desire to attend the university had summoned the worst in white Mississippians.

Silver later wrote, in a book he entitled *Mississippi: The Closed Society*:

> Like many observers, I was alternately enraged and heartsick that my fellow Mississippians, particularly the students, felt called upon to engage in a mad insurrection against their government. To me it was and still is nothing less than incredible.

But it was also true that Meredith had won. As Fleming would note years later, "The whole force of the United States—physical, legal, and moral—had been brought to bear to protect the constitutional right of one tiny black man. And that was something extraordinary to witness, and to be proud of as a citizen."

Not everyone agreed with that assessment. White politicians all over the South decried the federal "invasion" of Mississippi, and on the other side, among civil rights leaders, there was a feeling that Kennedy had been too timid, too willing to negotiate with a Mississippi governor who never intended to negotiate at all. Martin Luther King, already unhappy with Kennedy's failure to introduce a new civil rights bill, was one of those most critical. As historian Taylor Branch later put it, "King knew that Kennedy and Ross Barnett still had more in common with each other than either had with him."

Thus, in the fall of 1962, King was convinced that the movement must continue to exert pressure on the president. He was also determined to move on from his failure in Albany, Georgia, earlier in the year. More and more, he was thinking about a campaign in Birmingham, perhaps the most segregated city in the South, where Police Commissioner Eugene "Bull" Connor ruled with an iron and racist hand. In 1961, Connor had personally approved the beating of freedom riders at the Birmingham bus station, keeping his policemen away so the Klan could stage its bloody attack. If Police Chief Laurie Pritchett in Albany had refused to play the role of villain, King was certain Bull Connor would be unable to resist. He hoped a confrontation with Connor would make it clear to the country—and to Kennedy—that strong civil rights legislation was needed.

As a prelude to involvement in Birmingham, King decided to hold a convention in that city, an annual meeting of his organization, the Southern Christian Leadership Conference. By coincidence, he and other SCLC members were meeting at precisely the time that Meredith was trying to register at Ole Miss. On Friday, September 28, a day when Meredith had been turned away, King was speaking to about three hundred delegates, going through a series of routine announcements, when a white man rose from the audience and began walking toward the stage. Nobody thought much about it at first, but then the man, Roy James, an American Nazi sympathizer, lunged at King and began to hit him in the face. King's lieutenants, including Ralph Abernathy, rushed to his defense, and seemed ready to tear James apart when something truly remarkable happened. King took the white man gently in his arms to shield him from the rage of Abernathy and the others.

Lola Hendricks, one of Birmingham's most committed civil rights advocates, was in the crowd that day, and like many others she was astonished at this display of nonviolence. Even Roy James began to weep, for this quite clearly was not just a tactic, or even a philosophy, but an instinct that ran so deep in King that those who saw it could only consider the implications with awe.

"It gave me faith in nonviolence," remembered Mrs. Hendricks many years later. "Dr. King was something special."

In the coming year many thousands of Americans, black and white, would come to share Mrs. Hendricks's view. Martin Luther King would achieve a status that no black leader in the country ever had.

12

The Missiles and the Making of JFK

As the Ole Miss crisis came to an end in early October, President Kennedy had other urgent things on his mind.

In July, Raul Castro, brother of Cuban Prime Minister Fidel Castro, had traveled to Moscow to meet with Nikita Khrushchev. At about that time, and perhaps in that meeting, the governments of Cuba and the Soviet Union agreed to install Soviet missiles in Cuba. These were to be medium and intermediate-range weapons armed with nuclear warheads that could target most of the eastern United States almost without warning. It was an extraordinary decision, putting U.S. security at such obvious risk that American officials were moved to wonder, as one put it, "whether Khrushchev had lost his mind."

Partly because of the sheer improbability of the plan, U.S. intelligence did not discover it right away. Reconnaissance flights over Cuba detected unusual construction in August, but not until a U-2 flight on October 14 were intelligence experts able to identify what was going on. Analysts spent the following day and part of the evening poring over the U-2 photographs, concluding unmistakably that the installation of medium and intermediate range missiles would soon be complete.

Kennedy was dismayed when National Security Adviser McGeorge Bundy presented the news on Tuesday morning, October 16—angry that a change so radical in the status quo had been accomplished through elaborate Soviet deception. It was true that tensions were rising. Both sides had resumed nuclear testing, and Kennedy, in April, had reached the reluctant decision to restart above-ground testing, as well as underground, to match the Soviets stride for stride. But he assumed that they had reached a plateau.

In September, Khrushchev himself had sent a personal message to Kennedy affirming that any "armaments and military equipment sent to Cuba are for defensive purposes." Khrushchev had included an ominous boast: "Our nuclear weapons are so powerful in their explosive force, and the Soviet Union has so powerful rockets to carry these nuclear warheads, that there is no need to search for sites for them beyond the boundaries of the Soviet Union."

But if Kennedy was "furious" about the lie (that was the description by Arthur Schlesinger), participants in the urgent meetings that followed described him as "calm." Schlesinger, Attorney General Robert Kennedy, Defense Secretary Robert McNamara, and speechwriter Ted Sorensen all would offer their accounts of the crisis, and all were filled with admiration for the president. At the same time, those recollections were free of personal aggrandizement, as if the participants were humbled and awed by the magnitude of the moment. If the world had skated to the nuclear edge in the Berlin crisis of 1961, this time it peered into the abyss. In retrospect, it now seems likely that an all-out nuclear war was averted, incredibly, by a matter of seconds—and only because cooler heads prevailed.

Almost certainly, the coolest and most important was John Kennedy.

From the moment he learned of the missiles' existence, Kennedy insisted they would have to be removed. Militarily, they represented an unacceptable threat, but more than that, in Kennedy's mind, they were a political provocation so extreme that, if accepted, it would shred America's credibility in the world. But was it possible to compel their removal? And if so, how and at what cost? Would an escalation lead inexorably to nuclear war?

Those were the questions that had to be addressed, and as the president assembled an executive committee of advisers he knew they didn't have much time. Ongoing U-2 flights over Cuba made it clear that construction at the launch sites was proceeding rapidly. Once the weapons were ready to fire, the stakes were exponentially increased.

In the early hours, there seemed to be two choices. The United States could either accept the nuclear missiles in Cuba or it could attack the installations and bring a military end to the threat.

In his book, *Kennedy*, Ted Sorensen recalled how troubling both of those courses seemed to be. From the beginning, the president had rejected acquiescence. U.S. credibility and security demanded a resolute response. But a surprise attack on the missile installations, however decisive it might be, carried great risk. For one thing, even those pushing for a military strike acknowledged there was no way to be sure that all of the missiles could be destroyed. And if one missile, already armed with a nuclear warhead, survived the initial American barrage, the Soviets might well decide to launch it. There was, in addition, the question of storage sites for warheads that were not yet attached to Soviet missiles. Those sites, too, would have to be destroyed. Thus the military operation grew more complex.

But the dilemmas the executive committee faced were more than strategic. There were issues of diplomacy as well. Would a direct American attack on Cuba weaken our position in Latin America? Would neutral nations see the United States as a bully? Would America lose the moral high ground when Soviet and Cuban civilian workers died in the blast of U.S. bombs? And what about the European response? With the killing of Soviet citizens in Cuba, would Khrushchev suddenly seize Berlin, as he had threatened in the past? If so, would our allies blame us for putting them at risk? And how would America respond?

All of this weighed on the men in the room. But as they agonized over what to do next, there was even then another dimension to their debate. In this crisis, as the fate of the world hung in the balance, there was a life and death concern about the *right* thing to do—about the ethical choices that lay before them and about the moral judgments of history. Robert Kennedy was perhaps the most outspoken on these points. He argued for some middle ground, some alternative between acquiescence and a surprise attack on a nation much smaller than the United States.

Kennedy was heartened on Wednesday when Defense Secretary Robert McNamara, former president of Ford Motor Company and a man who was known for his energy and drive, began to lobby for a naval blockade. This, as McNamara noted, would prevent the introduction of additional missiles and send a clear signal to the Soviet Union that the United States was serious, that it would not accept such a threat to its security. Opponents in the executive committee argued strongly that a blockade would not be enough. It did nothing, for example, to address the missiles already installed. But it did offer hope that innocent lives would not be lost, and thus Robert Kennedy supported that plan.

In his book, *Thirteen Days,* in which he offered his own account of the crisis, the attorney general recalled a turning point in the committee's deliberations. It began, ironically, with a brilliant presentation by former Secretary of

State Dean Acheson, an eloquent Cold War hard-liner, in favor of an all-out attack. Kennedy wrote:

> With some trepidation, I [responded] that whatever validity the military and political arguments were for an attack in preference to a blockade, America's traditions and history would not permit such a course of action. Whatever military reasons he and others could marshal, they were nevertheless, in the last analysis, advocating a surprise attack by a very large nation against a very small one. This, I said, could not be undertaken by the U.S. if we were to maintain our moral position at home and around the globe. Our struggle against Communism through the world was far more than physical survival—it had as its essence our heritage and our ideals, and these we must not destroy.

McNamara, especially, listened to Kennedy's words with respect. He understood the role the president's younger brother would play in the crisis. John Kennedy decided on the first day that he would not attend every meeting of the executive committee. He knew his presence might inhibit free discussion. Some of those present might—consciously or unconsciously—say what they thought he wanted to hear, rather than offering their best ideas, and the president wanted nothing but the best. Thus, he delegated to his brother the task of keeping the committee on track.

But the attorney general's role was, as McNamara noted,

> . . . far more than administrative. On the basic policy question of whether to force the missiles out by massive air and ground attack or by the far less risky application of a maritime quarantine, he strongly favored the quarantine.
>
> He did so because he saw that air and ground strikes favored by so many would have brought death to thousands of innocent Cuban civilians and to thousands of U.S. military personnel. He saw, too, that such attacks ran the risk of triggering the launch of nuclear weapons from Cuba against the U.S. and the risk of Soviet retaliatory attacks on Berlin or other vulnerable points on the periphery of NATO.

By Thursday, October 18, most of the committee favored a blockade, though they struggled with the arguments against that position. They knew most importantly that a blockade would not eliminate missiles already in Cuba, at least not directly. And if Soviet ships ignored it, the United States would have to fire the first shot, which might prompt much of the world to blame America, not Khrushchev, for creating a crisis. The Soviet leader, moreover, would retain the same range of options in answer to a blockade that he would to a bombing raid or invasion of Cuba. He could blockade Berlin, or fire the missiles already in Cuba, or he could launch an all-out nuclear attack. The blockade, in short, might trigger a military confrontation without eliminating the Soviet missiles that caused it.

When John Kennedy met with the committee Thursday night, it was clear that major divisions remained, and Kennedy was convinced that time was running out. As the tension mounted within these highest councils of government, Kennedy worked to maintain his normal schedule. He did not want word of the crisis to leak before the U.S. was ready to act. Thus he kept his speaking commitments for the Congressional elections coming up in November, and on Thursday afternoon, October 18, he also met with Soviet Foreign Minister Andrei Gromyko. Kennedy wondered, as the previously scheduled meeting approached, if Gromyko intended to use that occasion to acknowledge the Soviet missiles in Cuba. With U.S. policy still uncertain, the president did not intend to bring it up, and he hoped Gromyko would not force his hand.

Remarkably enough, when the conversation turned to Cuba, Gromyko simply repeated the assurance that nothing unusual was going on. "As for Soviet assistance to Cuba," he said, "I have been instructed to make it clear, as the Soviet government has already done, that such assistance pursued solely the purpose of contributing to the defense capabilities of Cuba and to the development of its peaceful economy."

In *Kennedy*, Ted Sorensen recalled that the president remained poker-faced, betraying no emotion at all in response to this ongoing distortion: "Kennedy remained impassive, neither agreeing nor disagreeing with Gromyko's claim. He gave no sign of tension or anger . . ." For JFK it was, of necessity, a week of steely self-control, a reminder of Theodore White's observation in *The Making of a President*: "The man behaves in any crisis as if it consisted only of a sequence of necessary things to be done that will become complicated if emotions intrude."

Thus Kennedy, when the crisis broke, proceeded as if his job were a mental checklist. He ordered more reconnaissance flights over Cuba to be as certain as possible of the dimensions of the missile buildup. He ordered his advisers to tell no one what was happening until a course of action was clear. He also set the broad parameters, making it clear to his team of advisers that nuclear war was "the final failure," but the missiles in Cuba had to go. Together, they must find a path to that result.

There were moments when his emotion broke through. During one particularly intense discussion, when it was clear that Kennedy was leaning toward a blockade rather than an attack, Air Force Chief of Staff Curtis LeMay made a belligerent case for the latter. Kennedy knew LeMay's reputation. As an Air Force general in World War II, he had ordered the firebombing of Japanese cities, including Tokyo where at least 100,000 civilians died in a single night. Now he was arguing for an all-out attack on Cuba.

"I think that a blockade, and political talk, would be considered by a lot of our friends and neutrals as being a pretty weak response to this," LeMay insisted, "and I'm sure a lot of our own citizens would feel that way too. In other words, you're in a pretty bad fix at the present time."

Kennedy turned to the general with annoyance. "What did you say?"

When LeMay repeated his last sentence, Kennedy responded with an ironic chuckle. "You're in it with me," he said, and according to some of those in the room, there was ice in his voice.

On the other side of the emotional spectrum, Kennedy seemed eager to spend extra time with his family, and while on his way to the Libyan embassy, another routine appointment he kept while he was moving toward a decision on Cuba, he asked his driver to stop at St. Matthew's Cathedral. "We're going in here to say a prayer," he said. "Right now we need all the prayers we can get."

Throughout, he understood clearly his lonely burden. He had confidence in the men of the executive committee—in some more than others as the week wore on. But in the end, he knew it was up to him, and by Saturday morning he had made up his mind.

Early in the week, General Maxwell Taylor, head of the Joint Chiefs of Staff, had acknowledged there was simply no way to be sure that bombing raids, however intense, would destroy all the missiles. Almost certainly, there would have to be an invasion. Undersecretary of State George Ball urged the others not to underestimate the Soviet response to such an attack. "I think the price is going to be high," Ball maintained. "It may still be worth paying to eliminate the missiles, but I think we must assume that it's going to be high." And on Saturday morning, as Larry Sabato noted in *The Kennedy*

Half-Century, Deputy Secretary of Defense Roswell Gilpatric offered a final, respectful "nudge" in the direction Kennedy was already leaning: "Essentially, Mr. President, this is a choice between limited action and unlimited action, and most of us think it's better to start with limited action."

Thus did Kennedy make the most difficult decision of his presidency, seeking to balance resolution and restraint. They would begin with a blockade—a "quarantine," they decided to call it, since a blockade legally was an act of war. The president would address the nation Monday night, October 22, and in preparation for that speech, and whatever confrontation might follow, a flurry of diplomatic activity began. There were European allies to be informed (Dean Acheson was dispatched to France for a personal meeting with Charles de Gaulle) and Assistant Secretary of State Edwin Martin prepared for a meeting of the Organization of American States, seeking that group's support for the quarantine. At the United Nations, U.S. Ambassador Adlai Stevenson was drafting his own speech to that body, and on the afternoon of the presidential address, Kennedy himself met with leading members of Congress.

That particular meeting did not go well. Most of those present thought the president's response was weak, and two of the most outspoken were Richard Russell and J. William Fulbright, senators from Kennedy's own party. They argued that the blockade was irrelevant to the fundamental problem—removing nuclear missiles from Cuba—and they were essentially unmoved by Kennedy's reply. The president stood firm in the face of last-minute second-guessing. The bottom line, he said, was that the missiles in Cuba would have to be removed, and he intended to make that clear in his speech. For now, the approach he had chosen gave both sides the time and the room to maneuver as they searched for a peaceful resolution. The invasion the senators seemed to prefer could well set off a nuclear exchange in which millions of Americans might die. Perhaps in the end, it would come to war. But that was not the place he intended to start.

Kennedy emerged from the meeting angry, his speech to the nation less than an hour away. "If they want this job they can have it," he muttered to Ted Sorensen, as he walked toward his quarters to change his clothes. "It's no great joy to me." Within a short time, however, he was more philosophical, knowing that the senators' reaction was not very different from his own when he first learned of the missiles' existence. The members of Congress had not been tempered by the five days of discussion he and his executive committee had endured.

By 7 p.m., as he took his place before the television cameras, Kennedy once again was calm. In his address to the nation, which he knew also was an address to the world, he revealed the discovery of the missiles in Cuba, announced the U.S. naval quarantine, and then outlined the broader stakes:

> This nation is opposed to war. We are also true to our word. Our unswerving objective, therefore, must be to prevent the use of those missiles against this or any other country, and to secure their withdrawal or elimination from the Western Hemisphere. . . . We will not prematurely or unnecessarily risk the costs of worldwide nuclear war in which even the fruits of victory would be ashes in our mouth; but neither will we shrink from that risk at any time it must be faced . . .
>
> The cost of freedom is always high, but Americans have always paid it. And one path we shall never choose, and that is the path of surrender or submission.

All in all, these were chilling words, their meaning crystal clear to heads of state around the world and to ordinary citizens in the United States. Nuclear war between the two superpowers was a distinct possibility, and it could begin within a matter of days, unless Nikita Khrushchev could find a graceful way to retreat. No one knows precisely what Kennedy was thinking as he concluded his speech. But according to Arthur Schlesinger, the president returned immediately to his living quarters at the White House, and sought out his daughter Caroline, who was four. He told her stories until dinnertime, then dined alone with the First Lady. As Schlesinger reported it,

> "If anything happens," she told him firmly, "we're all going to stay right here with you. I just want to be with you, and I want to die with you, and the children do, too—than live without you."

The following day, the Organization of American States, representing the nations of the Western Hemisphere, passed a unanimous resolution of support for the quarantine. Prime Minister Harold Macmillan of Great Britain, Chancellor Konrad Adenauer of Germany, and President Charles de Gaulle of France also stood firmly with Kennedy. "If there is a war, I will be with you," said de Gaulle. "But there will be no war."

On Tuesday afternoon, October 23, the diplomatic offensive continued with a UN address by Adlai Stevenson, always a man of extraordinary eloquence:

> Since the end of the Second World War, there has been no threat to the vision of peace so profound, no challenge to the world of the Charter so fateful. The hopes of mankind are concentrated in this room. . . . Let [this day] be remembered, not as the day when the world came to the edge of nuclear war, but as the day when men resolved to let nothing thereafter stop them in their quest for peace.

After watching the speech on television, President Kennedy dictated a telegram of praise: "DEAR ADLAI: I WATCHED YOUR SPEECH THIS AFTERNOON WITH GREAT SATISFACTION. . . . THE UNITED STATES IS FORTUNATE TO HAVE YOUR ADVOCACY. YOU HAVE MY WARM AND PERSONAL THANKS."

There had always been a curious unease between the two men, a generational difference, some observers thought, or perhaps it was more a matter of personality—Kennedy so crisp and cool, Stevenson so intellectual and refined. But in the course of the Cuban missile crisis, their gap in personal understanding was replaced by a warm and mutual respect.

Meanwhile, a fleet of one hundred and eighty naval vessels under the command of U.S. Admiral Alfred Ward was now in the Caribbean, prepared to enforce the quarantine. In Cuba, preparations on the missile sites continued at a frantic pace, hastening the day when they would be operational. The tension mounted and became worldwide. In England, pacifist philosopher Bertrand Russell, who had won the Nobel Prize for Literature, was one of a number of British intellectuals who blamed the United States, not Khrushchev, for the threat of war. "YOUR ACTION DESPERATE," he wrote in a telegram to President Kennedy. "NO CONCEIVABLE JUSTIFICATION. WE WILL NOT HAVE MASS MURDER. . . . END THIS MADNESS." While to Khrushchev, Russell wrote: "YOUR CONTINUED FOREBEARANCE IS OUR GREAT HOPE."

From the Soviet Union the signals were mixed. Even as work continued on the missile sites, there were reports that Soviet ships on their way to Cuba, bearing additional missiles and military hardware, were slowing down, perhaps even turning around. But on the floor of the United Nations the Soviet government pushed its case. Its UN ambassador, V. A. Zorin, refused to acknowledge that the missiles represented an offensive threat. In a UN Security Council debate, Zorin's position prompted outrage, steely and eloquent, from Adlai Stevenson:

> "Do you, Ambassador Zorin, deny that the USSR has placed and is placing medium and intermediate-range missiles in Cuba? Yes or no? Don't wait for the translation. Yes or no?"

When Zorin complained that he was not a witness in a U.S. courtroom, Stevenson's tone turned even colder:

> "You are in the courtroom of world opinion. You have denied they exist, and I want to know if I understood you correctly. I am prepared to wait for my answer until hell freezes over. And I am also prepared to present evidence in this room—now!"

Stevenson brought in aerial photographs, which he displayed for the diplomats in the room, and then he turned again to the Soviet ambassador.

> "We know the facts and so do you, sir, and we are ready to talk about them. Our job here is not to score debating points. Our job, Mr. Zorin, is to save the peace. And if you are ready to try, we are."

This happened late on Thursday, October 25, and as the hours crept past, tensions neared a breaking point. Construction on the missile sites continued, and U.S. troops were massing in Florida, preparing to invade unless some other solution was found. In *Thirteen Days*, Robert Kennedy wrote of a complicating factor for the men in charge. These mere mortals, now staring potentially at the end of civilization as they knew it, were not getting enough sleep.

Measured by "impatience" and "fits of anger," Kennedy wrote, "The strain and the hours without sleep were beginning to take their toll."

On one of those nights, the attorney general had asked a friend to drive him home. John Jay Hooker, a young Tennessee lawyer with political ambitions of his own, worked in the Justice Department, and had even lived with

Kennedy and his family when he had first moved to Washington. As they were driving through the darkened streets of the city, Hooker turned to Kennedy, who appeared even more exhausted than usual, and told him he had to get some rest. Kennedy responded with obvious irritation. How the hell could he sleep under these circumstances?

They rode along in silence until Hooker, never a man at a loss for self-confidence, began to push from a different direction. "Do you think Khrushchev will fire the first shot?" he asked. Once again, Kennedy looked annoyed. How could anybody know? he snapped.

And what about the president? Hooker insisted. Did Robert Kennedy think his brother would push the button? The answer, Hooker added quickly, was of course not. Neither leader would be the first to push the button. Neither leader was insane. Therefore, the crisis essentially came down to diplomacy, and it was crucial for the men in charge to think clearly.

"So get some sleep," he told his friend. And Robert Kennedy did.

The tension, however, continued to build. On Friday morning, October 26, a Soviet ship bound for Cuba was stopped and boarded by the U.S. Navy. No missiles or military hardware was found and the ship continued on. Not far away, depth charges were dropped, forcing Soviet submarines to surface and identify themselves, and on the U.S. mainland preparations continued for an all-out invasion of Cuba if construction on the missile sites did not stop. Kennedy told his advisers,

> "We're going to have to face the fact, that if we do invade, by the time we get to these sites, after a very bloody fight, they will be pointed at us. And we must further accept the possibility that when military hostilities first begin, these missiles will be fired."

Thus the mood was appropriately grim as Kennedy and his team waited anxiously for Khrushchev's answer to a personal communiqué from the president. On Tuesday, the Soviet chairman had accused the United States of "outright banditry or, if you like, the folly of degenerate imperialism," after Kennedy had announced the naval quarantine. In his reply on Thursday to Khrushchev's letter, Kennedy had been firm while inviting once again a peaceful resolution of the crisis.

> "I ask you to recognize clearly, Mr. Chairman, that it was not I who issued the first challenge in this case. . . . I repeat my regret that these events should cause a deterioration in our relations. I hope that your government will take the necessary action. . . ."

At six p.m., Khrushchev answered. In a long, impassioned letter he proposed a peaceful solution—a pledge from the United States not to invade Cuba and to end its blockade, and in return his country would remove the missiles. Khrushchev wrote,

> If indeed war should break out, then it would not be in our power to stop it, for such is the logic of war. I have been in two wars and know that war ends when it has rolled through cities and villages, everywhere sowing death and destruction. [And now in the age of nuclear war], only lunatics or suicides, who themselves want to perish and to destroy the whole world before they die, could do this.

Friday, October 26, thus ended on a note of hope, as Kennedy contemplated his response.

But the following morning brought a series of deeply disturbing events. The first was the arrival of a new communique from Khrushchev, far more defiant and obviously not written by the chairman himself, adding unexpected conditions to the search for peace. To resolve the crisis, the new letter said, the U.S. must not only dismantle its blockade and pledge never to invade the island of Cuba, it must also remove its own missiles from Turkey. Oddly, Kennedy already wanted those missiles removed, believing they were obsolete, but accepting this additional demand, he thought, might be seen as a sign of weakness. Photographs from the latest reconnaissance flights indicated Soviet technicians in Cuba were working day and night on the missile installations, which was not the sign of a nation seeking peace. Then came the devastating report that another U-2 flight—piloted by Major Rudolph Anderson, whose flight on October 14 had first confirmed the presence of the missiles—had been shot down, and Major Anderson had been killed.

Suddenly, everything seemed bleak. The State Department drafted a response to Khrushchev's second letter, flatly rejecting his linkage of missiles in Turkey with those in Cuba, and the military leaders in Kennedy's inner circle began pushing harder than ever for an attack. The quarantine was not enough, they declared, as events that morning had clearly shown. Now the time had come to get tough.

This was the moment in which, hyperbolic as it sounds, the brothers Kennedy may quite literally have saved the world—along with a now-forgotten officer on a Soviet submarine. First, the president refused to be stampeded by his Joint Chiefs of Staff, these formidable men in uniform who were sure that the time had come for war.

"It isn't the first step that concerns me," Kennedy told them, "but both sides escalating to the fourth and fifth step—and we don't go to the sixth because there is no one around to do so."

Kennedy's second important decision that Saturday was to accept a simple suggestion from his brother, that instead of brusquely rejecting the demands in Khrushchev's second letter, as the State Department urged, the president should simply ignore it. Answer the first letter, Robert Kennedy said, the one in which the Soviet leader had spoken so passionately about the need for peace. Ambassador Llewellyn Thompson, who knew Khrushchev as well as anybody, agreed with that approach. So did the president. As far as he could tell this was their only glimmer of hope. He ordered his brother and Ted Sorensen to draft such a response, which he immediately signed and sent by diplomatic cable.

"Dear Mr. Chairman," the letter began, "I have read your letter of October 26 with great care and welcomed the statement of your desire to seek a prompt solution of the problem. The first thing that needs to be done, however, is for work to cease on the offensive missile bases in Cuba and for all weapons systems in Cuba capable of offensive use to be rendered inoperable, under effective United Nations arrangements.

"Assuming this is done promptly," the letter continued, the United States would agree, as Khrushchev had suggested, to remove its naval blockade and "give assurances against an invasion of Cuba."

As soon as the letter was on its way, the attorney general met with Soviet Ambassador Anatoly Dobrynin and told him President Kennedy expected an answer by the following day to avoid getting to the point where the path to war would be irreversible.

In *Thirteen Days*, Robert Kennedy wrote of a moment that same afternoon, just the two brothers in the president's office, sharing the agonized hours of waiting. JFK, his brother remembered,

> . . . talked about Major Anderson [the U-2 pilot] and how it is always the brave and the best who die. The politicians and officials sit home pontificating about great principles and issues, make the decisions, and dine with their wives and families, while the brave and the young die. He talked about the miscalculations that lead to war. War is rarely intentional. The Russians don't wish to fight any more than we do. They do not want to war with us nor we with them. And yet if events continue as they have in the last several days, that struggle—which no one wishes, which will accomplish nothing—will engulf and destroy all mankind.

Apparently, Khrushchev had similar thoughts. The following morning he agreed to dismantle the missiles in exchange for guarantees against a U.S. invasion of Cuba. Thus, at the moment when it seemed least likely, a peaceful resolution was found.

President Kennedy praised Khrushchev for his statesmanship and ordered that there be no gloating, no claims of victory over the missiles' removal, by anybody in the United States government. Instead, there was simply an overwhelming relief that the most dangerous crisis any of them had faced—or had ever imagined—was ending without a catastrophic loss of life.

It is one of the terrible ironies of history that neither John nor Robert Kennedy would live long enough to fully understand how close the world had come to disaster. In *The Cuban Missile Crisis at 50*, one of the definitive retrospectives on the subject, Harvard political scientist Graham Allison offered this most sober assessment:

> We now know . . . that in addition to nuclear-armed ballistic missiles, the Soviet Union had deployed 100 tactical nuclear weapons to Cuba, and the local Soviet commander there could have launched these weapons without additional codes or commands from Moscow. The US air strike and invasion . . . would likely have triggered a nuclear response against American ships and troops, and perhaps even Miami. The resulting war might have led to the deaths of 100 million Americans and over 100 million Russians.

Nor was that all. On October 27, the same morning that Kennedy resisted the urgings of his Joint Chiefs of Staff, an argument broke out among the officers on a Soviet submarine. An American warship, the *USS Beale*, had tracked the sub and dropped small depth charges, the size of hand grenades, as a warning for the Soviet vessel to surface. The captain, Valentin Savitsky, became angry and ordered the submarine's nuclear torpedo readied for firing. One of his officers, Vasili Arkhipov, argued desperately against that course, and the captain changed his mind. A nuclear exchange on the open seas was thus averted by a matter of seconds.

Arkhipov has been forgotten, while John Kennedy, of course, has not. The president's strength and wisdom under the withering pressure of the crisis have become a cornerstone of his legacy—his "finest hour," as one historian later put it. Even at the time, many Americans knew that something remarkable had happened. In *Kennedy,* Ted Sorensen recalled the Sunday morning meeting of Kennedy's advisers after news that the crisis had been resolved: "John F. Kennedy entered and we all stood up. He had, as Harold Macmillan would later say, earned his place in history by this one act alone."

But there would be more. It was as if Kennedy himself were suddenly imbued with a heightened sense of possibility. Certainly, for many of us, it was true that in the year just ahead, Kennedy's voice, along with Dr. Martin Luther King's, would resonate powerfully and fill us with inspiration and hope.

But there would be other voices as well, competing for the heart and soul of the country.

13

Setting the Stage

In November, George Wallace was elected governor of Alabama. It was an event little noticed outside the state, and few would have guessed that this gifted politician, whose style suggested the pugnacity of the bantamweight boxer he once was, would take his place on the stage of history alongside John and Robert Kennedy or Martin Luther King. Indeed, some of us who later would write about them would wonder if Wallace's legacy wasn't more lasting than the others'.

But none of that was visible in 1962. All anybody could really say was that Wallace won the governorship after making a Faustian bargain with his conscience. He had first run for the office in 1958 as a racial moderate. That is probably who he was in his heart. In his early career he had been a disciple of Big Jim Folsom, a New Deal populist who was elected in 1954 for a second term as Alabama's governor. The next year, as white resistance to *Brown v. Board of Education* was mounting, Folsom scandalized some Alabamians by having drinks in the governor's mansion with Adam Clayton Powell, the African American congressman from Harlem. Wallace apparently was not among the upset segregationists. In fact, while serving as a circuit judge, Wallace was often praised for his fairness, not only by whites but also by blacks who appeared in his court. Civil rights attorney J. L. Chestnut, an African American, called Wallace "the most liberal judge I ever practiced in front of. He was the first judge in Alabama to call me 'Mister' in his courtroom."

In his 1958 run, Wallace produced a television ad in which he declared with conviction: "I want to tell the good people of this state . . . if I didn't have what it took to treat a man fair regardless of the color of his skin, then I don't have what it takes to be the governor of your great state."

But hard-line segregationist John Patterson beat Wallace, and shortly afterward he came to the office of his friend and supporter, Seymore Trammell, the district attorney of Barbour County, where Wallace was from. "Seymore," he said, "I was outniggered by John Patterson, and I'll tell you here and now, I will never be outniggered again." In that moment Wallace became a spokesman for the racism he had once rejected, and in the coming years he would play the role more effectively than anybody else. He learned to avoid the *n-word*—as it came to be called—and to use instead a political code that touched the anger and alienation of many thousands of white Americans. He helped them believe that the worst instincts harbored in their hearts were actually their best. It was a powerful tonic, and for the next fifty years and maybe beyond, U.S. politics would not be the same.

Hardly anybody saw this coming. Outside Alabama, Wallace was perceived as merely another Ross Barnett, a caricature of Southern backwardness. Indeed, when it came to national headlines, his election was overshadowed on November 7 by the death of a great American liberal. Eleanor Roosevelt had become an icon, a larger-than-life former First Lady, recently appointed by Kennedy to chair the Presidential Commission on the Status of Women.

A few years earlier, it would have seemed unlikely that she and Kennedy could work together on anything. Among the Democrats then jostling for the presidency, Mrs. Roosevelt strongly preferred Adlai Stevenson, the thinker-politician from Illinois, a liberal who was committed to principles in a way she feared John Kennedy was not. She found the young senator from Massachusetts to be disturbingly pragmatic, more concerned about his own advancement than the betterment of the country. In particular, she worried about his failure to take a tougher stand against Senator Joseph McCarthy, the red-baiting Republican from Wisconsin who dealt in guilt-by-association lies in his crusade against communism. But even more, Mrs. Roosevelt worried that Kennedy was weak on civil rights, one of the great passions of her life.

As First Lady, she had well-publicized friendships with distinguished African American women such as opera singer Marian Anderson and educator Mary McLeod Bethune. She crusaded for anti-lynching legislation even when her husband the president was reluctant to give his support for fear of alienating Southern congressmen whose backing was needed for New Deal legislation. Mrs. Roosevelt rejected that political calculus. She criticized New Deal programs she thought were discriminatory against blacks, and when FDR's

Executive Order 9066 created internment camps for Japanese-Americans, she took a public stand against it.

Her life's commitment was to build a more inclusive society, not only in America but around the world. In December 1945, FDR's successor, President Harry Truman, chose her as a delegate to the United Nations General Assembly, where she helped draft the Universal Declaration on Human Rights, ratified in 1948. She called it "the international Magna Carta of all men everywhere."

In her independence as First Lady and afterwards, she embodied a new definition of womanhood that would resonate powerfully in the 1960s.

To the end of her life, she remained active in domestic politics, where she nursed a distaste for John F. Kennedy until finally, on August 14, 1960, the two sat down for a meeting. The setting was Hyde Park, the Roosevelt estate about which FDR once said, "All that is within me cries out to go back to my home on the Hudson River." Kennedy understood the pull of such a place, the history of it, and the beauty—knew the anchor it must have provided to a man whose life belonged to the world. Perhaps it was that reflective quality Mrs. Roosevelt sensed for the first time. Whatever the case, she was clearly impressed. She later wrote:

> When he came to see me at Hyde Park, I found him a brilliant man with a quick mind, anxious to learn, hospitable to new ideas, hardheaded in his approach. Here, I thought, with an upsurge of hope and confidence, is a man who wants to leave behind him a record not only of having helped his countrymen but of having helped humanity as well. He was not simply ambitious to be president; he wanted, I felt convinced, to be a truly great president. He neither desired nor expected his task to be easy. He saw clearly the position of the United States in the world today as well as the shortcomings at home and was both too honorable and too courageous to color these unpalatable facts or distort them . . .
>
> If my observation is correct, I have more hope for the solution of our problems than I have had for a long time.

So began a new friendship marked by mutual admiration. After Kennedy's inaugural address on January 20, 1961, Mrs. Roosevelt wrote a letter of warm congratulations:

> Dear Mr. President . . . I think "gratitude" best describes the sense of liberation and lift to the spirit which you gave. I have re-read your words several times and am filled with thankfulness. May we all respond to your leadership and make your task easier.

Later that year, as he was putting together the Presidential Commission on the Status of Women, an official inquiry into the barriers that still affected half of the U.S. population, Kennedy could think of no better chair than Mrs. Roosevelt. When she died in 1962 before that work was complete, Kennedy did not name a new chair—a gesture in recognition of her singular importance. But when the commission issued its official report—on what would have been her seventy-ninth birthday—it became a critical part of a new wave of feminism. In a sense, Mrs. Roosevelt's legacy would become enmeshed with the work of two women writers, Betty Friedan and Gloria Steinem, who were soon to emerge.

And there was more. Mrs. Roosevelt's concern for equality and justice for African Americans would also move to center stage in America.

14

'A Line in the Dust'

On a cold winter morning in Montgomery, Alabama, George Wallace gazed with evident satisfaction across the sea of faces before him. This was the moment he had dreamed about—and, more remarkably, had expected to happen—since he was a boy in Barbour County. As a teenager serving as a legislative page, he had stood on the brass star at the Alabama capitol marking precisely where Jefferson Davis had taken his oath as President of the Confederacy. Even then, Wallace longed for the day when he too would take an oath on that spot, and he thought it was only a matter of time. "I knew then," he later explained, "that I would be governor."

Among his many talents, Wallace had that sense of the past that skillful politicians employ to tap the psyche of the people. In addition to overt racism, there was also the historical DNA—a feeling of being invaded, wronged, treated with a kind of regional condescension—that went back to the Civil War. Perhaps even more, that collective resentment that Wallace understood was rooted in the era of Reconstruction, when the defeat and loss that overwhelmed white Southerners was measured in their minds by the rising fortunes of African Americans.

Throughout his second campaign for governor, Wallace's fiery speeches were sprinkled with bitter historical allusions. His political opponents were cast as "no good carpet-bagging, scalawagging liars," and sometimes worse. But now that he had won and at last was taking the oath of office, Wallace adopted a slightly different tone. The old defiance was there, the sense of a man who was spoiling for a fight, for that was now his political trademark. But on this day in January 1963, as he gave his inaugural address, there was also an eloquence that set him apart as a political orator:

> In the name of the greatest people that have ever trod this earth, I draw the line in the dust and toss the gauntlet before the feet of tyranny, and I say segregation now, segregation tomorrow, segregation forever!

Those words, however, were not written by Wallace. They came from the pen of speechwriter Asa Carter, a man with a most unusual resume. For one thing, he was a leader of one of the most vicious branches of the Ku Klux Klan. In 1957, in what was apparently intended as a brutal warning to Birmingham civil rights leader Fred Shuttlesworth, Carter's followers randomly kidnapped and castrated a black man. Later in his life, Carter bizarrely recast his identity, changing his name to Forrest Carter and writing a popular book, *The Education of Little Tree*, about growing up as a Native American. But in 1963, as a Wallace speechwriter, he was a swarthy and brooding white supremacist. That apparently was just fine with the governor. Such was his commitment to the politics of race.

Over the next several years, Wallace would learn to broaden his appeal to touch the alienation of whites even outside the South. But first, as he established his political base in Alabama, he served as a foil for the civil rights movement. Ironically, in his role as snarling segregationist villain, he helped that movement reach the conscience of the country.

As it happened, civil rights leaders had already chosen Alabama as a national battlefield, the place where they intended to draw their own line in the dust. In January, Martin Luther King and his top lieutenants met on the Georgia coast, not far from Savannah. In this place of soothing beauty and quiet, with its live oak trees and Spanish moss and great blue herons wading in the marsh, King and his staff mapped plans for Operation C—C for Confrontation. Their target was Birmingham; they knew that nowhere else in America was segregation meaner or more pervasive.

The looming showdown was in part the story of three larger-than-life historical figures. The first was MLK, who had had a bad year. In 1962, he helped lead protests in Albany, Georgia, where Police Chief Laurie Pritchett refused to play the role of villain, the national media lost interest, and the movement failed to achieve its goals. King and the others planning Operation C were sure that Birmingham would be different.

Fred Shuttlesworth, one of the planners, had spent his whole life in

Birmingham and knew there would be no shortage of villains. For one thing, the city had an active Ku Klux Klan, and Shuttlesworth himself had been the target of multiple attacks. His home and his church had been bombed, and when he tried to register his daughter at an all-white public school, a mob attacked him with baseball bats and bicycle chains. Only the heroism of a little-remembered white policeman, E. T. Rouse, saved his life.

Shuttlesworth's confidence that the meanness of his city could sustain the attention of the national media, and thus perhaps touch the conscience of the country, centered on a single man: Eugene "Bull" Connor was the police commissioner in Birmingham, a man of such savage hostility to blacks that by explicit arrangement he had withdrawn his policemen from the city's bus station when he knew the freedom riders were coming, giving the Klan fifteen minutes to beat and maim. King and Shuttlesworth knew Connor could be counted on to overreact when massive demonstrations began in his city.

In the beginning these three men were the defining public figures in the drama. Each had his own agenda. King was eager to bring pressure on Congress and the Kennedy administration to pass a meaningful civil rights bill. Shuttlesworth was determined to see everything change in Birmingham itself, where the daily insult of segregation was everywhere—in separate rest rooms for black and white, separate lunch counters, segregated schools, segregated parks, segregated everything, all symbols of oppression intended to remind African Americans that they were inferior. Connor, meanwhile, was willing to do whatever it took to make sure nothing changed.

WHEN THE DEMONSTRATIONS BEGAN on April 3, Connor was in an even more foul frame of mind than usual. The previous day, he had lost his bid to become Birmingham's mayor, and when the votes were counted, the difference had come in the black precincts. Connor had split the white vote evenly with Albert Boutwell, a businessman more moderate in his views on race. But African Americans were overwhelming in their repudiation of the police commissioner, whose hostility they had come to understand well.

Spoiling for a fight, Connor appeared almost disappointed when the first day's protests were smaller than expected. The plan had been for demonstrators—trained in nonviolence by the Reverend James Lawson, who three years earlier had trained the sit-in students in Nashville—to take their places and ask to be served at segregated restaurants downtown. Four of those establishments promptly closed. Twenty-one people were arrested without incident at the fifth restaurant, and the sit-in barely made the local papers. At the time, Birmingham had its mind on other things.

There was, first of all, the Alabama premiere of *To Kill a Mockingbird*, the movie adaptation of Harper Lee's novel, starring Gregory Peck as Atticus Finch. On April 8, Peck won the Academy Award for Best Actor, edging out Peter O'Toole for his role in *Lawrence of Arabia*. Both performances were iconic, but Peck's depiction of a decent white man in the racist South resonated powerfully in 1963. The film was especially big news in Birmingham where young Mary Badham, a native of the city who had played Scout Finch, was also nominated for an Oscar. Even though Badham did not win, the movie at first was a bigger story than the local demonstrations. But that began to change on April 9, a week before Easter, when three black ministers, including Martin Luther King's brother, the Reverend A. D. King, led a downtown march. This marked the first appearance of the police dogs—Bull Connor's corps of German Shepherds who were trained to tear at human flesh. On this Palm Sunday afternoon, as police began to arrest the marchers, a crowd of black onlookers gathered to jeer at Connor and his men. The TV news that night showed one of the dogs attacking Leroy Allen, an African American teenager, and now the Birmingham movement had its villain—its media melodrama of right versus wrong.

Even so, the demonstrations lagged. A Birmingham judge issued an injunction against future protests just as King and Shuttlesworth were running out of money to bail the marchers out of jail. At a strategy session on Good Friday, April 12, some of King's lieutenants urged him to embark on a national speaking tour, using his considerable gifts as an orator to raise more money. King decided instead to go to jail. He hated the idea; he had always suffered from claustrophobia, and once in Montgomery when he had been arrested he was sure the police intended to kill him. But he pushed his fears and his phobias aside to lead, he said, by example. How could he ask others to go to jail if he was not willing to go himself?

For me, this particular moment in history has a deeply personal dimension. I lived in Mobile, but I was in Birmingham that day on a high school field trip. I had little idea of what was going on, but as I was leaving the hotel there was Dr. King, barely three feet from where I was standing. Two Birmingham policemen were shoving him roughly up the sidewalk. I remember thinking that he looked so small, and there seemed to be a sadness in his deep, expressive eyes. At my impressionable age of sixteen, the moment shattered an illusion that everything was fine, that the racial problems in the South would subside if not for "agitators" like King.

Somehow in this instant he embodied the truth, a reality white Southerners were seeking to deny. The racial problems in our region ran deep in our hearts and deep in our history. I had no idea what to do with this epiphany, one that was not uncommon in my generation, and though I might have tried to shove it from my mind, I could not. Looking back, I'm certain that it set me on the path to becoming a writer. Though I could not have put it into words at the time, it was clear to me that this was history, and history had a face, and a face had the power to touch a conscience.

As I began to struggle with these ruminations, which were initially nothing more than a deep discomfort, King seized the moment, as great men do. On scraps of paper later smuggled from his cell, he wrote his famous "Letter from Birmingham Jail," a cornerstone document of the civil rights struggle that he composed in response to some local white clergymen who had published a letter asserting that the Birmingham protests were premature. He wrote:

> I guess it is easy for those who have never felt the stinging darts of segregation to say, "Wait." But when you have seen vicious mobs lynch your mothers and fathers at will and drown your sisters and brothers at whim; when you have seen hate-filled policemen curse, kick, brutalize and even kill your black brothers and sisters with impunity; when you see the vast majority of your twenty million Negro brothers smothering in an air-tight cage of poverty in the midst of an affluent society; when you suddenly find your tongue twisted and your speech stammering as you seek to explain to your six-year-old daughter why she can't go to a public amusement park; . . . when you have to concoct an answer to a five-year-old son asking in agonizing pathos: "Daddy, why do white people treat colored people so mean?"; . . . when you are harried by day and haunted by night by the very fact that you are a Negro, living constantly on tip-toe stance, never quite knowing what to expect next, and plagued with inner fears and outer resentments; when you are forever fighting a degenerating sense of "nobodiness"; then you will understand why we find it difficult to wait.

One of King's great gifts as a civil rights leader was his ability to frame the debate, something he would do again and again in the course of his career. But others were more adept at movement strategy, and while King languished in the Birmingham jail until April 20, they, not he, discovered a radical path to success. James Bevel, for example, was a veteran of the Nashville sit-ins who had come to Birmingham as one of King's lieutenants and begun talking to college and high school students, even a few in junior high school. He found in them a level of enthusiasm that the Birmingham movement had lacked.

"Let the children march!" he proposed, and King, among others, was startled by such a dangerous idea. What if children were hurt or even killed? While King was struggling to make up his mind, the more decisive leaders in the movement—Bevel and Shuttlesworth, Andrew Young and Dorothy Cotton—simply went ahead without him. On May 2, student demonstrators by the hundreds poured out of Sixteenth Street Baptist Church, the primary staging ground for the protests, and marched into nearby Kelly Ingram Park. More than a thousand were arrested by the end of the day, filling the jails in Birmingham and surrounding municipalities. The following morning, it was more of the same.

Bull Connor was enraged. At his command the police and the dogs were reinforced by firemen, who turned their hoses on peaceful demonstrators, knocking children to the ground, rolling them along "like a pebble at high tide," as a movement leader put it. And still the demonstrations didn't stop. After the spectacle on May 3 and the horrifying images on the television news, King, still deeply troubled, agreed it was time to turn up the pressure. On May 7, more than two thousand demonstrators, most of them young, faced off against police in Kelly Ingram Park. The protesters themselves were trained in nonviolence, but other blacks in Birmingham were not, and a crowd of onlookers, angered by the fire hoses and dogs, began to throw rocks at Connor and his men. Fred Shuttlesworth, a man of astonishing physical courage, waded into the fray, doing his best to calm the rioters and lead the youthful marchers to safety. A fireman saw him and took aim with his hose, knocking Shuttlesworth against a wall, breaking a rib with the first blast of water.

At the same moment, the Chamber of Commerce was meeting a few blocks away, and the white Birmingham businessmen decided that enough was enough. The city was spinning out of control. Terrible damage had been done to its national reputation, and the time had finally come to seek a truce. In Washington, the Kennedy Administration agreed, and the president dispatched Burke Marshall, assistant attorney general for civil rights, to help the two sides negotiate a settlement.

Marshall turned out to be perfect for the job. Quiet and taciturn, speaking most often in a monotone, he had a sort of anti-charisma that leaders in Birmingham, black and white, found somehow reassuring. After three days of talks, an agreement was reached. Shuttlesworth was not especially happy about it. He thought the timetable for change was too slow—ninety days to completely desegregate the city's restaurants and other public facilities—but King was delighted to claim a victory. The movement, he thought, needed such a boost, and now there was added pressure on President Kennedy to introduce a strong civil rights bill.

The forces of racism, meanwhile, were enraged. The Klan staged a night rally on May 11, and in the flickering shadows of a burning cross, Grand Dragon Robert Shelton aimed his fury not only at African Americans but at white businessmen willing to compromise. "Martin Luther King has not gained one thing in Birmingham," he shouted, "because white people are not going to tolerate the meddlesome, conniving, manipulating moves of those professional businessmen." As cheers rang out through the Birmingham night, he surrendered the podium to one of his KKK associates who called for "stiff-backed men . . . willing to go out and fight the battle for the Lord Jesus Christ."

That night two bombs exploded in the city. The first was at the home of the Reverend A. D. King, Dr. King's brother. Incredibly, no one was hurt. But windows were shattered and a door was blasted into splinters, and within a few minutes a crowd of angry blacks gathered in the street, threatening policemen who arrived on the scene. As his more famous brother had done in similar circumstances seven years earlier in Montgomery, Reverend King confronted the crowd, gently prodding them to go home. There had been enough violence, he said. He was making progress—the people were singing "We Shall Overcome"—when the sound of a second explosion split the night. The target this time was the Gaston Motel, where Dr. King had been staying while in Birmingham, and though he was in Atlanta that night, the bomb exploded right beneath his room. Word quickly spread that the Klan had tried to kill King, and Birmingham erupted into full-fledged riots. By dawn, fires were burning in a dozen places, and more than sixty people were hospitalized before the violence subsided.

Dr. King rushed back to Birmingham and began working his way through the honky-tonks and bars, the places where alcohol could lubricate rage. As he pleaded for peace among these angry, long-suffering people, he could feel—perhaps more powerfully than he had felt it before—what a razor-thin line he was seeking to walk.

For George Wallace, meanwhile, there was a certain perverse satisfaction, or at least a sense of opportunity, in the tension that now engulfed his state. He was mastering the politics of rage, and as summer approached he was preparing to make good on a campaign promise. In 1962, he had pledged to "stand in the schoolhouse door, if necessary," to bar black students from the University of Alabama.

There had been a U.S. District Court order to admit two students, and Wallace thought that if he played it just right, the whole country would have to pay attention. His adversary, as he framed it in his mind, was not just the students but the federal government—once again those invaders from the North, threatening the Southern way of life. He knew the narrative would play in Alabama, and he was about to discover there were other places where the anger and alienation also ran deep.

In Washington, the Kennedy brothers were worried. Memories of Ole Miss—two people dead, dozens of federal marshals wounded—were fresh in their minds. Already, on April 25, knowing a confrontation with Wallace was looming, Robert Kennedy had gone to Alabama to meet with the governor. When he arrived, he discovered the stately Capitol ringed with state troopers—for security, Wallace said, but Kennedy thought it was a show of force. As Kennedy was about to enter the capitol building, one of the troopers jabbed him in the stomach with the end of a nightstick, and the Attorney General of the United States thought the Alabama lawman would have relished killing him on the spot.

Once inside, Kennedy found the conversation bizarre. Wallace seemed to be living in a different world, oblivious to the inevitability of desegregation, and certainly to the justice of the civil rights cause. The governor did promise there would be no violence, but Kennedy thought the pugnacious little man was enjoying himself, as if he were both the director and the star of an upcoming piece of political theater.

The outcome of the showdown between state and federal authority was never in doubt. The two black students—Vivian Malone and James Hood—*would* be admitted to the University of Alabama. The troubling unknown for Robert Kennedy was what George Wallace was trying to prove and what he was willing to do to prove it.

For Wallace, the objective was clearer. He was running for President. This was not something he was willing to say on the record, but on June 2, nine days before the confrontation he was carefully orchestrating in his mind, Wallace eagerly accepted an invitation to appear on *Meet the Press*. For an hour on national television, he played the matador to a panel of reporters who were trying to paint him as a Southern demagogue. Wallace deftly sidestepped. He portrayed himself not as a bigot, but as a politician comfortably in command, raising important constitutional questions. One of the panelists, Anthony Lewis, an eloquent columnist for the *New York Times*, suggested that the courts had settled those questions already, and that Wallace's plan to stand in the doorway was "a political gesture to try to arouse violence."

Wallace responded with innocent calm. There would be no violence, he said. "I am against that as much as anybody."

As events would prove, the governor was telling the truth. On June 11, the day of his stand, the University of Alabama had seldom been quieter. There were no demonstrations, no mobs of Klansmen waiting to harass. Wallace's aides had put out the word to members of the Klan that they would not be allowed on campus. Troublemakers would be arrested on sight.

For his part, Wallace came early to the university. He waited in air-conditioned comfort inside Foster Auditorium, the administration building where the two black students were scheduled to register later that morning. Outside was sultry, the temperature soaring into the nineties, when Nicholas Katzenbach, Deputy Attorney General of the United States, arrived with the two black students. It was 10:48 a.m. As Katzenbach, dripping with sweat, approached, Wallace took his place at a podium in front of the door and read a statement about federal "usurpation of power." Katzenbach waited uncomfortably, arms folded across his chest, barely able to suppress his contempt.

"I do not know what the purpose of this show is," he said as soon as Wallace finished. "From the outset, Governor, all of us have known that the final chapter of this history will be the admission of these students. . . . I ask you once again to reconsider."

When Wallace simply stood there, Katzenbach turned and walked away. In Washington, President Kennedy immediately ordered in the National

Guard, and a little before 3:30 p.m. a line of infantrymen with M-1 rifles took up positions at Foster Auditorium. Faced with a ceremonial show of force, Wallace stepped aside, having delayed the inevitable for approximately four hours and forty minutes. But his popularity soared in Alabama, and for a while at least mail poured in from around the country praising his stand against the federal Goliath.

Lost in the drama were the two African American students, who were treated by the media at the time—and by many historians in the years since—as an afterthought. But Vivian Malone, who came from Mobile, would become the first black graduate of the University of Alabama. She was a young woman of extraordinary poise, always popular among her peers. She dressed conservatively, but with her high cheekbones and soft brown eyes, some people said she looked like a model. James Hood, raised in the industrial city of Gadsden in northeast Alabama, was a high school athlete, a football player who had run the hundred-yard dash in less than ten seconds. He was a student leader who had already graduated magna cum laude from historically black Alabama A&M College. He wanted to take additional courses in math. Except for the color of their skin, these were clearly the kinds of students their new university would otherwise recruit.

In Washington, D.C., President Kennedy was beginning to see the issue of civil rights in precisely these terms—as a problem that affected flesh-and-blood human beings, his fellow citizens whose humanity was constricted by laws and customs that were simply unjust. On the evening of Wallace's stand in the schoolhouse door, Kennedy decided at the last minute to address the subject on national television. In a message that was partly extemporaneous—highly unusual for a television address—Kennedy announced the introduction of a civil rights bill to overturn the practice of legal segregation. More than that, he cast the issue as a question of morality:

> It is as old as the Scriptures and as clear as the American Constitution. If an American, because his skin is dark, cannot eat lunch in a restaurant open to the public, if he cannot send his children to the best public school available, if he cannot vote for the public officials who represent him, if, in short, he cannot enjoy the full and free life which all of us want, then who among us would be content to have the color of his skin changed and stand in his place? Who

> among us would then be content with the counsels of patience and delay. One hundred years of delay have passed since President Lincoln freed the slaves, yet their heirs, their grandsons, are not fully free . . . And this nation, for all its boasts, will not be fully free until all its citizens are free.

Until that night, no President had addressed the subject in quite this way, or had allied himself so completely with the civil rights movement. After watching the speech on television, Martin Luther King sent a telegram to Kennedy, complete with the errors of his own hasty typing: "It was one of the most eloquent profound and unequival (sic) pleas for Justice and Freedom of all men ever made by any President."

Many Americans agreed with King. But it often seemed in the 1960s that for every shimmering moment of hope, there was always a price to be paid in blood.

15

Murder and Dreams

Medgar Evers did not get home until after midnight. On the evening of June 11, he had been at a strategy meeting in Jackson, Mississippi, where he was a field secretary for the NAACP. His wife, Myrlie, and their three small children were waiting up for him, still excited about the president's address. Myrlie, especially, was always relieved by the sound of his car pulling into the driveway. She knew it was dangerous work he was doing, leading the civil rights struggle in Mississippi. Suddenly, as she waited near the door, a shot rang out from just beyond the carport, and she and the children dove for the floor. After a moment, when the night was still, she gathered herself and rushed outside. She found her husband lying near the steps, shot through the back with a massive exit wound near the sternum. Within the hour, Medgar Evers was dead.

Across town, author Eudora Welty heard the news and almost immediately she began to write, seeking to imagine the voice of a man who could even conceive of such a crime. She had written before on the subject of race. In 1940, her short story, "A Worn Path," anchored her first book of fiction; many readers had found it remarkable that a white writer from Mississippi could create an African American heroine who was simultaneously so fragile, sympathetic and strong.

> She wore a dark striped dress reaching down to her shoe tops, and an equally long apron of bleached sugar sacks, with a full pocket: all neat and tidy, but every time she took a step she might have fallen over her shoelaces, which dragged from her unlaced shoes. She looked straight ahead. Her eyes were blue with age. Her skin had a pattern all its own of numberless branching wrinkles . . . as though a whole little tree stood in the middle of her forehead, but a golden color ran underneath, and the two knobs of her cheeks were illumined by a

> yellow burning under the dark. Under the red rag her hair came down on her neck in the frailest of ringlets, still black, and with an odor like copper.

For the next twenty years, Welty was part of a literary movement, not especially deliberate, but an emergence, nevertheless, of white women writers who tried to push past the old boundaries of prejudice. Carson McCullers, Lillian Smith, Flannery O'Connor, Harper Lee—all had made their distinctive contributions. And now in 1963, on the pages of *The New Yorker* magazine, Welty offered an imagined window into the mind of a killer.

> As soon as I heard the wheels, I knowd who was coming . . . It was the right nigger heading in a new white car up his driveway towards his garage with the light shining, but stopping before he got there, maybe not to wake 'em. That was him. I knowd it when he cut off the car lights and put his foot out and I knowd him standing dark against the light . . .
>
> I'd already brought up my rifle, I'd already taken my sights. And I'd already got him, because it was too late then for him or me to turn by one hair.
>
> Something darker than him, like the wings of a bird spread on his back and pulled him down. He climbed up once, like a man under bad claws, and like just blood could weigh a ton he walked with it on his back to better light. Didn't get no further than his door. And fell to stay. . . .
>
> I says, ". . . Now I'm alive and you ain't. We ain't never . . . going to be equals and you know why? One of us is dead."

As events would prove, Welty's portrait was chillingly accurate. On the evening of June 11, Byron De la Beckwith, a white supremacist from Greenwood, Mississippi, had waited in a patch of darkness-shadowed honeysuckle just a few yards from Medgar Evers's carport. When Evers drove in just after midnight, De la Beckwith raised his 30.06 rifle and squeezed the trigger. Police found the gun, complete with fingerprints. But a pair of all-white hung juries left him free to brag about his crime for three decades. He was finally convicted in 1994 and died in prison at the age of eighty, unrepentant for the only notable moment in his life.

IN THE RUSH OF events in 1963, the Evers murder was, if anything, overshadowed by another headline from half a world away. On June 11, the same day George Wallace stood in the schoolhouse door and President Kennedy delivered his seminal address on civil rights, a Buddhist monk in Vietnam set himself on fire. As more than three hundred followers watched in silence, Thich Quang Duc assumed the lotus position at a busy intersection in Saigon. Another monk doused him with gasoline, a five-gallon can poured over his head, and Duc himself struck the fatal match. "Nam mo Adida Phat," he said, "Homage to Amitabha Buddha."

Duc also left a message in a letter:

> Before closing my eyes and moving towards the vision of the Buddha, I respectfully plead to President Ngo Dinh Diem to take a mind of compassion towards the people of the nation and implement religious equality to maintain the strength of the homeland eternally.

Malcolm Browne of the Associated Press, one of a handful of journalists on the scene, won a Pulitzer Prize for his photo of Duc's burning body, and David Halberstam of the *New York Times*, who would soon win a Pulitzer of his own, did his best to describe it in words:

> I was to see that sight again, but once was enough. Flames were coming from a human being; his body was slowly withering and shriveling up, his head blackening and charring. In the air was the smell of burning human flesh; human beings burn surprisingly quickly. Behind me I could hear the sobbing of the Vietnamese who were now gathering. I was too shocked to cry, too confused to take notes or ask questions, too bewildered to even think . . . As he burned he never moved a muscle, never uttered a sound, his outward composure in sharp contrast to the wailing people around him.

In Washington, JFK was deeply distressed. The photo itself was horrible enough. "Jesus Christ!" he exclaimed, when he saw it in one of the morning newspapers. Later he added, "No news photograph in history has generated so much emotion around the world as that one." But there was more to Kennedy's reaction than shock. Like most American policymakers, he accepted the domino theory belief that in the global competition with Communism, the fall of one country in a particular region could lead inevitably to the fall of another. In Southeast Asia, the new battle line was Vietnam, and Kennedy, like Eisenhower before him, had pledged American power and support to the anti-Communist government of South Vietnam.

Now, however, this incredible act by a single monk had placed the U.S. policy in jeopardy. If the American-backed regime of Ngo Dinh Diem was so oppressive as to inspire a sacrifice this horrific, then what were the implications for the United States? This question had to be addressed, but Kennedy had his mind on more noble things. There was, first of all, the civil rights bill he had sent to Congress. Many of his advisers had warned him against it, fearing that it would not pass, but the president was determined to push ahead. His proposal called for a ban on discrimination in places of public accommodation—hotels, restaurants, theaters, and retail stores. It also gave the attorney general the power to initiate school desegregation lawsuits, instead of waiting for citizens who might lack the means or might face reprisals for challenging the status quo. On June 19, in a statement that accompanied the bill, Kennedy wrote:

> I ask every member of Congress to set aside sectional and political ties, and to look at this issue from the viewpoint of the nation. I ask you to look into your hearts—not in search of charity, for the Negro neither wants nor needs condescension—but for the one plain, proud and priceless quality that unites us all as Americans: a sense of justice.

But if Kennedy put forth the strongest civil rights bill in history, his greater passion was the pursuit of peace. On June 10, the day before his civil rights speech, and in that hugely eventful forty-eight hours that also included George Wallace's stand, the self-immolation of Thich Quang Duc, and Medgar Evers's murder, Kennedy delivered the commencement address at American University. It was a talk that explored the evolution of his thinking in the aftermath of the Cuban missile crisis—a time of massive relief and reflection about living with the dangers of a nuclear age. As Arthur Schlesinger explained it, "Only two men on the planet had been exposed to the absolute pressure of nuclear decision; and even for them it was not till the missile crisis that what was perceived intellectually was experienced emotionally."

Kennedy's immediate goal, though he knew it would face opposition in the Congress, and among his adversaries in Moscow, was a nuclear test ban treaty, which he saw as a step toward peaceful coexistence. At American

University, he sought to change the context—political, diplomatic, emotional, and moral—for the pursuit of that goal. Speaking in a voice so calm and clear, Kennedy declared,

> No government or social system is so evil that its people must be considered as lacking in virtue. As Americans, we find communism profoundly repugnant as a negation of personal freedom and dignity. But we can still hail the Russian people for their many achievements—in science and space, in economic and industrial growth, in culture and in acts of courage.
>
> Among the many traits the peoples of our two countries have in common, none is stronger than our mutual abhorrence of war. Almost unique among the major world powers, we have never been at war with each other. And no nation in the history of battle ever suffered more than the Soviet Union suffered in the course of the Second World War. At least 20 million lost their lives . . .
>
> Today, should total war ever break out again—no matter how—our two countries would become the primary targets. It is an ironical but accurate fact that the two strongest powers are the two in the most danger of devastation. All we have built, all we have worked for, would be destroyed in the first 24 hours. And even in the Cold War, which brings burdens and dangers to so many countries, including this Nation's closest allies—our two countries bear the heaviest burdens. For we are both devoting massive sums of money to weapons that could be better devoted to combating ignorance, poverty and disease. We are both caught up in a vicious and dangerous cycle in which suspicion on one side breeds suspicion on the other, and new weapons beget counter-weapons. . . .
>
> So, let us not be blind to our differences—but let us also direct attention to our common interests and to means by which those differences can be resolved. And if we cannot end now our differences, at least we can help make the world safe for diversity. For, in the final analysis, our most basic common link is that we all inhabit this planet. We all breathe the same air. We all cherish our children's future. And we are all mortal.

Soviet Premier Nikita Khrushchev was said to be deeply moved by the speech. He allowed the whole text to be reprinted in the Soviet press, and in this singular moment of mutual understanding the climate for negotiation was changed. Kennedy appointed former New York Governor Averell Harriman as his chief negotiator for a test ban treaty, and his Russian counterparts understood immediately that the president was serious. Harriman was a seasoned diplomat, a U.S. Ambassador to Russia during World War II known for his resolution and toughness. Kennedy, for his part, wanted nothing but the best. He regarded the issue as supremely important; the earth was already being poisoned by atmospheric testing, and there was new evidence that even tests conducted underground leaked radioactive residue. There had been seventeen confirmed "ventings," or leaks, of iodine 131 from the Yucca Flats Proving Ground in Nevada.

More than that, Kennedy saw peace as a process, a series of incremental steps in which each side increased its commitment to diplomacy instead of war. A nuclear test ban would not, of course, remove vast nuclear arsenals from the planet, or even prevent the construction of new weapons. But it would represent a careful step away from an arms race that had no bounds. Whatever its limitations, it would be a concrete symbol of good intentions, proof to the world, among other things, that Kennedy meant what he said at American University.

As preparations for the talks continued, though without a clear sense of the possibility of success, the president set off on a trip to Europe, seeking to reassure Germany in particular that negotiations would not occur at its expense. On June 26 in West Berlin, Kennedy delivered his third historic address in a month. *"Ich bin ein Berliner,"* he proclaimed before an audience estimated at more than 150,000 people. Though his German was flavored with the accents of his native New England, his message of solidarity was clear. The crowd responded with thunderous applause, a roar of approval so loud and sustained that Kennedy was almost shaken by its force. "We'll never have another day like this one as long as we live," he said, as he boarded Air Force One for home.

Six days later, Khrushchev answered with a piece of statesmanship of his own. He also chose Berlin for his stage. Speaking on the eastern side of the Berlin Wall, he announced his support for a ban on nuclear testing—in the atmosphere, the oceans, or in outer space, all those places where the nuclear poisons spread most freely.

Thus, the task for Averell Harriman and his team of negotiators in Moscow was more a matter of ironing out details than resolving a fundamental disagreement. By July 15, the work was done. In Moscow, a treaty was initialed by

Khrushchev and the U.S. delegation, and the following evening in the United States, Kennedy went on television to announce the results.

> I speak to you tonight in a spirit of hope," he said. [Since] the advent of nuclear weapons, all mankind has been struggling to escape from the darkening prospect of mass destruction on earth. . . . Yesterday a shaft of light cut into the darkness. . . .
>
> This treaty is not the millennium. . . . But it is an important first step—a step toward peace, a step toward reason, a step away from war. . . . This treaty is for all of us. It is particularly for our children and grandchildren, and they have no lobby here in Washington . . .

Kennedy knew the agreement still faced ratification in Congress, no easy task. But at this point, not a lot of people would have bet against him. The President of the United States was on a roll.

THERE WERE, OF COURSE, still multiple problems on Kennedy's plate. In Vietnam, which would soon come to dominate the decade, he had not yet confronted a basic dilemma. The side the United States had chosen in that country's civil war—a war with roots in imperialism carried out by people very much like ourselves—was deeply unpopular with many Vietnamese. And on the homefront he worried about the election of 1964. He knew he had alienated much of the South with his strengthening stand on civil rights, and indeed George Wallace and other Southern leaders would often invoke the specter of "those Kennedys"—the President and his Attorney General brother—in denunciations of the civil rights movement. There was no doubt now whose side the Kennedys were on.

I was, by this time, fully aware of such things—soon to be a senior in high school and surrounded by a few extraordinary friends, some more perceptive than I, but all deeply intrigued by the President, as if he were somehow leading us personally, along with many thousands of others, in the direction of something we couldn't quite define. We knew it was something decent and good, some shining possibility for the country, which we already thought was the greatest on earth. "He's a great president," declared my friend, Frank Moore, who was a year ahead of me in school and seemed much wiser. He went on to speak with feeling about Kennedy's intelligence, his leadership, his steady hand on the wheel. For those of us inching slowly toward manhood, Kennedy seemed to provide an example, a model, for larger possibilities. All of this went beyond politics or social change, though the threat to the status quo in the South was clear, and we wrestled—tentatively at first, and quietly, privately—with issues of justice.

All around us, our parents' generation was clearly digging in, or trying to, asserting with greater ferocity than ever that the changes being proposed by the civil rights movement, and supported by the President, simply wouldn't work in a region such as ours. My father, himself an elected official, an Alabama judge, wrestled in particular with his feelings about Kennedy. He often spoke with admiration about the President's leadership abilities, his courage and wisdom in the realm of foreign policy. But he disagreed vehemently with Kennedy's embrace of civil rights, of changes that would tear at the fabric of *our place.*

Many others, less measured, now hated the president—and even more viscerally, perhaps, his brother—in a way that unsettled those of us from another generation.

Ironically, many civil rights leaders, including Dr. King, remained wary of and unhappy with President Kennedy, despite his powerful speech of June 11. They thought he could and should have done more, and they wondered in view of the mounting Southern opposition how hard he would push the civil rights bill. In the summer of 1963, King and other black leaders rallied around an old idea: a massive march on Washington in support of jobs and civil rights—and the bill that Kennedy had put before Congress. Kennedy worried that the plan would trigger a backlash, particularly if something went wrong and the day devolved into violence. He invited several key backers of the march to meet with him at the White House, where he lobbied mildly against their plan. But he did not prevail.

"The Negroes are already in the streets," argued A. Philip Randolph, the veteran union leader of the Brotherhood of Sleeping Car Porters. It was not Randolph's first time facing off against a president. In 1941 he had met with Franklin D. Roosevelt, who also wanted him to call off a march, a protest in the nation's capital against discrimination in hiring. With a war coming on, Roosevelt wanted nothing that might raise questions about national unity. Randolph, however, refused to cancel the march without specific concessions from FDR. The demonstration would go forward, he said, unless Roosevelt issued an executive order barring discrimination in wartime industries. Roosevelt issued the order, and the march was canceled. But Randolph had dreamed ever since about a nonviolent show of force in Washington, demanding equality and greater opportunity for Negroes.

Now the date was set for August 28, and this time it was Randolph who made a solemn promise to a president. There would be no violence to mar the day.

THE TASK OF ORGANIZING the event and making good on Randolph's promise fell to Bayard Rustin, an African American activist with a resume like nobody else's. He was a tall, thin man of fifty-one with dark-rimmed glasses and graying hair that he combed straight up. He was also a pacifist, socialist, homosexual, and a former member of the Communist Party. He was resolutely committed to nonviolence and was known in the ranks of the civil rights movement as a brilliant organizer. In planning for the March on Washington, no detail was too small to escape his attention. He knew a crowd of 100,000, the minimum number the leaders were expecting, could become surly and restless for the smallest of reasons: too few bathrooms, not enough food, too little water if the day turned hot.

When August 28 arrived and the crowd began to gather on the Washington mall, Rustin had arranged for the installation of hundreds of portable toilets, extra water fountains, first aid stations, and more than 80,000 free lunches for anybody who didn't bring their own. The thing over which he had no control was the possibility of murderous heat, which could happen in August, and could take its toll on the mood of the marchers. But the weather could not have been better. The predicted high for the day was eighty-five. The only thing now was to keep things moving—the march, the speeches, the soaring beauty of the music. Joan Baez was there, looking as lovely as she sounded, her voice so pure, her face so alive with innocent emotion, and she brought along her lover and friend, a twenty-two-year-old songwriter named Bob Dylan. He sang two of his original songs, one inspired by the death of Medgar Evers, the other an anthem called "Blowin' in the Wind," which was already a hit for the singing trio known as Peter, Paul and Mary. His voice was nasal and piercing, almost as if he were talking the words, but it changed when he joined Baez for her rendition of "We Shall Overcome." His singing was suddenly more mellow, more harmonic, and as one of Dylan's biographers noted, the two never sounded better together.

The great black artists were there as well—Harry Belafonte and the folk singer, Odetta, a native of Birmingham, so recently the site of demonstrations and riots. And perhaps most memorably there was Mahalia Jackson, Dr. King's favorite. It was said that in the troubled days in Montgomery, when his life was threatened and his house was bombed, he would sometimes retreat to his study and play over and over her rendition of "A Balm in Gilead," finding comfort in it that seemed to come from nowhere else. At the March on Washington, before this racially mixed crowd of 250,000, Jackson sang "I Been 'Buked and I Been Scorned," then stood at King's side as he began to speak.

He started slowly, glancing at his notes. In the sonorous baritone that was now his trademark, he said,

> In a sense, we have come to our nation's capital to cash a check. When the architects of our republic wrote the magnificent words of the Constitution and the Declaration of Indepdendence, they were signing a promisory note to which every American was to fall heir. This note was a promise that all men—yes, black men as well as white men—would be guaranteed the inalienable rights of life, liberty and the pursuit of happiness . . . We refuse to believe that the bank of justice is bankrupt. We refuse to believe there are insufficient funds in the great vaults of opportunity in this nation . . . And so we have come to this hallowed spot to remind America of the fierce urgency of now. . . . There will be neither rest nor tranquility in America until the Negro is granted his citizenship rights. The whirlwinds of revolt will continue to shake the foundations of our nation until the bright day of justice emerges.

It was a brilliant start. King, as always, anchored his call for radical change in the most conservative ideas from the nation's founding. And though he was unwavering in his support of nonviolence, his demands and warnings rang out across the vast sea of faces—the tens of thousands, black and white, spreading from the base of the Lincoln Memorial. But something was missing, some emotional resonance that he always seemed to find in such moments.

"Tell them about the dream, Martin," said Mahalia Jackson, standing nearby. And so he did.

> I say to you today, my friends, even though we face the difficulties of today and tomorrow, I still have a dream. It is a dream deeply rooted in the American

> dream. I have a dream that one day this nation will rise up and live out the true meaning of its creed—we hold these truths to be self-evident, that all men are created equal. I have a dream that one day on the red hills of Georgia, the sons of former slaves and the sons of former slave-owners will be able to sit down together at the table of brotherhood. . . . I have a dream that one day down in Alabama . . . little black boys and little black girls will be able to join hands with little white boys and little white girls as sisters and brothers.
>
> I have a dream today!

It was a vision that became his gift to the country, a legacy that would echo down through the years, and watching on television at the White House John Kennedy turned to the others in the room. "He's damn good," the president declared. And later in a face-to-face meeting with King, Kennedy's greeting was a quote from the speech: "I have a dream."

Thus did a glorious summer come to an end, the weeks so filled with promise and hope, the words so grand, the feeling so contagious that the best days of America lay just ahead.

16

Women's Voices

Already, the rising expectations had spread.

As summer gave way to fall, the Presidential Commission on the Status of Women was hard at work on its final report. Released in October, the commission's findings documented discrimination against women in the workplace and thus became part of a tide of feminism sweeping the country. It was less visible initially than the quest for freedom among African Americans. But in February 1963, Betty Friedan published *The Feminine Mystique*, a book that addressed the sterility of mind and spirit imposed upon middle-class women. Her opening chapter, "The Problem That Has No Name," began with these words:

> The problem lay buried, unspoken, for many years in the minds of American women. It was a strange stirring, a sense of dissatisfaction, a yearning that women suffered in the middle of the twentieth century in the United States. Each suburban wife struggled with it alone. As she made the beds, shopped for groceries, matched slipcover material, ate peanut butter sandwiches with her children, chauffered Cub Scouts and Brownies, lay beside her husband at night—she was afraid to ask even of herself the silent question—"Is this all?"

And a few pages later she added:

> If I am right, the problem that has no name stirring in the minds of so many American women today is not a matter of loss of femininity or too much education, or the demands of domesticity. It is far more important than anyone recognizes. It is the key to these and other new and old problems that have been torturing women and their husbands and children, and puzzling their doctors

> and educators for years. It may well be the key to our future as a nation and as a culture. We can no longer ignore that voice within women that says: "I want something more than my husband and my children and my home."

In explaining the origins of her manifesto, Friedan pointed to her own middle-class life in the 1950s and more specifically to a 1957 questionnaire answered by some of her Smith College classmates as they prepared for their fifteenth reunion. As she pondered the undercurrents of their discontent, she decided to write on the subject for *Redbook*. The article was rejected. "Betty has gone off her rocker," the magazine's editor wrote Friedan's agent. "She has always done a good job for us, but this time only the most neurotic housewife could identify."

Friedan concluded in response to that rejection that she would simply have to write a book. Caught in the flow of her own ideas, she was often surprised, she remembered later, at where they were leading. The implications seemed so radical. She wrote,

> . . . I and every other woman I knew had been living a lie, and all the doctors who treated us and the experts who studied us were perpetuating that lie, and our homes and schools and churches and politics and professions were built around that lie. If women were really *people*—no more, no less—then all the things that kept them from being full people in our society would have to be changed. And women, once they broke through the feminine mystique and took themselves seriously as people, would see their place on a false pedestal, even their glorification as sexual objects, for the putdown it was.

As millions of women bought her book and identified instinctively with her conclusions, the women's movement that took shape around it was largely white and middle class. But as Friedan biographer Daniel Horowitz noted, that had not always been her focus. While she was editor of the student newspaper at Smith College, Friedan (Betty Goldstein before she was married) defended the rights of maids and others who worked at Smith to unionize for better pay. During that time, she had spent part of a summer at the Highlander Folk School in Monteagle, Tennessee, where a generation of labor and civil rights activists came to learn the techniques of nonviolent change. In his biography Horowitz argued—more emphatically than Friedan herself—that her early concern for social justice was a shaping force in *The Feminine Mystique.*

Almost certainly in the 1960s, the women's movement that the book helped trigger drew a part of its energy from a broader discontent, especially the civil rights struggle. Notions of equality were simply in the air. But among the cultural forces that came into play, at least one connection was even more direct. Black women were emerging as civil rights leaders. Rosa Parks was already an icon, Mahalia Jackson was a celebrity-confidante to Martin Luther King, and within the ranks of movement strategists, Ella Baker, Diane Nash, Dorothy Cotton, and Septima Clark, among others, played critical roles, sometimes in uneasy alliance with men.

In addition, white folk singers Joan Baez and Mary Travers of Peter, Paul and Mary were equal parts activist and entertainer, and in their support of racial justice these two performers—both young and beautiful women—projected feminine strength. This, too, became part of a culture of change, and by early 1963 even country music had its first woman superstar. Some might have argued that Mother Maybelle Carter attained that status in the 1920s, or perhaps Kitty Wells in the 1950s, but almost everybody agreed that there had never been anybody like Patsy Cline.

"She didn't just open doors for women," said her fellow country singer, George Hamilton IV. "She kicked them in."

Born in the Appalachian town of Winchester, Virginia, Cline first attracted national attention in 1957 when she appeared on *Arthur Godfrey's Talent Scouts* on CBS. As the applause meter soared, she sang "Walking After Midnight," her most recent recording, which soon reached number two on the country charts and number sixteen on the pop. From that moment on, she displayed an uncanny ability to pick songs by some of country music's best writers, including "Crazy" by Willie Nelson and "She's Got You" by Hank Cochran; both were major crossover hits. Her unmistakable contralto voice was deeply emotional, but her success was also a matter of personal style, which was always tough and edgy and brash.

Hamilton remembered a time in the 1950s when he and Cline and a then little-known Jimmy Dean, who later won a Grammy with "Big Bad John," were on their way to a performance. The three were riding in the back of a car when Cline pulled out a flask of whiskey. She drank from it and offered it to Hamilton, who was sitting in the middle. He politely declined.

"What's the matter, Hoss?" she demanded. "You too good to drink with the Cline?"

With that she passed the flask to Jimmy Dean, who took a sip and passed it back across Hamilton to Cline. After a few such exchanges, Hamilton finally agreed to a drink and did his best to keep up with Cline. When the three reached their destination, Hamilton was nearly too tipsy to walk.

"Patsy," he remembered, "was just fine."

Despite that toughness, Cline was better known for her generosity of spirit, especially her support for other female artists. Dottie West and Loretta Lynn were two of her closest friends, and both were devastated on March 5, 1963, when Patsy died in the crash of a small private plane. After her burial in Winchester, West and Lynn arranged for the building of a bell tower in Cline's honor. Every day at the cemetery, the tower plays hymns at 6 p.m.

Over the years, these female relationships became the subject of country music lore. As one newspaper wrote in a story about Loretta and Patsy:

> When Lynn first arrived in Nashville . . . the young singer-songwriter knew little about the town or the music business, but Patsy Cline took Lynn under her wing, sharing advice, friendship and even undergarments.
>
> "I didn't have hardly any clothes, so [Patsy] took care of me and gave me hers," Lynn remembers. "She gave me a pair of panties that, I swear, I wore for four years. I don't know what I've done with them, but they never did wear out."

Even before Cline's death, Nashville minister Will Campbell, a staunch supporter of the sit-in movement, made a donation to the Student Nonviolent Coordinating Committee (SNCC) in her name. Partly, he said, he just liked her music. But more than that, she was a woman who shared his hatred of walls—all those barriers that held people back.

IN MAY 1963, TWO months after the death of Patsy Cline and three months from the publication of *The Feminine Mystique*, another new writer appeared on the scene. Gloria Steinem was not yet an icon, as she would become before the end of the decade, but on the pages of *Show* magazine she took the first public steps of her feminist journey. She had written for *Esquire* the previous year about the choice many women felt forced to make between a marriage and a career. But the *Esquire* story was tame compared to the expose she wrote for *Show* about working conditions in a Playboy club. On assignment for the entertainment magazine, Steinem had answered an ad which read:

> Yes, it's true! Attractive young girls can now earn $200–300 a week at the fabulous New York Playboy Club. Enjoy the glamorous and exciting aura of show business, and have the opportunity to travel to other Playboy Clubs throughout the world. Whether serving drinks, snapping pictures or greeting guests at the door, the Playboy Club is the stage—the Bunnies are the stars.

Steinem, who was then twenty-eight but passed for twenty-four, the maximum age for a Playboy bunny, was hired immediately and wrote a pair of articles, matter-of-fact in their disdain, about the shameless exploitation of young women. Her revelations should have come as no surprise, for the Playboy empire was sexism per se. It was the hedonistic fantasy of Hugh Hefner, a journalist from Illinois, who, in 1953, scraped together $8,000 from a group of investors, including his mother, to launch *Playboy* magazine. Marilyn Monroe was on the first cover. As the magazine became more successful, Hefner, who made a habit of dating his centerfold girls, began to establish Playboy clubs around the country, where attractive young women known as bunnies dressed in skimpy costumes, including bunny ears, and served as waitresses, greeters, and coat-checkers to the delight of men who were members of the club. Members allegedly were not allowed to date the bunnies, but as Steinem revealed in her article for *Show*, exceptions were made for "number one key holders"—members with sufficient influence or wealth to rate special privileges.

Steinem's revelations were devastating. There were, first of all, the clumsy, unrelenting flirtations of the customers. "If you're my bunny can I take you home?" That was the most persistent pickup line. During her first evening waiting tables, two men offered her a one-dollar tip. "I thanked them," Steinem wrote, "and told them they were my first customers." One doubled over with laughter. "This girl," he said, clearly delighted by his wit, "this girl's a *virgin bunny*."

Much worse were the oppressions of the club itself. Earnings almost never approached the $200–300 mentioned in the ad. On Steinem's first night as a "hat check bunny" she learned that her pay would be twelve dollars for an eight-hour shift, no tips. Tips went to the club. In addition, she wrote, the costumes were nearly unbearable, usually a couple of sizes too small, and the bunnies were pressured to pad their busts—with gym socks, laundry bags, absorbent cotton; the managers didn't care as long as the feminine curves were enhanced.

Steinem was proud of the article when it appeared, happy to expose sexism at its most outrageous. But in the weeks that followed, it was hard for her to get other magazine assignments. If she could pass for a Playboy bunny, how seriously could she be taken as a writer? "I had now become a Bunny," Steinem wrote later, "and it didn't matter why."

She was, of course, a journalist of substance with a concern for major issues in American life, including racial justice. She had not yet experienced what she called "the click"—the sudden convergence in her mind of issues that affected the lives of women. That would come later, especially in 1969, when, among other things, she would coin the phrase, "women's liberation." But the raw materials of feminism were present in her own life and in the story of her family.

Her grandmother, Pauline Perlmutter Steinem, had been a suffragist, a leader in the push for the Nineteenth Amendment. Her mother, Ruth Steinem, had been a spirited young woman, ambitious enough to pursue a career in journalism at a time when the field was dominated by men. But the pressures mounted. Her husband wanted her to quit her job. She fell in love with another man at work but was afraid to act on it, or consider a divorce, and eventually she had a "nervous breakdown." By the time Gloria came along, Ruth was in and out of mental hospitals and suffered periodically from agoraphobia, the fear of venturing outside her home. In an essay she called "Ruth's Song (Because She Could Not Sing It)," Gloria Steinem wrote:

> In retrospect, perhaps the biggest reason my mother was cared for but not helped for twenty years was the simplest: her functioning was not that necessary to the world. Like women alcoholics who drink in their kitchens while costly programs are constructed for executives who drink, or like the homemakers subdued with tranquilizers while male patients get therapy and personal attention instead, my mother was not an important worker. She was not even the caretaker of a very young child, as she had been when she was hospitalized the first time. My father had patiently brought home the groceries and kept our household going until I was eight or so and my sister went away to college.

> Two years later when wartime gas rationing closed his summer resort and he had to travel to buy and sell in summer as well as winter, he said: How can I travel and take care of your mother? He was right. It was impossible to do both. I did not blame him for leaving once I was old enough to be the bringer of meals and the answerer of my mother's questions. ("Has your sister been killed in a car crash?" "Are there German soldiers outside?") I replaced my father, my mother was left with one more way of maintaining a sad status quo, and the world went on undisturbed.

Later, Steinem realized that even her Suffragette grandmother, who died when Gloria was five, lived a life more constricted than it might have been:

> . . . I knew Pauline had once been a suffragist who addressed Congress, marched for the vote, and was the first woman member of a school board in Ohio. She must have been a courageous and independent woman, yet . . . I finally realized that my grandmother never changed the politics of her own life. . . . She was a feminist who kept a neat house for a husband and four antifeminist sons, a vegetarian among five male meat eaters, and a woman who felt so strongly about the dangers of alcohol that she used only paste vanilla; yet she served both meat and wine to the men of the house and made sure their lives and comforts were continued undisturbed. After the vote was won, Pauline seems to have stopped all feminist activity.

By the 1960s, Steinem wanted more—for herself and for all women regardless of their race, nationality or class. Slowly, steadily she was coming to terms with what it might take to achieve such a goal.

ON JUNE 10, 1963, President Kennedy signed the Equal Pay Act, which made it illegal to pay men and women different wages for similar work. Bills to achieve that goal had languished in Congress since World War II, when thousands of women went to work in factory jobs previously held by men. Kennedy supported the notion that wage discrimination on the basis of gender was not only bad for women, but bad for the economy.

This was, of course, the concrete side of the feminist awakening, more measurable, certainly, than the broader concerns of Steinem and Friedan—those issues of fulfillment, or the pursuit of happiness, as the founding fathers put it—that were no less real than the size of a paycheck. But in ways a politician could understand, Kennedy put his stamp of approval on at least a part of the feminist yearning, the notion that forced inequality was un-American. On October 11, which would have been Eleanor Roosevelt's seventy-ninth birthday, Kennedy accepted the report of the President's Commission on the Status of Women, which called for an end to discrimination in hiring, for paid maternity leave, and for universal child care. The Commission also concluded that a U.S. Supreme Court ruling was "urgently needed" to affirm women's equality under the Fourteenth Amendment.

Thus, the momentum grew. The New Frontier that President Kennedy had proclaimed was becoming as real in the minds of many Americans as President Roosevelt's New Deal. If Roosevelt offered during the Great Depression the hope for an economy with room for everyone, Kennedy now offered possibilities that felt even larger. Those enlightenment ideals of the Declaration of Independence *that all men are created equal* might soon include black men as well as white, and American women as well as men. There was work to be done before such changes were real, or even before they were fully defined. But for many people caught up in those times, it felt like a glorious moment to be alive.

17

Birmingham and Dallas

But there was also the darkness, always the darkness, and in the autumn of 1963 it descended again on a bright Sunday morning. September 15 began so beautifully in Birmingham, with clear blue skies and the singing of hymns. At the Sixteenth Street Baptist Church, it was supposed to be a special day in which young people in their Sunday finest would act as ushers and sing in the choir at the main church service. The lesson for the day was "The Love That Forgives." But at 10:29 a bomb went off and four girls were killed when a basement wall caved in. This was no random attack. The church was a staging ground for the Birmingham movement, the place where people of all ages came to learn the philosophy and techniques of nonviolence, and where many of the demonstrations began.

Its minister, John Cross, a man of eloquence with an air of gentle certainty, would remember how, when he first heard the explosion, he thought the hot water heater must have blown, for they had been having trouble with it. But then he recognized the smell of dynamite and rushed outside. He saw a gaping hole in the wall and immediately began to dig through the rubble. A church layman, M. W. Pippin, was working beside him when they came to a patent leather shoe.

"That's Denise's shoe," said Pippin. He knew his granddaughter Denise McNair had been wearing a similar pair that morning.

"Mr. Pippin," said Cross, "that could be anybody's shoe. A lot of little girls wear shoes like that."

But then they came to the tangle of bodies—first Denise and then three friends, Cynthia Wesley, Addie Mae Collins, and Carole Robertson. Addie Mae's little sister, Sarah Jean, was there also, blinded by the flying debris but alive. She was among the fourteen wounded.

In Birmingham, it was too much. Riots erupted in the city that night. Black people were roaming the streets with their guns, others were throwing rocks at police, and in the course of the violence two more African American children were killed. Johnnie Robinson was shot by a Birmingham policeman and Virgil Ware by a pair of white Eagle Scouts. By the following day, when the violence finally ran its course, the painful recriminations began. Alabama Attorney General Richmond Flowers, more liberal than many officeholders in the state, argued courageously that examples set in very high places almost certainly influenced the bombers. "In their way," said Flowers, "the individuals who bombed the Sixteenth Street Church were standing in the schoolhouse door."

African American leaders reached a similar conclusion. George Wallace may not have wanted to see a church bombed and children killed, but that did not absolve him of responsibility. His snarling rhetoric of white supremacy had poisoned the political climate of his state and had set the stage for this unspeakable violence. That was the view of Martin Luther King and many others. "The blood of our little children is on your hands," King wrote in a telegram to the governor. Strategically, movement leaders decided that voting rights must become their focus—the political power to elect people of decency, including African Americans, and thus to change the moral mood of the country.

And there was also this. King returned to Birmingham in the aftermath of the bombing to preach the eulogy for the murdered girls. This is what he said:

> History has proven over and over again that unmerited suffering is redemptive. . . . So in spite of the darkness of this hour we must not despair. We must not become bitter, nor must we harbor the desire to retaliate with violence. We must not lose faith in our white brothers. Somehow we must believe that even the most misguided among them can learn to respect the dignity and worth of all human personalities.

As a young reporter a few years later, I was moved to wonder about that eulogy, trying to imagine how it must have sounded in the moment. Was it too lofty, too forgiving and generous for people still trying to cope with such a crime?

In pursuit of an answer, I spoke with a man who would know, the father of one of the murdered girls. Of all the interviews in a long career, it remains the most moving and profound—a testament to the human spirit at its finest. Trying as hard as I could to be objective, dispassionate, trying to stay out of the way of the story, but swept up nevertheless in this encounter with the very heart of the civil rights movement, this is what I wrote, after I had quoted the words of Dr. King:

> I had always wondered how the sermon was received. How could the people in the church . . . including the shattered families of the children, possibly have listened to such noble words? On a magazine assignment . . . I came to Birmingham to interview Claude Wesley, father of Cynthia. Mr. Wesley was a principal in the Birmingham schools, a thin and wispy, gray-haired man who wanted his students to understand black history, the taproots of freedom going back a hundred years. We took our seats in his living room, and he explained that he saw the bombing that way, as a terrible, heartbreaking, personal loss that was nevertheless part of a much bigger story. As he talked, he glanced at a portrait on the wall, a radiant smile on the round, pretty face.
>
> "Such a beautiful girl," I said.
>
> "Yes," he replied, "she was a very happy child. She always liked to be in the forefront. Her teachers used to say if they could get Cynthia on their side, they could get the whole class."
>
> We talked for a while about the Birmingham movement and the changes he had seen in the city. "Birmingham is now a good town," he said. "It wanted to be a good town then, but there were forces standing in the way."
>
> Finally, I came to the question I had driven all the way to Birmingham to ask. What about the eulogy? How did it feel to be called to forgiveness when bitterness and rage were the natural inclinations?
>
> Wesley's answer was quick and emphatic. "We were never bitter," he said. "That would not have been fair to Cynthia. We try to deal with her memory the same way we dealt with her presence, and bitterness had no place in that. And there was something else we never did. We never said, 'Why us?' because that would be the same thing as saying, 'Why not somebody else?'"
>
> When I heard Claude Wesley speak those words I thought I had never encountered a faith so profound . . . such a startling contrast that the hideous act that put it to the test.

This was the essence of the civil rights struggle, I thought—the idealism of the 1960s, powerful and pure, but no longer innocent, for it had now come face to face with its opposite, in a way that all of us would know soon enough.

In the autumn, President Kennedy was looking ahead to his reelection one year away. He knew his embrace of the civil rights movement had already complicated his prospects. He had won the South in 1960, most of it at least, for that was the pattern in those days. The white South nearly always voted Democratic. It was a throwback, oddly, to a different time when the Democrats were the party of slavery, secession, and civil war. During Reconstruction and its aftermath, when Republicans were still the party of Lincoln, Southern Democrats passed the laws of segregation and adopted new state constitutions designed to disenfranchise African Americans. They were aided by the naked terror of the Ku Klux Klan, and some of that hatred had been rekindled in the 1950s and '60s. Jack Kennedy, of course, represented the opposite, certainly in the minds of many white Southerners, and as he pondered his path toward reelection he knew he could no longer count on the South.

As Arthur Schlesinger remembered in *A Thousand Days*, this was a time of general reflectiveness for Kennedy. The summer had ended on a difficult note. On August 7, Jacqueline Kennedy gave birth to a son, Patrick Bouvier Kennedy, who was born prematurely and weighed less than five pounds. Two days later, the baby died. Many people close to the Kennedys, including White House Press Secretary Pierre Salinger, thought their grief brought them closer together as a couple. Whatever his personal thoughts, Kennedy was also in an introspective mood about his presidency. On a speaking tour of the Rocky Mountain West, an area in which he was eager to shore up support, he was heartened by the apparent popularity of his nuclear test ban treaty. In Montana and other stops in the West, it brought more applause than any other subject. Kennedy's approval rating stood at 59 percent (and had been even higher before opposition hardened in the South), and he hoped he could channel that personal popularity into major accomplishments in his second term.

He was determined to expand the emerging détente with the Soviet Union, to broaden the ban on nuclear testing and limit the growth of nuclear arsenals. That was his major foreign policy objective, to steer the world from the kind of nuclear showdowns that had loomed so precipitously in Cuba and Berlin. But he apparently knew in the fall of 1963 that his greatest policy failure had come in the form of an afterthought. Preoccupied by the Cold War, he had not yet confronted the fundamental dilemmas of Vietnam. Since the Eisenhower Administration, the United States had cast its lot with the South Vietnamese government of Ngo Dinh Diem.

From the beginning there were problems with this policy that neither Eisenhower nor Kennedy would publicly acknowledge, much less address. Beginning in 1954, Vietnam, which had been a single country, was divided temporarily by international agreement—communist government in the North, anti-communist in the South—pending reunification in 1956 through internationally supervised elections. Diem, however, refused to participate in the elections, knowing he would lose to Ho Chi Minh, the leader of North Vietnam. First under Eisenhower and then under Kennedy, the United States supported Diem, even as opposition to his government increased. There was, first of all, a civil war against the Viet Cong—communist insurgents in the South, supported by the government of Ho Chi Minh. According to the stream of official reports from the U.S. Embassy in Saigon, the war was going well for Diem. But young American journalists such as David Halberstam of the *New York Times* and Malcolm Browne of the Associated Press filed stories from the countryside that sharply contradicted the official line. Then came the Buddhist crisis in 1963 and the horrifying image of a monk setting himself on fire in Saigon, and suddenly the dilemmas came into focus.

In addition to the partition of Vietnam, unilaterally extended by Diem, in South Vietnam itself there were multiple rebellions against its U.S.-supported government. Finally, on November 2 there was a coup, with apparent CIA involvement. Diem and other members of his family were killed, and Kennedy was left to begin a gloomy reassessment of his policy. Arthur Schlesinger wrote:

> I saw the President soon after he heard that Diem and Nhu were dead. He was somber and shaken. I had not seen him so depressed since the Bay of Pigs. No doubt he realized that Vietnam was his great failure in foreign policy, and that he had not given it his full attention. . . . He had always believed there was a point at which our intervention might turn Vietnamese nationalism against us and transform an Asian civil conflict into a white man's war. When he came into office, some 2,000 American troops were in Vietnam. Now there were 16,000. How many more could there be before we passed that point?

As Kennedy pondered that question, bombarded by the conflicting advice of his advisers, there were more hopeful things on his plate. On the domestic front, there was the civil rights bill making its way through Congress, and he had begun to think about that issue in a broader context, specifically its ties to the U.S. economy. The civil rights legislation was aimed at the South's long and bitter history of legal segregation, but, as Kennedy understood, there were also racial problems in the North. Many were, he thought, tied to a lack of economic opportunity. The economy was doing well overall, growing at a rate of 5.6 percent a year. Profits, wages, and salaries were up and costs were stable, but unemployment was still nearly six percent, and Kennedy was contemplating tax cuts in the hope of creating more jobs. But he had also read *The Affluent Society* by John Kenneth Galbraith and *The Other America* by Michael Harrington which together gave a face to a structural, multi-generational poverty that crippled the lives of too many Americans. There would have to be programs, Kennedy believed, aimed at areas like the coalfields of Appalachia or the inner-city ghettos of the North. Schlesinger wrote:

> He was reaching the conclusion that tax reduction required a comprehensive structural counterpart, taking the form, not of piecemeal programs, but of a broad war on poverty itself. Here perhaps was the unifying theme which would pull a host of social programs together and rally the nation behind a generous cause.

At a cabinet meeting on September 29, Kennedy, as usual, was doodling on a yellow legal pad, writing the same word multiple times—the latest preoccupation of perhaps the most powerful man in the world—"poverty . . . poverty . . . poverty . . ."

BUT IF ALL OF this was the emerging agenda for his second term, there remained the problem of getting reelected. In November, he decided on a good-will trip to Texas, with stops in San Antonio, Houston, Ft. Worth, Dallas, and Austin. Some people close to him were worried about Dallas. On October 24, UN Ambassador Adlai Stevenson had gone to Dallas to deliver a speech on United Nations Day. He was attacked by a handful of hecklers at the end of his address, and although uninjured he told Arthur Schlesinger, his long-time friend, ". . . there was something very ugly and frightening about the atmosphere. Later I talked to some of the leading people out there. They wondered whether the President should go to Dallas and so do I."

Stevenson knew, however, that Kennedy would never cancel the trip out of fear, and in fact at the start it seemed to be going well. In San Antonio the president talked about space and the new frontiers of human understanding in a country with its sights now set on the Moon. Speaking at the Aerospace Medical Health Center, he declared, "There will be, as there always are, pressures in this country to do less in this area as in so many others . . . But this research must go on. This space effort must go on. The conquest of space must and will go ahead. That much we know."

On his stop in Houston the reception was warm, and it was again in Ft. Worth, where he told the leaders of the Chamber of Commerce, "No one expects that our life will be easy. . . . History will not permit it. . . . But we are still the key in the arch of freedom. . . ."

And then came Dallas.

"We are headed into nut country today," he told his wife. "But Jackie, if somebody wants to shoot me from a window with a rifle, nobody can stop it, so why worry about it?"

At 11:40 a.m. on November 22, Air Force One landed at the Dallas Airport. Jackie stepped from the doorway first. The president wanted everybody to see her, so radiant and lovely in her pink Chanel suit, her image captured on film by Ward Warren, a fifteen-year-old high school student who was excited to be in the crowd that day. Larry Sabato, a political scientist at the University of Virginia, whose assessments of Kennedy are so objective as to be almost cold, nevertheless spoke for many of us when he wrote in his book, *The Kennedy Half Century*,

> Fifty years later, we can look at Warren's film and see the Kennedys at the height of their power. Jackie looks stunning in her iconic outfit, and JFK appears tan, rested, and supremely confident. Even after so many years, a viewer's first reaction is to wish someone on the scene had an inkling of what was to come. We want a time tunnel to 1963 so we can shout, "Get back on Air Force One! Don't climb into the limousine!" But the celluloid figures cannot hear a warning. The grief and tears will just have to flow.

After he disembarked from the plane, Kennedy frightened his Secret Service protectors with unscheduled stops to shake hands with the crowd—twice with children who had caught his eye. The weather in Dallas was clear and a pleasant 63 degrees, and thus the bubble top on his limousine was down. The president had no shield against the sniper who was waiting at the Texas School Book Depository.

At 12:30 p.m., shots rang out. Kennedy lurched forward in his seat and blood and bone and bits of brain blew from a gaping wound in his head. Less than two seconds later, Texas Governor John Connally, sitting in the seat in front of Kennedy, groaned as a bullet struck him in the chest. Jackie Kennedy, now covered in blood, cradled the limp body of her husband in her arms. Even at the emergency room, as the limo pulled into Parkland Hospital, she refused to let him go. One of the Secret Service agents spoke to her gently: "Mrs. Kennedy, let us get the President."

At 12:40, the first news bulletin flashed across the television screen, and in the years since I have never met a person who was alive that day who didn't remember where they were and what they were doing when they first heard the news. I was a senior in high school in Mobile, Alabama, walking down an empty hallway on an errand for a school administrator. Suddenly, a boy I knew came running past.

"Kennedy's been shot," he gasped. I knew this boy was a practical joker with a sense of humor often crude and outrageous, and I remember even now with a searing shame that my first reaction to his words was to laugh.

"He must have pissed somebody off," I said.

I meant it as a joke, a teenaged quip, intended to be cynical and cool, for it simply never occurred to me that my friend could be serious. But now he stopped, turned and said, "No, really, Kennedy's been shot."

The next few minutes are a blur of memory, but I rushed back to the principal's office where people were gathering around a TV. Even then, denial refused to loosen its grip. The president shot . . . what a terrible thing. I wondered where the bullet had hit. Probably the arm. It had to be some kind of flesh wound, but what an awful thing anyway. Whoever did it, I hoped they put him away for life. Those were the thoughts that were spinning through my head—replayed now as if in slow motion—when the image of Walter Cronkite appeared on the screen. He was always the consummate newsman with his dark-rimmed glasses and tiny mustache, and that resonant baritone that commanded such trust every time you heard it. But now he looked both shaken and tired, removing his glasses, wiping his eyes. And then the words:

"From Dallas, Texas, the flash, apparently official, President Kennedy died at one p.m. Central Standard Time, two o'clock Eastern Standard Time, some thirty-eight minutes ago." Cronkite paused, choking back tears, before he made himself push ahead. "Vice President Johnson has left the hospital in Dallas, but we do not know where he has proceeded. Presumably he will be taking the oath of office shortly and become the thirty-fifth President of the United States."

The next image I remember, though it barely seemed real, was Johnson taking the oath. Jacqueline Kennedy in her blood-smeared dress was standing at his side, a symbol of continuity and courage.

"I will do the best I can," Johnson said. "That is all I can do."

I remember thinking it would not be enough.

A short time later, Robert McNamara, the secretary of defense, received a call on behalf of Mrs. Kennedy. As a cabinet member, McNamara had earned the president's trust. He had performed so beautifully during the Cuban missile crisis, pushing for a naval blockade instead of an attack—an idea that may have averted a nuclear war. Forty years later with a choke in his voice, McNamara told the story in a documentary film, *The Fog of War,* of Jackie's call, asking that he go to Arlington Cemetery and select a gravesite for her husband. McNamara remembered:

> We took the body to the White House . . . it was 4 a.m. . . . and called the superintendent of Arlington. And he and I walked over those grounds. They're hauntingly beautiful grounds. White crosses, row and row. And finally, I thought I had found the exact spot, the most beautiful spot in the cemetery. I called Jackie at the White House and asked her to come out there. She immediately accepted. And that's where the President is buried today. A Park Service ranger came up to me and said that he escorted President Kennedy on a tour of those grounds a few weeks before. And Kennedy said that was the most beautiful spot in Washington.

It was no accident that the place McNamara had chosen aligned precisely with the Lincoln Memorial, the Washington Monument, and the U.S. Capitol. Jacqueline Kennedy, with her impeccable sense of symbolism and taste, arranged for an eternal flame to burn on the grave, constructed to withstand any kind of weather. She lit the flame herself at the funeral ceremony, and it was one of many gestures that day that imbued the moment with unbearable sadness.

In the depth of her grief, she choreographed a period of mourning that would link her husband to the greatest leaders in American history. Within hours of the assassination, Civil War historian James Robertson was summoned to the East Room of the White House, where Lincoln's body had lain in state. With Robertson's guidance, the room was prepared as it had been for Lincoln, draped in black bunting, and Kennedy's coffin was placed on the stand—the *same one,* retrieved from storage—that had once held Lincoln's. On Sunday, November 24, after twenty-four hours at the White House, the casket was moved to the Capitol, transported by a team of horses through streets now lined with silent mourners—more than 300,000, according to one count. The only sounds were hoof beats, muffled sobs, and the slow and somber beating of drums.

And there was one more moment on Monday, the day of the service at St, Matthew's Cathedral, perhaps the most pure and heart-wrenching moment of all. As the President's casket was carried from the church, Jacqueline Kennedy stooped down and whispered to her son, John Kennedy Jr., who had turned three years old that day. The boy stepped forward, and as his father had taught him, raised his tiny hand in salute.

I don't know anyone who didn't weep.

Inevitably, of course, later generations would begin to acknowledge John Kennedy's faults—a "darker side," as one scholar put it, which included most obviously his voracious sexual appetites. But Jacqueline Kennedy, through the imagery of a funeral, and in her own quest for dignity and meaning, shaped our remembrance in a way that reinforced what we already knew. From the beginning of his short presidency to the end, her husband had the ability to inspire. In these extraordinary times, there were others, too, who possessed that gift, and many Americans, reeling with grief, turned to them now more desperately than before.

18

The Warren Commission

Almost immediately, the new president made a fateful decision. Lyndon Johnson was worried about the country. He could imagine a wave of hysteria arising out of the murder of a president by a left-wing loner. Then on the Sunday after the assassination, the nation watched in real time as the Dallas police—their ineptitude staggering in so many ways—allowed nightclub operator Jack Ruby to shoot Lee Harvey Oswald at point-blank range while he was in police custody.

The shooting occurred at 11:21 a.m. as two detectives were transferring Oswald from police headquarters to the county jail. Security had been already been shockingly lax. Incredibly, the press had talked with Oswald —surely the highest-profile prisoner in the world at that moment—*before* the police had finished their own interrogations. Lonnie Hudkins of the *Houston Post* was actually invited to sit in as officers questioned their double-murder suspect (Oswald was now also accused of killing Dallas policeman J. D. Tippit).

In *The Kennedy Half Century*, political scientist and author Larry Sabato described with astonishment Hudkins's conversation with Oswald as official investigators looked on:

> "'Why did you kill Officer Tippit?' And he threw the question right back at me and said, 'Someone get killed? Policeman get killed?' And at that time he had this little smirk on him and I wanted to hit him, but I didn't. And all of a sudden it dawned on me that he wasn't sweating; not a drop of sweat on him. He was cooler than all of the people around him—Secret Service, police, FBI, district attorney . . . *everybody* was in that office."

As the tainted investigation continued, virtually everybody else in the world, it seemed, was glued to the television. Political scientist Benedict Anderson of Cornell University would later write of *The Imagined Community*, a national identity forged among people too geographically diverse to know each other personally. In Anderson's view, that kind of identity began historically with the printed word, especially newspapers. But as others have noted, with television that connection became exponentially stronger. And we now know precisely the moment it happened—on this terrible November weekend when the bitter combination of incredulity and grief made it impossible to tear our eyes from the screen. For the first time in such a sweeping way, television brought us all together, creating a sense of national community intimately, immediately connected to the news.

Even Robert Kennedy, the shattered, grieving brother of the president, was a part of this audience, this community of people transfixed by a tragedy that all of us shared as we watched the live coverage of the aftermath of the assassination. When his friend and Justice Department colleague John Seigenthaler knocked on his door, hoping to offer some words of comfort, or at least to *be there* for a man he admired, Kennedy's greeting took him by surprise. "Obviously in pain," Seigenthaler remembered, "he opened the door and said something like this, 'Come on in, somebody shot my brother, and we're watching . . . on television.'"

In time, Robert Kennedy would have to pull himself together, to find an identity and a meaning for his life beyond one simply attached to his brother. Until November 22, that had been enough. But this wrenching process of rediscovery would have to wait, at least for a while. In the moment, there was only his grief. "He was the most shattered man I had ever seen in my life," remembered Pierre Salinger. "He was virtually non-functioning. He would walk for hours by himself."

Lyndon Johnson, meanwhile, understood the difficulties of his own position. For so many years he had wanted to be president, but not like this. It was true enough that he despised Robert Kennedy, a political nemesis both before and after the assassination. But he had always genuinely admired the President, respected his style and grace and intellect, and he knew his own rough-hewn Texas manner, so effective in the corridors of the U.S. Senate, would take some getting used to for the nation at large. It would not be easy to follow a martyr. He told historian Doris Kearns:

> I took the oath. I became President. But for millions of Americans I was still illegitimate, a naked man with no presidential covering, a pretender to the throne, an illegal usurper. And then there was Texas, my home, the home of both the murder and the murder of the murderer. And then there were the bigots and the dividers and the Eastern intellectuals, who were waiting to knock me down before I could even begin to stand up. The whole thing was almost unbearable.

But Johnson took the reins, firmly and with a humility that took his detractors by surprise. On November 27, five days after the assassination, he made his first major speech as president. He chose as his forum the U.S. Congress, the place he was always most at home. He spoke slowly, thoughtfully, sounding more and more presidential as he went along, and specifically about civil rights, an issue on which he had long urged Kennedy to act:

> "John Kennedy's death commands what his life conveyed—that America must move forward. First, no memorial or oration or eulogy could more eloquently honor President Kennedy's memory than the earliest possible passage of the civil rights bill for which he fought so long. We have talked long enough about equal rights in this country. We have talked for one hundred years or more. It is time now to write the next chapter and to write it in the books of law."

As one of his biographers later put it, Johnson suddenly "sounded like a president."

But an early Johnson decision seemed in retrospect to foreshadow the qualities of his own undoing. Whatever his strengths—and Johnson had many—he possessed an inclination toward secrecy, toward manipulating the instruments of power and playing his hand so close to the vest that his critics would later accuse him of deception. Thus he acted with mixed motivations when he created a commission to study the assassination of his predecessor. Certainly, he wanted to know what had happened. But he also wanted to calm the country's fears. Four days after the assassination, knowing that Americans had been watching constantly on TV, witnessing the murder of the assassin himself after public speculation of Oswald's ties to the Soviet Union, the new president summoned Chief Justice Earl Warren to the White House. He wanted Warren to lead an official inquiry into the death of President Kennedy.

In William Manchester's book, *The Death of a President*, Warren is quoted as giving this account of his meeting with Johnson:

> The President told me how serious the situation was. He said there had been wild rumors, and that there was the international situation to think of . . . He said that if the public became aroused against Castro and Khrushchev there might be war. "You've been in uniform before," he said, "and if I asked you, you would put on the uniform again for your country." I said, "Of course." "This is more important than that," he said. "If you're putting it like that," I said, "I can't say no."

The Warren Commission would begin its inquiry the following February and issue its final report in October. Many have argued since then that the commission's work raised as many questions as it answered, and that the flaws in its findings were tied in part to the flawed motivations of its creation. "The Warren Commission," wrote Larry Sabato, "was . . . the first damaging government whitewash in the 1960s."

If it was true that Lyndon Johnson wanted to soothe the anxious feelings of the nation as much as he wanted to get to the truth, there would be other moments in the next five years when he would fall victim to the same temptation. It was an inclination that served him badly—and served the country he loved even worse.

PART II

Inspiration/Loss

1964—"Sick and Tired": *LBJ makes his mark, Wallace for President, the British Invasion, Motown, Sam Cooke and Johnny Cash, the Civil Rights Act, Freedom Summer, Free Speech at Berkeley, the Goldwater insurgency, the Johnson landslide, the agony of RFK, Dr. King and the Nobel Prize*

1965—"The Arc Is Long": *The murder of Malcolm X, the Selma march, Escalation in Vietnam, the teach-ins, Billy Graham, Rioting in Watts and Chicago, Cesar Chavez, the Byrds, Julie Andrews, Doctor Zhivago*

1966—"Power": *War and peace, RFK, Governor Wallace and Governor Reagan, Banning the dunk, Black Power, Percy Sledge, the Beach Boys, Staff Sergeant Barry Sadler, God Is Dead, In Cold Blood, NOW, Miranda, Federal registrars and Black Panthers, Desegregating the Senate, the Supreme Court and Julian Bond*

1967—'In the Heat of the Night': *The war rages on, homestretch to the Moon, Martin Luther King and RFK, the Six-Day War Black Power, riots and academic freedom, Summer of Love, summer of rage, Interracial marriage, breaking the color barrier on the court, Joplin, Ronstadt, and Charlie Pride, Norman Rockwell, Mister Rogers and The Graduate*

1968—'Drop by Drop': *LBJ and the politics of war, Tet, My Lai, King and Kennedy: the last campaigns, Assassinations, death on campus, Farewell to Helen Keller, Resurrection City, Chicago, the Mexico City Olympics, Nixon Again, The first Earthrise*

19

LBJ

As the new year dawned, Lyndon Johnson was working on his first State of the Union Address as president, and he felt great clarity about the stakes. This was his chance to assume the mantle of leadership and offer his own vision to the country. It would not be a repudiation of what had come before, for that was not necessary to make his own mark, nor was it what he wanted to do. Every great leader had his own style, his gifts, his specific strengths. Johnson understood this. If John F. Kennedy's great gift had been to inspire, Johnson prided himself on getting things done. And rightly so. Probably nobody in Washington was more formidable or impressive one-on-one, nor more persuasive. LBJ was large and imposing, and if he was not classically handsome like Kennedy had been, there was something impressive about his face. Johnson biographer Doris Kearns, recalled her first meeting with him:

> His appearance startled me. The picture in my mind had been a caricature: the sly televised politician, his features locked into virtual immobility, eyes squinting, ears that seemed to dangle like thick pendants affixed to the sides of his head. Now I saw a ruddy giant of a man with a strong mobile face, and a presence whose manifest energy dominated an entire room filled with Senators, Representatives, Cabinet officials, White House staff members, and reporters.

Before his meetings with men of power (in those days it was nearly always men), Johnson always did his homework. He acquired a commanding grasp of detail that often took others by surprise. Sometimes by himself, sometimes with the help of one or more of his staff, he studied the character of the leaders he would meet. What made them tick? What were their strengths and vulnerabilities? What did they *want?* By the time they arrived, he usually had a sense of how to find common ground, of how to listen and how to persuade. And within days of his tragic rise to the presidency, the meetings began.

He was determined, first of all, to reach out to a constituency of civil rights leaders, for that issue, he hoped, would be the centerpiece of his legacy, along with the related issue of poverty. He knew he faced an uphill challenge to win the leaders' trust. Even John Kennedy was still viewed with some skepticism, especially by young activists toiling in the dangerous backwaters of the South and a growing cadre of northern militants about whom he was scarcely aware.

Louis Lomax, one of the country's fine African American journalists, wrote in the pages of *Look* magazine about the suspicion many blacks felt toward the new president:

> As we listened to him talk, the cracker twang in his voice chilled our hearts. For we knew that twang, that drawl. We have heard it in the night, threatening in the day, abusing; from the pulpit, sanctifying segregation in the market place, denying us opportunity; everywhere, abrogating our human dignity. Yes, we knew that twang. And we reacted.

Lomax, however, was one of many prominent African Americans who believed early on that Johnson might be a pleasant surprise. For one thing, he wanted to hear what they had to say. Shortly after the Kennedy assassination, he met alone with Martin Luther King, spending an hour, as historian Taylor Branch later put it, "in the close embrace of noble dreams as big as Texas." But the civil rights leaders with whom Johnson seemed most at home were Roy Wilkins of the NAACP and Whitney Young of the National Urban League. These men, in Johnson's estimation, understood politics, understood the mechanisms for getting things done. For more than half a century, the NAACP had done the painstaking work of filing lawsuits to establish the legal foundations of progress. Roy Wilkins, a man of such intelligence and dignity, was the capable heir to that leadership tradition, a man with whom Johnson could talk with candor. In their private sessions, he told Wilkins frankly that passage of the civil rights bill would require Republican support in Congress. He urged Wilkins to meet with Senate Minority Leader Everett Dirksen of Illinois, letting him know that African American political loyalty was not a monopoly held by the Democrats, that Republican support for equal rights would not be forgotten. Wilkins, apparently, was deeply impressed by

Johnson's candor, what seemed to be such extraordinary fairness in the new president's acknowledgment that neither party was *entitled* to black support; each would have to earn it.

Johnson had many conversations like that. He met with business and labor leaders as well, seeking their embrace not only of civil rights, but a comprehensive national war on poverty. This was an issue he understood well, for it took him back to his own hard-scrabble boyhood in Texas. As a politician, he was given to exaggerating his own family's deprivations, embracing the rags-to-riches American narrative that so appealed to voters. But he did know poverty. He saw it as a young schoolteacher in his native state, and in his early days as president he made frequent visits to the poorest areas of the country. Wrote Kearns:

> To Johnson, the poor would never be "the disadvantaged," an abstract class whose problems must be solved. They were familiar men and women suffering a circumstance he well understood.

In transforming poverty to a national priority, Johnson sought to make it clear that he was no presidential Robin Hood taking from the rich to give to the poor. He envisioned an economy that worked for everybody, an ever-growing "pie" with slices enough for all—the rich, the poor, the American middle class. Like Kennedy, he favored tax cuts for the wealthy to serve as an economic stimulus, but he was already fleshing out Kennedy's notions—those abstract doodlings on a legal pad, "poverty . . . poverty . . . poverty"—into a programmatic assault on the causes of economic deprivation. And now, after the whirlwind weeks of meetings, he stood before a Joint Session of Congress to deliver his State of the Union Address.

On January 8, 1964, he announced what he hoped would be the cornerstone of his legacy as president, a legacy tied deliberately to that of John Kennedy, but surpassing it, for Johnson intended to get more done:

> Let this session of Congress be known as the session which did more for civil rights than the last hundred sessions combined, as the session which enacted the most far-reaching tax cut of our time; as the session which declared all-out war on human poverty and unemployment in these United States; as the session which finally recognized the health needs of all our older citizens; . . . as the

> session which helped to build more homes, more schools, more libraries, and more hospitals than any single session of Congress in the history of our Republic.

This was Johnson's view of government, nurtured during the New Deal when he was still a young politician, absorbing a notion that began with George Washington and reached fruition under Franklin Roosevelt—that a strong central government was good for the country, for it was, in effect, the voice of the people with a shape and a focus provided by their leaders, shrewd, intelligent men like himself, ambitious in what they intended to accomplish, but schooled in the art of principled compromise. Thus did Johnson, as he seized the presidential moment for himself, deliver a State of the Union Address as historic as any in the twentieth century. He declared an all-out war on poverty. No other president had ever done that, and for very good reason. There had never been a time in American history when the U.S. economy seemed strong enough, or *large enough*, to make a place for everybody at the table.

But Johnson thought that now was the time, and he intended for history to remember his vision:

> Unfortunately, many Americans live on the outskirts of hope—some because of their poverty, and some because of their color, and all too many because of both. Our task is to help replace their despair with opportunity.
>
> This administration today, here and now, declares unconditional war on poverty . . .
>
> Very often a lack of jobs and money is not the cause of poverty, but the symptom. The cause may lie deeper—in our failure to give our fellow citizens a fair chance to develop their own capacities, in a lack of education and training, in a lack of medical care and housing, in a lack of decent communities in which to live and bring up their children.
>
> But whatever the cause, our joint Federal-local effort must pursue poverty, pursue it wherever it exists—in city slums and small towns, in sharecropper shacks and migrant worker camps, on Indian Reservations, among whites as well as Negroes, among the young as well as the aged . . .

Soon the new president would submit a bill to Congress fleshing out the details. And in this time of soaring possibility still shadowed by grief, there was another piece of government business begun under Kennedy, now coming to fruition under President Johnson, that was aimed at improving the health of the nation. United States Surgeon General Luther Terry, a small-town Alabamian who graduated from Tulane Medical School before taking a position at Johns Hopkins University, released a report on the health hazards of smoking. The previous year, Terry had read the findings on smoking by the Royal College of Physicians in the United Kingdom. He decided with the blessings of President Kennedy to chair a U.S. commission to study the literature on the subject. After poring through more than 7,000 scientific articles, the Surgeon General's Advisory Commission on Smoking concluded that tobacco was linked to lung cancer and chronic bronchitis, and probably to heart disease and other cancers.

Terry released the report on a Saturday, partly, he explained, to avoid a stock market plunge and partly to assure widespread coverage in the Sunday newspapers. The strategy worked. The findings, he said, "hit the country like a bombshell. It was front page news and a lead story on every radio and television station in the United States and many abroad." Despite a ferocious counter-attack by the tobacco industry, the Surgeon General's report triggered a wave of reform that continued for the next fifty years. In June 1964, the Federal Trade Commission voted to mandate health warnings on cigarette packages, and the following year Congress made that requirement a law. By the end of the decade, cigarette advertising was banned on radio and television.

Terry's efforts added to a feeling of momentum that surrounded the Johnson Administration early in 1964. In February, the president signed the Revenue Act of 1964, which cut income taxes by twenty percent across the board, and slightly more for the highest tax bracket. Corporate taxes were reduced by four percent. Over the next two years the economy soared, as unemployment dropped from 5.2 percent in 1964 to 3.8 percent in 1966, while federal tax revenues increased.

On March 16, in a special message to Congress, Johnson introduced the Economic Opportunity Act of 1964, detailing his plans for an assault on poverty that he hoped would make a difference. In January, he had asked Sargent Shriver, brother-in-law to President Kennedy, to draft the major components of a bill. Shriver proposed a broad and coordinated approach that included education and jobs programs, as well as something he called Volunteers in Service to America, or VISTA, the domestic equivalent of the Peace Corps that he had helped to launch under Kennedy.

As the Economic Opportunity bill began to make its way through committee, Johnson turned his attention to civil rights. During his own time in the Senate, he had helped water down civil rights bills in 1957 and 1960. He was determined to see that it didn't happen this time. He met with Senator Richard Russell, Democrat of Georgia, one of the most prominent opponents of the bill, to let him know there would be no compromise. It was not an easy meeting for the two old friends; at sixty-seven Russell was a senior member of the Senate, and Lyndon Johnson had been his protégé. They still talked often about foreign policy and other matters of state, but on the issue of civil rights legislation, Johnson told his former mentor, "If you get in my way, I'm going to run you down." Russell, for his part, prepared for an all-or-nothing filibuster, aimed at talking the bill to death.

"We will resist to the bitter end," Russell declared, "any measure or any movement which would have a tendency to bring about social equality and intermingling and amalgamation of the races in our [Southern] states."

As the controversy swirled, both in the Congress and in the country, Johnson seemed undaunted by the rumblings of a racial backlash—a term that only recently had entered the political lexicon. (In 1963, columnist Eliot Janeway, who wrote primarily about the economy, voiced concern that white workers would "lash back" against African Americans competing for their jobs.) By the spring of 1964, the chief apostle of backlash was George Wallace. The Alabama governor had decided his time had come to run for president. For the moment he was only testing the waters, entering three presidential primaries outside the South. Almost immediately, however, it was clear that Wallace struck a chord and touched a nerve in some unexpected places.

His presidential run began in Wisconsin, where his detractors simultaneously dismissed his importance and attacked him with a furious disdain that made him seem important indeed—how else could he strike such fear in their hearts?

On February 19, 1964, Wallace charmed a hostile crowd at the University of Wisconsin, using a combination of humor and a speech that skirted the issue of segregation to disarm what one historian called "a raucous band of demonstrators." One student who found Wallace harder to hate than he expected would grumble later that the governor's "Southern charm oozed out."

Shortly after that performance, Wallace and his staff received a call from Lloyd and Delores Herbstreith, a Wisconsin couple active in conservative politics. Their agenda included, among other things, abolition of the federal income tax in order to "destroy the welfare state." They urged Wallace to enter their state's presidential primary. With his raging ambition, he did not require a lot of persuasion. When his announcement came a few days later, the national media mostly ignored it (the *New York Times* ran a small story on page 76), but Wisconsin Governor John Reynolds sounded the alarm.

Reynolds himself was running in the primary as a "favorite son" stand-in for Lyndon Johnson, a common practice in those days, and to rally his own base, he predicted that Wallace might get as many as 100,000 votes. That, said Reynolds, would be a "catastrophe." He called for a "moral crusade" to repudiate the Alabama governor and "all he stands for." "Churches were bombed and children were killed in his state," Reynolds continued.

In *The Politics of Rage*, historian Dan T. Carter noted that the governor's voice was one of many in Wisconsin denouncing Wallace in the harshest possible terms. Labor leaders called him a "carpetbagger, a bigot, a racist, and one of the strongest anti-labor spokesmen in America." An interfaith coalition declared that Wallace was a "threat to the moral quality of our nation." And Governor Reynolds weighed in again, urging voters to go to "Vicksburg in Mississippi and . . . visit the graves of Wisconsin men who gave their lives to destroy the institution of slavery."

To all of this, Wallace responded with injured innocence. "I have tried to speak the truth, nothing more," he told his followers in Milwaukee. Liberals, he said, were the ones engaging in the politics of hate with their "express train of rhetorical abuse."

It was a brilliant response, delivered with a matador's grace, as Wallace deftly sidestepped the attacks and positioned himself as the voice of sweet reason. But there was also the rage. On an April 1 visit to Milwaukee's south side, Wallace addressed a rally of white ethnic voters at the Serb Memorial Hall, where a local band played "Dixie" and the people sang along in a mixture of Serb and Polish and English. Despite the exuberant incongruity of the singing ("'Dixie' sounds mighty good in Polish," Wallace declared), this was not a happy crowd. The tension mounted as a black protester shouted at the governor, "Get your dogs out!" Bronko Gruber, an ex-Marine and master of ceremonies that night, became irate. In *The Politics of Rage*, Carter described what happened next:

> *. . . Gruber grabbed the podium microphone. "I'll tell you something about your dogs, padre!" he shouted. "I live on Walnut Street and three weeks ago tonight a friend of mine was assaulted by three of your countrymen or whatever you want to call them . . ." Thunderous applause downed out the rest of his sentence. Gruber, fists clenched, barged ahead. "They beat up old ladies 83-years-old, rape our womenfolk. They mug people. They won't work. They are on relief. How long can we tolerate this: Did I go to Guadalcanal and come back to something like this?"*

Wallace again was the voice of calm. "My message is for all," he said, "and I want all of us to be in good humor tonight." But then his juices began to flow as he talked in a code that the crowd well understood. He did not mention racial segregation, as he often had in Alabama. At least not directly. But he denounced Lyndon Johnson's civil rights bill, which had recently passed the House of Representatives and was now making its way through the Senate. This "nefarious legislation," he said, would "destroy the union seniority system and impose racial quotas," and would render it impossible for a homeowner "to sell his house to whomever he chose." He railed against the U.S. Supreme Court, which had ordered the desegregation of schools and "outlawed Bible reading" in them. For good measure with this intensely anti-communist audience—so many of them with relatives in Eastern Europe—he expressed his pride that the communist newspaper, the *Daily Worker*, had called him "America's No. 1 Criminal."

"I am glad I have their opposition!" he boasted.

When the votes were counted on April 7, Wallace had won 266,000, more than a third of those cast, and more than two and a half times the number Wisconsin's hyperbolic governor had said would represent a "catastrophe." ("There must have been three catastrophes in Wisconsin," gloated Wallace.) In the expectations game of American politics, he was suddenly a winner on the national stage, even though he had lost two to one. On May 7, he won 30 percent of the vote in Indiana, and in Maryland on May 19, he did even better, with 43 percent of the total vote and a clear majority of the white vote. Even though he had entered only three primaries and lost them all, Wallace had sent a message to the nation. There was a rising discontent in the land, a skillful politician could bend it to his will, and there would be other elections down the line. One way or the other, George Wallace intended to be a part of it.

Lyndon Johnson was undismayed. Largely because LBJ knew it had teeth, he genuinely believed in the civil rights bill that produced such fear and loathing in Wallace. The measure outlawed discrimination based on race, color, religion, sex, or national origin in the workplace and in places of public accommodation such as theaters and restaurants. It further outlawed segregation in schools and authorized the U.S. Attorney General to file lawsuits on behalf of citizens whose rights were abridged.

Its prohibition against gender discrimination came almost as an afterthought, in the form of an amendment by Representative Howard Smith of Virginia. Smith was a segregationist who opposed the civil rights bill as a whole and voted against it. But he was also a longtime supporter of an equal rights amendment to prevent discrimination against women. Historians and even some of Smith's congressional colleagues disagree about his motivation in adding the amendment. Was he trying to kill the whole bill by introducing a controversial component? Or did he intend to embarrass Northern Democrats who opposed racial discrimination in the South but were unconcerned about women?

"Smith didn't give a damn about women's rights," asserted Representative Carl Elliott of Alabama. "He was just trying to knock off votes either then or down the line because there was always a hard core of men who didn't favor women's rights."

In *Pillars of Fire*, civil rights historian Taylor Branch notes that some of the men in Congress clearly regarded Smith's amendment as a joke. Indeed the *Congressional Record* reported laughter in the House chamber when it was introduced. And yet there it was, an added dimension to a bill aimed essentially at expanding the meaning of American democracy—to include as equals the people whose rights had been denied, whether by race or gender or national origin.

Not everybody saw it that way, of course. In the Senate, eighteen Southern Democrats began a filibuster against the bill that lasted fifty-four days. "This is the worst civil rights package ever presented to the Congress," fumed Senator Strom Thurmond of South Carolina, "and is reminiscent of the Reconstruction proposals and actions of the radical Republican Congress." On the morning of June 10, Senator Robert Byrd of West Virginia completed a marathon, fourteen-hour filibuster speech, a heroic effort in the eyes of segregationists. As soon as Byrd was finished, however, Senator Hubert Humphrey of Minnesota, a long-time champion of civil rights, introduced a motion to cut off debate. With the support of Senate Republican leader Everett Dirksen, the motion passed by a vote of 71–29. The filibuster ended, the bill passed 73–27, and on July 2, Lyndon Johnson prepared to sign it into law.

At the official ceremony, before an overflow crowd in the East Room of the White House, Johnson spoke of prejudice and discrimination, those historic stains on the national character, and then declared:

> We can understand without rancor or hatred how all this happened, but it cannot continue. . . . Morality forbids it, and the law I will sign tonight forbids it.

The president used multiple pens for the signing, sometimes more than one on each letter of his name, then gave them out as souvenirs to the civil rights leaders gathered in the room. One of the first went to Martin Luther King, another to Robert Kennedy, a man Johnson personally disliked but who had nevertheless helped ally the federal government with the cause of equality.

When the ceremony was over, he called several of the leaders aside, including King, and he told them almost sternly, as a father might speak to a wayward child, that this great legislative victory now ended the necessity for demonstrations in the streets. King and the others were not sure what to say; this did not seem like the time to argue with the president, but they were astonished. Did Johnson really think that all the racial problems in the country had been erased by the stroke of a pen? Obviously, he was trying to avoid a backlash that could damage his chances of reelection in the fall. This was understandable enough, but the naiveté of this wily politician, not to mention his presumption, did not sit well with the civil rights leaders, and they wondered privately what the future might hold. Did this encounter foreshadow a shaky alliance?

For the moment the question lay submerged in celebration. The black leaders sensed that this would be one of the most effective civil rights bills ever passed, ending more quickly than they could have dreamed the practice of legal segregation in the South. Less than two months later, on August 20, Johnson signed the Economic Opportunity Act, officially launching the War on Poverty, and the consensus among political commentators was that this new president was on a roll.

"There is no word less than superb to describe the performance of Lyndon

Baines Johnson as he became President of the United States," wrote journalist Theodore White. *Fortune* magazine, normally a friend to Republicans, was equally effusive in its praise: "Lyndon Johnson . . . has achieved a breadth of public acceptance and approval that few observers would have believed possible when he took office. . . . Without alienating organized labor or the anti-business intellectuals in his own party, he has won more applause from the business community than any President in this century." And in the *New York Times,* James Reston concluded: "The lovers of style are not too happy with the new Administration but the lovers of substance are not complaining."

Despite a few storm clouds building in the summer of 1964, including scattered racial violence and an ominous turn in the war in Vietnam, there seemed to be a feeling in the country that the business of government was humming along, and people turned their attention to other things. Those of us who were young were especially distracted, and had been for months, by a euphoria we had not seen coming.

20

The British Invasion

Ed Sullivan was a television icon. His variety show on CBS ran for twenty-three years, beginning in 1948, and for a while critics were mystified by its appeal. Sullivan, born in Harlem in 1901 before the neighborhood was all black, had been a newspaperman. His style as he introduced his television guests struck many observers as wooden and awkward, though his popularity was undeniable. In 1955, *Time* magazine wrote that Sullivan

> moves like a sleepwalker; his smile is that of a man sucking a lemon; his speech is frequently lost in a thicket of syntax; his eyes pop from their sockets or sink so deep in their bags that they seem to be peering up at the camera from the bottom of twin wells. . . . Yet instead of frightening children Ed Sullivan charms the whole family.

Sometimes the critics were more dismissive, and Sullivan, understandably, was not amused. When Harriet Van Horne wrote, "he got where he is not by having a personality, but by having *no* personality," Sullivan fired back, "Dear Miss Van Horne: You bitch. Sincerely, Ed Sullivan."

But if Sullivan could be irascible, and sometimes imperious with his guests offstage, he was also historic. In the 1950s, long before it was fashionable, he invited black artists onto his show and greeted them warmly. The list was long—Louis Armstrong, Pearl Bailey, Sammy Davis Jr., Pigmeat Markham, Bo Diddley, Fats Domino, Brook Benton, Jackie Wilson, the Platters. Thanks to Sullivan, all of these enjoyed a national television presence that might otherwise have been denied. In the days of segregation, white viewers were frequently enraged when Sullivan kissed Pearl Bailey on the cheek or draped his arm across the shoulders of Sammy Davis Jr., but the TV host would not back down. Nor was it just the black artists he defended. Early in Elvis Presley's career when critics sometimes treated him harshly, Sullivan assured the national TV audience, "this is a real decent, fine boy."

And so it was that on February 9, 1964, Sullivan prepared for what would soon become famous as the most-watched television episode in history, at least to that point. A British rock group known as the Beatles had made the journey across the Atlantic, and the excitement they elicited among youth was astonishing.

The band traced its roots to a summer night in 1957 when John Lennon met Paul McCartney. Lennon was sixteen, McCartney fifteen, and both were avid fans of rock 'n' roll and all the musical ingredients that enriched it. From Fats Domino to Arthur "Guitar Boogie" Smith, these two teenagers were drawn to the musical explosion taking place in America. According to Lennon, a single moment stood out from the rest—a night in 1956 when he heard Elvis Presley's "Heartbreak Hotel" beaming across the English Channel from a radio station in Luxembourg. "There were a lot of other things going on," Lennon said, "but that was the conversion. I kind of dropped everything."

"Heartbreak Hotel," recorded in Nashville, was Presley's first single for RCA, a top-five hit simultaneously on the pop, country, and rhythm and blues charts. This was in itself a feat so rare that the record quickly became iconic. Written by Mae Boren Axton and Jimmy Durden, the song was inspired by a *Miami Herald* story of a man who jumped to his death from a hotel balcony, leaving behind a note that said, "I walk a lonely street." The record that resulted was darker than anything Elvis had done, an eight-bar blues recorded in an empty hallway at RCA, adding an echo effect to the soaring emotion of the vocals.

Since my baby left me
I found a new place to dwell
Down at the end of lonely street
At Heartbreak Hotel

Lennon was captivated by the sound—by the energy of it and the exuberant artistic freedom it suggested, and he found a kindred spirits in McCartney and later in guitarist George Harrison and drummer Ringo Starr. The four came from Liverpool, a coastal city much less homogenous than many in England, and the blending of influences came to them easily. For a three-year period beginning in 1962, they played the clubs in Liverpool and Hamburg, and late in 1962 their first hit, "Love Me Do," began to climb the British charts.

By the following year, they were international stars, though in the United States the critics and record labels were dubious. At Capitol Records, the licensing partner of the Beatles' British label, EMI, executive Dave Dexter rejected the first several recordings EMI sent him, including such major British hits as "Please Please Me." As one Capitol insider put it, Dexter found the Beatles' music "generally amateurish and unappealing . . ." Journalists were equally obtuse. "They look like shaggy Peter Pans," wrote *Time* magazine. "The precise nature of their charm remains mysterious even to their manager." On the CBS Morning News, Alexander Kendrick declared: "They symbolize the 20th century non-hero as they make non-music, wear non-haircuts. . . . Meanwhile, yeah, yeah, yeah, the fan mail keeps rolling in and so does the money."

A few weeks later, *Newsweek* chimed in:

> Visually they are a nightmare: tight, dandified Edwardian beatnik suits and great pudding-bowls of hair. Musically they are a near disaster, guitars and drums slamming out a merciless beat that does away with secondary rhythms, harmony and melody. Their lyrics (punctuated by nutty shouts of 'yeah, yeah, yeah!') are a catastrophe, a preposterous farrago of Valentine-card romantic sentiments.

Such voices were quickly obliterated by the screaming ecstasy of teenaged girls and the durable judgments of a growing fan base. When the Beatles appeared on the Ed Sullivan Show, an unprecedented seventy-three million people were watching, and what they saw was four young men in their early twenties, possessing enormous energy and talent. They ended their five-song performance with "I Want to Hold Your Hand," already a number one hit. It was, as Mikal Gilmore put it in *Rolling Stone*,

> a blockbuster performance—a manifesto of a new creed of confidence and openness. The first time one hears the song, it's impossible to gauge where the melodic line, harmonic construction, vocal revelation and rhythmic impetus are headed: from colloquial opening, to blues turnaround, through a meditative interim that explodes in an outrageous, soaring exclamation—"I can't hide! I can't hide!"—in three-part harmony, Ringo slamming away, until it all detonates again.

Most of us who were watching at the time understood immediately that this was something different, even if we couldn't quite say what it was. "The Beatles," said *Rolling Stone*, "would help incite something stronger in American youth that night—something that started as a consensus, as a shared joy, but that in time would seem like the prospect of power." Beatles biographer Jonathan Gould aimed for a description that was more poetic and even more vague. "In America," he wrote, "like princes in a fairy tale, they seemed to awaken some great, slumbering need."

One of those needs, almost certainly, was simply a yearning to escape our grief. The Beatles arrived on American shores less than three months after the assassination of President Kennedy, and they too shared in the sense of loss. "From my point of view," said Paul McCartney, "and a lot of people in England's point of view, he was the best president that America had had for an awful long time." But now here they were, the original band of brothers, clowning their way through press conferences filled with the most ridiculous kinds of questions:

> "How many are bald, that you have to wear those wigs?"
> Ringo: "All of us."
> Paul: "I am. I'm bald."
> "You're bald?"
> John: "Oh, we're all bald, yeah."
> Paul: "Don't tell anyone, please."

For sure, their appearance was a major part of the whole. In *Can't Buy Me Love*, author Jonathan Gould wrote of

> the matching clothes and hair that tied them to one another and set them apart from everybody else. . . . The Beatles, were a vision of self-sufficiency, interdependence, and shared ambition that supplied popular music with the archetype of a "rock group."

And they seemed to be having so much fun. In Miami, where they traveled to tape a live concert for broadcast on the *Ed Sullivan Show*, they met a young boxer named Cassius Clay, who was scheduled a few days later,to fight Sonny Liston, one of the most feared heavyweight champions in history. Liston was widely regarded as a thug, a ferocious bear of a man with ties to the Mafia and a prison record for armed robbery. Twice in 1963, Liston had recorded first-round knockouts of former heavyweight champion Floyd Patterson. Many observers shuddered to think what he might do to Cassius Clay, a relatively untested twenty-two-year-old who had recently struggled against lesser opponents.

From all appearances, Clay himself was brimming with confidence, projecting a kind of exuberant brashness that fit with the Beatles. Publicists who arranged their meeting had sought a photo-op with Liston as well, but he declined. "I'm not posing with those sissies," he said. Clay, on the other hand, was delighted. He led the Beatles to the boxing ring where the four musicians lined up, with Ringo Starr on the end. When Clay playfully tapped Ringo on the chin, all four fell domino-style to the canvas.

On February 25, Clay shocked the world, punishing Liston for six brutal rounds, before winning the fight when the champion failed to answer the bell in the seventh. When it was over, Clay stood on the ropes and proclaimed: "I'm the greatest! I shook up the world!" The following day, in a more sober mood, he announced that he was a member of the Nation of Islam, a black separatist group headed by the Hon. Elijah Muhammad, who proclaimed among his other teachings that white people, based on the evidence, were apparently some kind of devils. A few weeks later, Clay changed his name to Muhammad Ali, a name chosen by Elijah Muhammad, and immediately became a complicated figure in American culture. He was initially reviled by many whites, who disliked his brashness and his politics (though, improbably and gradually, he would become almost universally beloved).

The Beatles liked Clay/Ali right away, or at least they enjoyed the moment of their meeting, for he seemed to have the same freshness of spirit, as if together they were a part of something new that was essentially beyond their power to explain. They loved the limelight—what was not to love?—but just as Ali took pride in his craft, the Beatles were ultimately focused on theirs. They were *musicians*, young men with flaws and complications of character, and a depth of talent that became apparent over time. But in the moment they were apostles of joy.

NOR WERE THEY ALONE in this quality. In the city of Detroit, 1964 was a breakthrough year for Motown Records, an independent label established by songwriter Berry Gordy Jr. five years earlier. Gordy was already successful at his craft, having written such hits as "Lonely Teardrops" for Jackie Wilson, "You Got What It Takes" for Marv Johnson, and "Money" for Barrett Strong. The grandson of a white planter and his female slave, Gordy came from a family that was part of the Great Migration from South to North in pursuit of freedom and better-paying jobs. For many thousands of African Americans, bitter disappointments accompanied that journey, and dreams of a promised land in the North morphed into a reality of sweltering slums. Gordy, however, was determined to construct—for himself and for other black writers and performers—an oasis of creativity and success.

He assembled a group of top songwriters, including himself, Smokey Robinson, and the writing trio of Eddie and Brian Holland and Lamont Dozier. Gordy's studio musicians were some of the best in the country, and promising young artists flocked to the label, drawn by the lure and possibility of success, and also, in the early years, by an all-for-one-and-one-for-all mentality that Gordy worked hard to instill in his team. There were even a few, like Levi Stubb, the gifted lead singer for the Four Tops, who felt they were all on a kind of mission.

"Motown was responsible for black and white music merging," he said. "The people there were concerned with excellence and there was a concerted effort to create music for a certain purpose. They wanted to reach everybody. I've never seen a company come together with such a common purpose and a kind of love—that's what made Motown."

Gordy himself may or may not have shared that view. As music historian Kevin Phinney later wrote,

> Gordy seemed to regard selling to whites as a marketing strategy rather than a roadmap to integration, and harbored few illusions of fostering racial unity through music. Perhaps he felt that guiding a black-owned company from inception to major label status in less than five years was statement enough. Martin Luther King was the one with the dream; Gordy had a *plan*.

Whatever the case, high school students such as myself thrilled to the latest Motown releases. In 1964, those included "Baby, I Need Your Loving" by the Four Tops; "Dancing in the Streets" by Martha and the Vandellas; "Where Did Our Love Go?" by the Supremes; and perhaps the greatest Motown record of all, "My Girl," by the Temptations. At a time when the Beatles dominated the charts, Motown provided their stiffest competition. And the competition was friendly, with the Beatles covering several major Motown hits as part of their instinctive, ongoing tribute to the power of black music in America.

Mitch Ryder, a white rhythm and blues artist from Detroit who was not a part of the Motown stable, summed up the label's achievement this way: "Motown was more sophisticated rhythm and blues, more pop-oriented, polished and accessible . . . Berry had a brilliant idea, obviously, and it sold and sold. . . ."

For those of us who bought and bought, the explanation seemed simple enough: This was music that made us smile.

That was not true of all music in 1964. Other artists set out successfully to make us think. On February 7, a Friday night two days before the Beatles debut on the *Ed Sullivan Show*, Sam Cooke was preparing to appear on a stage that was almost as big. Johnny Carson's *Tonight* show, a staple by now in most American households, generally featured at least one musical guest, and Cooke was ready to unveil a song he had not yet recorded. He had recently written "A Change Is Gonna Come," and it carried a message that came from his heart, even though he knew he was taking a risk.

Cooke was not a Motown artist; he had his own deal with RCA, but his marketing philosophy was very much the same. His roots were gospel and rhythm and blues, even a little bit of country, but whatever the subject matter of his lyrics he had polished his act into a smooth and accessible brand of pop. His fans were as likely to be white as black, and now he was preparing to debut a song on national television that was, in effect, a civil rights anthem. It was something he had wanted to do for a while. In October 1963, he had felt the personal sting of segregation when he was turned away from a Shreveport hotel because of his color. Perhaps more importantly, he admired Bob Dylan's "Blowing in the Wind," an act of poetic bravery, Cooke thought, in which a white artist echoed the question being raised by the civil rights movement.

How many roads must a man walk down
Before you call him a man?

Cooke began performing Dylan's song in his own live shows, and moved by a mixture of inspiration and shame (why had he not done it sooner?), he was ready to risk the loss of white fans by writing his answer to "Blowing in the Wind." His biographer Peter Guralnick reported that the words and the music came easily:

> It was less work than any song he'd ever written. He grabbed it out of the air and it came to him whole, despite the fact that in many ways it's probably the most complex song he ever wrote. It was both singular—in the sense that you started out, "I was born by the river"—but it also told the story both of a generation and of a people.

. . . I go to my brother
And I say "Brother help me please"
But he winds up knockin' me
Back down on my knees
There been times that I thought I couldn't last for long
But now I think I'm able to carry on
It's been a long, a long time coming
But I know a change is gon' come, oh yes it will

Many years later, former freedom rider John Lewis would remember lonely nights in the Mississippi Delta when he and other civil rights organizers, working the most dangerous reaches of the South, would huddle together in sharecropper cabins, listening to Cooke's song again and again, drawing inspiration and courage from the words, finding in the raw and haunting beauty of Cooke's voice a bulwark against their own fear. By this time, however, Sam Cooke was dead. On December 11, 1964, eleven days before the official release of his record, he was shot and killed under mysterious circumstances at the Hacienda Motel in Los Angeles. Motel operator Bertha Franklin claimed she shot Cooke in self-defense after he broke into her office and attacked her, wearing only a shoe and a sports coat. Cooke's family disputed the tawdry claim, but Franklin was never charged with a crime.

In the chronicle of tragedy in the 1960s, this one seemed especially bleak. Given the circumstances, it was hard to think of Sam Cooke as a martyr. He was simply a young singer—a prodigious talent, beloved by his fans—killed at the age of thirty-three for reasons that made no sense at all.

FOR MUCH OF 1964, two other artists traveled musical paths not altogether different from Cooke's. The first was Nina Simone, an African American singer-songwriter born in 1933 in Tryon, North Carolina. Simone was a jazz singer who loved classical music and the blues, with a bit of folk music thrown in for good measure. She began playing piano at age three, performed her first recital at age twelve, and had hoped to study at the Julliard School before discovering that her family could not afford it. Her recording career began in the 1950s and turned increasingly political in the 1960s. In 1964, she wrote a signature song called "Mississippi Goddam," in which she expressed her rage at the murder of Medgar Evers the previous summer and the Birmingham church bombing that killed four black girls.

On March 21, 1964, she performed the song at Carnegie Hall before a mostly white crowd, delivering her personal warning about the torrent of black rage she knew would soon come:

Alabama's got me so upset
Tennessee's made me lose my rest
And everybody knows about Mississippi Goddam

Her delivery of the words was taunting and hard, making clear her delight in the shock-value of it, as the anger grew more intense with every verse:

Oh but this whole country is full of lies
You're all gonna die and die like flies
I don't trust you any more

Simone's performance was recorded live and became part of her album, "Nina Simone in Concert," released in September 1964. The first single was "Mississippi Goddam," and though it was frequently banned in the South, Simone was willing to pay that price. Like Sam Cooke, she was angered by the reality of racism and offered her music to the cause of civil rights. But there was a difference. Simone was embarked on a journey of disillusionment and rage that would lead her by the end of the decade to turn her back on America altogether. She left the country in 1970, and died in France in 2003.

Though never as alienated as Simone—he was white, after all—Johnny Cash, too, was moved by the darkness of racial oppression. In 1964, he recorded an album called "Bitter Tears: Ballads of the American Indian." Cash, who began his recording career in the 1950s, was well on his way to becoming an icon, one of the greatest country singers of all time, and it was a status rooted primarily in his identification with the American underdog. In 1955, at Sam Phillips's Sun Studio in Memphis, he recorded "Folsom Prison Blues," telling the story of a convicted murderer who yearns to be free but is tortured by the knowledge of his guilt. Cash would go on to perform the song many times at prison concerts for which he never got paid. He was simply trying, as he said in an interview years later, to live up to the faith on which he was raised.

Cash was born in Dyess, Arkansas, and his Church of God family was part of a socialistic farmer's cooperative in the cotton country west of the Mississippi River. His boyhood began in the Great Depression, and if times were hard, his father, Ray Cash, always seemed to make enough of a crop to feed his own family and bail out needy neighbors. Johnny Cash thought for a while that he might have a little bit of Indian blood—Cherokee, it was said—and even when he learned it wasn't true he continued to brood over the tragic history of Native Americans. He was drawn to the music of Peter LaFarge, a singer-songwriter who was part of the Greenwich Village folk scene which also included Bob Dylan, Phil Ochs, and Pete Seeger. LaFarge traced his personal history to the Narragansett Tribe and wrote often of American Indian issues.

One of his songs caught Cash's attention. "The Ballad of Ira Hayes" told the story of a war hero—a Pima Indian from Arizona, who joined the Marines in World War II and during the Battle of Iwo Jima was one of a handful of men who made it to the summit of Mount Suribachi and planted the American flag. The moment was captured in a Pulitzer Prize-winning photograph by Joe Rosenthal of the Associated Press, and Hayes became temporarily famous. After the war, however, he returned to the reservation where jobs were scarce and water that once flowed into ancient Pima irrigation ditches was diverted to serve the growing city of Phoenix.

Hayes became an alcoholic, tormented by the loss of close friends in the war, and by the chronic lack of hope in Indian country. On January 24, 1955, after a night of heavy drinking he died. Some said it was alcohol poisoning, or perhaps he froze to death in the desert; but others said he passed out and drowned in two inches of water in an irrigation ditch.

This is how Peter LaFarge told the story:

Ira returned a hero
Celebrated through the land
He was wined and speeched and honored; everybody shook his hand

But he was just a Pima Indian
No water, no crops, no chance

At home nobody cared what Ira'd done
And when did the Indians dance

Call him drunken Ira Hayes
He won't answer anymore
Not the whiskey drinkin' Indian
Nor the Marine that went to war . . .

Yeah, call him drunken Ira Hayes
But his land is just as dry
And his ghost is lyin' thirsty
In the ditch where Ira died

For Johnny Cash, the song was a hit, reaching number three on the country charts, and becoming part of a musical canon in America intended to call attention to our flaws. Cash understood that music was more. Like the Beatles, he had cut his share of songs that made people smile. But he also saw the larger possibilities—the ability of music to touch the conscience or sound the alarm in a way that almost nothing else could.

21

Freedom Summer

Everything turned dark, or so it seemed, that summer. Young people from all over the country were preparing to descend on Mississippi. They were answering a call from SNCC, the Student Nonviolent Coordinating Committee, and CORE, the Congress of Racial Equality, to help register African American voters. As innocuous as it sounds in retrospect, at the time it was a life and death proposition, and SNCC and CORE did not try to hide that fact.

At a training meeting for the volunteers, held in the college town of Oxford, Ohio, the speakers talked of the dangers they had seen in Mississippi. John Lewis was one of those speakers, a former freedom rider and founding member of SNCC, and so was Bob Moses, who had been the organization's point man in Mississippi. In his memoir, *Walking with the Wind*, Lewis laid out the moral calculus behind Freedom Summer, as this volunteer effort would come to be called.

In 1961, he noted, Bob Moses had moved to Mississippi to try to organize a voting rights movement. Like some of the other young leaders in SNCC, Moses seemed an unlikely radical. Born in Harlem, he had attended mostly white schools before earning his master's in philosophy from Harvard. He taught school before coming to the South to join the civil rights movement. Gentle and soft-spoken, Moses began his registration efforts in Amite County, farming country in the southwest corner of Mississippi. Amite, as it happened, was the birthplace of Will Campbell, the white Baptist preacher who had supported the sit-in students in Nashville and worked as a Southern troubleshooter for the National Council of Churches.

Campbell knew Moses faced a difficult road. "I thought he was a mighty brave man," he said. "Either that or he was crazy."

Many shared that assessment. For civil rights workers, maintained reporter

Jack Newfield, "Amite County is a synonym for the Ninth Circle of Hell." It was even worse for the African American people who lived there, especially if they tried to rock the boat. And a few did try to rock it—men and women of such courage that Moses came to regard them with awe.

Not that they were abundant at first. Fewer than twenty people attended his earliest registration classes in Amite, and some of them were still too young to vote. But Moses didn't mind. It was important, he thought, to plant the seeds of possibility and hope. In 1961, of 5,500 African Americans who lived in the county, only one had managed to register. The others were afraid and rightly so, for it was simply the case in that part of Mississippi that an African American man or woman could be killed with impunity for simply offending a white person. Voter registration, with its implicit proclamation of equality, was almost certain to give offense.

Nevertheless, on August 15, 1961, Moses drove three aspiring voters to the county courthouse in the town of Liberty. One was an elderly farmer named Ernest Isaac, and the other two were middle-aged women, Bertha Lee Hughes and Matilda Shoby. The three filled out application forms, but were not allowed to take a literacy test which they were required to pass before they could register.

On the way home, their car was stopped by a Mississippi highway patrolman, and Moses was arrested and taken to jail. Two weeks later, after a barrage of threats, he was beaten by a man named Billy Jack Caston, the son-in-law of state legislator E. H. Hurst.

"I didn't recognize Bob at first, he was so bloody," remembered E. W. Steptoe, a Mississippi farmer who offered Moses sanctuary at his house. "I just took off his T-shirt and wrung out the blood like it had just been washed."

Then the beatings turned to killings. Herbert Lee was also a farmer, as most black people were in that part of Mississippi—a short, stocky man of fifty-four who owned a piece of land, where he grew his crops and tried to make his way in the world. In the summer of 1961, he began to attend voting rights classes, recruited by Moses himself, and on September 25 he was shot and killed by E. H. Hurst. It happened at noon in the town of Liberty, and there were at least a dozen witnesses. But an official inquest held the same day concluded that Hurst, the state legislator, had acted in self-defense.

From all accounts, Moses was devastated by the shooting. He blamed himself for putting Lee at risk, but he and other SNCC organizers decided there was nothing to do but push ahead. By 1962, they were beginning to see the first glimmers of progress, measured mostly by the growing number of grassroots leaders who were willing to put their lives on the line. Perhaps the most important was Fannie Lou Hamer, a sharecropper from Sunflower County who would soon emerge as a legendary figure, compared by some to Rosa Parks. Mrs. Hamer—and she always insisted on the courtesy title—was less educated and rougher-edged than Mrs. Parks, but her bravery was unsurpassed.

On August 18, 1962, she was one of eighteen blacks who traveled to the Sunflower County courthouse in Indianola, seeking to register as Mississippi voters. Mrs. Hamer and one other person were allowed to take the literacy test, but back in the community of Ruleville, on the sprawling plantation where she worked—and where she lived with her family in a rented cabin—the owner was waiting when she returned.

He told her sternly: "If you don't go down and withdraw your registration, you will have to leave. . . . We are not ready for this in Mississippi."

"I didn't try to register for you," Mrs. Hamer replied, with the kind of defiance that became her trademark. "I tried to register for myself."

She was evicted that same night.

She was then fully committed to the movement. The following summer, on June 9, after attending a voter registration workshop in South Carolina, she was part of a group returning to Mississippi by bus when she and the others were arrested in the town of Winona. Later, in her jail cell she could hear the cries of her friends being beaten, some of them screaming, others actually praying for their tormentors.

Then two white men came to her cell, and one of them told her, "We are going to make you wish you were dead." They dragged her off to another part of the jail where two black prisoners were ordered to beat her. "After the first Negro had beat me until he was exhausted," she remembered, "the State Highway Patrolman ordered the second Negro to take the blackjack." Telling the story in 1964 at the Democratic National Convention, Mrs. Hamer added, to place her own ordeal in time sequence, "I was in jail when Medgar Evers was murdered."

John Lewis was one of many in SNCC who regarded Mrs. Hamer as a grassroots hero. He wrote:

> She had been beaten by policemen who called her a "nigger bitch," and

> she would pay for that beating every day for the rest of her life with constant pain in her back and hips and a permanent limp. Her family was continually harassed—they received a $9,000 water bill one month, and her house did not even have running water—but Mrs. Hamer refused to back down . . .
>
> We became friends, and she was not afraid to speak up, not to white Mississippians, and not to black civil rights leaders either. "*Now, John Lewis*," she would say, "let me tell you all, if you're going to come to Mississippi, you can't just come here and stay for one day or one night. You've got to stay here for the *long* haul.
>
> "I *know* Mississippi," she would say, "and you'd better be ready to move *in*."

SNCC was ready. By the summer of 1963, young organizers, including national leaders like Lewis and the first group of college-aged volunteers, were scattered through the state. They were busy making plans for a mock election, an idea conceived by Bob Moses and a white activist, Allard Lowenstein. As president of the National Student Association when he was an undergraduate at the University of North Carolina, Lowenstein began a long association with liberal causes, and when he came to Mississippi in 1963 just after the murder of Medgar Evers, conditions there reminded him of what he had seen on an earlier visit to South Africa.

With Mississippi's black citizens systematically excluded from the political process, Lowenstein proposed an unofficial election "with real candidates and real ballot boxes," as John Lewis put it, an exercise that would simultaneously give African Americans who had never voted a taste of what it was like and dramatize to the rest of the country the massive scale of their disenfranchisement. The winners and losers were beside the point. Neither Aaron Henry, the African American candidate for governor, nor his white running mate, Ed King, would assume office when the campaign was over. But in the fall of 1963, when more than 85,000 black Mississippians turned out to vote in an election that did not even count, the depth of their democratic yearning was clear. African Americans in this most oppressive of all Southern states were determined to assume a place as first-class citizens.

ALL OF THIS SET the stage for Freedom Summer, and now the goal was much more real—not an exercise in mythical democracy, but a plan to elect an interracial delegation to the 1964 Democratic National Convention. Moses and the other Mississippi leaders wanted to bring in as many as a thousand volunteers to try to register black voters in unprecedented numbers—hoping to create a political system that had simply never existed in the South, one fully open to people of both races. They knew it was a monumental challenge, full of danger and moral complications.

For one thing, they understood that some of the young volunteers might die. People had already died in Mississippi—black people mostly, murdered for daring to proclaim their rights, even their fundamental humanity, in a place that was bitterly determined to deny it. The latest of those was Louis Allen, a Mississippi farmer gunned down at his home on January 31, 1964. Three years earlier, Allen had witnessed the shooting of Herbert Lee, and originally kept silent in fear for his life. Finally, however, he told Bob Moses what he had seen, and Moses urged him to come forward and tell his story to the FBI. Allen agreed, and now he was dead, and once again nothing happened—no arrests, no charges, just another black man killed in Mississippi.

Moses felt responsible for Allen's death, as he had for Lee's, but it left him more determined than ever to change the balance of political power. If African Americans were able to vote, he reasoned, they might be able to elect a sheriff who would actually investigate such a crime. He saw Freedom Summer as a crucial part of that journey, more ambitious than anything the movement had tried.

"For this campaign, we knew we needed help," remembered John Lewis. "Moses knew it. And that help, we decided, should come from *white* America—not in the form of money, not in the form of moral support, but in the flesh-and-blood form of their own sons and daughters."

There was debate about the idea within SNCC—a simmering resentment that these white students might get all the credit, and more substantially, a fear of generating a sense of dependence, a feeling that nothing would change unless white people helped make it happen. For Lewis and Moses, negatives were outweighed by the goal of letting African American people in Mississippi know that they were not forgotten, as it so often seemed. And there was one reason more chilling than the rest: "If white America would not respond to the deaths of our people," said Lewis, ". . . maybe it would respond to the deaths of its *own* children."

Nobody doubted that deaths might occur. But in Oxford, Ohio, when training of the volunteers began, Moses and the other leaders in SNCC were surprised by the number of students—most, but not all, white—who were willing to risk their lives. Many cited the inspiration of John Kennedy, his eloquence certainly, but also his message of service, his belief in the larger possibilities of America. On June 15, more than three hundred volunteers—"the first wave," as Lewis put it—gathered at Oxford's Western College for Women for a five-day briefing on the challenge ahead. These were, in part, sensitivity sessions on working with Mississippi's black population, people who were desperately poor and sometimes illiterate, but who were also extraordinarily brave, asserting their rights in the face of oppression so violent and complete that the volunteers were almost certain to find it terrifying.

"We were told," recalled Stephen Bingham, a white Yale graduate, "of murders which had occurred in the recent past, of which the press had taken no cognizance, or murderers who roamed at large, untouched by the law, and perhaps, in the society which is Mississippi, untouchable."

One who was there to issue the warning as well as to offer his moral support was John Doar, a civil rights troubleshooter for the U.S. Department of Justice. Doar, who was deeply admired by his boss Robert Kennedy as well as by most people who knew him, was a lifelong Republican in a fading time when Republicans were as likely as Democrats to be staunch advocates of civil rights. Doar was a Wisconsin native who had been in Alabama in 1961 to do what he could to protect the Freedom Riders, and who had escorted James Meredith when he desegregated the University of Mississippi in 1962. Now, when one of the volunteers asked what the federal government could do to protect them that summer, Doar's reply was characteristically blunt. "Nothing," he said. "There is no federal police force. The responsibility for protection is that of the local police."

By now the volunteers understood that the police most often were on the side of the Ku Klux Klan. In fact, sometimes they *were* the Klan, and with that sobering reminder these mostly middle-class students headed off to Mississippi.

THEY ARRIVED ON JUNE 21, and that same day three of the activists went missing. Mickey Schwerner and James Chaney had actually been in Mississippi for a while. Schwerner, twenty-four, was a field secretary for the Congress of Racial Equality, a young man both funny and intense who was known by the

Klan as "the Jew boy with a beard." Chaney was black, a native Mississippian who was also a veteran field organizer for CORE.

But the third member of their group, Andrew Goodman, was a summer volunteer who had come to Mississippi just hours before he went missing. He was a twenty-year-old anthropology major from Queens College in New York City, and some of his fellow volunteers would later wonder with horror what he must have been thinking when he and the others were arrested outside Philadelphia, Mississippi. They were charged with speeding and taken to jail, then released after paying a twenty-dollar fine.

It was the last time anyone saw them alive.

As word of their disappearance spread, Neshoba County Sheriff Lawrence Rainey insisted with a cynical sneer, "If they're missing, they just hid somewhere, trying to get a lot of publicity out of it, I figure."

Two days later, on Tuesday, June 23, Choctaw Indians from a nearby reservation discovered the burned-out shell of the civil rights workers' Ford station wagon in a swamp not far from the holiest of sites—a burial mound called Nanih Waiya, the ancient center of the Choctaw Nation. Not long after the recovery of the car, a Mennonite mission to the Choctaws was bombed, serving notice to the Indians to remember their place. More than a dozen other churches burned that summer, the rest of them black, and as a reign of terror gripped the state, the activists who had come to Mississippi pushed grimly ahead, battling a mixture of fear and depression that would haunt many for the rest of their lives.

One of their number, Jane Stembridge, a white SNCC staff member in the town of Greenwood, sustained herself in part by maintaining a kind of desperate correspondence with Lillian Smith, the white Southern author who had challenged segregation with her courageous book, *Killers of the Dream*. Stembridge was the daughter of a Baptist minister in Georgia known for his liberal views on race. As a student at Union Theological Seminary in New York, Stembridge met civil rights leader Ella Baker, who persuaded her to join the movement, and in 1960 she began working for SNCC. A poet, Stembridge admired Smith's writings, and in a heart-wrenching series of letters, she shared the bitterness and depth of her own disillusionment.

"For here, there has been no breakthrough," she had written the previous winter, "not one scrap of evidence that we are overcoming . . . The masses are huddled around tiny gas stoves. They are poor. They are hungry. And they are cold." And now on June 23, she added: "The beginning of freedom summer in Mississippi is that three people are missing and have been for forty-eight hours somewhere out in Neshoba County where they say the sheriff killed six Blacks last year."

"Mississippi is hell," she concluded. "My life here has been hell—goddam fucking hell of a nowhere of death."

During that summer of anguish in Mississippi, the racial revolution also moved north. In Harlem on July 16, two weeks after President Johnson signed the Civil Rights Act of 1964, police lieutenant Thomas Gilligan shot and killed James Powell, a fifteen-year-old African American. Gilligan said he fired in self-defense after Powell attacked him with a knife. Some witnesses said there was no knife. Whatever the case, four nights of rioting erupted in Harlem and nearby Bedford-Stuyvesant.

The city had seen these moments before. In *Notes from a Native Son*, author James Baldwin wrote of August 2, 1943, when the funeral procession for his father passed through the riot-torn streets of Harlem. It began as it would twenty-one years later, with the shooting of a black man by a white police officer, and Baldwin described the scene this way:

> We drove my father to the graveyard through a wilderness of smashed plate glass. . . . He had lived and died in intolerable bitterness of spirit and it frightened me, as we drove through those unquiet, ruined streets, to see how powerful and overflowing this bitterness could be and to realize that it was now mine.

His words rang true in 1964, but much of white America seemed not to understand. Theodore White, who had written so brilliantly about the presidential election of 1960, suddenly sounded woefully out of touch when he wrote about the riots in Harlem. How could it be, he wondered in 1964, that Negroes outside the South could behave in such an uncivilized way?

"Why had Negroes," he continued, "chosen to disrupt New York first? No city had made greater effort to include Negroes in its community life—or succeeded better."

Lyndon Johnson, alarmed that racial unrest was spreading from the South, thus raising the possibility of a backlash, summoned the major civil rights leaders to Washington. He told them sternly that they must help put a stop to such things, and he also ordered in the FBI. The agency's director, J. Edgar Hoover, promised a diligent search for conspiracies—whether from the Communist party, which he saw as a force within the civil rights movement, or from sinister political forces on the right.

Amid the voices of official self-delusion and the liberal hand-wringers such as Theodore White, one white journalist became a source of unrelenting truth. Charles E. Silberman, a writer and editor at *Fortune* magazine, published *Crisis in Black and White*, which spent nine weeks on the *New York Times* bestseller list. In reviewing the book, *Time* magazine declared that Silberman "marches in no-nonsense fashion to a number of hard truths that are not meant to comfort or console."

In his introduction, Silberman opened with a measured urgency that grew stronger as the book went on.

> For a hundred years, white Americans have clung tenaciously to the illusion that . . . time alone would solve the problem of race. It hasn't, and it never will. For time, as Rev. Martin Luther King points out, is neither good nor bad; it is neutral. What matters is how time is used. Time has been used badly in the United States—so badly that not much of it remains before race hatred completely poisons the air we breathe. . . .
>
> What we are discovering is that the United States—all of it, North as well as South, West as well as East, is a racist society in a sense and to a degree that we have refused so far to admit, much less face.

In his searing pages, made all the more so by a writing style in which the passion was submerged beneath a relentless cascade of facts, Silberman wrote of the people—black people, mostly—who instinctively understood these truths. One of his examples was Malcolm X, a Black Muslim leader whose simmering rage struck fear in the hearts of many whites.

In 1962, during a sermon to a group of his followers in Los Angeles, Malcolm had received word that a chartered plane on its way from Paris to Atlanta had crashed, killing the passengers on board. White passengers. "I would like to announce a very beautiful thing that has happened," said Malcolm. "Somebody came and told me that [God] had answered our prayers in France. He dropped an airplane out of the sky with over 120 white people in it because the Muslims believe in an eye for an eye and a tooth for a tooth.

But thanks be to God, or Jehovah or Allah, we will continue to pray and we hope that every day another plane falls out of the sky."

It was a horrifying sentiment, as Silberman noted, made more so by the fact that it resonated in black America. In *Crisis in Black and White*, Silberman quoted a conversation between a Harlem cabdriver and *Life* photographer Gordon Parks.

"I don't know how many followers he's got," the cabdriver said of Malcolm X, "but he has sure got a hell of a lot of well-wishers. Those Muslims or Moslems, 'ever what you call 'em, make more sense to me than the NAACP and Urban League and all the rest of them put together. They're down on the good earth with the brother. They're for their own people and that Malcolm ain't afraid to tell Mr. Charlie, the FBI or the cops or nobody where to get off. You don't see him pussyfootin' 'round white folks like he's scared of them."

When Parks asked whether Muslims hated all white people, the driver was blunt: "If they don't, they should, 'cause [whites] sure don't waste no love on us."

As it happened, I read these words not long after the book came out—part of my own journey of discovery about an issue that seemed to be engulfing us all. There would be other books—*The Fire Next Time* or *Black Like Me*—that stirred my imagination and conscience, but for me at the time, no writer had a greater effect than Silberman. More than anything, I was struck by the fact that he was fearless. Rather than cringing at the philosophy of Malcolm X, Silberman set out to understand its appeal—this emerging alternative in the minds of many blacks to the nonviolent message of Dr. Martin Luther King.

Part of it was simple. Whatever the hyperbole of his anger, Malcolm was mostly telling the truth. Kenneth Clark, a respected African American sociologist, argued in the early 1960s that Muslim leaders "are not inventing nor for that matter are they even exaggerating or distorting the basic fact. White America has permitted a system of cruelty and barbarity to be perpetrated and perpetuated on citizens of dark color . . ." But in Silberman's view, there was a fundamental honesty in the Muslim message that went beyond an indictment of whites—an acknowledgment that the centuries of discrimination had, in fact, created a pathology in black America. As Malcolm X put it, "the worst crime the white man has committed has been to teach us to hate ourselves."

That kind of self-hatred, Silberman wrote, "has produced the crime, the drug-addiction, the alcoholism that infest the Negro community; self-hatred is responsible for the apathy that keeps Negroes ignorant and poor and that makes them blame every failure on 'the man' . . ." And perhaps also it helped produce the riots that summer that began in Harlem and quickly swept through eight other cities—desperate eruptions of bitterness and rage in which destruction was greatest in black neighborhoods. Silberman, almost alone among white reporters, saw beyond the rhetoric of Malcolm X to a deeper urgency that burned in his heart.

Malcolm was trying to find a better way.

BACK IN MISSISSIPPI, MEANWHILE, the violence remained so raw and personal that it confirmed every assertion of white barbarity that Malcolm X and the others ever made. On August 4, the missing civil rights workers were found, shot to death and buried in a pond dam. Mickey Schwerner and Andy Goodman each died from a single bullet to the heart. James Chaney, the black Mississippian, had been beaten and shot three times.

Eventually, the whole sordid story emerged. Late on the night of June 21, after their release from the Neshoba County jail, the three young men headed south toward Meridian on Highway 19. They were pursued immediately by a lynch mob of Klansmen—at least ten men who had been inspired by a speech from their Imperial Wizard, Sam Bowers, about the "nigger-Communist invasion" of Mississippi and the need for an "extremely violent" response. One member of the mob was Cecil Price, the deputy sheriff who had initially arrested the activists. Another was Alton Roberts, a dishonorably discharged Marine who stood 6-foot-3 and weighed 270 pounds, an ill-tempered bear of a man with jet-black hair that he combed straight back.

"Are you that nigger-lover?" Roberts demanded of Mickey Schwerner.

"Sir, I know just how you feel," replied Schwerner, trying to calm the ex-Marine.

Roberts shot him through the heart. He shot Goodman also and when another member of the mob shot James Chaney, Roberts finished the job by shooting Chaney in the head. The bodies were taken to the farm of Olen Burrage, where they were buried in the dam. The autopsy revealed red clay in Goodman's lungs and clenched in his fist. Almost certainly, he was buried alive.

At the funeral of James Chaney, CORE organizer David Dennis, a former freedom rider, addressed the mourners and let free a torrent of heartbreak and rage:

> I've got vengeance in my heart tonight, and I ask you to feel angry with me. I'm sick and tired, and I ask you to be sick and tired with me. The white men who murdered James Chaney are never going to be punished. I ask you to be sick and tired of that. I'm tired of the people of this country allowing this thing to continue to happen. . . . If you go back home and sit down and take what these white men in Mississippi are doing to us . . . if you take it and don't do something about it . . . then God damn your souls!

At Andy Goodman's funeral, Rabbi Arthur Lelyveld delivered a very different kind of eulogy. Lelyveld was a friend of the Goodman family who had been to Mississippi that summer and experienced the violence of the state firsthand. He was attacked and hit on the head with a pipe. But at the funeral he praised the ideals of the civil rights movement:

> Not one of those young people who are walking the streets of Hattiesburg or Camden or Laurel or Gulfport or Greenville, not one of them, and certainly neither Andy nor James nor Michael, would have us in resentment or vindictiveness add to the store of hatred in the world. They pledged themselves in the way of nonviolence. They learned how to receive blows, not how to inflict them. They were trained to bear hurts, not to retaliate. Theirs is the way of love. . . .

At Schwerner's service, John Lewis echoed the words of the rabbi. But as he acknowledged in his book, *Walking with the Wind*, he understood the rage of David Dennis. In the upcoming struggle between vengeance and love, he knew his side had a hard road ahead.

22

Cynicism and Free Speech

It would be years before any of the killers were tried and sentenced to prison for their crimes, but the work in Mississippi went on. Lewis, Bob Moses, and their resolute army of student volunteers had their minds set on Atlantic City. So did Fannie Lou Hamer. Despite the terrible events of that summer—the murders, the beatings, the epidemic of church burnings by the Klan—this was a moment as full of hope as any she had known in her life.

She intended to lead a delegation—an *integrated* group—to the Democratic National Convention to unseat the white delegates sent by the regular Mississippi Democratic Party. Even two or three years earlier, she would barely have imagined such a thing. But all summer she had worked with the volunteers in a scattergun assault on segregation. In addition to the massive voter registration efforts, there were more than fifty freedom schools across the state, coordinated by Yale historian Staughton Lynd, who was beginning to emerge as a major activist. More than three thousand black students attended the classes, some seeking remedial work, but most studying things not offered in the black public schools—poetry and art, foreign languages and black history, even a few practical skills such as typing.

For their parents, there were literacy classes and healthcare screenings by volunteer doctors, and there were libraries filled with donated books. But the heart of the Freedom Summer effort was voting. More than 17,000 African Americans filled out voter registration forms, seeking to participate in Mississippi's official elections. Only 1,600 were allowed to register, but more than 80,000 took part in unofficial precinct, county, and statewide balloting conducted by the Mississippi Freedom Democratic Party. As lawyers from all over the country came in to document the barriers to black involvement in Mississippi's regular Democratic Party, the MFDP chose its delegation to the

DNC. Among the leaders were Aaron Henry, an African American pharmacist from Clarksdale who headed the state's NAACP, and Ed King, the white chaplain at historically black Tougaloo College. And of course there was Mrs. Hamer, the most powerful orator in the Mississippi movement.

In the spring of 1964, she had polished her rhetorical skills through what was seen in the state as her astonishing decision to run for Congress. No black person in the Mississippi Delta had done such a thing since Reconstruction, and her opponent, incumbent Democrat Jamie Whitten, had grown accustomed to running unopposed.

Whitten was an old-school advocate of agricultural policies that favored the wealthiest Mississippi landowners, not the small farmers—black and white—who struggled to eke out a living. Mrs. Hamer not only opposed that record; she *mocked* it. "Jamie Whitten is up there in Washington," she said, "trying to get the Congress and the president to keep the price of beef high so the big cattlemen in the district can make more money. He calls this 'aiding the livestock industry.' He doesn't seem to care what this does to poor people who have to get along on rice and beans and fatback because the price of beef is just too high."

Mrs. Hamer knew she would not get elected. There were not yet enough blacks registered to vote, even though they represented a majority in the district. But she intended to inspire a sense of possibility—a vision, perhaps, of what first-class citizenship might look like. She did it not only by talking about nuts and bolts issues, like the price of beef, but also by linking the struggles of African Americans to the Biblical stories on which many had been raised. Again and again, she told the story of her jailhouse beating in the town of Winona, using her personal suffering as a symbol of injustice, and her survival as proof of a loving God.

"I have been through the valley of the shadow of death," she would say, and then most often she would break into song—a capella renditions of Negro hymns delivered in her powerful alto voice that throbbed with certitude and conviction. *Go tell it on the mountain to let my people go.* As biographer Maegan Parker Brooks has noted, she gave an Old Testament force to the moral imperative of black freedom. Martin Luther King, of course, did the same, quoting Amos, Isaiah, or Jeremiah, along with the Sermon on the Mount, but nobody made it more real than Mrs. Hamer.

In June, when she lost as expected in the Democratic primary, she turned her full attention to the MFDP. She had considerable faith in the team of people who supported this grassroots effort—the leaders from SNCC like Lewis and Moses and Ella Baker in Washington, and there were others too who were deeply impressive in their commitment. Joseph Rauh, a prominent lawyer, a white man wise in the ways of politics, served as the Freedom Democrats' legal counsel. Rauh understood, perhaps more clearly than the MFDP delegation itself, that they faced an uphill climb. As one of the nation's leading civil rights lawyers for more than twenty years, he had worked with Lyndon Johnson in support of the Civil Rights Act that summer. He knew the President, now that that piece of business was finished and as he prepared to run for reelection, wanted to heal the growing rift in the Democratic party—the potential defection of the South.

Already, one Southern governor had privately warned him, speaking specifically about the MFDP and its challenge to the regular Mississippi delegation, "If you seat those black buggers, the whole South will walk out." Johnson thought the governor was right, and to keep that from happening, he was willing to play hardball.

The first battleground in Atlantic City was a hearing before the Credentials Committee, a group of delegates from around the country charged with recommending which Mississippi delegation to seat. At first the president's men made sure the hearing would be in the smallest possible room—too small for a phalanx of television cameras, too small even for the two competing delegations to sit. Rauh was irate. These sixty-eight members of the MFDP, all but four of them African American, had traveled 1,200 miles by bus to participate in American democracy, many of them for the first time, and the President of the United States would not *even let them see what was going on!*

Johnson relented. "I don't give a damn if he puts on a little show," the President told one of his aides. "Just as long as he don't wreck us."

On Saturday, August 22, the hearing opened in a larger room, the proceedings televised to the nation, as Joseph Rauh began to speak. "We have only an hour to tell you the story of tragedy and terror," he began. He quickly laid out the facts, how the Democratic Party in Mississippi systematically excluded black citizens, then called on members of the delegation. Aaron Henry spoke first, then Ed King. Both rose to the occasion, but everybody in the room understood that the show-stealer was Fannie Lou Hamer. She told the story of her ordeal in Winona, and then she added, with indignation rising in her voice:

> If the Freedom Democratic Party is not seated now, I question America. Is this America, the land of the free the home of the brave, where we have to sit with our telephones off the hooks because our lives be threatened daily . . .

Suddenly, in mid-sentence, Mrs. Hamer disappeared from viewers' televisions, and correspondent Edwin Newman came on-screen to announce: "We will return to this scene in Atlantic City, but now we switch to the White House and NBC's Robert Goralski." As historian Taylor Branch later wrote,

> President Johnson mounted a diversion with the cooperation of news outlets massed on alert for revelation of his vice presidential choice. He stepped before White House correspondents, with several governors in tow, and stretched the moment with small news and a sympathetic reference to [Governor John] Connally—still suffering from rifle wounds inflicted in the Dallas motorcade . . .

That was it. No news at all. Just a personal decision by the President to remove Mrs. Hamer from the nation's televisions.

Nevertheless, the powerful testimony continued in the room. With customary eloquence, Martin Luther King concluded the Freedom Democrats' presentation by telling the members of the credentials committee:

> I say to you that any party in the world should be proud to have a delegation such as this seated in their midst. For it is in these saints in ordinary walks of life that the true spirit of democracy finds its most profound and abiding expression . . . For all the disfranchised millions of this earth, whether they be in Mississippi or Alabama, behind the Iron Curtain, floundering in the mire of South African apartheid, or freedom-speaking persons in Cuba who have now gone three years without elections, recognition of the Freedom Democratic Party would say to them that somewhere in this world there is a nation that cares about justice. . . .

That night, the network newscasts featured large segments of Mrs. Hamer's testimony, introducing her to a much larger audience than the one the president had preempted in the afternoon. Telegrams of support began pouring in from all across the country, and John Lewis, among others, was elated. "We had momentum now," he remembered thinking. "It was working. Johnson's attempt to stem the tide had not stopped it." Even Rauh, more seasoned in politics, was cautiously optimistic. In past conventions, there had been similar disputes in which delegates vied for official recognition. As a young congressman in 1944, Johnson himself had been part of one such wrangle between New Deal supporters of President Roosevelt and a group of Texas regulars who opposed him. That delegate challenge and several others like it had been resolved by a fifty-fifty compromise. Though Rauh did not yet tip his hand, he expected something similar for the Freedom Democrats.

Johnson, however, had other ideas. The president was juggling two separate fears. If he supported the Mississippi regulars outright, offering nothing to the MFDP, he worried that King and the civil rights forces, riding a sudden wave of sympathy, might trigger a convention stampede to Robert Kennedy, the ambitious brother of a martyr. Johnson's dislike of RFK tortured his imagination, even as he considered a more realistic possibility. If he appeared to cave in to Fannie Lou Hamer and her band of insurgents, he feared a mass walkout by more Southern delegations than just Mississippi's. As Taylor Branch noted in *Pillars of Fire*, all of that was driving Lyndon Johnson to distraction.

In the end, the President dispatched the liberal Hubert Humphrey to talk with the MFDP leaders. Humphrey's proposed compromise was in effect an ultimatum. For the Mississippi regulars to be seated, he said, they would have to sign a loyalty oath to the party. For the party's next convention in 1968, there would be no segregated delegations, and for this convention the MFDP would be welcomed as honored guests. But they would not be allowed to vote.

Mrs. Hamer and the others were stunned. "Senator Humphrey," she said, "I have been praying about you, and I been thinking about you, and you're a good man. The trouble is, you're afraid to do what you know is right."

It was said that Humphrey wept at her words.

Finally, in this escalating drama of Atlantic City, Johnson's men added one other offer. The convention was prepared to seat two MFPD delegates, specifically Aaron Henry and Ed King—and specifically *not* Fannie Lou Hamer, this wholly unpredictable sharecropper woman who had such a gift for stirring up a crowd. Emotion was strong as the sixty-eight Freedom Democrats met to discuss the possibility. "There had been too much blood," said John Lewis. "We've come too far to back down now." And Mrs. Hamer added: "We didn't come all this way for no two seats."

The next day, the all-white delegation of Mississippi regulars walked out, rather than sign a loyalty oath to the party. The MFDP immediately occupied their seats, but security forces quickly removed them from the hall. There would be no Mississippi delegation at all.

Soon enough the convention went on about its business. Lyndon Johnson became the nominee with Hubert Humphrey as his running mate, and the tearful delegates watched a film tribute to John F. Kennedy. But, as John Lewis wrote, the Mississippi Freedom Democrats,

> . . . packed up and went home. As far as I'm concerned, this was the turning point of the civil rights movement. . . . Something was set in motion that week that would never go away. It was a major letdown for hundreds and thousands of civil rights workers, both black and white, young and old people alike who had given everything they had to prove that you could work through the system. They felt cheated. They felt robbed.

Bob Moses was one of the most disillusioned—all those years of bloodshed and patience, the hard work sustained by his existential philosophy and the hope of people redefining their lives. But this time he had hoped for some tangible triumph, and the hope was crushed by a cynical game, a heartless display of politics as usual by a president who professed to be on their side. For a while, Moses vowed never to work with white people again, and the anger and cynicism he felt went surging through the ranks of SNCC, turning protesters into radicals and revolutionaries.

Lyndon Johnson, meanwhile, understood none of this. In the world of politics, sometimes you won and sometimes you lost. He had given black America the Civil Rights Act, and now he needed something in return—their full support in his quest for reelection. That was simply the way things worked.

Why was that so hard to grasp?

At the end of Freedom Summer, most of the college students left Mississippi. Harvard psychiatrist Robert Coles, who wrote powerfully about social problems in the sixties, concluded that many of the volunteers suffered from PTSD, like survivors coming home from a war. But some were even more determined—more idealistic—than when the summer began.

One of the latter was Mario Savio, a twenty-one-year-old philosophy major from the University of California at Berkeley. Savio was a native New

Yorker and a student of literature and science—really of any intellectual pursuit that fed his restless curiosity. He came from an immigrant, working-class family—Italian Catholics in the borough of Queens—and during his days as an altar boy he had thought often of entering the priesthood. From that aspiration, he began a sometimes troubled journey that led him to become, in the autumn of 1964, the face of the Free Speech Movement at Berkeley—a student radical as eloquent, cerebral, and for a time as influential as any in the country. Even a few scholars—students of rhetoric—argued that Savio's oratory represented some of the finest in a decade that included the Kennedys and Martin Luther King.

It was hard to see any of that coming when Savio was growing up in Queens. He spent the first several years of his life speaking mostly Italian in a home presided over by his immigrant grandparents. When his father came home from World War II and insisted on English as the family language, Mario developed a paralyzing stammer. "It is painful even to describe," he remembered. "It was nightmarish to live through it."

He was also the victim of sexual abuse by a member of his extended family, and for the rest of his life he would suffer from depression and panic attacks. But he was a brilliant student. When he graduated first in his high school class, the school principal, in deference to Mario's stammer, said he could skip the valedictory address if he thought it might be too traumatic. But Savio insisted on going ahead, and an auditorium full of classmates and parents seemed astonished at what happened next. After the first sentence, Savio did not stutter at all.

"God has certainly looked kindly upon us," he declared, adding however that "we must free ourselves from obsession with the material. . . . Having once again become master of things . . . we must never again allow things to become our masters."

Savio was never much interested in material possessions, but he had a love-hate relationship with his faith. The Catholic understandings on which he was raised stamped his thinking for the rest of his life, and yet there was something so narrow about the church—its rigidity of thought, its tendency to guard its own self-interests, and its guilt-ridden agony of the confessional booth. Seeking broader truth, Mario became a student of science, though his fascination with physics or any other field was essentially an exercise in philosophy. What did it reveal about the nature of things?

He tried two colleges in New York City before winding up at the University of California at Berkeley, and there he discovered the civil rights movement. That was not his plan. He intended to concentrate on his studies. But in 1963, he spent the summer in Mexico working in a village so poor it shocked him, and he was appalled by the wealthy landowners and bureaucrats who didn't seem to care. He returned with a growing awareness of class discrimination and racism, and on March 6, 1964, he joined a sit-in at the Sheraton Palace Hotel in San Francisco. For the first time, Savio was arrested. While in jail, he and his cellmate began to talk about Freedom Summer, this call for volunteers in Mississippi, and after a bit of soul-searching he decided to go.

He met Bob Moses at a training session in Ohio, and was there when word arrived that Goodman, Chaney, and Schwerner were missing. Savio never forgot what happened next. "People have been killed," Moses told the assembled volunteers. "You can decide to go back home and no one will look down on you for doing it." Mario was amazed. Here was leadership so clear and transparent, so deeply and fundamentally democratic, that Moses became a role model for him—really, a hero in a way that no one else had ever been. "I wanted to be like Bob Moses," he remembered later. "I wanted to *be* Bob Moses if I could do it."

In a summer most easily remembered for its dangers (Savio himself was attacked by a Klansman with a baseball bat), what he talked and wrote about when it was over was the wisdom, courage, and sense of community that he encountered again and again in Mississippi. "You felt it in the black church, especially," Savio told an interviewer. "The singing. You really felt cradled. It's impossible to convey to someone who hasn't experienced it. As much as someone could who, by that time, was very much a secular person, you felt in the bosom of the Lord."

As the summer unfolded in McComb, Mississippi, Savio taught in a Freedom School, finding young black students who were eager to learn about things that never came up in their regular schools, including black history. Savio proved a popular teacher. "He was singular in his capacity to engage the kids and really gain their love," said a fellow volunteer, "and it was more than respect. You could see they loved him. He was followed around by the kids as if he was the pied piper. . . ."

One Mississippi moment stood out from the rest. In addition to his time as a teacher, Savio worked on voter registration, a much more double-edged proposition. Every time he urged an African American to register, he was, quite literally, asking that person to risk his life. The sheer presumption was something that Savio could not evade, and yet there were people who were willing to do it. That was the most amazing thing.

One whose story he told was that of an old man in the Mississippi Delta who stood before the voter registrar—a woman who was also the wife of the sheriff—and told her he had come to the courthouse to "redish." In the black dialect of rural Mississippi, "redish" was a synonym for register, but the woman pretended not to understand.

"What's that you say, boy?"

"I want to redish, ma'am."

"What's redish? What are you talking about boy?"

Despite the humiliation and abuse, the old man quietly stood his ground and the registrar eventually gave him a form. Savio was deeply moved. The deliberate cruelty was appalling, but Savio remembered even more the old man's silent courage. He returned to Berkeley at the end of the summer determined not only to pursue his studies, for he was still a serious student, but also to continue his support for the civil rights movement, doing whatever he could from afar.

He was amazed to discover that such support was forbidden by the university. The Board of Regents had adopted a policy, now implemented aggressively by the Berkeley administration, banning political activism on campus. In *Freedom's Orator*, biographer Robert Cohen noted that Savio was offended by this on multiple levels. His fresh memories of Mississippi made it unthinkable that he and others who shared his views could not proclaim them on campus. But as his writings and speeches would soon make clear, Savio processed his visceral feelings about civil rights through a matrix of philosophical notions that had taken shape over time. He had read Karl Marx and loved the phrase, "from each according to his abilities, to each according to his needs." It sounded so profoundly Christian to him, like something that could have come from the Sermon on the Mount, and even if he had become agnostic—no longer certain who or what God was—he was moved by the ideals of compassion and justice. There were also the Greek philosophers, those champions of the mind, and Immanuel Kant, who spoke so eloquently of a moral imperative; for Savio, such ideas were never far removed from experience.

Thus in the fall of 1964, as a movement emerged against the free speech ban, Savio quickly became its spokesman, offering an intellectual grounding that took his adversaries by surprise. But he was not the "leader" of the protest. No single person claimed that role, least of all Savio. At the age of twenty-one, he saw himself as simply a player in a great historic movement, an authentic upsurge in a yearning for democracy that was then taking shape on the Berkeley campus.

It began in September and escalated on September 30 with a student sit-in at Sproul Hall, the administration building. After difficult negotiations, the students agreed to leave the building. But the following day, Jack Weinberg, a former student who had become an organizer for CORE, was passing out literature on Sproul Plaza just outside the administration building. Students gathered as police arrived and shoved Weinberg roughly toward the squad car.

"Sit down!" somebody yelled from the crowd.

The students circled the police car and sat, and their numbers quickly swelled to the hundreds. Leaning against the hood of the car, Savio was struck by a simple idea. What about using the squad car—this symbol of power and oppression—as a podium to proclaim the moral necessity of free speech? His heart racing, Savio slipped off his shoes—he didn't want to scratch the paint—and climbed first to the hood and then to the roof, where he began to speak. He was acutely aware of his presumption. He said later he thought he might be "hooted down." But he was not. By all accounts, he spoke with passion and intellectual depth, invoking the wisdom of the ancient Greeks. Suddenly the Free Speech Movement had a voice.

Weinberg remembered the moment clearly. He had seen Savio on other occasions almost paralyzed by the stammer that still haunted him periodically. But there was no stammer this time. As Weinberg pointed out, Savio was not talking about himself, which always seemed to give him trouble, because "what right do you have to even waste anybody's time making noise so that they should listen to you?" But when Savio was speaking for a cause, especially one as noble as free speech, he was, said Weinberg, "an agent of history . . . In that capacity he was a very powerful person."

As the police car remained surrounded on the plaza, intense negotiations began between the students and the administration—a process that proved as central to the Free Speech Movement as all the oratory and demonstrations. There had already been a few conversations, sometimes pleasant, sometimes not, but now the discussions became almost a matter of life and death. That was certainly how it seemed as police began massing by the hundreds on the plaza. Student leaders feared a bloodbath.

Jackie Goldberg, who would later serve as a city council member in Los Angeles, was the student negotiator most determined to avoid a violent confrontation with police. Savio was more hard-line, believing university administrators were engaged in a high-stakes game of chicken and could be pressured into major concessions. Goldberg and others were terrified of taking that chance, and in this tension-filled moment, the administration and students simply agreed to keep on talking, during which time the students would "desist" from illegal demonstrations. Savio reluctantly supported the agreement and climbed once again to the roof of the police car, asking the demonstrators "to rise quietly and with dignity to walk home."

The standoff had lasted thirty-two hours.

THE NEGOTIATIONS THAT CONTINUED that fall were complicated by mutual disdain. The administrators regarded the Free Speech Movement leaders, especially Savio, as rude and immature and full of ideas that represented a threat to the university. Chancellor Edward Strong said after his first meeting with Savio, "I had him sized up as an intractable fanatic." Clark Kerr, president of the University of California system, quickly concluded that Savio "could not be restrained or controlled," but Kerr also mistrusted other free speech leaders. He told a press conference shortly after the police car blockage that the protesters included "persons identified as being sympathetic with the Communist Party and Communist causes." It was a tactic widely used by Southern politicians in their quest to discredit the civil rights movement. But now here was Kerr, widely regarded as a West Coast liberal who had opposed red-baiting in the 1950s, engaging in a bit of it himself, almost certainly knowing it was nonsense.

Mario Savio saw the tactic for what it was. He assumed Kerr must be referring to Bettina Aptheker, a Berkeley student and free speech leader whose father, Herbert Aptheker, was, in fact, a Marxist historian and a member of the American Communist Party. But Aptheker was also a veteran who had served with distinction in World War II, and within the ranks of the Free Speech Movement, his daughter, Bettina, was one of the moderates, especially in her negotiating stance. Savio despised what he thought was the cynicism and cowardice of people like Kerr, but as biographer Robert Cohen makes clear, Savio's differences with the Berkeley administration went deeper. Savio regarded free speech—especially the right to protest for civil rights and other causes that would soon include opposition to the war in Vietnam—as a moral issue rooted not only in American values but in the wisdom of the greatest philosophers in history.

In an interview, he quoted the Greek philosopher Diogenes, who regarded free speech as "the most beautiful thing in the world. Those words," said Savio, "are burned into my soul, because for me freedom of speech represents the very dignity of what a human being is. That's what marks us off from the stones and the stars."

Bettina Aptheker, who sometimes disagreed with Savio over tactics, summarized his character this way: "Mario was appalled by injustice . . . Personally appalled. Mario's great strength was his absolute and transparent integrity. He never wavered from his bedrock principles of freedom of speech, justice and equality."

Thus, at Berkeley that fall, though increasingly uncomfortable with the limelight, Savio provided the movement with a backbone, and when negotiations stalled with the university administration, his eloquence stirred a broad cross section of students. He thought the university under Kerr's leadership had become not a forum for ideas but a training arm for corporate America—the military-industrial complex, as Dwight Eisenhower had called it. To Savio it was no wonder, given those priorities, that the administrators sought to stamp out dissent.

At a December 2 rally on the steps of Sproul Hall, he told the assembled students:

> There's a time when the operation of the machine becomes so odious, makes you so sick at heart, that you can't take part. You can't even passively take part. And you've got to put your bodies upon the gears and upon the wheels, upon the levers, upon all the apparatus, and you've got to make it stop. And you've got to indicate to the people who run it, to the people who own it, that unless you're free the machine will be prevented from working at all.

Six thousand students heard Savio's speech. Some were drawn to the plaza by the presence of Joan Baez, who sang her gentle protest songs, including Bob Dylan's "The Times They Are A-Changin'," then proclaimed her support for a sit-in at Sproul Hall:

> The only thing that occurs to me, seeing all you people there—I don't know how many of you intend to come inside with us—but that is that you muster up as much love as you possibly can, and as little hatred and as little violence, and as little "angries" as you can . . . The more love you can feel, the more chance there is for it to be a success.

As the rally ended, at least a thousand students marched into Sproul Hall, singing "We Shall Overcome" and bearing witness, in Savio's words, to "a growing understanding in America that history has not ended, that a better society is possible and that it is worth dying for." At 3:30 a.m., more than four hundred police officers began dragging protesters roughly from the building. The arrests, however, only generated sympathy for the Free Speech Movement, as thousands of students boycotted classes. The Academic Senate—the governing body of the Berkeley faculty—met on December 8 and voted 824–115 in favor of ending the free speech ban. Savio and the others had won, but in his victory speech he did not gloat. He cautioned his fellow students to "exercise their freedom with the same responsibility they've shown in winning their freedom."

In other parts of the country, many of us just entering college, who would soon enough have our own encounters with the issue of free speech, were left to marvel at Savio and his friends, wondering perhaps if we would have the nerve. When I read later that he regarded his movement as fundamentally conservative, making demands that were rooted in the founding ideals of the country—indeed, in the most ancient wisdom of Western civilization—I remember thinking that he was right. With his clean-shaven face and rhetoric as earnest as it was poetic, he seemed more like an activist-scholar than the stereotype of a student radical. But it was clear enough that many people did not agree.

In southern California, actor Ronald Reagan was deeply disturbed by events in Berkeley, believing that somebody should "clean up the mess." At the time, he was known to most Americans as the avuncular host of a television series sponsored by the General Electric Corporation. But he was beginning to aspire to a career in politics—to play his part in a conservative movement that in the presidential election of 1964 was getting ready to try out its wings.

23

Landslide

In the fall of 1964, Lyndon Johnson was a man with a lot on his mind. In addition to the matter of getting reelected, there was also the war in Vietnam. He knew already that it was going to be a problem. He had talked about it with his friend Richard Russell, the venerable senior senator from Georgia, who had been his opponent on the civil rights bill. This was how it worked in Washington, especially in the Senate. Sometimes you found yourself locked into opposition with a friend, and the rhetoric that either of you might use could soar with a passion that ordinary people might regard as personal. But it was not personal. Not to Johnson and not to Russell, who had been the best of political friends, and when it came to foreign policy—particularly *military* policy—Johnson was happy to seek Russell's advice.

Russell was chairman of the Senate Armed Services Committee, and he knew that terrain as well as anyone. In private, the two could talk with candor and freedom.

"What do you think about this Vietnam thing?" Johnson asked Russell early in his presidency.

"It's a mess," said Russell, "and it's going to get worse."

As Taylor Branch recounted in *Pillar of Fire,* Russell suggested that perhaps the United States could engineer another coup—"get some fella in there that would say they wished the hell that we would get out. Then that would give us a good excuse for getting out."

Short of that unlikely prospect, both men agreed the choice for Johnson was impossibly hard. "They'd impeach a president that would run out, wouldn't they?" Johnson asked. But on the other hand, he said, "when I think about making this decision and sending that father of six in there, and what the hell are we going to get out of his doing it, it makes the chills run up my back."

"It does me, too," said Russell.

"I just haven't got the nerve to do it," said the president. "But I don't see any other way out of it."

"It's one of those things, heads I win, tails you lose," replied Russell. ". . . We're in the quicksand up to our neck, and I just don't know what the hell to do about it."

"I love you," said Johnson, and with that the conversation ended.

On August 2, 1964, the dilemma became more real. In the Gulf of Tonkin, North Vietnamese torpedo boats unsuccessfully attacked a U.S. destroyer, the *Maddox*, after American shelling of two islands off the North Vietnamese coast. The Johnson Administration, maintaining that a second attack had occurred on August 4, sent a resolution to Congress authorizing the president to repel any assaults on U.S. forces and to do whatever was necessary to assist the government of South Vietnam. On August 7, the resolution was approved overwhelmingly—unanimously in the U.S. House of Representatives and with only two votes against it in the Senate.

Johnson assured the public, however, that he had no intention of escalating the war, "sending American boys to do what Vietnamese boys should be doing for themselves." In the upcoming general election he intended to run as the peace candidate, the steady alternative to his bellicose Republican opponent, Barry Goldwater. In the short run, the strategy worked. Johnson won reelection overwhelmingly, but his credibility suffered in the coming months when he in fact began a massive escalation of the war.

The deeper irony was that Goldwater, while suffering a landslide defeat, helped change the course of American politics. He became for a time the face of a conservative movement at least as durable as any of the others that were sweeping through the country, including those—civil rights and free speech—that many of the rest of us found more appealing. During the presidential primaries in the spring, the standard-bearer of the right had been George Wallace, with his racism bubbling beneath a new façade. But now it was Goldwater, a rock-ribbed idealist whose contrarian views were genuinely rooted in the world of ideas.

There were others like him—the students, for example, in Young Americans for Freedom who drew inspiration from the writings of William Buckley and Ayn Rand. Rand herself, the bestselling author of *Atlas Shrugged*, had just released a new book, *The Virtue of Selfishness*, the title of which meant exactly what it said. Selfishness was a good thing. "Concern with one's own interests," she wrote, was the rational basis for human behavior, and fashionable attempts to deny that truth were not only futile, but misguided. For many Americans, this was a resonant notion in 1964, when the quest for change had become a signature of the times, and demonstrators from Mississippi to California were roiling the waters and risking their lives in a desperate attempt to make it happen.

Rick Perlstein wrote in *Before the Storm: Barry Goldwater and the Unmaking of the American Consensus*:

> Millions thrilled to the moral transcendence of those heroic warriors for freedom. Millions of others decided that rabble-rousers—perhaps Communist dupes—were spitting on law and order, overturning tradition, and might not stop until they had forced their way into their own Northern white neighborhoods.

Goldwater sensed in this gathering discontent an opening for his cherished notions of conservatism, an incipient movement that had languished for years in the paranoid delusion of fanatics. As the 1950s drew to a close, one of the most ambitious fanatics was Robert Welch, founder of the John Birch Society, who regarded Eisenhower as a Communist sympathizer, and was certain the Southern civil rights movement was a Communist plot to start a race war in the United States. Goldwater did not go that far. But he praised the patriotism of John Birch members, and Robert Welch was one of his admirers. So was Clarence Manion, a former law school dean at Notre Dame who became a weekly radio commentator and discerned, like Welch, "left-wing Communists" in the Eisenhower Administration. And one of Goldwater's most fervent propagandists was Phyllis Schlafly, who identified herself as a Wisconsin housewife and mother (she was pregnant with her sixth child) but was also a savvy and outspoken lawyer with a right-wing vision for the future of America.

In 1964, she self-published her first book, *A Choice Not an Echo*, which in less than two months sold a remarkable 600,000 copies. Accusing Democrats of being soft on Communism, and Republican "kingmakers" of offering only "me-too" alternatives, she posed this question in the run-up to the Republican National Convention:

> At this crucial point in American history, will we send in our bat boy? Or will we send in our Babe Ruth—a man who is not afraid or forbidden to take a good cut at all major issues of the day.

For the Republicans, it was a watershed moment. The party had no shortage of able politicians, some of whom were bona fide heirs to the party of Lincoln. Nelson Rockefeller, for example, though he came from one of the richest families in America, was an outspoken advocate of civil rights. For years, his family had supported Negro colleges in the South, trying to help African Americans secure the tools to build better lives for themselves. Nelson's social conscience was stirred in 1937 when he was twenty-nine and made a trip to South America where his family's company, Standard Oil, had extensive holdings. He was shocked by the poverty he saw, the squalor in the towns surrounding the oil fields, and when he returned he appeared before the company's board of directors. "The only justification for ownership," he said, "is that it serves the broad interest of the people. We must recognize the social responsibilities of corporations and the corporation must use its ownership of assets to reflect the best interests of the people."

In 1960, during the presidential primary season, he had sought his party's nomination. Now he was ready to try again. As governor of New York, an office he won in 1959, Rockefeller had a strong political base, and of course he had the money to support his ambition to accomplish even greater good in the world. In many ways, he was the consummate liberal patrician, aware of his privilege, determined to use it wisely and well, but nursing his own political aspirations, dead certain of his ability to lead. His views were broad, nuanced, complex; when it came to foreign policy, he was a dedicated cold warrior, committed to stopping the spread of Communism and strengthening America's military might. But he favored John Kennedy's test ban treaty and vigorous diplomacy within the United Nations. He wanted to balance the federal budget, but he favored social welfare programs. More than anything, however, it was his racial liberalism that set him apart from other Republicans, made him sound too much like Democrats Kennedy or Johnson, and caused GOP leaders to fear that he would lose.

Rockefeller's undoing came in an unexpected way. Toward the end of an empty marriage, he fell in love with Margaretta Murphy, known as "Happy" to her friends, though she too was trapped in loveless matrimony. Rockefeller and Murphy divorced their spouses and on May 4, 1963, married each other. Better that, Rockefeller believed, than carrying on a clandestine affair. He preferred to live his life aboveboard, sunny in the hope that he would be understood. In any case, wrote journalist Theodore White, "He would not give up the woman he loved even for the presidency."

Former Senator Prescott Bush, father and grandfather to future presidents, had been a longtime friend, but now he denounced Rockefeller as a home-wrecker. As the chorus of disapproval grew louder and more people questioned Rockefeller's morality (for reasons that today seem remarkably tame), the door was opened for Barry Goldwater.

Suddenly the stakes seemed higher. Goldwater was not a typical candidate. He was a man of the West with silver hair and sun-tanned face, and when he posed for pictures in the Arizona desert, often with a rifle or a shotgun across his knee, he looked more like a Hollywood sheriff than a U.S. senator. He shared a bit of Nelson Rockefeller's sense of corporate responsibility, rooted in his own family's example. As author Rick Perlstein noted, the Goldwaters thought "private citizens should take care of their own," and they ran the family department store accordingly.

"Goldwater's paid higher than the industry wage," Perlstein wrote, "provided health, accident, life, and pension benefits; provided profit sharing, a store psychiatrist, and a formal retirement plan. Later came a twenty-five acre farm for employee recreation, and a day camp for children. The family allowed employees to examine the company's books whenever they wished."

With Goldwater, however, there was also a sense of entitlement, of the prerogatives of ownership, and he hated the notion that workers might demand even more, heaven forbid with the help of a labor union. One of his least favorite people was Walter Reuther, whose aggressive leadership of the United Auto Workers had helped transform the working class in the United States into a new, expanding middle class. Goldwater thought Reuther had too much power and was always demanding more and more of American corporations, until sooner or later the whole arrangement would collapse. There was also the 1964 Civil Rights Act—a government overreach, in Goldwater's view, that undermined states' rights. Not that he favored racial oppression. From all indications, he did not. But the philosophical abstraction of limited government held sway in his mind, and civil rights leaders, quite understandably, regarded Goldwater as an enemy.

Later in his life, the Arizona senator came to admire Dr. Martin Luther King, and he did speak for the rights of people on the margins, including gays. But he mistrusted the radicals of the 1960s and a government that sometimes seemed to support them with civil rights measures. Goldwater was standing against the tide, and his way of doing it worried the Republican establishment even as it cheered the hard-line conservatives. For years, people like Robert Welch and Phyllis Schlafly had argued that conservatives could create a new truth, a new body of mainline American assumptions, if they simply hammered away at their message, no compromise, no backing down. Goldwater seemed to be that kind of man.

And yet there was something else about him. Despite his bedrock challenge to a consensus in which the difference between Republicans and Democrats often seemed mostly a matter of degree—Goldwater brought a civility to the task. Before November 1963, he had looked forward to running against John F. Kennedy, in part, ironically, because he liked him. He thought Kennedy, like himself, was a man of principle, and the two were political friends. They talked half seriously about traveling together on the same campaign plane and debating at every stop, as Abraham Lincoln and Stephen Douglas had done. Both knew it would not happen, but their amity was a remarkable thing, especially from today's vantage point.

Then came Dallas, and Goldwater entered a kind of Hamlet phase, brooding, indecisive, no longer certain that he wanted to run. Part of it was simply self-doubt. Perlstein wrote:

> He had a favorite Western maxim, a good man knows the length of his rope. "Doggone it," he told the *Chicago Tribune*, "I'm not even sure I've got the brains to be President of the United States." He worried whether he had the courage to do what he wanted to do in the White House. And what if lightning struck and he won? What would he be then but master of the world's most byzantine bureaucracy?

That was all part of it, but there was more, an emotion more personal and more deeply felt. "His heart was sick within him," wrote Theodore White in *The Making of the President—1964*. "Poison-pen letters and hate letters poured across his desk in hundreds as if he, personally, were responsible for the killing of the man he was so fond of. ('Are you happy now?' asked one letter.) And so for a period of about ten days, Goldwater gave up politics. To his wife he said, 'The heck with the Presidential thing,' and somberly withdrew into himself." There were plenty of capable Republicans—not only Rockefeller, but Henry Cabot Lodge, the U.S. Ambassador to Vietnam, and William Scranton, the bright young governor of Pennsylvania, even Milton Eisenhower, a respected economist and brother of the former president. Let one of them do it.

In December, however, after months of cajoling, Goldwater's inner circle finally persuaded him to run. For the sake of all he believed, it was time to test his mettle against the other strong men in the party. In the spring of 1964, he plunged into the task, barnstorming through the primary season, and it was clear from the start that the nation was in for something new.

For one thing, Goldwater was a shoot-from-the-hip candidate, given to hyperbole in private conservation that could sound terrifying on the campaign trail. "Let's lob one into the men's room of the Kremlin," he might say, mostly joking, and voters were left to wonder if he really intended to start a war with Russia. Before a group of reporters in New Hampshire, he suggested that Social Security should be voluntary, and speaking about the causes of poverty, he declared, "The fact is that most people who have no skills have no education for the same reason—low intelligence or ambition."

Some hard-line conservatives agreed, but others wondered if Goldwater was really that heartless. Did he actually think that stupidity was the main cause of poverty? And was he willing to jeopardize Social Security, the crucial safety net for the elderly? "If he doesn't mean what he says, then he's just trying to get votes," one New Hampshire Republican told Theodore White. "And if he does mean what he says—then the man is dangerous."

That was the problem Goldwater faced, and in the coming months it worsened. There were times, to be sure, when he spoke from the depths of his heart about his hopes and fears for the country. At a Memorial Day rally, he declared:

> We are gathered here in memory of those boys who gave their lives for us . . . and wherever they are in heaven they are trying to warn us. . . . Some wobbly thinkers think that laws will stop you from hating, laws will make you generous. But when I read about street crimes, about hatred covered in blood, I ask what's happening to the principles these men died for. Did they die in vain? Sometimes I think they did.

In such moments the crowds were stirred to a patriotic fervor; but there were other occasions when Goldwater generated alarm, and some of the most venerable men in his party thought he was leading it to ruin. In June, during the final run-up to the Republican convention, he had a huge lead in the delegate count and had just beaten Rockefeller in the California primary. The nomination looked to be his, all his rivals now safely vanquished. In the Senate, however, the time arrived for a vote on the civil rights bill—the historic piece of legislation that John F. Kennedy had introduced and Lyndon Johnson was pushing toward passage. Barry Goldwater voted against it.

One of those most appalled by Goldwater's vote was William Scranton, the governor of Pennsylvania, who could not imagine the standard-bearer for the party of Lincoln voting, in effect, for continued racial oppression in America, no matter what words he might use to explain it. Scranton's own family had stood beside Lincoln and had been stalwarts in the party when it pushed through the Thirteenth, Fourteenth, and Fifteenth amendments, ending the abomination of slavery and enshrining more deeply in the Constitution the notion of equality in the law. Scranton had not yet declared his candidacy for president—he was happy enough to be governor of Pennsylvania—but now he decided he must try. Somebody had to stop a man who betrayed the soul of what the Republican Party stood for.

Nelson Rockefeller agreed. His own ambitions had ended with his loss in California, but now he offered his support to Scranton, and he hoped for the same from Dwight Eisenhower. Nobody else commanded such respect. Eisenhower shared Scranton's and Rockefeller's concerns about Goldwater, but he was curiously tepid in his response. In *The Making of the President—1964*, Theodore White gave this account of the tension backstage, beginning with a phone call from Eisenhower to Scranton:

> He wanted to know what Scranton thought of Goldwater's vote. Scranton replied that the vote had made him sick—that it, more than anything else, had made him want to run for the presidency. Eisenhower responded that he was certainly glad to hear that. . . . But Eisenhower would not move publicly. Nelson Rockefeller, battling as valiantly for the Pennsylvania governor as he had for himself, telephoned the former President to plead for support. The former President said he could not come out publicly, he had to preserve his influence. Acidly, Rockefeller inquired: For what?

It was clear very soon that Scranton's challenge was too little, too late, and at the Republican convention in San Francisco, against a backdrop of deep division, Goldwater steamrolled to the nomination. On the final night, as the bands played and balloons of patriotic colors tumbled from the rafters, as the delegates cheered and sang "The Battle Hymn of the Republic," Goldwater gathered himself to deliver a speech that he and his staff had worked on for weeks. He had been over every word. He knew exactly what he wanted to say, and he assumed the mantle of conservative prophet, delivering hard truth to the people of his country.

> The Good Lord raised this mighty Republic . . . not to stagnate in the swamplands of collectivism, not to cringe before the bully of Communism. . . . Our people have followed false prophets. . . . Rather than useful jobs . . . people have been offered bureaucratic make work; rather than moral leadership, they have been given bread and circuses; they have been given spectacles and, yes, they've been given scandals. . . .
>
> Tonight there is violence in our streets, corruption in our highest offices, aimlessness among our youth, anxiety among our elderly, and there's a virtual despair among the many who look beyond material successes toward the inner meaning of their lives. . . .
>
> The Republican cause demands that we brand Communism as the principal disturber of peace in the world today. Indeed, we should brand it as the only significant disturber of the peace. . . . Communism and the governments it controls are enemies of every man on earth who is or wants to be free. . . .
>
> Anyone who wants to join us in all sincerity we welcome. Those who do not care for our cause, we don't expect to enter our ranks in any case. And let our Republicanism, so focused and so dedicated, not be made fuzzy. . . . Extremism in the defense of liberty is no vice! Moderation in the pursuit of justice is no virtue!

In the San Francisco streets outside the convention center, demonstrators, mostly African American, joined hands and sang "We Shall Overcome," their voices soft and strong in the California night. Elsewhere in the country, millions of citizens watching on television wondered what in the world was going on. Who was man who had issued such a stern and stirring challenge? And what exactly did he mean?

Extremism in the defense of liberty . . . What was Goldwater talking about?

THAT QUESTION HOVERED OVER the election, and Lyndon Johnson, among many other Democrats, was absolutely delighted that Goldwater had posed it. They would hang him with his own words. When the Republican nominee talked about cuts in government spending, the Democrats quoted his musings on Social Security and how, perhaps, it could be privatized. What kind of cold-hearted man would risk the financial security of the elderly, or for that matter, vote against a bill aimed at ending segregation?

It was the issue of war and peace, however, that the Democrats used to greatest effect. Back in May, Goldwater had appeared on ABC's television show, *Issues and Answers.* The always well-informed host, Howard K. Smith, asked Goldwater what he would do if elected president to stop the resupply of Communist forces in South Vietnam. From the north, the Communist troops of Ho Chi Minh had cut trails through the jungles skirting the borders with Cambodia and Laos, and munitions poured south in a steady stream. What could the United States do to stop it?

"It's not as easy as it sounds," Goldwater replied. "There have been several suggestions made. I don't think we would use any of them. But defoliation of the forests by low-yield atomic weapons could well be done. When you remove the foliage, you remove the cover."

When Smith asked if such an action might provoke a war with neighboring China, Goldwater's answer was chilling. "You might have to," he said. "Either that, or we have a war dragged out and dragged out. A defensive war is never won."

As it happened, Goldwater's comments came against a cultural backdrop provided by *Dr. Strangelove*, a satirical movie telling the story of unhinged Americans launching the first strike in a nuclear war. It was unfair, of course, to compare Goldwater to the lunatics in the film, but ridicule poured forth nevertheless. Robert Kennedy joked about a Goldwater approach to crime in Central Park. "He would use conventional nuclear weapons and defoliate it." And so it went until November 3, when Lyndon Johnson won in a landslide. Goldwater carried only six states, all of them in the Deep South, and the pundits were quick to write him off. In 2001, Rick Perlstein looked back at the Goldwater campaign and wrote in *Before the Storm*:

> The wise men weighed in . . . Reston of the *Times*: "He has wrecked his party for a long time to come and is not even likely to control the wreckage." Rovere of *The New Yorker*: "The election has finished the Goldwater school of political reaction." "By every test we have," declared James MacGregor Burns, one of the nation's most esteemed scholars of the presidency, "this is as surely a liberal epoch as the late 19th century was a conservative one." . . . It was one of the most dramatic failures of collective discernment in the history of American journalism.

Goldwater might never run for president again, but the movement he led was far from finished. This was the time, as Perlstein wrote, when true believers on the right learned,

> . . . how to *act*: how letters got written, how doors got knocked on, how co-workers could be won over on the coffee break, how to print a bumper sticker and how to pry one off with a razor blade; how to put together a network whose force exceeded the sum of its parts by orders of magnitude; how to talk to a reporter, how to picket, and how, if need be, to infiltrate—how to make the anger boiling inside you ennobling, productive, *powerful*, instead of embittering. How to feel bigger than yourself.

In addition, Washington columnist E. J. Dionne maintained that conservatives discovered in the 1964 election season the champion who would lead them into the future. In *Why the Right Went Wrong* (in which he argued against a meanness creeping into the movement), Dionne recalled the night of October 27 when Ronald Reagan delivered a television address in support of Goldwater.

> "You and I have a rendezvous with destiny," Reagan proclaimed. "We'll preserve for our children this, the last best hope of man on earth, or we'll sentence them to take the last step into a thousand years of darkness."
>
> It is in no way an exaggeration to say that Reagan's speech, titled "A Time for Choosing," changed the course of history. When Ronald Reagan appeared in conservative living rooms . . . a week before Goldwater's coming rout, millions in their ranks realized that they had found a leader who would pick up where Goldwater left off—and could deliver their message far more powerfully than the man they were about to vote for.

Perhaps more importantly, there was also something in the times—an emerging sense of grievance in America. No longer was it simply African Americans, or dissident students demanding free speech, all those voices resonating from the left. Now there were protests from the other side: entrepreneurs who saw government regulation as the enemy, and people who feared the Communist menace and detected its presence in the movement for change; there were those who nursed their demons of prejudice and conflated easily the restless demands of the civil rights movement with crime, and later riots, in the inner city. There were many who believed with Ayn Rand (or who had simply concluded on their own) that self-interest should be the engine of politics, not a soft-headed sympathy for people on the margins. In the United States of America, a land brimming over with opportunity, people should be able to make it on their own. George Wallace had talked about these things, and so had Goldwater, and that actor, Reagan, was waiting his turn, and the sources of energy they tapped seemed to be growing stronger. Soon enough, Christian evangelicals would raise their voices. All of these passions ran strong and deep.

To some of us, however, this conservative message that was suddenly all around us seemed cold and heartless at its core—a politics of selfishness and fear. Most of the conservatives, as far as we could tell, didn't care about justice at all.

24

Keepers of the Dream

That same November, Robert Kennedy was elected U.S. Senator from New York. The twelve months since the death of his brother had been excruciating. Never in his life had he felt so shattered, so adrift. Always an avid reader, he became more of one, searching for answers to the question he had uttered aloud on the night after the assassination: *Why God?* He was still a Catholic, a man of faith, but faith had become more an agonizing mystery than a consolation as he confronted an ancient dilemma: *The innocent suffer—how can this be possible and God be just?*

That was how he posed it in his private scribblings, as he turned his attention to the Greeks, seeking in their ancient wisdom, and in the words of other philosophers, some fortification against his pain. Even in the depths of his own despair Kennedy understood that he was born into privilege and wealth, with the means to make a difference in the world. It occurred to him now, as he moved from the Greeks to the existentialist philosophers, especially Albert Camus, that a man must shape the meaning of his life.

On the day of his brother's funeral, he had written notes to his own children: *Remember all the things that Jack started—be kind to others that are less fortunate than we—and love our country.* In the end, that seemed like good advice to himself, for what other meaning could he find, what other redemption, for a moment more painful than he thought he could bear?

Eventually, as some of his friends would observe, a measure of freedom came with his grief. If he had loved his brother perhaps more deeply than anybody on earth, he had also sublimated his own identity, finding purpose in serving the career of John Kennedy. Then in a split second, a bullet he gladly would have taken himself propelled him on an existential journey, a five-year span in which he came to embody—more viscerally than any politician of his time—an identification with people who hurt. Wrote Arthur Schlesinger,

> He was now the head of the family. The qualities that he had so long subordinated in the interest of others—the concern under the combativeness, the gentleness under the carapace, the idealism, at once wistful and passionate, under the toughness—could rise freely to the surface. He could be himself at last.

His pulpit became the U.S. Senate. There was talk for a while about the vice presidency, but he and Lyndon Johnson both knew it wouldn't work. If LBJ and Jack Kennedy had liked each other, and by most accounts they did, Johnson and Bobby Kennedy did not. The new president was known to fly into a rage at the mention of Bobby's name, and Kennedy, for his part, once told Schlesinger, "he lies all the time. . . . He lies even when he doesn't have to lie."

At Johnson's urging and in the interest of an orderly transition, Kennedy stayed on for a while as attorney general, but his heart was no longer in the job. On August 22, two days before the Democratic Convention in Atlantic City, he announced his candidacy for the Senate. The following Thursday he stood before the convention, and in the wake of all the controversy regarding the Mississippi Freedom Democratic Party, he presided over what may have been the only authentic moment of unity that the Democrats shared all week. The occasion was a film tribute to his fallen brother. As Kennedy prepared to say a few words of introduction, a twenty-two minute ovation swept the cavernous auditorium. Every time Kennedy attempted to end it, the cheering soared and overwhelmed his voice. After a while, he simply let it happen, standing there red-eyed and silent and understanding with a bittersweet certainty, a certainty rooted in his own sense of loss, exactly who the cheering was for.

In the weeks that followed, his Senate campaign was not easy. His opponent was Kenneth Keating, a Republican incumbent who at age sixty-four somehow seemed much older. At first, Kennedy ran an awkward, uncertain race, afraid that he would come across as a bully. His stump speeches were stiff, yet with flashes of a new possibility, a candor in his answers to questions, which often disarmed skeptics. And he found a growing enthusiasm in the crowds, especially among young voters.

"If I had my way," he quipped at one stop, "I'd lower the voting age to six."

Some called him a carpetbagger, since he had only recently moved to New York, and some of the state's most dedicated liberals viewed him harshly as an opportunist. In the end he won by more than 700,000 votes, though Lyndon Johnson won the state's presidential vote by a much larger margin.

Kennedy, however, now had his Senate platform, and for advice he turned to his younger brother Edward, who in 1962 had been elected the junior senator from Massachusetts. Already Teddy Kennedy was winning the esteem of his Senate colleagues, liberal or conservative, Republican or Democrat, for the respectful way he carried himself. This would come much harder for Robert, who was moody, impatient, still consumed by the hurt of his older brother's murder. Nevertheless, he plunged into the task of being a senator, turning his attention to the hurt in the country, and more and more as the months went by he spoke about it with a passion that took many by surprise.

Some young activists on the left—the SNCC organizers in Mississippi, the Free Speech Movement advocates in California—were skeptical of charismatic leaders, preferring instead a leadership by consensus, where ordinary people were sufficiently empowered that decisions could flow from the grass roots upward. In the Port Huron Statement, the founding document of the Students for a Democratic Society, Tom Hayden had called it "participatory democracy"; it was an idea embraced by leaders as diverse as Mario Savio and Bob Moses. Even Savio, however, understood the importance of a spokesperson who could frame the debate, bring ideas alive in a way that offered inspiration where there had been none.

For many of us, beginning as early as 1964, Robert Kennedy began to play that role, taking his place beside Martin Luther King, even if Kennedy might not have put it this way, as one of America's great apostles of hope. Dr. King, meanwhile, was stepping once again to center stage as the tumultuous year was coming to an end. In December, he was awarded the Nobel Peace Prize, and even as he traveled to Oslo to receive it—at thirty-five, the youngest person ever so honored—his mind was already on other things. His organization, the Southern Christian Leadership Conference, had turned its attention to voting rights in the South, and King was planning demonstrations in Selma, Alabama, a place still crippled by the legacy of hate. In his acceptance speech he proclaimed:

> I experience this high and joyous moment not for myself alone but for those devotees of nonviolence who have moved so courageously against the ramparts

> of racial injustice and who in the process have acquired a new estimate of their own human worth. Many of them are young and cultured. Others are middle aged and middle class. The majority are poor and untutored. But they are all united in the quiet conviction that it is better to suffer in dignity than to accept segregation in humiliation. These are the real heroes of the freedom struggle: they are the noble people for whom I accept the Nobel Peace Prize.
>
> This evening I would like to use this lofty and historic platform to discuss what appears to me to be the most pressing problem confronting mankind today. Modern man has brought this whole world to an awe-inspiring threshold of the future. He has reached new and astonishing peaks of scientific success. He has produced machines that think and instruments that peer into the unfathomable ranges of interstellar space. . . . His airplanes and spaceships have dwarfed distance, placed time in chains, and carved highways through the stratosphere. This is a dazzling picture of modern man's scientific and technological progress.
>
> Yet, in spite of these spectacular strides in science and technology, and still unlimited ones to come, something basic is missing. There is a sort of poverty of the spirit which stands in glaring contrast to our scientific and technological abundance. The richer we have become materially, the poorer we have become morally and spiritually. We have learned to fly the air like birds and swim the sea like fish, but we have not learned the simple art of living together as brothers.

Most of us did not know, as we read and pondered these lofty words, that the FBI under the direction of J. Edgar Hoover was working hard at that very moment to plant a story in the press about King's pattern of marital infidelity. The Bureau had documented this particular frailty by consistently bugging King's motel rooms. The media, for the most part, was resistant to the leak, finding it too grubby and distasteful, but if the smears in general went unreported, it was clear that other opposition was building. In the wake of Goldwater's run for the presidency, new voices were emboldened to compete with Dr. King's, offering a very different vision for the future.

The battle for the soul of America was joined.

25

The Blood of Malcolm

As the new year began, Alex Haley was worried about Malcolm X. Haley was an African American writer embarked on his most ambitious assignment, a book he was calling *The Autobiography of Malcolm X.* Haley had already published magazine articles about Malcolm in *Reader's Digest* and the *Saturday Evening Post* and an at-length interview in *Playboy*, and each time Malcolm was pleased, surprised, in fact, that mainstream magazines owned and edited by whites would print with accuracy his blistering denunciations of white America.

"I think my life story may help people to appreciate better how Mr. Muhammad salvages black people," Malcolm replied, when Haley first broached the subject of a book. "This is the book's dedication," he added, pulling from his wallet a piece of paper on which he had scrawled: "This book I dedicate to the Honorable Elijah Muhammad, who found me here in America in the muck and the mire of the filthiest civilization and society on this earth, and pulled me out, cleaned me up, and stood me on my feet, and made me the man I am today."

As the interviews for the project began, for months Haley and Malcolm engaged in long, difficult conversations. Malcolm rarely strayed from proclamations of Black Muslim orthodoxy, a ritual homage to Elijah Muhammad, founder of this curious movement called the Nation of Islam that was so bitter in its condemnation of whites and yet so demanding of its adherents. Muhammad was a shadowy figure, shy and soft-spoken, but among his followers, including Malcolm X, he was the object of messianic devotion. He was born in Georgia to sharecropper parents and while still a child witnessed three lynchings. As a young man in Detroit, Muhammad (then known as Elijah Poole) became a black nationalist sympathizer. Slowly his separatist philosophy became intertwined with his own renegade version of Islam, in which the white race was the great, irredeemable villain of history.

That was what Malcolm X believed when he and Haley first met, and for a time it was all he wanted to talk about. Haley, of course, wanted the rich details of Malcolm's own life and grew frustrated, wondering if he would have to tell his publisher that the project was not going to work after all. Malcolm X was simply too guarded, too programmed with Muslim ideology to share his own story. Finally, one night when they were talking late, Malcolm was pacing the floor, tense and exhausted from the rigors of the day. On impulse Haley suddenly asked, "I wonder if you'd tell me something about your mother?" In what became the book's epilogue, Haley told what happened:

> Abruptly he quit pacing, and the look he shot at me made me sense that somehow the chance question had hit him. . . . Slowly, Malcolm X began to talk, now walking in a tight circle. "She was always standing over the stove, trying to stretch whatever we had to eat. We stayed so hungry that we were dizzy. I remember the color of dresses she used to wear—they were a kind of faded out gray . . ." And he kept on talking until dawn, so tired that the big feet would often almost stumble in their pacing. From this stream-of-consciousness reminiscing I finally got out of him the foundation for this book's beginning chapters.

In this marathon session, Malcolm told the story of his childhood, beginning with what he called "my earliest vivid memory"—a night of terror when he was six years old:

> I remember being suddenly snatched awake into a frightening confusion of pistol shots and shouting and smoke and flames. My father had shouted and shot at the two white men who had set the fire and were running away. Our home was burning down around us. We were lunging and bumping and tumbling all over each other trying to escape. My mother, with the baby in her arms, just made it into the yard before the house crashed in, showering sparks.

Malcolm's family was living in Lansing, Michigan, having moved from Omaha after threats against his father by the Ku Klux Klan. The father, Earl Little, was a proud and angry man, and white supremacists—both the Klan in Nebraska and a splinter group in Michigan called the Black Legionnaires (their robes were black instead of white)—correctly saw him as a troublemaker.

Little certainly intended to be. He was an itinerant Baptist preacher, capable of stirring black crowds to a frenzy, and he was also a follower of Marcus Garvey, a Pan-African leader from Jamaica who urged blacks in the United States and the Caribbean to return to Africa and "redeem" the continent from European control.

It was unclear when that redemption would come. In the meantime, Earl Little was a troubled person, his rage occasionally aimed against whites, but all too often against his family. As Malcolm recounted in his autobiography, his father often lashed out physically—beating Malcolm's mother and brothers, though for some reason never Malcolm. Violence became a staple in the family's life, and on the day that Earl Little died there had been a terrible argument and he had stormed away in a rage. The police came later and said his body was found on the streetcar tracks, cut almost in half by the train. An accident, they said. But Malcolm told Haley:

> Negroes in Lansing have always whispered that he was attacked, and then laid across the tracks for a streetcar to run over him. . . . I was six. I can remember a vague commotion, the house filled up with people crying, saying bitterly that the white Black Legion had finally gotten him.

Later, his mother was committed to a mental hospital, and out of such anguish Malcolm slid easily into a life of crime. He was known on the streets as "Detroit Red," and after a while he wound up in Harlem, running numbers, selling dope, burgling homes, sustained, he said, by "cocaine courage." In 1943, with World War II raging, he was ordered to report to his draft board. "In those days," he said, "only three things in the world scared me: jail, a job, and the Army." He reported as ordered, wearing the wildest suit he could find, along with yellow shoes, and set out to behave as strangely as he could, speaking loudly, demanding to be sworn in on the spot. Within a few minutes, he was led down the hall to be interviewed by an Army psychiatrist. In the doctor's office, as he told Haley:

> I kept jerking around, backward, as if somebody might be listening. . . . Suddenly, I sprang up and peeped under both doors, the one I'd entered and another that was probably a closet. And then I bent and whispered fast in his ear. "Daddy-o, now you and me, we're from up North here, so don't you tell

> nobody. . . . I want to get sent down South. Organize them nigger soldiers, you dig? Steal us some guns, and kill up crackers!" That psychiatrist's blue pencil dropped, and his professional manner fell off in all directions. He stared at me as if I were a snake's egg hatching, fumbling for his red pencil. . . . A 4-F card came to me in the mail.

That was Malcolm—hustler, hoodlum, con man, thief. For a while he managed to make it work, but eventually the drugs and danger took their toll, and his life grew wilder and more erratic. There were times he almost cracked from the strain.

Eventually he served seven years in prison after a series of home burglaries in Boston, mostly targeting rich white families. In Massachusetts's Charlestown State Penitentiary, redemption came from an unexpected source. From a fellow inmate and then from his brother, Reginald Little, Malcolm learned of the teachings of Elijah Muhammad. Some of those teachings were downright bizarre. According to Muhammad, more than six thousand years ago a black man named Mr. Yacub, a mad scientist with an oversized head, rebelled against Allah and created a devil race of people whose skin was a hideous, bleached-out white. For six thousand years, Allah had allowed the white devils to rule, but now the moment of black liberation was at hand.

Mythology aside, Malcolm found the story compelling. All he had to do was look around. White people *did* behave like devils, and their greatest transgression had been to make black people hate themselves. The depravity of his life was a prime example of that self-hate, but Muhammad offered an antidote to the shame. It was not an easy path, requiring a renunciation of the white man's poison—drugs and alcohol, for starters, but also the lies and the self-deception, the willingness to wallow in their own oppression, which crippled the lives of so many blacks.

For Malcolm, the message carried the force of revelation, like Saul's on the road to Damascus, he thought, for he had no doubt that Elijah Muhammad was speaking for God.

Malcolm jettisoned his surname Little, his father's name, and replaced it with X. This was a ritual among Elijah's followers, a repudiation of "slave names," with an X standing in for African ancestries lost to slavery. Following his parole in 1952, Malcolm X became a minister for the Nation of Islam, placed in charge of Temple #7 in Harlem. With a convert's zeal, he began speaking to crowds all over the country, condemning the racial sins of white America. He soon emerged as a folk hero, especially among the African American masses.

AS THEIR INTERVIEWS MORPHED into warm friendship, Haley began to accompany Malcolm on his regular strolls through the streets of Harlem. He was struck by the ease of Malcolm's connection to the people.

> Malcolm X here was indeed a hero. Striding along the sidewalks, he bathed all whom he met in the boyish grin, and his conversation with any who came up was quiet and pleasant. "It's just what the white devil wants you to do, brother," he might tell a wino, "he wants you to get drunk so he will have an excuse to put a club up beside your head." Or I remember once he halted at a stoop to greet several older women. "Sisters, let me ask you a question," he said conversationally, "have you ever known *one* white man who either didn't do something to you, or take something from you?" One among that audience exclaimed after a moment, "I sure *ain't*" whereupon all of them joined in laughter. . . . Malcolm X loved it . . . the man had charisma, and he had *power*.

Because of that, Haley was one of many who wondered at Malcolm's subservience to Elijah Muhammad—his constant repetitions of the phrase, "The Honorable Elijah Muhammad teaches," while taking none of the credit for himself. By the 1960s, it was clear that Malcolm, not Muhammad, was the most charismatic figure in the Nation of Islam—arguably, in fact, the most trusted African American leader, even including Dr. King, in the big-city ghettos of the North.

M. S. Handler, a white reporter for the *New York Times* whose honesty Malcolm came to trust, argued ironically that one reason for Malcolm's standing among blacks was the fear and loathing he inspired among whites. "The white man sensed an implacable foe," Handler wrote, "who could not be had for any price—a man unreservedly committed to the cause of liberating the black man in American society . . ."

Given all that, many people wondered, how did Malcolm and Muhammad work it out? How could Malcolm muster such deference, and how did Muhammad endure Malcolm's fame?

By the end of 1963, it was becoming clear that the tension was greater than had been known. On December 1, Muhammad announced that Malcolm

X had been suspended from the Nation of Islam. The reason, ostensibly, was Malcolm's public statement calling the death of John Kennedy "chickens coming home to roost," by which he meant that the violence of white America had now been turned on one of its own. Many people, black and white, found the statement insensitive, and even Muhammad, despite his separatist instincts, sensed the affection that African Americans held for Kennedy. He suspended Malcolm for sixty days, ordering a moratorium on his statements and speeches.

At first, Malcolm publicly acknowledged the authority of Muhammad. "I'm in complete submission to Mr. Muhammad's judgment," he said. Privately, he chafed, particularly when he began to hear rumors that Muhammad had a habit of fathering children among some of the women who had been his secretaries. Malcolm was shocked. Muhammad's message had long been strict and ascetic, a rejection of drugs, alcohol, and sexual immorality, and when Malcolm tried to talk to him about it, Muhammad spoke defensively of spreading his "seed."

On March 8, 1964, Malcolm broke with the Nation of Islam, forming a new group, the Organization of Afro American Unity. It was clear that his philosophy was in flux. Beneath his aura of charisma and charm, he had always been a seeker, a restless intellectual, and now he began to travel internationally, first to Mecca, the holiest site in the Muslim world, and then to Africa and Europe. His religion became more orthodox, an acceptance of the doctrines of Sunni Islam, and he began to consider the possibility of respect among people of all races. He had seen them come together in Mecca, Muslims of multiple ethnicities and colors, united in faith. And the truth was, he had always enjoyed the speeches he gave on college campuses, where most of his listeners were white.

As Malcolm struggled with these changes, Elijah Muhammad's rage turned deadly. Soon after Malcolm's break, Muhammad had told Louis X, one of his ministers who would later become known as Louis Farrakhan, that "hypocrites like Malcolm should have their heads cut off." The April 10, 1964, edition of *Muhammad Speaks*, the Black Muslims' official newspaper, carried a cartoon depicting Malcolm's severed head.

BY EARLY 1965, AS Malcolm and Haley were poring over the manuscript for the *Autobiography*, Malcolm confessed that he did not expect to see the book published. Nevertheless, he kept pushing forward. On February 3, he made his first trip to the American South, visiting Selma, Alabama, to offer his support to Martin Luther King. Several years earlier, he had publicly referred to King as a "chump" and scoffed at the philosophy of nonviolence. Now he wanted to heal that breach.

King at the time was in the Selma jail. Since January, he had been leading demonstrations in that part of Alabama, which had succeeded Mississippi as the new battleground for the voting rights movement. At first, King's lieutenants were alarmed by the news that Malcolm was coming to town.

They were to be pleasantly surprised. Malcolm met first with Coretta King, and he seemed gentle as he assured her that he simply wanted to help. Whatever his criticisms of the past, he would not complicate things now for her husband.

That night he spoke at Brown Chapel A.M.E. Church, a modest brick church within a housing project that was named for the scientist George Washington Carver. Malcolm freely admitted that he did not share the philosophy of nonviolence, but neither did he advocate its opposite. He merely believed in self-defense—the right of a man to hit back, or *shoot* back, as the case might be, depending on the level of provocation.

Few listening to him that night knew that even as he spoke he was waiting for assassins sent by Muhammad, knowing they might appear at any moment. He seemed calm enough, however, sharing the podium with Mrs. King and the Reverend Fred Shuttlesworth, the fiery, nonviolent leader from Birmingham.

"I think the people in this part of the world," Malcolm declared, "would do well to listen to Dr. Martin Luther King and give him what he's asking for and give it to him fast, before some other factions come along and try to do it another way."

On the night of February 14, less than two weeks after his return to New York, he awakened suddenly to the screams of his children as flames spread through his Long Island home. It was *déjà vu*, a frantic replay of the night when he was six years old and his family's home had burned to the ground, collapsing in a final shower of sparks. The attackers that night had been white. Now they were not, but what difference, really, did it make? Hate was hate.

On February 19, he told the African American photographer Gordon Parks, a man he had come to trust and admire, that he did not expect to live much longer. The Nation of Islam was trying to kill him, and he thought it was only a matter of time. Two days later, he was giving a speech at Harlem's Amsterdam Ballroom. He had barely started when a trio of black gunmen rushed the stage, firing point-blank with a sawed-off shotgun and two semi-automatic handguns. Malcolm reeled backward and lay in a spreading pool of his blood. An autopsy revealed twenty-one wounds, including the fatal shot to his chest.

At the funeral on February 27, before an overflow crowd at one of Harlem's biggest churches, actor Ozzie Davis delivered the eulogy. Speaking in his resonant, deep voice, he set out to answer a question being posed in other places:

> Many will ask what Harlem finds to honor in this stormy, controversial and bold young captain—and we will smile. . . . They will say that he is of hate—a fanatic, a racist—who can only bring evil to the cause for which you struggle!
>
> And we will answer and say unto them: Did you ever talk to Brother Malcolm? Did you ever touch him, or have him smile at you? Did you ever really listen to him? Did he ever do a mean thing? Was he ever associated with violence or any public disturbance? For if you did you would know him. And if you knew him you would know why we must honor him. Malcolm was our manhood! This was his meaning to his people. And in honoring him, we honor the best in ourselves. . . .

Soon after the murder, Haley's publisher, Doubleday, backed out of its deal, fearing, a company spokesperson said, for the safety of its employees if it released *The Autobiography of Malcolm X.* Grove Press picked up the contract and the book appeared later in 1965. Haley, still grieving, could take a bittersweet satisfaction in helping to expand the legacy of Malcolm, the public understanding of the meaning of his life. By the end of the decade the book would enter its eighteenth printing. Sales soon totaled more than six million copies.

Three Black Muslims were convicted of the murder.

Malcolm X lived to be thirty-nine.

26

Marches and Martyrs

On the day Malcolm X was murdered, another black man lay fighting for his life in a hospital down in Alabama. Jimmie Lee Jackson was twenty-six years old, an Army veteran and deacon in his church. On the night of February 18, he was shot at close range by Alabama State Trooper James Fowler during a civil rights march in the town of Marion, just a few miles up the road from Selma. On February 26 Jackson died, becoming one of the most unlikely martyrs of the civil rights era.

He never expected to play a major role. Jackson, in fact, was the definition of a movement foot soldier, just an average man in a small Southern town who had come out to a rally with members of his family. His grandfather, Cager Lee, was eighty-two and had never once voted in an election. Like most African Americans in the Black Belt—the fertile crescent of rich, dark soil curving through central Alabama—the old man was not a registered voter, not because he didn't want to be, but because white people would not allow it. He wanted to change that before he died, and at last he thought he saw the chance.

Martin Luther King had come first to Selma, and then to Perry County where Mr. Lee lived, and to Wilcox County just a few miles south, and Dr. King had said things that filled him with hope—things nobody else had ever said. He said black folks were just as good as white. Maybe they should have known it already, but there were so many negative reminders in that part of the world that Mr. Lee and others who scratched out a living on Alabama farms were not really meant to be first-class citizens. They had heard all their lives that they were not *ready* to vote, not educated, not prepared to make decisions about the things that mattered in their community. But Dr. King said all of that was a lie.

"I've come to tell you that you are God's children," King declared. "You are as good as any white person . . . and you've got to believe that."

In early 1965, as the voting rights movement spread through the Black Belt, King had sent the Reverend James Orange, one of his young staff members, to work with local leaders in Marion. Orange was a veteran of the 1963 children's crusade in Birmingham—those brave and frightening demonstrations in which young people, many in high school, some even younger, confronted Bull Connor's fire hoses and dogs. Now, in Marion, Orange began to lead similar demonstrations, and more than seven hundred protesters were arrested. Orange himself was charged with contributing to the delinquency of a minor, an allegation that could lead to hard prison time, and there were rumors on February 18 that the Ku Klux Klan intended to drag him from the jail that night and lynch him.

In response, Albert Turner and other local activists quickly organized an evening protest rally at Zion Methodist Church, only a block up the street from the Perry County Jail, and then a march. It was a dangerous idea. Night marches were rare in the civil rights movement, for the cloak of darkness often brought out the worst. The night was a time that belonged to the Klan.

Nevertheless, the church was packed as the Reverend C. T. Vivian, a former freedom rider and now a member of Dr. King's staff, delivered a fiery, eloquent call to nonviolence. At the end of his speech, the people left the sanctuary and began to march in the direction of the jail. They wanted James Orange to know they were there.

The marchers made it less than a block before they were stopped by a police force consisting of officers from Marion, a contingent of Alabama Highway Patrolmen, and even a few deputies who had driven up from Selma, where Dallas County Sheriff Jim Clark said things had gotten "too quiet." Marion Police Chief T. O. Harris ordered the demonstrators to return to the church. When one of their leaders, James Dobynes, knelt to pray, a policeman hit him in the back of the head. Other lawmen followed with a full-scale assault on every protester they could get to, and in the *New York Times* the following morning reporter John Herbers described the scene this way: "Negroes could be heard screaming, and loud whacks rang through the square."

Cager Lee and his daughter, Viola Jackson, tried to find safety in a little café behind the church, but troopers followed them inside and began to beat

Mr. Lee. When his grandson, Jimmie Lee Jackson, tried to intervene, Trooper James Fowler shot him in the stomach. Eight days later, Jimmie Lee died.

THERE ARE DIFFERING ACCOUNTS of who came up with the idea for a protest march that would take the body of Jimmie Lee Jackson to Montgomery and lay it on the State Capitol doorstep of Governor George C. Wallace. The Reverend James Bevel, another former freedom rider and King staffer at the Southern Christian Leadership Conference, was one of the idea's proponents. Bevel was regarded by many as a wild-eyed mystic with a flair for the dramatic. Eventually, of course, he and others began to tone it down, for Jimmie Lee deserved a decent burial and to rest in peace. But the idea for a march—a protest unlike any in the past, lasting for days, stretching all the way from Selma to Montgomery—swept like wildfire through the Black Belt.

The first attempt came on March 7, a day that would become known as "Bloody Sunday." It was a moment for which the marchers were remarkably unprepared. "We weren't equipped for a march of that distance," remembered the Reverend L .L. Anderson, one of Selma's civil rights leaders. "We had no supplies, no arrangements for quarters along the way. All we had was our enthusiasm. . . ."

John Lewis, marching at the head of the line, carried a knapsack on his back. In it were a toothbrush and a book by the Trappist monk Thomas Merton. Lewis was fascinated by the writings of Merton, finding in them sustenance for his own spiritual journey that had led him into the civil rights movement. He was amazed that a man like Merton, who lived in a monastery in Kentucky, writing from the solitude of a cinder-block room, could speak with such authority about the ways of the world. Merton wrote often about racial oppression, and he corresponded with Dorothy Day, a founding editor of the *Catholic Worker*, about the realities of poverty in America. After the assassination of John Kennedy, Merton had offered his own benediction: "There will be another solemn requiem today, this time for the President." He saw in Kennedy's death the "same blind idiot destructiveness and hate that killed Medgar Evers in Mississippi, the Negro children in Birmingham. . . . The country is full of madness and we are going to know this more and more."

The prophecy was about to come true in Selma.

As a long line of marchers reached the summit of the Edmund Pettus Bridge on the highway leading to Montgomery, they saw a phalanx of deputies and state troopers—some on horseback, many wearing gas masks—waiting for them at the base of the bridge. The demonstrators were marching in silence, two by two. John Lewis shared the first row with Hosea Williams, a member of King's staff, and in the next row were Albert Turner and Bob Mants, a SNCC organizer in neighboring Lowndes County.

In the television footage from that day, Lewis looked so young—he was barely twenty-five—as he came to a stop before the state troopers, hands thrust deeply into his pockets. The officer in command, Major John Cloud, gave the marchers two minutes to disperse, but the attack began almost at once. "Troopers, advance!" Cloud commanded, and Lewis quickly lost his footing in the crush. Amelia Boynton, one of Selma's grassroots leaders, was standing just behind Lewis when a state trooper clubbed her in the head. She staggered, but did not fall, so immediately the trooper hit her again. This time, she crumpled unconscious to the pavement, but the trooper kept pounding her and screaming, "Get up, nigger! Get up and run."

Many did run, choking and gasping through a cloud of tear gas, but even those who made it to Brown Chapel A.M.E. where the march had begun were chased and beaten as they rushed inside. On national television that night, ABC was showing *Judgment at Nuremberg*, a film about Nazi persecution of Jews. When the network switched to news footage from Selma, many viewers thought it was part of the movie.

Martin Luther King was in Atlanta when he heard the news, having preached that Sunday at his church. He rushed back to Selma to assess the damage and meet with leaders of the Alabama movement to decide what to do next. He found things suddenly more complicated. The terrifying parable in black and white—of good versus evil—that had flashed across the nation's television screens was abruptly giving way to a torrent of anger. People were talking about taking up arms. They had tried the way of nonviolence and look where it had gotten them. Remarkably enough, nobody had been killed that morning on the Edmund Pettus Bridge, but dozens were seriously injured—John Lewis himself had a fractured skull—and now the time had come to fight back.

The Reverend Andrew Young, one of King's closest SCLC advisers, began to work the crowd, trying to make the case for nonviolence. He knew the usual arguments wouldn't work—all those ideals of redemptive suffering and loving your enemies that Dr. King had talked about so often. This time he simply noted the obvious: black people would be outgunned. As the African American citizens of Selma weighed their options, fighting through feelings of hurt and rage, a remarkable thing began to happen. Through his network of civil rights contacts, King put out a plea for men and women of good will from all over the country to come to this small Alabama town and join forces with people who were trying to be free. By the next day, volunteers were arriving in such startling numbers that the wounded marchers could hardly believe it.

"That saved the nonviolent method," said the Reverend F. D. Reese, one of the local civil rights leaders. "After the beatings on the bridge when I got back to the church, I looked into the eyes of those marchers and I could see a question mark. Should the nonviolent method really be pursued? But that same night, when we were still in the sanctuary, a group of people arrived from New Jersey. They said, 'We have heard the call of Dr. King. We are here.' That was the most exhilarating thing. I looked into the eyes of the people again, and I saw renewed hope."

Many of those who came were members of the clergy. There were Unitarians and Catholics and Episcopalians, and there was the well-known Jewish rabbi and author, Abraham Heschel. Three years earlier Heschel had written a book called *The Prophets*, a book that Dr. King admired. It told the story of the ancient champions of justice—of men like Micah, Isaiah, Amos and Jeremiah. Heschel offered this summary of their calling: "The prophet is a lonely man. His standards are too high, his stature too great, and his concerns too intense for other men to share."

King knew that feeling, and it moved him deeply when Heschel also declared: "Where in America today do we hear a voice like the voice of the prophets of Israel? Martin Luther King is a sign that God has not forsaken the United States of America."

Heschel later said that in coming to Selma he was "praying with my feet," and more and more there were people in the Judeo-Christian community who understood exactly what he meant. For many the pursuit of simple justice was becoming an important measure of their faith. King was heartened by all of that, but less than twenty-four hours after Bloody Sunday he was also torn, caught in the pull of competing imperatives.

On Monday morning, King and a team of civil rights lawyers filed a motion before U.S. District Judge Frank M. Johnson Jr., asking for an injunction against state interference with a second march that was now called for March 9. King was hopeful about the motion. Johnson was known as a fair judge who, among other things, had ruled in 1956 against the segregation of Montgomery buses. He agreed to a full hearing on the matter the following Thursday, March 11, but issued a restraining order against a march before that time. King had never defied a federal judge. He viewed the U.S. federal courts, particularly in the South, as an important ally of the civil rights cause. But activists in Selma were impatient. They wanted to march again the next day, Tuesday, March 9.

All Monday night, King agonized about what to do. He was feeling the greatest pressure from young SNCC workers who had rushed to Selma from Mississippi and Atlanta after hearing the news of Bloody Sunday. SNCC officially had not been a part of the events of March 7—John Lewis had acted on his own—but now they were fanning the flames of defiance. To hell with the federal judge, they said. To hell with anybody white who counseled patience, even for a matter of days. They had lived through the bloodshed of Freedom Summer and the bitter disappointment of President Johnson's rejection of the Mississippi Freedom Democrats. They were angry, ready to march, and they criticized King for his indecision.

At the same time, in the interest of preventing more bloodshed, President Johnson sent an emissary to Selma to meet with King and try to stop the march. LeRoy Collins proved a good choice for that extremely delicate assignment. In 1960, as governor of Florida, Collins had set himself apart from other Southern governors by declaring that he represented every person in his state—"whether that person is black or white, whether that person is rich or poor, or whether that person is influential or not influential." In 1964, President Johnson had picked Collins as the first director of the Community Relations Service, a mediation agency created by the Civil Rights Act.

In Selma, Collins argued in conversations with King that another march before Judge Johnson had a chance to rule was an invitation to more police brutality. This time, Collins said, people might die. Why not wait a couple of days to let the federal court do its job?

King understood the rationality of the argument, but he also believed that if he refused to lead a march, someone else would do it anyway and the civil rights movement would begin to come apart. On Tuesday morning, Collins proposed a compromise. He would secure from George Wallace and the volatile

Alabama Public Safety Commissioner Al Lingo a promise that there would be no violence. King, in return, would agree to lead marchers across the bridge, but no further. He would turn around and lead the marchers back into Selma once they had reached the line of state troopers on the Montgomery side of the bridge. Two days later, Judge Johnson would issue his ruling, and he was almost certain to side with the movement.

King and Collins both knew the deal made sense, and King said he would try to keep the situation under control. That afternoon, the march began, with King in the lead; few of the marchers knew of his agreement with Collins. When the marchers reached the foot of the Edmund Pettus Bridge, nervous about what would happen next, a line of state troopers again blocked the highway. This time, however, when King and the leaders knelt to pray, the troopers waited for them to finish. When King then rose and began a solemn walk back across the bridge, many of the marchers were startled and confused. What was King doing? Why was he leading them away so meekly?

Some in the ranks were more than confused. They were enraged, especially the delegation from SNCC, and the divisions that simmered beneath the surface of the movement now erupted into the open. For some time now, many young radicals in SNCC had resented the "grandstanding" of Dr. King, all the acclaim that seemed to follow the marches he led and the speeches he gave as he flitted from place to place—Birmingham, the March on Washington, Selma—grabbing headlines, but never digging in with local black communities and sharing their burdens the way SNCC people did. Now in Selma they denounced his "trickery" and derided his march as "Turnaround Tuesday." Some vowed never to work with him again.

Again, John Lewis was an exception. He had not yet recovered from his injuries, but on Tuesday night he checked himself out of the hospital and went to the rally at Brown Chapel A.M.E. He said he was "overjoyed" to be there, and he told reporters, when they asked him about divisions in the movement, "SCLC is not the enemy. George Wallace and segregation are the enemy."

Then came one of those moments that put the divisions into perspective, at least temporarily. Later that night, once the singing and the preaching were over, three white ministers who had come to Selma to support Dr. King, decided to get something to eat. They had heard of a little soul food place called Walker's Café, where the Southern cooking was said to be the best. They ate their fill and started back toward the church, but took a wrong turn. They passed another café called the Silver Moon, which was only a couple of blocks away but was a Klan hangout. The ministers suddenly found themselves surrounded. The Reverend James Reeb, a Massachusetts Unitarian, was clubbed in the head with a baseball bat—a roundhouse swing that drove shattered fragements of his skull into his brain. Two days later, he died.

That same day, Thursday, March 11, Judge Johnson heard arguments in federal court about banning state interference with a march. King thought the hearing went well, but Johnson did not immediately rule as King had hoped. On Saturday, amid the grief and tension after the death of James Reeb, President Johnson introduced a voting rights bill that he wanted Congress to pass. The following Monday he addressed a Joint Session of Congress:

> At times, history and fate meet at a single time in a single place to shape a turning point in man's unending search for freedom. So it was at Lexington and Concord. So it was a century ago at Appomattox. So it was last week in Selma, Alabama. . . .
>
> Rarely in any time does an issue lay bare the secret heart of America itself. . . . The issue of equal rights for American Negroes is such an issue. And should we defeat every enemy, and should we double our wealth and conquer the stars and still be unequal to this issue, then we will have failed as a nation. . . .
>
> It is wrong—deadly wrong—to deny any of your fellow Americans the right to vote in this country. . . . Their cause must be our cause too. Because it is not just Negroes, but really it is all of us who must overcome the crippling legacy of bigotry and injustice. And we shall overcome.

King was watching on television in Selma. He had gathered with a group of his friends in the living room of Sullivan Jackson, an African American dentist who had offered his home to leaders of the movement. John Lewis was there, and C. T Vivian, and they were watching King's face as the president spoke. Many years later, they still remembered the glistening of a tear on King's cheek as Johnson ended his speech with the words of the famous civil rights anthem. In all the years they had spent together, in all the joy and heartbreak of those days, none had ever seen King weep.

Two days later on March 17, Judge Johnson finally issued his ruling approving the march:

> The extent of the right to assemble, demonstrate and march peaceably along the highways and streets in an orderly manner should be commensurate with the enormity of the wrongs that are being protested against. In this case, those wrongs are enormous.

ON MARCH 21, THE third attempt to march from Selma to Montgomery began. This time the marchers would make it all the way.

It was Sunday afternoon when they set out together from Brown Chapel, more than three thousand strong with Dr. King marching in the lead. Beside him were some others whose names were well-known, but for John Lewis the greatest dignitaries in the column were not the Nobel laureate Ralph Bunche, nor the renowned Rabbi Abraham Heschel, nor even the venerable labor leader A. Philip Randolph. To Lewis, the celebrities were the everyday people who had struggled so long in the Black Belt. Cager Lee was there, the grandfather of Jimmie Lee Jackson, whose murder had prompted the march in the first place. James Armstrong, a foot soldier from Birmingham, was carrying the American flag, and there was Amelia Boynton, the unofficial first lady of the Selma movement who had worked for the cause since the 1930s.

It took five days to make it the fifty miles to Montgomery. A bitter northerly wind blew in on Sunday night, and on Tuesday a cold rain drenched the demonstrators. On Wednesday night, they camped at a Catholic Church complex on the outskirts of Montgomery, where they were entertained by an all-star cast. Odetta was one of the headliners, along with Joan Baez and Peter, Paul and Mary, Tony Bennett, and Harry Belafonte.

On Thursday morning, they set out on the last few miles of their walk to the Capitol, their ranks swelling to twenty-five thousand as people poured out of the black neighborhoods they were passing through and joined the procession. Their route took them up Dexter Avenue, past the Baptist church where King was pastor in the days of the Montgomery bus boycott, and then to the base of the gleaming white marble steps where Jefferson Davis took the oath of office to become president of the Confederacy in 1861.

His back to the Capitol, Dr. King looked out across the faces, black and white together, and he delivered what many of his followers have said was one of the finest speeches of his career. In the tones and cadence that had now become so familiar, he said:

> I know that some of you are thinking, "How long will it take?" I come to say to you this afternoon, however difficult the moment, however frustrating the hour, it will not be long, because truth pressed to earth will rise again. How long? Not long, because no lie can live forever. How long? Not long, because you still reap what you sow. How long? Not long, because the arc of the moral universe is long, but it bends toward justice!

In the crowd, Annie Cooper, a veteran activist from Selma, wept at the reassuring power of his words. She had heard him so many times in the pulpits of her town, urging people like herself to keep on pushing, but there was something different about him this day. "His eyes were just a' twinklin'," she said, and more than thirty-five years later, with a catch in her voice, she repeated her favorite line from the speech: "The arc is long, but it bends toward justice."

OVER THE YEARS, MANY historians have shared her assessment, and some have said that moment in Montgomery—and the voting rights legislation that followed—represented the high-water mark of the nonviolent movement.

At the time, however, the euphoria was soon overshadowed. That same night, Viola Liuzzo, a mother of five who had driven down from Detroit to be a part of the march, was helping to ferry some of the participants back to Selma. Mrs. Liuzzo was white, and when a carload of Klansmen spotted her Oldsmobile sedan, the passenger in her front seat was black. They chased her down Highway 80, the route of the march, and when they finally pulled alongside, one of the Klansmen shot her dead.

According to Leroy Moton, her young passenger, who survived, at the moment just before the bullet struck, Mrs. Liuzzo was softly singing "We Shall Overcome."

27

Billy Graham Speaks

In June, with racial tension still running high, Billy Graham came to Montgomery, having been urged by President Johnson to do what he could to help calm the waters. Some observers might have seen Graham as an unlikely choice. He was the most famous evangelist in the world, a man who had spoken to enormous crowds on every continent except Antarctica. But he did his best to avoid controversy. "The gift of an evangelist is a very narrow gift," he told one reporter, and Graham seldom strayed far from his calling.

On the issue of race, however, he occasionally made an exception. He was proud of the fact that in 1953, at a "crusade" in Chattanooga, Tennessee, he had "personally and physically" pulled down the ropes that separated whites and African Americans in the huge crowd of people who had turned out to hear him. Four years later, in his hometown of Charlotte, North Carolina, he had written a personal letter of support to Dorothy Counts, a fifteen-year-old African American girl who had attempted, with dignity, to enroll in a previously all-white school and was harassed by an ugly mob. "Be of good faith," Graham urged her. "God is not dead. He will see you through."

He regarded Martin Luther King as a friend, not close perhaps, but a fellow Christian trying to make a difference in the world, and in 1957 invited him to deliver a prayer at a Billy Graham Crusade in New York. Regarding the fundamental lesson of the Scriptures, Graham was clear. "All men are created equal under God," he said. "Any denial of that is a contradiction of holy law." And speaking in Jackson, Mississippi, he framed the issue with even greater eloquence. "The ground at the foot of the cross is level," he said. "It touches my heart when I see whites stand shoulder to shoulder with blacks at the cross."

In Birmingham, not long after the 1963 church bombing, Graham conducted an integrated rally where he spoke of the "Great Reconciliation"—a plea for racial understanding and peace. A week later, he addressed the National Association of Evangelicals and told them bluntly: "We should have been leading the way to racial justice but we failed. Let's confess it, let's admit it, and let's do something about it."

It came as no surprise, therefore, that when President Johnson asked for his help in the summer of 1965, Graham pushed other commitments aside. He had deep reservations about civil disobedience and a moderate's fear of moving too fast. There was always a caution at the heart of his character, a resolute mildness when it came to social or political issues. But speaking to a group of students in Honolulu before he began his trip to Alabama, Graham offered an oblique endorsement of King's methods.

"It's true I haven't been to jail yet," he said. "I underscore the word *yet.* Maybe I haven't done all I could or should do."

In Montgomery, one of the people who most looked forward to Graham's coming was the Reverend Stephen Dill, a prominent Methodist minister in the city who had had his own encounter with the issue of race. On April 11, a Sunday morning not long after the Selma march, a member of his church read a statement to the congregation. C. H. Lancaster was a segregationist and a leader in the White Citizens Council, and he spoke with passion against racial integration in the pews. Lancaster insisted,

> The present controversy raging within Dalraida Methodist Church is over a basic question: Shall we remain a White Christian church or a Racially Mixed body? I do not intend to remain in any service while a member of the African race is present. . . . They come not to worship but to mock. They are part and parcel of the immoral mob aided by the National Council of Churches that staged the infamous march from Selma to Montgomery. As for me, I will not suffer my wife and children to sit among them.

In the South in 1965, this was how raw the issue could be, and Dill was one of a handful of Montgomery ministers who decided to address it head-on. He respected Dr. King's witness and the moral necessity of a voting rights march, and he made it clear to the members of his church that the brotherhood of man must be color-blind. When the board of directors of Dalraida Methodist supported his view that Sunday worship was open to anyone, Lancaster, the white supremacist, called it a "craven acquiescence," and withdrew from the church.

The experience was fresh enough in Dill's mind for him to look forward to Billy Graham's visit, and he took his place on the welcoming committee. Not everyone felt the same. Civil rights leaders were understandably disappointed by Graham's tone when he first came to town. Eager not to offend, the evangelist conceded that while Alabama had its racial problems, there were many other places "where the problem is just as acute." Searching for some middle ground, Graham went on to question the movement's reliance on civil disobedience, while criticizing resistance by whites to federal court rulings on desegregation.

"If the law says that I cannot march or I cannot demonstrate," he said, "I ought not to march and I ought not to demonstrate. And if the law tells me that I should send my children to a school where there are both races, I should obey that law also. Only by maintaining law and order are we going to keep our democracy and our nation great."

Where, some critics asked, was the Graham who had mused in Honolulu, far from the pressures of his native South, about one day joining Dr. King in jail? Why, some African Americans wondered, had Graham come to Alabama in the first place?

In *A Prophet With Honor*, Graham biographer William Martin maintained that however equivocal his public statements, Graham worked hard behind the scenes:

> Unable to countenance any kind of unseemly behavior, and equally unable to denounce his fellow Southerners as particularly wicked people, Graham nevertheless took a firm position on the side of civil rights and racial integration. Behind the scenes, he met with hundreds of pastors, laypeople, civic leaders, and even with Governor George Wallace, repeatedly calling for tolerance and understanding and confidently reporting signs of "great progress" on every hand. If blacks found this too tame, segregationists found it too radical, but Graham received an enthusiastic rating from the man who sent him to the troubled region. In a warm and effusive letter, President Johnson assured him that "you are doing a brave and fine thing . . ."

Stephen Dill was inclined to agree. Billy Graham, he knew, was a man who lived and worshipped in the heart of the American mainstream. Now, in these most turbulent times, he had spoken gently and clearly in support of racial understanding and justice. In Montgomery, Alabama, that was no small thing.

28

Vietnam

For many in the civil rights movement, Lyndon Johnson's finest hour may well have been his speech about events in Selma. No other president, not even John Kennedy, had spoken with greater clarity or force about racial justice in America. Certainly, Johnson himself wanted to be remembered this way—as a president who did great things about the greatest issue of his day.

He had introduced a voting rights bill that would send federal registrars to the South, making it possible for African Americans to register and vote. In its broadest terms his goal was nothing less than to create, for the first time, a genuine multi-racial democracy that would include all fifty states. At the same time, he was pushing legislation for the Medicare and Medicaid healthcare programs for the elderly and poor.

But there was another issue on his mind—one that had filled him with dread even before his reelection as president—and now he was faced with a grim reality. The civil war in Vietnam was not going well. Early in 1965, after another round of agonizing and extensive consultation with his advisers, Johnson made a fateful choice. In February, he launched Operation Rolling Thunder, a sustained bombing campaign against North Vietnam, and on March 8, the first American soldiers officially designated as combat troops arrived in the Vietnamese port of Da Nang.

Johnson later told biographer Doris Kearns:

> I knew from the start that I was bound to be crucified either way I moved. If I left the woman I really loved—the Great Society—in order to get involved with that bitch of a war on the other side of the world, then I would lose everything at home. All my programs. All my hopes to feed the hungry and shelter the homeless. All my dreams to provide education and medical care to the browns

> and the blacks and the lame and the poor. But if I left that war and let the Communists take over South Vietnam, then I would be seen as a coward and my nation would be seen as an appeaser and we would both find it impossible to accomplish anything for anybody anywhere on the entire globe. . . .
>
> Losing the Great Society was a terrible thought, but not so terrible as the thought of being responsible for America's losing a war to the Communists. Nothing could possibly be worse than that.

This was the way Johnson framed the issue, and even in those early days of escalation there were those who believed the seeds of tragedy lay in the president's misunderstanding. On March 11, three days after the arrival of combat troops in Da Nang, a group of faculty at the University of Michigan organized the first teach-in against the war. Their instrument of protest would be information. As Marilyn B. Young wrote in her splendid history, *The Vietnam Wars, 1945–1990,*

> [T]he initial assumption among many of the protesters was that the government had simply gotten it wrong. Neither Johnson nor his advisers fully understood Third World nationalism, the link between nationalism and social revolution, the specific history of anti-colonialism in Vietnam, the impact of the raging Sino-Soviet split on the world Communist movement, or the history of the Cold War. Mired in hopelessly anachronistic concepts that saw the beginning of all evil in "appeasement," and communism as monolithic, militaristic, and ruthlessly expansionist, the leaders of the United States had foolishly pursued a misguided policy in Vietnam. It was time to educate them and the American people. Who better to do so than professors?

The teach-in began on March 24, and as mild as it may have sounded to some, it became a controversial event. The initial idea was a faculty strike; professors would call off classes for a day and spend the time leading discussions about the war. Strong objections emerged in the state legislature, the university administration, and even among the faculty. In response, the plan was changed to off-hour discussions that would last all night, an idea embraced by the university's SDS chapter.

The campus was tense as the 8 p.m. start arrived. "Somehow we had set off a bombshell," remembered Thomas Mayer, a sociology professor and one of the organizers. Several times during the evening, that seemed like a literal possibility. Even before the first sessions began, there was a bomb threat, and another one several hours later.

Despite the tension and freezing temperatures, more than three thousand people, most of them students, spent all night debating the war—twelve straight hours of spirited discussion. They heard from professors who had studied the issue and some who just had strong opinions, and a few spoke in favor of the war. Hecklers and helmeted policemen searching for bombs added to the tension. As the *Michigan Daily* student newspaper reported the next day:

> Two bomb scares last night interrupted what was described as the biggest demonstration in university history. The first occurred at 7:25 p.m.
>
> . . . Police strode up to the lecture stage to inform students and protesters that the buildings would have to be cleared . . . In the bitter cold, an estimated 1,000 students gathered to hear speakers after the bomb scare . . . Protesting groups picketed the teach-in, backing administration foreign policy; they marched around the midnight rally waving flags with "Drop the Bomb" and "Peace Through Strength."

But the idea spread. Like the 1960 sit-ins, the protests captured the imagination of the young, and there were teach-ins that spring at more than thirty other colleges. Even Vanderbilt, a Southern university where I was a freshman, had its own chapter of SDS, whose leaders included some of the brightest students on campus. I remember their earnestness, and their patience, as Lee Frizzell and his friends tried to explain to the rest of us that the United States was on the wrong side of history—that the North Vietnamese and the Viet Cong, the people the president had defined as our enemies, were not the surrogates of the Soviet Union—and certainly not of Vietnam's ancient enemy, China. They were fighting to free their nation from invaders, just as they had been forced to do for centuries, and they would keep on fighting until they finally outlasted us all.

The following year, I would write a story about SDS for the Vanderbilt student newspaper, giving wider voice to these ideas which seemed to me to be so compelling. But in the beginning I mostly listened, bewildered that Lyndon Johnson, a man I had supported for reelection because of his support for civil rights, might be so wrong about a faraway war.

At the time, of course, most people disagreed with the antiwar critique. Most Americans supported the president, and some of the campus teach-ins that spring were exercises in favor of his policy. Professors from prestigious universities spoke out in the media, eager to challenge assumptions that most academics were opposed to the war.

"These fellows make an awful racket, a lot of noise," said David Rowe, professor of political science at Yale University, speaking of his antiwar colleagues. "But they are in an absolute, unmitigated minority." In the same article in the *New York Times*, Ernest Griffiths, dean of the School of International Service at American University, said a petition calling for U.S. withdrawal from Vietnam was circulated on his campus, "but less than one fifth of the 250 faculty members subscribed to it."

Still, opposition to the war was growing. In April, SDS called for an antiwar march in Washington. The call was supported by SNCC, whose young civil rights activists had become deeply cynical about Lyndon Johnson after the Democratic Convention in Atlantic City. Organizers hoped for a turnout of as many as a few hundred people. On April 17, they were amazed. Crowd estimates ran as high as 25,000, and the *New York Times*, which used a lower number, described the demonstration this way:

> *More than 15,000* students and a number of their elders picketed the White House in the spring sunshine today, calling for an end to the fighting in Vietnam. Walking three or four abreast in orderly rows and carrying printed white signs, the students clogged the sidewalk. The principal occupant of the White House was at his ranch in Texas. In early afternoon, the marchers paraded to the Sylvan Theater, on the grounds of the Washington Monument, for a series of speeches. Then they walked down the Mall to the Capitol, bearing a petition for Congress . . .
>
> Many marchers appeared to be newcomers to the "peace movement," and some had only a hazy idea of how they might go about ending the fighting. Sundy Smith, a 19-year-old student at Michigan State University, was dressed in a fashionable maroon-and-black suit, and she carried a sign reading, "War on Poverty, Not War on People." Miss Smith, who said she had never before participated in a public demonstration, said "I feel the President responds to public opinion—look what he did on civil rights—and I want him to know that public opinion is behind him if he sees the possibility for negotiations."

The march in Washington was followed by the largest demonstration of the spring, a teach-in on the Berkeley campus. On May 21, an all-star cast of dissident speakers gathered for the thirty-six hour event. Phil Ochs was there, the folksinger-activist whose anthem of empathy, "There But for Fortune," had been recorded beautifully by Joan Baez; and there was Benjamin Spock, a pediatrician and author, whose *Baby and Child Care* was one of the bestselling books of all time. Spock was beginning to use his renown in support of the emerging antiwar movement, as were Yale's radical historian Staughton Lynd, a veteran of Freedom Summer in Mississippi, and the author Norman Mailer, who would soon write an entire book about a single act of antiwar protest. At Berkeley, before crowds that may have reached 30,000, they joined former Free Speech Movement spokesman Mario Savio, civil rights leader Bob Moses, and journalist I. F. Stone, who offered this summary of their mission: "The polls show that, while the majority is prepared to support Johnson wherever he leads—in the sheeplike way that human herds always move toward war—the educated minority question his course. Our job is, by the widening of debate, to increase their number."

This was the article of faith when the teach-ins began—that a national dialogue would matter, that if people only knew the history and the facts they could make their voices heard, and Lyndon Johnson might listen to reason. Johnson, however, had no patience with these pseudo-academic exercises, which he suspected were traitorous at their core. "At the President's request," wrote historian Marilyn Young, "the FBI ran name checks on anyone signing antiwar telegrams or letters and briefed congressmen on the probable Communist source of demonstrations. Johnson was insistent that Communist governments were financing the growing protest movement. When CIA director Richard Helms failed to come up with any proof, Johnson was furious."

In *Lyndon: An Oral Biography*, reporter Merle Miller described what happened next: "Johnson shook that gigantic finger in Helms's face and said, 'I simply don't understand why it is that you can't find out about that foreign money.'"

By the summer of 1965 it was clear. Johnson had no interest in a national dialogue—no interest in debating the backstory of Vietnam, or the promise of catastrophe it contained.

THIS WAS THE HISTORY the president dismissed:

On September 2, 1945, Ho Chi Minh stood before a half million people in Hanoi and proclaimed the independence of Vietnam. Carefully paraphrasing the words of Thomas Jefferson, he said:

> All men are created equal. The creator has given us certain inviolable Rights: the right to Life, the right to be Free, and the right to achieve Happiness. Do you hear me distinctly, fellow countrymen? These immortal words are taken from the Declaration of Independence of the United States of America in 1776. In a larger sense this means that: All the people on earth are born equal. All the people have the right to live, to be happy, to be free.

For Ho this glorious autumn day—this moment of hope—was something he had worked for all of his life, but he knew the struggle went back much further. Since the fifteenth century, the history of his country had been filled with martyrs and heroes who had fought against foreign invaders. For the past eighty years, the hated colonial power had been France, a long-time U.S. ally. At the end of World War I, Ho, then a twenty-eight-year-old revolutionary, reached out to President Woodrow Wilson in Versailles, asking for his support in Vietnam for the freedom he espoused in other places. Wilson was the man, after all, who had renounced imperialism as a cornerstone of U.S. foreign policy, and now spoke of World War I as a "war to end all wars." Surely a leader with such ideals could understand the yearning of the Vietnamese.

From Wilson, Ho received a chilly rebuff, and he turned his attention to the writings of Vladimir Lenin. Ho found new hope in those ideas. In a French translation of Lenin's "Thesis on National and Colonial Questions," he discovered in the turgid prose a call for nationalist revolutions in the colonial world, and a promise of help from the Soviet Union.

Ho became a Communist. He spent most of his early life in exile—in the Soviet Union, China, and various parts of Europe, dodging arrest, making plans, until finally in 1941 he was able to slip back into Vietnam. Meeting in a cave in Cao Bang Province on the Chinese border, Ho and his compatriots established the Viet Minh, a group of nationalist revolutionaries that included Communists, but other dissidents as well. In the complicated world of global politics, France by now had surrendered to Germany in the early months of World War II; a French puppet government now ruled Vietnam with

Germany's wartime ally, Japan. Famine ensued in northern Vietnam, but even in the midst of the terrible suffering Ho saw new possibilities for resistance.

In a call to the citizens of Vietnam, he wrote:

> The hour has struck! Raise aloft the insurrectionary banner and guide the people throughout the country to overthrow the Japanese and the French! The sacred call of the fatherland is resounding in your ears. . . . He who has money will contribute his money, he who has strength will contribute his strength, he who has talent will contribute his talent. I pledge to use all my modest abilities to follow you, and am ready for the last sacrifice.

In a brief biography entitled *Ho*, journalist David Halberstam, who won a Pulitzer Prize for his coverage of Vietnam, assessed the subject of his book this way:

> Ho Chi Minh was one of the extraordinary figures of this era—part Gandhi, part Lenin, all Vietnamese. He was, perhaps more than any other single man of the century, the living embodiment of his own people. . . . He was the gentle Vietnamese, humble, soft-spoken, always seen in the simplest garb, his dress making him barely distinguishable from the poorest peasant—a style that Westerners for many years mocked, laughing at the lack of trappings of power, of uniform, of style, until one day they woke up and realized that this very simplicity . . . this capacity to walk simply among his own people was basic to his success.

Actually, a few Americans did understand these qualities in Ho. During World War II, agents for the OSS (Office of Strategic Services), the forerunner of the CIA, developed an alliance with Ho in the fight against their common enemy, Japan. He helped them in their intelligence gathering and in their search for downed American flyers, and they made him an agent of the OSS. (Officially, he was Agent 19.) The OSS "thought he was 'an awfully sweet guy,'" wrote Marilyn Young, but it was a sweetness tied to a ferocity of purpose, a willingness to fight to the very last man to rid his country of foreign invaders.

As Ho later put it, in a warning to the enemies of Vietnam, "You can kill ten of our men for every one we kill of yours. But even at those odds, you will lose."

THE FRENCH LEARNED THAT lesson first. Soon after Ho's declaration of independence for Vietnam, French troops returned to Southeast Asia, supported logistically by their allies, including the United States. Ho appealed this time to President Harry Truman. In a long letter, he pointed out that the Viet Minh had joined the United States in the war against Japan, and he condemned French "aggression on a peace-loving people." He also urged the United Nations—with moral leadership from the United States—"to show that they mean to carry out in peace-time the principles for which they fought in wartime."

Truman did not reply.

The war that followed lasted eight years, ending with the startling French defeat in the Battle of Dien Bien Phu. When hostilities began in December, 1946, the United States offered uncomfortable support to its ally, France, understanding the anachronism of French colonial policy, but providing money nevertheless for the French war effort. On the ground in Vietnam, State Department officials warned their superiors in Washington that Ho Chi Minh was not only the most popular nationalist leader in Vietnam; he was the *only* leader most people in the country were willing to follow. Moreover, there was no evidence that Ho, though a Communist, took his marching orders from Moscow or intended to be an agent of Soviet expansion. On the contrary, he was still reaching out to the United States, still seeking aid and moral support. But the ambivalence of American policy ended with an edict from Secretary of State Dean Acheson, a hard-line Cold Warrior who saw in the Communist control of Eastern Europe a warning against a similar disaster in Southeast Asia. Ho was a "Commie," Acheson said. His nationalism was a secondary matter, and thus a facade; it simply did not matter.

As Marilyn Young noted, U.S. policy thus became a syllogism that would not change for the next thirty years:

> By definition, Communists could not be genuine nationalists; by definition, America supported genuine nationalism. Therefore, those people the United States supported were nationalists, the rest were Communist stooges.

Nevertheless, the struggle went on in Vietnam. At the Battle of Dien Bien Phu, which began on March 13, 1954, the French were determined to end an eight-year stalemate, a guerilla war in which casualties mounted on both sides. They fortified a village near the Laotian border with thirteen thousand troops, ten tanks, and six fighter-bombers, and dared the Vietnamese to attack. They hoped General Vo Nguyen Giap, the Vietnamese commander, could be enticed from a pattern of attack-and-retreat to fight the way armies fought in Europe. The way people fought in the civilized world.

Giap obliged, but on his own terms. For three months leading up to the battle, more than 200,000 peasants loyal to Ho Chi Minh began carving trails through a jungle landscape that the French had thought would be impassable. Women and men working side by side carried multiple tons of ammunition and supplies, as well as artillery pieces—many of them U.S. weapons captured by the Chinese Army during the Korean War and made available now to the Vietnamese.

When the battle began, the French were stunned by the strength of Giap's artillery barrage. As the Vietnamese army seized control of the highlands surrounding Dien Bien Phu, the French were trapped with mounting casualties. In the United States, there was growing concern about the impending Communist victory, and some of President Eisenhower's advisers, including Vice President Richard Nixon, urged intervention on behalf of the French. A few even lobbied for nuclear weapons—two or three tactical bombs, they said, ought to teach the Communists a lesson—but Eisenhower rejected that advice. On May 7, the French garrison surrendered. The United States urged the French to fight on in the rest of the country, but they were done.

In Geneva, the great nations gathered to consider the future of this faraway place. There were pundits and thinkers who wondered whether the Vietnamese—these colonial people—were ready for such an audacious thing as self-government. For long and bitter weeks, the nations wrangled—France, Great Britain, the Soviet Union, the People's Republic of China, the United States, Cambodia, Laos, and the two governments of a now divided Vietnam—Ho Chi Minh's Democratic Republic of Vietnam and the State of Vietnam, which had supported the French. Ho wanted full and immediate independence, but for the sake of peace he compromised. He knew his people were weary of war.

Under the Geneva Accords, supported by Ho and signed in July, the fighting would end and Vietnam would be divided temporarily, North and South, with free, internationally supervised elections two years later to achieve a final reunification. All the great powers signed except the United States, which found, instead, another surrogate to continue the struggle against Asian Communism.

Ngo Dinh Diem was a Vietnamese nationalist who disliked the French as well as Ho Chi Minh—the perfect choice to create a new government in South Vietnam. With U.S. backing, Diem immediately set about that task, and after consolidating his power, refused to participate in elections to reunify the country. The United States supported that decision, and again Vietnam—this gentle land where the people lived simply in the lush countryside, wishing mostly for the space and the peace to grow their own rice—drifted inexorably toward war.

The inconvenient truth for American policy was the growing unpopularity of Diem. "Cruel like the French," concluded one peasant, amid a wave of executions and torture in which the victims numbered in the tens of thousands. By 1960, Diem's opposition came together in the National Liberation Front (or National Front for the Liberation of Vietnam,or NLF), an umbrella group that Westerners called the Viet Cong. Many of its leaders were Communist, but there were also professionals, architects, teachers, and others who, though non-Communist, were allied comfortably with Ho Chi Minh. Their goal was an independent Vietnam, and as one non-Communist explained it later, "Of this movement, Ho Chi Minh was the spiritual father, in the South as well as the North, and we looked naturally to him and to his government for guidance and aid . . . And yet this struggle was also our own."

Having embraced Diem, the United States faced difficult choices. How far could it go in support of a man regarded by so many Vietnamese as the enemy?

John Kennedy, a devout anti-Communist, raised the American investment. He increased the number of U.S. advisers from 900 to 16,000, while deferring the decision that would have to be made—"all in or all out?" If Kennedy had lived would his cool pragmatism have prevailed? Would he have assessed the cost-benefit of a faraway war in defense of a deeply unpopular government? Or would he have marched to his own inaugural drum, willing to pay any price and bear any burden in defense of liberty as America understood it?

Those questions will remain unanswered. Kennedy was murdered, and about the same time so was Diem. When the dust settled after the coup, a new South Vietnamese strongman, General Nguyen Khanh, emerged from the rubble, ready to escalate the war.

Ho Chi Minh, meanwhile, still hoped for peace. In a fall 1963 letter to a Polish diplomat, Ho revealed, once again, a dogged faith in the rationality and good will of Americans:

> Neither you nor I know the Americans well, but what we do know of them, what we have read and heard about them, suggests that they are more practical and clear-sighted than other capitalist nations. They will not pour their resources into Vietnam endlessly. One day they will take pencil in hand and begin figuring. Once they really begin to analyze our ideas seriously, they will come to the conclusion that it is possible and even worthwhile to live in peace with us. Weariness, disappointment, the knowledge that they cannot achieve the goal which the French pursued to their own discredit will lead to a new sobriety, new feelings, and new emotions.

In this assessment, Ho Chi Minh was wrong. Even more than John Kennedy, his new adversary Lyndon Johnson saw only through a Cold War lens: *Losing a war to the Communists . . . Nothing could possibly be worse than that.* In 1965, having secured reelection as the candidate of peace, Johnson made the decision for war. In the next eight years, more than 58,000 Americans would die, and many, many more Vietnamese. If body counts were a measure of might, it was a war the United States should have won. But we did not. Ho and his followers simply would not quit, and young Americans were sent to fight in a bewildering land where they could never be sure who the enemy was. Indeed the enemy seemed to multiply like mushrooms in a shadowy place, and eventually the day would come when, despite all the bravery and sacrifice, it was necessary to stop. But that would be later, much later. For now, Lyndon Johnson had made up his mind.

29

Rebellion in California

Summer came and found the president immersed in the part of the job he loved. Not that he had disengaged from the war; far from it, but his massive political skills were absorbed in pushing important legislation through Congress. First of all, there were the Medicare and Medicaid bills, expanding health care for people in need. Medicare was essentially an amendment to Title 18 of the Social Security Act, to provide health insurance for all Americans over the age of sixty-five. The measure faced stern opposition from the American Medical Association (AMA) and from many Republican leaders. Rising political star Ronald Reagan warned that Medicare was "a foot in the door of a government takeover of *all* medicine."

Medicaid was even more controversial. The measure pending before the Congress added Title 19 to the Social Security Act, under which matching funds would be offered to states to provide health coverage for the poor. When the two amendments passed together on July 30, the president signed them immediately, for this was government as he understood it—a force to improve the lives of citizens in measurable and concrete ways. Together, Medicare and Medicaid became a cornerstone of his Great Society, a vision rooted in Roosevelt's New Deal, extended now to become the heart of Johnson's own legacy.

There were other measures in the president's flurry of new legislation—federal aid to education, including Head Start for low-income preschoolers, and an immigration bill that carried the seeds of future controversy. The latter, championed by Senator Edward Kennedy, abolished a quota system that had limited immigration from Asia, Africa, and the Middle East, thus giving preference to white Europeans. Senator Sam Ervin, a segregationist from North Carolina, argued unapologetically for the old ways. "With all due respect to the people of Ethiopia," he said, picking a random African country, "I don't know of any contributions that Ethiopians have made to the making of America."

Lyndon Johnson dismissed such fears. When he signed the act in a ceremony held at the Statue of Liberty, he insisted it was "not a revolutionary bill . . . It does not affect the lives of millions." In that regard, the president was wrong. Almost immediately, once the quotas were gone, the number of Asian immigrants increased, and as others followed from disparate parts of the world, the complexion of the country quite literally changed. Steadily, inevitably, and within a generation, America became less white.

Johnson, however, had more immediate questions on his mind, especially when it came to the issue of race. In the summer of 1965, his voting rights bill was also approaching a vote in Congress, having received an unexpected boost from somber events taking place in Alabama. In early May, Collie Leroy Wilkins, the accused killer of Viola Liuzzo, went on trial in the town of Hayneville. The case against him was open and shut, many people would have said, for FBI informer Gary Thomas Rowe was in the car with him when Wilkins aimed his pistol at Mrs. Liuzzo during a high-speed chase between Montgomery and Selma. Rowe was a credible witness when the case came to trial, a stocky, red-haired man, neatly dressed in a dark blue suit, and he seemed proud of his work with the FBI. He testified that he had been with a group of Klansmen on the day of the Selma to Montgomery march. They had been inspired, Rowe said, by a chance encounter with the man who killed the Reverend James Reeb, another of Selma's martyrs.

"God bless you men," Reeb's killer told Rowe and the others. "You do your job—I've already done mine."

Arrests came quickly in the wake of Mrs. Liuzzo's death, and it was clear to many who attended the trial that Alabama solicitor Arthur Gamble prosecuted the case conscientiously. On the day of the verdict, the *New York Times* offered this account: "The square-jawed solicitor, drawing himself up to his full 6-feet-3 inches, urged the jury in a slow, commanding voice: 'Don't put the stamp of approval on chaos, confusion and anarchy.'" It was perhaps a measure of Gamble's effectiveness that the all-white jury in one of the most segregated towns in Alabama voted 10–2 to convict. But conviction, of course, required a unanimous vote, and with a hung jury Collie Leroy Wilkins went free.

In Washington, President Johnson saw opportunity in that dismal result—further proof that a Voting Rights bill was needed. "The vote," Johnson said, "is the most powerful instrument ever devised by man for breaking down the walls of injustice."

As historian David Carter has noted, this was a time when Johnson was thinking beyond any single piece of legislation, formulating in his mind a new and broader definition of equality. On June 4, at a commencement speech at Howard University, Johnson presented his evolving thoughts. The address was one of Johnson's most far-reaching, drafted by speechwriter Richard Goodwin, though the ideas it contained were the president's own. Johnson paused and gazed across the upturned faces at the predominantly African American university as he declared that the nation's goal must be for every citizen

> . . . to be treated in every part of our national life as a person equal in dignity and promise to all others. You do not wipe away the scars of centuries by saying: Now you are free to go where you want and do as you desire and choose the leaders you please. You do not take a person who, for years has been hobbled by chains and liberate him, bring him to the starting line of a race and then say you are free to compete with all the others, and still . . . believe that you have been completely fair. Thus it is not enough just to open the gates of opportunity. All our citizens must have the ability to walk through those gates. This is the next and the more profound stage of the battle for civil rights. We seek not just freedom but opportunity. We seek not just legal equity but human ability, not just equality as a right and a theory but equality as a fact and as a result. . . .
>
> The great majority of Negro Americans—the poor, the unemployed, the uprooted and the dispossessed . . . are still another nation. For them the walls are rising and the gulf is widening.

In *The Music Has Gone Out of the Movement,* David Carter argued that with this speech Johnson pushed the civil rights issue to a new and more complicated place—more realistic, perhaps, in its assessment of the problems that still lay ahead, but more controversial as well. This was, in effect, a merger of civil rights and the Great Society, two ideas which Johnson had pursued with equal fervor. Now he was saying that poverty and racial inequality were connected, and the barriers to freedom and fairness in America were more fundamental than legal discrimination in the South. As many black leaders had been saying for years, racism was a *national* problem far more vexing than the morality plays taking place in Alabama or Mississippi.

For many white Americans, these were troubling ideas, for if whites in the North believed this president with a Southern accent, then they, too, would be affected by the issue of race. Northern whites might share in Johnson's satisfaction when, on August 4, Congress passed the Voting Rights Act, sending federal registrars to the South to make sure all Americans could vote. That was only fair in a place where bigotry had been a matter of law. But what did Johnson want to do next? What did he mean when he spoke of "results" and not merely "opportunity" as a measure of America's racial progress? In his metaphor about "the starting line of a race," did he want to give blacks some kind of head start?

For many whites, this had the ring of presidential favoritism—a whole new policy of "affirmative action," favoring one race over another. Was that what Johnson intended? And now that he had raised the subject, what did black people want, anyway?

As the debate began rippling through American life, quietly at first, the moment came quickly when it was not a theoretical question.

ON AUGUST 11, IN a part of Los Angeles known as Watts, a traffic arrest in the early evening escalated into a roadside argument, then to pushing and shoving between police and African Americans, and soon to a full-scale riot that lasted six days and left thirty-four people dead. It began simply enough. Marquette Frye, a twenty-one-year-old black man driving his mother's 1955 Buick, was stopped by a highway patrolman for driving erratically. Frye failed a field sobriety test, and his brother, Ronald, who was a passenger in the car, walked to their house, which was not far away, and returned with their mother, Rena Price. Accounts differ about what happened next, but according to one newspaper report a crowd of about two dozen people gathered while Price began to berate her son, who in turn blamed the incident on police. The crowd grew, more police arrived on the scene, and by 10 p.m. the rock throwing began. The violence escalated quickly into the looting of stores, and police cordoned off a twenty-square-block area in what some officials were calling the worst racial violence Los Angeles had ever seen.

"Officials were at a loss to explain the cause of the rioting, which started last night after a routine drunken driving arrest," reported the *New York Times*.

"The unusually hot, smoggy weather was doubtless a contributing factor. Many Negroes at the scene complained about alleged police brutality but few cited specific instances to support their charges."

One reporter less baffled by the unrest was Karl Fleming, the Los Angeles bureau chief of *Newsweek*. Fleming, who reveled in his role as a tough, hard-drinking chronicler of the news, had been in California for less than a year. At the age of thirty-seven, he was a veteran of the civil rights beat in his native South, having covered the desegregation of Ole Miss, the bombing of the Sixteenth Street Baptist Church in Birmingham, and the voting rights demonstrations in Selma. One of the first things he did when he began his new job in Los Angeles was to tour Watts. At first glance, he thought, it had the look of a pleasant neighborhood with single-family homes, neatly trimmed lawns, and a few scattered apartment buildings.

But outward appearances were deceiving. More than 450,000 African Americans lived in South Central Los Angeles, and Watts was the epicenter of an urban segregation favored by most of California's voters. In 1964, some 65 percent of the electorate had voted in support of Proposition 14 that overturned California's fair housing law and affirmed the "absolute discretion" of property owners to refuse to sell or rent to anybody they chose, including, of course, African Americans. Blacks were embittered by the slight, and their anger was fueled by high unemployment and poverty rates and by ongoing tension with the police. In his memoir, *Son of the Rough South*, Karl Fleming described his first encounter with the area:

> As a part of learning about my new beat, I got the sheriff's department public relations man to drive me around South Central and was stunned when he repeatedly said "nigger" as casually as any redneck counterpart in deepest Mississippi. When I visited the Seventy-Seventh police precinct station in the heart of Watts I saw a prominently displayed picture of Eleanor Roosevelt hanging on the wall with the inscription "nigger lover" beneath it. Billy clubs were laughingly known among LAPD cops as "nigger knockers." South Central's big public housing projects had large numbers painted on their separate building roofs—like prison camps I thought—for easy identification by police helicopters.

In the riot of 1965, Fleming was one of those who covered the story as the violence spread and grew more intense. Hundreds of businesses, especially those known to be white-owned, were looted and burned, and white motorists passing nearby were dragged from their cars and beaten. Gangs of shirtless black men roamed the streets, some laughing as they took what they wanted from the ravaged storefronts, others cursing and threatening any white person they saw.

"The fuck you doing down here, Whitey?" one young man yelled at Karl Fleming.

"I'm a reporter," Fleming replied.

"You gonna be a dead muthafuckin' reporter you don't get your honky ass out of here," the black man shouted. As Fleming remembered, "I retreated quickly toward the cops."

Some of the most vivid reporting on the violence came from Robert Richardson, who became, that week, the first black staff writer for the *Los Angeles Times*. Richardson had been a low-level *Times* employee, nursing dreams of becoming a reporter, when the editors plucked him out of the advertising department and sent him into the fray. It was a dangerous assignment for a light-skinned black man with reddish hair—someone who might pass for white—but Richardson's work was sufficiently fearless that he became a kind of urban legend at the newspaper, perhaps the first reporter from any publication to document cries of "Get Whitey!" and "Burn, baby, burn!"

As Richardson and Fleming understood, however, the racial fury cut both ways. Fleming witnessed one policeman screaming at an old black man, "You goddamn niggers gave up all your rights this week. One fucking move and I'll kill you." There was no doubt that the officer meant it. Police, sheriff's deputies, and eventually some 10,000 National Guardsmen stormed the neighborhood, their military convoys led by Jeeps mounted with machine guns. Of the thirty-four who died that week, thirty-one were killed by law enforcement.

By official estimates, more than 30,000 participated in the riots; there were 1,032 injuries and 3,438 arrests. Property damage totaled $40 million ($310 million in 2018 values).

WHEN THE WATTS REBELLION began, Martin Luther King was on his way to Puerto Rico to deliver a speech and hoping for a few days of rest. But he knew he had to go to Watts. He waited until the violence subsided, then flew to California to do what he could to help heal the wounds. He met with California Governor Edmund "Pat" Brown, whom he found to be a reasonable man, and with Otis Chandler, publisher of the *Los Angeles Times*. Both meetings were cordial enough, but King was amazed later in the day by a three-hour session with Los Angeles Mayor Sam Yorty and Police Chief William Parker. In comments to reporters during the violence, Parker had compared the rioters to "monkeys in a zoo," and he later told the *New York Times*: "When you keep telling people they are unfairly treated, and teach them disrespect for the law, you must expect this kind of thing. . . ."

In the meeting with Yorty and Parker, the police chief bristled when King urged the creation of a civilian review board to consider complaints of police brutality. In Los Angeles, Parker insisted with evident scorn, racism was simply not a problem—and certainly not with the members of his police force. King left the meeting convinced that Parker's bigotry was a match for Bull Connor's in Birmingham, or that of any other Southern sheriff he had known.

But as King biographer David Garrow explained in his Pulitzer-winning book, *Bearing the Cross,* the most important moment on the trip was King's first visit to Watts. The devastation alone was almost more than he could process—wrecked cars still littering the streets, entire city blocks reduced to smoldering rubble. The epiphany came when King addressed a crowd of a few hundred people at the Westminster Community Center in Watts. He was jeered by some. One young man shouted, "Hell, we don't want no damn dreams. We want jobs." That evening, King brooded over what he had seen with civil rights strategists Bayard Rustin and Bernard Lee, who had made the trip to California with him. Garrow wrote:

> King expressed to Rustin and Lee how his visit to Watts had brought home to him more than ever the material and spiritual desolation that shattered the lives of millions of black citizens trapped in America's ghettos. Rustin had been telling King for nearly two years that the most serious issues facing the movement were economic problems of class rather than race, but on this evening Rustin sensed that the day's experiences convinced King of the truth of that analysis. "That struck Martin very, very deeply," Rustin explained. "I think it was the first time he really understood."

As King took stock of how far they had come, he realized that the movement's first two goals had been achieved. Together, they had overturned the laws of segregation, and they had ended the disenfranchisement of blacks in the South. It might take some time to fully implement the Voting Rights Act, but they were on their way. The same month as Watts, with the arrival of federal registrars in Alabama, Mississippi, and Louisiana, more than four thousand African Americans had registered to vote in a three-day period. Now, however, the movement faced a more difficult challenge—confronting poverty and despair in black communities outside the South. King was not yet certain what it would take, though it would clearly require some affirmative effort going far beyond the current "War on Poverty"—some basic shift in the nation's priorities, and the pressure to make it happen would have to come from every part of the country. His mind aswirl, King began to consider how he might carry nonviolence to the cities of the North. He knew it would not be easy.

At the same time King worried about a backlash, a fear he knew was growing nationwide as many white Americans took stock as well. There was suddenly a pattern of long hot summers, the riots in Harlem in 1964, and then the deadly upheaval in Watts, followed immediately by looting and burning in Chicago. There, "the straw that broke the camel's back," as one African American put it, was what appeared to be a fluke accident in the Garfield Park neighborhood. On July 12, a fire truck veered out of control and hit a street sign, which fell on and killed a young black woman. The problem was that the black residents of Garfield Park had come to dislike the all-white fire department because of a pattern of disrespectful service.

Only two years earlier, the neighborhood itself had been white. But in 1963 a black family moved in and whites moved out—a massive demographic shift that African Americans regarded as racist. By 1965, there were no whites left in Garfield Park. The riot that began on July 12 lasted three days, until the National Guard moved in to stop it. But bitterness lingered—on both sides of the racial divide.

White fear and black rage were becoming a toxic combination in America. Martin Luther King hoped against hope that the country could find a way to make it through.

30

Grapes of Wrath

Late that summer in another part of California, a union organizer named Cesar Chavez was beginning to develop a King-like reputation. Perhaps not yet in the nation at large, but certainly among Mexican Americans. Chavez had embarked on a quixotic quest, doomed to failure, many people said, to organize migrant farm workers in California. Most of them, by the 1960s, were Mexican, Filipino, or members of other minority groups, and Chavez knew their world very well. It had been his world since he was twelve, and his family, having lost its Arizona farm to foreclosure, moved to California seeking work in the fields.

The year was 1939, the same year John Steinbeck's novel, *The Grapes of Wrath*, reached number one on the bestseller lists. Steinbeck, a former journalist, wrote of the Dust Bowl refugees, dirt farmers driven from their homes by drought in Oklahoma, desperately seeking work in California. His book was one of two bestsellers that year describing life in the migrant labor camps. The other, *Factories in the Field*, was by journalist Carey McWilliams and recounted the history of California agriculture from the Gold Rush to the Great Depression. During that ninety-year span, the color of the faces in the fields might change—American Indians replaced in succession by Chinese, Japanese, Mexican, Filipino, and white—but the conditions under which they worked did not. As Steinbeck and McWilliams made clear, there was a steady loss of something fundamental as the love of the land gave way to simple greed and farms became agricultural factories where the goal of the owners was to hold down costs, no matter the price in human pain.

For a time in the 1930s, the migrants fought back, organizing to demand better wages and safer, more sanitary places to work. The response was a mixture of official repression and vigilante violence, and by the time the Chavez family arrived the resistance had virtually collapsed.

The family spent the winter in a tent in the town of Oxnard north of Los Angeles. In Arizona, the Chavez family owned its own subsistence farm. Though indisputably poor, they never went hungry, and Cesar and his brother played together in the semi-desert, safe in a world of extended family. But in California everything was different, not only the damp, inescapable chill of winter, but a cold emotional landscape as well. As Miriam Pawel wrote in her heralded biography, *The Crusades of Cesar Chavez*:

> The physical hardships left fewer scars than the emotional burden of adjusting to an alien, often hostile world. Where they once roamed the Gila Valley, knowing everyone they met, Cesar and Richard now found themselves in a land of fences, locked doors, and strangers. . . .
>
> For the first time, they experienced pervasive discrimination and prejudice. Decades later, they remembered the insults: the teacher who scolded children for not lining up straight by saying, "You remind me of the Mexican army"; the stores that refused to serve ethnic Mexicans; the segregated seating in restaurants and movie theaters that nurtured a life-long instinct to check where they sat; the rural towns controlled by white growers, bankers, and lawyers, each town divided by the railroad tracks—Mexicans on one side, Anglos on the other.

For a time, Cesar joined other members of his family in the fields, picking grapes, cotton, cauliflower, and cabbage, whatever the season called for. In 1946 he joined the Navy, and after he served his two-year enlistment, he returned to California and soon to the fields with his brother Richard, first picking apricots, then hauling lumber. He married Helen Fabela, a young Mexican American who worked in agricultural packing sheds earning seventy cents an hour. They began to raise a family.

For Cesar, who like so many others felt trapped in meaningless, dead-end jobs, everything changed on the night of June 9, 1952. He met Fred Ross, a community organizer who had come to California to work with the poorest of the poor. Cesar had heard of this gringo who held meetings in Sal Si Puedes, a barrio on the eastern side of San Jose, where Cesar, Helen, and their four children lived. He was skeptical at first, wondering what Ross was really up to, but Chavez discovered in Ross a kind of realistic hope that he had never encountered. Ross was a disciple of Saul Alinsky, a community activist from Chicago who believed that poor people knew what they needed and with the help of a professional organizer—a person who understood the levers of power—had the ability to change their own lives. Alinsky, by then the executive director of the nonprofit Industrial Areas Foundation (IAF), had successfully organized the meatpacking district in Chicago that Upton Sinclair wrote about in his muckraking masterpiece, *The Jungle*. In the 1950s, Alinsky had turned his attention to the Mexican American communities in California, and when Chavez went to work for Ross's Community Service Organization, the IAF paid his salary.

In his scattergun assault on the problems of his people, from voter registration to police brutality, Chavez developed a handful of friendships that he would rely on for most of his life. In addition to Ross, there was Father Donald McDonnell, an activist priest whose ministry was the Mexican American community, and Bill Esher, a radical from New York who came to California and became the first editor of Chavez's newspaper, *El Malcriado*. Perhaps most important was Delores Huerta, a college-educated Californian who hated the oppression of workers in the fields.

Chavez's allies saw in him a relentless commitment and drive, measured in danger and constant travel and nights of three or four hours sleep, that they had never seen in anybody else. On May 28, 1962, Chavez signed one of his letters to Ross, *Viva La Causa*—words that became not only his slogan but the definition of his life. Helen Chavez, mother of eight, understood her husband's sacrifice—and her own—and willingly accepted the burden. Thus armed, Chavez worked and brooded and struggled and dreamed, and by the 1960s he thought he knew what the people needed most. Those who labored in the California fields, whose lives were unchanged from Steinbeck's portrayal in *The Grapes of Wrath*, needed a union to represent them against a three-billion dollar agribusiness industry that was the most powerful economic force in California.

The leaders of that vast enterprise were contemptuous at first of this unimposing little man, barely five-foot-six, with his deep, sad eyes, olive brown skin, and a shock of black hair that always seemed to fall toward his forehead. In 1965, when Chavez and cofounder Delores Huerta's brand new union, the National Farm Workers Association, with its mostly Mexican American membership, joined a strike of Filipino grape pickers in Delano, California, the growers' contempt took the form of harassment. As journalist Miriam Pawel wrote:

> They blasted music to drown out the pickets' chants, ran trucks to stir up dust clouds, and sprayed strikers with the sulfur used to fertilize the fields. . . . Cars were forced off the road. Fights broke out. Growers unleashed dogs, hired armed guards, and used physical and verbal threats, trying to provoke a violent response from the strikers. Chavez insisted that pickets resist the temptation to fight back. . . . Whether nonviolence was a core belief, a tactic, or both, Chavez used the doctrine to great advantage.

Chavez had learned from the civil rights movement in the South, the melodrama created for the country when Bull Connor's fire hoses and dogs were loosed on the ranks of peaceful demonstrators. Like Martin Luther King, Chavez understood the power of the media and was savvy enough to use it. When the local sheriff announced that he would arrest people for shouting *Huelga!,* the Spanish word for "strike," on the grounds that they were disturbing the peace, Chavez asked Helen, his wife, to lead a group of women to the picket lines, where they would shout the forbidden word and subject themselves to arrest. He timed the protest to coincide with a speech he was giving on the campus of Berkeley—at Sproul Plaza where the Free Speech Movement had made its mark.

The media covered both the speech and the arrests, and slowly but surely the word began to spread beyond California. In December, the AFL-CIO, the umbrella organization for labor unions nationwide, endorsed the farm workers' strike. Walter Reuther, perhaps the nation's most powerful labor leader, called working conditions in the fields of California "the one remaining blot on American democracy in an economy of abundance."

By the end of the year an idea emerged that further assured a national audience for Cesar Chavez and his crusade. The Reverend Jim Drake, a new staff member at California's Migrant Ministry, a Protestant group whose director Chris Hartmire was a steadfast supporter of Chavez, suggested a national consumer boycott of grapes as a way of supporting the field workers' strike. Civil rights activists, especially West Coast leaders of SNCC, began to publicize the boycott, making the connection between their movement and *La Causa.* As Hartmire wrote in a letter to supporters,

> There is no relevant middle ground on a moral issue that is as clear as the farm workers' fight for opportunity and self-respect . . . The issue of human worth is as central in Delano as it was in Selma.

Victory would be a long time coming, but the battle was joined, and in a season of rising discontent, the nation discovered a nonviolent hero to take his place beside Dr. King. As events in California made clear, the issue of racial justice in America was no longer merely Southern, no longer as simple as it may have once seemed, no longer black and white. For many of us coming of age on college campuses—places that were, in the biblical paraphrase of Mario Savio, "in the world, but not of the world"—all of these things, plus the War in Vietnam, made it harder to remain indifferent.

31

The Sounds of Music

On October 1, as the fighting continued in Vietnam, and the protest against it gained momentum at home, a folk-rock band known as the Byrds released a new single. We knew the group had already had a number one hit with the Bob Dylan song, "Mr. Tambourine Man," and now they returned to the great well of folk writers with Pete Seeger's "Turn, Turn, Turn." Seeger admitted he was proud of the song. After all, he said with trademark wry humor, "I did write six words." The rest consisted of quotes, or minor paraphrases for the sake of meter, from Ecclesiastes, regarded by many as one of the most curious and enigmatic parts of the Bible. At once an ode to the virtue of wisdom, these verses attributed to Solomon, the sexually promiscuous son of King David, also acknowledge a kind of ultimate futility: *All streams flow into the sea, yet the sea is never full . . .* The great American novelist, Thomas Wolfe, once called the poetry of Ecclesiastes perhaps the finest piece of writing in history:

> "Of all I have ever seen or learned, that book seems to me the noblest, the wisest, and the most powerful expression of man's life upon this earth—and also the highest flower of poetry, eloquence, and truth. I am not given to dogmatic judgments in the matter of literary creation, but if I had to make one I could say that Ecclesiastes is the greatest single piece of writing I have ever known, and the wisdom expressed in it the most lasting and profound.

Pete Seeger, too, was drawn to the text, especially the notion that in the unpredictable unfolding of life everything has its season. In the words of Ecclesiastes 3:1–8:

> To every thing there is a season, and a time to every purpose under the heaven:
>
> A time to be born, and a time to die; a time to plant, and a time to pluck up that which is planted;
>
> A time to kill, and a time to heal; a time to break down, and a time to build up;
>
> A time to weep, and a time to laugh; a time to mourn, and a time to dance;
>
> A time to cast away stones, and a time to gather stones together; a time to embrace, and a time to refrain from embracing;
>
> A time to get, and a time to lose; a time to keep, and a time to cast away;
>
> A time to rend, and a time to sew; a time to keep silence, and a time to speak;
>
> A time to love, and a time to hate; a time of war, and a time of peace.

To the final verse, Seeger added his own affirmation, the six original words for which he claimed wry credit: "I swear it's not too late." With this line he became more intentional, perhaps more idealistic, than the Old Testament writer, transforming the Biblical fatalism into a deliberate cry for peace, despite the odds and the indifference of history.

The song was a favorite of Roger McGuinn, the gifted lead singer and guitarist for the Byrds. As a veteran of the Chicago folk music scene, McGuinn had admired earlier versions (recorded under the title "There Is a Season") by artists that included the Limeliters and Judy Collins. By that time, McGuinn was also listening to the Beatles and incorporating into folk music the unmistakable sound of British rock 'n' roll. For the Byrds' rendition of "Turn, Turn, Turn," he played a 12-string Rickenbacker guitar (the Beatles' John Lennon played a Rickenbacker, too), and the song became a folk-rock anthem, a gentle and melodic plea for peace in a country descending rapidly into war.

Other forms of protests were becoming more strident. There were national demonstrations October 15–17, and Attorney General Nicholas Katzenbach threatened legal action against the dissidents. "There are some Communists involved in it," Katzenbach maintained. "We may very well have to prosecute." In response, more than a hundred clergy from across the country, led by Rabbi Abraham Heschel and Jesuit priest Daniel Berrigan, issued a sharp rebuttal. "To characterize every act of protest as Communist-inspired," the clergy members declared, "is to subvert the very democracy which loyal Americans seek to protect."

In the escalating debate, more than 25,000 people marched in New York

City in favor of the war on October 30; on November 27 a slightly smaller crowd marched against it in Washington. In between came a moment of horror. On November 2—election day in many states—Norman Morrison, a thirty-two-year-old pacifist, husband, and father of three, stood beneath the Pentagon window of Defense Secretary Robert McNamara, doused himself with kerosene, and lit a match. It was, of course, shockingly reminiscent of the self-immolation of Buddhist monk Thich Quang Duc two years earlier in Saigon. Morrison had read about the U.S. bombing of a South Vietnamese village in which small children were killed. He decided quite literally to share their fate. As the flames engulfed his body, Air Force Staff Sergeant Robert Bundt, who was leaving work at the Pentagon, rushed to try to smother the fire, sustaining burns of his own on his neck and his hands. But it was too late. Earlier that day, Morrison had asked his wife Anne, "What can we do that we haven't done?" He did not tell her what he was planning, which left the family, as Anne wrote later, "in a state of frozen grief."

Amid the mounting tumult, the Catholic Church reassigned Daniel Berrigan to Latin America in an effort to silence his antiwar protests, and in December the Catholic publications *Commonweal* and the *National Catholic Reporter* condemned the church's decision. Senator Robert Kennedy called for a Christmas truce, a modest proposal that nevertheless irritated Lyndon Johnson. And finally, in a year that was ending in a rush of headlines, three American activists, Tom Hayden, Staughton Lynd, and Herbert Aptheker flew to Hanoi to see for themselves the effects of the U.S. bombing raids.

As some of us wrestled with all of this, our views on the war, our response to the escalating protests against it, we did not wrestle with "Turn, Turn, Turn." We were drawn, comfortably and easily, to the harmonies of the Byrds and the lyrics by Pete Seeger and the ancient author of Ecclesiastes. We absorbed this, just as we had absorbed Seeger's other anthem, "If I Had a Hammer," recorded so movingly by Peter, Paul and Mary. We knew of Seeger's past membership in the American Communist Party, but listening to his music it was hard to imagine an artist more patriotic or full of good will.

The whole year had been punctuated by music set against a backdrop of war, some of it coming to us in the movies. There was a sweetness at first—the soaring voice of Julie Andrews and the flowered hillsides of the Austrian Alps—as *The Sound of Music* became the most popular film of the year, even if the critics had a field day with it. Bosley Crowther of the *New York Times* called it "saccharine pudding," and added:

> Except for Julie Andrews in the crucial role of the governess who reestablishes singing and happiness in the Von Trapp home, the cast is generally stiff and mawkish. In the case of Christopher Plummer, it is both. He is painfully posey and pompous as the handsome widower who succumbs to the governess' cheer and vivacity and finally breaks into wistful song himself.

I remember thinking some of the same things. I had always been a dubious consumer of musicals, too literal-minded to suspend disbelief when characters on the screen burst suddenly into song. At first, that was especially true of *The Sound of Music*, which told, at its core, the story of a family's frightening escape from the Nazis, as the world moved inexorably toward the bloodiest war in human history. Captain Georg Von Trapp was in life, as in the movie, the widowed father of seven who summoned a nun, Maria Kutschera, to work as a governess. They did, in fact, marry in 1927, and because Von Trapp opposed the Nazi agenda of Adolph Hitler, they fled from Austria, which had fallen under German control, to seek asylum in a safer part of the world. In real life, they traveled by train to Italy, rather than by foot across the mountains to Switzerland as in the movie. But the essence of the story was true.

In this final collaboration between composer Richard Rodgers and lyricist Oscar Hammerstein before Hammerstein died of cancer, the two artists embellished Maria Von Trapp's memoir, *The Story of the Trapp Family Singers*, with a collection of soon-to-be-classic songs. The voice of Julie Andrews made it work. The public overwhelmingly rejected the response of curmudgeons like Bosley Crowther and me, and so did the Oscars. The movie was nominated for ten Academy Awards, winning five, and it was clear that it was destined to become one of the most beloved films of all time.

In the March 12 issue of *Life*, for which Miss Andrews graced the cover, the magazine's editors put it this way: "Julie's radiance floods the screen, warms the heart and brings back the golden age of the Hollywood musical."

But in the same issue of *Life*, there were stories also about Vietnam, where U.S. combat troops had just arrived. As the weeks went by and similar articles became more numerous, the cultural reflections of our mood grew darker. With Stanley Kubrick's *Dr. Strangelove* nominated for four Academy Awards, we encountered again the power and the irony of the film's final scene—the actual footage of nuclear explosions with English songwriter Vera Lynn singing, "We'll Meet Again." It was a song of romance recorded in 1939, its poignancy magnified by the painful separations of World War II, and now by those of 1965.

Then in July, a gravelly-voiced singer named Barry McGuire recorded "Eve of Destruction," a bitter song of protest that offered little consolation or hope.

Think of all the hate there is in Red China
Then take a look around to Selma, Alabama
You may leave here for four days in space
But when you return it's the same old place
The pounding of drums, the pride and disgrace . . .
Ah, you don't believe
We're on the eve of destruction

The song, written by P. F. Sloan, made a quick climb up the *Billboard* charts, reaching number one by the end of September. "Turn, Turn, Turn," released a few days later, also made it to number one, providing at least a glimmer of redemption: *I swear it's not too late.*

Finally, in December there was *Dr. Zhivago*, another film about love and war in which music played a major role. The movie was based on the novel by Nobel Prize winner Boris Pasternak, who had to smuggle the manuscript out of Russia. Pasternak was sixty-seven when the novel was first published in Italian, and he told one colleague who expressed an interest in it, "You are hereby invited to watch me face the firing squad." He knew the book would be controversial, almost certain to be condemned by Soviet censors for its lack of sympathy with the Bolshevik revolution. Pasternak, like his protagonist Yuri Zhivago, a doctor and a poet, rejected the revolutionary article of faith that human history—perhaps even human nature—could be remade, reshaped to conform to the Communist Party's concept of justice.

> The remaking of life! Those who talk this way . . . have not once come to know life, not felt its spirit, its soul . . . Life is never a material, a substance. It you want to know, it is an uninterruptedly self-renewing, eternally self-working principle . . . infinitely grander than the obtuse theories held by you or me.

That was, perhaps, the fundamental moral of *Dr. Zhivago*, a warning against the hubris of power, regardless of its initial intent. But it was the humanity of the book, the epic story of love and loss, set against the turmoil of war, that caught the attention of director David Lean. He saw, as critic Angela Livingstone wrote, a "depiction of an important period of history reflected in individual lives." Lean was certain he could capture the heart of the story on film, and his timing could not have been better.

With a powerful cast of Omar Sharif, Julie Christie, and Rod Steiger, and with Academy Award-winning cinematography and music, this was a movie that made us think. Perhaps more than that it made us *feel.* It may have been set in an unfamiliar place, against the frozen backdrop of the Ural Mountains, but the epic love story—lives torn apart by the remorseless march of human history—touched a nerve in our time, too. Some critics did not like it. Bosley Crowther discerned a "passivity" in the leading characters. Others thought the film was too long; "sprawling," one scholar said. But every time I heard "Lara's Theme," the musical heart of the movie, I was caught in the sadness of lost possibilities—a feeling, many of us discovered, that would only grow stronger in the unfolding drama that we were living through.

32

A Nation at War

The new year dawned with Vietnam at center stage. For better or worse, this was Lyndon Johnson's war, with all its vast and varied implications both for our country and for the world.

The still-outnumbered opponents of his policy were certain the president had rejected numerous opportunities for peace. After the fall of Diem in 1963, the first government to emerge from the chaos, headed by General Duong Van Minh, supported American disengagement from the war. Van Minh and other members of his council promised to pursue a "government of reconciliation" in South Vietnam, open to "peaceful coexistence between Saigon and Hanoi." French President Charles de Gaulle offered his services to help make it happen. But the United States threw its support behind the more bellicose General Nguyen Khanh, who wanted to fight the Viet Cong and seemed open to advice about how to do it.

Soon after Khanh seized power, however, U.S. policy makers were dismayed to discover his government was at least as unpopular as Diem's. Johnson's response was more military support for Khanh. In 1964, United Nations Secretary General U Thant had called for direct negotiations between the U.S. and North Vietnam. Bringing the credibility of the United Nations to his efforts, Thant delivered a private message to Secretary of State Dean Rusk, letting him know that Hanoi was prepared to talk. The United States did not respond. In February 1965, Thant delivered a stinging rebuke.

> I am sure the great American people, if only they knew the true facts and background to the developments in South Viet-Nam, will agree with me that further bloodshed is unnecessary. And that the political and diplomatic methods of discussions and negotiations alone can create conditions which will enable

> the United States to withdraw gracefully from that part of the world. As you know, in times of war and of hostilities the first casualty is truth.

Within the U.S. government, at least one high-ranking official urged Johnson to pursue the path of "graceful" extrication. Undersecretary of State George Ball, a holdover from the Kennedy Administration, argued for a political solution for what was ultimately a political problem. Propping up an unpopular government with ever-increasing military support was a recipe for disaster, Ball said, and probably doomed to failure. And while it was true that negotiations were also an uncertain path, Ball pointed out that the possibility had not been explored. "We have given almost no attention," he noted in a State Department memo, "to the possible political means of finding a way out without further enlargement of the war." Ball was, in the words of historian Marilyn Young, a lone voice in "a wilderness of war makers."

Johnson made the decision to escalate. In the political shorthand of Washington, the president did not want to be accused of "losing" Southeast Asia, as Harry Truman had "lost" China, and Dwight Eisenhower had "lost" Cuba. Like most Americans of his generation, Johnson's views were shaped by World War II, when the United States, both mighty and righteous, had conquered the menace of Adolph Hitler. Now it was ready to fight once again, for in the Cold War communism had replaced fascism as the enemy of freedom all over the world.

That was the way Johnson saw it, and the idea that for tens of thousands of Vietnamese—communist and non-communist alike—the United States had become the enemy of *their* freedom was purely a fantasy of the left. In the president's mind, no patriotic American would make such a claim.

As the war raged on into 1966, there were continued overtures for peace. From North Vietnam, the newest feeler came during a visit to Hanoi by three American activists, Staughton Lynd, Tom Hayden, and Herbert Aptheker. Lynd was a history professor at Yale. As a pacifist, he had committed his energy to the civil rights movement, until a moment in Mississippi fused the war and the movement in his mind. In August 1964 at the funerals of James Chaney, Andrew Goodman and Michael Schwerner, SNCC organizer Bob Moses noted bitterly that their bodies were found on the day the president ordered the first bombing of North Vietnam. This was more than an irony, Moses said. It was also a lesson that "men simply have to stop killing."

For Lynd that simple declaration reinforced everything he knew in his heart. He had studied the writings of Henry David Thoreau, especially his dissent during the Mexican War, linking the injustice of that war, as Thoreau understood it, with the parallel evils of slavery and genocide. Lynd soon began quoting Thoreau in his speeches about Vietnam: "It is in jail that the fugitive slave, and the Mexican prisoner on parole, and the Indian come to plead the wrongs of his race, should find the honorable American."

Lynd assumed he and his traveling companions to North Vietnam might themselves wind up in jail. Under U.S. law, their trip was clearly illegal. But he thought it was a chance that they must take.

As he and Hayden later wrote in *The Other Side*, a published diary of their trip, Lynd had already begun taking risks, crossing the line into civil disobedience—a willful violation of the law to protest a war that he saw as immoral. He refused to pay taxes beyond those deducted by his employers at Yale, and he urged young men who shared his views to refuse to serve in an unjust war.

Lynd had also been friends and a fellow Quaker with the pacifist Norman Morrison, who had burned himself to death outside the Pentagon in 1965. For Lynd, Morrison's act was a terrible reminder of the stakes. He knew that U.S. bombers were using napalm as a part of their arsenal, a flammable liquid with a gelling agent that stuck to the skin, and women and children were among those killed by it. Morrison, he thought, had brought the spectacle home, and he and others had the responsibility to do the same—not necessarily by self-immolation, but in whatever other ways they could find.

When Lynd's fellow historian, Herbert Aptheker, a leading theoretician of the American Communist Party, was invited to travel to Hanoi, and to bring non-communists on the trip with him, Lynd was eager to go. He invited Tom Hayden, a founding member of SDS, who was then working as a community organizer in Newark.

In December, just before the three activists arrived in Hanoi, the United States declared a Christmas pause in its bombing campaign against North Vietnam. The bombing, as Johnson explained, was designed to pressure Hanoi into submission, by which he meant an unconditional acceptance of the pro-Western government in South Vietnam. In defending his policy to individual members of Congress, the president often used a coarse sexual imagery that left his some of his visitors dismayed. "I'm going up her leg an inch at a time," he told Senator George McGovern, who had worried that increased bombing would force Hanoi into an escalation of its own. "I'll get to the snatch before they know what's happening." He extended the metaphor with newspaper columnists Rowland Evans and Robert Novak, explaining that his graduated escalation was more like seduction than rape.

Johnson's other symbolism was "the carrot and the stick." Even as the bombs rained down on North Vietnam, he dangled the possibility of a billion-dollar foreign aid package as soon as the war was brought to an end.

"If Ho Chi Minh had been George Meany," mused former Johnson aide Bill Moyers, "Lyndon Johnson would have had a deal."

But Ho was not George Meany, the wily U.S. labor leader who headed the AFL-CIO. He was, instead, a revolutionary head of state who had been fighting for most of his life to free his country from foreign occupation. He no longer trusted American words and saw the Christmas bombing pause as insufficient proof that the U.S. intended to negotiate seriously. Nevertheless, his government sent its own peace feeler through the three American visitors, Lynd, Aptheker, and Hayden. Really, it was more a reaffirmation of North Vietnam's *desire* for peace and a negotiating position that included the withdrawal of U.S. forces.

In a meeting with Hayden, Lynd, and Aptheker, North Vietnamese Prime Minister Pham Van Dong told his visitors,

> If we understand each other more fully it is a good thing. Your visit marks a new step . . . The Vietnamese people feel they are fighting a just cause against barbarous aggression . . . It is not true that we do not desire peace. We desire it more than anybody. The war is happening in our country and killing our people. . . . But peace at what cost? We must have independence. We would rather die than be enslaved. . . . We know there are very complex questions, but . . . if the United States really wants peace everything complicated can be settled.

Upon their return to the United States, the three were not optimistic about peace talks, but they wanted at least to put a human face on a people and a country they called "The Other Side." Hayden and Lynd began working on a book with that title, and the two began making speeches. Describing their flight to Hanoi, Hayden reported:

> Below rolled miles of delicately manicured fields interrupted by areas of dense vegetation, a countryside developed with obvious care by generations of people. As we drove into Hanoi from the city's airport (too small for jets), the fields on both sides of the road were tended by people working actively in the huge paddies. If they were the quaking targets of the U.S. Air Force, it did not show in their appearance. In fact, if anyone was feeling an emotional shock it was ourselves as we entered this little world forbidden to Americans, so unknown to our people and so exposed to our military power.

The visitors did encounter the effects of U.S. bombs—a damaged factory, a school in ruins, a Buddhist pagoda that was hit. But they were continually surprised by the atmosphere of calm. And they discovered something else as well, something poignant, startling, maybe even macabre, depending on a person's point of view. North Vietnam had a new national hero to take his place beside Ho Chi Minh and all the other martyrs from the past. Everywhere Hayden and the others went, people paid homage to Norman Morrison, the American Quaker who burned himself to death as the ultimate gesture of solidarity in suffering.

There was a folk song about him, performed at public gatherings, the lyrics published in one of the country's largest newspapers, and a poster in a factory in Hanoi with an inscription that read: "The flames of Morrison will never die." A village chief in the rural countryside told Hayden and his friends: "We extend our thanks for your calling upon us, and we wish you to convey to the American people, especially laboring people, our best wishes, and also our best wishes to Mrs. Anne Morrison."

It seemed clear enough, as pro-war critics in America would claim, that the people of North Vietnam did take heart from the antiwar movement in the United States. It was, after all, a foreshadowing of peace.

CERTAINLY, IT WAS ALSO clear to Hayden and Lynd that they faced an uphill climb in their attempt to humanize the other side. All around them the anecdotal evidence reflected the polls: In early 1966, most Americans were in favor of the war. For some it was a case of tight, circular logic. They supported the war because the country was at war, and thus a patriot had no choice. Others applauded more explicitly the president's resolve to stop the spread of communism.

One indicator of the national mood occurred in Atlanta, where a young SNCC activist named Julian Bond faced opposition as he prepared to take his seat in the Georgia House of Representatives. He had been elected the previous year, one of eight black candidates in that state to reap the benefits of the Voting Rights Act. For the first time in more than half a century, the Georgia House was now a biracial body. But in the case of Bond there was a problem. He opposed the war in Vietnam.

Ironically, it was not a major preoccupation. Bond served as communications director for SNCC, and the civil rights group the previous week had issued a statement opposing both the war and the military draft. Bond said he supported SNCC's position, and as a pacifist himself he urged people who shared his views to seek another form of public service. A Georgia legislator called him a traitor.

"Anyone who gives aid and comfort to the enemies of the United States or the enemies of the State of Georgia is guilty of treason," declared Representative Jones Lane of Statesboro.

On the afternoon of January 10, Bond dutifully appeared before a hearing of his fellow legislators to consider whether he was too subversive to be in their midst. His manner took many by surprise. As one politician told the *New York Times*, he expected somebody "bearded and unkempt." Instead, here was Bond, only four days short of his twenty-sixth birthday and looking even younger with his boyish, clean-shaven face, his dark suit, gray vest, and a demeanor that was easy-going and calm. He was a college president's son, and even within the ranks of SNCC, he was always seen as a little different—his soft-spoken manner tempered by a wicked sense of humor, full of irony and irreverence. Once, at the organization's headquarters, a group of the activists began to muse, half-seriously, about what would happen if the racists could somehow reestablish slavery.

"Well," said Bond, deadpan, "if it does come back, I want to own Ray Charles."

I got to know him soon after that, not quite well enough to call him a friend, but we were cordial in our acquaintance. I had invited him to speak at Vanderbilt, where I was then a student, and perhaps to debate a prominent conservative.

"Sure," he said, "That sounds fine."

"Great," I replied. "We've invited William Buckley."

There was dead silence on the other end of the line.

"*Buckley*?" he finally asked, with what sounded like a mixture of incredulity and alarm. "You want me to debate William Buckley?"

"Sure," I said. "He's one of the great conservative minds of our time."

All of this was true. Buckley was the founding editor of *National Review*, a syndicated columnist, and one of the great debaters in the country. He had a gift for multi-syllable words and arched eyebrows that radiated a withering contempt.

"I'm not debating Buckley," Bond said.

"Aw, c'mon," I told him. "You have the truth on your side." And we both laughed.

In the end, despite this humanizing flash of insecurity, the debate did happen and Bond held his own. But that is getting ahead of the story.

On the night of January 10, after a contentious afternoon hearing, the Georgia House of Representatives voted 184 to 12 not to seat young Julian Bond. By refusing to condemn those who resisted the draft, Bond was guilty in the legislators' eyes of "giving aid and comfort to the enemy." Even his defenders were cautious. The *New York Times*, while suggesting that the legislature had gone too far, called Bond "a misguided young man . . . It is unfortunate that a man in whom his neighbors have placed such trust should advocate illegality, even by implication."

THE CRITICISM ESTABLISHED BOND as a martyr for civil rights and peace, a quiet hero of the American left. But the war went on. In the streets of Saigon and other cities, a Buddhist peace movement, backed by one of South Vietnam's most effective generals, held marches in the streets, demanding an elected, coalition government and the withdrawal of U.S. troops. But General William Westmoreland, the American commander, pursued his strategy of "search and destroy," which meant killing as many of the enemy as possible, thus winning a bloody war of attrition. The body counts were encouraging from Westmoreland's point of view, always greater losses for the Viet Cong than for the Americans, but the other side's resolve seemed never to waver. For the U.S. forces, whose numbers in 1966 stood at 385,000 and counting, it was often hard to tell who the enemy was. They were everywhere.

My friend John Slattery was a U.S. Marine in 1966. I didn't know him then, but later he shared his personal story of the war. It was not an easy story to tell, but Slattery knew it was not uncommon.

He was a drill sergeant's son, small and wiry, and he knew from the start he had to be tough. His father, after leaving the Marines, became a police officer in Boston—"an honest cop," in Slattery's words, who was fair and fearless as he walked the beat. "I never admired anybody more than my father," he said. "There was nobody with more integrity." But the younger Slattery, like many of his generation, also found inspiration in the life and grace of John F. Kennedy—a feeling that this handsome president who stirred such hope was "a symbol of what America could be. When they shot him, it was like a trap door opened under you and you started falling. I was going to Boston College when it happened. I figured, 'the hell with it,' and dropped out."

Slattery joined the Marines, following in his father's footsteps, determined if anything to outdo him. "When I shot expert on the firing range, I made sure he knew about it." He threw himself into basic training, crawling on his stomach under barbed wire while live bullets whistled just above him, laughing off a drill sergeant's sadism, feeling like he could "take on the world." When orders came to deploy to Japan, Slattery began a cross-country drive to California where he would catch a flight overseas. In South Dakota, his car skidded off the road in a blizzard and wound up deep in a snow bank. It was impossible even to see the highway, but he finally managed to find it again and hitched a ride into town on a snowplow. Later, he retrieved his car and kept heading west. Just one more adventure for a young Marine.

From San Francisco, he boarded a military transport and flew the Arctic route to Okinawa. Once there, he learned from a gunnery sergeant that despite his Japan orders he was headed instead for Vietnam. Slattery didn't mind. He was a Marine, and Marines went to war. He soon deployed to the U.S. airbase at Chu Lai, where in the summer of 1965, General Westmoreland had launched a major offensive on a Viet Cong stronghold north of the city. The attack was staggering in its firepower—jets, destroyers firing from just offshore, artillery pounding from the Chu Lai base, bombs, napalm, 6,000 Marines, and when it was over, by American count, 573 Viet Cong lay dead. Another 122 were captured, and the VC fighters were forced to retreat. Westmoreland claimed a major victory, and the Marines returned to their base at Chu Lai. The Viet Cong moved right back in.

That was the way it went in this war, so different from those the United States had won in the past, where strategic territory was critical. But the Marines at

Chu Lai did their jobs. Slattery's assignment in those first months was air traffic control, guiding in the Phantom jets in one of the busiest airports in the world.

Sometimes he would forge a few passes so he and his buddies could go to the villages nearby, places officially off limits to Marines. He was shocked by the poverty—shacks with dirt floors, walls made out of refuse including flattened Coke cans. But the people, he thought, were friendly and generous. Once at dinner with a Vietnamese family, he was treated as "a guest of honor. We sat together on the ground and they brought out a large fish." But he wondered what they did on other nights. Were some of these people, so gentle and kind, fighters for the Viet Cong? An American could never be sure.

Occasionally, he went out on patrol, and there was a night in 1966 that changed his life. The Viet Cong had been firing on planes near the end of the runway at Chu Lai. Slattery and two other Marines waited in ambush, while a larger patrol circled from another part of the base to drive the enemy in Slattery's direction. In the darkness, he said, "we saw the shapes of about five people coming toward us. We opened fire. They fired back. The shooting went on for about five minutes, which seemed like an hour, before it finally stopped. I knew I had hit somebody, and after everything was quiet I went out with my flashlight and shined it down."

He saw an enemy soldier lying dead in the sand, armed only with a bolt-action carbine. He had been shot once through the head.

When his flashlight beam fell on the face, Slattery suddenly felt sick to his stomach. "I threw up," he said. "I started crying. He looked like he was about twelve years old, like he had lain down on the sand and fallen asleep. He was probably only a few inches more than five feet tall. He looked like a child asleep. And that's the first thing I thought, that I'd killed a child."

By the time the other Marines came up, Slattery had pulled himself together. This was war, after all, and you had to move on. But two or three weeks later, he was sick. "I felt really terrible," he said. "I went over to the sick bay and collapsed. I woke up on a table and they were arguing over what I had. They sent me to a MASH unit, which got mortared while I was there, and I was feeling so bad I kind of hoped they would hit me. They flew me to Japan, where they told me I was not going back to Vietnam. They offered me a forty percent disability and a discharge. I turned it down. I saw people with no legs, people completely covered with bandages who had been hit by napalm—napalm dropped on our own troops."

After finally being diagnosed with ulcerative colitis, Slattery was reassigned to Okinawa. He was feeling better, working again as an air traffic controller, but he also began to drink heavily. He was spending time in the red light district, getting drunk every night, and once he punched a Military Policeman.

"He was giving me a hard time," said Slattery, "and I wanted to hit somebody."

Over the years, his demons grew worse. "Nothing mattered," he said. "I was acting that way more than thinking that way. You tamp feelings down. I don't think it's a conscious thing." After leaving the Marines, he got a "lousy job" and as his downward spiral continued, he began to steal from the store where he worked, giving away what he stole. "Like Robin Hood," he said. He also began to do drugs, especially mescaline and other hallucinogens, and finally, after years of trying to hold back the guilt, doing whatever he could to escape it, Slattery had a psychotic break. He went into his bathroom one night and turned on the faucet, which began to speak: "The faucet told me it was on my side, but there were others who were against me. The next thing I remember, I was in the living room sitting on my couch." Slattery said he saw before him a row of monsters, Dracula, Frankenstein and others, seated like a panel of judges. "I was on trial," he said. There was a lawyer who was assigned to defend him, and Slattery knew the face very well. It was the boy he had killed in Vietnam.

It was a long road from that moment to the life John Slattery finally built for himself—as a teacher of English as a second language, working for a while in Saudi Arabia, and later at a community college in Santa Fe. He spent some time in a mental hospital, but went AWOL because he didn't trust the doctors. He was still terrified, feeling as though he was "an inch away from being crazy." He turned to literature and philosophy, the poetry of Yeats among other readings, and slowly but surely he convinced himself that his mind was going to come back strong. In the end it was philosophy more than psychiatry that saved him—a belief developed over time, through all the pain he had inflicted and known—that all of us ultimately are connected, every human being, every piece of creation.

"I believe," he explained, "that the universe is an infinite web, and that the slightest movement on any strand of that web affects it all. If you kill and survive, unless you are a sociopath, you also are grievously, often mortally, wounded, although it can be a slow death. The guilt of taking another's life consumes you, and makes your life a hell you can try to lessen temporarily, through drugs and alcohol. But for many, suicide presents itself as the only real escape.

"Yet the irony is that the hell you are in can also be your salvation. If you can come to understand that what you're going through reveals how all of us are a part of one another, that it so clearly shows that when we hurt others, we hurt ourselves as well, and that when we help others, we are also helped, then you can begin your redemption by atonement. Nothing can undo what you did, but you can make amends by kindness to others, by caring for the unfortunate, by loving even the unlovable. . . .

"There is salvation, redemption, in the knowledge that by living, we can—actually, we must—change both time and space, that our presence here is not meaningless, that we can be a force for what is good and what is true."

John Slattery's friends have come to understand that this is the witness he bears every day to a truth with its roots in Vietnam.

OTHERS TOLD A DIFFERENT story, young Americans who came home proud, confirmed in a sense of patriotic duty, and the valor of the soldiers with whom they served. Major Jim Bowman was one of those. He was a Cherokee Indian who became a Special Forces commander, leading his men on midnight missions, when the moon was new or hidden by clouds. They traveled in silence through the bamboo forests, scrambling along ridge tops steeper than those in his native Smoky Mountains. As Bowman explained, they were grimly prepared for the kind of bloody, hand-to-hand combat that sometimes haunted his dreams at night.

Some in his unit were Montagnards, a tribal people from the central highlands, who could live for days on sumac roots and sometimes drank the blood of a tiger. Together they would search out the Viet Cong, slipping into their huts or trenches, doing most of their killing with knives, because it was quieter. Later, Bowman said, he would think about the Cherokee fighters of his Indian past as he tried to put the ugliness out of his mind—the stifled screams, the terror on the faces of those being killed. These were brutal missions he led, but this was the duty for which he was trained. He came home knowing he had done his best.

There were some, however, no matter how brave, for whom the war took a lasting toll. Slowly at first, then later in a torrent, we began to hear their voices of dissent. One soldier wrote to his hometown newspaper, the *Akron Beacon-Journal*, describing the horrors of things he had seen. One day, he said, on a sweep through a village, a fellow GI had tossed a grenade into what he assumed was an empty hut. Just as the GI pulled the pin, "an old man started jabbering and running toward my buddy." Before the explosion they heard a baby crying, but it was too late. A mother and two children died in the blast.

"We looked at each other and burned the hut," the soldier concluded. "The old man was just whimpering in disbelief outside the burning hut. We walked away and left him there."

In February 1966, *Ramparts* magazine published a veteran's indictment of the U.S. policy that caused such suffering. In an article entitled, "The Whole Thing Was a Lie," Master Sergeant Donald Duncan, a decorated member of the Special Forces, wrote in detail about his own disillusionment. He had come to Vietnam a devout anti-communist but concluded sadly that the United States was on the wrong side of history. Ho Chi Minh and his surrogates had won the hearts and minds of the people.

"The Viet Cong soldier believes in his cause," Duncan wrote. "He believes he is fighting for national independence. He has faith in his leaders, whose obvious dedication is probably greater than his own. His officers live in the same huts and eat the same food. . . . In the long run I don't think Vietnam will be better off under Ho's brand of communism. But it's not for me or my government to decide. The decision is for the Vietnamese."

Among the ranks of American politicians, only a few even considered such a possibility. One of the exceptions was a freshman member of the U.S. Senate, a man who saw the war as a problem and now admitted his share of the blame.

33

RFK

By early 1966, Robert Kennedy was fully immersed in his work as a senator. The previous year he had climbed a mountain—metaphorically, of course, from the depths of his grief, but also literally. Canada's fourteen-thousand-foot Mount Kennedy had been renamed in honor of his brother, and Robert Kennedy's decision to climb it was remarkable for at least two reasons. He had never climbed a mountain before, and Mount Kennedy, rising stark and alone in the distance reaches of the Canadian Yukon, had never been climbed.

"Don't slip, dear," his mother told him as he set off on his adventure, and Kennedy later revealed what the members of his family already knew. He was terrified of heights. Fortunately, he made the climb with Jim Whittaker and Barry Prather, both of whom had climbed Mount Everest. For most of the climb, Kennedy was roped between Whittaker and Prather, but for the final two hundred feet he took the lead and stood alone for a time on the summit, lost in his thoughts.

"I didn't really enjoy any part of it," he admitted after his descent. "Henceforth, I'm going to stay on the first floor of my house."

The truth was that politically and physically Robert Kennedy had a love-hate relationship with risk. As a senator, his evolving views on Vietnam showed caution, tilting increasingly toward political courage. The war was a delicate issue for him. As a member of the National Security Council, he had helped shape his brother's policies of a steady, reluctant escalation. By 1965, however, as Lyndon Johnson made the decision to go all in, Kennedy was certain the president was wrong. The future of Vietnam, he believed, could not be settled by force alone, and that was where Johnson seemed to be headed.

In November 1965, Kennedy created a brief firestorm when he was asked by a student reporter at the University of Southern California if he favored sending blood to the victims of war in North Vietnam. Kennedy answered on impulse.

"I think that would be a good idea," he said.

"Is that going too far?" the reporter asked.

"If we've given all the blood that is needed to the South Vietnamese, I'm in favor of giving anybody who needs blood—I'm in favor of them having blood."

"Even to the North Vietnamese?"

"Yes."

The John Birch Society called the idea treason, and George Wallace labeled Kennedy "that fellow who advocated giving blood to the Viet Cong." As his own constituents demanded an explanation, Kennedy clarified that he was talking only about civilian non-combatants. But he continued to speak about Vietnam, and controversy dogged the things he said. When President Johnson ended the Christmas bombing pause after thirty-seven days, Kennedy criticized the decision.

"Obviously," he said, "the resumption of bombing in the North is not a policy, and we should not delude ourselves that it offers a painless method of winning the war. For if we regard bombing as the answer in Vietnam we are headed straight for disaster."

On February 19, he called a press conference in his Senate office and while he opposed the unilateral withdrawal of U.S. forces, he began to challenge—cautiously, at first—the fundamental assumptions of American policy. The solution, he said, must be political, negotiations involving all factions in South Vietnam, including the Viet Cong:

> Whatever the exact status of the National Liberation Front—puppet or partly independent, any negotiated settlement must accept the fact that there are discontented elements in South Vietnam, Communist and non-Communist, who desire to change the existing political and economic system in the country. There are three things you can do with such groups: kill or repress them, turn the country over to them, or admit them to a share of power and responsibility. . . . It may mean a compromise government fully acceptable to neither side.

He favored the latter possibility, and as historian Joseph Palermo wrote in *Robert F. Kennedy and the Death of American Idealism*, this was dangerous political territory. "The President's hard line had the solid backing of a formidable coalition," Palermo noted, both in the Congress and among the pundits. Thus, when Kennedy proposed a coalition government, Vice President Hubert Humphrey led a chorus of scorn: "I do not believe we should write a prescription for Vietnam which includes a dose of arsenic." The *Chicago Tribune*, one of the largest newspapers in the country, called him "Ho Chi Kennedy."

At least for a while, Kennedy concluded he had pushed the issue as far as he could—a fact that frustrated such antiwar journalists as I. F. Stone and Jack Newfield ("While Others Dodge the Draft, Bobby Dodges the War," read the headline on one of Stone's critiques). But for many of us, Kennedy continued to emerge as a political voice of possibility and hope. In many ways he was reminiscent of his brother; he was a *Kennedy* after all. But there was something different about the eyes and the smile. There was always a trace of sadness, it seemed, a hint of pain, a sense of the tragedy in the world, even as he walked among the crowds, and there were always crowds. From New York to California, he was a magnet for the dispossessed, for those seeking change—and then as later, for journalists and skeptics trying to pick him apart.

After the riots of 1965, Kennedy had begun meeting with some of the young and idealistic members of his staff, particularly Adam Walinski and Peter Edelman. *Newsweek* journalist Evan Thomas later described one of those meetings at Hickory Hill, Kennedy's residence in Virginia. Kennedy invited his aides to go for a swim as they talked about the link between poverty and inner-city violence—and innovative ways to bring about change. In the biography, *Robert Kennedy: His Life*, Thomas wrote that Kennedy was "oblivious, in his way, to the incongruity of discussing anti-poverty policy while working on his tan." But others saw a different incongruity—that a man who was born to such power and privilege was becoming increasingly obsessed with the problems of other people who were not.

Jack Newfield was one of the skeptics who began almost despite himself to see in Kennedy an authenticity lacking in other politicians. Newfield was a staff writer at the left-leaning *Village Voice*, and after his first encounter with Kennedy, in 1963, he was emphatically unimpressed. On that occasion, Newfield was one of about 3,000 demonstrators massed outside the Justice Department, demanding that the attorney general protect the activists in Birmingham who had been the victim of fire hoses and dogs. Kennedy soon emerged from the building to talk to the demonstrators face-to-face. That, itself was impressive enough. A lesser or a more arrogant man might have simply hidden inside.

But when a protester shouted, "We haven't seen many Negroes come out of there," Kennedy grew defensive and shouted back, "Individuals will be hired according to their ability, not their color."

"It was," wrote Newfield, "exactly the sort of impersonal, legalistic response, blind to the larger moral implications of our protest, that we felt made Kennedy such an inadequate attorney general."

But in 1966, Kennedy seemed different, so much so that Newfield wondered about his earlier impressions. "His blue eyes were now sad rather than cold," Newfield remembered, "haunted rather than hostile. The freshly carved lines of sorrow in his brow, around his eyes, near his mouth, made him look ten, not five years older" than when he became attorney general. On a visit that stretched out over a period of hours, ending in Kennedy's Manhattan apartment, the two sipping bourbon and talking about literature and poetry, Newfield was impressed by Kennedy's intellectual curiosity. He had become an avid reader, drawn to the wisdom of the ancient Greeks, the poetry of Ralph Waldo Emerson, the philosophy of Albert Camus. Especially Camus. Not only did the French existentialist write about suffering and unpredictability and a man's responsibility to shape his own life, he possessed a passionate concern for justice. As Evan Thomas later reported, Kennedy carried this passage from Camus in his daybook.

Perhaps we cannot prevent this world from being a world in which children are tortured. But we can reduce the number of tortured children.

The more he and Kennedy came to know each other, the more convinced Newfield became that Kennedy's mission—the new and fundamental definition of his life—was to struggle against the suffering he saw in the world. He walked with Kennedy through the crime-ridden streets of Bedford-Stuyvesant, one of the poorest neighborhoods in New York, and saw the awkward show of affection as Kennedy stopped to talk to a child.

"You know something?" Kennedy said. "My little girl has glasses just like yours. And I love my little girl very much."

His friends never doubted the depth or honesty of his compassion. "One thing I know for sure," said John Jay Hooker, a protégé from the Justice Department, "Bob Kennedy was who he said he was." As Hooker and Newfield both pointed out, Kennedy was not content with acts of kindness, or even with speeches about economic justice. In the case of Bedford-Stuyvesant, Kennedy set out in 1966 to make the neighborhood a laboratory in the fight against poverty. He found allies among Republicans, most notably Jacob Javits, the senior senator from New York, and John Lindsay, the charismatic mayor of New York City. Kennedy was always a little wary of Lindsay, a handsome patrician, articulate and poised, but they shared concerns about poverty and race. Lindsay was comfortable walking the ghetto streets of New York, chatting with the people, listening to grievances, promising to do what he could to help. "You are the most beautiful cat," a young black man told him on one of those walks, for he sensed in Lindsay an uncommon empathy, at least by the standards of white politicians.

Kennedy saw the mayor as a formidable opponent in some future election, but the two put that possibility aside when it came to the problems of Bedford-Stuyvesant. The neighborhood had once been white and middle class, but by the 1960s the residents were black or Puerto Rican, and the symptoms of poverty were extreme. Eighty percent of the teenagers were high school dropouts and more than a fourth of the population had incomes of less than $3,000 a year. Half the housing was "dilapidated or insufficient," and the anecdotal reality was worse.

Wrote Jack Newfield, whose own Jewish family had been one of the last in Bedford-Stuvesant:

> Diseased debris rotting under a halo of mosquitos in a vacant lot. Teenage girls feinting and punching with the fluent fury of grown men. Burned-out houses with families still living behind the boarded-up windows. Roaches so bold they no longer flee from the light. A shabby record store loudspeaker blaring Aretha Franklin singing, "I can't get no satisfaction," while a junkie shoots up with heroin in the doorway. Bedford-Stuyvesant's everyday reality is filled with the surreal imagery of a bad LSD trip.

Kennedy was convinced that if he could make a difference in Bedford-Stuyvesant, it could be a model for change anywhere. Never an apostle of liberal orthodoxy, Kennedy was a critic of the Great Society. Not its intent or the necessity of the effort, or even many of its programs, but he thought it gave too little attention to jobs, which he saw as the key to the problem. He had grown especially skeptical of welfare, and he confessed to a group of New York editors that conservative critics of the system had a point.

> Most of us deprecated and disregarded these criticisms. People were in need; obviously, we felt, to help people in trouble was the right thing to do. But in our urge to help, we also disregarded elementary fact. For the criticisms of welfare do have a center of truth, and they are confirmed by the evidence. Recent studies have shown, for example, that higher welfare payments often encourage students to drop out of school, that they encourage families to disintegrate, and that they often lead to lifelong dependency . . .

But Kennedy was not content to leave it at that. He called on the private sector to join with government to solve a problem that was not only immoral, but dangerous. In 1964, when rioting began in Harlem, it quickly spread to Bedford-Stuyvesant, and for anyone who had walked those streets, as Kennedy had, it was easy to see how the violence could happen. From early 1966 until his death in 1968, he worked on the problems of this neighborhood, putting together a massive project that faced its share of obstacles and setbacks, including bitter infighting within the community. But Kennedy pushed ahead with a doggedness that became his trademark. The plan he developed with members of his staff was to create two nonprofit boards, one of leaders from Bedford-Stuyvesant to lay out plans for neighborhood development—who better to do it than the people who lived there?—and the other composed of white business leaders who were willing to invest in the inner city.

Kennedy, always impatient with bureaucracy and regarded by many fellow senators as arrogant, secured $7 million in start-up money from the Labor Department and another $750,000 from the Ford Foundation. ("Don't worry about it," he said, when a lawmaker pressed for details about how his project would alleviate poverty. "It's going to do it.") It was clear at least that his goals were ambitious. Newfield wrote:

> The initial plan included coordinated programs for the creation of jobs, housing renovation and sanitation, . . . the conversion of an abandoned bottling plant into a town hall and community center, a mortgage consortium to provide low-cost loans for homeowners, the starting of a private work-study community university geared toward dropouts, and a campaign to convince industry to relocate in the community.

As Evan Thomas and other biographers have noted, Kennedy did not eradicate poverty in Bedford-Stuyvesant. By 1969, however, more than a dozen new black-owned businesses, which were able to get credit from a consortium of banks, had opened their doors, creating 570 new jobs. More than four hundred houses and tenements had been restored, with local residents doing much of the work, and 250 of those neighborhood carpenters went on to full-time construction jobs. Two community centers had opened, IBM put a computer cable plant in the heart of the neighborhood, the City University of New York agreed to open a campus in the area, and more than three thousand residents had worked on plans for two "super blocks" that would include renovated housing, as well as new street lighting and parks. All of that was a start, and the work continued, but the progress still seemed dwarfed by the need.

"The ghetto is too big," Newfield wrote in 1969, "and the project has touched the lives of perhaps only 25,000 of Bedford-Stuyvesant's 450,000 inhabitants. The corporate community and the Congress have not responded adequately. If Robert Kennedy were still alive, he would probably walk through the dark ghetto and mutter, *This is still unacceptable. We can do better.* Robert Kennedy gave a damn, but Bedford-Stuyvesant is still hell."

AS HE WORKED ON the problems of the Brooklyn ghetto, Kennedy found himself drawn almost by accident to another crusade across the country. In March 1966, he flew to California to participate in Senate hearings on the problems of migrant farmworkers. He did it as a favor to Walter Reuther, the U.S. labor leader who had begun to champion the farmworkers' cause. Kennedy was busy with other things, and on the flight to Delano, where Cesar Chavez was embroiled in a strike and a grape boycott, he turned to aide Peter Edelman and muttered, "Why am I dragging my ass all the way out to California?" However, as soon as he saw conditions in the fields, his attitude changed. He was appalled by the arrogance of California growers and public officials, especially a sheriff who explained that he routinely arrested strikers as they walked the picket lines in order to avoid the possibility of a riot.

"This is the most interesting concept," Kennedy replied with cold fury. "How can you go arrest somebody if they haven't violated the law? I suggest that during the luncheon period that the sheriff and the district attorney read the Constitution of the United States."

Cesar Chavez was amazed. He turned to his fellow organizer Delores Huerta and whispered with a mixture of admiration and alarm, "He shouldn't go so far because it's only going to hurt him." But a bond was formed. Evan Thomas wrote:

> Kennedy sized up Chavez, a gentle, soft-spoken man about his own age—at once steely and beatific—who had been fighting wealthy farmers for fifteen years. "Time stopped," recalled Edelman. "The chemistry was instant." Each man immediately admired the other, saw in each other the same qualities of suffering and pride. Chavez had never seen such honest anger and sympathy in a white public official. Kennedy promised to help Chavez. He did, raising money, pushing for legislation to protect migrant workers, and badgering the IRS to stop using deportation threats to break the farmworkers' union.

Kennedy was developing a public identity as a fierce and passionate champion of justice, but it may not have been until the following summer, during a trip to South Africa, that he began to see himself that way. In June, he delivered a series of speeches in a country suffocating under apartheid, a system of official white supremacy that was even more complete than its counterpart in the American South. Kennedy was invited to South Africa by the anti-apartheid National Union of South African Students (NUSAS), and he arrived at a time of extraordinary tension. The South African government, though reluctantly allowing the visit, refused all diplomatic courtesies; not a single government official would meet with this unwelcome visitor from the United States. Among the citizenry, however, the reception was intense.

He arrived around midnight on June 4, 1966—uncharacteristically nervous, the people close to him thought—and plunged into a waiting crowd of 1,500 people. Some hecklers shouted "Yankee go home," but they were outnumbered by people pressing in around him, calling his name, tearing at his clothes (he lost a pair of cufflinks). Outside the terminal, he climbed to the top of a car and spoke briefly to the crowd, amazed by its hunger, though for what he wasn't quite sure. Did these white South Africans want somebody to tell them they were wrong about apartheid, to reassure them that they could do better? Or were they merely curious—or worse, ready to respond with anger to his words?

Whatever their collective expectations, he wanted to do more than scold or condemn. He was determined to challenge the decency within them, to preach the necessity of racial justice and change. Again and again, he spoke of "the full human equality of all our people" and "a shared determination to wipe away the unnecessary sufferings of our fellow human beings." His most celebrated speech came at the University of Cape Town:

> Few will have the greatness to bend history itself; but each of us can work to change a small portion of events, and in the total of all these acts will be written the history of this generation. It is from numberless diverse acts of courage and belief that human history is shaped. Each time a man stands up for an ideal, or acts to improve the lot of others, or strikes out against injustice, he sends a tiny ripple of hope, and crossing each other from a million different centers of energy and daring those ripples build a current which can sweep down the mightiest walls of oppression and injustice.

Over the next several days, Kennedy stepped beyond the cloister of that nation's universities to visit the ghetto streets of Soweto, where people rushed toward him, shouting "Master, Master."

"Please don't use that word," Kennedy said gently, his discomfort apparent.

Wrote Arthur Schlesinger:

> He made speeches from the roof of the automobile, from the steps of the Catholic cathedral, from a chair in the middle of a school playground. Later the inhabitants papered their shacks with Kennedy photographs cut from the newspapers.

For Kennedy himself, the highlight may have been his visit with Chief Albert Luthuli of the Zulu tribe, an anti-apartheid advocate who won the Nobel Peace Prize in 1961. In his personal diary of the trip, Kennedy wrote at length about Luthuli:

> A most impressive man, with a marvelously lined but kind face. What did one notice first? The white goatee, perhaps, so familiar in his pictures, but then quickly the smile that lit up his whole presence, the eyes which danced and sparkled, and then, when he talked of the future of his country, of his people, of the relationship between the races, became intense and hurt and hard all at once.

"What are they doing to my country?" Luthuli asked in his visit with Kennedy. "Can't they see that men of all races can work together—and that the alternative is a terrible disaster for us all."

As the Kennedy trip went on, the crowds grew larger and more sympathetic, white and black South Africans by the thousands cheering the idealism of his words. "Perhaps the most attractive and compelling feature of Senator Kennedy's speeches," wrote the *Cape Times*, a South African newspaper, "was the insistence that he and all South Africans he spoke to belonged to the same world. . . . There was a common humanity, he insisted, which went beyond all superficial differences of race and culture." The *Rand Daily Mail* added, "Senator Robert Kennedy's visit is the best thing that has happened to South Africa for years. It is as if a window has been flung open and a gust of fresh air has swept into a room in which the atmosphere has become stale and fetid. Suddenly it is possible to breathe again without feeling choked. . . ."

Some voices were more cynical and gloomy. An editorial in the *Cape Argus* concluded: "Like a meteor, Mr. Kennedy has flashed across the South African sky, and has gone. . . . South Africa remains as it was."

Anti-apartheid activist Margaret Marshall disagreed. As she told Evan Thomas:

> He reminded us—me—that we were not alone. That we were part of a great and noble tradition, the re-affirmation of nobility in every human person. We all had felt alienated. It felt to me that what I was doing was small and meaningless. He put us back into the great sweep of history. Even if it's just a tiny thing, it will add up. He reset the moral compass, not so much by attacking apartheid, but simply by talking about justice and freedom and dignity—words that none of us had heard in, it seemed like, an eternity. He didn't go through the white liberals, he connected straight—by standing on a car. Nobody had done that. How simple it was! He was not afraid.

On the flight home to the United States, Kennedy knew that he had struck a chord. But even in the afterglow of his triumph, he worried about the people he was leaving behind—and if it was clear by now they were cheering for more than the memory of his brother, a part of him was left to brood again over the bittersweet meaning of it all.

IN 1966, ROBERT KENNEDY was not the only politician determined to make his mark on the country. From the other end of the political spectrum, George Wallace was eager to preserve his national standing, achieved in 1964 when he entered three presidential primaries and won more attention and votes than anyone had expected. He was planning to run for president again but he faced a problem. He was entering his final year as governor of Alabama and under the state's constitution was not allowed to succeed himself. He thought he needed an ongoing political platform, continued access to the levers of power, and he finally arrived at an unexpected solution—he would run his wife for governor as his proxy.

That was not his original plan. Initially, he tried to browbeat the legislature into amending the state's constitution so a governor could succeed himself. A handful of stubborn senators, however, some of whom had come to see Wallace as a demagogue, blocked the measure. He turned reluctantly to plan B. The decision astonished many political observers. "The idea of Wallace running his wife is so bizarre," wrote veteran Alabama reporter Bob Ingram, "and so very difficult to take seriously that it is not easy even to comment on it."

Only one woman, Miriam Ferguson of Texas, had ever been elected a governor in the United States, and although she too was a stand-in for her husband, "Ma" Ferguson enjoyed the limelight. Lurleen Wallace did not. Known to friends as soft-spoken and shy, she yearned for a quieter life than the one she had known with George Wallace. But there was another obstacle that was far more urgent. Lurleen had cancer. On January 10, 1966, she underwent surgery for a uterine tumor, and her doctors were veiled about her prognosis. Nevertheless, she agreed to run. Her second daughter, Peggy, was worried about her—not only her physical health, but also her gentle disposition amid the roar and passion of Alabama politics.

"Why do you need to do this?" Peggy asked.

In later years, after her marriage to Mark Kennedy, a Democratic lawyer who became a liberal justice on the Alabama Supreme Court, Peggy Wallace would chart a course fiercely independent of her father's legacy, supporting the candidacy of Barack Obama to become the nation's first black president. But as a teenager in 1966, she was simply concerned about her mother, bewildered by her parents' decision—and by the self-centeredness of her father's ambition. There was no doubt George Wallace loved his wife, but it was equally clear that this would never have been her choice. As Lurleen told a member of the governor's staff, "I did it for George."

She won the election in 1966, carrying herself with dignity and grace, as she became Alabama's first woman governor. When she died in office on May 7, 1968, George Wallace was running, more seriously than ever, for the presidency of the United States. "I'll shake the eye-teeth of the liberals in this country," he said, and it was clear that he meant every word.

At the same time, in California, another conservative with a remarkably similar set of priorities announced his candidacy for governor. As his political career progressed, Ronald Reagan's great gift was reassurance, his ability to make the country feel better about itself. In 1966, however, he ran on the politics of fear. In the wake of the student demonstrations at Berkeley and race riots in Watts, Reagan cast himself as a "law and order" candidate. He promised to put "the welfare bums back to work," and "to clean up the mess at Berkeley." His biographer Matthew Dallek summarized his appeal this way:

> In the mid-1960s revolution was in the air. Leaders of the New Left spoke of revolt against the Establishment; leaders of the Far Right echoed them in talk of toppling the liberal order. Media images were filled with violence: frightened National Guardsmen brandished fixed bayonets in Watts, where burned-out buildings lay in ruin; angry activists marched on military bases; protests erupted against segregated hotels and businesses; students turned out by the thousands to fight for free speech on campus. . . . The real Reagan revolution . . . began as a debate about retaking control of a society in chaos. What Ronald Reagan stood for above all was law and order.

It was also true that in a stunning victory over incumbent Governor Pat Brown, Reagan and his team demonstrated a command of political strategy—an organizational "ground game," as some pundits put it, learned by conservatives through the trial and error of Barry Goldwater's presidential campaign. Reagan's team knew how to get their voters to the polls.

In 1966, however, the complementary appeals of Reagan and Wallace were rooted ultimately in divisions—racial at their core—that ran as deep in California as they did in Alabama.

34

Black Power

There were multiple measures of the great divide, one of which was a basketball game. On March 19, the University of Kentucky, a perennial power, was to play for the national championship against an underdog team from Texas Western College. The David versus Goliath match-up was one of the story lines, but another reality resonated strongly in these troubled times. The Kentucky team was all-white. Texas Western was all-black. A few white TWC players had ridden the bench, and one played, and played well, in the national semifinals, but all seven who would play against Kentucky were black.

Texas Western coach Don Haskins said his decision on which players to put on the floor wasn't based on color, and probably it wasn't. But Haskins knew and had told his players about the racial attitudes of Kentucky's legendary coach Adolph Rupp, who had been under pressure from the university's president to recruit black players. "Harry," Rupp reportedly told one of his assistants, "that sonofabitch is ordering me to get some niggers in here. What am I going to do?" Rupp was not alone in his approach to recruiting. In 1966, every basketball team in the Southeastern Conference, the one in which Kentucky played, was all-white, and only one coach in the conference, Vanderbilt's Roy Skinner, was earnestly recruiting black players. But Kentucky under Rupp was something more, it was a symbol of white supremacy.

"No five blacks are going to beat Kentucky," Rupp vowed privately before the game.

In public, Haskins took it in stride. Rupp was not only an Old South racist, he was also one of the greatest coaches of all time. His teams had won four national championships, and were heavily favored to win a fifth, especially after beating Duke in the national semifinals—a game that most observers thought would be the one that really counted.

Texas Western had other ideas. They played so *fast*, particularly on defense where they kept stealing the ball from Kentucky's all-American guard, Louis Dampier. And on offense there was David Lattin—"a cross between Michael Jordan and a gorilla," recalled Perry Wallace, an African American player who had scrimmaged against Lattin in pickup games and offered the comment as an expression of awe, not derision.

On the second play of the championship game, after Haskins told him, "Just dunk it like they ain't ever seen it dunked," Lattin slammed the ball over the outstretched arms of Kentucky's Pat Riley (a future NBA coaching legend). "Take that, honky," Lattin snarled, or at least that's now a part of the legend. Whatever the specific trash talk, there was no doubt that players on both teams understood the history at stake in the game. No team with five black starters had ever won the national championship, but it was the *way* the Texas team went about it—the speed, the intensity, and most obviously, the *dunks*—that changed the face of college basketball.

After Texas Western won 72–65 (and some said it was not that close), Rupp's nightmares continued the following fall when two black freshmen began their careers at Vanderbilt. Perry Wallace had played against Lattin and patterned his own game after Lattin's. Not the taunting, trash-talking part, for Wallace was a quiet, respectful young man, the valedictorian of his high school class, who would major in engineering at Vanderbilt and go on to become a law professor at American University. Wallace was a collegiate Jackie Robinson, relentless in his dignity even in the face of the racist hostility of white Southern sports fans.

And it did get ugly. In a game at Mississippi State in the fall of 1966, the fans in the sweltering small arena, sitting on bleachers so close to the floor that Wallace could hear every taunt, every curse, every racial slur, eventually became so abusive that he feared being physically attacked. He remembered that at halftime he and Godfrey Dillard, the other black Vanderbilt player, sat together on the locker room bench, holding tightly to each other's hands.

"We were trying to be in denial," Wallace said. "We didn't want it to be this bad."

That season, Ole Miss cancelled both of its freshman games with Vanderbilt (in those days, freshmen could not play on the varsity) rather than compete against black players.

But perhaps the strangest reaction came at Kentucky. Wallace, who stood six-foot-five, small for a college center, was known for his powerful leaping ability, and his favorite shot in those days was the dunk. In the Kentucky game, he slammed one over Kentucky freshman Dan Issel, and when Wallace glanced at the bench, he noticed the scowl on Coach Rupp's face. The following spring, the NCAA banned the dunk—a decision most observers thought was aimed at UCLA's seven-foot center, Lew Alcindor (later to be famous as Kareem Abdul-Jabbar). "Clearly, they did it to undermine my dominance in the game," wrote Kareem in his autobiography. "Equally clearly, if I'd been white they never would have done it."

Vanderbilt's Roy Skinner had a different view. Everybody knew Rupp hated the dunk, hated the taunting play of David Lattin and the whole Texas Western championship team, and now here was Perry Wallace, threatening to bring the same style to the Southeastern Conference. Skinner was sure that Rupp had played a role behind the scenes in the NCAA's ban, and he was equally sure that Wallace was Rupp's unspoken target.

"The NCAA," Skinner said, "crapped on Perry."

In retrospect, the short-lived ban on the dunk seems silly, but at the time the African American pioneers in college basketball became a metaphor for the tensions and fears that pervaded the country. Almost every day, it seemed, there were headlines and media reminders of the depth and volatility of our problems.

On May 17, U.S. newspapers ran a photo of Karl Fleming, Los Angeles bureau chief of *Newsweek*, lying bloody on a Watts sidewalk. He had been knocked to the pavement by a group of black youths in another flare-up of inner-city violence. A black security guard came to his rescue, told him not to move, that an ambulance was on its way. Fleming was left with a fractured skull, both jaws broken, and multiple bruises where he had been kicked. Some observers noted the irony of such violence on the anniversary of the U.S. Supreme Court's landmark ruling in *Brown v. Board of Education*. *Newsweek* saw a different incongruity. For its "Top of the Week" summary of the news, the magazine wrote:

> That he was beaten by Negroes in the streets of Watts was a cruel irony. Fleming had covered the landmark battles of the Negro revolt from Albany,

> Ga., to Oxford, Miss., to Birmingham, Ala., and numberless way stations whose names are now all but forgotten. He ducked bullets and brickbats, whiffed tear gas, brazened out threats on his life—and never was seriously injured. And, a North Carolinian by birth, he reported the black man's march down Freedom Road with insight and compassion. No journalist was more closely tuned in to the Movement . . .

Fleming was moved by the testimonial but perhaps a bit embarrassed too, for he understood that the violence against him was not personal. His inner-city attackers were filled with rage, and he was white and in their path. Even at the time, Fleming told interviewers from his hospital bed, "If I was a young black man growing up on the streets of Watts, seeing what they had seen and going through what I know they went through to survive, I might feel like hitting some white guy in the head, too." Later, he wrote:

> It was harder to feel angry at the young black men of Watts who had attacked me and rebelled so terribly against the world in which they felt trapped. They had grown up walled off from the rest of the world in their freeway-encircled ghetto, without fathers, without education, without jobs or hope. Most of them, I strongly suspected, had never had human contact with a white person, and if they had, it had likely been with a white cop bent on showing them who was boss.

Many whites in California and other parts of the country could not muster the same sympathy. To those, for example, who supported the law-and-order candidacy of Ronald Reagan, these black Americans were thugs—destructive, menacing, ready to kill, and it might be only a matter of time until they broke free from their sweltering ghetto and rampaged through the California countryside. This was the mood of fear and dread building steadily in the suburbs.

THAT SAME SUMMER, VIOLENCE spread to another part of the country. On June 5, James Meredith, who, four years earlier, had become the first black student at Ole Miss, set out on a one-man "March Against Fear" from Memphis, Tennessee, to Jackson, Mississippi. On June 6, he was shot. Meredith survived, and the shooter was caught, but in the wake of this attempted murder, civil rights leaders rushed to Mississippi to pick up the march where Meredith left off. Martin Luther King came not because he was a fan of Meredith's; most people in the movement were not. Meredith was always a lone wolf, unpredictable and erratic, but his attempted murder could not be ignored. King had recently taken his movement north and was embroiled in complicated protests in Chicago, but he flew to Memphis, where James Lawson met him at the airport.

Lawson, mentor to the student activists in Nashville during the early sit-ins, was now a Methodist minister in Memphis. He was still involved in civil rights, still friendly with King, and eager to help in the coming protests. They were joined at the airport by Floyd McKissick, the new and militant leader of CORE, and the three drove to Meredith's hospital room. They found him in surprisingly good spirits, recovering from his shotgun wounds, and happy they wanted to continue the march.

Stokely Carmichael soon arrived, too. Carmichael was flush with the feeling of victory, having just engineered an organizational coup within SNCC that deposed John Lewis as chairman. Lewis, though dogged and brave in his pursuit of equality, was resolutely nonviolent, while Carmichael and a growing number of militants were beginning to drift in another direction. In the coming days, these simmering disputes within the movement would burst dramatically into the open.

Since the early sixties, Carmichael had been one of the boldest SNCC organizers, "a hip, fear-no-evil type of guy," said fellow SNCC worker Bob Mants. He had accepted nonviolence as a tactic, though never a way of life, as Lewis, King and James Lawson had. Now Carmichael had grown impatient, tired of the violence aimed at the movement, tired of measuring words for fear of giving offense to white allies; tired, in fact, of white people generally. It was time, he thought, that blacks took control of their own movement, and he began a steady purge of white organizers from the ranks of SNCC, no matter how devoted they had been.

"The crazies are taking over," confided Julian Bond in a rueful conversation with Lewis. But there seemed to be nothing they could do.

For his part, Lewis joined the others who were ready to resume Meredith's march near the town of Hernando, Mississippi, where he had been gunned down. As always, it was important not to let white violence carry the day, and the leaders now were working on a plan to register black voters along the way. All of that was good. Lewis worried, however, about deep divisions within the ranks. He was afraid this march would make them public in a way the media could not ignore, in a way, in fact, that would distract from the issues they were trying to raise—the pattern of racial violence in the South, the intimidation of black voters, the ongoing defiance of civil rights laws.

It didn't take long for the angry young SNCC militants to make John Lewis look like a prophet. On Thursday, June 16, the marchers reached Greenwood, a past site of bitter civil rights struggles. Willie Ricks, one of the most militant members of SNCC, who had been an activist since the age of seventeen (he was now twenty-three), urged Carmichael to use a new phrase in addressing the crowd. "Black Power!" said Ricks, had struck a chord in small advance rallies he had been a part of. He thought it fit the mood of the times, a growing conviction among movement militants that power was the only thing white people understood. Carmichael was happy to give it a try. Just a few hours earlier, he had been arrested and charged with trespassing for helping the marchers set up camp on the grounds of an African American school. Released on bond from the Greenwood jail, he was steaming mad when he returned to the march.

"This is the twenty-seventh time I've been arrested," he yelled to the crowd, "and I ain't going to jail no more!"

Carmichael was a gifted orator, angry and brash, able to read the mood of the people. "What we're gonna start saying now is 'Black Power!'" he shouted. And then:

"What do you want?"

And the crowd yelled back: *"Black Power!"*

"What do you want!"

"Black Power!"

Again and again.

Carmichael had never seen anything like it—such euphoria, a cathartic delight, interwoven with the rage, as if the words were self-fulfilling; as if the act of shouting them aloud carried a certain kind of truth. Not surprisingly, Martin Luther King had a different response. "Immediately," he said, "I had reservations." Not that the concept of power was irrelevant. Clearly, it was not. The absence of power among African Americans in the South was the cornerstone of their oppression. But there was something divisive about the phrase, something easily misunderstood by African Americans as well as whites. Almost certainly, among the latter, the slogan would feed a mood of resentment—of fear—that was already building in much of the country. And among black people? It would depend entirely on what they did with it.

Not far away in Lowndes County, Alabama, the route of the Selma to Montgomery March, where not a single black citizen had been registered to vote as late as 1965 (such was the power of white intimidation), African Americans were now preparing to assert their political power at the polls. They had paid a heavy price to get to that point. The previous winter, more than forty families were evicted from their tenant shacks after the passage of the Voting Rights Act. Many white landowners in Lowndes and other counties let it be known that any fieldworker who tried to register to vote would no longer have a place to live. Or a job. But blacks registered anyway, and some spent the early winter months of 1966 shivering in tents near Highway 80, the route of the Selma march. One young woman, Josephine Mays, gave birth in one of the tents.

SNCC organizer Bob Mants, who was raised on a farm in rural Georgia, was moved by the bravery of these people—sometimes whites in passing cars fired random shots in their direction. Along with Carmichael and local leaders like John Hulett, who would eventually become the county's first black sheriff, Mants wanted to make sure the collective sacrifice paid off. In the spring, SNCC helped organize an all-black political party after the white-controlled Democratic Party increased the filing fee for candidates to five hundred dollars—a prohibitive sum for the black people of Lowndes. Their new party, the Lowndes County Freedom Organization, chose a black panther as its symbol—because, said Hulett, "a panther won't bother anybody, but push it into a corner, and it will do whatever it takes."

That was the philosophy among the Lowndes County activists. They knew they were living in a dangerous place. Mants recalled that on the day he first arrived in the county one of the local men took him aside and warned him sternly: "You can't come here talking that nonviolence shit. You'll get yourself killed, and other people killed." Thus, in 1965, after a white man murdered Jonathan Daniels, an Episcopal seminarian who had come to the county in support of the civil rights movement, John Hulett put out the word to local whites: "You kill one of us, we'll kill three of you."

As most people knew, Hulett was a not a man looking for a fight. He was small and wiry, "a gentle soul," in the words of one journalist, but he was instinctively more a follower of Malcolm X than of Martin Luther King. He had never met Malcolm, and he loved Dr. King, but in the place where he lived, Hulett believed in the philosophy of self-defense.

One man who was moved by the example of the people of Lowndes was Huey Newton, a handsome law student from Oakland, California. Like many African Americans there, Newton was angry, and the primary target of his discontent was the Oakland police. He saw them as racist and disrespectful—often brutal—toward the black community they were supposed to serve. In 1966, Newton came to Alabama and worked for a while as a volunteer with the Lowndes County Freedom Organization, which was now often called the Black Panther Party. Newton was impressed by the bravery he saw in this place, and when he returned to Oakland, he took with him the Black Panther symbol—an emblem of ferocity that might offer new focus to the anger in the ghetto.

Later in 1966, Newton and fellow activist Bobby Seale organized the Black Panther Party for Self-Defense and began to make headlines of their own. Meanwhile, the quieter work went on in Lowndes County. On May 3, more than nine hundred African Americans from every corner of the county voted in the Black Panther primary. For most of them, it was the first time they had voted for anything, and it was transformative. As Carmichael later wrote in his book, *Black Power*, this was an existential moment—an affirmation of citizenship, but more than that of *personhood*, a redefinition of what it meant to be alive.

In the general election the following November, the results were disappointing. In Lowndes County, not a single black candidate was elected. There were reports of voter fraud, and there still too many African Americans who had not yet mustered the courage to vote. But Hulett and the others were not dismayed. "We won't quit," he said. "We won't give up."

To Carmichael, all of this was a part of the meaning of Black Power, the transformation of a people once oppressed, a new understanding of their place in the world. But did Carmichael mean something more? Something more violent and menacing perhaps? These were bitter times in America, and there was reason to fear, in this transitional year for the country, that the bitterness was only going to get worse.

35

Music in Alabama

In this time of tension, which had been building steadily for most of the decade, there was a little oasis in northern Alabama. Nobody could quite say why it was there. Maybe it was just the blind luck of history. But in the nearly contiguous small towns of Florence, Muscle Shoals, Tuscumbia, and Sheffield—in the heart of a vast agricultural plateau—there was a place where music was an antidote to prejudice. Or at least that was how it seemed.

W. C. Handy came from this place—the Father of the Blues, whose wide-ranging musical tastes included a vast cross-section of beauty, from the symphonies of the great European masters to the singing of ordinary African Americans. Early in the twentieth century, he established a music publishing company in Memphis, where he began to write sheet music for the blues. "The primitive southern Negro, as he sang, was sure to bear down on the third and seventh tone of the scale, slurring between major and minor," Handy wrote. "I tried to convey this effect by introducing flat thirds and sevenths, now called blue notes . . ." His publishing company helped legitimize the artistry of the blues. Quite intentionally, he also published the work of white artists, for music, he thought, could be the universal reprieve from the crippling prejudice he saw all around him.

Sam Phillips, who was white, thought the same thing. Like Handy, he was born and raised near Florence, and he made the same musical pilgrimage to Memphis where he produced records by white and black artists, from Bobby "Blue" Bland to Elvis Presley. By the 1960s, however, the visionary artists and producers no longer felt the need to leave this part of Alabama. There were studios now in Muscle Shoals, and in March 1966 a young Alabamian named

Percy Sledge, who worked in Sheffield as a hospital orderly, cut a record on his home turf that quickly soared to number one in the nation. "When a Man Loves a Woman" became, in fact, one of the legendary ballads in American music, as Sledge, who sang more comfortably in the lower registers, pushed his voice to the breaking point, achieving a level of plaintive urgency that made the rock 'n' roll world take notice. Within a few weeks, another Alabamian named Wilson Pickett, who had already had a major hit with "The Midnight Hour," came to Muscle Shoals and recorded "Land of a Thousand Dances," which went to number six on the charts.

Soon Aretha Franklin would lead a parade of national artists to this same backwater (she was quickly followed by Bob Dylan, Paul Simon, and Willie Nelson) and music historians generally agree, Aretha found her voice in north Alabama. Her first top ten hit on the Billboard charts, "I've Never Loved a Man (The Way That I Love You") was recorded there, followed by the country-soul ballad, "Do Right Woman, Do Right Man." What most of us didn't know as we listened to these songs, such triumphant performances by black artists, was that their splendid studio bands were white. There were musicians in Muscle Shoals like Spooner Oldham, Donnie Fritts, and Dan Penn, and producers like Quin Ivy and Rick Hall, all of them white and many of them coming from the same kind of rural, hard-scrabble backgrounds as their artists. Together, they shared a love of the black and white music of the South—blues, country, and now rock 'n' roll, but their sensibilities went deeper than that. They understood, for how could they not, that the world around them was a turbulent place, so filled with racial tension and hatred, and all of those things began to seem absurd—self-inflicted, unnecessary—from the vantage point of Muscle Shoals.

In that place, remembered Percy Sledge, "We were like brothers, like family. We were as one."

Most of us did not think about it this deeply, but amid the mounting troubles of 1966 we did find an escape in great records. This was the year the Righteous Brothers, who had their musical roots in California, released their second number one hit, "Soul and Inspiration." These were white guys who had sounded black when we first heard them in 1964 with their debut release, "You've Lost That Lovin' Feelin'." There was something explosive in the mixture of Bill Medley's baritone-bass and Bobby Hatfield's tenor, both singers pushing their voices to the limits the way that black artists did. The critics called it "blue-eyed soul," and though the term became a cliché it was true enough as far as it went.

It was a little more difficult to pigeonhole the Beach Boys, another California band that had been making hits since 1962. In the beginning they sang about the beach, with songs like "Surfin' Safari" and "Surfin' USA," and there was a kind of innocence about the sound that belied the subtlety of its production. Most members of the band were only marginally interested in surfing, but they did love music, especially the vocal harmonies of groups like the Everly Brothers and the Four Freshmen. Three brothers, Brian, Dennis, and Carl Wilson, and their cousin Mike Love, formed the heart of the band, and though Brian later suffered from drug and mental problems, he was the driving force for a sound that became increasingly complex.

During the Beach Boys' early years, they sang about girls and cars and the joys of summer, but their biggest hit of 1966—indeed, their biggest hit ever—was "Good Vibrations." Lyrically, it was still a boy-girl song with a chorus written by Love that sounded like a quirky throwback to their earlier records. *I'm picking up good vibrations/She's giving me excitations.* But the verses were more introspective.

Close my eyes, she's somehow closer now
Softly smile, I know she must be kind
When I look in her eyes
She goes with me to a blossom world

Love said later, in an interview with *Uncut* magazine, that the song foreshadowed the psychedelic era of rock 'n' roll, and if that described the lyrics, it was even more true of the musical production. The trademark vocal harmonies were there, the high falsetto blended with Love's lead vocals, but the instrumentation was radical and new: a cello, a clarinet, a harp, and an electronic instrument known as a theramin—all blended into a sound that was spinning intricately in Brian Wilson's head. Music critic Tom Pinnock called it "a new kind of writing and production . . . a preoccupation with webs of sound, complex arrangements and classical textures. As Wilson's consciousness bloomed—a spiritual awakening fueled by acid and weed—so had the music."

Rolling Stone pronounced "Good Vibrations" one of the greatest records in the history of rock 'n' roll, but it was not the biggest hit of 1966. That distinction went to a song on the other end of the artistic spectrum, a patriotic anthem about the Vietnam War, called "The Ballad of the Green Beret." Staff Sergeant Barry Sadler, the singer-songwriter, had been a Special Forces soldier himself and had fought in the jungles of Vietnam. Once he was wounded by a punji stick tipped with human feces, and when the flesh on his leg began to rot, the military surgeons were forced to enlarge the wound, cutting the fetid tissue away.

Sadler did not write about that in his song. Instead, he wrote about the glory of war, the honor and the sacrifice of it, in a way that stirred the American public.

Fighting soldiers from the sky
Fearless men who jump and die
Men who mean just what they say
The brave men of the Green Beret

On January 30, 1966, Sadler debuted the song on the *Ed Sullivan Show*, and with the release of the record the following month, it became a phenomenon of the times. The sergeant's song spent five weeks atop the *Billboard* charts, the official index of commercial popularity. There was nothing especially artful about it; the vocals and instrumentation were plain, mechanical almost, the lyrics admiring to the point of being mawkish. But people loved it. As the record made clear, most Americans still supported the war, and perhaps there was even more to it than that. They wanted to believe—and did believe—in the fundamental goodness of their country.

36

'In Cold Blood'

In early 1966, an American novelist with deep Southern roots was beginning to make a bit of literary history. Truman Capote was already a celebrity, but now his newest and most ambitious book, which told the true story of the murder of a farm family in Kansas, was climbing quickly up the bestseller lists. *In Cold Blood* reached number one on February 6 and remained there until May 8, and there was already talk of a full-length movie. Success was nothing new to Capote. He had emerged in the 1940s as a publishing wunderkind.

His first novel, *Other Voices, Other Rooms,* appeared with great literary fanfare when he was only twenty-three years old. This was the same age as his friend Carson McCullers when she had published her debut novel, *The Heart Is a Lonely Hunter.* Capote was inclined to notice such things. He regarded himself as the kind of extraordinary talent whose achievements should take a back seat to no one's:

> I had to be successful, and I had to be successful early. The thing about people like me is that we always knew what we were going to do. Many people spend half their lives not knowing. But I was a very special person, and I had to have a very special life. I was not meant to work in an office or something, though I would have been successful at whatever I did. But I always knew I wanted to be a writer and that I wanted to be rich and famous.

Later, he added two other qualities that set him apart: "I'm homosexual. I'm a genius."

This sense of himself as superior and different, which he knew could be double-edged, was nurtured during a lonely boyhood spent primarily in Alabama. He was born in New Orleans to a mother who concluded that she was not meant to be a mother, and when Truman was still a toddler she sent him to live with relatives in Monroeville. In that small Alabama village, his next-door neighbor was Nelle Harper Lee, who would, herself, grow up to be a writer of renown. She became a character in Capote's first novel, and when her own *To Kill a Mockingbird* was published, Miss Lee returned the favor, immortalizing Capote as Dill, an enigmatic little boy filled with bright, insatiable curiosity.

Capote saw himself more or less that way:

> You see, I was so different from everyone, so much more intelligent and sensitive and perceptive. I was having fifty perceptions a minute to everyone else's five. I always felt like nobody else was going to understand me, going to understand what I felt about things. I guess that's why I started writing. At least on paper I could put down what I thought.

Capote biographer Gerald Clarke recounts how the young author, with the moral support of Carson McCullers, threw himself into the writing of *Other Voices, Other Rooms*. The book was partly a work of catharsis, an attempt to exorcise his demons—"an unconscious, altogether intuitive attempt," Capote admitted, "for I was not aware, except for a few incidents and descriptions, of its being in any serious degree autobiographical. Rereading it now, I find such self-deception unpardonable."

In Capote's story, Joel Knox, a boy of thirteen, is sent to live in the decadent household of Southern relatives. Some members of this extended family are grotesque characters physically and emotionally, and the boy must find his way in their world. The prose itself set the novel apart, elegant, stylish, a match for the sensitivity of the story. In the end, wrote Clarke,

> Joel accepts his destiny, which is to be homosexual, to always hear other voices and live in other rooms. Yet acceptance is not a surrender; it is a liberation. "I am me," he whoops. "I am Joel, we are the same people." So, in a sense, had Truman rejoiced when he made peace with his own identity.

There was a touch of irony in the rush of acclaim that followed publication of the novel. First impressions focused as on the cover of the book, the jacket photo of the author, and only later did people talk seriously about the story inside. The *New York Times* described the image as "an androgynously pretty Mr. Capote, big eyes looking up from under blond bangs, and wearing a Tattersall vest, reclining sensually on a sofa." Over the years, this became Capote's persona, a lisping, effeminate, contrarian presence, charismatic and charming—an extra layer of celebrity for his writing.

Other books followed, including the novel *Breakfast at Tiffany's*, soon adapted into a movie starring Audrey Hepburn, but Capote wanted something more, something bigger. He wanted to invent a new literary genre. He began to consider the possibility that a writer could, if he or she chose, write nonfiction in the shape of a novel. All the literary ingredients were there—character, plot, dialogue, theme; the difference was that in nonfiction they were *discovered*, not invented. There had been other books by American journalists—John Hersey's *Hiroshima*, for example—that told powerful stories relying entirely on the literal facts. Capote wanted to push it one step further, researching his subject in such depth and detail that he could tell the inner story of his characters, as well as the outer.

"I wanted to produce a journalistic novel," Capote remembered, "something on a large scale that would have the credibility of fact, the immediacy of film, the depth and freedom of prose, and the precision of poetry."

He found his subject on November 16, 1959, on page thirty-nine of the *New York Times*. In an article of three hundred words, the newspaper reported:

> A wealthy wheat farmer, his wife, and their two young children were found shot to death today in their home. They had been killed by shotgun blasts at close range after being bound and gagged. The father, 48-year-old Herbert W. Clutter, was found in the basement with his son, Kenyon, 15. His wife Bonnie, 45, and a daughter, Nancy, 16, were in their beds. There were no signs of a struggle and nothing had been stolen. The telephone lines had been cut. "This is apparently the case of a psychopathic killer," Sheriff Earl Robinson said.

For the next six years, Capote made multiple visits to Holcomb, Kansas, the unlikely setting for such a terrible crime—a windswept town on the western plains that he described this way in his masterwork, which he decided to call *In Cold Blood:*

> The village of Holcomb stands on the high wheat plains of western Kansas, a lonesome area that other Kansans call "out there." Some seventy miles east of the Colorado border, the countryside, with its hard blue skies and desert-clear air, has an atmosphere that is rather more Far West than Middle West. The local accent is barbed with a prairie twang, a ranch-hand nasalness, and the men, many of them, wear narrow frontier trousers, Stetsons, and high-heeled boots with pointed toes. The land is flat, and the views are awesomely extensive; horses, herds of cattle, a white cluster of grain elevators rising as gracefully as Greek temples are visible long before a traveler reaches them.

This was what Capote was seeking, novelistic detail made more immediate by the writer's bargain he struck with his readers—that every single bit of it was true. In gathering the raw ingredients for his story, Capote had help. His friend Harper Lee, who shared his lonesome Alabama childhood, and who was, herself, fresh off the completion of *To Kill a Mockingbird*, traveled to Kansas with him. Together, they conducted the interviews—with law enforcement and the people of Holcomb—and in the coming months, Capote alone would interview the killers, who were captured after he began his research.

Miss Lee made careful notes throughout, meticulously typed and turned over to Capote, whose own methods were unorthodox. He said he had "a talent for mentally recording lengthy conversations, an ability I had worked to achieve . . ., for I devoutly believe that the taking of notes, much less the use of a tape recorder, creates an artifice and distorts or even destroys any naturalness that might exist between the observer and the observed, the nervous hummingbird and its would-be captor." When the interview was over, as the *New York Times* reported, Capote would "rush away . . . and immediately write down everything he had been told."

Whatever their combined methodology, this was the story that he and Harper Lee pieced together. The murders of Herbert William Clutter and his family were carried out by a pair of drifters, neither of whom, almost certainly, would have had the gumption, the twisted temerity, to commit such a hideous crime on his own. Perry Smith was an ex-con—a half-blood Cherokee with a heavily-muscled upper torso and scarred and stunted legs, the result of a motorcycle wreck on a rain-slick road. When he was a child, his Indian mother, who rarely even asked the names of the multiple men with whom she slept, sent him away to live in an orphanage; later, when he was still a young man, his father attempted to shoot him, execution-style, only to discover that the gun was unloaded. Even in prison, Perry was a bed-wetter.

His cellmate in the 1950s, for crimes committed before the Clutter murders, was a petty criminal named Dick Hickock. Hickock was drawn to Perry because he thought he might be, despite his problems with bladder control, "a natural-born killer," and Hickock had some killing in mind. One of his other cellmates, first-time offender Floyd Wells, who was doing time for stealing lawnmowers, told him about the year he worked on Herb Clutter's farm. Clutter was a good man, Wells said, generous and fair: "If you were a little short before payday, he'd always hand you a ten or a five." When Hickock began asking questions, Wells acknowledged that Clutter was wealthy and may have kept a safe in his office.

> Next thing I knew, Dick was talking about killing Mr. Clutter. Said him and Perry was gonna go out there and rob the place, and they was gonna kill all witnesses—the Clutters and anybody else that happened to be around. He described to me a dozen times how he was gonna do it, how him and Perry was gonna tie them people up and gun them down. . . . I never for a minute believed he meant to carry it out. I thought it was just talk.

But it was not. On November 15, 1959, shortly after midnight, Dick and Perry, having served the time for their earlier crimes, pulled a stolen Chevrolet into the tree-lined drive of the Clutters' farm, and doused the headlights. It was a cloudless, full-moon night, a bit chilly as they entered the house through an unlocked door. Armed with a shotgun and a knife, they surprised the Clutters—Herb, his wife Bonnie, and two teenaged children, Nancy and Kenyon. They locked them first in a downstairs bathroom, and Dick began searching for the safe, certain despite Mr. Clutter's denials that there must be one, and that it would be stuffed with thousands of dollars in cash. Perry cut the phone wires in the house.

Soon enough it was clear that there was no safe, that the whole escapade had been a fool's errand from the beginning, and it was not over. Having promised themselves there would be no witnesses, Smith and Hickock bound and gagged the Clutters and took them to separate rooms of the house.

They killed them methodically, one by one. Mr. Clutter was first. Smith cut his throat, and the sound, he remembered, "was like somebody drowning. Screaming under water."

"Then I aimed the gun," he told Alvin Dewey of the Kansas Bureau of Investigation in a rambling confession after being captured. "The room just exploded. Went blue. Just blazed up. Jesus, I'll never understand why they didn't hear the noise twenty miles around."

Capote would spare no detail in recounting the rest of Smith's confession, and the cold satisfaction it gave lawman Dewey, who had known and admired Herb Clutter and his family, who could scarcely believe that such good people had met such a cruel and mindless fate:

> Dewey's ears ring with it—a ringing that almost deafens him to the whispery rush of Smith's soft voice. But the voice plunges on, ejecting a fusillade of sounds and images: Hickock hunting the discharged shell; hurrying, hurrying, and Kenyon's head in a circle of light, the murmur of muffled pleadings, then Hickock again scrambling after a used cartridge; Nancy's room, Nancy listening to boots on the hardwood stairs, the creak of the steps as they climb toward her, Nancy's eyes, Nancy watching the flashlight's shine seek the target ("She said, 'Oh, no! Oh, please. No! No! No! No! Don't! Oh, please don't! Please!'. . .")

The story could not have been more terrible, or more vividly told. Capote had conceived it first as the story of a town, small, isolated, content with the ordinary rhythms of life, now faced with this bloody, unspeakable moment. How would the people respond? Would they turn on each other in suspicion and fear, certain that the killer was still in their midst? Would they pull together in grief, even if, for the first time in their lives, they slept behind locked doors at night? Or would it be, as Capote discovered, a little of both?

And what about the victims? Capote wanted their stories, too; wanted, in a sense, to bring them once again to life: Herb Clutter, forty-eight, strong, successful, a pillar of the community, almost universally admired; Bonnie, his wife, who suffered with bouts of clinical depression, and the two teenagers, Kenyon and Nancy; Kenyon, a quiet and solitary boy, and Nancy, just a few weeks short of her seventeenth birthday, a cheerful, outgoing girl, whose father thought she was getting too serious about a boy who lived just up the road.

Gerald Clarke wrote:

> *In Cold Blood* was not just the chronicle of a gruesome crime; it was a tale of a good and virtuous family being pursued and destroyed by forces beyond its knowledge or control. It was a theme that reverberated like Greek tragedy, a story that Aeschylus or Sophocles might have turned into a drama of destiny and fate.

In the beginning stages of his research, Capote was fortunate to have Harper Lee as his traveling companion. The stolid inhabitants of western Kansas were initially unimpressed by this lisping little man from New York City, who stood barely five-foot four and seemed to be so effeminate and strange. Some wondered if he might, in fact, be the killer, returning to Holcomb to taunt and to gloat. But Harper Lee was a different matter. She came to Kansas from Monroeville, Alabama, and she understood the ways of rural America, how the people thought and talked. She helped smooth the way for her eccentric friend until finally he was able to break through on his own—to charm these suspicious farmers as he did nearly everyone he met.

He had been in Kansas a little more than a month when the story became suddenly more complex, more intricate and layered, darker even than it had been at the start. On December 30, 1959, Perry Smith and Dick Hickock were captured in Las Vegas, and quickly confessed to their hideous crime. When Capote had first come to Holcomb, they were still on the run, but now he needed to know them too, to come as close as he could to the answer: What in the world had made them do it?

In the coming months, he was able to visit them multiple times in the disconcerting confines of death row, and when he was not in Kansas, to strike up a steady stream of correspondence. He connected most easily with Perry Smith. Both were uncommonly short, Smith an inch or two taller than Capote, and both came from troubled, alcoholic backgrounds. In Smith, speculated one biographer, Capote "recognized his shadow, his dark side, the embodiment of his own accumulated angers and hurts." Smith, for his part, had nursed aspirations of becoming a writer, and saw in Capote "the successful artist he might have been."

Nevertheless, Smith threatened to kill him.

"I've half a mind to do it," he said in the middle of one interview. "It would give me pleasure. What do I have to lose?"

These were the characters who made up the story. The American author, Norman Mailer, would later insist that Perry Smith was one of the great villains in contemporary letters, and clearly the reading public was enthralled. Some critics, however, were not. What kind of book was this anyway, and whoever heard of a "nonfiction novel," the genre Capote now claimed he invented?

"This isn't writing," sniffed Stanley Kauffmann of *The New Republic*. "This is research." Tom Wolfe attributed the book's suspense mostly to "the promise of gory details." But others took a wholly different view. Biographer Gerald Clarke noted that Capote had mostly kept his bargain with the reader—that every word he wrote was true, based on years of meticulous research. His only lapse into fiction came in the final scene of the book. He decided not to end with the grisly execution by hanging of the killers, and instead contrived a chance encounter between investigator Al Dewey and a friend of Nancy Clutter's. A "peaceful" ending, Capote later said.

Other than that, wrote Clarke, "Everything he set out to do, Truman succeeded in doing. On a superficial level, *In Cold Blood* is a murder story of riveting vitality and suspense. On a deeper level, it is what he had always known it could be, a Big Work—a masterpiece."

As columnist Jimmy Breslin wrote: "This Capote steps in with flat, objective, terrible realism. And suddenly there is nothing else you want to read."

As Capote absorbed his shower of acclaim, disappointed that he did not win the Pulitzer Prize, something shocking happened in the country. If he had chiseled a work of literary art from the stuff of real life, suddenly, in a way that no one had imagined, real life began to imitate his art. On July 13 in Chicago, a drifter named Richard Speck—a man whose random fascination with violence was not altogether different from the killers in Kansas—broke into a dormitory and murdered eight student nurses with a knife. In the flood of national news that followed, we learned that Speck had lived a bloody life. His alcoholic stepfather beat him often when he was a boy growing up in Texas, and Speck followed in that path of abuse. In January 1966, he and his wife divorced after she accused him of physical assault, including rape, and in the months after he was trailed by suspicions of murder and violence—a woman raped in Monmouth, Illinois, where Speck was living, then a barmaid murdered a few days later.

Speck was questioned about both crimes, but left for Chicago where he took a job on a Great Lakes freighter, *The Russell.* He was fired for fighting, and during the second week of July went on a three-day binge of drinking and drugs. At 11 p.m. on July 13 he lurched toward a two-story brownstone building where the student nurses lived. He knocked on the door, and Corazon Amurao answered. She was a dark-haired, slightly built woman from the Philippines and the only survivor of the terror that followed. She testified later she found herself face-to-face with a greasy-haired man of about 160 pounds, armed with a knife and a gun. He had a tattoo on his left arm—BORN TO RAISE HELL—and reeked of whiskey. At the door, he said he didn't want to hurt anybody, he just wanted money, and the nurses at first tried to cooperate, tried to keep him calm.

He ordered them upstairs, tied them with strips of bed sheet cut with his knife, then took them one by one to another room, where he stabbed and strangled each one. He washed his hands after every murder.

At the end of his spree, Speck tried to rape Gloria Davy, while Amurao watched from under her bed. She had rolled there and managed to hide until all her friends were dead and Speck was gone. Later, at the trial she described the ordeal in gruesome detail, and at one point rose from the witness stand and, in the words of a wire service reporter, "walked to within two feet of the chair where the lanky, twenty-five-year-old drifter . . . slouched. 'This is the man,' she said, pointing her finger directly at Speck.

It was a morbid moment in American life, widely reported throughout the country. Incredibly, another one followed just a few weeks later that was even more chilling and more prophetic. In Austin, Texas, beginning in the early hours of August 1, a University of Texas architecture student (whose autopsy revealed a brain tumor), killed his wife and mother, leaving a note near the body of his wife: "I love her dearly . . . I cannot rationally pinpoint any specific reason for doing this."

Later that morning, Charles Whitman, a former Marine, assembled an arsenal of weapons and drove to the UT campus. He took an elevator to the top of a tower which was the university's most famous landmark. At 11:48, he opened fire from an observation deck, eventually killing fourteen people. A United Press International dispatch offered this account:

> Students, professors and visitors ran for cover. A student on a bicycle was shot and toppled off. Passers-by ran to help him and began to fall. A small boy

> was shot. Three bodies lay on the campus for nearly an hour in the 98 degree heat. Rescuers could not reach them until an armored car was brought up.

At 1:24 p.m. Austin police officers Ramiro Martinez and Houston McCoy reached the observation deck and opened fire, killing Whitman. The mass murderer thus became the seventeenth fatality and the forty-seventh person shot that day.

A student I knew at Vanderbilt, who was home in Austin on summer break, barely missed being the forty-eighth. He said he had driven his convertible to the Texas campus a few minutes before the shooting began. When he heard the first volley and saw people fall, he slammed on brakes and dove from the car, just as a bullet tore through the seat. As he told his story a few weeks later, all of us wondered at how surreal the whole thing seemed. Richard Speck was a serial killer whose murderous spree was bloody and personal. We had heard of people like him. Whitman was something new, something colder and more detached, more in the realm of a natural disaster, except of course it was not.

As we tried and failed to understand what had happened, it never even crossed our minds that one day in America—a nation that would arm itself to the teeth—this would become an everyday thing.

37

'Is God Dead?'

The cover headline from *Time* practically made the magazine jump off the newsstand with its bold red letters against a background of black: "Is God dead?" Even in the heart of the sixties, when the times were a'changing and the news turned dark at the drop of a hat, this was a startling idea. One of the people mentioned in the story was a man whose answer to *Time's* question was yes. Thomas J. J. Altizer was a theologian at Emory University, a Methodist institution in Atlanta, where—as his academic renown began to morph into public notoriety—the administration felt compelled to defend his presence.

Altizer's theology was subtle, the product of an upbringing in which freedom of inquiry was encouraged. He was raised in West Virginia, a descendant and namesake of Confederate General Thomas Jonathan "Stonewall" Jackson. As a boy, Altizer was fascinated by the Christian faith and found a sanctuary in books, supported in that pursuit by his father. It was a part of family lore that his grandfather once became so enraged while reading Friedrich Nietzsche's *The Antichrist*, which condemned the "lies" of Christianity, that he slammed it shut and hurled its heresies into the fire.

Thomas Altizer was no Nietzche, was never a hater of the Christian faith, which remained the central focus of his life. However, in those formative years when he pursued his doctorate at the University of Chicago, his faith was a source of personal anguish—the object of competing revelations, including on the first occasion, an epiphany in which he was convinced that Satan had entered his body and soul. It was a wretched experience, but soon it was followed by another that was more reassuring:

> I had what I have ever since regarded as a genuine religious conversion, and this was a conversion to the death of God. Never can such an experience be

> forgotten, and while it truly paralleled my earlier experience of the epiphany of Satan, this time I experienced a pure grace, as though it were the very reversal of my experience with Satan.

In a revealing retrospective on the university's most famous theologian, *Emory Magazine* summarized his theories this way:

> On a most basic level, Altizer studies God not as a separate presence but as a historical force that has been transformed by death. This God began giving himself to the world at its creation and ultimately died through Jesus Christ, whose earthly demise in turn poured the spirit of God into the world. Altizer calls for a dialectical form of faith that acknowledges the coincidence of opposites: through God's death, the sacred becomes profane, and vice versa; one cannot exist without the other. Only in modernity, Altizer believes, can we fully realize the paradox of the death of God—that the very absence of God signifies God's presence in all things.

As the controversy swirled around him, some of Altizer's Emory colleagues, who admired his integrity, suggested that he simply choose different words. Was he not saying that the spirit of God is everywhere in the world? Could he not proclaim, as Jesus did in the Gospel of Luke, that "the Kingdom of God is within you?" But Altizer was stubborn, and following the article in *Time* and a television appearance on *The Merv Griffin Show*, he found himself, as he later put it,

> one of the most hated men in America. Murder threats against me were almost commonplace, savage assaults against me were widely published, and the churches were seemingly possessed by a fury against me. . . . You have to go through the depths of darkness to realize the joyous glory of the light. My work really means just the opposite of what everyone thinks. I'm violently misunderstood.

Misunderstood or not, in the spring and summer of 1966, Altizer represented a dilemma for Emory University, where the president, Sanford Atwood, had just embarked with the Board of Trustees on a $25 million capital campaign. Some of the trustees wanted Altizer fired, and hate mail poured into Atwood's office, demanding that he protect the reputation of his university.

Atwood did not flinch. This was a moment not altogether different than the one at Berkeley two years earlier, where students demanded the right to speak freely on the issues that mattered most in their lives. Atwood believed in that kind of freedom, even when it was institutionally inconvenient, and he sprang to the defense of Thomas Altizer, Emory's brash and handsome theologian who was causing such a stir at the age of thirty-nine.

"Altizer is a professor who feels he has an idea worth discussing," Atwood said. "He has the right to do so."

In the end, Emory suffered little for Atwood's stand. On the contrary, it emerged with its national reputation enhanced, recognized as a beacon of academic freedom. In the coming years, other universities would follow, while some did not, as the freedom to say unpopular things became a theme of the 1960s. For Altizer, meanwhile, the hatred continued, and the question was why? Why, first of all, did his proclamations stir such rage, and on the other side, what was it about these times that led to the rise of such a controversy—to a movement proclaiming that God is dead?

Altizer was not alone in uttering those unsettling words. In 1966, he worked with William Hamilton of the Colgate Rochester Divinity School on a book, *Radical Theology and the Death of God.* Hamilton's journey of faith—and he insisted that's what it was—was different from Altizer's. Born in 1925, Hamilton found after learning of the Holocaust that he could not reconcile such massive suffering with "the image of all-powerful God."

"I wrote out my two choices," he said. "'God is not behind such radical evil, therefore he cannot be what we have traditionally meant by God' or 'God is behind everything, including the death camps—and therefore he is a killer.'"

As the *Los Angeles Times* wrote about Hamilton, "He discovered that he no longer believed in an active God," though he still believed in Christian principles like the truth and beauty of the Sermon on the Mount.

In this same time of religious ferment, Harvard theologian Harvey Cox, who also believed in the Sermon on the Mount, published his book, *The Secular City*, in which he argued that like it or not, an urbanized world was entering "an age of 'no religion at all.' It no longer looks to religious rules and rituals for its morality or its meanings." But none of this, as Cox understood it, implied the death or irrelevance of God. "God came *into* this world," he wrote, "and that is where we belong as well." He rejected pious words of faith "so tarnished by misuse," and argued that the pursuit of justice is the Christian's "appropriate response to God."

"Like Moses," he concluded on the book's final page, "we must simply take up the work of liberating the captives . . ."

In its cover story of April 8, remarkable for its depth as well as its startling red-letter headline, *Time* reflected on these ideas, these affronts to the comfort of Sunday School certainty. This was, after all, an unsettled era when the yearning of the spirit took many forms, when multiple currents of belief surged through the consciousness of the country. It was clear in a sense that the theologian Paul Tillich, who died in 1965, was right when he proclaimed a gospel of Christian existentialism. Just as Jesus ended his parables with a question, forcing his listeners to decide what they meant, the realities of life in the twentieth century forced the same kind of choice.

"What's it all about, Alfie?" asked a character in a 1966 movie, and it felt like a question for us all. As *Time*'s editors wrote, 97 percent of Americans still proclaimed a belief in God, but what exactly did that mean? When Billy Graham, the world's most famous evangelist, stood before the crowds and called them forward, gently cajoling, filled with certitude and reassurance *. . . you come now, men and women, black and white, there's something about coming forward that helps to settle it in your mind* . . . what, precisely, did he want them to *do*?

If those were the questions we found troubling, it was not because of a shortage of answers; there were, in fact, multiple examples of men and women of extraordinary faith. Dr. Martin Luther King was one. He led a movement firmly rooted in the church, and biographer Lewis Baldwin argues that King's leadership of the civil rights struggle was as surely a powerful expression of his Christianity as it was a quest for social change.

"King believed in a personal God," says Baldwin, a divine presence at the very heart of the movement, capable of offering in moments of crisis the strength that he and others might need.

Once in Montgomery, in the early days of the bus boycott, King was sitting alone in his kitchen, feeling despondent. He was only twenty-seven, too young and inexperienced, he feared, too riddled with doubt, to be an effective leader of the cause. A few days earlier, he had been arrested downtown, and as the police car drove through the streets of the city with King handcuffed in the back seat, he noticed with a surge of fear that the car was headed out of town. He did his best not to panic, but he knew what could happen to black people in the South. When they crossed the bridge at the Alabama River, he could imagine himself floating face down, perhaps with a bullet in his brain. He took a deep breath and gathered himself, did his best to stop the trembling in his hands, realizing finally that the policemen merely intended to scare him.

A few nights later, he was brooding in his kitchen at about midnight, staring at a pot of coffee on the stove when the telephone rang. "Nigger," said a voice on the end of the line, "we are tired of you and your mess now. If you aren't out of town in three days . . ." King hung up the phone and poured a cup of coffee. It wasn't just the fear that he was feeling in the moment; it was the barrage of decisions the movement forced upon him, so many occasions when he had to make a choice with too little time to think about it, and he knew that if he made the wrong one the whole thing might come apart. And what chance, really, did they have for success, this whole quixotic crusade they were on with so much power arrayed against them?

In describing these moments later, King said he could feel a prayer taking shape in his mind—not quite a plea for divine intervention, just a few words of desperate resignation, shared with a God he hoped was there: "Lord, I must confess that I'm weak now. I'm faltering. I'm losing my courage. And I can't let the people see me like this."

King said he heard an inner voice reply, telling him that he would never be alone. The following Monday he was speaking at a church when an old woman everybody called Mother Pollard rose from the pew to say that the preacher looked troubled that night. She put her arms around him and told him not to worry, not to be afraid: "God's gonna take care of you."

To Dr. King all of this was real, evidence he could feel in his heart of a God immersed in the history of the world. But it was also true, as Lewis Baldwin and others have noted, that in addition to these moments of emotional truth, King's faith was buttressed by his intellect. King, said Baldwin, drew from a wide variety of readings:

> He had a Ph.D. in systematic theology. At Boston University, he wrote his dissertation on Paul Tillich and Henry Nelson Wieman. He read Plato, he read the existentialists, and he felt it necessary to keep abreast of the theological trends of the 1960s. He struggled with the Death of God theology—Hamilton, Altizer,

> Paul Van Buren. He said, "My problem is not with theoretical atheism, with people not believing in God, as much as it is with practical atheism—people who live as if God is dead." King was a theologian. That was his training. You've got to view him as a spiritual leader, and not just the leader of a movement.

More than anything else, perhaps, King and other thinkers in the civil rights movement believed in a radical idea of love. That was the heart of their faith, the core of their belief in nonviolence. Jesus had talked about it often. *Love your enemy. Turn the other cheek. Love your neighbor as yourself.* As King made clear on multiple occasions, this was not just a tactic, but a way of life. It was not just King, however, and not just the leaders like Nashville's James Lawson. I remember a conversation with Theoda Smith, an African American woman in Selma, who told this story of the demonstrations there:

> People were scared. We had good reason to be scared, but I remember very well the thing that turned me around. Dr. King and the other organizers had used some children in the picketing and demonstrations. One day my daughter was with a group, and a white man in a car started heading straight for them. He was going to run them down. But this nun, I don't even know her name, had come in from out of town, and she stepped between the car and the kids. The driver didn't want to run over a white lady, a nun at that, so he stopped. Well, I figured then, "If these people I don't even know can take that kind of risk for my children, it's time for me to do something myself."

For King, there was nothing surprising about the heroism of a nun. Catholic activists had long been involved in civil rights and related issues of poverty and peace. The monk and philosopher Thomas Merton wrote about such things, often in *The Catholic Worker*, and the paper's editor, Dorothy Day, had herself conducted a ten-day fast for peace, not far from the Vatican. In 1965, she had also stood with young Catholics who burned their draft cards, protesting the War in Vietnam, and she spoke in defense of Roger LaPorte, a twenty-two-year-old Catholic layman who set himself on fire outside the United Nations building—just as the Quaker, Norman Morrison, had done at the Pentagon.

LaPorte and Morrison, wrote Day in *The Catholic Worker*, were "trying to show their willingness to give their lives for others, to endure the sufferings that we as a nation were inflicting on a small country and its people by our scorched-earth policy, our flamethrowers, our napalm. . . ." Inevitably, she admitted, there would be Catholics who regarded LaPorte's death as a sin, a suicide forbidden by the church, "but all of us around the *Catholic Worker* know that Roger's intent was to love God and to love his brother."

In 1966, Day was serving with Merton and a priest named Daniel Berrigan on the advisory board of the Catholic Peace Fellowship, a group of laypeople opposed to the war. Berrigan and his brother Phillip, also a Jesuit priest, were emerging as the most prominent activists in the Catholic church, men who believed in peace and social justice and were willing to go to jail for their faith. In an interview for the book, *Generation on Fire*, Dan Berrigan told author Jeff Kisseloff that the roots of his protests probably traced to the generous Catholicism of his family. He was the fourth of six children, raised on a family farm in Minnesota, and in his interview with Kisselhoff he offered this memory from his boyhood:

> We were raised during the Great Depression. We didn't have much, but we had acreage and food from a big garden, a lot of which ended up at the neighbors, given away. That was just the way we grew up. The benefits of a family who had land and food belonged to others who had nothing. And it was very quietly done; it wasn't talked about.
>
> There were always people around us who were hungry. Hoboes, who had gone on the road looking for work, would come by for a handout or to stay over. One of them put a mark on our barn, which we never noticed. That mark was a sign to other hoboes that you could get a meal and a night at our place, so they came, and some of them stayed quite a while. When they did come, my mom would take them in, put them at the table, and make a meal for them.

For Berrigan, the jump-start from that example of kindness to a radicalism rooted in faith may have been the atomic bomb. "I just couldn't believe it," he said of his reaction to the bombing of Hiroshima and Nagasaki. A poet and an avid reader, he said he came upon a book by Ronald Knox, a Catholic writer in Great Britain, who regarded the bombing as unnecessary.

"His thesis was that this was a monstrous crime," remembered Berrigan, "and if they wanted to use that thing, why didn't they shoot it off on some abandoned island and say, 'This is what we can do.'"

His brother Phillip served with distinction in the war, but the specter of nuclear war, and a sense of shame that America was the only nation on earth that had actually unleashed such abominable fury, united both Berrigans in a pacifism rooted quite literally, in the Bible. As Jeff Kissiloff wrote:

> The Berrigans could not understand a church that refused to back up its own teachings with action. If Isaiah decreed, "Turn your swords into plowshares," that was enough for them to commit civil disobedience against nuclear weapons. If the Fifth Commandment said, "Thou shalt not kill," then killing—all killing—was wrong, they reasoned. This placed them at odds with powerful figures in the church, including New York's Cardinal Francis Joseph Spellman, a cold warrior who publicly supported the Vietnam War. The Berrigans replied by saying that as far as they knew, there were no exceptions made for killing Viet Cong.

For Dan Berrigan, certainly, this represented a journey of the mind as well as the heart, shaped and guided by other Catholic writers he admired. One was Dorothy Day, "a person of uncommon courage and intelligence," and the other was Thomas Merton, who wrote a late-1950s article about nuclear war that Berrigan regarded as one of the most powerful essays he had ever read. The two men began a correspondence, and in 1965 Berrigan led a group of Catholics to the Gethsemani monastery in Kentucky, where Merton was cloistered. They talked about the war in Vietnam, and soon afterwards the Berrigans began an escalating series of protests that landed both brothers in prison.

As it happened, other protestors not as devout as the Berrigans also traced their roots to the church. SDS founder Tom Hayden and Berkeley Free Speech Movement leader Mario Savio were both raised Catholic, and both took seriously the church's teachings that related to justice. Savio, especially, as he immersed himself in philosophy and science in a quest to discover meaning, still found himself drawn to old patterns of thought—to the notion, for example, that the civil rights movement in the South, so rooted in the church, felt like the spirit of God in the world. Savio was not unlike the student at Yale who told the university's chaplain, William Sloane Coffin, "I don't know whether I'll ever believe in God, but Jesus is my kind of guy."

By the mid-sixties all of this was part of the ethos, a willingness to embrace uncertainty, to experiment with new ways of thinking. In San Francisco in

1966, a group of American Buddhists led by a Japanese priest, Shunryu Suzuki, began searching for land in California's mountains to establish the first Buddhist monastery in the United States. They chose a spot near the edge of Los Padres National Forest, which became the Tasujara Zen Mountain Center, a fixture in the spiritual life of California.

In the cutting-edge world of San Francisco, others picked a different path, attending, for example, the "Acid Tests" of novelist Ken Kesey, exploring what they maintained were the spirit-enriching, mind-expanding qualities of LSD. Within a couple of years Tom Wolfe, a gifted magazine writer out of New York, would be chronicling the exploits of Kesey and his friends in a groundbreaking work of new journalism called *The Electric Kool-Aid Acid Test.*

Meanwhile, amidst all the upheaval and drama, all the experimentations of thought, there was in other parts of America a simultaneous quest for something quite different—a yearning for certainty, for some fixed point in the constellation of faith. One of the most popular movies of 1966 was *A Man for All Seasons*, winner of the Academy Award for Best Picture. The film told the story of Sir Thomas More, an English lawyer who became a Catholic saint. He opposed the Protestant Reformation, and in a fatal display of personal integrity he rejected King Henry VIII's claim to be the leader of the Church of England and the annulment of Henry's marriage to Catherine of Aragon. Convicted of treason and then beheaded, More famously declared just before his death: "I die the King's good servant, but God's first."

Shakespearean actor Paul Scofield played the role of Sir Thomas with such uncommon grace that he won the Academy Award for Best Actor. In the closing scene, Scofield's More added a word of reassurance to his executioner: "You send me to God." There was, many of us felt as we filed from the theater, a noble certitude about this pronouncement, a telling contrast to the swirling ambiguity we saw all around us.

In the end, of course, it was just a movie. But the need for certainty in the country was real, and many people turned to religion to find it. There was already, although it had not yet come to fruition, an emerging alternative to the Christian left—to the Berrigans and Martin Luther King—and to the doubters and the "Death of God" theologians.

In 1966 in Lynchburg, Virginia, a young minister named Jerry Falwell launched the Lynchburg Christian Academy, which opened its doors as an all-white school. In 1958, Falwell had preached a sermon at his rapidly growing Thomas Road Baptist Church that he called "Segregation and Integration: Which?" His emphatic answer was segregation, and in the 1960s Falwell nursed a deep distaste for his fellow Baptist, Martin Luther King (Much of the anti-King propaganda Falwell distributed at his church was furnished by J. Edgar Hoover's FBI.)

In March 1965, Falwell had delivered a widely circulated sermon called "Ministers and Marches" in which he questioned

> the sincerity and nonviolent intentions of some civil rights leaders such as Martin Luther King, Jr. . . . It is very obvious, that the Communists, as they do in all parts of the world, are taking advantage of a tense situation in our land, and are exploiting every incident to bring about violence and bloodshed. . . . Believing the Bible as I do, I would find it impossible to stop preaching the pure saving Gospel of Jesus Christ and begin doing anything else—including the fighting of communism or participating in the civil rights reform. . . . Preachers are not called to be politicians, but to be soul winners.

In his book *With God on Our Side*, religious historian William Martin pointed out that Falwell's position was self-refuting. "Falwell's distribution of material attacking Martin Luther King and preaching against integration and the Civil Rights Act were fully as political as supporting the movement would have been," Martin wrote. But it was also true, he noted, that Falwell's views on race were changing. In later years, Falwell often told the story of a black man who shined his shoes every week asking with utter straightforward sincerity, "When will I be able to join your church?"

Falwell said the question hit him "like a boxer feels a bad blow to the stomach."

But if Falwell began to grow queasy about segregation, he and many members of his church believed that society somehow was coming loose from its moorings. Bill Godsey, for example, was a member of the Thomas Road church who taught in public schools and had no trouble adjusting to a student population that was half black, half white, but he worried about a world of changing values. "When I was growing up," he told William Martin, "you not only had values, you had limits. . . ."

Those values and limits were based fundamentally in the teachings of the Bible, and it was time for the nation to learn them again. For Christian conservatives, the rebellions of the sixties only added urgency to that message, and whether it was Falwell, or the more moderate Billy Graham, or Bill Bright and the Campus Crusade for Christ, which grew to have chapters at more than forty U.S. colleges, this was another version of the faith, competing with those that *Time* wrote about. Soon enough, it became more political, injecting the fervor of religion into the fight against abortion and gay rights. It was, finally, the political opposite of the peace and justice Christianity of King and the Berrigans, anchored in a radical sense of God's love.

If it was really true, as national polls indicated, that most of us believed in God, not much unity came with that belief. In these middle years of the 1960s, faith was one more source of division, one more battleground of the heart.

38

'You Have the Right'

In the secular world, there also were powerful changes in the wind, unsettling to some, highly promising to others. There was, first of all, an evolution in the law that felt at the time like a tectonic shift in democratic values. "The courts," said one federal judge, "are places where people can come, where they should come, and where other measures of power recede and the playing field is leveled."

A reminder of that possibility came in the form of *Miranda v. Arizona*, a June 13 ruling by the U.S. Supreme Court overturning the rape-kidnap conviction of Ernesto Miranda. At the time of his arrest three years earlier, Miranda, a Mexican-American from Arizona, had just gotten off work at a loading dock in the town of Mesa. It was the only steady job he had ever held. By all accounts, Miranda had lived an unenviable life, quarreling with his stepmother as a little boy, skipping classes at his elementary school, quitting altogether after eighth grade.

He soon began a life of violent crime, with convictions in Arizona and California ranging from attempted rape to armed robbery. He joined the army for a while, but went AWOL and was dishonorably discharged. He met Twila Hoffman, who was eight years older and the mother of two, and after Miranda moved in with her, they found steady jobs in Mesa. For the first time in his life, this wiry, dark-haired ex-convict seemed to be on a promising path.

But then in 1963, an eighteen-year-old woman was walking home by herself from a movie, when a man pulled up in a car beside her, forced her inside and warned her with ominous reassurance, "Don't scream and you won't get hurt." She told police he drove her to the desert where he raped and robbed her of four dollars. He then drove back to her neighborhood, where, curiously, he asked as he let her go, "Pray for me."

A week later, one of the victim's relatives saw a 1953 Packard driving slowly through the neighborhood. Based on the license number, police discovered the car belonged to Twila Hoffman. They arrested Miranda that same night, and although the victim was unable to pick him out of a lineup, the Mesa detectives began a two-hour interrogation, during which time Miranda confessed. He testified later they threatened to "throw the book" at him, not only for the rape, but for a host of other crimes he may have committed. They did *not* tell him, as the Supreme Court would later require, that he could remain silent, or that he had the right to legal counsel, even if he could not afford it.

Miranda was convicted, based largely upon his confession, and after multiple appeals his case came to the U.S. Supreme Court. There, it was combined with three others from Missouri, New York, and California, and argued on February 28 and March 1, 1966. In a 5–4 opinion written by Chief Justice Earl Warren, the court concluded that Miranda's rights had been violated. He may have been poor and uneducated, may have had a checkered past, but his Constitutional rights were undiminished. They were precisely the same as those of the most respected and well-informed citizen in the country, and Miranda was entitled to know what they were.

Warren required police to make known, in stilted but now familiar language, to every person accused of a crime "that he has the right to remain silent, that anything he says can be used against him in a court of law, that he has the right to the presence of an attorney, and that if he cannot afford an attorney one will be appointed for him prior to any questioning if he so desires."

I was home from college that summer and I remember a political discussion in the family in which a relative of mine, an aunt who lived in the house next door, said it certainly came as no surprise to see Earl Warren "turning Mexican rapists loose." Technically, this was more or less true. The Supreme Court did, as its bottom line, overturn Ernesto Miranda's conviction, based on the violation of his rights. But he was soon retried and again found guilty, even without admission of the tainted confession.

My aunt, of course, was far from alone in her distaste for Chief Justice Warren. In 1954 in Alabama and other places, billboards with screaming letters—IMPEACH EARL WARREN—flanked by the image of an American flag had sprouted like mushrooms when a unanimous Warren court ruled that segregated schools were unconstitutional. That was the first in a string of rulings that infuriated conservatives and identified the court with the nation's dispossessed. Before *Miranda*, there was the case of *Gideon v. Wainright*, in which Clarence Earl Gideon, a white man who had spent much of his life as a homeless drifter, was accused of stealing five dollars in change from a Florida pool hall. He had a long history of petty crime, and when his case came to trial the presiding judge, Robert McCrary, was eager to dispose of it quickly. As was common in those days when the case involved a lesser offense, the judge refused to appoint a lawyer for the indigent Gideon.

Gideon was convicted and sentenced to five years in the Florida penitentiary. While there, he began to visit the prison library, where he studied the U.S. Constitution, and concluded that under the Sixth and Fourteenth Amendments he should have been afforded legal counsel. He scrawled a five-page petition, hand-written, and mailed it to The Supreme Court of the United States, asking Warren and the other eight justices to consider his case. Remarkably, they agreed to do it.

At the Supreme Court hearing, Gideon was represented by nationally prominent attorney Abe Fortas, who later served on the court himself, and on March 18, 1963, the highest judicial body in the land ruled unanimously in Gideon's favor. In an opinion written by Justice Hugo Black, the court affirmed that if all Americans are equal before the law, even indigent defendants must have an attorney. Gideon was soon retried *with* a lawyer, and this time he was acquitted.

Attorney General Robert Kennedy was one of those who reflected on how remarkable all of this was:

> If an obscure Florida convict named Clarence Earl Gideon had not sat down in prison with a pencil and paper to write a letter to the Supreme Court; and if thc Supreme Court had not taken the trouble to look at the merits in that one crude petition among all the bundles of mail it must receive every day, the vast machinery of American law would have gone on functioning undisturbed. But Gideon did write that letter; the court did look into his case; he was re-tried with the help of competent defense counsel; found not guilty and released from prison after two years of punishment for a crime he did not commit. And the whole course of legal history has been changed.

Many historians have argued that not since the term of John Marshall, the nation's fourth chief justice, had the court played a bigger role in American life. Some of its rulings were deeply emotional. In its 1962 *Engel v. Vitale* ruling, the Warren Court outlawed state-sponsored prayer in public schools, prompting a bitter outcry from conservatives. "The First Amendment is being turned on its head," fumed Ronald Reagan, and many others agreed.

On the other end of the political spectrum, civil rights leader Fred Shuttlesworth remembered his response in 1954 when he saw a headline about the *Brown* decision: SUPREME COURT OUTLAWS SEGREGATION. It made him feel, he said later, as if "God was moving in the world."

Somewhere in the middle of all those emotions was a fundamental truth. In its stream of rulings from *Brown* to *Miranda*, the Warren Court had changed the political discussion in America. Part of it was subtle, even psychological, for it was not just the rights of minorities or criminal defendants that the court was prompting us to consider. We could sense a larger commitment to equality—racial, political, but above all else, equality in the eyes of the law. Warren was not the only source of this commitment. In the South, especially, appellate judges like Elbert Parr Tuttle of the Fifth Circuit and district judges like J. Skelly Wright of Louisiana and Frank Johnson Jr. of Alabama followed bravely where the high court led. "Judges Elbert P. Tuttle, John Minor Wisdom, Richard T. Rives, and John R. Brown operated in the eye of a storm," wrote historian Jack Bass, "making the Fifth Circuit Court of Appeals the institutional equivalent of the civil rights movement itself. For a decade and a half after the Supreme Court's basic school desegregation decision, they translated it into a broad mandate for racial justice and equality under law." But the initial vision, indisputably, was Warren's. He was a strong-willed man, a Republican liberal from California, handsome, persuasive, skilled in his pursuit of consensus, undaunted by the controversies that followed.

"Everything I did in my life that was worthwhile," he said, "I caught hell for."

Perhaps as much as anything, Warren was moved by his own understanding of the concept of *rights*. "Earlier courts had stressed property rights," wrote one historian. "Under Warren the emphasis shifted to personal rights." This soon became embedded in the language of the country: The crusade for racial justice in the South called itself the *civil rights* movement, and taking their cues, perhaps unconsciously, from this climate created by the court, there were those who pushed the idea even further. Ralph Nader, for example, was a Washington lawyer who emerged in 1966 as the nation's leading advocate of *consumer* rights.

He made the case that the average American had a right, essentially, not to be harmed by the things he or she might buy. The year before, Nader had published *Unsafe at Any Speed*, a book that was sharply critical of the auto industry. He singled out the Chevrolet Corvair as one of the least safe cars on the road, and as the owner of one of those myself, it occurred to me as I read Nader's book that I should try very hard not to hit anything. The auto industry was enraged. On March 22, 1966, General Motors CEO James Roche admitted at a U.S. Senate hearing that his company had hired a private investigating firm to search for damaging information on Nader, even going so far as to tap his phone.

Nader sued for invasion of privacy, and used his subsequent $425,000 settlement to support his work on behalf of consumers. Partly because of that work, by 1968 federal law required lifesaving seat belts in all vehicles except buses.

In June 1966 another group of Americans assembled in Washington, D.C., to assert their rights. They came together as part of the Third National Conference of Commissions on the Status of Women, the successor group to President John Kennedy's Commission on the Status of Women. Many of the delegates were angry. As they understood clearly, the Equal Employment Opportunity Commission had not enforced Title VII of the 1964 Civil Rights Act, which prohibited job discrimination against women. On June 30, after the Conference refused to issue a statement criticizing the EEOC, a group of dissenters gathered in the hotel room of Betty Friedan.

Friedan was a natural leader of the group. In 1963, her book, *The Feminine Mystique*, had stirred a new wave of awareness among American women—a willingness, first, to talk about their own empty lives, but also to push for concrete change. More and more they began to draw inspiration from the feminist heroes of the past—women like Susan B. Anthony, who pursued the right to vote, and Emma Goldman, who wrote in 1909 "A New Declaration of Independence," proclaiming equal rights for all Americans "irrespective of race, color, or sex," and Margaret Sanger, who led the crusade for women's contraception. In 1964, when women demanded a place in the Civil Rights Act, or in 1966 when twenty or more gathered in Friedan's hotel room to create a national organization, some saw themselves as part of a long and courageous history.

Friedan had scribbled the word NOW on a napkin, and it became both a title and an acronym for a new organization: the National Organization for Women. In October, the group met officially for the first time, again in Washington, where it chose its first officers (Friedan as president) and began to map an ambitious agenda. The founders pushed first for enforcement of Title VII of the Civil Rights Act, demanding equal pay for equal work, and soon expanded to other issues—maternity leave, child care, and most ambitiously an Equal Rights Amendment to the U.S. Constitution.

In a report in 1966, Friedan summarized the spirit of those early days: "We shared a moving moment of realization that we had now indeed entered history."

As NOW was beginning to marshal its forces, there was another development not specifically related to the women's movement, but curiously relevant in those times. In 1966, researchers William Masters and Virginia Johnson published their groundbreaking text, *Human Sexual Response*, based, they said, on at least 10,000 laboratory observations of men and women having sex. Between 1957 and 1965, 382 women and 312 men participated in the study. Most were married couples, but in the beginning Masters and Johnson also used female prostitutes. Ultimately, the book was clinical, but the authors clearly regarded sex—for women and well as men—as a healthy and natural part of life. This frank acknowledgment by Masters and Johnson was unsettling to many people. Even in a scientific context, an open discussion of such matters as the frequency and intensity of the female orgasm touched another dimension of the new feminism, broader, more intimate, more deeply personal, namely, a new, emergent understanding of sex.

In 1961, Lillian Smith had written in a revised edition of *Killers of the Dream* about the cold and lifeless pedestal on which many women had been placed, especially, she said, in the American South where the joys and intimacy of fulfilling sex might lead them astray; might conceivably, to be more specific, lead *white* women to cross forbidden barriers of race. Less than a decade later, in *The Female Eunuch*, Australian-born feminist Germaine Greer framed the argument in a different way. In an interview with the *New York Times*, Greer offered this summary of her intent:

> The title is an indication of the problem. Women have somehow been separated from their libido, from their faculty of desire, from their sexuality. They've become suspicious about it. Like beasts, for example, who are castrated

> in farming in order to serve their master's ulterior motives . . . women have been cut off from their capacity for action. It's a process that sacrifices vigor for delicacy and succulence, and one that's got to be changed.

For many women in the 1960s, the issue was complicated by the Playboy philosophy of Hugh Hefner—his magazine, his clubs—which sought to loosen sexual mores and cast itself as an ally of fulfillment, for women as well as men. To feminists, of course, Hefner's empire was not that at all; it was, instead, the shallow hedonism of Hefner himself, an exercise in exploitation, and anybody who doubted that fact had only to read Gloria Steinem's expose of the Playboy clubs, published in 1963.

And so the issue swirled, often just below the surface, sometimes painfully, and for a long time. More than thirty-five years later, Becky McLaughlin, a feminist writer at the University of South Alabama, published an essay entitled "Sex Cuts," in which she reflected on

> a body brimful of warring desires and self-policing reflexes. Like a path through narrow and twisting city streets, my stories meander, wander in one direction for a while, and then another, looking for the self I mean to be, experimenting with novice navigational skills, recognizing my own (speed) limits, but driving on.

If feminism thus became a durable force in American life, this journey that gained momentum in the 1960s became part of a larger groundswell of change. It included at a minimum the political objectives of NOW—especially the position, still radical, that women should not be paid less or excluded from jobs because of their gender. But there were other issues coming into focus, and even more basic was the idea that connected feminism with, among other movements, the African American quest for equal rights.

These dissenters were saying, simply and above all else, that every single person in the country deserved to be treated as a human being.

39

'We Are All Mississippians'

In the summer and fall of 1966, the racial struggle in America continued—often bitterly, and on many fronts. The latest riot had occurred in Cleveland, in an African American neighborhood called Hough. The problem began on July 18 with racial altercations in two local bars, and erupted into six days of violence in which four people died and fifty were injured. Many of us barely noticed. There were mentions of it on the news, of course, but after a while it all ran together. From Selma to Chicago, from rural Mississippi to Watts, African Americans were making their demands, and the anger smoldered—and sometimes exploded—on both sides of the racial divide.

In Alabama, the civil rights focus shifted to political power, particularly in Selma where Dallas County Sheriff Jim Clark, the unrepentant and brutal obstructionist of black voting, was seeking reelection. Newly enfranchised African Americans rallied furiously against him.

Once the votes were cast, federal registrar Bill Meeks, himself the son of a white sharecropper and therefore wise in the ways of the South, stood guard all night in the Dallas County courthouse to make sure nobody tampered with the ballots. Meeks was one of the unsung heroes of history. He was part of a small, but intrepid delegation from the U.S. Civil Service Commission, sent after passage of the Voting Rights Act to some of the toughest hamlets in the South. Working with the Justice Department, they were charged first with the registration of new voters, and then with the prevention of election fraud. Partly because they did their jobs, acting with a quiet and steely resolve, Clark lost decisively to Wilson Baker, a relative moderate by Selma's standards, who had served as the city's chief of police.

It was a sign of things to come. Within the next four years, Alabama and Mississippi, two of the states with the fewest black elected officials, would lead the nation in that category, as African Americans by the tens of thousands took full advantage of the Voting Rights Act.

With the franchise won, Martin Luther King shifted his attention to the North. His visit to Watts immediately after the 1965 riots had convinced him that big city ghettoes needed attention and help. King believed in nonviolence, believed with all his heart that the movement could work in the North as well as the South, and he felt, as he had said many times, "the fierce urgency of now." He and his advisers picked Chicago, the nation's second largest city, as a test case. They felt that if they could build a movement there and make a dent in inner-city poverty, they could make a difference anywhere and everywhere.

The problem was—and this was hard for King to admit—they didn't really know what they were doing. What should a Northern movement look like? If the great racial problem in the North was slums, what kind of protests, what demands might actually result in meaningful change?

For months they floundered in search of an answer, and along the way they made some bad and hypocritical decisions. They announced that King, in solidarity with the people he wanted to serve, would live in an inner-city Chicago apartment. One of his lieutenants, Bernard Lee, found King a $90-a-month, four-room flat on South Hamlin Avenue, but as soon as it was rented, repairs began to make it more comfortable. As King biographer David Garrow wrote, "press wags suggested King's best bet for improving ghetto housing would be to move from building to building."

Even with its improvements, King did not stay at the drafty apartment except on scattered symbolic occasions. He preferred a warm hotel or the home of a friend. Within the movement, these were the things that drove critics crazy, particularly the young field workers of SNCC, who *did* move into the communities they served, assuming every hardship and danger of the people who were already there. King, these young militants contended, was a headline grabber who came and went as he pleased, leaving the dirty work to someone else. Even during the Selma to Montgomery march, one of the great triumphs of his career, King did not walk with the masses for the whole fifty miles. He was there ceremonially at the start and the finish, and he delivered his powerful address at the end. But he did not share the misery of a cold, rainy night camped alongside Highway 80. All of that might not have mattered if King had been upfront about it, or in Chicago, if his movement there had been better conceived.

But six months passed between SCLC's arrival in the city and the launch of the "action phase" of the protest. Even then, critics maintained the goals were unclear. King spoke grandly of a campaign "to bring about the unconditional surrender of forces dedicated to the creation and maintenance of slums." But what did this mean? What *forces* did he expect to *surrender* when he led a march on the mayor's office? King's appeal to Chicago's conscience was, said journalist Marshall Frady, "like trying to engage a vaguely malign smog" or, as David Halberstam wrote in *Harper's*, "an immorality with invisible sources."

Eventually, King did offer some specifics. On July 10, he led a march of five thousand people to city hall, where he taped a list of demands to the door. These included nondiscriminatory listings by real estate brokers, an end to racially biased mortgage lending, an increased supply of low-income housing, a civilian review board to consider allegations of police brutality, and meaningful desegregation of Chicago schools.

King and other movement leaders soon met with Chicago Mayor Richard Daley to discuss their demands. The meeting did not go well. Daley was a proud, irascible man, a veteran, rough-and-tumble politician who had his own plan for dealing with slums. He resented the implication that his administration was part of the problem. He was most put off by King's call for a citizen board to monitor the police. The whole business left him annoyed—"visibly angry," the media reported, especially after King announced, "We are demanding these things, not requesting them."

Daley complained that even with this written ultimatum, King didn't know what he wanted. His ideas were vague, lacking in substance, and while the mayor was certainly willing to listen, King had not offered any real solutions to the complicated problems of the inner city.

Soon after that unpleasant meeting, there was an unexpected moment when everything suddenly came into focus, when King's remarkable skills as a leader were summoned in a crisis. On a stifling hot July evening, after a dinner with their friend Mahalia Jackson, Martin and Coretta King were driving to a mass meeting where he was scheduled to speak. They saw a crowd of angry African Americans running wildly through the streets, and when King stopped to ask what was going on, he learned of a confrontation with police. On a day when temperatures reached the mid-nineties, a group of young people were playing in streams of water spewing from a fire hydrant, when police arrived to shut it off. Some black youths resisted, and six were arrested and taken to jail.

In other cities, lesser sparks had set off riots, and King feared the same for Chicago. He drove immediately to the jail and persuaded police to set the teenagers free. He took them with him to a church where a large crowd still awaited his speech, and when he began to plead for calm, some people jeered and walked away. For King it was a rare moment of rejection, and he brooded about what it meant. The problems in the North were so intricate and multilayered, and resources that might be used to address them—particularly funds from the federal government—were being spent on the war in Vietnam.

"A lot of people have lost faith in the establishment," King told a group of Chicago ministers. "They've lost faith in the democratic process. They've lost faith in nonviolence."

In retrospect, it was always a measure of his strength as a leader that even in moments of gloom, he made himself keep pushing on. Biographer David Garrow wrote that:

> King felt burdened by what he believed was a personal responsibility to do all he could both to end the violence and eliminate the wretched conditions that produced it. To some acquaintances, he seemed discouraged . . . but he allowed neither his emotional commitment not his physical strength to lag.

As Chicago teetered on the edge of a riot, King met again with Mayor Daley, who agreed to make fire hydrants and swimming pools available in the sweltering days to come. King also met with leaders of the city's youth gangs—the Cobras, the Roman Saints and the Vice Lords—and listened for hours to their complaints. They talked about police brutality and a lack of jobs and the rundown, rat-infested housing of the ghetto, the worst of it owned by absentee landlords. With King at the meeting were U.S. Justice Department officials John Doar and Roger Wilkins, longtime veterans of the civil rights struggle, who also listened to the young men's stories. After several hours of intense conversation, King began to make the case for nonviolence—not a moral case this time, but a tactical argument of necessity. Nothing else worked as well, he said. Sometime after 3 a.m., the gang leaders agreed to ask their members to help keep the peace.

King understood this was only a start, a band-aid solution to head off a riot. It was important now to keep the pressure on, to mount demonstrations that would not only call attention to inner-city issues, but provide an outlet for anger in the ghetto. Former freedom rider Bernard Lafayette, who was also in Chicago working for the American Friends Service Committee, a Quaker social justice organization, had been saying for weeks that segregated housing was a key to the problem, for it kept black Americans trapped and stifled in the inner city. King agreed. Both practically and morally, he decided, open housing was a good place to begin.

On Thursday, July 28, King announced a vigil for the following evening outside a real estate company known for discriminating against blacks. On Friday, when fifty demonstrators arrived at the company's office in the all-white neighborhood of Gage Park, they were forced to retreat by a violent band of an estimated thousand white hecklers. Five hundred demonstrators were back the next day and were met again by a rock-throwing mob, while police offered only token protection. One of the demonstrators struck during the volley was a young King staffer named Jesse Jackson, who would rapidly emerge as probably the most visible black leader in Chicago.

Jackson had joined the SCLC staff around the time of the Selma to Montgomery march. Named in 1966 as head of SCLC's Chicago branch of the Operation Breadbasket project, he was eager to prove his mettle, especially in the eyes of Dr. King, who had become a father figure to him. King was away that weekend, attending to other movement business, but was planning to return the following week, and Jackson used the time in between to increase his visibility in the movement. Handsome and charismatic at the age of twenty-four, he carried a chip on his shoulder, or perhaps more accurately, he wrapped himself in a private armor that he had developed in his native South Carolina. His mother, Helen Burns, pretty, almond-eyed, and unwed, was only sixteen when he was born. As Jesse grew up poor and illegitimate in the segregated South, he braced himself, his friends agreed, against a world that tried in so many ways to point at him and tell him he was nothing. That at least was how it appeared, and the movement offered a kind of salvation—particularly with the mentorship of Dr. King, who was secure and comfortable in his own skin in a way that Jackson could only admire.

In Chicago, as tensions mounted during King's absence, Jackson set out to up the ante. Apparently without consultation, he announced plans for several more open-housing marches through rigidly segregated white neighborhoods.

On Friday, August 5, shortly after his return to Chicago, King himself led one of those marches. A caravan of more than one hundred cars left New Friendship Church for the protest site near Gage Park. Once again, a huge crowd of whites was waiting, and almost as soon as King got out of his car he was hit in the temple with a rock. He fell to one knee and remained there for a few seconds before righting himself and proceeding with the march. Despite more serious efforts this time by Chicago police to provide protection, the shower of rocks and bottles continued. Thirty people were injured. Forty-one were arrested.

"I had expected some hostility, but not of this enormity," King told the press. Even in the South, he said, including Birmingham and Selma, he had "never seen anything so hostile and so hateful."

More marches followed, then tense negotiations that included Chicago's business and religious leaders, representatives of the real estate board, Mayor Richard Daley, and leaders of the Chicago movement, including King and local activist Al Raby. The first session, which lasted most of a day, resulted in a genuine search for consensus. Daley clearly wanted peace in his city and was willing to make concessions to achieve it, including an explicit support of open housing. But how would it happen? Would real estate companies in white neighborhoods really welcome black clients?

While the specifics were being worked out, Daley demanded a moratorium on future marches. Movement leaders balked. They were determined to continue the pressure, and negotiations were on the verge of breaking down until King began to speak. In his prize-winning biography, *Bearing the Cross*, David Garrow quoted at length from King's impassioned and unscripted words:

> This has been a constructive and creative beginning. This represents progress and a sign of change. I've gone through this whole problem in my mind a thousand times about demonstrations, and let me say that if you are tired of demonstrations, I am tired of demonstrating. I am tired of the threat of death. I want to live. I don't want to be a martyr . . . But the important thing is not how tired I am; the important thing is to get rid of the conditions that lead us to march. . . .
>
> Our humble marches have revealed a cancer. We have not used rocks. We

> have not used bottles. And no one today, no one who has spoken has condemned those that have used violence. Maybe there should be a moratorium in Gage Park. Maybe we should begin by condemning the robber and not the robbed . . . Our marching feet have brought us a long way, and if we hadn't marched I don't think we'd be here today. No one here has talked about the beauty of our marches, the love of our marches, the hatred we're absorbing. Let's hear more about the people who perpetuate the violence.
>
> We appreciate the meeting. We don't want to end the dialogue. We don't see enough to stop the marches, but we are going with love and nonviolence. This is a great city and it can be a greater city.

Inspired by King's soliloquy, the negotiators continued until finally an agreement was reached—a ten-point plan for open housing that included a promise by the real estate board to support it, and a promise by leaders of Chicago's banks to cease their discriminatory lending. For a while at least, King was pleased. If their movement had floundered in the beginning, it had found its focus with the issue of housing. The agreement achieved by Chicago's leaders did not go as far as he might have liked, but such negotiations rarely did. All in all King thought they had done pretty well.

His satisfaction, however, was short-lived. Almost immediately, black leaders in Chicago who had not been part of the negotiations began to criticize the results, a few even charging that King had sold them out. King was certain that he had not, but he was stung by the words; they began a kind of cascading disillusionment that gripped him for the next several months. It was soon apparent that many of Chicago's realtors had no intention of serving black clients, no matter what the city's leaders might have agreed to. Then from Washington there was more bad news. President Johnson had proposed a new civil rights bill with a strong open housing provision, and it was clear that the bill was dead on arrival. Illinois Senator Everett Dirksen, who had supported Johnson's civil rights measures aimed at the South, refused to do the same for a law with nationwide implications—one that might undermine the sanctity of neighborhood segregation in the North. He didn't put it that way, of course, but to King the message was unmistakable.

"White America," he said, with a bitterness that was rare in his public remarks, "never did intend to integrate housing, integrate schools, or be fair with Negroes about jobs."

In November his despair grew worse as he surveyed election results nationwide. In King's native Georgia, Lester Maddox was elected governor, which might have seemed merely a bad joke if the symbolism had not been so stark. Maddox was a buffoon, more akin to Mississippi's Ross Barnett than to Alabama's George Wallace, who was, despite his segregationist views, a talented, articulate politician. Maddox was simply a die-hard segregationist, a former Atlanta restaurant owner who had refused to serve black customers even after the passage of the 1964 Civil Rights Act. Once, when three young African Americans—students at nearby Georgia Tech—quietly, politely asked to be served, Maddox repelled what he called their "invasion" by threatening them with a club-like ax handle.

Two years later, Maddox was governor of the state.

The news was no better in other parts of the country. In Alabama, where, despite the presence of federal registrars, new black voters were sometimes physically attacked at polling stations, Lurleen Wallace was elected governor as a surrogate for her husband, who was forbidden by term limits from running again. She was, to be sure, a kinder, gentler presence than George—that was simply her nature—but the message of her election as his proxy was clear.

Even more significantly, in California, Ronald Reagan, the former actor and new rising star of the political right, defeated incumbent Governor Pat Brown, a liberal Democrat, in that state's November election. Reagan was as genial as George Wallace was pugnacious, and he was a man of much greater depth than his political opponents generally acknowledged. Reagan was always ready with a smile or a quip, often self-deprecating in a way that reassured and disarmed. But he opposed California's open housing laws, and though he vigorously denied any personal bigotry, he had also opposed the Civil Rights Act of 1964. Perhaps most importantly, Reagan was one of ten new conservative Republicans (in addition to Wallace and Maddox, who were both Democrats) elected in 1966. It was, in retrospect, a watershed moment, part of what journalist Rick Perlstein later called "the unmaking of the American consensus."

Not that liberalism was dead. But it was no longer the unchallenged heart of a powerful yearning, nursed since the start of the New Frontier, to make the country even greater by making it *just*.

If Martin Luther King had stirred our hearts by proclaiming a dream "deeply rooted in the American Dream," even he had to wonder in the closing months of 1966 if he had given the country too much credit. In his darker moments, he asked himself if he had accomplished anything. Of course he had. He had led a movement that ended legal segregation in the South and secured for black Southerners the right to vote. He had also taken his movement to the North, and, as Lyndon Johnson put it in another context, "laid bare the secret heart of a nation."

"Chicago nationalized race," wrote historian Taylor Branch from the vantage point of forty years later. ". . . The violence against Northern demonstrations cracked a beguiling, cultivated conceit that bigotry was the province of backward Southerners. . . ."

As the *Saturday Evening Post* concluded at the time, "We are all, let us face it, Mississippians."

40

Measures of Progress

The closing weeks of 1966 were not entirely bleak from Dr. King's point of view. There was heartening news from Massachusetts, where the state's attorney general, Edward Brooke, became the first African American since Reconstruction to be elected to the U.S. Senate.

The first black senator had been from Mississippi. Soon after the end of the Civil War, an eloquent black minister named Hiram Revels was picked to fill one of the Senate seats vacated by Jefferson Davis and Albert Brown when Mississippi seceded.

The remarkable Revels was born free in North Carolina, and as a young man moved to the North, where he studied theology in a Quaker seminary. As a traveling minister before the Civil War, he was jailed in Missouri for preaching the gospel to African Americans. During the war, he served as a chaplain in the Union Army, organized two black regiments, and later fought at the Battle of Vicksburg. In 1870, after being chosen by Mississippi's Reconstruction legislature to fill the open Senate seat, he faced opposition from (white) Democrats who argued on the basis of the *Dred Scott* decision—the pre-Civil War Supreme Court ruling that denied full citizenship to blacks—that Revels and other African Americans should never be allowed to serve in the U.S. Senate.

In a piece of historical symmetry, two senators from Massachusetts, the state that would later elect Edward Brooke, sprang to Revels's defense. Charles Sumner and Henry Wilson argued unequivocally that America's constitutionally sanctioned racism died at the end of the Civil War—what did the terrible bloodshed mean, if not at least that?—and Revels, therefore, should be welcomed as a member of the U.S. Senate. Sumner and Wilson prevailed. Revels was seated and served briefly and with distinction, supporting equal rights for African Americans, while opposing punishment for whites who had fought for the Confederacy.

Nearly a hundred years later, Edward Brooke embodied some of that same moderation. He was a Republican, which had been, after all, the party of Lincoln, at a time when many blacks were becoming Democrats. Described as "gentlemanly and charming" by the *New York Times*, he was a strong supporter of civil rights and open housing and resisted his party's retreat from those issues. As a military veteran, he was more conservative about foreign policy and was critical of Martin Luther King's comments against the Vietnam War.

King understood the importance of Brooke's election—no African American had ever held a higher office—but he was much more comfortable with the views of Julian Bond, who in December 1966 enjoyed his own moment of triumph. Because of his opposition to the war, Bond had been blocked from taking the seat he had won in the Georgia House of Representatives. He appealed that decision by his fellow legislators all the way to the U.S. Supreme Court. On December 5, the court ruled in his favor.

For Chief Justice Earl Warren and his colleagues, Bond's dilemma seemed an easy call. Writing for a unanimous court, Warren concluded:

> Legislators have an obligation to take positions on controversial political questions so that their constituents can be fully informed by them, and be better able to assess their qualifications for office; also so they may be represented in government debates. We therefore hold that the disqualification of Bond from membership in the Georgia House because of his statements violated Bond's right of free expression under the First Amendment.

King was pleased by the court's decision. It was one more reminder that the civil rights movement had a prestigious ally in this branch of government. More personally, King was happy for Bond, who had always been one of the most promising leaders in SNCC. Bond was handsome, calm, and quietly charismatic, and he had stood like a rock behind the organization's antiwar statement—risking his seat in the legislature.

In that, there might have been a lesson for King. He, too, was concerned about the war and had spoken about it on scattered occasions, criticizing the U.S. bombing, calling for a negotiated settlement. But he had tiptoed reluctantly across that minefield, wary of alienating friends of the civil rights movement who supported the policies of LBJ. In the closing months of 1966, during his time of brooding and gloom, he wondered if maybe he had been too calculating about the effect of his words on white America—or for that matter on the other side, as he struggled to retain the loyalty, and stir the hopes, of African Americans who were drawn to the rhetoric of Black Power. He thought it was an unnecessarily divisive term, and though he understood the anger behind it he feared that in the end it led nowhere beyond a momentary catharsis.

How could he, in this darkening climate, continue to preach the gospel of nonviolence and still be heard? As he pondered and prayed and conferred with his closest circle of advisers, there came a moment near the end of the year when his calculations became less strategic. This had happened before in times of crisis: in Birmingham, when the movement floundered and nobody knew what to do next, he had simply led a march in which he knew that he would be arrested, joining other protesters in jail, despite his own claustrophobic fears. He knew he needed to lead by example, by simply being who he was, who he felt himself called to be, and now he came to that place again. He was a preacher, first and foremost, and for whatever time he might be given (always, it seemed, he was acutely aware of the possibility of death) he would go forward in that way, preaching about the issues that mattered to him most.

He would speak about peace and economic justice. How could he do otherwise with this terrible war being waged in his country's name, sapping its resources, killing its spirit; and how could he ignore the disillusionment and rage in the big city ghettoes, where people suffocated from a lack of opportunity, so carefully, intricately, and invisibly constructed that white Americans managed not to notice?

None of this would be easy, he knew. But he would push ahead, no matter the resistance, no matter the cost. There was really nothing else he could do.

41

Dispatches

January began with the editors of the *New York Times* defending one of their own. For years, Harrison Salisbury had been one of the paper's toughest, most fearless correspondents, and in late December Salisbury had been reporting from Hanoi. One year earlier, three American critics of the war—Staughton Lynd, Tom Hayden, and Herbert Aptheker—had made their own trip behind enemy lines, recording the things they saw, honestly perhaps, as almost anyone who knew them could attest, but inevitably through the lens of their own dissent. This was different. This was a newspaperman, trained in the craft of objectivity, reporting on things that the U.S. government had never admitted.

On Christmas day, Salisbury had filed a dispatch from Nam Dinh, a city fifty miles southeast of Hanoi. In plain but gripping newspaper prose, he recounted an interview with the town's mayor, Tran Thi Doan, conducted in a bomb shelter while air raid sirens warned of approaching U.S. planes. There had been, he wrote, at least fifty-one attacks against this city which had no apparent military importance. This was a part of Salisbury's report:

> Christmas wasn't a joyous occasion for Namdinh although strings of small red pennants decorated the old grey, stucco Catholic church and a white Star of Bethlehem had been mounted on the pinnacle of the tower. Few Americans have heard of Namdinh, although until recently it was the third largest North Vietnamese city.
>
> Mayor Doan regards her city as essentially a cotton-and-silk textile town containing nothing of military significance. Namdinh has been systematically attacked by American planes since June 28, 1965.
>
> The cathedral tower looks out on block after block of utter desolation; the city's population of 90,000 has been reduced to 20,000 because of evacuation; 13 percent of the city's housing, including the homes of 12,464 people, have been destroyed; 89 people have been killed and 405 wounded.

> No American communiqué has asserted that Namdinh contains some facility that the United States regards as a military objective. It is apparent, on personal inspection, that block after block of ordinary housing, particularly surrounding the textile plant, has been smashed to rubble by repeated attacks by Seventh Fleet planes.

And another dispatch on December 27 about the bombing of a highway leading south from Hanoi:

> The results of American bombing of the route are readily visible—particularly in small villages and hamlets along the route. They have suffered severely, often being almost obliterated. But the effect on transportation has been minimal.

Some newspapers in the United States were harshly critical of Salisbury's mission, and accused him of "putting out Communist propaganda." The *Washington Post*, always a major competitor with the *Times*, echoed the charge and reported U.S. officials were "deeply irritated"—especially with Salisbury's use of damage figures provided by the North Vietnamese.

On January 6, the *Times*' editors responded that Salisbury was reporting what he saw, as any correspondent should, and that he also might be advancing the cause of peace. He met with North Vietnamese leaders who suggested, as they had on other occasions, that there was flexibility in their negotiating stance. This was important for the U.S. to know, the editors insisted.

Whatever the diplomatic potential, others saw a different meaning in Salisbury's work—most importantly, a reporter's inclination to be a thorn in the side of power. Neil Sheehan, another decorated writer at the *Times*, pointed out that Salisbury took delight in exposing lies and hypocrisy in high places, specifically, in this case, that "the Johnson Administration was killing thousands of civilians while claiming to be conducting a 'surgical bombing campaign' in North Vietnam."

Marilyn Young, in her history of the war, maintained that Salisbury's reporting normalized North Vietnam, made it "a real place, whose government handouts were therefore no less worthy than those of other capitals." If U.S. officials charged indignantly that Salisbury had reported Hanoi's statistics on civilian casualties, the answer was, of course he had. Who else would know? Certainly not the American government, which claimed there were no casualties at all.

All of this was part of a shift, glacial at first but then more rapid, in American attitudes about the war, particularly when it came to the credibility of the government. The U.S. commander, General William Westmoreland, was resolutely reassuring in his reports, offering casualty figures that pointed persuasively toward a U.S. victory. Every battle, it seemed, left a landscape littered with Viet Cong. One of the problems, however, for U.S. forces was that no matter how often they would "search and destroy," as Westmoreland put it, once the battle was won and the Americans returned to their base, the Viet Cong simply moved back in.

To combat this maddening departure from the way other wars had been fought, Westmoreland and the American commanders devised a new strategy. When an area was known to be under the control of Viet Cong, the United States and the army of the government of South Vietnam began systematically to bomb and bulldoze it to oblivion—"trees, houses, crops," wrote Marilyn Young, "taking the population out with the troops, leaving the burned-over district as a free field for bombs and artillery."

In early 1967, twenty-four-year-old Jonathan Schell, officially on assignment from the *Harvard Crimson*, observed one of these missions firsthand and wrote about it for the *New Yorker*. In an article of 32,000 powerful and gracefully understated words, he described the destruction of the village of Ben Suc, less than thirty miles southwest of Saigon. In the second week of January, Schell flew in with some five hundred U.S. soldiers, transported by a fleet of sixty helicopters—two rows of thirty, flying twenty yards apart. Schell was on Chopper 47, seated with six American soldiers, several of whom were about to see combat for the first time.

The mission was easy enough for the Americans. There was little resistance as the helicopter fleet dove suddenly to treetop level and swerved toward the village, flying at a hundred miles per hour. Soon after the landing, one villager was shot as he rode his bicycle toward the Americans, and he fell face down in a muddy ditch.

"You know," said a soldier, with a forced and husky defiance in his voice, "that's the first time I've ever seen a dead guy, and I don't feel bad. I just don't, that's all." Another added, "Yeah, he's dead. Ah shot him. He was a fuckin' V.C."

Over the course of the morning, the villagers were herded toward a central place in the hamlet where the interrogations began—some by the Americans, some by the South Vietnamese army, seeking information on the Viet Cong.

Schell wandered freely through these sessions, and he stopped at one where the South Vietnamese were torturing a suspect. An American adviser who was watching it all called Schell aside and tried to explain what was going on:

> "You see, they do have some—well, methods and practices that we are not accustomed to, that we wouldn't use if we were doing it, but the thing you've got to understand is that this is an Asian country, and their first impulse is force. Only the fear of force gets results. It's the Asian mind. It's completely different from what we know as the Western mind, and it's hard for us to understand. Look—they're a thousand years behind us in this place, and we're trying to educate them up to our level."

Schell continued to explore the village, then returned to the same interrogation hut, where the torture continued:

> After twenty seconds or so, the American looked up and said to me, "They've been usin' a little water torture." In the water torture, a sopping rag is held over the prisoner's nose and mouth to suffocate him, or his head is pushed back and water is poured down his nostrils to choke him.

In the end, after the interrogations and torture, and the removal of all the people from their houses, the village was burned, bulldozed, and bombed, "as though having decided to destroy it, we were now bent on annihilating every possible indication that the village of Ben Suc had ever existed."

The residents were sent to a refugee camp.

It was a policy that increasingly defined the U.S. war effort, and reporters continued to describe it to the world. One Japanese writer, Katsuichi Honda, thought this cavalier destruction of villages that were often hundreds of years old, inhabited by the same families, generation after generation, lay in a fundamental lack of understanding—a lack of regard—for the Vietnamese people and their agrarian way of life. In 1967, Honda described the plunder of a rice field by five American tanks:

> The ripe ears of rice, now ready to be harvested, were mercilessly trodden and kneaded in the muddy field under the caterpillars as they took their capricious way over the paddies. They did not even have the kindness to make one tank

> follow in the wake of the preceding one. The seed beds of rice plants, and the newly planted paddies—all these were nothing in their eyes.

All over the world, but especially in the United States, these kinds of articles—overflowing as they were with heart-wrenching specifics—combined with televised battles on the six o'clock news to create a new reality of war. Even the president began to have nightmares. Later, he told Doris Kearns of the nights he lay in his White House bed, caught in a haze between insomnia and sleep, and began to imagine scenes from the war:

> I would . . . begin to picture myself lying on the battlefield in Da Nang. I could see an American plane, circling above me in the sky. I felt safe. Then I heard a long, loud shot. The plane began to fall faster, faster, faster. I saw it hit the ground, and as soon as it burst into flames, I couldn't stand it any more. I knew that one of my boys must have been killed that night. I jumped out of bed, put on my robe, took my flashlight, and went into the situation room.

There, at any hour of the day or night, officials from the Pentagon and the CIA were processing a constant flow of battleground information—targets hit, bridges destroyed—and as Kearns wrote,

> the classified tickers and reports were endowing illusion with the appearance of precision. . . . Bombers, flying over hundreds of hamlets and hillocks and villages, could not even begin to separate enemies and innocents, soldiers and civilians. . . . This was combat by proxy; it was war waged at a distance. It looked impressive from the air. But on the ground one could see that it was like "trying to weed a garden with a bulldozer."

Attorney General Ramsey Clark, sometimes present in the Situation Room, recalled another troubling impression. Nobody appeared to care about the Vietnamese. "I never sensed any concern for the other side," Clark told author Merle Miller. "How many did the Vietnamese lose? How many people were killed in the villages? How many South Vietnamese, how many North Vietnamese, how many Viet Cong? It was our lives, our country; and they didn't figure, those people."

Clark was different from many Washington officials. The Texas-born son of a Supreme Court Justice, he was, as *Jet* magazine once described him, a resolute "New Frontier liberal," instinctively compassionate, committed to civil rights, and dubious about concentrations of power. Tall and soft-spoken with the gentle hint of Texas twang in his speech, he could sometimes be a minority of one, and didn't seem to mind when it came to issues like the callousness of war. He knew there were other good people in government, caught in the strategic urgency in the moment—"the fog of war," Robert McNamara called it—and later some of them were filled with regret. In 1967, however, if they thought about the Vietnamese at all, it was less the humanity of those on the ground, or the destruction of villages by napalm and bombs, as it was the maddening enemy resolve. As McNamara told a reporter from *Newsweek*, "I didn't think these people had the capacity to fight this way."

McNamara, of course, was simply not listening. He was not alone in that but the evidence was always explicit and clear. In December 1966, in a conversation with the German theologian Martin Niemoeller, Ho Chi Minh repeated the things he had said all along: "Everything depends on the Americans. If they want to make war for twenty years then we shall make war for twenty years. If they want to make peace, we shall make peace and invite them to tea afterwards."

There was no tea, just a test of wills, and after a while there was also this: The casualty figures were no longer abstract. Even those of us still watching from a distance, grateful perhaps for our college deferments, knew people willing to enter the fight. Some were drafted, others volunteered, and many of them paid a brave price. "The lamp of liberty lights my way," one friend said, announcing his decision to join the Marines. My friend was joking in his choice of words, deflecting with characteristic self-deprecation the disbelieving pleas from the rest of us who told him he had lost his mind. But of course he was serious; his country called and he was ready.

Later that year he was shot through the spine.

AMID THE DESULTORY HEADLINES of war and all the human cost they revealed, there *was* excitement on another front. In January, the United States was entering the homestretch of its race to the Moon. Since 1961, our successes in space had multiplied, each one building upon the last. The Mercury missions had progressed from the parabolic lobs of the first two flights to multiple orbits around the globe, one courageous astronaut at a time. Then came Gemini—a series of missions, two pilots each, in 1965 and '66 that produced spectacular demonstrations of prowess. One of those was the first American space-walk. Astronaut Ed White was so delighted by his time spent floating outside the capsule that he refused at first to come back in.

White was not the first human being to perform this feat. A Soviet cosmonaut had done the same thing a few days earlier, raising the possibility of a serious, two-nation race to the Moon. But after ten Gemini flights, the United States was clearly in the lead, and now at last it was time for Apollo. These would be flights with three-person crews, each one getting us closer to the Moon before a landing near the end of 1969.

Apollo 1 was scheduled for launch as a low-orbit flight on February 21, 1967, with a key dress rehearsal three weeks earlier. On January 27 the three Apollo pilots, spacewalker Ed White, rookie astronaut Roger Chaffee, and mission commander Gus Grissom climbed into the capsule, and almost immediately things began to go wrong. Grissom was particularly annoyed. In 1961, as the second American in space, he had nearly drowned in the Atlantic Ocean when the hatch blew and his capsule sank.

His Gemini mission went much better. In a mischievous reference to his Mercury flight, he named his Gemini capsule *Molly Brown* (after a 1964 Debbie Reynolds movie, *The Unsinkable Molly Brown*.) NASA officials were not amused and insisted that he change the name of the capsule. Grissom suggested *Titanic*. Appalled, NASA decided to go with *Molly Brown*.

Ordinarily, Grissom was not much of a comic. He was known around the space program as a man of few words who said what he meant and meant what he said, and one of the things he talked about in the weeks leading up to his Apollo mission was the poor design of the space capsule. Among other things, the hatch opened inward which made it much harder to maneuver, especially if there was ever a time when astronauts had to make a quick exit. The capsule was filled with pure oxygen, and there was reason to worry about the wiring and whether there was enough insulation. But the first thing to go wrong on the day of the test was the radio. The static was so bad it was hard to communicate with the control tower.

"Jesus Christ," Grissom snapped. "How are we going to get to the Moon if we can't talk between two or three buildings?"

Then came a spark underneath Grissom's seat. It was just a tiny arc at first, but in the capsule environment of undiluted oxygen, that was all it took.

"We've got a fire in the cockpit!" It was the voice of Roger Chaffee, tinged with urgency, and two dozen NASA workers rushed toward the capsule, trying desperately to open the hatch, which the astronauts were unable to do. This was the *New York Times* account:

> The fire lasted only four minutes before crews inside the gantry around the spacecraft and its rocket could open the hatch atop the spacecraft. Mr. Haney (NASA spokesman Paul Haney) said 26 workmen had inhaled smoke while trying to open the hatch. Two of the men were hospitalized. The Apollo spacecraft is not equipped with ejection seats, as were the Gemini spacecraft, which was flown in training missions in 1965 and 1966. Even if there were no fire inside the spacecraft, it would have taken a minimum of 90 seconds for the three astronauts to open the Apollo hatch and emerge, a NASA technician said.
>
> The astronauts were reported to have been fatally burned almost instantly by the sweeping fire.

For Americans accustomed to space flight successes, it was a nearly unbelievable moment. I remember as if it had just happened a radio broadcast in which a NASA spokesman acknowledged: "We've always known that one day astronauts would die." It was chilling to hear it put that way, but just a week before the fire, Gus Grissom had said the same thing: "If we die, we want people to accept it. We are in a risky business, and we hope that if anything happens to us, it will not delay the program. The conquest of space is worth the risk of life."

But was it? That was the question in the immediate aftermath of the tragedy, and for a while nobody knew what the answer would be. NASA cancelled Apollo 2 and 3, and the next three flights were unmanned, while the agency conducted a massive review and began to redesign the flawed capsule. Not until Apollo 7, an eleven-day, low orbit flight commanded by veteran Wally Schirra, did U.S. astronauts venture again into space. By then it was 1968, and barely fourteen months remained to meet President Kennedy's goal of a man on the Moon by the end of the decade.

Many people thought it was unrealistic, but NASA was moved by the voice of the president and perhaps by the voice of Gus Grissom as well.

They were not ready to give up yet.

42

The Road to Riverside

February came and found both Martin Luther King and Robert Kennedy agonizing over Vietnam. Both wanted to make a stronger case than either had in the past, and both faced enormous pressure not to.

King was "transfixed," in the words of one journalist, by the January issue of *Ramparts* magazine, which contained a condemnation of the war written by Benjamin Spock, the amiable and aging pediatrician who had become an antiwar activist. Spock had spent most of his professional life writing books about the care of America's children, but in *Ramparts* he wrote about the children of Vietnam. It was not his words, as fiercely eloquent as they were, that made the greatest impression on King. It was the twenty-four pages of accompanying photographs—heartbreaking images of children gravely wounded in the fighting. King could not stop returning to the pages, trying to fathom the things that were being done in America's name. The photographs were the work of William F. Pepper, a political scientist at Mercy College in Dobbs Ferry, New York. Pepper had gone to Vietnam to study the effects of the war on women and children, and in *Ramparts* he also wrote about the things he had seen:

> For countless thousands of children in Vietnam, breathing is quickened by terror and pain, and tiny bodies learn more about death every day. These solemn, rarely smiling little ones have never known what it is to live without despair.
>
> They indeed know death, for it walks with them by day and accompanies their sleep at night. It is as omnipresent as the napalm that falls from the skies with the frequency and impartiality of the monsoon rain.
>
> The horror of what we are doing to the children of Vietnam—"we," because napalm and white phosphorous are the weapons of America—is staggering,

> whether we examine the overall figures or look at a particular case like that of Doan Minh Luan.
>
> Luan, age eight, was one of two children brought to Britain last summer through private philanthropy, for extensive treatment at the McIndoe Burn Center. He came off the plane with a muslin bag over what had been his face. His parents had been burned alive. His chin had been "melted" into his throat so that he could not close his mouth. He had no eyelids. After the injury, he had no treatment at all—none whatever—for four months.

King could barely stand to read such words. For people like himself or Robert Kennedy, whose statements against the war had been so measured, restrained by their own strategic self-interest, these images could only be a sobering call to do something.

In the case of Dr. King, some of his closest advisers argued strongly against saying more. Bayard Rustin and Stanley Levison, two men in whom King placed great trust, had only to remind him of the reaction by U.S. Senator Thomas Dodd, a Connecticut Democrat, when King called for a halt in U.S. bombing back in 1965. Dodd not only blasted King for being out of his depth, he also cited an obscure federal law barring private citizens from meddling in foreign policy.

King was stung by the rebuke, for it was clear that Dodd was speaking for the president, who had been, by any reasonable estimation, a courageous ally of the civil rights movement. Rustin and Levison now tried their best to make King understand that he could not—*must not*—break with Johnson over Vietnam. King, however, had made up his mind. On February 25 in Los Angeles, he shared the podium with four antiwar senators—Republican Mark Hatfield and Democrats George McGovern, Ernest Gruening, and Eugene McCarthy—and spoke of America's "declining moral status in the world" and the "deadly western arrogance that has poisoned the international atmosphere for too long."

"Our nation," King continued, "which initiated so much of the revolutionary spirit of the modern world, is now cast in the mold of being an arch anti-revolutionary. We are engaged in a war that seeks to turn the clock of history back and perpetuate white colonialism."

Lyndon Johnson was said to be irate, but King pushed ahead. He began a series of meetings with members of Clergy and Laity Concerned About

Vietnam, an ecumenical antiwar group founded in 1965. Among its leaders were pacifist priest Daniel Berrigan, Yale chaplain William Sloane Coffin, and King's longtime friend and civil rights ally, Rabbi Abraham Heschel. King was eager to find just the right setting to deliver a fully fleshed-out address on the war, and the clergy leaders suggested Riverside Church. King was thrilled. There was no more majestic cathedral in the country than Riverside, which towered over the Hudson River from Morningside Heights in upper Manhattan. The church, paid for by John D. Rockefeller, opened its doors in 1930 with the great Christian orator Harry Emerson Fosdick as its pastor. In its thirty-seven-year history it had hosted guest sermons by some of the finest theologians of the twentieth century, including Paul Tillich, Reinhold Niebuhr and Dietrich Bonhoeffer. King was happy to be in such company, and he and the antiwar clergy agreed on a date of April 4.

On March 25, he and Benjamin Spock led an antiwar march through the streets of Chicago. Four days later, King met privately with heavyweight champion Muhammad Ali, who had announced as an act of conscience that he would refuse induction into the Army. Ali was a follower of Elijah Muhammad, the controversial head of the Nation of Islam, where a philosophy of black nationalism was enmeshed in a mutation of Muslim theology. Malcolm X had once been a leader in the Nation of Islam, but had broken with Muhammad just before his murder in 1965. Now Ali was about to do something similar. He told King he intended to defy Muhammad's ban on political activity by opposing the war in Vietnam. The two of them talked about the risks, not the least of which, in addition to crossing Elijah Muhammad, were being stripped of his heavyweight title and perhaps serving time in a federal prison.

Ali was prepared to pay the price.

On Sunday morning, April 2 King delivered a sermon on Vietnam at his own Ebenezer Baptist Church in Atlanta. He spoke with admiration about the moral courage of the heavyweight champion, and about the depth of his own misgivings regarding the war.

"I preach to you today on the war in Vietnam," he said, "because my conscience leaves me no other choice. . . . There comes a time when silence is betrayal."

Then it was on to Riverside. On April 4, accompanied by Rabbi Heschel, historian Henry Steele Commager, and John Bennett, president of Union

Theological Seminary, King ascended the pulpit beneath the great stone arches of what he called "this great magnificent house of worship." At times he sounded like the preacher he was: "The calling to speak is a vocation of agony, but we must speak. We must speak with all the humility that is appropriate to our limited vision, but we must speak."

But much of the time what he offered was a history lesson, which was fitting enough since the speech was drafted by the Harlem-born historian Vincent Harding. Having worked with Harding's words to make them his own, King talked of a war that undermined the national fight against poverty by sapping it of the necessary funds. He spoke of how the burden of battle in this faraway land fell disproportionately on African Americans. But much of what he talked about was a history of suffering in Vietnam:

> As I ponder the madness of Vietnam . . . my mind goes constantly to the people of that peninsula. I speak now not of the soldiers of each side, not of the junta in Saigon, but simply of the people who have been living under the curse of war for almost three continuous decades now. I think of them too because it is clear to me that there will be no meaningful solution there until some attempt is made to know them and hear their broken cries.
>
> They must see Americans as strange liberators. The Vietnamese people proclaimed their own independence in 1945 after a combined French and Japanese occupation, and before the Communist revolution in China. They were led by Ho Chi Minh. Even though they quoted the American Declaration of Independence in their own document of freedom, we refused to recognize them. Instead, we decided to support France in its re-conquest of her former colony.
>
> Our government felt then that the Vietnamese people were not "ready" for independence, and we again fell victim to the deadly Western arrogance that has poisoned the international atmosphere for so long. With that tragic decision we rejected a revolutionary government seeking self-determination, and a government that had been established not by China (for whom the Vietnamese have no great love) but by clearly indigenous forces that included some Communists. For the peasants this new government meant real land reform, one of the most important needs in their lives.
>
> For nine years following 1945 we denied the people of Vietnam the right of independence. For nine years we vigorously supported the French in their abortive effort to recolonize Vietnam.

Before the end of the war we were meeting eighty percent of the French war costs. Even before the French were defeated at Dien Bien Phu, they began to despair of the reckless action, but we did not. We encouraged them with our huge financial and military supplies to continue the war even after they had lost the will. . . .

After the French were defeated it looked as if independence and land reform would come again through the Geneva agreements. But instead there came the United States, determined that Ho should not unify the temporarily divided nation, and the peasants watched again as we supported one of the most vicious modern dictators—our chosen man, Premier Diem. The peasants watched and cringed as Diem ruthlessly routed out all opposition, supported their extortionist landlords and refused even to discuss reunification with the north. The peasants watched as all this was presided over by U.S. influence and then by increasing numbers of U.S. troops who came to help quell the insurgency that Diem's methods had aroused. When Diem was overthrown they may have been happy, but the long line of military dictatorships seemed to offer no real change—especially in terms of their need for land and peace.

The only change came from America as we increased our troop commitments. . . . Now they languish under our bombs and consider us—not their fellow Vietnamese—the real enemy. They move sadly and apathetically as we herd them off the land of their fathers into concentration camps where minimal social needs are rarely met. They know they must move or be destroyed by our bombs. So they go—primarily women and children and the aged.

They watch as we poison their water, as we kill a million acres of their crops. They must weep as the bulldozers roar through their areas preparing to destroy the precious trees. They wander into the hospitals, with at least twenty casualties from American firepower for one "Viet Cong"-inflicted injury. So far we may have killed a million of them—mostly children. They wander into the towns and see thousands of the children, homeless, without clothes, running in packs on the streets like animals. They see the children, degraded by our soldiers as they beg for food. They see the children selling their sisters to our soldiers, soliciting for their mothers. . . .

We have destroyed their two most cherished institutions: the family and the village. We have destroyed their land and their crops.

Now there is little left to build on—save bitterness. Soon the only solid physical foundations remaining will be found at our military bases and in the

> concrete of the concentration camps we call fortified hamlets. The peasants may well wonder if we plan to build our new Vietnam on such grounds as these? Could we blame them for such thoughts? We must speak for them and raise the questions they cannot raise. These too are our brothers . . .

Interrupted frequently by applause from an audience that filled the great cathedral, King called for an end to American bombing, a date for withdrawal of American troops, and a negotiated settlement that would include the Viet Cong. More than that, to prevent such future calamities he urged a rethinking of our national priorities, especially our affinity for colonialism—which he said was racist at its heart—and our failure to see the limits of military power.

In retrospect, the bravery and truth of King's speech are remarkable, and because it stands the test of history, and the test of fact, the response to it in the moments immediately after its delivery are even more amazing than the speech itself. If King had spoken the truth in 1963 when he proclaimed his dream at the Lincoln Memorial, and if much of the nation was stirred by his words, this was not the case with his address at Riverside. This time, the condemnation came in a torrent. *Life* magazine called the speech "a demagogic slander that sounded like a script for Radio Hanoi." The *New York Times* took special issue with King's labeling of "fortified hamlets" as concentration camps, and chastised him for "recklessly comparing American military methods with those of the Nazis." African Americans, including columnist Carl Rowan and Senator Edward Brooke, joined in the chorus of criticism, which culminated with the *Washington Post* all but dismissing King: "Many who have listened to him with respect will never again accord him the same confidence. He has diminished his usefulness to his cause, to his country, and to his people. And that is a great tragedy."

There were a few exceptions to this cascade of scorn. The *Detroit Free Press,* whose editor Mark Ethridge Jr. was widely respected among his peers, endorsed King's stand, and the *Christian Century* praised his "magnificent blend of eloquence and raw fact . . . of tough realism and infinite compassion."

King was stung by the criticism and grateful for those who stood beside him, but if he was given to occasional self-doubt, on a much deeper level he was certain this time that he was right. After the speech, Roy Wilkins of the NAACP, always a more cautious voice, called to goad King, telling him, "I saw your picture in the paper, Martin."

As David Garrow notes, King calmly returned the fire: "Yes, Roy, why weren't you there with me?"

IN THESE SAME WEEKS, Robert Kennedy found himself on a similar trajectory, with similar results. For some time, he had worried about Vietnam and the mounting evidence of a U.S. policy gone seriously awry. He knew that when his brother was president, viewing Vietnam through a Cold War lens, he had played a significant role in John Kennedy's mistake. Other senators had spoken much earlier against the war—Ernest Gruening, Frank Moss, Mark Hatfield, George McGovern—and though it was true that all had less to lose (unlike Kennedy, they were not regarded as presidential front runners for 1972), Kennedy had to admire their courage.

For months, his friends on the left, including journalist Jack Newfield and antiwar activist Allard Lowenstein, had been urging Kennedy to ally himself unapologetically with the peace movement. History, they said, was on its side. In January, Kennedy traveled to Europe for a speaking engagement, followed by meetings with foreign leaders. Everywhere he went, he encountered disillusionment and dismay toward American policy. In France Andre Malraux, the novelist who served as minister of cultural affairs, told him simply, "Vietnam is against American tradition." President Charles de Gaulle agreed, warning Kennedy that U.S. standing in the rest of the world was being undercut by the war.

"As I told your brother," said de Gaulle, "the United States is involved in a wrong course in Vietnam," and he reminded Kennedy of painful lessons learned by France: "History is the force at work in Vietnam, and the United States will not prevail against it."

In German and Italy, there was more of the same, and Pope Paul VI, citing "extremely reliable sources," told Kennedy the North Vietnamese were ready to talk and might be more flexible than the U.S. assumed. A French official had said the same thing; in a meeting with Kennedy and John Gunther Dean, a Vietnam expert in the U.S. Embassy, French diplomat Étienne Manac'h affirmed that Hanoi was prepared to negotiate if the United States stopped the bombing. The State Department leaked to *Newsweek* the story of a "peace feeler" sent through Kennedy, and Lyndon Johnson was enraged. He assumed that Kennedy was off on a freelance diplomatic mission, intended to undercut U.S. policy. On February 6, Johnson called

Kennedy to the White House and accused him of leaking the story as an act of political sabotage.

"I think," Kennedy answered coldly, "the leak came from your State Department."

"Goddamn it," Johnson snapped, "it's *your* State Department."

The conversation went downhill after that curious assertion, with Johnson insisting that military victory was not far away, and by giving aid and comfort to the enemy, Kennedy had American blood on his hands. Kennedy immediately rose to leave.

"I don't have to take that from you," he said.

In Kennedy's mind, the meeting was a turning point. He ordered speechwriter Adam Walinski to start drafting a major address on the war and told columnist Mary McGrory, "I'm going to escalate this." By now, more and more voices were being raised in dissent, including those of a dozen U.S. senators from both parties and every part of the country. Even traditionally conservative Southerners like J. William Fulbright of Arkansas and Albert Gore Sr. of Tennessee were joining with Frank Church of Idaho and Jacob Javits of New York to challenge with varying degrees of certainty the tragedy in Southeast Asia.

Nobody, however, had the clout of Robert Kennedy. For more than a month, he worked on various drafts of a speech with Walinski, Richard Goodwin, and Arthur Schlesinger. During that time, as Schlesinger recounted, Kennedy met with old friends in the Johnson Administration, including Robert McNamara and Averell Harriman, to learn what he could about the future direction of U.S. policy. He also met with critics of the war, including some of the most outspoken. Kennedy had recently read *The Other Side*, and asked Newfield to arrange a meeting with two of its authors, Tom Hayden and Staughton Lynd. According to Newfield's later account, the afternoon meeting on February 13 began with a kind of stiff formality, until Lynd's young son spilled Coke on the rug of Kennedy's apartment. Kennedy picked the little boy up and told him gently, "Don't worry about that. It makes the rug grow better." Immediately, everybody relaxed. Kennedy liked both Hayden and Lynd. He found them reasonable, and their point of emphasis was one he had heard before, most recently on his trip to Europe. It was also one with which he agreed: The United States must stop the bombing of North Vietnam, for if it did peace talks could proceed from there, and the agony might finally come to an end.

According to the latest Gallup Poll, however, only 24 percent of Americans favored an immediate end to the bombing. Lyndon Johnson, who shared the furious conviction of General Westmoreland that military victory was the way to end the war, still enjoyed broad public support. Nevertheless, a bombing halt became Kennedy's central policy recommendation, as he put the finishing touches on his speech.

On the morning of March 2, the day of the address, he joked with his wife Ethel at breakfast, using his sense of irony and self-deprecation, as he had so often with his late older brother, to help defuse the tension of the moment. "I spoke with Teddy last night," he said, referring to Edward Kennedy who was now the senior senator from Massachusetts. "He said to make sure they announce it's the Kennedy from New York."

At 3:40 that afternoon, he rose to speak in the Senate chamber, beginning with something that was rare among American politicians—an admission of his own culpability for the war. "I can testify," he said, "that if fault is to be found or responsibility asserted, there is enough to go around for all—including myself."

For many of us who watched him carefully back then, this was Kennedy at his most compelling, for there was, we felt, a kind of visceral honesty about him, followed immediately by a deep identification with people who hurt. He had seen the photographs of the war, and they moved him as powerfully as they had Dr. King. In his speech, Kennedy called us to imagine "the vacant moment of amazed fear as a mother and child watch death by fire fall from an improbable machine sent by a country they barely comprehend." This, he said, was something for which we all bore the blame, "not just a nation's responsibility, but yours and mine. It is our chemicals that scorch the children and our bombs that level the villages. We are all participants."

When he urged a unilateral end to the bombing, this became the nugget of "news," the focal point of political debate in the furious counterattack that followed. But for many of us, who were drifting inexorably toward our own dissent, Kennedy's great gift was his ability to humanize an issue. He did it in this speech against the war, and again in April when he paid a visit to the Mississippi Delta.

IN MISSISSIPPI THE ISSUE was poverty, part of the triumvirate of liberal concern that had firmly solidified in the country. In the parallel journeys of Kennedy and King, these two men who together embodied a sense of possibility against the ever-growing evils that threatened to engulf us, it was harder now to tell the issues apart. War, racism, economic injustice; each one seemed to bleed into the next. Poverty and prejudice were clearly part of a never-ending cycle, and the war was sapping our resources and spirit, and in Mississippi Kennedy saw the problem at its worst.

He went there because of Marian Wright, a twenty-seven-year-old African- American lawyer from South Carolina, who earned her law degree from Yale. Wright went to work in Mississippi for the NAACP Legal Defense Fund, and in March 1967 she testified before the Senate Labor Committee about the desperate poverty she had seen in the Delta. On the strength of her account, Kennedy and Committee Chairman Joseph Clark, a Democrat from Pennsylvania, flew to Mississippi. They arrived in Jackson on April 9, and the following day set out for the rural countryside. Details of their visit come from several first-person accounts. Reporter Nick Kotz filed a hard-hitting story for the *Des Moines Register* about a tenant shack the senators visited, which smelled of "mildew, sickness, and urine." Civil rights leader Charles Evers, whose brother Medgar had been murdered less than four years earlier, described what happened when Kennedy insisted on going inside.

> There was no ceiling hardly; the floor had holes in it, and a bed that looked like the color of my arm—black as my arm—propped up with some kind of bricks to keep it from falling. The odor was so bad you could hardly keep the nausea down. . . . This lady came out with hardly any clothes on, and we spoke to her and told her who he was. She just put her arms out and said 'Thank God' and then she just held his hand.

As Arthur Schlesinger wrote later, there was a child sitting on the floor "rubbing grains of rice round and round." Evers picked up the story from there:

> His tummy was sticking way out just like he was pregnant. Bobby looked down at the child, and then he picked him up and sat down on that dirty bed. He was rubbing the child's stomach. He said, "My God, I didn't know this kind of thing existed. How can a country like this allow it? Maybe they just

> don't know . . ." Tears were running down his cheek, and he just sat there and held the little child. Roaches and rats were all over the floor.

Marian Wright was also amazed. She expected that Kennedy, like any national politician, was there for the publicity, but later she told the Justice Department's Roger Wilkins,

> He did things that I wouldn't do. He went into the dirtiest, filthiest, poorest black homes . . . and he would sit with a baby who had open sores and whose belly was bloated from malnutrition, and he'd sit and touch and hold those babies . . . I wouldn't do that! I didn't do that! But he did. . . .

The day after they returned to Washington, Kennedy and Clark went to see Secretary of Agriculture Orville Freeman and began to pressure the Johnson Administration to provide free food stamps for the poorest of the poor. The hard truth was, Kennedy had seen this kind of desperation in other places—in upstate New York where he and Senator Jacob Javits found a migrant family living in a rotted out school bus, in Bedford-Stuyvesant where he met a child whose face had been mutilated by a rat, on Indian reservations where one Sioux leader, Vine Deloria, was so impressed by Kennedy's compassion that he offered the highest compliment he could think of: "Spiritually, he was an Indian."

But nothing was worse than Mississippi. In June, Harvard psychiatrist Robert Coles, a gifted, empathetic writer, traveled to the Delta and reported that he and his party "found it hard to believe we were examining American children in the twentieth century." They returned to Washington with an urgent plea for emergency funding, but received a cold shoulder from the Johnson Administration. "You don't have to take that," Kennedy told them, and with his encouragement they continued to apply the political pressure. In July, Senator John Stennis, a Mississippi conservative, finally introduced a bill to send food and medicine to the most wretched parts of his state. The Senate passed it within ten days, but a final bill didn't pass both houses until November. Even then, Johnson resisted spending the money. "On at least 12 specific occasions," wrote the *Des Moines Register*'s Nick Kotz, who continued to follow the story, "his aides and Cabinet officers had recommended food aid reform and Lyndon Johnson had said 'no.'"

Even Hubert Humphrey, Johnson's remarkably loyal vice president, wrote critically to a prominent Democrat who was concerned about the malnutrition of children. "There are ways the President could have helped. . . . But he has not."

Was it Johnson's hatred for Robert Kennedy? Had the war begun to poison his heart? Or was there some more rational reason? Historian Arthur Schlesinger later suggested that Johnson may have feared inflation if he increased the size of the federal budget. Whatever the case, Schlesinger concluded, by the spring of 1967 Johnson's War on Poverty "was a fading memory. Johnson even banished the phrase from his speeches."

As journalist Jack Newfield wrote, the president was becoming a hated figure—the "Anti-Christ of the New Politics," while Martin Luther King and Robert Kennedy were rapidly emerging as its heroes.

43

Rockwell and the Power of Art

On May 16, *Look* magazine appeared on the newsstands with a cover that promised an examination of "SUBURBIA: The Good Life in Our Exploding Utopia." The magazine intended to take a broad view, exploring such topics as "Parties and Prejudice," "Morals and Divorce," and "Teenagers in Trouble." Included in the mix was an article entitled "The Negro in the Suburbs," written by journalist Jack Starr and set in Chicago, the site of Dr. King's open housing marches. It began this way:

> "Being a Negro in the middle of white people is like being alone in the middle of a crowd," says Mrs. Jacqueline Robbins, a young Negro housewife who lives in the Chicago suburb of Park Forest, Ill. In December, 1962, Mrs. Robbins, her chemist husband Terry, 32, and their two sons moved into the then all-white suburb, whose first, and only Negro family had just recently moved out. . .The Robbins are not alone. Although Negroes are still a rarity in the green reaches of suburbia, they are emerging from nearly all the large metropolitan ghettos with increasing frequency. In Chicago last year, 179 Negro families moved into white suburbs—more than twice as many as in the previous year, seven times as many as in 1963, and 45 times as many as in 1961 and 1962 combined.

The article made an important point. Segregation in the suburbs was beginning to break down, and Americans were divided about that fact. But it may well be that the readers of *Look* were as intrigued by the illustration of the story, as they were by Starr's well-crafted article. The art came from the brush of Norman Rockwell in the form of a painting he called *New Kids in the Neighborhood.* Among America's visual artists, Rockwell was certainly one of the best known. Then 73, he had spent forty-seven years painting covers for the *Saturday Evening Post*, a competitor of *Look*, and his work at the *Post* consisted primarily of all-American scenes of everyday life. Art critics were often underwhelmed, regarding Rockwell's work as simply too sweet to be taken seriously. But the American public loved him, seeing perhaps a reassuring reflection of themselves, and for nearly fifty years the editors at the *Post* knew they had a good thing.

Rockwell, however, was a man with a conscience, which had flickered periodically throughout his career, showing itself in paintings such as *Freedom of Speech*, in which a lone, blue-collar dissenter with a plaid shirt and open jacket rises to speak to a white-collar crowd. By the 1960s, Rockwell was ready to address the issue of race, a dangerous topic in the eyes of his editors, and the *Saturday Evening Post* resisted this turn toward social relevance. Rockwell decided to jump ship, finding greater freedom at *Look*, and almost immediately there was a power in his painting that many readers may not have expected.

On January 14, 1964, *Look* published his iconic *The Problem We All Live With*, depicting a moment from four years earlier when Ruby Bridges, a six-year-old African American girl, flanked by four federal marshals to ensure her safety, entered the first grade in a previously all-white school in New Orleans. On the wall behind her, in Rockwell's painting, we can see the hate-filled graffiti—the word "Nigger" and the initials "KKK"—and on the ground is a splattered tomato recently hurled in her direction. Ruby Bridges never met Norman Rockwell, but in 2005 she joined the board of his museum, and was instrumental, in 2011, in arranging a loan of the painting to the Obama White House.

For Rockwell, other social commentary followed, including *New Kids in the Neighborhood*, his haunting, enigmatic portrait of two black children, a boy and a girl, who have just moved into a white, suburban neighborhood. Three white children have come to see them, their body language suggesting curiosity, perhaps a vague uncertainty and tension, but more than that we cannot tell. There is a geographic distance on the sidewalk between them, and we are left to wonder how or whether it will be closed. But as the title of the painting suggests, these are kids, and so there is hope.

With these two works, along with another entitled *Murder in Mississippi*, Rockwell earned a place—improbably for some, who knew him only through the *Saturday Evening Post*—among the ranks of the great civil rights artists of the 1960s. Many of the others were African Americans whose passion for the subject was more visceral than Rockwell's. Jacob Lawrence, for example, was already an icon—a celebrated figure in the Harlem Renaissance, born in New Jersey in 1917 to parents who were refugees from the South. They were part of the *Great Migration* that Lawrence painted at the age of twenty-three—a sixty-panel masterpiece depicting conditions that drove black people north: the random violence, the capricious possibility of police brutality, the daily insults of Southern segregation. There were panels also that suggested hope for a better life in the North, and for the rest of his long and distinguished career, Lawrence sought to capture the history and struggle of African Americans.

He called his style "dynamic cubism," and the influence of Picasso was clear. But the greater influence, he often said, was the vibrant culture in which he was raised, including memories from his own childhood. "People of my mother's generation," he explained, "would decorate their homes in all sorts of color . . . so you'd think in terms of Matisse." By the 1960s, when people saw vivid splashes of color in a painting, many of them thought in terms of Jacob Lawrence, such was his standing in the world of art.

In 1962, he produced a taut, emotional work called *Soldiers and Students*, which reflected a double inspiration from the civil rights years. Part of it was the memory of Little Rock in 1957—the nine black students who broke the color barrier at that city's Central High School, threatened by mobs and protected finally by the National Guard. Then in 1962, there was a similar scene, only worse, when James Meredith enrolled at the University of Mississippi. The painting that Lawrence created in response was, as one critic described it, a "menacing" depiction of students and soldiers braced for the possibility of violence, the intensity enhanced by "bright colors and partially filled in characters." This was not the artistic realism of Norman Rockwell, utterly intriguing, but emotionally restrained; rather it was an attempt by Lawrence to capture with his brush and canvas (or, in this case, woven paper) the emotion that defined a moment in history.

A short time later, another Harlem Renaissance artist who was also moved by the civil rights struggle began to experiment with a new medium. In 1964, Romare Bearden, a native Southerner from North Carolina, turned from oil painting to collage, and for the next two decades produced a stream of iconic work. For years, Bearden had been a strong and gentle presence in the New York art scene. He had moved north with his parents when he was still a boy, and from the beginning his art was stamped by the place he lived and the place he remembered—by New York City, so teeming with people and throbbing with life, and by Charlotte, North Carolina, where his relatives were sustained by a sense of community against the vagaries of segregation.

Most people who knew him held him in extraordinary esteem. One of Bearden's biographers, Myron Schwartzman, wrote in his book, *Romare Bearden: His Life and Art*:

> He struck me as taller somehow and even more substantial than his 5'11", 210-pound frame would warrant, smiling with a gaze in his hazel green eyes that was at the same time congenial, approachable, yet detached and distant—and there was a decidedly special aura about him. Although Bearden was a remarkably fair-skinned black American, he was also what Albert Murray had called an Omni-American—part frontiersman, part Cherokee, part Southerner, part urbane Harlemite, and part blues-idiom hero, fully capable of improvising his way through the briar patch. He was a man whose presence charged a room with intelligence, not that he ever put on airs: he had no need to.

In the summer of 1963, at about the time of the March on Washington, Bearden met with a group of black artists, including the famous painter Hale Woodruff, to discuss the role of art in a time of unrest. Bearden's answer was different from many others, including Jacob Lawrence. He focused less on the movement itself, or the anger that produced it, than on the culture that gave it strength. In his remarkable collages, fashioned (literally) from a bag full of photographs clipped from magazines and cut into unexpected shapes, often splashed with color, he set out to capture the heart of a people.

"The subjects," wrote a gallery owner who displayed his work, "range from burials and cotton fields to jam sessions [and] Harlem streets. . . . In these days of civil right strife they are . . . a unique statement of pride in tradition, dramatic in many instances but never a form of protest or agitation. Artistically they are most remarkable. . . ."

A wave of other black artists followed—people like Jack Whitten, Emma Amos, Jeff Donaldson, and Elizabeth Catlett—adding their own aesthetic passion to the racial revolution in America.

There was one more development at about this time, one more expression of bravery and beauty in the face of the country's history of oppression. It was, in a sense, an unexpected merger of art and commerce that sprang from a most improbable place, the village of Gees Bend, Alabama. Sometime around the end of 1965, a white Episcopal priest named Francis Walter found his way to this all-black community. He came in support of the civil rights movement after another activist priest, Jonathan Daniels, was shot to death in a nearby town. Despite eyewitness testimony against him, Daniels's killer was acquitted by an all-white jury, and in Walter's view it was crucial that the movement not be deterred.

When he came to Gees Bend and the area around it, he discovered a curious thing. Almost every woman made quilts, lovely creations intended to keep their families warm when the winter winds blew cold on the sharecropper cabins. Few of them meant to create art, but Walter was amazed by the beauty of their work. With a grant from the Episcopal church, he bought some quilts for ten dollars each and sold them to art lovers in New York. He brought the profits back to Gees Bend, and there the women used the money to launch the Freedom Quilting Bee, a collective enterprise that became a cornerstone of economic independence. For this tiny village in the Alabama Black Belt, it was one more step on the journey toward freedom.

Living on a bend in the Alabama River, they depended on a ferry to get to the county seat of Camden, and after 1965, when many of them tried to register to vote, white leaders in the county cut off ferry service entirely. "We didn't close down the ferry because they were black," said Sheriff Lummie Jenkins. "We did it because they *forgot* they were black."

Such was Alabama in the 1960s, but now they could feel the beginnings of change. Martin Luther King had been to Gees Bend and told them they were as good as anybody, and many of them were starting to believe it. They were voters now, full participants in the political process, and suddenly these quilts they had made for generations, going all the way back to the days of slavery, were seen as precious works of art. Given the evidence, it was easy to hope in this most oppressive part of the South that better days might be ahead.

But that was not the case everywhere.

44

'Burn, Baby, Burn'

The long hot summer began in April. We knew it was coming sooner or later; for the past three years, riots had erupted in one or more big-city ghettos as soon as the weather turned hot. This time the violence began in Nashville, long before the dog days of summer frayed the nerves of angry young men. I was a witness to this first conflagration—from a distance, true, but a distance that did not seem quite safe. I suppose you could say it was my first full immersion into the sixties, though I had certainly been an interested observer, writing occasionally for the campus newspaper on issues that seemed to matter in the country.

By the spring of 1967, I was deeply involved with an organization called Impact, a student-run symposium that had brought an impressive array of speakers to the Vanderbilt campus. In earlier years, we had heard the great Southern journalists, Ralph McGill and James J. Kilpatrick, and back-to-back speeches by Roy Wilkins of the NAACP and Alabama's segregationist governor George Wallace, who went out of his way to insult black students. Barry Goldwater came in 1966, still pushing a hawkish foreign policy agenda, and his views were countered by Tran Van Dinh, an antiwar diplomat from Vietnam.

These were thought-provoking moments, giving many of us the feeling that the whole world was passing through our campus. But none of it compared to 1967, when Impact chairman Bob Eager, a bold and energetic senior from Valdosta, Georgia, put together the most provocative lineup we could imagine. Martin Luther King was the apparent headliner, coming to Vanderbilt only three days after his antiwar speech at Riverside Church. U.S. Senator Strom Thurmond might have been expected to stir some controversy as well; his unreconstructed racial views were infuriating to anybody with a conscience. But he and King were both overshadowed. Eager and his student committee had also invited Allen Ginsberg, an openly homosexual, counterculture poet, who had been writing about sex and drugs long before these things were freely discussed. But Impact's most outrageous decision, certainly in the eyes of the Nashville community, was its invitation to Stokely Carmichael, who had begun winning fame the previous summer as the nation's leading proponent of Black Power.

Carmichael had been a busy young man. At twenty-five, he was chairman of the Student Nonviolent Coordinating Committee (SNCC), having led an organizational coup the year before to depose his predecessor, John Lewis. In the eyes of many, Lewis was a movement hero. As a freedom rider and later at Selma on Bloody Sunday, he had been arrested and beaten on multiple occasions, regarding each as a badge of honor. Lewis had never hit back, never even permitted himself that thought, for he was a committed disciple of nonviolence—a "freedom fighter," yes, in his own estimation, even a revolutionary perhaps, for he refused to compromise with segregation or the broader implications of racism. But violence, he believed, was an evil in itself regardless of who the perpetrator was.

Carmichael had grown impatient with that view. They were living in a violent time, he argued, and both at home and around the world there was no force more menacing than white America, no institution more deadly than the U.S. government. His was an angry and radical critique, shared increasingly by the members of SNCC, and in the summer of 1966 Carmichael reduced it to a revolutionary slogan, Black Power!

It was a message he carried to every corner of the country.

At about that time, SNCC itself began to fall apart. By a narrow margin the following December its black staff voted to purge white members, "cutting the umbilical cord," they said, turning their most committed allies into symbols of dependence on white America. Months of disarray quickly followed. Contributions began to dry up, divisions deepened, and ideological bickering became more intense. Stokely, however, was a star—brash and charismatic, seen by some as the next Malcolm X. He was younger than Malcolm had been, and less focused in his rage as he barnstormed the country from college campuses to big-city ghettos, preaching a gospel of Black Power with increasing intimations of revolutionary violence.

"To hell with the laws of the United States!" he told an audience of black students in Birmingham. "If a white man tries to walk over you, kill him. One match and you can retaliate. Burn, baby, burn!"

THERE WAS ANOTHER SIDE to Carmichael. In fact, there may have been several other sides. Before his sudden onset of fame (or notoriety, depending on his listener's point of view), he had spent his time as a SNCC organizer in some of the toughest corners of the South. Almost everywhere he went, he left a trail of people who admired him—grassroots leaders like John Hulett, who would soon become the first black sheriff of Lowndes County, Alabama.

Then and later, Hulett viewed Stokely as a warm-hearted man, as gentle with rural African Americans as he was bold in his confrontations of power. Hulett saw him once with a .25-caliber pistol, but never heard him advocate violence, not even in private. SNCC organizer Bob Mants agreed: "Stokely's public persona was this hip, articulate, fear-nothing guy. But he was not the violent radical he was perceived to be. He would rather talk his way out of a situation than fight."

In 1967, Carmichael collaborated with political scientist Charles V. Hamilton on a book, *Black Power: The Politics of Liberation*. By the time it came out, Hamilton acknowledged, Carmichael was "a full-fledged proponent of violent revolution." But the book itself was a call for *political* power, especially the power of the vote in places where blacks were in a majority. I interviewed Hamilton a few years later, and this is what I wrote about his view of Carmichael:

> Hamilton thought he saw an incongruity between Carmichael's rhetoric and his private personality. He remembered a time when they were working on the book and had gotten together in southern Pennsylvania. Ivanhoe Donaldson was there also, an old SNCC hand, and Carmichael had taken center stage, regaling his friends with tales of Lowndes County. After a few minutes, the telephone rang, and it was James Reston of the New York Times, looking for Stokely. When the interview was over, Carmichael returned to the group, looking pensive and subdued.
>
> "What's the matter, fellow?" Hamilton asked him.
>
> "I'm too young for this," Carmichael muttered. "I don't know enough yet."
>
> That was how Charles Hamilton saw him, a young man deeply committed to the cause who was also aware of his own limitations. His rhetoric would take on a life of its own, particularly the media catchphrase Black Power, and his political theories would continue to evolve, moving eventually down an esoteric path that took him far from the American mainstream. But in the year or more he spent in Lowndes County, what Carmichael wanted was to get

> people to vote, and within the local black leadership he was widely regarded as one of the heroes.

In 1967, Carmichael was still a riveting enigma, and at Vanderbilt the Impact committee was eager to hear what he might have to say. Amazingly, as we came to understand, we were supported in this aspiration by the university's chancellor, Alexander Heard. At a time when students at Berkeley and other places were demonstrating in support of free speech, the top administrator at Vanderbilt was as committed to that principle as we were, willing, in fact, to risk his own job.

We soon realized it might come to that. The American Legion was the first to express outrage, when the members of Post 5 passed a resolution calling Carmichael a "demagogue" and a "rabblerousing denouncer of the United States and its policies." The resolution went on to allege that Carmichael's "treasonable antics" were a "reflection on, and demoralizing to, all citizens of the United States regardless of race, color or creed . . ." The Tennessee legislature quickly followed, passing a proclamation that declared: "Mr. Stokely Carmichael has, under the guise of the free speech provision of the constitution of a government he despises and urges others to disobey, spread his racist poison and his anti-American doctrine throughout the length and breadth of the U.S."

The *Vanderbilt Hustler*, our student newspaper, responded with a strong front page editorial:

> It became very obvious this week that many influential people in Nashville do not understand what a liberal arts university is all about. To survive, a free society must tolerate—and even encourage—a wide spectrum of ideas. . . . A liberal arts university has a special obligation to offer a forum for all points of view, no matter how unpopular. . . .

Chancellor Heard, I later discovered, observed all this with quiet satisfaction, for he thought it was education at its finest—a real-world debate in the semi-protective cloister of a college, where students could explore ideas, not only in the abstract, but in their flesh-and-blood competition for space and validation in society. Thus, in a bracing swirl of controversy, Vanderbilt went forward with the Carmichael speech, and on the day before it happened, it fell to me as a member of the Impact Committee to meet with a group of Stokely's advisers—his advance team, as it were—to talk about the details. This group turned out to consist of three SNCC organizers and a radical journalist from California, all black and all armed. Although some of my memories of the moment have faded, there is a grainy recollection of bandoliers crisscrossing chests and cold, hard stares aimed at a skinny white boy from Alabama.

The conversation went well enough until we came to a delicate matter. There had been death threats against Carmichael (and for that matter, against the student sponsors of his visit), and we were working with the Nashville police to protect him. Our liaison was Lieutenant J. T. Hill, a consummate professional who happened to be African American, a fact that I thought might be reassuring to these young men who represented Stokely. It was not.

"Wait a minute," said George Ware, who seemed to be the spokesman for the group. "We don't want police protection. The police, man, we think of them as the *occupying army!*"

I had the feeling that Ware was trying to be patient, trying to cross the inevitable gaps of understanding and perspective that existed between us. I tried to do the same, explaining that while we thought the threats were probably all talk, we were committed to Carmichael's safety. We trusted Hill, who was a good man, and those of us who had taken at least a little heat for inviting Stokely to visit our campus would not subject him to a trap or harassment by police. We just wanted him to be safe.

I was relieved to see Ware smile. "Well," he said, "it'll be nice, for a change, to have them on our side."

Before I could answer, I heard a voice to my left, cold and quiet—"I don't like it"—and I turned to face the hardest pair of eyes I had ever encountered. I discovered they belonged to Eldridge Cleaver, a convicted rapist and now the author of a searing memoir, *Soul on Ice*. Cleaver had written the book from prison. I had not read it yet, but later I would and it was riveting.

Cleaver recounted a time in 1955 when he was a very young man in a California prison and learned the story of Emmett Till, who was lynched that year in Mississippi for the crime of flirting with a white woman. Till was fourteen, and his mutilated body was tossed like garbage into a river. When Cleaver saw a magazine photo of the woman whose delicate sensibilities had triggered such a crime, he said he had a "nervous breakdown." He remembered the time a prison guard had torn down the pinup from his wall because the naked woman was white, and he thought of slave masters having their way with black women, and for several days, he said, "I ranted and raved against the white race, against white women in particular, against white America in general. When I came to myself, I was locked in a padded cell. . . ."

After his release from prison he became a rapist, taking a kind of revolutionary pleasure in attacking white women: "It delighted me that I was defying and trampling upon the white man's law, upon his system of values, and that I was defiling his women. . . ." Inevitably, he was caught and sentenced once again to prison, and this time he began to read—voraciously—Voltaire, Malcolm X, Thomas Merton, Plato; every piece of philosophy, every source of wisdom, became fodder and antidote to his anger. Soon enough he began to write, his words a mixture of reflection and rage.

> I'm perfectly aware that I'm in prison, that I'm a Negro, that I've been a rapist, and that I have a Higher Uneducation. I never know what significance I'm supposed to attach to these factors. But I have a suspicion that, because of those aspects of my character, "free-normal-educated" people rather expect me to be more reserved, penitent, remorseful, and not too quick to shoot off my mouth on certain subjects. But I let them down, disappoint them, make them gape at me in a sort of stupor, as if they're thinking: "You've got your nerve! Don't you realize that you owe a debt to society?" My answer to all such thoughts lurking in their split-level heads, crouching behind their squinting bombardier eyes, is that the blood of Vietnamese peasants has paid off my debts; that the Vietnamese people, afflicted with a rampant disease called Yankees, through their sufferings . . . have canceled all my IOUs.

And in another place he added:

> All society shows a convict its ass and expects him to kiss it: the convict feels like kicking it or putting a bullet in it. A convict sees man's fangs and claws and learns quickly to bare and unsheathe his own. . . .

These were the words of a bitter man, the one whose eyes were staring at me on the Vanderbilt campus, cold and impenetrable, empty of feeling, as far as I could tell, and I had the sense that our discussion of logistics about the Carmichael speech was about to come apart—that a mixture of ideology and suspicion might cause Cleaver and Ware and all of Stokely's team to decide that they had better things to do. All I could think to do in the moment was meet Cleaver's stare and affirm that on this curious occasion, we were in it together. Nobody knew what would happen with the speech, but it was at least an attempt at understanding—for Stokely and for us—and it was critical to move forward with trust.

After a second or two that seemed much longer, Eldridge Cleaver lowered his gaze and the Carmichael speech went ahead as planned. A crowd of more than 4,500 awaited him at the Vanderbilt basketball arena, where he spoke at the base of an American flag, said to be the largest in the world, hanging from the rafters to the base of the stage. Almost as soon as he began to speak, a white student in the balcony draped a much smaller banner—a Confederate battle flag—from the top of the railing, and Carmichael's response was immediate and calm. "I respect your flag," he said, "just as long as you don't burn down any of my churches."

As I remember it, most of us clapped, for Stokely was a mesmerizing figure, tall and handsome in his own way, with a pointed nose and eyes that were softer somehow than his words. He spoke with the trace of a Caribbean accent, and he was fiercely intelligent as he explained the idea of institutional racism—the notion that oppression is so embedded in the life of the country, from economics to education, politics to our system of justice, that it no longer requires deliberate bigotry to sustain it. Not that he spared any scorn for the bigots.

"When we were marching in Selma, Alabama," he said, clearly beginning to enjoy himself, "we were not marching to integrate. That was what the TV kept saying: 'Oh the Negroes are marching to integrate.' But that was not what we were doing. We were not marching to sit next to Jim Clark. We were marching to render that honky *impotent* over our *lives*! And there's a big difference. There's a big difference."

All in all, most of us found him reasonable enough, as compelling perhaps as Martin Luther King, who had spoken the night before. But Stokely also visited the other side of town, and there he struck a different tone.

"Honkies can't stop us!" he shouted to a crowd of black students. "The world runs on power. We are going to have complete liberation or we are going to tear this nation *up*!"

"Black Power!" the crowd screamed in reply.

Then a frenzied chant, again and again, becoming more fervent with each repetition:

"Black Power!

"Black Power!

"Black Power!"

THERE WAS NO RIOTING during Carmichael's speeches. There were reports, in fact, that he had left town before the violence occurred. But around 9 p.m. on Saturday, there was an altercation at a north Nashville nightclub, and the tension escalated when police were called to the scene. According to accounts in the *Nashville Tennessean*, blacks began throwing rocks, and reporter Frank Sutherland, who would later become the newspaper's editor, was one of those injured—knocked to his knees by a volley of rocks. At predominantly black Fisk University, students barricaded themselves behind a low stone wall surrounding the campus, and as the *Tennessean* reported, "the rock throwing increased." Police charged the wall and the students dispersed, but "roaming gangs" surged through the area, throwing rocks, breaking windows until sometime after 2 a.m.

The following night was worse. Sniper fire erupted from another black Nashville campus, Tennessee A&I College. At least two people were wounded in the gunfire and thirty-six were arrested, and while all this was going on, the telephone rang on the floor of my dorm. It was Eldridge Cleaver asking for me.

"How are things where you are?" he asked.

"Okay," I said. "Just words on this side of town. I know it's worse in north Nashville."

"Yeah," he said, "it's pretty bad. I just wanted to make sure you guys are okay."

I remember that conversation almost verbatim because I was taken so completely by surprise. What had prompted this angry African American man to place such a call? It was true that we had chatted pleasantly enough both before and after Carmichael's speech, and he had asked if I meant what I said about trust. I told him yes, and he had nodded. But this seemed to be an extraordinary gesture, a genuine, unexpected expression of concern, and I made a mental note never to underestimate the value of good will.

BOTH IN NASHVILLE AND the rest of the country, controversy continued to rage. The *Nashville Banner*, the city's conservative afternoon paper which once ran a front-page column calling for a nuclear strike against China, was moved again to editorialize on page one. Under the indignant headline, "What Price Folly?," the newspaper left no doubt about where it stood:

> Nothing that could be said by way of public apology . . . can remove the stench of the Stokely Carmichael visit to Vanderbilt University. . . . The stupidity of a campus group's explanation that he was brought here as a part of a "search for truth" was more than matched—it was exceeded—by Vanderbilt administrative officers who so far disregarded a duty to the campus, the institution, and the community itself, as to publicly endorse the appearance of Carmichael. . . . It is colossal stupidity indeed, to suggest that one must lift the lid of a garbage can to discover that there is garbage in it. . . .
>
> In the final analysis, the ultimate responsibility for what occurred lies at the door of the Chancellor. . . .

From all accounts, Chancellor Heard never flinched. Deftly, by standing on principle and a spotless reputation in the academic world, he deflected an attempt by conservatives among the Vanderbilt trustees to demand his resignation, or at the very least that he "eat crow," as one historian later put it. When the board met on May 5, Heard rejected an offer by some of his allies to push through a resolution of support, contending instead that the Carmichael visit was simply routine, a case of the university "being a university."

"It hardly seems necessary," he told the board, "to burden you with a defense of the free exchange of ideas, or of the freedom to hear and the freedom to read for our students, or of the educational value of those freedoms."

And the board moved on to other business.

Three days earlier, far from the cloister of a Southern university, another group of men with whom Carmichael would soon develop a close association marched into the California Assembly in Sacramento. They were armed. Huey Newton, Bobby Seale and their friends were members of a new organization called the Black Panther Party for Self-Defense. Newton, who had worked for voting rights in Alabama, had carried the panther symbol of an all-black political party in Lowndes County back with him to California. John Hulett and other grassroots leaders in that part of Alabama had chosen the panther as their emblem, because, Hulett said, "A panther won't bother anybody, but push it into a corner and it will do what it takes."

Newton loved the spirit of these rural people, their willingness to stand up for themselves, and in California he and Seale planned a dramatic introduction for their organization. To the horror of the assembled legislators, two dozen black men led by Seale, their rifles and shotguns pointed toward the ceiling, marched into the second-floor chamber to oppose the adoption of a gun control law. In the confrontation that followed, the Panthers agreed to stand down if Seale was allowed to read a manifesto against "the racist power structure of America."

"The Black Panther Party for Self-Defense," he declared, "believes that the time has come for Black people to arm themselves against this terror before it is too late."

On May 12 in Atlanta, Carmichael resigned as chairman of SNCC and soon affiliated with the Black Panther Party. His successor was H. Rap Brown, a native of Baton Rouge, Louisiana, who was not well-known to the general public but soon would be. To many whites in the months to come, he was at least as frightening as Carmichael, speaking openly in defense of violence.

At that same SNCC meeting, native Alabamian Bob Zellner, who had been the organization's first white staff member and would soon become its last, delivered a heartfelt appeal to continue his affiliation with SNCC. He agreed to end his work with the black community, honoring a new SNCC policy of a black revolution organized only by African Americans. He said he would shift his attention to whites, trying to organize for progressive causes, but he wanted to do it under the auspices of SNCC.

His plea was rejected. Among some veteran members of SNCC who were Zellner's friends, this was a bitter pill. They knew his story—how he was the son and grandson of Ku Klux Klansmen, but how his father, a Methodist minister named James Abraham Zellner, had rejected the Klan after a mission trip to Europe. Many people in SNCC had heard Bob Zellner describe what happened:

> My father was part of a scheme to establish a Christian fundamentalist organization in the middle of Europe. The idea was to convert Jews to save their souls and save them from the Nazis. Later, I asked him if he converted any Jews, and Dad said, "No, but they converted me." I said, "Dad, I could see you could have an intellectual conversion—the Klan, the Nazis—but something changed you in your heart." He said, "I had been traveling in the Soviet Union in the

> dead of winter by sled. Our little group joined with a group of gospel singers from the South. We were white, they were black, but we talked about ham and biscuits and okra; we played the same songs, we prayed the same prayers. And one day I forgot they were black."

Zellner was always a cheerful and colorful raconteur, sharing his tales and sharing the dangers with his friends in SNCC—sharing the fear that all of them felt as they ventured into places like rural Mississippi. "We were terrified," he admitted. But Zellner and the others were willing to die if that's what it took, and the bonds that were forged under those circumstances were not easy to break.

"It hurt," he said.

Publicly, Zellner never complained. He went to work in Mississippi as a kind of wildcat labor organizer, getting whites and blacks to work together against companies that were trying to divide and exploit them. But SNCC had been his life since 1961, and his primary solace at the time of the split was that many of his brothers and sisters who were black—people like John Lewis, Julian Bond, and James Forman—did not want to see him go. They had simply been outvoted.

Rap Brown, meanwhile, became the face of an all-black SNCC. Even some of his allies agreed that Brown was a cold and angry man who made it clear what he meant when he spoke of revolution. "I say violence is necessary," he said. "It is as American as cherry pie."

45

Long, Hot Summer of 1967

By summer, amid growing fears of racial unrest, public sentiment was beginning to shift regarding the war in Vietnam. It was not so much the damage done by the 128,000 tons of U.S. bombs that had already fallen on North Vietnam. Nor, outside the antiwar movement, was there any widespread awareness of the planners in the Pentagon who were contemplating bombing dams and dikes, flooding the rice fields, and triggering a famine that might bring Ho Chi Minh to his knees. For many ordinary Americans, the straw that broke the camel's back was taxes. With the war costing $20 billion a year, the Johnson Administration was forced to seek a 10 percent surcharge on individual and corporate income taxes. Almost immediately, the number of citizens who thought the war was a mistake became greater than those who supported it—by a margin of 46 to 44 percent.

But the war went on, and at first the only distraction in a bloody summer was the specter of war in other places. On June 5, fighting broke out between Israel and three of its Arab neighbors, Egypt, Syria, and Jordan. In only six days, Israel inflicted heavy casualties and seized the Sinai Peninsula from Egypt, the Golan Heights from Syria, and the west bank of the Jordan River from Jordan.

Some years later, I had a chance to talk to General Mattiyahu Peled, one of Israel's military heroes. Born in 1923 in the port city of Haifa, Peled grew up in Jerusalem. In 1948, during the war for Israel's founding, he was a member of the Palmach, among the most elite and dedicated of Jewish freedom fighters. He was a Zionist, and after the horrors of the Holocaust, he was one of those most determined to create a safe haven for Jews. In the years that followed, he rose to the rank of general in the Israeli army, served for a time as governor of the occupied Gaza territory, and in the Six-Day War of 1967 was coordinator of logistics in Israel's swift and stunning victory.

But on what he called "the seventh day of the Six-Day War," he began to find himself at odds with his government. As one of the country's most respected generals, Peled proposed that Israel adopt "the principle of partition"—the basic 1948 proposal by the United Nations to divide the old area of Palestine into two contiguous states, one Jewish and the other Palestinian. When the Arab countries rejected that idea in 1948 and launched a war to eradicate Israel, Jordan seized control of what became the West Bank. But Israel took it away in 1967, and Peled saw a golden opportunity—to pursue on this contested piece of ground the creation of a Palestinian state, which could serve as a buffer between Israel and Jordan. More importantly, the Palestinian people, who had been Peled's neighbors for all of his life, could begin to build a country of their own, and this land on the bank of the Jordan River could become the key to a Middle East peace.

Peled lost the argument. The Israeli government wanted the land, and tensions in the region became more intense. It foreshadowed something new for American diplomacy—a challenge from another part of the world that one day would replace Vietnam as a central agony of U.S. policy. For American Jews, this place for which they felt a connection nurtured by the blood of the Jewish people added another moral preoccupation—and began subtly to alter their role in American life. Many still supported such causes as the civil rights movement (some had even given their lives), but now the future of Israel gradually became a more urgent concern for them and their country.

MOST OF US SAW none of this coming. We were too absorbed with Vietnam and, by midsummer, with what seemed like a war in our own backyard. It began in Newark on July 12 with another confrontation—there had been so many in our inner cities—between a black citizen and the police. A cab driver named John Smith passed a police car that was double-parked. He was pulled over, arrested, and beaten when police discovered that his license had expired. Police said Smith cursed and attacked them, but at a bail hearing Smith gave a different account:

> There was no resistance on my part. That was a cover story by the police. They caved in my ribs, busted a hernia, and put a hole in my head. After I got into the precinct six or seven other officers along with the two who arrested me

> kicked and stomped me in the ribs and back. They took me to a cell and put my head over the toilet bowl. While my head was over the toilet bowl I was struck in the back of the head with a revolver. I was also being cursed while they were beating me. An arresting officer in the cell block said, "This baby is mine."

Word spread. Witnesses in the housing project where Smith was arrested saw him being dragged—"paralyzed," according to one account—to the police car, and other black cab drivers who worked for Smith's company reported the incident on their car radios. In his book *Rebellion in Newark*, Tom Hayden, who had been a community organizer in Newark, pieced together a detailed account of what happened next.

A group of civil rights leaders, he said, went to the police precinct, and after an angry verbal exchange, were allowed to visit Smith in his cell. They were alarmed by his condition, and insisted that he be examined at a hospital. The police agreed. At the same time, a crowd gathered outside the precinct, and three Newark civil rights leaders spoke to them through a bullhorn. Bob Curvin, an organizer for CORE, accused the police of waging war on the black community. Timothy Still, a resident of the Hayes Homes housing project, denounced the "sadists" in the department, but urged the crowd to remain peaceful. Oliver Lofton of the Newark Legal Services promised that his office would aggressively defend John Smith.

The crowd cheered, but in the nearby darkness a group of young men gathered bricks and bottles, which they began to hurl at the station house. Police rushed out in riot gear but were driven back by the fury of the barrage. By midnight, the crowd had grown to five hundred, and two Molotov cocktails exploded against the wall of the precinct. "A stream of fire curled fifty feet down the wall," wrote Hayden, "flared for ten seconds, and died." More than a hundred windows were broken.

About 2 a.m., the looting started. Crowds of young men, mostly between the ages of fifteen and twenty-five, began smashing windows and taking whatever they wanted from stores, and the police were confronted with a disconcerting problem. The projects were, in Hayden's words, "a useful terrain for people making war":

> The police station is well lit, but the projects are dark, especially the rooftops a hundred yards above the streets. Each room in the projects can be darkened

> to allow people to observe or attack from their windows. There is little light in the pathways, recreation areas, and parking lots around the foot of tall buildings. The police thus were faced with the twin dangers of ambush and searching through a shadow world where everybody and everything appears to be alike.

In their frustration, police lashed out and reports of brutality stoked the fury of the crowd: a black policeman, dressed in plain clothes as he reported for work, was attacked by white officers who did not recognize him in the dark; a black woman was struck with a billy club; a black man was punched and kicked by as many as fifteen officers at the entrance to the building where he lived.

The violence finally subsided about 4 a.m., but the next night was worse. As the *New York Times* reported,

> Negro mobs spilled from their Central Ward ghetto into the heart of the downtown business district. Mayor Hugh J. Addonizio telephoned Governor Richard J. Hughes at 2:20 a.m. and told the Governor that the rampaging Negroes who had looted, burned and smashed their way through the city on the second straight night of violence had produced an "ominous situation."

The *Times* described fires raging in the heart of downtown, as Hughes ordered in the National Guard and a plea came over the police radio: "We're sitting ducks out here. They're hitting us with everything. Give us the word. Let us shoot."

Mayor Addonizio gave that order, gun battles followed, and again there were charges of police brutality. Bill Lowe, a black reporter from *The Trentonian*, the daily newspaper in New Jersey's capital, said he was clubbed by three white policemen, and when he fumbled for his press credentials, one officer told him, "Don't show me that," and hit him again. Not far away, a white reporter was attacked by the mob. Hundreds were injured that night, and the rioting continued for four more days.

"The line between the jungle and the law," said Governor Hughes, "might as well be drawn here as well as any place in America."

In the official attempt to draw that line, armored personnel carriers rumbled through the streets of Newark, exchanging fire with snipers on the rooftops. Police reported gunshots aimed at City Hospital where the wounded were being taken for treatment. Community organizers recounted cases of African

American citizens—several of them women with children in their care—killed in their homes by random fire from police. Newark Police Commissioner Dominick Spina acknowledged later that much of the reported sniper fire did, in fact, come from police, as well as from state troopers and the National Guard. By the time the violence was finally over, 1,200 people were jailed, six hundred were injured, and twenty-three were dead. Most of the dead were black men, but as historian Taylor Branch later noted, the fatalities included "two white officers and two small children."

Among the national media, the *New York Times* took the lead in trying to understand what had happened—the fundamental causes of this deadly violence in a U.S. city. The *Times* rejected the governor's conclusion that "it was plain and simple crime and not a civil rights protest." Governor Hughes, said the paper's editorial board, was "too able and sensitive" to offer such a loaded, simplistic analysis. The editors went on to say:

> Many of the causes of Newark's agony are all too common in the black ghettoes of this country. Newark's Negroes are predominantly poor people who are unemployed or have low-paying jobs. Their housing is shameful in many cases, their education usually grossly deficient, and their prospects for improvement virtually invisible. They feel cheated that they are not full fledged participants in the affluent society. . . . The central political fact about Newark is that half or more than half of its population consists of Negroes. Yet the great majority of the levers of political and economic power in that city are in the hands of white men who, many Negroes are convinced, do not want to share that power equitably with black men. . . .

Perhaps most dramatically, the newspaper interviewed more than 150 white residents in and around Newark and found among them a sprinkling of sympathy mixed with a torrent of fear and loathing. One young man who had served as a member of the National Guard boasted of shooting a looter in the leg. "I didn't shoot to kill," he said, "but next time I will." Many whites said they were buying guns, while others—already a minority in Newark—admitted they were planning to move. Journalist Richard Reeves, who wrote the story, offered this summary of the city's mood: "Most of the white people interviewed spoke of Negroes with open hatred."

And then came Detroit.

On July 23 just before dawn, city police raided five "blind pigs," or unlicensed bars, and a confrontation at one escalated from pushing and shoving to rock-throwing, then to looting and arson. In the next day's papers, it was *déjà vu* as the Associated Press recounted a now familiar story.

> Thousands of rampaging Negroes firebombed and looted huge sections of Detroit last night and early today. Gov. George Romney ordered 1500 National Guardsmen, backed by tanks, to quell the riot. Violence spread uncontrolled over most sections of the city. Destructive fury swept along three-mile and four-mile sections of streets crisscrossing the heart of Detroit and ranging seven miles outward almost to the city limits. A warm, sultry wind fanned scores of fires, and in at least one area the fire raged in a solid sheet for more than 10 blocks. At least four persons were reported killed. . . . The police arrested more than 600 adults and 100 juveniles.

Flying over Detroit in a helicopter, Governor Romney called it "a war zone." The riot lasted five days, one less than Newark, but the death toll this time stood at forty-three. Shaken by the carnage, President Johnson appointed a commission headed by Illinois Governor Otto Kerner to determine what was wrong. Johnson did not put it this way, but why was the toll of killing in these two cities—sixty-six—nearly half that from a week's worth of war in Vietnam?

There were people in Detroit who thought they already knew the answer. The Reverend Albert Cleage was a radical African American minister who had installed a painting of a black Madonna in his church, which he then renamed The Shrine of the Black Madonna. In his sermons and in other pronouncements, he spoke with passion about the desperate lives of men in the ghetto.

> At every meeting some young black man jumps to his feet screaming, "I can't stand it any longer. Let's take it to the streets and get it over with!" We all know how he feels and why he feels that way. Each of us has felt that same sense of powerlessness that makes us ache with helplessness and hopelessness and drives us to seek death as an easy way out. Those of us who cry out think of ourselves as revolutionists and participants in the Black Revolution. But a revolution seeks to change conditions. So each day we must decide. Either we

> are trying to achieve the power to change conditions or we have turned from the struggle and are seeking a heroic moment when we can die in the streets.

Not long before the riot, Cleage brought H. Rap Brown to his church. There was, as always, a coldness in Brown's voice when he spoke of violence. "Let America know," he said, "that the name of the game is tit-for-tat, an eye for an eye, a tooth for a tooth, a life for a life. Motown, if you don't come around, we are going to burn you down!"

There was at the same time, like distortion in a carnival mirror, anger in other quarters, including most significantly the police. Even before the explosion in Detroit, the city's officers, 93 percent of whom were white, had seen the TV footage out of New Jersey, the burning buildings, the rattle of gunfire. They knew that Newark police officer Frederick Toto (of course by now they knew his name, had seen his face in the papers) had been killed by a sniper on the streets of that city. Soon the story hit closer to home. On July 25, Detroit policeman Jerome Olshove was shot to death by a looter. From all accounts he was a good man, and his friends in blue clearly saw him that way. After seven years on the force, he was planning to leave for a job at IBM, and Thursday, July 27, was to be his last day in uniform. He was killed on Tuesday. There was open weeping when Olshove's death was announced at roll call.

Soon it seemed that a kind of madness gripped the city. In the streets, the tension was worsening. President Johnson sent in federal troops, a combination of mostly white, inexperienced National Guardsmen and a veteran, racially integrated force of Army regulars, who were said to be tightly disciplined and efficient. As they struggled to contain the violence, tragedy struck at one of Detroit's rundown motels. In his book, *The Algiers Motel Incident*, Pulitzer Prize-winning writer John Hersey set an eloquent literary stage for a deadly moment of police brutality.

> Detroit is a vast flat sprawl of houses planlessly intermixed with schools and colleges and great automobile factories and little works and warehouses and stores and public buildings, and in this sprawl the resident nations of black and white had for years been encroaching and elbowing and giving way to each other; there was no great ghetto; there were pockets of prosperity, of ethnic identity, of miserable poverty, of labor, of seedy entertainment and sometimes

> joy. The Algiers had had a habit of reaching into several of these pockets; its management had changed a few years back, and it was now run by Negroes mainly for a pleasure-loving black clientele.

During the riot, a group of black teenagers had taken rooms there, and in a singular act of bad judgment, seventeen-year-old Carl Cooper was on the motel porch firing a starter pistol into the air. He was shooting blanks. It was not yet dawn on the morning of July 26, and Cooper was having fun with his friends, seven young black men and two young white women. Not far away, a group of National Guardsmen, jumpy from the tension of the night, reported the shots and a call went out on police radios: "Army under heavy fire."

The police arrived and began a brutal interrogation. By the time it was over, three of the seven young men were dead and the others were beaten. So were the women. Nobody was ever convicted of a crime, but multiple conflicting accounts of the incident reverberated through the country, and among many black Americans the Algiers Motel became a symbol of everything that was wrong.

John Hersey gave the moment a face, just as he had more than twenty years earlier when he was one of the first journalists to enter Hiroshima after the atom bomb was dropped. Writing then with customary restraint, he described the suffering and dignity of the wounded, thanking caregivers for sips of water, and now in Detroit, he quoted the words of a grieving mother:

> All the police knew Carl. Beginning when he was thirteen, fourteen, they began to pick Carl up, they'd take him to the police station and keep him overnight or maybe two days, there was never any charge, just suspicion, they never put a finger on anything he actually did, you know. One of the detectives told me once, "Carl isn't a bad guy, he just doesn't like people to talk nasty to him, call him 'nigger,' 'punk,' all like that." Once he come home with a black eye, they'd picked him up and drove him round in their car and took him in a dark street and just beat him up. I wanted to get a lawyer, but Carl said, "No, Momma, it would just be their word against mine, and you know how that would end up."

That was one reality in Detroit, one that as much as any other fueled the fury of an insurrection. But there were others which once had seemed to offer hope. The city had a large black middle class, wages in the auto industry were good, and black workers benefited as well as white. Under the leadership of Walter Reuther, the United Auto Workers union was planning major redevelopment of inner-city slums, working with progressive mayor Jerome Cavanaugh. John Conyers, a black Democrat, represented the city in Congress. The morning newspaper, the *Detroit Free Press*, (which would soon win a Pulitzer for its coverage of the riots) was one of the most civic-minded in the country. Not long before the city exploded, the *New York Times* concluded editorially that Detroit had "more going for it than any other major city in the North."

Now as he surveyed the numbers and the ruins—43 dead, ten white, 33 black; 1,189 injured, 7,200 arrests, more than 2,000 buildings destroyed—Mayor Cavanaugh offered an epitaph for his city:

> Today we stand amidst the ashes of our hopes. We had hoped against hope that what we were doing was enough to prevent a riot. It was not enough.

There were other voices in other places. Rap Brown proclaimed that the riots were merely "a dress rehearsal" for the revolution soon to come. Ronald Reagan, the newly installed governor of California, called the rioters "mad dogs against the people," and Martin Luther King told members of his staff, "There were dark days before, but this is the darkest." King canceled a scheduled trip to Jerusalem, where in the aftermath of a Six-Day War—one that had flared and ended with the fury and speed of an American riot—the message of nonviolence would be an "awkward" one to deliver. King feared the same was true in the United States, but he knew he had to try.

All across the country, on both sides of the great divide, many Americans found themselves in flight-or-fight mode. Others simply wanted to change the subject, while a few—particularly young people in the city of San Francisco—had their minds on sweeter things.

46

Summer of Love

That summer a song came on the radio that I immediately and instinctively liked, mostly because of the singer's voice. Scott McKenzie was a folk artist. He was raised in the mountains of North Carolina (where, according to one profile that I read, he used to mow Billy Graham's lawn). From 1961 to 1964 he was part of a group called the Journeymen, recording three albums and seven singles with his friends John Phillips and Dick Weissman. When the Journeymen disbanded, Phillips moved to California and started a popular band called the Mamas and the Papas, while McKenzie set off on a solo career.

McKenzie's first hit, written and produced by Phillips, who remained a close friend, made a quick climb up the Billboard charts:

If you're going to San Francisco
Be sure to wear some flowers in your hair
If you're going to San Francisco
You're gonna meet some gentle people there

This was a curious message, I thought, delivered in a high, melodic voice, but what in the world was he talking about? In retrospect, it does seem odd that I didn't know, for I was, by now, fully and forever a child of the sixties. But it was a decade of so many parts, and I was wholly immersed in the idealism of social change, the pursuit of racial justice, an end to the war in Vietnam. Now came something called the Summer of Love, the subject of Scott McKenzie's song, which revealed a restlessness of the spirit. The caricature understanding of it, both at the time and later, was solely as a moment of hedonism—"sex, drugs, and rock 'n' roll"—but many of the participants saw it as more.

"My experience was a spiritual quest," said one of my friends, Pamela Smith, who headed west from the University of Missouri. "I just wanted to see the world and see what was happening."

Admittedly, at the start, it was a journey fueled in part by marijuana: "It changed my perspective on life. It opened up a whole different realm of reality." In San Francisco, Pamela began attending "Monday Night Classes" led by Stephen Gaskin, a former Marine and writing instructor at San Francisco State University, who was emerging by 1967—the year he lost his teaching job—as a guru to hundreds of disaffected young people who were streaming west in search of something not all of them could name.

Gaskin was one of the people they found. He would sit lotus-style on a raised platform, surrounded by admirers whose hair in most cases was as long as his. With a charisma that many found mesmerizing, he would hold forth on topics from mysticism to mathematics. The setting was usually the Family Dog, a concert-lecture venue overlooking San Francisco Bay, where radical politics mixed with rock 'n' roll.

More and more as time went by Gaskin talked about the land. "I can't put my attention into a city scene anymore," he said on one occasion. "Because the worst thing happening on the planet is the cities."

By the early 1970s, Gaskin became a leader in the back-to-the-land movement. He and his followers set out in a caravan of old buses and bought a farm in the hills of Tennessee. They built a counterculture community called The Farm, a refuge for hard-working hippies that was still in existence more than forty years later.

Gaskin, of course, was only one of the prophets and searchers who populated San Francisco in the mid to late sixties. The youthful pilgrims who flocked to the city—seekers of wisdom or hedonistic pleasure, refugees from the horrors of the world as it was—always seemed to find somebody. In *The Haight-Ashbury: A History*, journalist-historian Charles Perry, who was once a part of the scene, chronicled what he saw as the rise and fall of one of the great experiments of the decade.

It began in a sense at an urban crossroad, the corner of Haight and Ashbury streets that marked the heart of an old neighborhood. It was a place of seedy-looking shops and Victorian houses, some of them in a state of disrepair. Sometime around 1965, it began to develop a kind of critical mass of disaffected young people, numbed by the assassination of John Kennedy, weary of living in the shadow of the bomb, repulsed by the scandal of racism and war. They discovered that in The Haight, as they called it, they could rent two floors of an old Victorian, constructed after the 1906 earthquake, for the appealing sum of $175 a month. They began to dress in "flashy mod clothes," as Perry put it, but some set aside their miniskirts for Victorian dresses purchased on the cheap at local thrift shops.

Viewing the world through a lens of desolation, many sought escape in marijuana and music and soon the mind-altering substance known as LSD. In addition to escape, they also found a sense of community. "Taking LSD," wrote Perry, "was like being in a secret society." The drug was not illegal when it had first begun to make the rounds in San Francisco, but it felt like it should be, wrapped as it was in a secret aura. Timothy Leary, a former professor at Harvard, had become its champion, writing about it in his own journal, which he called the *Psychedelic Review*. But publicly, at first, most people didn't talk about it much.

Over the next year or two, the hip neighborhoods in San Francisco became not only havens for drugs but places of radical creativity. The egalitarian poet Lawrence Ferlinghetti ran his City Lights bookstore, selling only paperbacks, at 261 Columbus Avenue. He also published books on the side, and one of the titles he carried in his store was an eight-page chapbook of four poems by Lenore Kandel. One poem in *The Love Book* was called "To Fuck With Love," and it included this couplet:

> I kiss your shoulder and it reeks of lust
> the lust of erotic angels fucking the stars

In November 1966, with newly elected governor Ronald Reagan promising to root out radicalism and immorality, police raided City Lights and another store, the Psychedelic Shop, and seized Kandel's book from the shelves. Up until that time, it had sold fifty copies. As the author became a celebrity, a defiant, meteoric symbol of free speech, sales of the book soared to twenty thousand copies.

In her moment of local renown, many in the Bay area discovered that Lenore Kandel was a serious poet. Born in New York in 1932, she came to California around 1960, a beautiful woman who found acceptance among the celebrated writers of San Francisco. Her friends included Allen Ginsberg, Jack Kerouac, and Gary Snyder, and they admired her ability to write of erotic love as a manifestation of the human spirit. In 1967, while her legal challenge to the seizure of her chapbook was making its way through the courts, she published a second volume of poems, *Word Alchemy*, and in the introduction she offered thoughts on the essence of her craft:

> Poetry is never compromise. . . . If you compromise your vision you become a blind prophet. . . . Two poems of mine, published as a small book, deal with physical love and the invocation, recognition, and acceptance of the divinity in man through the medium of physical love. In other words, it feels good. It feels so good that you can step outside your private ego and share the grace of the universe . . . A large part of the furor was caused by the poetic usage of certain four-letter words of Anglo-Saxon origin instead of the substitution of gentle euphemisms. . . . Euphemisms chosen by fear are a covenant with hypocrisy and will immediately destroy the poem and eventually destroy the poet.

On January 14, 1967, she read her poetry in Golden Gate Park as part of an event called the Human Be-In. Its name was inspired by the civil rights sit-ins and the teach-ins against the war, and there was an element of protest in this gathering as well. In addition to the threats of censorship, the California legislature had passed the previous fall a bill to outlaw LSD. But the Be-In was also a massive party with music by bands like the Grateful Dead and Jefferson Airplane and exhortations by counterculture heroes. Ginsberg was there, brave and outrageous, having already written without fear or shame about subjects off-limits in the mainstream culture, including his own homosexuality. Timothy Leary was present as well, and his Harvard colleague Richard Alpert, who would soon set off on a pilgrimage to India and change his spiritual name to Ram Dass. They were joined by the gentle Buddhist thinker Alan Watts, and just before it all began, an activist named Jerry Rubin explained the meaning of the moment to reporters. They were gathering, he said, to reject "the games and institutions that oppress and dehumanize." He mentioned napalm, the Pentagon, Ronald Reagan, and the rat-race frenzy of suburban life.

In the immediate run-up, the *Berkeley Barb*, a counterculture paper, waxed ecstatic about the possibilities:

> The spiritual revolution will be manifest and proven. In unity we shall shower the country with waves of ecstasy and purification. Fear will be washed away, ignorance will be exposed to sunlight, profits and empire will be drying

> on deserted beaches, violence will be submerged and transmuted in rhythm and dancing.

Even those on the political left, the dissenters against war and injustice, were trying to figure out what to make of all this. In the March issue of *Ramparts* magazine, two months after the Be-In, where crowd estimates ran to 20,000, journalist Warren Hinkle offered what he called a "Social History of the Hippies." In his article he reflected on the mixture of turned-on antics in Haight-Ashbury, lyrical pronouncements from counterculture publications, and the radical pursuit of change.

> Hippies are many things, but most prominently the bearded and beaded inhabitants of the Haight-Ashbury, a little psychedelic city-state edging Golden Gate Park. There, in a daily street-fair atmosphere, upwards of 15,000 unbonded girls and boys interact in a tribal, love-seeking, free-swinging, acid-based type of society where, if you are a hippie and you have a dime, you can put it in a parking meter and lie down in the street for an hour's suntan (30 minutes for a nickel) and most drivers will be careful not to run you over . . .
>
> Hippies have a clear vision of the ideal community—a psychedelic community, to be sure—where everyone is turned on and beautiful and loving and happy and floating free. But it is a vision that, despite the Alice in Wonderland phraseology hippies usually breathlessly employ to describe it, necessarily embodies a radical political philosophy: communal life, drastic restriction of private property, rejection of violence, creativity before consumption, freedom before authority . . .

The subtleties of the hippie worldview included a psychedelic naïvete shading from innocence to something very different. As the Human Be-In came to a close, here was Allen Ginsberg leading the throngs in a Buddhist chant, then organizing volunteers from the massive crowd for a careful cleanup of a day's worth of trash. But to some of us who were learning about these things from a distance, reading, for example, the flamboyant journalism of Hunter S. Thompson or Tom Wolfe, there were competing spectacles that gave us pause—especially those of Ken Kesey and his newly discovered friends, the Hell's Angels.

In the early sixties, Kesey was the heralded author of *One Flew Over the Cuckoo's Nest.* But by the middle of the decade he was the leader of the Merry

Pranksters, a traveling road show of LSD parties that he called "acid tests." For one of those parties at his home in La Honda, a six-acre retreat in the hills outside of San Francisco, Kesey invited the Angels, the notorious, sometimes violent biker gang that was now well established in San Francisco and Oakland. "The party lasted two days and two nights," wrote Charles Perry, "and continued off and on for a month and a half. It was almost routine: you'd come over the footbridge to Kesey's woodsy retreat, get your LSD-dosed pill, watch the Angels gang-bang some willing girl, chip in for spaghetti, wander around the woods among the sculptures . . ." Some of these outrageous works of art depicted men and women having oral sex or a naked woman formed from piano wire and emitting various musical notes if you fingered the area near the vagina.

Tom Wolfe wrote about this with what can only be described as awe, despite the artful cynicism of the prose. In *The Electric Kool-Aid Acid Test,* Wolfe recounted, among other things, Kesey's decision after being arrested for drugs to fake his own suicide and flee to Mexico—hiding in the back of a friend's car. One of his other friends drove Kesey's truck to northern California and a cliff overlooking Humboldt Bay, and Wolfe picked up the story from there:

> Always nice to have some help to commit suicide. Next Dee dropped Kesey's distinctive sky-blue boots down to the shore below—but they hit the water and sank without a bubble. Next, the goddamned romantic suicide desolate foaming cliff was so goddamned desolate, nobody noticed the truck for about two weeks, despite the Ira Sandperl for President sign on the rear bumper. Apparently people figured the old heap had been abandoned. The Humboldt county police finally checked it out on February 11. Next, the suicide note, which seemed so ineluctably convincing as Kesey and Mountain Girl smoked a few joints and soared into passages of Shellyan Weltschmerg—it gave off a giddy sense of put-on, even to the straight cops of the Humboldt.

Hunter Thompson struck a similar tone with the Hell's Angels, chronicling in prose that was slightly more measured the aura of menace that made the gang a legend. One day in 1965, Thompson had ridden with the Angels and their leader Sonny Barger to a mountain resort known as Bass Lake, where they confronted the local sheriff, a man who stood about six-foot-six, and did not want the bikers around. Thompson wrote:

> Barger is barely six feet, but not one of his followers had the slightest doubt that he would swing on the sheriff if things suddenly came down to the hard nub. I don't think the sheriff doubted it either, and certainly I didn't.

The California rebellion was in part an escapist adventure powered by adrenaline and LSD. But in San Francisco, there was more to it. In addition to a cat-and-mouse drug trade, intermittently interrupted by the local police, Haight-Ashbury was developing a sense of community, sustained by its own peculiar institutions. In the fall of 1966, a newly established psychedelic newspaper, *The San Francisco Oracle*, offered its first editorial opinions: "Protest has not gained any meaningful change because we are psychologically and materially dependent on the system we're changing." The solution, said the paper, lay in the wisdom of Timothy Leary: "Turn on, tune in, drop out." About the same time, a group calling itself the Diggers (a name taken from a sect of seventeenth-century radical, anarchistic Protestants who rejected the notion of private property) began to stage a series of street "happenings," including the Death of Money Parade. One of the founders, Peter Coyote, the son of a New York investment banker, said the Diggers intended "to invent a new culture from scratch."

"I was interested in two things," Coyote recalled, "overthrowing the government and fucking. They went together seamlessly."

Among other things, the Diggers became the apostles of "free"—free love, free food, free medical care, even free stores where those in need could simply help themselves. Sheila Weller described the "burgeoning group" in *Vanity Fair*:

> The Diggers wore animal masks and held up traffic in down-with-money demonstrations. They drove a flatbed truck of belly dancers and conga drummers into the financial district and passed out joints to the crowd. They dispensed fake dollar bills printed with winged penises. They cadged day-old food from markets and fresh food from farmers and turned them into Digger Stew.

ALL THE WHILE THE bands played on—Country Joe and the Fish, the Grateful Dead, Grace Slick and Jefferson Airplane. In the spring, following the success of the Human Be-In, everybody had braced for what was coming that summer. The word had spread, and by the middle of May with the release of Scott McKenzie's song of invitation, "If You're Going to San Francisco," it was already clear that the Summer of Love would be a watershed event. The Diggers had persuaded a local doctor, David Smith, to open a free clinic, treating whatever needed to be treated, especially venereal disease and bad drug trips. More than 75,000 people from other parts of the country, most of them young, flooded into Haight-Ashbury. The psychedelic pilgrims were followed immediately by busloads of tourists gawking at the hippies, and by representatives of the mainstream media who tried to find words for what was going on.

Harry Reasoner was there from CBS, and William Hedgepeth, a respected writer from *Look* magazine, who discovered something wonderful in the scene. "I never wore a suit or tie again," he remembered. "Consciousness is irreversible. It changed my life."

Nicholas von Hoffman of the *Washington Post* offered a more sober assessment. The exuberant promiscuity was only part of it, beautiful girls bedding down with boys who could barely believe their own good luck, all in the name of human freedom. What really bothered von Hoffman were the drugs. Not only did these kids use them freely, but there were self-appointed, psychedelic prophets, not to mention assorted rock stars, who spread the word to a whole generation. Looking back on it in *Vanity Fair*, von Hoffman was certain that the damage was basic.

"This was when American blue-collar and working-class kids became drug users," he said. "This was the beginning of the Rust Belt rusting."

BY THE END OF The Summer of Love, the scene was beginning to collapse, at least the heart of it in Haight-Ashbury. There were simply too many people in too small a space. The crime rate rose and many young people returned to college, taking lessons of love and liberation with them (and sometimes the drugs.) The Diggers staged a Death of the Hippie march on Haight Street, a final funereal act of street theater. But something in the spirit of the place lived on.

"The bulk of what was happening in the summer of love was the exchange if ideas and attitudes and feelings," wrote Bob Weir, a founding member of the Grateful Dead. "It wasn't drugs that made me decide I wasn't going to let the powers that be send me to war. It was the reality of war and the wrongness of that war in particular."

So the young people kept drifting west, perhaps no longer in a fad-driven mass, but a steady flow, seeking a place where they felt free to think. One of my friends, poet and artist Anne Kent Rush, was a part of that post-summer wave. Her search led her not so much to the Haight, though she did spend some time there, but to destinations like the San Francisco Zen Center. The Center's founder, Shunryu Suzuki, a priest who had come to California from Japan, gave frequent talks on the principles of Zen Buddhism, which were soon compiled into a little book, *Zen Mind, Beginner's Mind.*

Rush found herself moved by the precepts.

I vow not to kill.

I vow not to take what is not given.

I vow not to misuse sexuality.

I vow to refrain from false speech.

I vow to refrain from intoxicants.

I vow not to slander.

As the months went by she discovered other wisdom simply in conversation with her neighbors. She lived for a time in a converted goat barn in Muir Woods, an area of hills and old-growth redwoods north of San Francisco. It was an idyllic place, named for John Muir, a turn-of-the-twentieth-century conservationist who founded the Sierra Club and lobbied to create more national parks, including Yosemite. Immediately across a winding lane from Rush's cabin, philosopher-theologian Alan Watts kept a library of books on Asian religion. In 1966, he published *The Book: On the Taboo Against Knowing Who You Are* and in 1967, a collection of what he called "literary nonsense" entitled, not surprisingly, *Nonsense.* Watts wrote often about the natural world, its beauty and grace, and this dimension of his work struck a chord with the youthful backers of environmentalism. They were beginning to emerge in this part of California, combining adventure with a love of the land, as they climbed El Capitan and the other rock faces of Yosemite, and joined in the work of the Sierra Club.

Down the lane a little further from Rush's goat barn stood the rustic dwellings of Elsa Gidlow, a lesbian poet born in Canada, and Margo St. James, a feminist who lobbied for the rights of prostitutes. St. James, especially, did her best to promote a sense of humor among those who confronted hard issues of the day. Convicted of prostitution in 1962, though she had not yet worked in that profession, she sometimes wore a nun's habit given to her by comedian Dick Gregory, as she promoted what she called "sex-positive" feminism. She once ran naked in the annual Bay to Breakers race, slipping into the bushes of Golden Gate Park before the police could arrest her. Far more seriously in those same years, she performed abortions for women who were desperate (including, she said, one on herself, during which she almost died).

Amid all this, Anne Kent Rush published her poems, began to research a book about the Moon, and reveled in a rush of spiritual freedom. Theirs was a powerful mix of ideas—feminism, environmentalism, Eastern philosophy—which she was certain would leave a hopeful, indelible mark.

"We were trying to make a new world," she said. "And we did."

FINALLY, INEVITABLY, THERE WAS the music.

On October 17, the nation's first rock musical, *Hair*, opened Off-Broadway, its creators, James Rado and Gerome Ragni, having been inspired by the antiwar movement and the Summer of Love. Some three weeks later, on November 9, a new publication appeared in San Francisco. Jann Wenner and Ralph Gleason called it *Rolling Stone*, and on page 2 of that first issue, Wenner explained both the name and the publication's purpose:

> You're probably wondering what we're trying to do. It's hard to say: sort of a magazine and sort of a newspaper. The name of it is *Rolling Stone* which comes from the old saying, "A rolling stone gathers no moss." Muddy Waters used the name for a song he wrote. The Rolling Stones took their name from Muddy's song. "Like a Rolling Stone" was the title of Bob Dylan's first rock and roll record. We have begun a new publication reflecting what we see are the changes in rock and roll and the changes related to rock and roll.

Wenner, a veteran of the Berkeley Free Speech Movement, and Gleason, a music critic, both understood that in America in the 1960s, music was more than entertainment or escape. It *was* both of those things, of course, but it was also a reflection of the times, sometimes an anthem against injustice, other times a cry from the heart. They had heard it all in the Summer of Love, and now they knew what they wanted to do. They would write about the music and everything it touched.

They could see how much it mattered.

47

Joplin and Ronstadt

June 18 was one of the high points of the summer, a pinnacle in the history of rock 'n' roll. It was the third and final day of the Monterey Pop Festival, a jubilant celebration of music thrown together in only seven weeks, largely through the efforts of John Phillips. Phillips's own band, the Mamas and Papas, was one of the headliners. So were Otis Redding (who would die in a plane crash by year's end), Jimi Hendrix, Jefferson Airplane, Eric Burdon, the Grateful Dead, Ravi Shankar, and the Who.

But on the final Sunday, a band from San Francisco stole the show. Big Brother and the Holding Company featured as their lead singer a girl from Texas, twenty-four years old, and there had never been anybody like her. Certainly, nobody white. Janis Joplin sang with a raw, urgent edge, a mesmerizing mixture of vulnerability and strength that was jaw-dropping to the crowd at Monterey. She was a white girl singing the blues, and as the people in the audience could tell, she knew exactly what she was doing.

From all accounts she carried wounds from her adolescent years in Port Arthur, Texas. Growing up there, she was smarter than most, not classically pretty, and she resisted the tides of casual racism. Even at the peak of her musical stardom, when she was asked about the place she was from, her voice would often grow pensive and quiet, her answers evasive; watching her even on television you waited for tears she was holding inside. The tears didn't come, for there was also a toughness about her, a rough, hard-drinking, hard-living exterior to go along with a tenderness of heart.

Soon after Monterrey, all of this found perfect expression in her first hit song. She heard an earlier version on the radio, sung by Erma Franklin, Aretha's older sister, in a rendition that was nominated for a Grammy. "(Take Another Little) Piece of My Heart" was written by a man, but it was made for a woman, and in 1967 Erma Franklin's version reached the top ten on the rhythm and blues chart.

The following year, Joplin made it a different song. She sang it with such abandon, such raw and reckless pain, that Franklin, for one, barely recognized it.

Didn't I make you feel like you were the only man—yeah!
An' didn't I give you nearly everything that a woman possibly can?
Honey, you know I did!
And each time I tell myself that I, well I think I've had enough
But I'm gonna show you, baby, that a woman can be tough

Even on the radio, it sounded like the words were being ripped from her heart. Yet there was a feminine defiance and strength that also became Janis Joplin's trademark. The song reached number twelve on the Billboard charts and was Joplin's biggest hit before she left Big Brother and the Holding Company to begin her solo career. Other signature performances followed, including her remake of the Garnet Mimms's soul hit, "Cry Baby," and the Kris Kristofferson country love song, "Me and Bobby McGhee." With success came a high-rolling life, the thrill of the stage and people calling her name, and drugs to fill the empty spaces in between. As the months went by, one of the drugs she turned to was heroin. At the age of twenty-seven she took a fatal dose. She died alone in a Hollywood hotel, fully intending, one biographer believes, to end her on-again, off-again addiction. She was excited about the record she was making, preparing on the following day to cut a song that became heart-breaking in the irony of its title: "Buried Alive in the Blues."

Her friend and biographer Myra Friedman wrote:

> She was a rock 'n' roll woman to her toes, a blues singer of unparalleled passion, and the greatest female performer to emerge from the tempest of the late 1960s. Ecstatic on stage and emotively sublime, she went through life like a superbly visible comet streaking across the sky: quick, brilliant, gone. More than any performer of her day, she symbolized the mental condition of the decade that molded her genius, and out of its theatricalities, its eye-popping colors, its peaks, its overdrive sex, its impatience, excitements, and, dammit, its dangers, too, she made herself a complete and dazzling original."

Even some of us who merely followed her music, sensing perhaps, even from a distance, some of the sadness and danger in her life, were moved all along by a vague sense of dread. We watched her on the *Dick Cavett Show*, talking about music, talking about life, with this most intelligent of late night hosts. Joplin's own intellect was on display as well, her reflectiveness about the music she made, and something even more subtle, I thought: a struggle for emotional authenticity, a self-protectiveness sometimes in her answers, and yet a sense that she was baring her soul. She seemed to embody the vulnerability of the artist, even as she reveled in growing tidal wave of her acclaim. For the rest of us in the 1960s, absorbed in the sounds and the statements she was making, all we could do was marvel at the music.

During the earliest flash of Janis Joplin's stardom, another young singer in California began to make her own mark. She and Janis knew and liked each other, but then almost everybody liked Linda Ronstadt. She came from a musical family in Tucson, with roots reaching into Mexico. Her music was very different from Joplin's, the product of multiple influences, many of which were absorbed through her family. Her father introduced her to Mexican songs that came from the mountains where his family lived before they made the move to Arizona. Linda said later the greatest influence on her own vocal style was almost certainly the Mexican artist Lola Beltran, who sang south-of-the-border country songs in a way that reminded one of the opera star Maria Callas.

"She was a belter," Ronstadt said of Beltran. "She had an enormous, richly colored voice that was loaded with drama, intrigue, and bitter sorrow."

But there were other influences on Ronstadt—her sister's love of Hank Williams, and her own discovery of the sixties' folk singers, including the Canadian group, Ian and Sylvia. The founder of that duo, Ian Tyson, was literally a cowboy, a swashbuckling refugee from the plains of Canada, who wrote about the spirit of his place in the classic folk ballad, "Four Strong Winds." For a while, Linda played these songs—she had a special place in her heart for the ballads—with family and friends in the little folk clubs scattered around Tucson. She decided, however, after her freshman year in college to strike out on her own for California.

In Los Angeles, she found a different music scene than the one in San Francisco where Janis Joplin was becoming a star. By 1967, Linda and her friends Kenny Edwards and Bobby Kimmel formed a folk-rock group called the Stone Poneys, its name taken from a Delta blues song by the great Mississippian Charlie Patton. More than Joplin, Ronstadt was drawn to strong lyrics, the ability of a song, like any other work of literature, to touch the heart of the human condition.

She recorded "Different Drum," a song written by transplanted Texan Michael Nesmith before he joined a sixties rock group called the Monkees. It was clearly written for a guy asserting his freedom to a lover who wants to tie him down: *I'm not ready for any person, place or thing to try and pull the reins in on me.* Linda Ronstadt turned it around, and in her rendition the song became something more—a proclamation, perhaps bittersweet, of feminine independence and strength.

Oh, don't get me wrong
It's not that I knock it
It's just that I am not in the market
For a boy who wants to love only me

For many of us when we first heard the song, it was not just the lyrics that caught our attention; it was the power and beauty of this young woman's voice. Linda Ronstadt was only twenty-one, and in this country-flavored folk song, innovatively arranged with a harpsichord, she sounded so confident and sure of her message. Actually, she wasn't, as we later learned. In the studio, she sang the song only twice, trying to adjust to a new arrangement, and at the end of the session she was sure that she had failed. Ronstadt was like that. She was always her own worst critic, a lover of the music who sometimes wondered if she had done it justice.

Only a few people had the same doubts. Even her friends tended to see her as iconic—one of the pioneers of California country-rock, unfailingly supportive of others involved in that pursuit: singer-songwriters like Gram Parsons and Emmylou Harris, as well as the members of her backup band who later set out on their own as the Eagles. Drummer Don Henley, a member of that band, praised Ronstadt for her "insight, dignity and grace." (More than forty years later, he would acknowledge that "I'm still learning from her.")

As a young reporter about her age, I interviewed her once in those early days, briefly, just before a concert. She was wearing a pair of baggy overalls, having not yet changed into the tighter-fitting jeans she would wear on stage. I was powerfully struck by her beauty, her soft, dark eyes and even darker hair, and by her understated sexuality. There was, I thought, a shy vulnerability about her, balanced comfortably by a keen intellect, as we discussed the currents in American music. I remember that I mentioned the strength of her voice, juxtaposed as it so often was by the tenderness of a good country song. I asked about her love of tradition, her appreciation of artists from Woody Guthrie to Merle Haggard. She seemed happy enough to talk about the old songs, but deflected discussion about her own role with effusive praise for her contemporaries, especially Emmylou Harris.

Despite her instinctive humility, she was a critical figure in that particular moment in American music. If Janis Joplin embodied—reflected—the wild abandon of life on the edge, Ronstadt—as suggested in the title of her first hit song—traveled to the beat of a different drum. She was a leader among the California artists who embraced the interplay of tradition and change, a creative blending of the old and the new. The Californians were not alone in this, for echoes were coming out of Nashville as well. In 1967, George Hamilton IV of the Grand Ole Opry had a top ten hit called "Urge for Going," a song written by Canadian folk-singer Joni Mitchell. It was far more lyrical than the standard fare on country radio.

I awoke today and found
the frost perched on the town
It hovered in a frozen sky
then it gobbled summer down
When the sun turns traitor cold
and all the trees are shivering in a naked row
I get the urge for going
But I never seem to go

Hamilton's record helped introduce Mitchell to a national audience (it was the first chart hit with one of her songs, preceding by a year the Judy Collins single, "Both Sides Now," which became a signature Mitchell composition). In the aftermath of Hamilton's hit, Mitchell came to Nashville where she met and jammed with some of the most promising songwriters in town, including Mickey Newbury and Kris Kristofferson. On the night of her first visit, rock 'n' rollers David Crosby and Michael Nesmith were there, along with Hamilton and maybe one or two others—all sprawled on the floor and the beds of a motel room, passing around a guitar and playing their favorite songs for each other. Remembered Hamilton:

> It was quite a night, one of those famous exchange-of-song sessions that were pretty common in Nashville back in those days. Every time people like

> Joni would come through, they would get together with some local pickers, often out at Johnny Cash's house, but someplace, and they would listen to each other's songs. . . . It was a beautiful period in Nashville.

What made it so, Hamilton explained, was not simply the camaraderie—in some ways not even the music itself, impressive as it was—but the reminder it offered of common ground at a time when the world seemed so divided. Not everybody would have put it that way, but there they were, coming from different backgrounds, different musical traditions that now overlapped and enriched each other. Thus, as the country met and embraced new artists—Joplin, Ronstadt, Joni Mitchell—the music became, in the minds of some, a metaphor of hope in troubled times.

There was one more example in Nashville this year of the ability of music to help people see differently. In 1967, Charley Pride made his first appearance on the Grand Ole Opry, an important step on his road to country stardom. Pride was not the first African American to play the Opry, nor the first black star in country music. That distinction belonged to DeFord Bailey, a harmonica player extraordinaire, who was an Opry regular from 1925 to 1941. Bailey was, however, dropped from the cast for reasons he was certain had to do with his color, and no black artist had performed on the Opry in the following quarter century. Until the 1960s, African Americans were not even allowed in the audience. Rock 'n' roller Chuck Berry, who loved country music, remembered bitter nights in the fifties listening to the Opry from the alley out back, wishing he could be on stage.

Now came Pride, handsome, unassuming, gifted with a mellow, sunburned voice that was country to the bone. He was born and raised in Sledge, Mississippi—cotton country in the heart of the Delta—and he sang country music not to make a social or political statement, but simply because he loved it.

"I guess it's kind of funny, me being up here with this permanent tan," he would say to the all-white crowds, and most would smile with unexpected reassurance that the talented young singer who stood before them loved the music as much as they did. For some who listened with admiration to his songs, the discovery was as simple as it was profound. Charley Pride was one of *them*.

48

Mr. Justice Marshall

On August 30, in a time of falling barriers, the U.S. Senate confirmed the appointment of Thurgood Marshall as a Justice of the United States Supreme Court. This was no ordinary confirmation, no ordinary appointment by President Johnson. Not only was Marshall the first African American ever to serve on the court, he was also the most important civil rights lawyer of the twentieth century. Among other things, he was the lead attorney in *Brown v. Board of Education*, the landmark 1954 case that outlawed segregation in public schools and provided the legal underpinning for black Americans' push for equal rights.

In this pursuit, Marshall embodied a great leap of faith—that the third major branch of the U.S. government, the federal courts, could be transformed into an ally of racial justice. For much of the nation's history, that had not been the case. In 1857, the Supreme Court in its *Dred Scott* decision referred to blacks as "that unfortunate race" which had, under the moral and legal assumptions of slavery, "no rights which the white man was bound to respect." In 1896, in the case of *Plessy v. Ferguson*, the same court upheld the laws of racial segregation, and the history of that particular decision had to be chilling to those who hoped somehow to reverse it.

Plessy was a test case, brought by an interracial group in New Orleans—black, white, and Creole—who opposed a new law requiring segregated railroad cars. Homer Plessy, for whom the case was named, had been a shoemaker before becoming a civil rights activist. He was himself a man of mixed descent (seven-eighths white, one-eighth black), but was considered black under Louisiana law. On June 7, 1892, Plessy bought a first-class ticket from New Orleans to Covington, some thirty miles away. By pre-arrangement with the railroad company, which also opposed the law (partly because providing separate cars for blacks and whites would require the purchase of additional cars), Plessy took a seat in the whites-only coach and was promptly arrested when he refused to move. He was fined $25. With the backing of the citizens group, he appealed his punishment all the way to the U.S. Supreme Court, losing at every stop on the way.

His lawyers argued before the high court that his arrest was plainly unconstitutional under the equal protection clause of the Fourteenth Amendment. The court disagreed. Writing for the majority, Justice Henry Billings Brown put forth the notion of separate but equal, which became a cornerstone of American law for more than fifty years. Brown wrote:

> We consider the underlying fallacy of the plaintiff's argument to consist in the assumption that the enforced separation of the two races stamps the colored race with a badge of inferiority. If this be so, it is not by reason of anything found in the act, but solely because the colored race chooses to put that construction upon it.

Alone among the members of the court, Justice John Marshall Harlan issued a passionate dissent, arguing that the equal protection clause of the Constitution meant exactly what it said: "In respect of civil rights, all citizens are equal before the law. The humblest is the peer of the most powerful." More than that, Harlan predicted, the majority opinion would be misused. It would almost certainly "stimulate aggressions" of white against black, thus making it as infamous in its own way as the *Dred Scott* decision. Harlan concluded:

> The destinies of the two races . . . are indissolubly linked together, and the interests of both require that the common government of all shall not permit the seeds of race hate to be planted under the sanction of law.

Harlan's warning was prophetic, as Thurgood Marshall understood very well. Born in Baltimore in 1908, he came from a proud and successful family, which asserted and expected equal rights for blacks. Baltimore was a good place to do it. Neither Northern nor Southern, it was home to more free people of color than any other city before the Civil War, and now to an emerging black middle class. Thurgood was taught by his father, William Marshall, to believe he was as good as anybody—and to fight any person who suggested otherwise. "Either win or lose right then and there," the elder Marshall said. In 1923, at the age of fifteen, Thurgood was arrested during a flailing fist fight with a white man who had called him a "nigger." Some people said he never stopped fighting for the rest of his life.

From the beginning, he understood the fiction of "separate but equal"—the cynical application of the Supreme Court mantra handed down in the case of *Plessy v. Ferguson*. All over the American South and beyond, "separate" was a fact but "equal" was a lie, and Marshall intended to do something about it. He graduated first in his class from Howard University Law School and wrangled a job as a junior attorney with the NAACP. His first major civil rights case was *Murray v. Pearson*, which he won in the Maryland Court of Appeals. On behalf of the NAACP, Marshall represented Donald Gaines Murray, an African American graduate of Amherst College who wanted to study law at the University of Maryland. Murray was denied admission under the state's segregation laws, which required him to attend an all-black law school.

Marshall was able to demonstrate to the court's satisfaction that the available black institutions were inferior, thus failing the test of "separate but equal." For a while that remained Marshall's strategy—not a frontal assault on segregation, but a whittling away at it, forcing states at least to improve conditions at black schools.

The strategy changed in an unexpected place. In 1947 in Clarendon County, South Carolina, farming country in the state's coastal plain, a group of black citizens wanted a school bus. The Reverend J. A. DeLaine was braver and more educated than most, and he clearly recognized the need for a change. Students in the little community of Jordan lived nine miles from the Scott's Branch School, the one to which they were assigned, and the one in which DeLaine's wife Mattie worked as a teacher. The DeLaines both knew that during certain seasons of the year when a nearby lake overflowed its banks, the children from Jordan had to row a boat across the swollen waters and then embark on their nine-mile walk because the white school board refused to provide a bus for black children. DeLaine persuaded a courageous farmer, Levi Pearson, to file a lawsuit seeking a bus, but the suit was thrown out because part of Pearson's small farm lay on the other side of the county line. After the case was dismissed, a white legislator in the capital city of Columbia was heard to mutter, "Our niggers don't even know where they live."

That was when Thurgood Marshall came to the state, invited by leaders of the NAACP. It was always dangerous, Marshall said, to rely on a single plaintiff in a lawsuit, especially one with broad implications. He told the leaders in South Carolina, including DeLaine, that if they wanted his help they would have to come up with at least twenty plaintiffs, black citizens who had felt the sting of inferior schools and were brave enough to stick their necks out. Otherwise, said Marshall, he would find other cases. He was gruff and convincing when he said such things, a large man, more than six feet tall, with a little mustache that slowly turned gray as the years went by. He could be tactless and arrogant, some people thought (although he generally softened those qualities with humor). But nobody doubted his solid track record as a civil rights lawyer.

Marshall knew already that if DeLaine found the plaintiffs he would file a suit that went far beyond the provision of a school bus. They would demand an end to the appalling conditions in all-black schools—the hand-me-down books, the pot-bellied stoves, the overcrowded buildings with leaky roofs. But as the 1940s drew to a close, Marshall was wrestling with a dilemma. Did he dare raise the issue of desegregation? That was what Homer Plessy had done, and when the Supreme Court finally ruled against him, the racial discrimination Plessy had sought to undo instead became more deeply enshrined into law. Now that half a century had passed, would the court reconsider? Was it worth risking another setback?

By the time Reverend DeLaine found his twenty plaintiffs and the Clarendon County case went to federal court, Marshall and the NAACP had decided on a dual strategy. They would begin to make the case that segregated schools could never be equal, while hedging their bets by documenting the most flagrant deprivations in all-black schools that violated the standard set forth in *Plessy*.

That was when a white judge intervened.

U. S. District Judge J. Waties Waring had been on the bench since 1942, a reward for his uneventful career as a patrician lawyer in Charleston, South Carolina. During the first sixty-one years of his life, Waring had rarely rocked any boats, quietly enjoying his local prominence. But all of that changed when he became a judge. One of the early cases to come before him, one that offended his *noblesse oblige* sensibilities, was a peonage dispute: a white man accused of detaining a black and forcing him to work for almost nothing, treating him essentially as a slave. Unlike some Southern judges who winked at the practice, Waring ordered the white man to jail. As the cases kept coming, from voting rights to the deprivations of black schools, Waring came to understand that racial fairness could not be achieved simply by ameliorating the cruelties of individual hate; rather, a solution would require more systemic remedies. African Americans, contrary to the spirit of the Constitution, were not equal citizens in the eyes of the law. That was clear in so many ways.

Billie Fleming, a grassroots leader in South Carolina, remembered the day Marshall began presenting the Clarendon County case to the judge. In his carefully crafted arguments, Marshall raised the possibility of desegregation while clinging to the safety net of *Plessy*, a motion to make the black schools equal. Fleming remembered the response of Judge Waring, how he peered from the bench with an expression that seemed both somber and friendly, and summoned Marshall forward.

"He told us," said Fleming, in an interview that I did with him later, "'You're going down the wrong road. If you really want the courts to declare segregation unconstitutional, you need to draw your arguments exactly that way.'"

IN HIS BRILLIANT BOOK, *Simple Justice*, historian Richard Kluger recounts how Marshall seized the opening, shepherding the Clarendon County case along with four others through the federal courts, and adding a bit of legal innovation. Marshall secured the services of Kenneth Clark, a social psychologist who was, like himself, a graduate of Howard University, where the faculty included such scholars as the soon-to-be Nobel laureate Ralph Bunche.

"The whole atmosphere of the place was heady," remembered Clark, "and every scholar was eager to relate classroom work to social action."

Clark set out to do the same. He was thrilled for the chance to work with Marshall to demonstrate not just the physical inferiority of black schools but the damage done by segregation itself. He was offended by the sophistry of the *Plessy* decision, its dubious finding that enforced separation was not a declaration of white superiority except in the minds of African Americans. For some time now, he and his wife Mamie, who, like her husband, had earned her doctorate from Columbia University, had been embarked on a sociological study, publishing their findings in the *Journal of Social Psychology* and the *Journal of Experimental Education*. The Clarks used a group of dolls, some brown, some white, purchased for fifty cents each at a five-and-dime store in Harlem. They asked black children which dolls were good, which were bad, which they liked, and which they didn't, seeking to explore the children's sense of self-worth.

These simple tests, wrote Richard Kluger, "disclosed how early in life black children came to understand that success, security, beauty, and status all wear white skin in America."

Although some of his colleagues thought he was crazy—using *dolls* in a federal court case!—Marshall wanted to introduce these results into the record. Even if the scholarship was not especially sophisticated, merely the beginning point of a long inquiry into the damage done by American racism, its emotional impact was immediate and strong. It gave a face to the problem—the face of a child. Marshall said:

> I told the staff that we had to try this case just like any other one in which you would try to prove damages to your client. If your car ran over my client, you'd have to pay up, and my function as an attorney would be to put experts on the stand to testify to how much damage was done . . . When [civil rights attorney] Bob Carter came to me with Ken Clark's doll test, I thought it was a promising way of showing injury to these segregated youngsters. I wanted this kind of evidence on the record.

In the end, it was difficult to measure the precise impact of the dolls. But when the Supreme Court agreed to consider the Clarendon County case in a group with four others—beginning alphabetically with *Oliver Brown, et al. v. Board of Education of Topeka, et al.*—the justices did conclude that segregation *itself* was the problem, not simply the manifestly unequal facilities that had long been the norm in Southern school systems.

On behalf of a unanimous court, Chief Justice Earl Warren wrote:

> Segregation of white and colored children in public schools has a detrimental effect upon the colored children, The effect is greater when it has the sanction of law. . . . We conclude that, in the field of public education, the doctrine of "separate but equal" has no place. Separate educational facilities are inherently unequal."

In *Thurgood Marshall: American Revolutionary*, journalist Juan Williams argues that when the decision was announced on May 17, 1954, that moment alone was enough to secure Marshall's place in history. But there were so many other cases through the years, legal opinions secured by Marshall that built the foundation for civil rights progress. Because of that remarkable record, Williams contends, Marshall stands with Martin Luther King and Malcolm X in a triumvirate of the nation's most important black leaders.

A man of rock-solid confidence, Marshall himself was certain of the role he had played, and by the summer of 1967 a new ambition burned in his heart. He wanted to be the first black justice on the U.S. Supreme Court. His opportunity came when Justice Tom Clark, who had been on the court when *Brown* was handed down, decided to retire. Attorney General Ramsey Clark, son of the judge, urged his fellow Texan, President Lyndon Johnson, to nominate Marshall to fill the vacancy, but the president was curiously resistant. In his biography of Marshall, Juan Williams described the drama surrounding the appointment. Some of it was pure gamesmanship, Johnson's delight in asserting his power. On the night before he made his announcement, the president called Marshall aside at Tom Clark's retirement party and told him privately that he had decided on somebody else. Marshall was bitterly disappointed, but held his tongue and brooded later—in the privacy of his own home—on the moment when history had passed him by.

Johnson did have genuine reservations. He had heard rumors that Marshall had become lazy in the looming shadow of his sixtieth birthday, and others who had the president's ear argued curiously that there were more capable black lawyers. But the most important consideration was political. Johnson was afraid that a Senate dominated by Southern conservatives, as it was in 1967, would not approve Marshall's nomination.

Marshall, however, had powerful advocates. Nicholas Katzenbach, Ramsey Clark's predecessor as attorney general, was horrified when Johnson told him in private, "Marshall's not the best—he's not the most outstanding black lawyer in the country." Katzenbach grimaced. "Mr. President," he said, "if you appoint anybody, any black to that court but Thurgood Marshall, you are insulting every black in the country. Thurgood is *the* black lawyer as far as blacks are concerned—I mean there can't be any doubt about that."

In the end, Johnson succumbed to his own sense of history. With the appointment of Marshall, not only would he, as president, be remembered for breaking the color barrier on the court, he would do it by appointing the country's greatest legal champion of civil rights. This would be more than a historic first. It would be yet another affirmation of Johnson's own greatness—his willingness to lay his prestige on the line, to risk a rejection by the U.S. Senate, and appoint the man who most clearly deserved it. Thus, on the morning after Tom Clark's party, Johnson called Marshall to the White House (to salve the wound, Marshall assumed) and told him with what appeared to be delight: "You know something, Thurgood? I'm going to put you on the Supreme Court."

"Marshall was stunned," wrote Juan Williams. "All he could say was 'Oh yipe!'"

The reaction in the U.S. Senate seemed at first to be precisely what Johnson had feared—an ugly resistance that was racist at its core. Williams recounted investigations by the FBI at the behest of Southern senators about whether Marshall hated whites, or had ties to communists, or drank too much, or slept with women other than his wife—anything that might disqualify this history-making black lawyer from taking his place on the U.S. Supreme Court. In the end, these attempts failed.

Marshall was confirmed by the Senate and ascended to the bench precisely at a time when the court was dealing with anachronisms.

On June 12, 1967, in the aptly named case of *Loving v. Virginia*, the justices had ruled 9–0 that state laws banning interracial marriage were unconstitutional. At the time of the decision, sixteen states still maintained such bans, asserting governmental control over this most personal of human institutions. The case began as an epic story of injustice. On a hot July night in 1958, Sheriff Garnett Brooks of Caroline County, Virginia, burst into the bedroom of Richard and Mildred Loving, armed with warrants for their arrest.

"I woke up," Mildred remembered, "and these guys were standing around the bed. I sat up. It was dark. They had flashlights. They told us to get up and get dressed. I couldn't believe they were taking us to jail."

The Lovings' offense was getting married, something they had done on June 2 in Washington, D.C., where their union was legal. Richard Loving was white, and Mildred was black, at least according to the laws of Virginia, where the couple wanted to live. Mildred later told Arica Coleman, author of the book *That the Blood Stay Pure*, that she was a Rappahannock Indian, though almost certainly her heritage was mixed. The state of Virginia was not the least bit interested in Mildred's genealogy. Under the state's Racial

Integrity Act passed in 1924 (the latest in a line of anti-miscegenation statutes dating to 1691), anybody with "one drop" of black blood was black. Nor did it matter if the couple had married elsewhere. They had taken up residence in Virginia, living in the basement of Mildred's family home, and thus were in violation of the law.

They were tried, convicted and sentenced to a twenty-five-year probation—no prison time as long as they stayed out of Virginia. They could return, of course, one at a time, but never together without risking arrest. As the years went by, they occasionally violated those terms, mostly to visit members of their family, fearful every time that they might get caught. Mildred, especially, grew weary of this, and in 1963 she wrote a letter to Attorney General Robert Kennedy, knowing the administration's civil rights record, and asked what Kennedy could do to help. The Justice Department referred her to the American Civil Liberties Union (ACLU), where attorney Bernard Cohen jumped at the chance to represent her.

"The name of the case itself enthralled him," wrote historian Peter Wallenstein. "Loving versus Virginia."

Cohen knew the U.S. Supreme Court had refused to consider miscegenation cases in the 1950s after strenuous internal debate. Two of its most brilliant members, Justice William O. Douglas and Justice Felix Frankfurter, disagreed on the wisdom of addressing such an emotional topic in the wake of its landmark ruling in *Brown*. Frankfurter, the advocate of caution, temporarily prevailed, but by the mid-sixties the legal landscape had changed. There had been a wave of the civil rights cases, as the Warren Court made its mark on history, and the justices were beginning to consider other, more delicate issues relating to the institution of marriage.

In 1965, in the case of *Griswold v. Connecticut*, the court struck down a state ban on contraception for women, even if they were married. The issue arose on November 1, 1961 when Estelle Griswold, executive director of the Planned Parenthood League in Connecticut, opened a birth control clinic with Dr. Lee Buxton, a gynecologist at the Yale School of Medicine. The two of them were quickly arrested under the Comstock Law, a Connecticut statute passed in 1873 and still on the books, prohibiting the use of "any drug, medicinal article, or instrument for the purpose of preventing conception."

When the case reached the U.S. Supreme Court, Justice Douglas delivered the 7–2 majority opinion, ruling that the Comstock Law represented a pointless government intrusion, thus violating a constitutional right to privacy. Douglas was an activist judge, often criticized by conservatives for his alleged willingness to make new law. In his critics' eyes, the *Griswold* decision was an example. Nowhere in the Constitution or its amendments was there any mention of a "right to privacy." The words were not there. Douglas might have answered in his own defense that neither were the words "separate but equal" when the court established that standard in *Plessy*. But Douglas was not interested in arguing with his critics. The Constitution, he thought, was brilliantly crafted to cover issues the founders had not imagined. History evolved and so must the law.

Thus in 1965, the court sent a signal in the *Griswold* case that in matters of personal intimacy and marriage, the government must tread more lightly. This was good news to the lawyers representing Mildred Loving. On April 10, 1967, as they prepared to deliver their oral arguments to the Court, they asked their clients if they wanted to attend. The Lovings declined. "Mr. Cohen," wrote Richard Loving, "tell the Court I love my wife, and it is just unfair that I can't live with her in Virginia."

In many ways, it was really that simple. For the most mean-spirited and archaic of reasons, two people who had fallen in love and committed their lives to each other were denied equal protection under the Fourteenth Amendment. On June 12, writing for a unanimous court, Chief Justice Earl Warren called the Virginia law "repugnant," and went on to explain: "The clear and central purpose of the Fourteenth Amendment was to eliminate all official state sources of invidious racial discrimination in the States."

The legal aftershocks continued for several more years, as states like Alabama and Mississippi maintained implausibly that the Supreme Court ruling applied to Virginia, but not to them. They lost those arguments, and more and more it began to appear that the courts had driven a stake through the heart of Jim Crow. Finally, one hundred years after the Civil War, legal segregation was dead.

Racism, of course, lived on.

The *Loving* case reached the court before Thurgood Marshall took his seat. But there were others on the way that would broaden the definition of individual freedom and continue the march of civil rights progress. One of those involved contraception for unmarried women, which was, despite

FDA approval of the pill in 1960, still illegal in many states. The case began in Boston. In March, 1967, the student newspaper at Boston University, the *B.U. News*, announced that it had invited a man named William Baird to visit the campus and "distribute free lists of abortionists and birth control devices to interested coeds." Baird was a birth control activist and former medical student from Brooklyn, who displayed, in the words of historian David Garrow, "a highly developed taste for publicity." He had picketed St. Patrick's Cathedral in Manhattan to protest the Catholic opposition to birth control, and had demonstrated against Planned Parenthood, protesting fees he said were too high.

Baird came to Boston University on April 6, where he appeared before a crowd of nearly two thousand people, 65 percent of whom were women. Seven Boston police officers waited patiently as Baird delivered a sixty-minute lecture, during which he told the women in the crowd that they were being "enchained by men who have no right to dictate to you the privacy of your bodies." Garrow, in his book *Liberty and Sexuality*, recounted how Baird began to distribute free packages of Emko vaginal foam and "called upon the watchful officers 'to do their duty.'"

"The only way we can change the law," Baird said, "is to get the case into a court of law."

Baird was arrested and his case began a seven-year journey to the U.S. Supreme Court, which eventually extended its *Griswold* precedent from women who were married to those who were not. Birth control, the Court declared in 1972, was a matter of individual intimacy and freedom, and not a proper realm for the government. Soon enough, other women's rights activists would push that precedent to include abortion, generating a whole new level of controversy and division, as the women's movement continued its advance.

More immediately for Marshall and other members of the court, there was an ongoing flow of civil rights cases, including another from Virginia involving the desegregation of schools. Civil rights leaders had grown impatient with the lack of progress. On October 1, 1967, the day before Marshall was officially sworn in, his replacement at the NAACP Legal Defense Fund, a Jewish lawyer named Jack Greenberg, filed a Supreme Court brief in *Green v. New Kent County*, raising a critically important question. Was it enough for school systems simply to *desegregate*—to assign students to schools without specifically considering their color? Could they, for example, assign those students geographically, or simply allow them to choose their own schools (as New Kent County had done), even if mixing of the races was minimal?

Or were school systems required to *integrate*—to assign students in a way that actually put black and white students together, erasing every trace of past segregation?

To Marshall the issue was crucial. For all of his life he had been a passionate believer in integration. Only if people really knew each other, working toward a world of mutual respect, could the country find its way to racial harmony. Marshall was sure of that—and as a man of legendary practicality, there was one more thing he believed as well. As long as it was possible to identify a public institution as black—especially a school—that institution was almost certain to be shortchanged. That was simply the way of the world.

The following year, in the case of *New Kent County*, Marshall was happy to be part of a unanimous decision. In this rural part of Virginia there were only two high schools, one white, one black, and no particular pattern of residential segregation. In the words of one historian, "white and black farms were salt and peppered across the landscape," and black and white children were bused to separate schools that would have been easy enough to integrate if that had been the school board's goal. The Supreme Court ruled that this would not do. In an opinion written by Justice William Brennan, the court ordered school officials in the county—and by extension, in other parts of the country as well—to remove every remnant of legal segregation, "root and branch."

By the mid-seventies, in the face of mounting public controversy, the Supreme Court under new leadership would begin to pull back. But for a while at least in the nation's public schools, much to Thurgood Marshall's satisfaction, racial integration was the law of the land.

49

Jonathan Kozol and Mister Rogers

It was an important time in American education. At the beginning of October, respected publisher Houghton-Mifflin released a new book by a teacher in Boston. Jonathan Kozol's *Death at an Early Age* was a passionate account of his time at a school in the Roxbury ghetto, of the children he knew there and the terrible things that were being done to them. This was a segregated school, precisely the kind that had always worried Thurgood Marshall. Kozol was fired after six months, allegedly for introducing his fourth-grade students to the Langston Hughes poem, "The Ballad of the Landlord."

Landlord landlord my roof has sprung a leak.
Don't you 'member I told you about it
Way last week?
Landlord, landlord,
These steps is broken down.
When you come up yourself
It's a wonder you don't fall down.

Remembering the moment fifty years later, Thelma Burns, a parent at the school, told National Public Radio's *All Things Considered* how she and other parents tried to meet with school officials after Kozol was fired, tried to explain how this magna cum laude graduate of Harvard seemed to be the only teacher who genuinely understood their children. "No one at the school would talk to us," remembered Burns. "That's the way it was at the time." So the parents decided to picket. Kozol, meanwhile, set about writing *Death at an Early Age*, his subtitle brimming with indignation and grief: *The Destruction of the Hearts and Minds of Negro Children in the Boston Public Schools.*

I remember that I first encountered the book through an advance excerpt in the September 1967 *Atlantic Monthly*. This was barely two months after the deadly riots in Newark and Detroit, and for me the rage of those terrifying events suddenly took on the face of a fourth-grader. The cruelty that Kozol described was as blatant and as matter-of-fact—as routine and officially ingrained—as anything I had ever seen in the South; it was a portrait, I thought, of the institutional racism that I had heard Stokely Carmichael speak about at Vanderbilt. Critics would later say that Kozol oversimplified the problem, that the issues afflicting inner-city schools went deeper than the insensitivity of white teachers, and that those of us who were moved by his story were simply indulging our own liberal guilt. That may be true. But here in *The Atlantic* was Kozol writing about a little boy.

> Stephen is an eight-year-old pupil in the Boston public schools. A picture of him standing in front of a bulletin board on Arab bedouins shows a little light-brown person staring with unusual concentration at a chosen spot upon the floor. Stephen is tiny, desperate, unwell. Sometimes he talks to himself, or laughs out loud in class for no apparent reason. He is also an indescribably mild and unmalicious child. He cannot do any of his schoolwork very well. His math and reading are poor. In third grade his class had substitute teachers much of the year. Most of the year before that he had substitute teachers too. He is in the fourth grade now, but his work is barely at the level of the second.

In Kozol's account, Stephen is frequently abused at home, where he lives with foster parents who no longer want him. His great gift at school is his artwork, which is wildly imaginative and original, but his art teacher does not like him because he refuses to color within the lines. His math teacher does not like him either, treating him frequently with abusive contempt, though she describes herself as a liberal—a committed supporter of the civil rights movement, especially in the South. Kozol likes Stephen very much but is often reprimanded by his peers for treating his students too much like friends.

In one attempt to engage his class, Kozol asked them to write about a place that mattered in their lives, not worrying about the niceties of spelling. Ordinarily, those rules came first, but Kozol wanted his students to write from the heart. To the horror of the administration, one little girl wrote about conditions at the school, the fact that it was often dirty and the paint was chipping away in places, and a broken window was simply boarded up. To Kozol, the student's paragraph was impressive—observant, honest, a commentary her teachers should have respected. But the other teachers were appalled, not only by the child's lapses in spelling ("I see an old browken window"), but by her candor—and that Kozol would support it. There was something in the culture of the school, he thought, that compelled an obsession with authority and control, ultimately enforced by corporal punishment.

> Perhaps a partial explanation lies in the fact that segregated schools seem to require this kind of brutal discipline because of the bitter feelings which are so often present in the air. The children—enough of them anyway—are constantly smoldering with a generally unrecognized awareness of their own degradation. The resulting atmosphere is deeply threatening to teachers and administrators.
>
> Possibly in most cases, this is the entire story. Thinking of some of the teachers, however, I am convinced that something else was happening at times, and once you had watched it, you would know exactly what it was and would never deny that it was there. "This hurts me," goes the saying, "more than it hurts you." Yet there are moments when the visible glint of gratification becomes unmistakable in the white teacher's eyes.

Kozol became one of the leading thinkers in American education, winner of multiple prizes for his work, including the National Book Award. Like his peers in his first ghetto school, his critics thought he was too hard on administrators and teachers and too soft on students, undermining authority and hard-headed standards. But the number and quality of Kozol's admirers drowned out the critics and gave him comfort—particularly the support he received from a man who would soon become one of his best friends.

FRED ROGERS, TOO, WAS emerging as a national figure in education. He secured a grant from the Sears Foundation to begin taping a national television show that would gain renown as *Mister Rogers' Neighborhood.* Rogers, then thirty-nine, was a native of Latrobe, Pennsylvania (a birthplace shared with one of the great gentlemen golfers of the sixties, Arnold Palmer). He earned a degree in music composition from Rollins College and a divinity degree from Pittsburgh Theological Seminary and was an ordained Presbyterian minister. In the 1950s, he began a television show for children because, he said, he hated the crassness of television and the damage he thought it could do to children.

His own show aired locally in Pittsburgh and then in Canada before October 1967, when he began taping the first of more than eight hundred episodes that would be shown on the Public Broadcasting Service (PBS). Every program began in the same way—Mister Rogers entering the door of his home, singing his trademark song, "Won't You Be My Neighbor," and changing into sneakers and a zippered sweater. Everything about him was calm and reassuring, and over the years it became apparent that children of every cultural background, every conceivable advantage or disadvantage in life, instinctively trusted this tall, slender man, as if he were not just a television character but a crucially important part of their lives. Many adults felt the same.

Jonathan Kozol remembered a time when he and Rogers were on the No. 6 train headed to the South Bronx and a tutorial program at St. Ann's Episcopal Church. Kozol worked often with the children at St. Ann's, and he wanted Rogers to meet them, especially a little boy named Elio, who was six.

> It was a nice experience to ride with Mr. Rogers on the train. There he was, the same sweet guy that children have been learning from. . . . He even had on his sweater and his sneakers and a bow tie, and people on the train kept looking at him kind of strangely. We got off the train at Brook Avenue. We walked one block, and a garbage truck came to a screeching halt. The driver, a 50-year-old black man, jumped out and hugged Mr. Rogers. We went to St. Ann's, where Elio spotted Mr. Rogers from across the crowded room. He zoomed straight across the room with his arms spread wide. At the moment of collision, he gave him a big kiss on the forehead. He said, "Welcome to my neighborhood, Mr. Rogers.

Over the years, such stories became commonplace. Even a publication as urbane as *Esquire* magazine published a profile of Rogers that was tinged with unmistakable awe. Writer Tom Jurod recounted the time when Rogers went to visit a boy in California, fourteen years old and severely afflicted with cerebral palsy. The boy couldn't speak and communicated through a computer and sometimes with flailing gestures of self-hate, hitting himself with his awkward fists, telling his mother that he wanted to die. "He was sure," wrote Jurod, "that God didn't like what was inside him any more than he did." Over the years, the boy had endured stares of disgust nearly every time he left the safety of his home, and cruelty in the form of verbal abuse, but one thing gave him comfort each day: he watched *Mister Rogers' Neighborhood.*

When Mister Rogers came to see him, however, the boy was caught in a wave of self-doubt, feeling apparently that he was unworthy. He began flailing and hitting himself again, and his mother had to take him into another room to help him calm down. And then, wrote Jurod, this is what happened:

> . . . when the boy came back, Mister Rogers talked to him, and then he made his request. He said, "I would like you to do something for me. Would you do something for me?" On his computer, the boy answered yes, of course, he would do *anything* for Mister Rogers, so then Mister Rogers said, "I would like you to pray for me. Will you pray for me?" And now the boy didn't know how to respond. He was thunderstruck. Thunderstruck means that you can't talk, because something has happened that's as sudden and as miraculous and maybe as scary as a bolt of lightning, and all you can do is listen to the rumble. The boy was thunderstruck because nobody had ever *asked* him for something like that, ever. The boy had always been prayed *for.* The boy had always been the *object* of prayer, and now he was being asked to pray for Mister Rogers, and although at first he didn't know if he could do it, he said he would, he said he'd try, and ever since then he keeps Mister Rogers in his prayers and doesn't talk about wanting to die anymore, because he figures Mister Rogers is close to God, and if Mister Rogers likes him, that must mean God likes him, too.
>
> As for Mister Rogers himself . . . well, he doesn't look at the story in the same way that the boy did or that I did. In fact, when Mister Rogers first told me the story, I complimented him on being so smart—for knowing that asking the boy for his prayers would make the boy feel better about himself—and Mister Rogers responded by looking at me at first with puzzlement and then with surprise. "Oh, heavens no, Tom! I didn't ask him for his prayers for *him*; I asked for me. I asked him because I think that anyone who has gone through challenges like that must be very close to God. I asked him because I wanted his *intercession.*"

Jurod came away from writing his story—one of the most lovely that I have ever read—convinced that Rogers's life of reaching out to children was religious at its core, a ministry he had embarked upon even before he earned his divinity degree. Jurod ended his profile with another anecdote about a prayer. He and Rogers and a minister at his church were standing together and at Rogers's behest, they were praying for grace.

"What is grace?" wrote Jurod. "I'm not certain; all I know is that my heart felt like a spike, and then, in that room, it opened and felt like an umbrella."

I OFFER THIS STORY about Fred Rogers because he came to represent for me (particularly when I had children of my own) as pure an embodiment as I can imagine of the idealism I felt in the sixties—a colorblind generosity (and he was literally colorblind) and identification with those most vulnerable in our society. This was, of course, what many of us believed to be our values, before the anger and the echoes of war took over and everything began to veer off track.

But there is another point I wish to make here. This was a time of extraordinary writing. Jonathan Kozol was one example of that, a man duly honored with the National Book Award and other recognitions for the power of his work, and there were those like Tom Jurod who filled publications such as *Esquire, The Atlantic,* and *The New Yorker* with some of the finest prose of our time.

In that same October, another writer of considerable renown set off upon an ambitious project—one inspired by the war in Vietnam—that would make its way first to *Harper's*, another extraordinary magazine, in an article entitled "The Steps of the Pentagon."

We would soon come to know it better as a book, a Pulitzer Prize-winning bestseller called *The Armies of the Night.*

50

The War at Home

On the 21st of October—such an eventful month in America—Norman Mailer was arrested on the steps of the Pentagon. Mailer was not known for civil disobedience, though he had spoken at rallies against the war long before it was fashionable to do so. But he was not an activist. He was a writer, a novelist up to that point, famous for his book, *The Naked and the Dead*, and now, he decided, he wanted to bring a literary eye to the writing of history. He intended to use a March on the Pentagon—a demonstration that drew 100,000 people—to write about the war and the struggle against it. He had in mind a magazine article that might be as long as 10,000 words, followed by a book.

Willie Morris, the wunderkind editor of *Harper's*, got wind of Mailer's plan, tracked him down and offered to publish the piece. They agreed on a price of $10,000, and Mailer retreated to his house on Cape Cod and began to write his story in a sprawling longhand, working faster than he ever had in his life. He swore off alcohol as he wrote. Two weeks into the project, Mailer called Morris and told him the piece was running long and he needed a little more time. Morris agreed, but after another few weeks, having heard nothing more, he flew to Cape Cod with another *Harper's* editor, Midge Decter, to check on Mailer's progress. There, in a house set back in the dunes, he found a young typist trying frantically to sort through the scribbles and the scrawl and the crossed-out words, and Mailer upstairs locked in battle with the last several pages.

Assembling the scattered pieces of the story, Morris began to read. "It's marvelous," he thought to himself. When he came to the end, he decided to publish all ninety thousand words, making Mailer's piece the longest ever to appear in a magazine. This was journalism as Morris thought it should be, personal, stylish, a brilliant reflection on the times, though not everybody shared that opinion. *Time* magazine rebuked Mailer's role in what it called the "capers" at the Pentagon, and among the letters to the editor that poured in to *Harper's*, some criticized Mailer's self-indulgence. A few readers even canceled their subscriptions. But Morris knew the article had powerfully touched a nerve in the country. He later wrote:

> "The Steps of the Pentagon" . . . was one of the signal and most controversial events in the long history or American magazines: its impact on the country and the times on a variety of levels was stunning and instantaneous. It opened radical new ground in subject matter and in its uses of language in popular national journals.

I vividly remember my first reaction, an immediate comparison to *In Cold Blood* just in the sheer ambition of the project. By his explicit acknowledgment, Mailer made himself the protagonist, adopting the unexpected device of a third-person first-person narrative, referring to himself throughout as Mailer. The pretension of it, so obvious at first, was balanced by his habit of self-deprecation, but much more than that, by his novelist's understanding of tragedy. Like Morris, I was moved by how Mailer, in the magazine version, ended his epic of contemporary history.

> . . . he wrote of necessity at a rate faster than he had written before, as if the accelerating history of the country forbid deliberation. Yet in writing his personal history of those four days, he also delivered a discovery to himself of what the March on the Pentagon had finally meant, and what had been won, and what had been lost in that quintessentially American and most contemporary event—the scheduled happening which begins with the given and ends on the road to that mystery where courage, death, and the dream of love give promise of sleep.

Despite the grandeur of Mailer's prose, and his description of a flawed attempt to stop the killing in Vietnam, the war went on. That was the incontrovertible truth. And with war came the reflexive lying of our leaders that would then and forever taint our understanding of the government and our moral understanding of ourselves. The American commander, General William Westmoreland, became a legend for his clichés—"light at the end of the tunnel," "mopping up the enemy"—and for promises nobody believed.

"We have reached an important point," he told the National Press Club in Washington, "when the end begins to come into view." He based his generally sunny assessments on the grim reality of body counts—the mounting totals of dead Viet Cong, though some of his officers would later acknowledge that in their experience every dead Vietnamese "was considered VC." And there were so many dead Vietnamese. There was little doubt that the total reached more than a million men, women and children.

Reports also filtered back home of a routine reliance on torture. I knew a young man who returned from the war ruined by things he was ordered to do. Once, during an interrogation of suspected Viet Cong, the captives were taken up in a helicopter, and when they refused to talk, this boy I knew, who came home desperate in his addiction to drugs, was ordered by his sergeant to throw one of the Vietnamese out the open door of the helicopter. The others were left to consider their fate if they, too, refused to answer their interrogators' questions.

K. Barton Osborne, a military intelligence officer who came to Vietnam in September 1967, later testified before Congress about some of the harsher interrogation techniques. Among other things, he described

> the use of the insertion of the 6-inch dowel into the canal of one of my detainee's ears and the tapping through the brain until he died. The starving to death [in a cage] of a Vietnamese woman who was suspected of being part of the local political education cadre in one of the local villages . . . the use of electronic gear . . . attached to . . . both the women's vagina and the men's testicles [to] shock them into submission.

In response to reports of such cruelty, and the intransigence of the policies that produced it, the peace movement grew and its character changed. Todd Gitlin, a leader in SDS, remembered that:

> As the war became more militant, so did the antiwar movement—in demands, in spirit, in tactics. Between 1965 and 1967, as American troops in Vietnam doubled and redoubled and redoubled twice more, most antiwar movers and shakers shook off their leftover faith in negotiations and endorsed immediate withdrawal."

As Gitlin noted, the cutting edge of the movement no longer concerned itself with strategic solutions—a negotiating position to preserve American honor or prestige—as indeed it had in the past. Less than two years earlier, when Staughton Lynd and Tom Hayden returned from their visit to North Vietnam, they brought with them ideas, doggedly hopeful, about the possibility of a negotiated settlement. By the fall of 1967, such considerations had largely disappeared. The antiwar movement was angry, disillusioned, fed up, and the March on the Pentagon was a cry of "Enough!"

IT WAS ONE OF many that autumn. In Oakland, California, and the surrounding area, a series of escalating protests soon became known as Stop the Draft Week. On October 16, Joan Baez was one of those arrested, along with her mother, and spent forty-five days in jail for supporting young men who resisted the draft. In San Francisco, more than four hundred of those young men, many of them students, turned in their draft cards in a united act of protest. Soon after that the demonstrations turned violent. To be sure, much of the violence came from police. On a day the movement would come to call "Bloody Tuesday," referencing the outcome of the historic march across the Edmund Pettus Bridge, Oakland's men in blue attacked a group of protesters who were blocking access to a draft induction center. The following day, the *San Francisco Chronicle* described the moment in vivid detail:

> Police swinging clubs like scythes cut a bloody path through 2,500 antiwar demonstrators who had closed down the Oakland Armed Forces Examining Station yesterday for three hours.

There were at least forty confrontations that fall at college campuses across the country, including one at the University of Wisconsin aimed at a recruiter from the Dow Chemical Company, makers of napalm. When police moved in to disperse the demonstrators, many of them, led by SDS, fought back, throwing rocks and bricks and sending seven officers to the hospital. Sixty-five students were injured as well.

More fighting erupted at the Pentagon, where Norman Mailer was one of 179 people arrested. Twenty-seven people were injured, including six military personnel. On October 22, the *Washington Post* reported:

> More than 55,000 persons demonstrated here against the war in Vietnam yesterday in what started out as a peaceful rally but erupted into violence at the Pentagon late in the day.
>
> At one point a surging band of about 30 demonstrators rushed into the Pentagon, only to be thrown out by armed troops.
>
> Dozens of youthful demonstrators were arrested during two brief but angry melees at the Pentagon's Mall entrance. Several thousand demonstrators surged across boundaries that the Government had prescribed.
>
> In many isolated incidents, military police and U.S. marshals clubbed the jeering, rushing demonstrators who invaded forbidden spots or pushed against defensive lines. . . .
>
> The vast majority of the demonstrators were not involved in the attempt to storm the Pentagon. Among those arrested at the Pentagon area were author Norman Mailer . . . and Dave Dellinger, the self-styled radical who is chairman of the National Mobilization Committee to End the War in Vietnam, sponsor of the rally.
>
> In the most serious incident, 20 to 30 demonstrators slipped through lines of U.S. marshals and military policemen and into a small vestibule inside the office of the Pentagon's Mall entrance. Once inside they encountered heavily armed troops.
>
> The troops, carrying rifles with sheathed bayonets, used gun butts to force some outside and carried others out bodily. Blood was spotted on the floor.

By now such stories were familiar, and their collective meaning seemed to be this: the peace movement was no longer peaceful. "It was not revolution," Todd Gitlin wrote euphorically to one of his friends after a demonstration in Oakland, "but it *was* insurrection. . . ." There had been a fundamental change, he said, as frustration mounted against U.S. policy, and symbolic protest gave way to resistance, designed to disrupt the machinery of war.

In *The Sixties: Years of Hope, Days of Rage,* Gitlin looked back on it all with candor—the adrenaline rush that became almost an end in itself. "We deployed for two hours," he wrote of one demonstration against the draft, "against more than two thousand cops, in a kind of scrimmage, or was it warfare?" And then:

> The cops charged. Some got surrounded, some broke ranks to bash or Mace. The crowd retreated to seize more intersections. When the cops pulled back

> to redeploy, the crowd took back the block, sealed it off from traffic, spray-painted the pavement and sidewalks. People hauled parked cars into the streets (the U.S. attorney's, for one), disconnected their distributors, let the air out of their tires, punctured them; and hauled anything else that could be moved: benches, newspaper racks, parking meters, garbage cans, trees in concrete pots. . . . Crowds pulled the wires out of a public bus here, a Coca-Cola truck there. One bus was commandeered, emptied, and pushed into a line of cops. I saw a group mount a truck, stand one foot away from a line of Oakland cops, clubs at the ready, and burn draft cards in their faces. . . .

As the skirmish continued, this curious mixture of political purpose and spontaneous vandalism, one demonstrator pleaded with his peers, "For God's sake, stop it." That moment recorded by the *San Francisco Chronicle* was actually part of a much larger debate that erupted now within the antiwar movement. Leaders like David Harris, who had worked to organize opposition to the draft (and who would soon marry Joan Baez), knew instinctively that a lack of discipline in these demonstrations would provide opponents exactly what they needed—an easy reason to dismiss the larger purpose of the protests. It was true, of course, that these random acts of violence were trivial beside those of the U.S. government and its massive killing machine in Vietnam—the bombs and napalm and the ranks of young soldiers who could never be sure who the enemy was so that for some, in fear of their lives, the enemy became any Vietnamese. This was the larger truth, the hideous reality of the war, but the ethical absurdity of a violent peace movement suddenly gave average Americans an easy and convenient way to discount it. Nor was it only the vandalism and petty violence. As Gitlin noted, it was also the drugs—"especially LSD, whose glory and terror is precisely to suspend a sense of the real." And now, he said, it "percolated through the New Left. . . ."

In addition, there was one final lapse into self-destruction from which it would take the American left at least a half century to recover. The young men and women on the radical edge had developed by now an infatuation with North Vietnam and the Viet Cong. In his retrospective, Gitlin described the mounting disillusionment of the New Left, the transformation from idealism and compassion for the suffering in Vietnam to an elemental hatred of American policy—and an urgent frustration that nothing seemed to *work.* The war went on, and the patriotism that drove the early opposition—a bitter disappointment in their own country—gave way to an alienation so profound that the radicals searched desperately for something to believe in. If they could no longer love America, certainly not as they had in the past, then perhaps they could love its enemy—the target of its bombs.

"Strange partners indeed," wrote Gitlin, "these marijuana-smoking Americans and ascetic Asian revolutionaries, united by B-52s!"

There were occasional meetings between these groups, and invariably the representatives of North Vietnam or the National Liberation Front were dignified, polished, well-informed and humble, much like Ho Chi Minh, the gentle and ruthless revolutionary whose name was now a New Left chant: "Ho, Ho, Ho Chi Minh!"

After one such conference in Bratislava, journalist Christopher Jencks speculated wisely in *The New Republic* about the affinity between the U.S. radicals and the Vietnamese:

> The common bond between the New Left and the NLF is not, then, a common desire or a common experience but a common enemy: the U.S. government, the system, the Establishment. The young radicals' admiration for the NLF stems from the fact that the NLF is resisting The Enemy successfully, whereas they are not."

Whatever the motive, the damage in credibility was profound. For many Americans, their growing disillusionment with the war was matched, paradoxically, by an equal disdain with the movement that opposed it.

Even in a time of national anguish, patriotism was a powerful force.

Writing today with the hindsight of history, we can only wonder what the New Left radicals might have thought if they had known another story that was simultaneously unfolding. On October 26, U.S. Navy Lieutenant Commander John McCain III, an Annapolis graduate and the son of an admiral, was on his twenty-third bombing mission over North Vietnam. He dove low from the skies above Hanoi, flying his Skyhawk bomber five hundred miles per hour at 4,500 feet when a missile "the size of a telephone pole" knocked the right wing off his plane. As the aircraft began to spin, McCain ejected, which was always a dangerous procedure, and this time the force that sent him hurtling out of the cockpit broke both his arms and his right leg. He landed semi-conscious in a lake on the western side of Hanoi and sank to the bottom. Desperately, he swam to the top, sank again, then remembered to inflate a flotation device contained in his fifty pounds of gear. He made it to the shore where a crowd quickly gathered and began to curse and kick and beat him.

After a time—he wasn't sure how long—he was placed on a stretcher and taken to the main prison in the city, where he was left on the floor of a cell.

> For the next three or four days, I lapsed from conscious to unconsciousness. During this time, I was taken out to interrogation—which we called a "quiz"—several times. That's when I was hit with all sorts of war-criminal charges. This started on the first day. I refused to give them anything except my name, rank, serial number and date of birth. They beat me around a little bit. I was in such bad shape that when they hit me it would knock me unconscious. They kept saying, "You will not receive any medical treatment until you talk."

Some years later, after his release, McCain told his story to the *U.S. News and World Report*, a nightmarish account, chilling in detail, of his five and a half years as a prisoner of war. In the beginning, he said, he lay untreated in his cell, still lapsing in and out of consciousness, and it occurred to him through a haze of pain that he was slowly dying of a broken leg. After four days, however, his captors discovered that his father was an admiral, and he was rushed to the prison hospital. But again he languished for days until the doctors finally performed surgery on his leg. By then he had lost more than fifty pounds, and when he was moved from the hospital to a prison compound, his cellmates did not expect him to live.

Slowly, however, McCain regained his strength, stubbornly resisting Vietnamese demands that he confess his "crimes." In retribution for his "bad attitude," he spent the next two years in solitary confinement. Torture followed, often in the form of beatings, delivered with savage, sadistic delight, interspersed with offers to set him free. McCain refused. He would not consider it, he said, when others had been in captivity even longer. And so the cycle of torture continued, until finally, on March 14, 1973, the North Vietnamese sent him home.

All of this, too, was part of the truth, part of the cruelty of Vietnam, and there were people like Allard Lowenstein who simply wanted it to stop.

Born in 1929 in Newark and raised in an upper middle class Jewish family, Lowenstein was an energetic, inveterate leader of liberal causes. He studied at Yale, served as an assistant dean at Stanford, and taught at North Carolina State, where he became involved with the civil rights movement. In 1964, he had traveled the country recruiting college students for Mississippi's Freedom Summer, and now he had turned his attention to the war. Lowenstein drew his political inspiration from the lions of the American left—people like Eleanor Roosevelt and the Socialist leader Norman Thomas, who was still active at eighty-three, still a pacifist.

In the spring of 1967, Lowenstein launched what came to be known as the Dump Johnson Movement, a grassroots effort to channel the fury and disillusionment against the war into the realm of electoral politics. Specifically, he hoped to build support for an antiwar candidate to oppose Lyndon Johnson in the 1968 Democratic primaries. Most politicians thought he was crazy. But a few liberal leaders, including the economist John Kenneth Galbraith, offered their support to Lowenstein's crusade.

Lowenstein knew who he wanted as his candidate. Robert Kennedy was first on the list, and the other possibilities—George McGovern, Eugene McCarthy—were not a close second. Lowenstein knew Kennedy and admired him, understood instinctively the depth of his concern about issues like poverty or racial injustice. And, increasingly, Vietnam. The two met and talked on occasion, and there was a growing affinity that went both ways. Kennedy, who disliked sycophants, respected Lowenstein's directness, his willingness to criticize a politician's caution, while Lowenstein saw in Kennedy not only a man who opposed the war, but one who actually could win the presidency.

There was hard data to support that view. By the fall of 1967, the Gallup Poll had Kennedy up 51–39 in a head-to-head race against Johnson, even though Kennedy had not said he would run. The Harris Poll had it 52–32. Kennedy, of course, was seriously tempted, for he thought the situation in the country was dire. The rioting the previous summer had been the worst so far, U.S. troop levels in Vietnam had climbed to 525,000, and 7,484 Americans were killed in the fighting in 1967. Through his friend, Robert McNamara, who was still the Secretary of Defense, Kennedy knew something of the growing desperation within the highest councils of government.

"How can I hit them in the nuts?" President Johnson demanded fiercely in one Cabinet meeting. "Tell me how I can hit them in the *nuts*!"

McNamara, for his part, was becoming disillusioned, telling a Senate committee in August that militarily it made no sense to keep bombing the North. Johnson was furious and soon sent McNamara packing, choosing him to head the World Bank.

"Two months before he left," Johnson later said of McNamara, "he felt he was a murderer and didn't know how to extricate himself. . . . After a while the pressure got so great that Bob couldn't sleep at night. I was afraid he might have a nervous breakdown."

As Robert Kennedy reflected on the mounting toll of the war, he found it measured in unexpected ways. He spoke at a Catholic women's college and asked the students to vote by show of hands about America's role in the war. Should there be an end to the bombing, he asked, or should it be intensified? He was astonished to discover that these young women wanted to see the bombing increased.

"Do you understand what that means?" Kennedy demanded. "It means you are voting to send people, Americans and Vietnamese, to die. . . . Don't you understand that what we are doing to the Vietnamese is not very different from what Hitler did to the Jews?"

As Arthur Schlesinger wrote later, all of this was hard for Kennedy to grasp, a callousness in the face of mass killing—*unnecessary* killing inflicted on people in a distant land by the most powerful nation on earth; and now that indifference had seeped its way to the student body of an all-girl's college. It was one more reminder, Kennedy thought, of America losing the best of itself—a time when the President of the United States had squandered his ability to lead. There were so many reasons for Kennedy to step up, to accept the challenge of Allard Lowenstein, and run against Johnson—not waiting until 1972, when everybody said he would win, when it would be, according to the political wisdom of the day, the American equivalent of a coronation. The country needed him now. Kennedy was sure of that. But should he do it? Was it reckless to take such a chance, to challenge a sitting president in his own party? What if in the ensuing division, he weakened the Democrats and gave the White House to the Republicans—to *Richard Nixon*! Would the party forgive him? Would America?

David Halberstam, now writing for *Harper's*, became an observer of Kennedy's dilemma while researching a profile on Lowenstein, this enigmatic champion of political rebellion, unknown to most Americans, who sought to channel disillusionment with the war away from insurrection in the streets. In his *Harper's* article, Halberstam recounted a critical meeting between Lowenstein and Kennedy.

> They were friends now. . . . But in September Lowenstein, who had been urging the race all year, went to Kennedy and said that the moment of truth had come; it was past the time of writing magazine articles on the ghetto and making speeches in the Senate on Vietnam; the army was ready, it would march, the President was ripe to be beaten, it could all be done. The enemies Kennedy would make by running were enemies he already had. The friends he would make were more important, for they would be dominant in American life for the decade to come. By the time of the convention, the party, which was obviously badly shattered, would be very glad he was making the race, but most of all he had to run this year, the issue went far beyond normal party loyalty; it was a question of moral imperative. . . .
>
> Kennedy heard Lowenstein out and admired his sincerity and idealism and intensity, and then finally, reluctantly, said No, he could not go, he had just talked with Mayor Daley and Chairman X and Governor Y, and they had all said the same thing, you can't do it, it's not your year, you must wait. . . . Lowenstein had looked at him for a long time and then answered, "The people who think that the honor and the future of this country are at stake don't give a shit what Mayor Daley and Chairman X and Governor Y think. We're gong to do it and we're going to win, and it's a shame that you're not with us because you could have been President."

Journalist Jack Newfield, who had come to know Kennedy well, wrote in *RFK: A Memoir* that even after this fateful meeting with Lowenstein (which Newfield said occurred in October) Kennedy still thought actively about making the race. The political pros all advised him against it, but he found support among some people he trusted—Arthur Schlesinger, speechwriter Adam Walinski, and his wife, Ethel Kennedy, who did not hesitate to speak her mind. Newfield, too, was one of those voices, and in December he wrote a blunt column in *The Village Voice*:

> If Kennedy does not run in 1968, the best side of his character will die. . . . Kennedy's best quality is to be himself, to be authentic in the existential

> sense. . . . And it is this quality Kennedy will lose if he doesn't make his stand now against Johnson. He will become a robot mouthing dishonest rhetoric like all the other politicians.

"My wife cut out your attack on me," Kennedy said, the next time he saw Newfield. "She shows it to everybody."

Disarmed by the irony and self-deprecation, both of which were characteristic of Kennedy, Newfield asked what the senator himself had thought of the column.

"I understand it," Kennedy replied. "It was discerning. On some days I even agree with it. . . . It's all so complicated. I just don't know what to do."

As Kennedy remained caught in his Hamlet moment, Allard Lowenstein moved on. In his search for a candidate, he turned next to Senator George McGovern, an antiwar Democrat from South Dakota, who had earned a doctorate in history from Northwestern University. McGovern was a decorated hero of World War II who knew and understood the nature of war, and because of that, believed it must be a last resort, which was not the case with Vietnam. McGovern also understood the cost of this war, measured in all of its multiple dimensions, and he seriously considered entering the race if Kennedy himself was unwilling to do it. But McGovern had political considerations of his own. He faced a tough reelection fight in 1968 for his Senate seat in South Dakota, and in the end he concluded the Senate must be his priority. That, after all, was a race he could win.

So Lowenstein went to Eugene McCarthy, the junior senator from Minnesota, a cerebral Democrat and political intellectual who did not believe he could unseat the President. But for ethical reasons McCarthy said he would try, and on November 30, 1967, he announced he would enter the Democratic primaries.

Allard Lowenstein now had a candidate.

And the killing continued in Vietnam.

51

A Philadelphia Story

In November, Lyndon Johnson tried to change the subject. He was perpetually preoccupied by the war, and yet in his mind, his greatness lay in a whole different realm—his ability to translate a vision for America into specific acts of Congress. Nobody else, certainly not his predecessor, John Kennedy, had this gift; Johnson was certain of that, and on November 21 he called attention to his talent once again. At a ceremony in the East Room of the White House, he signed the Clean Air Act of 1967, a bill pushed through the Congress by Senator Edmund Muskie of Maine, setting aside more than $400 million to combat the problem of air pollution.

"Either we stop poisoning our air," Johnson said, "or we become a nation in gas masks groping our way through dying cities and a wilderness of ghost towns."

At the same ceremony, Johnson spoke of other legislation he intended to pursue as part of his domestic agenda. High on the list were such consumer protection measures as a meat inspection bill, a truth in lending bill, and a flammable fabrics bill. "If you can't give us everything we've asked for, we will understand," Johnson said with a smile. "Just give us ninety percent this year and we'll come back next year and ask for the rest." This was Johnson's version of charm, but more than that it was the essence of his understanding of government—a benevolent force that acted in specific, concrete ways to make life better for every American. It was the philosophy behind his civil rights legislation, his antipoverty program, his pursuit of Medicare and Medicaid. Now the environment and consumer safety had risen to the top of the president's agenda, and it galled him more than a little to know that the nation no longer seemed grateful.

Sadly for Johnson, as Jack Newfield noted, much of the country no longer believed in its president as it had when his hand seemed so steady on the tiller after President Kennedy's murder. If he did not, even then, stir the same kind of love or enthusiasm as Kennedy, at least he seemed to know what he was doing. But then came the war, and the summers of violence in the inner cities for which Johnson seemed to have no answer. His most vocal critics were on the left, like the hundred thousand people who marched on the Pentagon, but as Newfield wrote, the disillusionment was broad and multi-layered.

Most of all, there was the war, and Johnson's corollary failures of character, chiefly his inclination to lie, which the media came to call a "credibility gap." He had run for reelection as a peace candidate, and almost immediately after he won he began a steady escalation, bitterly rejecting every voice of dissent. "Johnson's political and personal idiosyncrasies gradually drove most of his more worldly and intellectual aides like Bill Moyers, Eric Goldman, and [Richard] Goodwin out of the White House," wrote Newfield. "And by the end, the White House came to resemble the Alamo. . . ."

Johnson began to feel he was haunted by a ghost, the idealized aura of his martyred predecessor. And the Washington press corps that in general had liked John Kennedy was increasingly put off by the style and substance of his successor. As their collective portrait of LBJ darkened, and as disillusioned demonstrators against the war came to regard him with open hatred, fewer defenders rallied to his cause. The masses of white conservative Americans, who did not like the antiwar movement (even if they also did not like the war), were increasingly fearful of the violence in the ghettoes, and they indirectly blamed Johnson. He was the one, after all, who had championed the cause of black America, passing all of those civil rights laws, and now look where it had gotten the country. So many things were spinning out of control, and Lyndon Johnson had helped set them in motion.

Not that the president was the primary focus of this disillusionment. The rebellion against him was more oblique, consisting chiefly of a steady drift from his liberal priorities. One illustration of that point occurred in Philadelphia, a microcosm, some people said, of the mood and politics of the time. On Friday, November 17, some 3,500 black students left their schools to march on the city's board of education. Some chanted black power slogans, as a small group of student leaders and their adult advisers met with the superintendent of schools, Dr. Mark Shedd. The superintendent was joined by Richardson Dilworth and the Reverend Henry Nichols, the president and vice president of the school board. By most accounts the meeting started well. The students presented their demands, and while there was an edge of militancy in the air, not uncommon during those times, their presentation was articulate and well-rehearsed. Their list of twenty-five demands included black history courses taught by black teachers and the appointment of black principals in all black schools.

The mood of the crowd outside was festive, and Dilworth, who had earned a reputation as a liberal reformer when he had earlier served as Philadelphia's mayor, was confident that peace would prevail. So was Superintendent Shedd. They had asked the police to send only its civil disobedience squad, trained to deal amicably with demonstrators, to monitor the situation in the streets.

There was disagreement about what happened next. But as police radios crackled with worry about the growing size of the crowd, a student demonstrator began jumping from the top of one parked car to another. His arrest sparked confrontation as other demonstrators tried to free him. Two protesters, including a white Episcopal priest, were beaten, and the crowd surged forward, playing, some said, to television crews, who by now had arrived on the scene. Bill Mathis, a Philadelphia leader in the Congress of Racial Equality (CORE), asked police to give him a few minutes to calm the students. Mathis felt he might be making progress, until Police Commissioner Frank Rizzo arrived.

A PHILADELPHIA NATIVE AND the son of an Italian immigrant, Rizzo was, in the words of historian Timothy Lombardo, "perhaps the archetypal example of late twentieth-century urban, white ethnic, populist conservatism." He was, for sure, a hard-line law-and-order man who had little patience with unruly demonstrations. He was reported to have said of one group, "When I'm finished with them, I'll make Attila the Hun look like a fag." Rizzo had joined the Philadelphia police force in the 1940s and risen through the ranks. On multiple occasions, he was accused of brutality, most often in the form of beatings with a blackjack, though the charges in every case were dismissed. He came to the office of commissioner early in 1967. He referred to the police as "my men, my army," and sometimes led them personally, billy club in hand, when they confronted disorder in the streets.

That was the case on November 17. Rizzo was at a swearing-in ceremony for new police sergeants when he received word that the student demonstrators might be getting out of hand. Rizzo and the new sergeants rushed to the scene on police buses, and, according to journalists and other witnesses, Rizzo issued the order to charge: "Get their black asses!" As the police attacked, the commissioner himself was in the melee, swinging his nightstick. Some officers, wrote historian Matthew Countryman, "laced their violence with racial epithets," and at least one adult organizer of the protest urged the students to fight back. Pandemonium ensued. Many students ran from the scene and raced through Philadelphia's downtown, attacking pedestrians at random. Police said at least twenty-seven victims of those attacks were treated for their injuries, along with a dozen police officers. Fifty-seven people were arrested.

Some people called it a police riot. Others praised Rizzo and his men.

In his book, *Up South: Civil Rights and Black Power in Philadelphia*, Countryman set out to sort through the complicated event. Philadelphia had a long history of civil rights activism going back at least to the 1940s, and the touchstones for many black Philadelphians were not events that happened in the South—not Birmingham or Selma or even Freedom Summer in Mississippi. For the young demonstrators on November 17, the seminal moments of triumph and tragedy were more apt to be the assassination of Malcolm X, or the Black Panthers' show of force in the California assembly and on the streets of Oakland, or Muhammad Ali's refusal to serve in the military even at the cost of his heavyweight title. Since the previous summer, many of these students—and their street-corner counterparts in the inner city, the members of gangs—had been involved in black power demonstrations, a lot of them aimed at police brutality.

More broadly, they and the adults who advised them, leaders of a group called the Black People's Unity Movement (BPUM), were demanding black community control over the institutions that affected their lives. This most certainly included the schools, and their demands and concerns ranged from black history courses to the freedom to wear dashikis—Afrocentric symbols of pride.

School system liberals like Superintendent Shedd or School Board President Dilworth believed the power of reason could prevail. But Frank Rizzo had a different view. He came from an ethnic family that fought to find its place in America—and found it through a mixture of toughness and sweat. He hated those people in the life of his city who would subvert the good order that he believed in. His record as commissioner was a curious one. His police force had more black officers than most (20 percent in 1968), and he often assigned black and white policemen to patrol black neighborhoods together, hoping to reduce friction with the community. During his five-year tenure, Philadelphia's crime rate was the lowest of the nation's ten largest cities, despite an increase in the number of murders. But Rizzo talked about "faggots," led Saturday night roundups of homosexuals, and once declared that Black Panthers "should be strung up . . . I mean, within the law." He loved to mix it up with demonstrators, and more and more, as his profile grew, white Philadelphians liked his approach.

It was "a populism of style," said Timothy Lombardo, author of *Blue-Collar Conservatism: Frank Rizzo's Philadelphia and Populist Politics*. A part of Rizzo's appeal, wrote Lombardo, was indisputably racist, or at the very least racial—a fear of civil disorder in the form of riots, demonstrations, or any other form of black discontent, which conflated easily with the fear of black crime. But there was something else at work in these times, an instinctive understanding among blue collar whites that Frank Rizzo was one of them, and so were the officers who worked on his force. Lombardo wrote:

> . . . Police officers were a model of cultural traits and shared values associated with blue-collar identity. It was a cultural class identity indebted to a sense of blue-collar authenticity based on the shared values of hard work, sacrifice, toughness, and tradition.

For many working class whites in Philadelphia, it was easy to believe—with a certainty nurtured in their white neighborhoods—that Rizzo's hard-line tactics were not a matter of race, but a necessary quest for law and order. What decent person could disagree with that? But to African Americans who listened to his inflammatory words, or personally witnessed this bear of a man—Rizzo was six-foot-two, two hundred and forty pounds—swinging his nightstick with ardor and resolve, his mission was clearly racist at its core. In this yawning gap of perception, Philadelphia in 1967 was a microcosm of the country, and Rizzo was a national symbol, not only of tough-guy policing, but of the very heart of our division.

At least one politician in the coming year would try to find a way to heal the breach, while others saw value, for themselves and their party, in trying to drive the wedge even deeper.

52

The Movies

In this decade of rebellion, a time when people searched for meaning, many did not find it, and some of those were the victims of prosperity rather than injustice. Hollywood occasionally addressed this theme, and never more memorably than in December with the Mike Nichols film, *The Graduate*. The plot and the dialogue of the film closely followed Charles Webb's 1963 novel with the same title; Webb was, in fact, a recent graduate of Williams College, as was the title character. Webb later worried that the soaring acclaim of the film overshadowed his seriousness as a writer. And indeed his remarkable accomplishment at the age of twenty-four was often overlooked, as Nichols's brilliant adaptation touched a powerful chord in the country.

The story itself was a big piece of it. Benjamin Braddock, a young Californian, returns to his upper-middle-class home after graduating from college, caught in a kind of purposeless malaise, having no plan for what to do next. He spends his days by the pool before being tempted into an affair with the wife of his father's business partner—then falls in love with the same woman's daughter. The tangled web and the unlikely ending—Ben and Elaine, the girl he loves, in desperate flight from her interrupted wedding to another man—require some suspension of disbelief. But most moviegoers didn't mind. Actress Anne Bancroft was so compelling in the role of Mrs. Robinson, Ben's older temptress, and her accomplishments on the screen were more than matched by the introduction of Dustin Hoffman as Ben.

Before *The Graduate,* Hoffman was a struggling New York actor who had won an Obie Award for his Off Broadway role in *The Journey of the Fifth Horse*. When Mike Nichols called and asked him to audition for *The Graduate,* Hoffman read the book and told him, "I'm not right for this part, sir. . . . This is Robert Redford." Redford, in fact, agreed. He and Nichols were friends and had discussed it. Redford, blond, handsome, and already a star, wanted the role. But as critic Sam Kashner later recounted in *Vanity Fair*, Nichols told Redford it just wouldn't work.

"You can never play a loser," he said.

"What do you mean?" said Redford, pushing his case. "Of course I can play a loser."

But the part went to Hoffman, and in the end the casting of the movie was a key to its successful blending of comedy, poignancy and social commentary. Hoffman's Ben was unforgettable, a character who was bumbling, stiff and awkward, but deeply sympathetic and true to himself. Anne Bancroft evoked in Mrs. Robinson not only a manipulative and predatory cynicism, but hints of desperation and sadness. Kashner wrote:

> Mrs. Robinson now seems the most complex and compelling character in the film, in part due to Anne Bancroft's stunning performance. That she's an alcoholic, that she's trapped in a sexless marriage, that she's predatory, cool, and ironic—those are the traits that make her dangerous. That she was once an art major, a fact she reluctantly reveals to Benjamin in his one attempt at pillow talk, makes her vulnerable. We suddenly understand her—her bitterness, her deep pool of sadness.

And Dustin Hoffman added, "I think Anne and Mike Nichols made a very critical decision, which was not to judge the character."

Nichols won an Oscar for Best Director for his skill at putting the pieces together, and Hoffman and Bancroft both won Golden Globe Awards for their acting. Even Katharine Ross, beautiful and radiant at the age of twenty-four, earned her share of critical acclaim for her portrayal of Elaine, a student at Berkeley, innocent and serious, a counterpart of warmth to the cold and jaded character of her mother. Most critics were effusive in their praise of the film, though one, oddly, waxed dismissive at one of the movie's most memorable qualities: its use of music.

Just before the filming began, Nichols's brother had sent him the album, *Parsley, Sage, Rosemary and Thyme* by Simon & Garfunkel. Nichols was already a fan, an admirer of poetic songs of alienation like "Sounds of Silence" and "Homeward Bound"—and of the sweet and intricate blending of voices that immediately became the duo's trademark. Paul Simon and Art Garfunkel had been singing together since they were kids growing up in Queens, listening to the Everly Brothers on the radio, inspired by the rockabilly harmonies of these brothers from Kentucky. By 1967, they were on a commercial and creative roll, and by some accounts, responded lukewarmly to Nichols's decision to feature their music in his film. But Simon did write a song for the movie that became, like others previously recorded, a kind of interior monologue for the characters. "Mrs. Robinson," later a hit on its own, included a wry and ironic couplet, which was, like the move itself, at once comedic and poignant:

Here's to you, Mrs. Robinson
Jesus loves you more than you will know

In the creativity of Paul Simon and the unexpected quirks of his lyrics, the movie somehow found its final evocation of life in the suburbs—a sterility that begged for some kind of rebellion. In any case, *The Graduate* took its place among the classic films of the decade.

It was, all in all, a good year for the movies. From the film adaptation of *In Cold Blood*, to Paul Newman's prison classic, *Cool Hand Luke*, to the Redford-Jane Fonda comedy, *Barefoot in the Park*, many of us found plenty to distract us when the news turned dark. For me, the year was defined by ambitious films of social commentary. In December, ten days before the release of *The Graduate* and six months after the Supreme Court decision in *Loving v. Virginia*, Columbia Pictures released the Stanley Kramer film, *Guess Who's Coming to Dinner.* This story of interracial marriage, featuring Sidney Poitier, was also the final film pairing of Katharine Hepburn and Spencer Tracy, one of Hollywood's great couples. Tracy died shortly after shooting his final scene, a monologue that often evoked open sobs in theaters, and Hepburn, in her grief, said she never watched the film, despite her Academy Award for Best Actress. Critic Roger Ebert wrote:

> Yes, there are serious faults in Stanley Kramer's *Guess Who's Coming to Dinner*, but they are overcome by the virtues of this delightfully old-fashioned film. It would be easy to tear the plot to shreds and catch Kramer in the act of copping out. But why? On its own terms, this film is a joy . . .

For Poitier, remarkably, it was one of three important films he starred in that year, each a commentary on the issue of race. In *To Sir, with Love*, he played a black teacher in an all-white British school, and in the most heralded of the three films, *In the Heat of the Night*, he teamed with Rod Steiger in a racial drama set in Mississippi. The movie won an Academy Award for Best Picture, and Steiger's iconic performance won for Best Actor. He played the role of Police Chief Bill Gillespie in the sleepy Mississippi town of Sparta, where there has just been a murder. In his toughness and swagger, Steiger's character could have been modeled after Birmingham's Bull Connor or Selma's Jim Clark (or for that matter, some thought, Philadelphia's Frank Rizzo with a Southern accent). Gillespie, however, possessed a quality of heart that seemed missing in his real-life counterparts, and the drama of *In the Heat of the Night* is driven as much by the chief's relationship to Virgil Tibbs, a black detective played by Poitier, as it is by attempts to solve the murder.

The movie in the end was a story of redemption that came at a time when the country needed to believe in such a thing. The ironic setting of Mississippi—in the minds of many, an unlikely source for such a message—only added to its force. The film's other theme, important to Poitier in a time of racial tension, was dignity and self-respect, culminating in a scene in which Eric Endicott, a rich white man, slaps Virgil Tibbs for suggesting Endicott might have motive for the murder. Tibbs slaps him back. It was said that after the film was released, Poitier and Steiger sometimes slipped into theaters together just to watch the audience reaction—the murmurs of satisfaction or shock at the moment of the slap, depending on the race of the viewer. Such was the visceral power of the film.

Fifty years later, I still remember these movies very well—the triumphs of Steiger, Hoffman, Poitier, of Anne Bancroft and Simon & Garfunkel. They were sources of reflection, but also of welcome escape. The hours spent in the theater were a respite from all that we knew was waiting outside.

53

Dump Johnson

With the coming of the new year, Eugene McCarthy was in New Hampshire campaigning for president against Lyndon Johnson. The national media was not paying much attention. With the possible exception of Allard Lowenstein and one or two others in the Dump Johnson Movement, almost nobody thought McCarthy had a chance. How could he? He was a little-known senator from Minnesota, detached and cool in his political style, running against an incumbent president in his own party. In early 1968, it seemed mostly a symbolic gesture.

On January 30, however, the Viet Cong confounded reassurances from official Washington that the war on the ground was under control. With strategic support from North Vietnamese regulars, the National Liberation Front launched coordinated attacks on five of South Vietnam's six largest cities, including the capital, Saigon, where fighting went on for three weeks in the streets outside the heavily fortified U.S. Embassy. The city of Hue quickly fell to the NLF, whose forces also attacked 36 of South Vietnam's 44 provincial capitals and more than fifty other towns.

For a specific historical reason, the NLF chose Tet, the Vietnamese new year, as the occasion to launch the surprise assault. In 1789, in the season of Tet, Nguyen Hue became a national hero when he led a surprise attack against an invading Chinese army, driving the foreigners back across the border. According to Vietnamese lore, as they marched toward battle, Hue's men were singing: "The heroic southern country is its own master."

Just a month before the 1968 Tet Offensive, U.S. Ambassador to Vietnam Ellsworth Bunker had invited his New Year's Eve party guests to celebrate "the light at the end of the tunnel." Both in Washington and Saigon, that holiday hope was shared by those who accepted the assurances of Bunker and the generals that "the military war in Vietnam is nearly won."

Suddenly, the lie was exposed. In the mountains just south of the demilitarized zone marking the boundary with North Vietnam, some twenty thousand NVA regulars crossed the border from the North and laid siege to the U.S. garrison at Khe Sanh. Its six thousand American troops were well-fortified but desperately outmanned. General Westmoreland sent reinforcements, and before the North Vietnamese withdrew in early March, U.S. troop strength reached fifty thousand. American warplanes, in the words of one historian, "denuded the mountainside with more than 60,000 tons of napalm." It was, despite the eventual outcome, a massive distraction from Viet Cong attacks throughout the rest of South Vietnam.

On the streets of Saigon, where urban warfare raged through much of February, especially near the embassy and in the city's Chinese neighborhood, it took nearly eleven thousand U.S. and South Vietnamese troops to dislodge a few thousand NLF guerillas. In Hue, the NLF seized control and set up its own coalition government. In its attempt to retake the former capital, a riverfront city in central Vietnam filled with nineteenth-century shrines, the United States bombed much of it to rubble. Nearly ten thousand of the city's seventeen thousand houses were completely destroyed and another three thousand seriously damaged. Thousands of civilians died in what one journalist called "the most hysterical use of American firepower ever seen." For those who saw it with their own eyes, it was a scene that lent itself to hyperbole.

But there was another side to the story. When the Viet Cong forces finally retreated after a month of ferocious fighting, victorious Americans found mass graves of civilians, many with their hands tied behind their backs. Varying estimates of the number of executions ranged from several hundred to five thousand, but regardless of the total it was clear that the NLF had perpetrated a massive war crime. For a while, U.S. and South Vietnamese officials sought to use the massacre as propaganda, citing the wanton brutality of the enemy. In parts of South Vietnam, it worked. For civilians simply trying to survive the war, it was clear there might be a deadly price if you found yourself on the losing side.

In the United States the story was generally obscured by the multiple shockwaves of Tet. For one thing, the Saigon government sent its own teams of assassins into Hue, searching for NLF sympathizers. For another, the dominant image coming out of the city was the devastation wreaked by American bombs. There was also a moment in Saigon that was captured by NBC news cameramen and by a still photographer for the Associated Press. On February 1, General Nguyen Ngoc Loan, the leader of the South Vietnamese National Police, raised his personal .38-caliber pistol to the head of Nguyen Van Lem, a captured Viet Cong suspect. The South Vietnamese said later that Lem was part of an assassination team. Whatever the case, AP photographer Eddie Adams was peering through his lens precisely at the moment when Loan pulled the trigger. In an image published immediately in newspapers worldwide, Adams captured precisely the moment of death—the casual indifference on the face of General Loan, the anguish frozen on the face of Lem, a tiny man, bound and barefoot, as the bullet tore a hole in his head.

For many Americans, it was as if the entire brutality of the war was captured in a single photograph. The shock of the image was soon compounded by a flurry of Orwellian pronouncements emanating from Vietnam. There was the U.S. general, for example, who announced when his men successfully drove the NLF from the provincial capital of Ben Tre: "We had to destroy the town in order to save it." A few weeks later, on February 27, CBS correspondent Walter Cronkite, the most trusted name in television news—he was, after all, the steady, resonant-voiced man who had wiped away tears when he reported the death of President Kennedy—delivered a rare editorial opinion from South Vietnam:

> We are mired in a stalemate. . . . To say that we are closer to victory today is to believe, in the face of the evidence, the optimists who have been wrong in the past.

As if to confirm that assessment, General Westmoreland asked the president for another 206,000 troops. Campaigning in New Hampshire, and buttressed by this flow of news, Senator Eugene McCarthy was honing his stump speech: "The Democratic Party in 1964 promised 'no wider war.' Yet the war is getting wider every month. Only a few months ago we were told that 65 percent of the population was secure. Now we know that even the American embassy is not secure."

Some U.S. military officials were dismayed by this reaction to Tet. Although the fighting lasted for more than a month, and though similar attacks followed in May and beyond, by the measure of body counts and strategic territory retaken, the whole operation had been a defeat for the enemy. But all of a sudden in the United States, nobody measured the news that way. According to a post-Tet Gallup Poll, only 33 percent of Americans thought their side was winning, and nearly half thought the country should never have gone to war in the first place.

On March 12, voters went to the polls in New Hampshire's Democratic primary. Lyndon Johnson, who had not campaigned in the state—had not even officially declared as a candidate, though everyone assumed he would run for reelection—won with 49 percent. But 42 percent cast their ballots for Eugene McCarthy, exceeding expectations, always a critical consideration in primary season, and his achievement altered the politics of war.

"Mr. McCarthy's strong showing," wrote Tom Wicker in the *New York Times*, "demonstrated that there is strong potential in the antiwar movement, and in opposition to President Johnson."

Even Johnson's closest advisers were shaken. There had been warning signs, chiefly the ever-increasing need for more troops. But the official optimism had been so strong, so consistent, and despite all the noise of the antiwar movement, most Americans had believed their president when he said the war was being won. This was America, after all, and America *always* won. Johnson fiercely, passionately, with all his heart, did not want to be the first president saddled with a loss. But now everything was turned on its head, and by the middle of March Johnson listened glumly to his inner circle, as one by one they expressed their doubts. They had just been briefed by a Pentagon spokesman who estimated that 45,000 enemy troops were killed in the Tet offensive, and at least three times that many had been wounded.

The problem was that before the offensive the Pentagon had estimated total NLF troop strength at 175,000. UN Ambassador Arthur Goldberg quickly did the math. "Well, if that's true," he observed sardonically, "then they should have no effective forces left in the field."

The meaning of the moment was clear. The president's top political and diplomatic advisers no longer believed the military men. Whatever the body counts of Tet, it was simply not clear that the war was being won or even that it could be, given the political climate. Even Dean Acheson, the former secretary of state and a dependable hard-liner, now told Johnson that the moment had come: "We must," he said, "begin to disengage."

MEANWHILE, ROBERT KENNEDY WATCHED miserably with a feeling that history was passing him by. His brother and fellow senator Edward Kennedy had made his own trip to Vietnam not long before the Tet offensive and was shocked. As Jack Newfield reported, the younger Kennedy told his brother "that American policy there was more tragic and vicious than even the harshest Senate critic imagined."

But RFK remained caught in what one friend called "morose introspection." He saw college students stumping for McCarthy in the snows of New Hampshire, energized by the hope that the war might actually come to an end; McCarthy, not Kennedy, was the source of that hope. On his own frequent visits to campuses—two or three a week—Kennedy sometimes encountered heckling signs: "HAWK, DOVE OR CHICKEN?" Nevertheless, he kept coming back, subjecting himself to the hecklers as if he wanted them to persuade him, or, perhaps more accurately in the view of people close to him, he was simply incapable of ducking his critics. It was as if they were somehow part of an existential quest that went to the core of who he was. Some of those critics—particularly the young and the idealistic—might just be speaking the truth.

During this time, he continued to visit people on the margins, factory workers who feared for their jobs, men and women who lived in the ghetto, and on one occasion a hospital for mentally and emotionally handicapped children. When he walked through the door of one crowded ward, an eight-year-old called out happily, "Look, there's President Kennedy." Newfield reported how Kennedy winced, then stooped and cradled the child in his arms, "caressing his neck and hands."

During his final days of indecision, Kennedy carried a letter in his pocket, reading it often, showing it to friends. It was written by Pete Hamill, a journalist, author, and tough Irish-Catholic who was a longtime admirer of the Kennedys. Hamill made the case for running, not only because of the war, but because of desperation in the ghettoes, which had spilled so often into self-destructive violence. Hamill spoke of the hope that John Kennedy had inspired among African Americans, and how Robert Kennedy was now the heir to that hope—and how the time might be running out.

> I don't think we can afford five summers of blood. I do know this: if a fifteen-year-old kid is given a choice between Rap Brown and RFK, he might choose the way of sanity. It's only a possibility, but at least there is that chance. Give that same kid a choice between Rap Brown and LBJ, and he'll probably reach for his revolver.

Finally, after the weeks of self-reproach, and after Tet and the strength of McCarthy's New Hampshire showing, Kennedy decided that he would run. He knew the timing of his decision preceded by all of his Hamlet hesitations would subject him to the charge of opportunism. But he suddenly acted like a man set free. In his official announcement on March 16, he praised McCarthy for his "valiant campaign," and expressed the hope that the two of them could work "in harmony" against the war in Vietnam. But the truth was that Kennedy and McCarthy didn't like each other. Kennedy still harbored deep resentments about McCarthy's reluctance to support his brother in 1960, and he doubted McCarthy's commitment to minorities or the poor. For his part, McCarthy regarded Kennedy as a ruthless opportunist who was, to put it bluntly, not McCarthy's intellectual equal.

Thus, a new curiously three-sided political battle was joined, with McCarthy and Kennedy running against each other but also against Johnson and the war. For Allard Lowenstein and the Dump Johnson forces, this was everything they could have hoped for—not one, but two candidates taking on the president and his long, bloody conflict. They knew the Tet offensive had been crucial. Hans Morganthau, a German-born political theorist and adviser to Presidents Kennedy and Johnson, maintained that Tet was one of the seminal events of the twentieth century. It undercut political support for Johnson's war and, even among policy makers, belief in the efficacy of escalation. The National Liberation Front and their allies in North Vietnam had achieved their political objective, despite an enormous military price.

For American fighting men on the ground, nothing really changed. The war went on, and some of the battles in February and March were as furious as any these soldiers could remember. On at least two occasions, a company from the 11th Brigade of the 20th Infantry Regiment had sustained heavy casualties in a coastal area they called Pinkville. Named for its color on a military map, the area was a Viet Cong stronghold, a cluster of villages on the northeast coast that included several small hamlets known collectively as My Lai. On March 16, more troops, including a platoon led by Lieutenant William Calley, set off on a mission of search and destroy in what they were told was a free fire zone. Leaflets apparently had been dropped urging civilians to evacuate, and anybody who was left was assumed to be Viet Cong. Calley's men, so it was said, were jumpy and angry as their helicopters landed outside of My Lai.

But on this day, March 16, 1968, the hamlet contained no Viet Cong. When the soldiers arrived, they found women, children, and a few old men, cooking their breakfasts of rice, preparing for a day at the market. Calley and his men began shooting anyway. Most Americans knew nothing of this until November 1969 when investigative journalist Seymour Hersh broke the story in the *St. Louis Post-Dispatch.* Later, in *The New Yorker*, Hersh offered a more comprehensive account:

> During the next few hours, the civilians were murdered. Many were rounded up in small groups and shot, others were flung into a drainage ditch at one edge of the hamlet and shot, and many more were shot at random in or near their homes. Some of the younger women and girls were raped and then murdered. After the shootings, the G.I.s systematically burned each home, destroyed the livestock and food, and fouled the area's drinking supplies.

At the time, the U.S. operation on March 16 was reported as a military victory, with 128 Viet Cong dead. Later, as many of us would see, it was a moment that challenged the nation's bedrock understanding of itself, the notion nurtured since World War II that America was both powerful *and* good. But even in March 1968, when almost no one knew that My Lai had happened, the seeds of doubt were already planted. In addition to the casualties among our soldiers, and the destruction of villages in Vietnam, the war had taken its toll at home, especially among those who spoke out against it.

For many of us, the "Ask Not" innocence of the early sixties—the soaring hope inspired by President Kennedy's inaugural—was lost even if a dogged idealism endured. Some of the young people who had demonstrated bitterly against the war, sometimes skirmishing with the police, were now working door-to-door for Senator McCarthy. Others of us were drawn to Robert Kennedy, or perhaps to Dr. Martin Luther King, who was addressing with a new and radical enthusiasm the interwoven issues of poverty and peace.

There was an inspiration that went with these crusades. These were the men, we thought at the time, who were keeping the best of America alive.

54

The Last Campaigns

In early March, just before he officially announced for president, Robert Kennedy made a trip to California. More than three weeks earlier, his friend Cesar Chavez had embarked on a fast in support of nonviolence. He had not eaten in twenty-five days. Chavez's decision, which had now begun to imperil his health, came at a time when many of his followers were growing frustrated. The farmworkers' strike in the fields of California had entered its third winter without much to show for it. Some grape growers were pulling up their vines rather than sign a contract with Chavez's union. In retaliation, acts of vandalism against the growers—sabotage, for example, against the refrigerated railroad cars that carried grapes to market—were becoming more common. Chavez decided to do something dramatic to stop it—and to call attention to his cause.

He took a room in a converted gas station at a place called Forty Acres, a barren patch of ground that soon became a kind of holy shrine. Every evening of the fast, Father Mark Day, a priest who firmly supported the union, said mass in a room that resembled both a union headquarters and a church. A union banner hung near a picture of the *Virgen de Guadalupe*, and somebody had placed a portrait of President Kennedy above a card table that served as an altar. As Chavez biographer Miriam Pawel recorded, the crowds increased exponentially—a hundred or so for the first mass, then two hundred, and eventually six hundred or more, invoking holy blessings upon the cause. Some were worried about Chavez, a few even angry that he would take such a risk, for who would be their leader if he died? But still they came.

From a distance in Washington, Kennedy was one of those who worried. He knew that when Chavez made up his mind, he was not apt to change it. Thus he was deeply grateful and relieved when word finally came that the great union leader—this small, disheveled giant of a man, for that was how

Kennedy thought of Chavez—had decided to break his fast. Chavez asked Kennedy to be there when he did it, and Kennedy did not hesitate. On March 10, he flew to California with John Seigenthaler, his longtime friend from the Justice Department who had been attacked during the Freedom Rides in Montgomery, and Peter Edelman, one of his most trusted advisers. He thought of announcing his candidacy for president right there in a dramatic moment with Chavez, but decided against it. The occasion, after all, was a mass, not a political rally, and Kennedy wanted to talk to McCarthy about his plans. It seemed the decent thing to do. But some of the people closest to him knew that he had already made up his mind, even before the primary vote in New Hampshire.

On March 10, Kennedy spoke publicly about none of these things. The day belonged to Chavez and four thousand of his followers who gathered for an emotional ceremony at the Delano Community Center. Too weak to walk on his own, Chavez leaned on the shoulders of two of his friends as he made his way to the altar and broke his fast with communion bread. He turned and offered the loaf to Kennedy, who accepted his own ceremonial taste, then spoke in tribute to Chavez and his movement:

> I am here today out of respect for one of the heroic figures of our time—Cesar Chavez. I congratulate all of you who are locked with Cesar in the struggle for justice for the farm worker, and in struggle for justice for Spanish-speaking Americans. . . . There are those of you who question the principle of everything you have done so far—the principle of nonviolence. Let me say to you that violence is no answer. . . .

As the ceremony ended and Kennedy left the building and started toward his car, the crowd surged forward, calling his name, reaching out to shake his hand or just touch him. It took thirty minutes for him to make it less than a hundred yards to the car. John Seigenthaler, observing, was not ordinarily a sentimental man. But he remembered thinking that when Robert Kennedy did announce for president, he would be no ordinary candidate.

After the announcement came on March 16, Kennedy began his campaign in Kansas. He chose this Republican state in the center of the country precisely because it seemed unlikely. In 1968, only fourteen states held Democratic primaries, and the path to the presidential nomination inevitably involved impressing the most powerful men in the party. Kennedy entered primaries that he knew would accomplish that goal if he won—Indiana, with its white ethnic voters who had turned out for Wallace in 1964; Oregon, where the polls showed McCarthy running strong; and California, where Ronald Reagan, the emerging champion of conservatism, was in his second year as governor. He also scheduled speeches in the South—in Tennessee and Alabama (where on a trip in 1963 to meet with Governor Wallace, his path had been blocked by a state trooper who jabbed him—the Attorney General of the United States—in the stomach with a nightstick).

Kennedy was determined in 1968 to demonstrate his appeal even in these most difficult places, but regardless of that, to deliver an urgent message to the country. There was so much anger and division, yet he believed in the sense of possibility that his brother had tapped in 1960. The message would have to be different now, more sober perhaps, more realistic, some people might say, and Kennedy wondered how it would go. According to the people closest to him, he was nervous as he set off for Kansas.

His plane touched down in Kansas City around 8:30 p.m. on March 17. It was a warm Sunday night and twenty-five hundred people were waiting for him at the airport. As the farmworkers had in California, they surged in his direction, pulling at his clothes, reaching to shake his hand, pleading for a speech. There were no microphones, for there had been no preparations for an airport event, but Kennedy teased and joked with the crowd, telling them he came from "a great farm state myself—Massachusetts." He told them he would need their help, then ended his brief remarks with a smile that struck some as shy.

"That was my very first campaign speech," he said. "Now let's all clap."

The following morning, he spoke to a crowd of fourteen thousand at the field house at Kansas State University, where the student body was said to be conservative. He decided to talk about the war, and began by admitting, as he had before, that he bore part of the responsibility. He was, after all, a party to his brother's decisions which had helped set the nation on its current course. "But past error," he said, "is no excuse for its own perpetuation." He spoke of the terrible costs of war, and said the time had come for hard questions.

> Can we ordain to ourselves the awful majesty of God—to decide which cities and villages are to be destroyed, who will live and who will die, and who will join refugees wandering in a desert of our own creation?
>
> . . . Let us think of the young men we have sent there: not just the killed, but those who have to kill; not just the maimed, but also those who must look upon the results of what they do . . . It must be ended, and it can be ended in a peace for brave men who have fought each other with a terrible fury, each believing that he alone was in the right. We have prayed to different gods, and the prayers of neither have been answered fully.
>
> Now . . . is the time to stop.

That afternoon he went to the University of Kansas, where he was greeted by twenty thousand. He spoke again of the war in Vietnam, but for most of his speech he talked about values, and how the most powerful economy on earth does not alone make a nation great.

> Our gross national product, now, is over eight hundred billion dollars a year, but that GNP—if we should judge America by that—counts air pollution and cigarette advertising, and ambulances to clear our highways of carnage. It counts special locks for our doors and the jails for those who break them. It counts the destruction of our redwoods and the loss of our natural wonder in chaotic sprawl. It counts napalm and the cost of a nuclear warhead, and armored cars for police who fight riots in our streets. It counts Whitman's rifle and Speck's knife and our television programs which glorify violence in order to sell toys to our children.
>
> Yet the gross national product does not allow for the health of our children, the quality of their education, or the joy of their play. It does not include the beauty of our poetry or the strength of our marriages; the intelligence of our public debate or the integrity of our public officials. It measures neither our wit nor our courage; neither our wisdom nor our learning; neither our compassion nor our devotion to our country; it measures everything, in short, except that which makes life worthwhile.

Three days later he came to Vanderbilt, where I was a student and a part of the committee that brought him to campus. I don't think we idealized Kennedy. We had already encountered the cynicism of his advance team as they tried to manipulate the optics of his visit. We had sold tickets to Kennedy's talk—for one dollar each—and as a result we knew precisely how many people would be in the crowd. In a gymnasium that held eleven thousand, every seat would be full. Kennedy's team, however, wanted us to open only half the arena so that the television cameras could record the thousands of people waiting outside, clamoring to get in, or merely to catch a glimpse of the candidate. We refused. We were young and brash, and we took offense at such manipulation. When the advance man threatened to move the speech to a different venue, I remember telling him that might work as long as no reporter asked why he had done it. But if the question arose, we would tell the truth. Kennedy himself knew nothing of this, and on the night of March 21 an overflow crowd on the Vanderbilt campus waited impatiently for his arrival. He was two hours late, having been delayed in Alabama where another huge audience turned out to hear him at the same university where George Wallace had stood in the schoolhouse door five years earlier.

At Vanderbilt, he talked about the necessity of dissent:

> There are millions of Americans living in hidden places, whose faces and names we will never know. But I have seen children starving in Mississippi, idling their lives away in the ghetto, living without hope . . . on Indian reservations. I have seen proud men in the hills of Appalachia, who wish only to work in dignity—but the mines are closed and the jobs are gone and no one, neither industry or labor or government, has cared enough to help . . . So I dissent, and I know you do too.

Reporters who covered Kennedy during those weeks searched for superlatives to describe the frenzied reaction of the crowds. Even now, nearly fifty years later, I struggle to describe it. I had never seen anything like it, nor have I since. Even at the Nashville airport, before his talk, thousands were waiting for him, and they surged forward with such force that he was trapped. He climbed to an unsteady perch on an escalator railing and delivered a brief, impromptu speech about the problems of the country and the values that still held Americans together. As soon he finished, the screaming press of bodies became more urgent, more intense, and because I was a part of his official welcome, I was walking beside him as he made his way, one deliberate step at a time, through the throng. Even now as I attempt to understand it, I know it had something to do with his brother, as if he were a reincarnation of hope. But John F. Kennedy's gaiety and elan were nowhere present in this slouched and slender man. For one thing, Robert Kennedy was shy. I saw this clearly after he and I took our seats in the car and waited for the others in his party to join us. I was struck by the odd and unsettling notion that I, as a college senior, had to say something to put the presidential candidate at ease.

"Feels a little safer in here," I said.

"Yes, it does," he replied, and we both laughed.

The irony, of course, given the assassin's bullet that awaited less than three months later, is difficult to bear, and I am certain Kennedy knew even then that dangers might lurk in the gleeful hysteria. On his return trip to the airport, he shared a car with John Jay Hooker, his friend from the Justice Department, and as the two talked in the back seat, Kennedy's twelve-year-old son, David, was sitting in Hooker's lap. Hooker, who had lived for nine months with the Kennedys when he first came to Washington, was especially fond of David, a little boy of sensitivity and sweetness, and did not want to give voice to the dread that was taking shape in Hooker's mind. But when David was looking in a different direction, Hooker formed his thumb and forefinger into the shape of a pistol and silently simulated the recoil.

"I can't think about it," said Robert Kennedy. "What happens, happens."

All of us know, in retrospect, that Kennedy was not the only great player on the stage of history moving in this moment toward an unexpected ending. Lyndon Johnson was also contemplating a destiny he had not thought possible. As historian Nick Kotz recounted in *Judgment Days*, Johnson in March 1968 was reeling from the Tet offensive and from General Westmoreland's astonishing request for an additional 206,000 troops. It was a number, the general admitted, that could only maintain the status quo. He was sure the North Vietnamese could match it. Abruptly, it was now apparent to the president—and to advisers like Secretary of Defense Clark Clifford—that it was "madness" to continue a policy of escalation. The war, quite simply, would not be won. The government of South Vietnam could not defend itself, and the burden would fall upon the United States, and more and more young Americans would die. Already, the president would sometimes awaken in the middle of the night and wander down to the Situation Room to check on the casualty totals for the day. There were times when the numbers made him weep. He could see as clearly as any of his critics what the war was doing to the country's resources, emotional as well as financial.

That same month the Kerner Commission, a presidential task force that Johnson had appointed after the 1967 riots, delivered its report, blaming the racism of white America. The Commission urged massive spending—a domestic Marshall Plan—to address the problems of the inner cities. Johnson understood immediately that Congress would never agree to such a measure. The federal budget was stretched to the breaking point by the war.

Johnson continued to do what he could. He introduced new civil rights legislation aimed in part at protecting civil rights workers in the South. But he also pushed, as he had in the past, for an open housing law, despite the unpopularity of such a measure among whites. "I don't give a damn about the election," he told his advisers. "I will be happy to just keep on doing what's right . . ."

It turned out that Johnson meant what he said. In late March, he began working on a speech to the country on the subject of peace in Vietnam. He set a date of March 31, and people close to him remember his restlessness in those days. In a conversation with historian Merle Miller, Johnson's wife Lady Bird recalled how they rose early that morning to greet their daughter Lynda at the White House. She had said goodbye to her husband Chuck Robb, who was on his way to Vietnam, and had flown from California to Washington to be with her parents. Lady Bird said:

> She looked like a ghost, pale, tall and drooping. We both hugged her and then we all went upstairs. I took her into her room, helped her get her clothes off, and put her to bed. . . . When I went back to Lyndon's room, his face was sagging and there was such pain in his eyes as I had not seen since his mother died. But he didn't have time for grief. Today was a crescendo of a day. At nine in the evening, Lyndon was to make his talk to the nation about the war. The speech was not yet firm. There were still revisions to be made and people to see.

The president had decided already that he would announce a halt in the bombing of North Vietnam, except for an area just north of the Demilitarized Zone, in hopes of starting serious peace talks. But he was thinking hard about adding a couple of paragraphs, announcing that he would not seek reelection.

All day he pondered that course of action, talking to a few close friends, and early in the evening he showed the final draft to Clark Clifford.

Clifford was stunned. "You've made up your mind?"

"I've made up my mind," said Johnson. "I'm actually going to do it."

Like most Americans, I was watching that night, curious to see if the speech would offer anything new. I was deeply cynical about Lyndon Johnson, and as I awaited his address with a group of my friends, some of the same students who had invited Robert Kennedy to Vanderbilt, most of us wondered what fresh lies this president would tell. As far as we were concerned, that had been his pattern with regard to Vietnam. Nevertheless, we found ourselves listening intently as he spoke to us, gravely, calmly, from the flickering black and white of the television screen.

"Tonight," he said, in the Texas twang we had come to dislike, "I have ordered our aircraft and our naval vessels to make no attack on North Vietnam, except in the area north of the demilitarized zone. . ." He pledged that the United States would send its diplomats, led by Averell Harriman, an ambassador so respected around the world that his very presence would signal our seriousness, "to discuss the means of bringing this ugly war to an end." This had the sound of a new and promising policy and we held our breath as the president continued:

> With America's sons in the fields far away, with America's future under challenge right here at home, with our hopes and the world's hopes for peace in the balance every day, I do not believe that I should devote an hour or a day of my time to my personal partisan causes or to any duties other than the awesome duties of this office—the presidency of your country.
>
> Accordingly, I shall not seek, and I will not accept the nomination of my party for another term as your president.

After a moment of stunned and disbelieving silence in our cluttered apartment, we began to cheer and dance and embrace each other, astonished by what we had heard. Could it really be that our warmonger president had finally seen the light?

There was, of course, a callous oblivion in our euphoria, springing as it did from our hatred of the war and Johnson's years of stealthy escalation. In this moment, we were ignoring everything else, the tragic story of greatness undone, for here was a deeply flawed politician who had aimed so high on behalf of his country—a son of the New Deal who believed that government could and should work in the service of ordinary people. He had pushed that notion further than any president in our history, building on the legacy of Franklin Roosevelt as well as John Kennedy. It was not just his landmark civil rights legislation or his Great Society programs, as important as those were. With his remarkable legislative agenda, he had erased legal barriers to racial equality, and in the first ten years of his War on Poverty, had cut the poverty rate from more than 17 percent to 11, its lowest level ever. There were other factors at work, of course, including the economic growth his policies helped to stimulate, but the bottom line was clear. Nor was that all. Environmental protection, consumer protection, and health care, including the bedrock programs of Medicare and Medicaid—all were a part of Johnson's mark on the country, the ways in which he made it better, and all were blotted from our short-term memory by the bitter reality of the war.

Willie Morris, who was editor of *Harper's* at the time of Johnson's fall, and who had spent his college years in Texas, recalled his feelings in that double-edged moment:

> Given my own time in Texas, as writer and editor, I always had mixed, even confused feelings about him, as did most who knew him then. "I was determined to be the greatest President of them all," he had said, "the whole bunch of 'em." He had known poverty and racism first-hand, considerably more so than all the Kennedys multiplied. His speeches as President on the American poor were heartfelt and powerful. He never really forgot his origins. His "We Shall Overcome" address had already entered history as one of the most forceful and stirring messages by any President. Years later Bill Moyers remembered observing the members of Congress in the joint session in the instant Johnson uttered those words; he saw the hands of white Southern segregationists suspended in mid-air as the rest of the chamber cheered and applauded, then they too began clapping, tentatively at first, then with vigor.

All of this deserved to be remembered, but there was no denying that when Johnson said he would not run again, many of us felt a new and elevated level of hope.

Martin Luther King shared the mood of ambivalence. He understood as clearly as anyone Johnson's record on civil rights, and after the passage of the 1965 Voting Rights Act, he had told the president, "You have created a Second Emancipation."

"The real hero is the American Negro," Johnson replied.

Such was the formal and gracious respect that they accorded each other for a while. By 1967, however, and even more in 1968, there was increasing tension between them. King had spoken out about the war, and he was calling for a radical commitment of resources to address the problem of American poverty. On March 31, the same day Lyndon Johnson announced that he would not seek reelection, King delivered one of his most far-reaching speeches at the Washington National Cathedral. The address is remembered for its most eloquent lines:

> One day we will have to stand before the God of history, and we will talk in terms of things we've done. . . . It seems that I can hear the God of history saying, "That was not enough! I was hungry and ye fed me not. . . ."

In this speech and others he delivered in 1968, King turned his attention from segregation and the right to vote to a broader appeal for economic justice, and a confrontation with the nation's racism, which went far deeper than most people acknowledged. "It is an unhappy truth," King said, "that racism is a way of life." This great American sin, he believed, was tied to poverty and the massive suffering it caused in the world, and these were not problems that would slowly take care of themselves with time.

> Somewhere we must come to see that human progress never rolls in on the wheels of inevitability. It comes through the tireless efforts and the persistent work of dedicated individuals who are willing to be co-workers with God. And without this hard work, time itself becomes an ally of the primitive forces of social stagnation. So we must help time and realize that the time is always ripe to do right. . . .
>
> I was in Marks, Mississippi, the other day, which is in Whitman County, the poorest county in the United States. I tell you, I saw hundreds of little black boys and black girls walking the streets with no shoes to wear. I saw their mothers and fathers trying to carry on a little Head Start program, but they had no

> money. The federal government hadn't funded them, but they were trying to carry on. They raised a little money here and there; trying to get a little food to feed the children; trying to teach them a little something.
>
> And I saw mothers and fathers who said to me not only were they unemployed, they didn't get any kind of income—no old-age pension, no welfare check, no anything. I said, "How do you live?" And they say, "Well, we go around, go around to the neighbors and ask them for a little something. When the berry season comes, we pick berries. When the rabbit season comes, we hunt and catch a few rabbits. And that's about it."
>
> And I was in Newark and Harlem just this week. And I walked into the homes of welfare mothers. I saw them in conditions—no, not with wall-to-wall carpet, but wall-to-wall rats and roaches. I stood in an apartment and this welfare mother said to me, "The landlord will not repair this place. I've been here two years and he hasn't made a single repair." Poor people are forced to pay more for less. . . . It becomes a kind of domestic colony.

Angered and hurt by these things he had seen, King announced plans for a Poor People's Campaign, a gathering of blacks, whites, Latinos, and Indians—for the poor included all of those groups—descending on the nation's capital, willing to disrupt the mechanisms of government, demanding as the price for their departure a massive investment in low-income America. Every citizen should be guaranteed a job, King insisted, with the federal government as employer of last resort. And for those unable to work, there must be a guaranteed annual income. All of this King demanded and more.

Writing in the *Journal of Ecumenical Studies* some twenty years after King's death, Christian ethicist Kenneth Lee Smith set out to document "the radicalization of Martin Luther King." During the final years of King's life, Smith concluded, King lost faith in the capitalist system, and while he cherished the good will of many white Americans, he came to believe whites of good will were a minority. "I am sorry to have to say," King declared, "that the vast majority of white Americans are racists."

As he wrestled with these ideas, struggling to formulate in his own mind how the ideals of democratic socialism might become a force for justice, King became involved in a struggle by garbage workers in Memphis. They were seeking a union contract with the city—one that might result in a decent wage and safer working conditions. In his offer of support, King was partly answering an old friend's call. James Lawson, now a Methodist minister in Memphis, had been a principal architect of nonviolence in the early years of the civil rights struggle. In Nashville, he had taught the philosophy and technique to the students in the sit-in movement, and he had later done the same in Birmingham. In Memphis, Lawson threw his support behind a wildcat strike of sanitation workers. Their slogan was, "I Am a Man." What they meant was simple. They worked hard at a thankless, dirty job that was essential to their city. For this, they expected to be paid a living wage. But the City of Memphis refused to budge. The mayor fired the strikers.

To King, this was precisely what he was talking about—economic exploitation compounded by racial condescension and prejudice—and with Lawson championing the workers, King was happy to get involved. On March 18, he flew to Memphis and spoke to a crowd of some fifteen thousand. He also agreed to return and lead a march.

Ten days later, the march began peacefully with King and Lawson at the head of the line. But as the procession stretched along Beale Street, young blacks at the rear began smashing the windows of neighborhood stores. Police arrived quickly and attacked not only the violent mob, but also the ranks of peaceful demonstrators. In the pandemonium, several of King's aides insisted on getting him to safety, and a shaken Dr. King agreed. He was already feeling emotionally drained—over-extended, unable to sleep, more obsessed than usual with continuing reports of threats on his life.

The next day, newspapers reported not only that the march had turned violent, but with information planted by the FBI, some pundits jeered at King's inglorious flight from the scene. The *Memphis Commercial Appeal* ran an editorial cartoon with the caption "Chicken a la King." In a conversation with Ralph Abernathy, his closest friend in the movement, King wondered if his time had passed. "Maybe," he said, "we just have to admit that the day of violence is here, and maybe we just have to give up, and let violence take its course."

Multiple biographers and historians, including Nick Kotz, David Garrow, Taylor Branch, and Lewis Baldwin, have sought to describe the depths of King's despair during this fateful Memphis crusade. But nowhere was his mood more evident than in his own words in the speech he gave on the night of April 3. He had not even wanted to be there. He had a sore throat and had sent Abernathy in his place, but the crowd would have none of it. They wanted Dr. King. So in a driving rainstorm, he made his way to Masonic Temple and delivered a dark and brooding speech, remembering the various attempts on his life, including in 1958 when a woman had stabbed him in the chest. And that very morning a bomb threat had delayed his flight to Memphis. He was tired of living with that weight, he said, but he was "happy"—that was the word he used—to be a part of this moment in history, "to see a community rally around those brothers and sisters who are suffering."

As King moved toward the close of his speech, it was as if the torrent of emotions inside him were welling simultaneously to the surface—the depth of his sadness about the state of the country, his doubts about his own leadership, and a fear that he might soon be killed. But there was also a faith that he was able to summon in what became known as his "Mountaintop Speech."

> Well, I don't know what will happen now. We've got some difficult days ahead. It doesn't matter what happens with me now. Because I've seen the mountaintop. And I don't mind. Like anybody, I would like to live a long life. Longevity has its place. But I'm not concerned about that now. I just want to do God's will. And he's allowed me to go up to the mountain. And I've looked over. And I've seen the promised land. I may not get there with you. But I want you to know tonight that we, as a people, will get to the promised land. And I'm happy tonight. I'm not worried about anything. I'm not fearing any man. Mine eyes have seen the glory of the coming of the Lord. His truth is marching on.

King spent the next day, April 4, waiting at the Lorraine Motel while his trusted lieutenant, Andrew Young, was at a court hearing, seeking modification of a federal injunction against another march. At the end of the day, when Young finally returned, King confronted him in mock anger: "Where you been? You're always running off without me knowing about it." He and Young each grabbed a pillow, and with Abernathy joining in, these three great leaders of the civil rights movement launched a spirited pillow fight, laughing like little boys. After a few minutes, with the tension relieved, the three of them and Jesse Jackson got ready to go to dinner. King's limousine driver, Solomon Jones, reminded him that it was going to be chilly that night and said he should definitely bring a coat. With that, they walked out onto the motel balcony.

The others heard a shot, or was it a firecracker? They glanced toward the building across the street and then at each other, and in the split second of confusion they wondered what had happened to King. He was no longer standing beside them. In the next split second, they saw him lying on his back, bleeding from a massive wound to his face. A piece of his jaw had been shot away.

Abernathy knelt and cradled his fallen friend in his arms. "Martin, this is Ralph. Martin, can you hear me? Everything is going to be all right, Martin. Everything is going to be all right."

Andrew Young, normally the most composed of the group, broke into sobs. "Oh my God, my God! It's all over."

55

Grief and Rage

Robert Kennedy was on his way to Indianapolis when he heard the news. He was beginning his campaign in Indiana, a primary he knew he had to win much as his brother in 1960 had needed to win in West Virginia (that economically ravaged backwater of Appalachia was where JFK laid to rest the idea that a Catholic could not win in the heartland). Now, in Indiana, the younger Kennedy would have to earn the votes of alienated whites, many of whom had voted for Wallace in 1964. RFK, as a champion of the poor and dispossessed—of blacks and Indians and Mexican Americans—knew he faced an uphill climb. But he also knew, both personally and politically, that he could not turn his back on the ghetto, and that was where he began.

On the flight to Indianapolis for a scheduled rally in the inner city, a *New York Times* reporter told Kennedy that King had been shot. By the time the plane landed, they knew King had died. Jack Newfield reported that Kennedy wept, perhaps for the country, perhaps in private memory of his brother, though his grief in a sense was more generic than personal. He did not know Dr. King well. The two, by most accounts, never quite understood or trusted each other. But Kennedy did understand King's importance for African Americans. When police officials in Indianapolis warned him not to venture into the ghetto, for on this night especially it would be too dangerous for any white man to be there, Kennedy brushed the warnings aside. Even when the police refused to go with him or to offer protection, Kennedy forged ahead.

He found a crowd of a thousand people waiting, milling around, hunched against the cold. Remarkably, in this era before the cable news/internet cycle, they did not yet know that King had been shot. It fell to Robert Kennedy to tell them.

Standing on a flatbed truck, wearing an oversized coat that once belonged to his brother, he began in a flat, somber voice:

> I have some bad news for you, for all of our fellow citizens, and people who love justice all over the world, and that is that Martin Luther King was shot and killed tonight.

As Kennedy biographer Evan Thomas recounted, "There was a collective gasp and shouts of 'No, no!'" Kennedy paused briefly, then continued to speak. He had scribbled some notes before he arrived, but he paid no attention to them now. The words simply came.

> Martin Luther King dedicated his life to love and to justice for his fellow human beings, and he died because of that effort.
>
> In this difficult day, in this difficult time for the United States, it is perhaps well to ask what kind of a nation we are and what direction we want to move in. For those of you who are black—considering the evidence there evidently is that there were white people who were responsible—you can be filled with bitterness, with hatred, and a desire for revenge. We can move in that direction as a country, in great polarization—black people amongst black, white people amongst white, filled with hatred toward one another.
>
> Or we can make an effort, as Martin Luther King did, to understand and to comprehend, and to replace that violence, that stain of bloodshed that has spread across our land, with an effort to understand with compassion and love.
>
> For those of you who are black and are tempted to be filled with hatred and distrust at the injustice of such an act, against all white people, I can only say that I feel in my own heart the same kind of feeling. I had a member of my family killed, but he was killed by a white man. But we have to make an effort in the United States, we have to make an effort to understand, to go beyond these rather difficult times.
>
> My favorite poet was Aeschylus. He wrote: "In our sleep, pain which cannot forget falls drop by drop upon the heart until, in our own despair, against our will, comes wisdom through the awful grace of God."
>
> . . . So I shall ask you tonight to return home, to say a prayer for the family of Martin Luther King, that's true, but more importantly to say a prayer for our country, which we all love—a prayer for understanding and that compassion of which I spoke.

THE NEXT DAY, KENNEDY spoke to a very different audience, a gathering of white business leaders in Cleveland. He spoke from a printed text this time, again in a voice both passionate and somber, the sound of it almost a monotone, which somehow only added to the force:

> This is a time of shame and sorrow. It is not a day for politics. I have saved this one opportunity to speak briefly to you about this mindless menace of violence in America which again stains our land and every one of our lives.
>
> It is not the concern of any one race. The victims of the violence are black and white, rich and poor, young and old, famous and unknown. They are, most important of all, human beings whom other human beings loved and needed. No one—no matter where he lives or what he does—can be certain who will suffer from some senseless act of bloodshed. And yet it goes on and on.
>
> Why? What has violence ever accomplished? What has it ever created? No martyr's cause has ever been stilled by his assassin's bullet. No wrongs have ever been righted by riots and civil disorders. A sniper is only a coward, not a hero, and an uncontrolled, uncontrollable mob is only the voice of madness, not the voice of the people. . . .
>
> But there is another kind of violence, slower but just as deadly, destructive as the shot or the bomb in the night. This is the violence of institutions; indifference and inaction and slow decay. This is the violence that afflicts the poor, that poisons relations between men because their skin has different colors. This is a slow destruction of a child by hunger, and schools without books and homes without heat in the winter.
>
> This is the breaking of a man's spirit by denying him the chance to stand as a father and as a man among other men. And this too afflicts us all. I have not come here to propose a set of specific remedies nor is there a single set. . . . Yet we know what we must do. It is to achieve true justice among our fellow citizens. . . .
>
> We can perhaps remember—even if only for a time—that those who live with us are our brothers, that they share with us the same short movement of life, that they seek—as we do—nothing but the chance to live out their lives in purpose and happiness, winning what satisfaction and fulfillment they can. Surely this bond of common faith, this bond of common goal, can begin to teach us something. Surely we can learn, at least, to look at those around us as fellow men and surely we can begin to work a little harder to bind up the wounds among us and to become in our own hearts brothers and countrymen once again.

As I read over these words now, words that I can almost recite, the historian's detachment disappears into memory. I feel again the sense so many shared at the time that this was the heart of America laid bare—the hope on the other side of our national inclination to violence; for we could see that inclination all around us. It was there in our policies and in our history, and we could sense that Kennedy understood it, felt its anguish in a personal way; and whatever his flaws as a human and a man, his petty resentments, his cold ambitions for his brother and himself, the people closest to him seldom doubted the authenticity of the message he delivered. Nor did many of the people in the crowds. There were no riots in Indianapolis on the night that Martin Luther King was shot, the night that Kennedy spoke in the ghetto, but in more than a hundred other cities there was a firestorm of rage. At least forty-six people were killed in the rioting, and another twenty-six hundred were injured. When Kennedy flew back to the nation's capital, billows of smoke hung over the city. He insisted on walking the ruined streets himself before flying to Atlanta for Dr. King's funeral.

More than one hundred thousand people, white as well as black, gathered on April 9, many of them weeping as King's good friend Mahalia Jackson sang "Take My Hand, Precious Lord," weeping again as a mule-drawn wagon carried King's casket through the streets of the city, and as Benjamin Mays, the former president of Morehouse College, delivered the eulogy. Mays spoke of the symbolism of King's death, of the least of these and the Biblical symmetry of the last being first. "There was no greater cause to die for," he said, "than fighting to get a just wage for garbage collectors." At the graveside, Ralph Abernathy offered a few final words:

> This cemetery is too small for his spirit but we submit his body to the ground. The grave is too narrow for his soul, but we commit his body to the ground. No coffin, no crypt, no stone can hold his greatness. But we submit his body to the ground.

As grief and catharsis offered a momentary respite from the rage in the streets, Lyndon Johnson responded in the way that he knew best. He began to push legislation through Congress. An open housing bill had languished for weeks in the House Rules Committee, and Johnson immediately applied pressure to bring it to the floor for a vote. His ally was House Speaker John

McCormack, a Massachusetts Democrat who had served in Congress since 1928. On Monday, April 8, McCormack summoned supporters of the bill to his office. Outside the windows, they could see a cloud of smoke from the riots, and the grief and the guilt and the fear of further violence became a tool in the legislative effort.

John Anderson, a Republican from Illinois, cast the deciding vote to get the housing bill out of committee. With strong bipartisan support, the House passed the measure by a roll call vote of 250 to 172.

"The proudest moments of my presidency," Johnson said, "have been times such as this when I have signed into law the promises of a century. . . . With this bill, the voice of justice speaks again."

Johnson biographer Nick Kotz, never reluctant to address the frailty of his subject, offered a stirring assessment of the president's triumph:

> Now, as cities burned, as black Americans raged and wept, as his own presidency lay in ruins, its lustrous accomplishments tarnished by cruel fate and by America's unwillingness to respond generously to the least among its number, tormented by his own flagrant flaws, weaknesses, and doubts, Lyndon Johnson sought again to rouse the spirit of brotherhood in the land. Out of the ashes of King's death and of cities now in flames, Johnson would . . . forge another legislative victory.

But the president added a caution: "There is much yet to do."

IN THIS TIME OF crisis, as the nation reeled from assassination and riots, another confrontation unfolded in New York. At Columbia University, beginning in March, demonstrators led by the Students for a Democratic Society began a series of protests with racial *and* antiwar dimensions. The students opposed Columbia's association with a weapons think-tank known as the Institute for Defense Analyses, and at the same time they were seeking to block the construction of a gymnasium on public land in Morningside Park. Columbia had long been an uneasy neighbor with the black community of Harlem, having evicted over the years some seven thousand mostly Puerto Rican or African American residents from properties owned or controlled by the university. Black Power advocates, including those in the New York chapter of SNCC, saw the new gymnasium as one more incursion by the Ivy League behemoth.

On April 23, the confrontation escalated, as students and their neighborhood allies clashed with police at the construction site. After a scuffle the students returned to campus and staged a sit-in at Hamilton Hall, a building that included the office of Henry Coleman, dean of the university's undergraduate school. Some three hundred students occupied the office, chanting slogans and refusing to leave. Tactically, the occupation resembled the 1965 Berkeley protests. But the spirit was different this time. Instead of the eloquent Mario Savio, the Berkeley Free Speech Movement leader whose oratory was laced with quotes from the ancient Greeks, Columbia's student spokesman was the not-so-eloquent Mark Rudd, who headed the university's SDS chapter and, among other things, referred to University President Grayson Kirk as "that shithead."

The *New York Times*, among other publications, intoned gravely against this student misbehavior. "The destructive minority of students at Columbia University," wrote the *Times*, "have offered a degrading spectacle of hoodlum tactics." The *Times*, as usual, covered the protests in careful detail, proving once again that it was the national paper of record. But my favorite account, then and now, came from one of the student protesters. James Simon Kunen was a nineteen-year-old Columbia undergraduate from Boston who made irreverent notes on the campus uprising. In 1969, he published his observations in a book, *The Strawberry Statement*, which I thought was honest and witty and wry. About the events of April 23, he wrote:

> I have been noncommittal to vaguely against the gym, but now I see the site for the first time. There is excavation cutting across the whole park. It's really ugly. And there's a chain link fence all around the hole. I don't like fences anyway so I am one of the first to jump on it and tear it down. Enter the New York Police Department. One of them grabs the fence gate and tries to shut it. Some demonstrators grab him. I yell "Let the cop go," partly because I feel sorry for the cop and partly because I know that the nightsticks will start to flagellate on our heads, which they proceed to do.

And about the occupation of Hamilton Hall:

> I am not having good times here. I do not know many people who are here, and I have doubts about why they are here. Worse, I have doubts about why

> I am here. (Note the frequency of the word here. The place I am is the salient characteristic of my situation.) It's possible that I'm here to be cool or to meet people or to meet girls (as distinct from people) or to get out of crew or to be arrested. Of course the possibility exists that I am here to precipitate some change at the University. I am willing to accept the latter as true or, rather, I am willing, even anxious, not to think about it any more. If you think too much on the second tier (think about why you are thinking what you think) you can be paralyzed.

By the following morning, the takeover spread to four other buildings, including the president's office, and for nearly a week faculty members tried to negotiate a solution. The negotiations stalled over a student demand for amnesty, and early in the morning of April 30, President Kirk summoned the police. As the officers massed near the occupied buildings, they were greeted by a mocking chant from the students: "Up against the wall, motherfuckers!" Tom Hayden, an SDS founder who had joined the Columbia protests—and who was known to his friends as a man with a wicked sense of humor—shouted to his fellow demonstrators, "Keep the radio on! Peking will instruct you!"

The police attacked. Their targets included faculty and bystanders as well as student radicals, and before it was over, more than seven hundred, many bloodied, were arrested and taken off to jail. In the coming months, as the protests spread to other campuses, many people knew—though some did not, for there had been an imbalance of media attention—that the attack at Columbia was far from the worst that occurred that year.

BY THE TIME OF the Columbia unrest, the most tragic campus confrontation of 1968 had already happened—at South Carolina State College in the sometimes sleepy town of Orangeburg, population twenty thousand. Oddly, there were two black colleges in that modest community, operating on contiguous campuses. South Carolina State was a public land-grant college, founded in the *Plessy v. Ferguson* era to give the appearance of separate-but-equal. Claflin College was older—established in 1869 with money from a prominent Massachusetts Methodist family to educate newly freed slaves. Under the terms of its charter, Claflin was open to anybody, regardless of race, but the segregation laws of South Carolina undercut that high-minded ideal.

In a town the size of Orangeburg, the two colleges created a critical mass of young African Americans—many bright and highly motivated and, by the latter half of the 1960s, increasingly militant. At South Carolina State, an early outburst of activism came in defense of a white professor. Dr. Thomas Wirth was a young Woodrow Wilson fellowship teacher who was shocked about how little his students knew of black history. He organized a trip to Atlanta so that some of these young men and women could visit with leaders of SNCC, an organization focused on black pride.

Protests followed when school officials refused to renew Dr. Wirth's contract. Not long afterward, SNCC organizer Cleveland Sellers, born and raised not far from Orangeburg, returned to the area and moved into a house near Claflin College. As journalists Jack Bass of the *Charlotte Observer* and Jack Nelson of the *Los Angeles Times,* both veterans of the civil rights news beat, later wrote in *The Orangeburg Massacre*, Sellers was twenty-three and "soft-spoken, polite," but with his goatee and Afro he struck fear in the hearts of many local whites.

He had been active on campuses across the state, organizing for such reforms as black history classes. At South Carolina State he helped promote an activist group, the Black Awareness Coordinating Committee, which took a leading role in student protests. Sellers also opposed the military draft. In April 1967, with his organizing work in full swing, his local draft board ordered him to report for induction into the army. He assumed this was not a coincidence. On May 1, he reported as ordered to an induction center in Atlanta but refused to take the oath for military service. Blacks, he contended, were generally excluded from local draft boards, and in Vietnam they bore a disproportionate share of the fighting. He was charged with violating the Selective Service Act and released on bond.

Many black students in Orangeburg were focused on a peculiar source of annoyance: a segregated bowling alley. Nearly four years after passage of the Civil Rights Act, Harry Floyd, the white proprietor of the All Star Bowling Lanes, still refused to serve black customers. He said it would be bad for his business.

On Monday, February 5, a group of about forty students led by John Stroman, a senior at South Carolina State, entered the bowling alley and refused to leave. Sensing danger, city officials ordered the facility closed for the night. On the evening of February 6, the students returned—an even larger group this time, and they were met by state and local police. At least fifteen protesters were arrested, as others shouted insults and black power slogans.

"Hey, honky!" "Burn, baby, burn!"

One demonstrator broke from the crowd and smashed a window, and another spat in an officer's face. The police attacked. Randomly, it seemed, with fists and batons, they began beating students, those who were peaceful and those who were not. Many in the crowd ran for the campus, some smashing windows as they went. Outrage simmered for more than a day, particularly as word began to spread of policemen beating female students.

On the evening of February 8, after they were denied a permit to march, students from both Claflin and South Carolina State built a bonfire on a nearby street. Several tried to firebomb a vacant house. Others threw rocks at passing cars, forcing police to reroute traffic, and a state policeman was hit in the face by a piece of bannister apparently ripped from the empty house. As the officer lay on the ground, bleeding badly, some policemen thought he had been shot. Minutes passed. Somebody heard the sound of a gun. The police then opened fire. Not all of them, but enough. With shotguns and pistols, they sprayed the students massed on the campus, wounding twenty-seven and killing three. Most of the young people were shot in the back or the side as they tried to run, others while they lay on the ground. None were armed.

In a story carried by newspapers across the country, the Associated Press reported the event as a shootout between police and black militants. Some publications, including *Time*, did not report it at all. The AP never corrected its mistake.

In the spring issue of *Columbia Journalism Review*, reporter Jim Hoagland of the *Washington Post* documented the errors of his peers and speculated that the shoddy coverage reflected a change in sympathies, even among journalists, in the wake of the riots of the previous summer. People were simply tired of the violence and no longer cared about the details. Will Campbell, the white Baptist minister who had been active in Mississippi and Nashville civil rights activities, conducted a memorial service for the Orangeburg victims; he lamented that in 1968, "there was a lull in the reporting of violent outbreaks . . . especially those committed by the state. . . ." Bass and Nelson subsequently wrote *The Orangeburg Massacre*, a book that was notably clear and even-handed. The Justice Department, under the leadership of Attorney General Ramsey Clark, launched its own investigation. Eventually, nine highway patrolmen were charged in the shooting. Their trial began on March 11, 1969. They were acquitted.

At the service he conducted in honor of the victims—and in grief for a country in which such things happened—Will Campbell ended his homily by reciting the names of the dead:

> Samuel Hammond, Delano Middleton, Henry Smith. Let us softly speak their names and pass on. Let us shed a silent tear and move on.

Most Americans did not shed a tear. But they did move on.

56

Indiana

Though the country's very understanding of itself was rapidly dividing along multiple lines, there was still, improbably, a feeling of hope. It was focused now on electoral politics—on Robert Kennedy and Eugene McCarthy, our dueling champions of justice and peace who wanted to be President of the United States.

May found Kennedy in Indiana and Nebraska. In Nebraska, where he would win the primary by twenty percentage points, Kennedy relied on charm and self-deprecating humor to leaven a serious discussion of the issues. Biographer Evan Thomas recounted a visit by Kennedy to the small farming town of Crete where a crowd laughed and cheered as Kennedy said:

> "You probably wonder why I come to Crete. When I was trying to make up my mind whether to run for president I discussed it with my wife, and she said I should, because then I could get to Nebraska. So I said why should I get to Nebraska and she said, 'Because then you might have a chance to visit Crete!' All those who believe that, raise your hands." When the children in the audience did raise their hands, everybody laughed and cheered again. It was corny, and it might have been condescending coming from a different political figure. But Kennedy so clearly liked the people he met, so obviously shared their hopes, that many were moved.

The more difficult challenge was Indiana. In the days that followed the killing of Dr. King, and Kennedy's speech in the Indianapolis ghetto, the candidate at first crisscrossed the country, taking reckless chances, his advisers thought, plunging into crowds, stopping his motorcade once in Michigan precisely at a place where police had spotted a man with a gun, standing on a nearby roof. Against the advice of his bodyguards, Kennedy began to work the crowd, as if deliberately tempting fate.

Always, it seemed, he was drawn to the children, to people in wheelchairs, sometimes stopping to talk to them quietly, as if he had nowhere to go. But in Indiana he began to focus. The crowds at first were small and lukewarm, particularly in the southern part of the state, and his campaign advisers were divided on how he should present himself. John Bartlow Martin, a former journalist and an Indiana native, argued for a conservative message. Kennedy, he said, should begin to talk about law and order, and remind white audiences that as attorney general in his brother's administration, he had been the country's chief law enforcement officer.

When Kennedy began to follow Martin's advice, some of his younger staffers, particularly speechwriters Adam Walinsky, Jeff Greenfield, and Peter Edelman, bitterly complained about the change in tone. But as Evan Thomas wrote, this was a part of who Kennedy was: "If he sounded more conservative on these matters, it was because he was more conservative . . ." Kennedy, however, was incapable of changing his message entirely, even when his more senior strategists pushed him to do it. In his own journal, Martin wrote with frustration, and then with amazement, about Kennedy's stubbornness on the campaign trail.

> He went yammering around Indiana about the poor whites of Appalachia and the starving Indians who committed suicide on the reservations and the jobless Negroes in the distant great cities, and half the Hoosiers didn't have any idea what he was talking about; but he plodded ahead stubbornly, making them listen, maybe even making some of them care, by the sheer force of his own caring. Indiana people are not generous nor sympathetic; they are hard and hard-hearted . . . but he must have touched something in them, pushed a button somewhere. He alone did it.

Multiple writers, including Evan Thomas and Jack Newfield, have recounted the moment in Indiana when Kennedy was speaking at a medical school to an audience that was overwhelmingly white. He talked of increasing Social Security benefits and improving health facilities in the slums, and his remarks were greeted with "chilly indifference." When the medical students began asking questions, many of them hostile, Kennedy listened with visible annoyance.

"Where are we going to get the money to pay for all these new programs you're proposing?" one student demanded.

"From you!" the candidate snapped. "Let me say something about the tone of these questions. I look around this room and I don't see many black faces. . . . Part of civilized society is to let people go to medical school who come from ghettos. I don't see many people here from the slums, or off the Indian reservations. You are the privileged ones here. It's easy for you to sit back. . . ."

And so it went. The audience hissed and booed that night, but there were others who admired his grit and toughness. Many were blue collar whites who had voted for his brother, and then for George Wallace, and now were drawn to a Kennedy again. On Monday, May 6, the last day of the primary campaign, Kennedy traveled to Gary, flanked, as he stood on the back seat of a convertible, by the boxer, Tony Zale, a hero to Gary's white ethnic masses, and on the other side, as the three men clung to each other for balance, thirty-four-year-old Richard Hatcher, Gary's first black mayor. It was a powerful image in a city where racial divisions ran deep—a piece of political showmanship that personified Kennedy's hopes for the country.

Later that night, as he waited for the votes to be counted, he went to dinner with a group that included some of his favorite journalists—Newfield, David Halberstam, and others—and he talked of the hectic days in Indiana.

> I like Indiana. The people here were fair to me. They gave me a chance. . . . I gave it everything I had here, and if I lose, then, well, I'm just out of tune with the rest of the country. . . .

Kennedy did not lose. In a three-way race that included himself, McCarthy, and Governor Roger Branigan, who was standing in for Lyndon Johnson, Kennedy won 42 percent of the vote. Branigan was second with 31, while McCarthy finished third with 27. Kennedy won the black vote overwhelmingly and carried seven counties that George Wallace had won in 1964. He finished first in seventeen of twenty-five farm counties in southern Indiana, and overall he won nine of the state's eleven Congressional districts. His victory, wrote historian Joseph Palermo, "pointed the way toward bridging the racial divide."

That same day, he trounced Vice President Hubert Humphrey in the District of Columbia primary, and he was feeling tired but satisfied that night when he came upon two young McCarthy volunteers sitting alone in a near empty airport. Kennedy stopped to talk.

"I don't know what happened," the young man said. "I canvassed Negro neighborhoods, and they wouldn't listen to me for five seconds."

"That's not your fault," replied Kennedy.

"But you're a Kennedy," the young woman said. "You have the name."

"Look, I agree I have a tremendous advantage with my last name. But let me ask you, why can't McCarthy go into a ghetto? Why can't he go into a poor neighborhood? Can you tell me that he's been involved in those areas? Why did he vote against the minimum wage for farm workers?"

The two young people remained unconvinced, and Kennedy told them, "You're dedicated to what you believe, and I think that's terrific." He offered to drive them to a hotel so they wouldn't have to spend the night in the airport.

The next morning, he arose to a news analysis in the *New York Times* concluding that he had underperformed. "Senator McCarthy," wrote columnist Tom Wicker, "the man who first challenged President Johnson, had done the most to advance his own cause." It was, of course, a journalistic non sequitur, one of those moments of reportorial presumption, in which the man who ran third—fifteen percentage points behind the leader—was proclaimed by the press to be the real winner. The Kennedy forces were angered by the arrogance of media math, but it had happened before—for instance, when McCarthy came in second in New Hampshire.

This was a time when there were only fourteen Democratic primaries, so in a sense it was a season of auditions—a time to impress the party pros who would choose the nominee at the Democratic National Convention. Kennedy knew that in the game of expectations, always a moving target, his campaign still had a long way to go.

57

'Is Everybody Okay?'

There was other news that May, as the candidates prepared to move on to Oregon. In Catonsville, Maryland, nine antiwar activists—all Catholics, led by the radical priests Daniel and Phillip Berrigan—seized a stack of files from the local draft board and burned them in the public parking lot, using a batch of homemade napalm. As one of the participants, George Mische, explained in an article he wrote for the *National Catholic Reporter*, all 378 files contained records of young men classified 1-A—those at the top of the list to be drafted. These Christian vandals prayed as the files went up in flames, and they waited for the police they knew would come and for the hard prison time they thought might follow. Daniel Berrigan offered their reasons in a poem:

Our apologies good friends
for the fracture of good order   the burning of paper
instead of children

On May 21, four days after the arrest of the Catonsville Nine, some three thousand poor people from across the country built a shantytown—dubbed Resurrection City—on the Washington Mall. The Poor People's Campaign had been in a sense the final dream of Martin Luther King—a gathering of America's most disadvantaged, demanding an end to poverty in a nation of plenty. Ralph Abernathy, King's successor as the head of the Southern Christian Leadership Conference, set out to fulfill his good friend's vision. The gritty and brave Abernathy lacked King's eloquence and leadership skills, but for a time at least, the Poor People's Campaign was hard to ignore.

In *Life* magazine, another venue of good writing in the sixties, John Neary sketched a scene of desperation and gloom, and, perhaps in deference to the ghost of Dr. King, tattered remnants of hope:

> They came, a gaudy pauper's army from every state, on foot, in auto caravans the like of which the country hadn't seen since the Dust Bowl Okie days. In buses and by plane they came, some for thrills and a taste of life on the wrong side of town, but most of them to slam down a clenched fist on the federal desk and demand an end to poverty and violence, to demand a meaningful job for every employable person, an end to the hunger and malnutrition that scarred their lives. They wanted help, freedom, their human rights, dignity, a future, a chance for their kids, a modicum of happiness, all the things they didn't have and so many other people did have in this nation of unprecedented plenty.

Campaigning in Oregon, Robert Kennedy found himself in a place curiously disconnected from the anguished demonstrations in Catonsville and Resurrection City, and he felt that his own style, his message so full of urgency and passion, was falling on deaf ears. Eugene McCarthy, however, felt right at home. He was a man of principle, particularly when it came to the war; he had stepped out first to challenge Johnson, and legions of college students admired his courage and followed him to Oregon, determined even now to make him their president. They called him "Clean Gene" and saw in him a purity that no other politician possessed.

In the afterword of *The Strawberry Statement*, James Simon Kunen wrote of McCarthy as a last and critical test for the country:

> Since the First Republic of the United States is one hundred ninety-two years old and I am nineteen, I will give it one more chance. But if the Democrats do not nominate Clean, whom against my better judgment I love . . . then I will have no recourse but to acknowledge that democracy is not only dead, but is also not about to be revived through democratic means.

In addition to having the unshakable support of many students, McCarthy's cool intellectualism played well in Oregon, a state in which only 1 percent of the population was black. Oregonians, it seemed, hardly knew what Kennedy was talking about when he spoke of unemployment in the ghetto, or suicides on Indian reservations, or the hardships of life in the migrant labor fields. Nor was that all. In a state where hunting was a popular sport, many looked askance at Kennedy's strong support for gun control. Kennedy with characteristic stubbornness refused to dodge or soft pedal the issue.

"Nobody is going to take your guns," he told a group of hunters in the town of Roseburg. "All we are talking about is that a person who's insane, or seven years old, or is mentally defective, or has a criminal record, should be kept from purchasing a gun by money order."

All in all, it was an uphill slog, made worse two days before the voting when syndicated columnist Drew Pearson published a revelation leaked by President Johnson. As attorney general, wrote Pearson, Kennedy had personally approved FBI wiretaps on Martin Luther King. That part was true. To the point of lunacy, FBI director J. Edgar Hoover had hated Dr. King, wiretapping his phones in hopes of proving that King had communist connections. For more salacious purposes, Hoover had also directed the bugging of King's motel rooms. Hoover came up dry in attempting to portray King as a communist; he was not. But the director's agents did record extramarital affairs, which the FBI tried to plant in national newspapers and eventually, in a singular act of cruelty, simply mailed to Coretta Scott King. The Kennedy Administration had approved the wiretaps, hoping to confirm or dispel rumors of foreign influence on King, but the Kennedys did not approve the motel bugging. Hoover ordered that on his own.

Fortunately for RFK, Pearson's story, carried by newspapers all over the country, reported erroneously that Kennedy had approved the motel bugging. The Kennedy campaign was thus able to castigate the bugging allegation as false, while fuzzily acknowledging that Kennedy had, like other attorneys general before and after him, approved wiretaps "in cases affecting the national security."

Despite the campaign's artful dodge, the column was a blow to Kennedy's momentum, and McCarthy won the Oregon primary by six percentage points. Kennedy was gracious in defeat, congratulating McCarthy and making jokes at his own expense about being the first Kennedy to lose an election.

He said, "I feel like the man Abraham Lincoln described who was run out of town on a steel rail: If it were not for the honor of the thing, I'd rather have walked."

All of this added new pressure to the already critical California primary. Not only were delegates directly at stake, but Kennedy knew that a defeat in California could doom his presidential ambitions—in 1968, certainly, but perhaps in 1972 as well. If he lost in back-to-back primaries, the most powerful men in the Democratic Party would have reason to doubt that Kennedy could win in the general election. Jack Newfield, one of the reporters closest to Kennedy, thought his friend was curiously liberated by this all-or-nothing moment. Kennedy told him:

> I can accept the fact I may not be nominated now. If that happens, I will just go back to the Senate, and say what I believe, and not try again in '72. Somebody has to speak up for the Negroes, and Indians, and Mexicans, and poor whites. Maybe that's what I do best. Maybe my personality just isn't built for this. . . .

Despite such musings, Kennedy threw himself into the California contest with a furious energy that astonished chroniclers of the campaign. Theodore White, researching *The Making of the President, 1968*, found himself so exhausted in those final days of chasing after Kennedy that he was unable to get out of bed.

White and the others—Newfield, Halberstam, and reporters from all the major newspapers—saw a campaign in disarray when Kennedy returned to California from Oregon. Jesse Unruh, Speaker of the California State Assembly, urged Kennedy to run a more traditional race—an appeal to white suburban voters conducted primarily on television. There were tensions between the Unruh faction of Kennedy supporters and grassroots leaders from minority communities, and Kennedy sent in two of his most trusted advisers, John Seigenthaler and Steve Smith, to solve the problem. Immediately, they began to organize the kind of campaign in which Kennedy thrived, maximum exposure to flesh-and-blood people, especially low-income voters.

In *The Last Campaign*, Thurston Clarke recounts a meeting Seigenthaler organized in Oakland between Kennedy and a group of angry black radicals, including members of SNCC and the Black Panther Party. On April 6, two days after King's death, Panthers led by Eldridge Cleaver, the erratic militant whose *Soul on Ice* had recently been published to great acclaim, shot it out with police in an Oakland neighborhood. Cleaver and two policemen were wounded, and Black Panther Bobby Hutton was killed—after he had surrendered. Cleaver later admitted, in an article written by Kate Coleman in *New West* magazine, that he and Hutton had ambushed two officers, Nolan Darnell and Richard Jensen, because Cleaver believed "it was necessary to drive police out of the community with guns." At the time, however, Cleaver claimed the police attacked without provocation, and the Panthers were in a surly mood when they met with Kennedy in May.

Kennedy invited former astronaut John Glenn, who had been campaigning on his behalf, to go to the meeting with him. He told him:

> This won't be a pleasant experience, John. These people have a lot of hostility towards whites and lots of reasons for it. . . . They're just going to tell me off, over and over. I've been through this before, and you don't do anything. You listen and try to respond thoughtfully. But no matter how insulting they are, they're trying to communicate what's inside them.

Glenn was astonished at what happened next. There was, as Kennedy predicted, a torrent of hostile questions.

"Why don't you take your family fortune and redistribute it to the people?"

"Why did you tap Dr. King's telephones?"

"What do you think about black people, Senator?"

To the latter question, Kennedy replied, "I like some. Some, I don't." He said he felt the same about whites. But when he tried to shift to policy concerns, including his efforts in the New York ghetto of Bedford-Stuyvesant, a black man shouted in response: "Look, man, I don't want to hear none of your shit! What the goddamned hell are you going to do, boy? . . . You want this vote? . . . Put up a black bank and let us borrow this money!"

After nearly two hours of abuse, California Assemblyman Willie Brown, moderator of the meeting, finally declared that enough was enough. But Kennedy saw a few more hands. "Can I answer those questions?" he asked.

Willie Brown smiled. He could not imagine another white candidate who would display such patience, while at the same time refusing to be cowed, refusing to make any kind of false promise.

"That's the kind of situation I really enjoy," said Kennedy when the meeting was over.

"We're going to do very well," said Brown.

In the coming days, the ghetto crowds began to swell. A. J. Cooper, a young black lawyer from Alabama who managed the Kennedy campaign in Watts, remembered a "quite remarkable" outpouring of support as Kennedy's motorcade inched through the streets. Theodore White, who was there taking notes, tried to capture the sense of delirium—the bedlam of spontaneity and joy—as the throngs of black people engulfed the candidate and called out his name.

> The hands would reach for him, grabbing for a thread, a shoelace, a shoe; in the near-hysteria, anyone in the car with Bobby would become a bodyguard, protecting him. If he stooped to shake a single black hand, six more would clutch at him, at his fingers, up his wrist, to the elbow, tugging. One learned to protect him, not by clubbing down on the gripping hands, but by thrusting up to break their grip. For they would not let go. . . .
>
> Over and over, his staff warned Kennedy of crowds; over and over, those who traveled warned of how close to the edge of violence he brought himself by exposing himself to mobs, friendly or otherwise. Yet he would not listen. When it came to blacks, or Mexicans, or Indians, or any underprivileged, there was no cold Bobby—he was the Liberator, on horse, screaming with every fiber of his being that this was the purpose of power and government, to take care of them; and he was careless of whatever danger, political or personal, might lurk on the way.

Day after day he pushed himself toward and beyond some point of exhaustion that those around him were sure he would reach—and finally on his last day of campaigning, he did. He simply collapsed, "racked with nausea," as Thurston Clarke put it. "His knees buckled, and he sat down on the edge of the stage and buried his head in his hands." Even then he gathered himself, after Rafer Johnson and Roosevelt Grier, two African American athletes who had come to love and admire him, helped him to the restroom and back.

As Kennedy began to speak again, Richard Harwood, a reporter for the *Washington Post* who had initially disliked him, pulled the plug on a television camera so that Kennedy, in a moment of vulnerability and illness, would not be embarrassed. It was about this time that Harwood asked to be reassigned. He told his editor, "I'm falling in love with this guy."

ON JUNE 4, THE day of the voting, Kennedy retreated to the beach with his family. He swam in the Malibu surf with his son, David, who in a frightening moment was swept away by the undertow. Kennedy dove after him and pulled the boy to the surface. As the two emerged from the waves, father and son held tight to each other's hands.

Meanwhile, all over California, voting was heavy in the black and Latino wards—nearly 100 percent in an Oakland precinct not far from where Kennedy had met with the Panthers. By the end of the day, the results were coming in from South Dakota as well, where Kennedy had campaigned sparingly. In one Native American precinct, he had received all but two votes. In the state as a whole, he won by 50 percent to 30 for Hubert Humphrey, and only 20 percent for McCarthy.

Later in the evening, as the numbers trickled in, it was clear that he would win California as well. In suite 511 at the Ambassador Hotel, Kennedy savored the sudden surge of momentum and talked future strategy with several of his aides. He led McCarthy in the delegate count but still trailed Humphrey. He said it was time "to chase Hubert's ass all over the country." Just before midnight, he and Ethel and other members of their entourage began to make their way to the Ambassador ballroom to address an overflow crowd of supporters. He joked about whether they should bring Freckles, their dog.

"McCarthy," he noted, "said I needed a dog and an astronaut to win."

As he passed through the kitchen, he paused to shake hands with the hotel staff, including Juan Romero, a seventeen-year-old busboy from Mexico. Two nights earlier, Romero had delivered a room-service meal to Kennedy's suite and was impressed by Kennedy's response—the strength of the grip as they shook hands, the respectful kindness of Kennedy's manner as the two chatted briefly.

"He made me feel like a regular citizen," Romero said later. "He made me feel like a human being."

Finally, around midnight, Kennedy arrived in the ballroom and began to thank everybody he could think of. With a grin he included Freckles, then Ethel. "I'm not doing this in any order of importance," he said. Then one by one, he talked about the members of his staff, about Jesse Unruh and Cesar Chavez, about the black and Latino citizens of California . . . the list went on like some kind of acceptance speech at the Oscars, until Kennedy finally ended with words that would soon be broadcast again and again:

"So my thanks to all of you, and on to Chicago, and let's win there."

As he turned and reentered the hotel kitchen, Sirhan Sirhan, an angry Palestinian whose motives for the deed were never clear, waited for him with a .22 pistol. Juan Romero, in a rush of exuberance, reached out to shake Kennedy's hand again, and in that moment he heard a popping sound. He saw the man who had made him feel human slump to the floor. While Rosie

Grier, Rafer Johnson and the writer George Plimpton wrestled the gun from Sirhan, Romero knelt beside Kennedy, who looked up at him and spoke his last words: "Is everybody okay?"

PEOPLE HAVE STRUGGLED IN the months and years since to describe the import of those final seconds. I remember thinking, like Romero, of a tiny personal moment—a time I shared the back seat of a car with Kennedy and his friend John Glenn on a twenty-minute ride to Vanderbilt University. Somehow, I had known that one of his sons—I think it was Matthew, but can't remember that for sure—had been sick, and I asked Kennedy how the boy was doing.

"He's better," the senator said. "He's had a rough time, but he's doing better." As the conversation began to drift to other topics, Kennedy turned back to me. "Thank you for asking that," he said.

It was, of course, a small and ordinary exchange, but it injected something personal into the hemorrhaging sadness I shared with millions—with the tens of thousands of every race and class who lined the tracks as his funeral train made its way into Washington; with Senator Edward Kennedy who choked out a eulogy at the funeral:

> My brother need not be idealized, or enlarged in death beyond what he was in life, to be remembered simply as a good and decent man, who saw wrong and tried to right it, saw suffering and tried to heal it, saw war and tried to stop it.

Willie Morris, the editor of *Harper's*, would soon reach for all the eloquence he could muster as he tried to describe the magnitude of loss.

> The sight of him on the television lying in the pool of blood on the floor of the hotel pantry in Los Angeles . . . was almost too much to bear. As he lay dying in the hospital the next morning with his shattered brain, like his brother Jack's, I wandered the streets of the Upper West Side, remembering the silent pavements of the village on the day of his brother's funeral, the smoke spiraling from Harlem on the night of King's death. I never felt more sorrow for my country. The Jewish widows spoke in small whispers from their benches, people walked along Upper Broadway with their heavy faces . . . the hush of death and the early Sabbath pierced every now and again by the squeal of a

> junkie, the supplication of a panhandler, the dirgeful echo of a boat's horn from down by the river.

Morris ended his reflections with a quote from Arthur Schlesinger, who had been a friend to both fallen Kennedys, and who wrote in the hours after this second murder:

> "We cannot take the easy course and blame everyone but ourselves for the things we do. We cannot blame the epidemic of murder at home on deranged and solitary individuals separate from the rest of us. For these people are plainly weak and suggestible men, stamped by our society with a birthright of hatred and a compulsion toward violence."

It may be that those who were not alive in that time will resist Arthur Schlesinger's doleful conclusion, will not share the feeling with him, as I do, of a retroactive stamp upon all of our history by these things that happened in the 1960s. Ours was a land, after all, that began its journey with the burden of chattel slavery, grew with the genocidal conquest of a continent, and in a flush of contemporary righteousness and power, drifted so easily into Vietnam. Even with all of the pain of that last mistake, we could not, in 1968, find a way to break free, nor to make peace with the racial sins of our past. Through all of this, we held to a powerful hope of redemption, nurtured, in part, by our founding ideals, but embodied by the men who had now been murdered.

For me at the time, and I believe even now, the truest, most wrenching summation came from Juan Romero—the busboy who knelt in the blood of Robert Francis Kennedy because, he said, "I wanted to protect his head from the cold concrete." Later, he told the *Los Angeles Times* the truth of what he learned in that moment—a truth from which the country has not yet recovered.

"No matter how much hope you have, it can be taken away in a second."

58

The Shadow of Death

There was a less noticed flicker of sadness in that excruciating first week of June. Helen Keller died in Connecticut. Her obituary made the front page of the June 2, 1968, *New York Times*, but I don't recall much discussion of her life. She was remembered primarily for a triumph that happened when she was a child, one immortalized in *The Miracle Worker,* a 1963 movie. Patty Duke played Helen, and Anne Bancroft, four years before her iconic performance in *The Graduate*, played Keller's teacher Anne Sullivan, who helped set her free from a prison of silence.

Keller was born with both hearing and sight, but a severe illness robbed her of both before her second birthday. For years as she was growing up in Alabama, the little girl raged against her affliction, its terrors and isolation, until her parents—her father Arthur Keller, a conservative newspaper editor, her mother Katherine, who stubbornly refused to allow their daughter to be institutionalized—hired Miss Sullivan to try to accomplish what nobody else could. The teacher herself was nearly blind, a graduate of the Perkins Institute for the Blind in Boston, but she possessed a gift for working with children. Because of the triumphant scene in *The Miracle Worker,* many could describe the dramatic moment when her latest charge was suddenly set free—when Anne Sullivan led her to the water pump outside a cottage on the Keller estate. The teacher began to pump cool water onto one of Helen's hands, while spelling out letters on her other: W-A-T-E-R. By the end of the day Helen knew thirty words.

Keller's obituary in the *Times* chronicled the remarkable achievements of a life that transformed her into a symbol of courage, tenacity, and the will to overcome almost any conceivable hardship. She attended the Perkins School for the Blind and the Horace Mann School for the Deaf; then in 1904, at age twenty-four, she became the first deaf and blind graduate of Radcliffe

College. Befriended by Mark Twain, with his encouragement she soon emerged as a writer of international renown and champion of handicapped people everywhere.

But another dimension to Keller's life, one largely overlooked at the time of her passing, was relevant to the idealism of the sixties. For the first half of the twentieth century and beyond, she was one of the country's most committed radicals. There was scarcely a public figure in America who saw more clearly the interconnectedness of the great social movements she embraced. In addition to speaking for the rights and dignity of the handicapped, Keller backed the crusade for women's suffrage and joined Margaret Sanger's birth control movement. In the early days of the NAACP, she supported its leader, W. E. B. Du Bois, and her work was published in the organization's magazine, *The Crisis*. In 1920, she was a founder of the American Civil Liberties Union, and for all of this time she spoke in support of the labor movement, including such radical unions as the International Workers of the World. She was also a socialist, an economic theory she found more compatible with the bedrock compassion of Christianity.

When she died at the age of eighty-seven, her connection to the roots of radical aspiration went largely unnoticed. As one of her admirers suggested, we live in a country that prefers to sanitize its heroes, to sweeten legacies so they will not give offense. But perhaps at the time we were simply too numb to care.

In that early summer of 1968, even the most flamboyant activists seemed primarily to be going through the motions. In Washington, D.C., Jesse Jackson and other leaders of the Poor People's Campaign still staged periodic protests at the Department of Agriculture and other federal agencies, demanding that the country feed its poor. But in the shadow of the death of Dr. King, every protest seemed only to emphasize his absence. Soon the rain began to come in torrents, three days and two nights in an unbroken stretch, transforming Resurrection City into what journalist Marshall Frady described as "a microcosmic ghetto of shoe-sucking mud."

"I think the poor people should probably go home," Senator Eugene McCarthy declared, the cool detachment of his pronouncement a stark reminder once again of absence—in this case, of the now-stilled voice of Robert Kennedy. Finally, on June 24, the day after a Park Service permit expired, police and National Guardsmen moved into Resurrection City to flatten its shanties and arrest anybody who refused to leave.

The gloom deepened.

But there was, I remember, a wistful reprieve that summer on newspapers' comics pages. Charles Schulz, the creator of *Peanuts*, introduced a new character in his iconic cartoons. On October 2, 1950, *Peanuts* had begun its half-century run, becoming easily the most beloved comic strip in history. Its central protagonist was Charlie Brown, a good-hearted, laconic boy who suffered from an inferiority complex but stubbornly persisted in doing things he was not good at, like playing baseball.

For nearly eighteen years, all of the children in the comic strip were white. Then in April 1968, Schulz received a letter from one of his readers.

Harriet Glickman, a mother of three from Sherman Oaks, California, wrote:

> Dear Mr. Schulz,
>
> Since the death of Martin Luther King, I've been asking myself what I can do to help change those conditions in our society which led to the assassination and which contribute to the vast sea of misunderstanding, fear, hate and violence. . . .
>
> It occurred to me today that the introduction of Negro children into the group of Schulz characters could happen with a minimum of impact. The gentleness of the kids . . . even Lucy, is a perfect setting. The baseball games, kite-flying . . . yea, even the Psychiatric Service cum Lemonade Stand would accommodate the idea smoothly.
>
> Sitting alone in California suburbia makes it all seem so easy and logical. I'm sure one doesn't make radical changes in so important an institution without a lot of shock waves from syndicates, clients, etc. You have, however, a stature and reputation which can withstand a great deal.

Schulz, a barber's son from St. Paul, Minnesota, who grew up reading the "funny papers" with his father, did not ordinarily pay attention to advice from his readers. It was not that he considered himself too good for other people's suggestions; he could be as self-effacing as the characters he created in *Peanuts*. But there was, he knew, a delicate balance to his particular art, this mixture of sadness, intellect and humor he was compelled to produce every day of the year.

In the heartbreaking spring of 1968, there was something different about Mrs. Glickman's letter, and Schulz decided to reply. He said he liked her suggestion, but worried about appearing presumptuous if he suddenly introduced a black character. Mrs. Glickman said she would share his concern with her black friends, and a short time later one wrote his own letter to Schulz:

> Though I doubt that any Negro would view your efforts that way, I'd like to suggest that an accusation of being patronizing would be a small price to pay for the positive results that would accrue!

When Schulz decided to go ahead, he faced resistance from some newspaper editors and even, briefly, from the distributor of the strip, United Feature Syndicate. To the latter, Schulz said, "Let's put it this way: Either you print it just the way I draw it or I quit. How's that?"

Thus, a little boy named Franklin, his skin tones shaded dark brown, made his debut on July 31, 1968. He approached Charlie Brown on a beach, carrying a beach ball in his hands.

"Is this your beach ball?" he asks.

"Hey! Yeah! Thank you very much!

"I was swimming out there, and it came floating by . . ."

"My silly sister threw it into the water."

"I see you're making a sand castle."

The two boys stand for a moment before Charlie Brown's lopsided creation.

"It looks kind of crooked," says Franklin gently.

"I guess it is," replies Charlie Brown. "Where I come from, I'm not famous for doing things right."

There was nothing racial in this exchange, just two children playing on the beach, approaching each other with honesty and kindness. It was a footnote of wisdom in a deeply troubled time.

59

Chicago

The Republicans made their decision first. Meeting on August 5 in Miami Beach, the loyal opposition—the party of Lincoln, seeking to return to the corridors of power—was hoping to find a presidential candidate who could lead them back from the devastation of 1964. Barry Goldwater had lost that election by sixteen million votes, and when the dust finally settled, Republicans held only a third of the seats in the U.S. Senate, the fewest seats in the House of Representatives at any time since the New Deal, and only seventeen governorships nationwide. Journalist Theodore White told the story of Goldwater's chief speechwriter Karl Hess, whose fall from political grace was a metaphor for his party's. In his search for employment after the election, Hess was forced to enroll in night school to find a job as a welder.

The Republicans' prospects had improved by 1966, but then the odds always got better in the midterm elections for the party not in power. Now the challenge was to find the right leader and message for a party that sensed opportunity—the Democrats' most charismatic candidate was dead, the darling of antiwar students and liberal idealists was stirring little excitement among the party professionals, and the establishment candidate was tainted by his dutiful support of LBJ's war.

The GOP had more than its share of talent. There were, for starters, John Lindsay, Charles Percy, and Ronald Reagan, a trio of handsome, articulate political newcomers from disparate parts of the country.

Lindsay was the mayor of New York—a charismatic patrician, liberal on poverty and race, a man who *looked* the part of a president, even if he was only a first-term mayor. Percy, the junior U.S. Senator from Illinois, possessed the same innate appeal; he was a telegenic former businessman who carried himself with a natural grace and had entered politics with the encouragement of none other than Dwight Eisenhower. Percy, too, was a racial moderate who supported affordable housing for low-income families and questioned U.S. policy in Vietnam. James Reston of the *New York Times* called him "the hottest political article in the Republican Party." But Percy removed himself from the presidential discussion for a reason that was rare among politicians: he did not believe he had enough experience.

The third of the Republican newcomers was easily the most ambitious. Less than ten days after his 1966 election as governor of California, Ronald Reagan gathered his brain trust to plot his run for the presidency.

As history later would attest, he was a talented politician often underestimated by his opponents, perhaps because a background as an actor did not then seem to be a steppingstone to higher office. But in the run-up to 1968, Reagan's presidential ambitions hit a snag when *Newsweek* reported in its political gossip column, "Periscope," that a "top GOP presidential prospect has a potentially sordid scandal on his hands. Private investigators he hired found evidence that two of his aides had committed homosexual acts. The men are no longer working for the GOP leader but the whole story may surface any day." On October 31, 1967, it did. Muckraking columnist Drew Pearson questioned "whether the magic charm of Governor Ronald Reagan can survive the discovery that a homosexual ring has been operating in his office."

Reagan biographer Lou Cannon wrote later that Reagan, a product of his times, did fire the aides suspected, but he did so quietly, refusing to release their names. The episode came and went, but in the short term the whiff of scandal damaged Reagan's presidential hopes.

THE REPUBLICANS SOON TURNED to more familiar faces. Michigan Governor George Romney was a Republican moderate who in 1964 had broken with Barry Goldwater on the issue of civil rights. Romney said,

> Whites and Negroes, in my opinion, have *got* to learn to know each other. Barry Goldwater didn't have any background to understand this . . . and I couldn't get through to him. I understand Barry and Ronnie Reagan, they come from the same background I did—they just can't understand what we have to do, how to reach Negroes with programs of their own, how we have to know each other.

Romney was also dubious about U.S. policy in Vietnam, and on August 31, 1967, he had spoken in a television interview about a trip he made to the war zone:

> Well, you know when I came back from Vietnam, I just had the greatest brainwashing that anybody can get when you go over to Vietnam. Not only by the generals but also by the diplomatic corps over there, and they do a very thorough job. And since returning from Vietnam, I've gone into the history of Vietnam, all the way back into World War II and before. And, as a result, I have changed my mind. . . . I no longer believe that it was necessary for us to get involved in South Vietnam to stop Communist aggression.

It was a candid statement, an explanation of evolving views by a politician whose bedrock quality, wrote Theodore White, was "a sincerity so profound that . . . one was almost embarrassed." In his hyperbolic reference to *brainwashing*, Romney was describing an experience common among U.S. dignitaries who visited Vietnam—a bombardment by military brass and diplomats that obscured the reality on the ground. Five days after Romney uttered the B-word, a headline appeared in the *New York Times*, reflecting, of course, such indifference to context as to be fundamentally misleading: ROMNEY ASSERTS HE UNDERWENT 'BRAINWASHING' ON VIETNAM TRIP.

The White House charged that Romney had impugned the integrity of General Westmoreland and U.S. Ambassador Henry Cabot Lodge. In the media frenzy that followed, Romney's candidacy was effectively derailed. For the first two months of 1968, he campaigned dutifully through the frigid countryside of New Hampshire, but the opinion polls tilted overwhelmingly against him. White wrote:

> Thus, since he who lives by the polls must die by the polls, George Romney took his decision forthrightly, openly, bravely, and on February 28th called an end to it, leaving behind the impression of an honest and decent man simply not cut out to be president of the United States.

Richard Nixon saw in all this an opportunity for himself. Early in 1967, he had entered a self-imposed exile from the political stage. He read philosophy and political memoirs—the works of Plato, John Locke, and St. Thomas

Aquinas, the autobiography of Winston Churchill. His own biographer, Evan Thomas, reported that one of Nixon's favorite quotes came from the lectures of Charles de Gaulle: "Powerful personalities . . . capable of standing up to the tests of great events frequently lack that surface charm which wins popularity in ordinary life."

In 1963, during a Nixon trip to Europe after he had lost both the 1960 presidential election and the 1962 governor's race in California, de Gaulle had toasted the former vice president's return to public life "in a very high capacity." He also talked to Nixon about the need for Western powers to reach out to Communist China, which had no diplomatic relations with the United States. (This idea of grand statesmanship—a history-making approach to China—germinated in Nixon's mind and was to become the greatest triumph of his career.)

Nixon officially announced his run for president on February 2, 1968, a little more than a month before the New Hampshire Republican primary, which he won with 80 percent of the vote. He stepped gingerly through the issues facing the country. About Vietnam, he said, "End the war and win the peace in the Pacific," a position deliberately both hopeful and vague. The issue of race was a bit more tricky, especially after the death of Martin Luther King. Remembering 1960 when King had been arrested and John Kennedy reached out to Mrs. King and won the black vote in the process, Nixon traveled this time to Atlanta to offer his sympathy to a grieving widow.

"How's it playing?" he asked his campaign staff. Evan Thomas wrote:

> He was told that his visit to the King family wasn't playing at all—because it had been kept secret. "Damn it!" Nixon exclaimed, "I'm going to have to go down there to that funeral."

Seeking to walk a delicate line, he met in June with Southern senators Strom Thurmond, the old segregationist from South Carolina, and John Tower, a rock-ribbed conservative from Texas. He assured both that in his view the Supreme Court had tilted too liberal and pledged his opposition to busing as a tool to desegregate public schools. Both senators seemed pleased.

Only one other question loomed large for Nixon: What would Nelson Rockefeller do? Theodore White wrote of Rockefeller:

> Rising high above all lesser figures on the national Republican scene, he was almost a force of nature, like a slumbering volcano, wreathed in clouds, occasionally emitting smoke which soothsayers attempted to interpret.

For ten years, Rockefeller had been an activist governor of New York, supporting civil rights, consumer protection, increases in the minimum wage, and guaranteed college loans for young New Yorkers. In many ways, he was the last liberal lion among the Republicans, hawkish on foreign policy, but determined to make America more inclusive. Rockefeller, however, had run for president before, and in 1964 his challenge to Barry Goldwater had divided the party and left a residue of bitterness within its growing conservative wing.

For months, he vacillated until, finally, on April 30, moved by the assassination of Martin Luther King, he announced that he would run. Even then his campaign languished until the summer when a second assassination, ironically, seemed to give it life. Crowds of young voters, mixed with African Americans seeking a champion to replace Robert Kennedy, lined the streets for his motorcades and cheered at his rallies. Polls showed Rockefeller running better than Nixon against the Democrats, but Nixon already led overwhelmingly in the delegate count.

Rockefeller's only hope lay in a desperate alliance with Ronald Reagan, his ideological opposite, who also had reignited his campaign after the killing of RFK. With Reagan preaching law and order to Rockefeller's message of progress, the two governors from opposite ends of the country hoped to block Nixon on the first Republican National Convention ballot, then "with one foot planted on Nixon's political carcass," in the colorful words of Theodore White, "duel to the death for the delegates left in his estate."

It did not work. Nixon won the nomination on the first ballot. His remarkable political resurrection was celebrated in an acceptance speech that promised a return to law and order and an end to the war in Vietnam. Before the cheers and the requisite cascade of balloons from the rafters, he reached for a rhetorical finish, the kind of eloquence that others had summoned in our troubled decade:

> Tonight I see the face of a child. He lives in a great city. He's black or he's white, he's Mexican, Italian, Polish. None of that matters. What matters is he's an American child. That child in that great city is more important than

> any politician's promise. . . . He sleeps the sleep of a child, and he dreams the dreams of a child. And yet when he awakens, he awakens to a living nightmare of poverty, neglect and despair. He fails in school, he ends up on welfare. For him the American system is one that feeds his stomach and starves his soul. It breaks his heart. And in the end it may take his life on some distant battlefield. . . .
>
> To millions of children in this rich land this is their prospect, but this is only part of what I see in America tonight.
>
> I see another child tonight. He hears a train go by. At night he dreams of faraway places where he'd like to go. It seems like an impossible dream. But he is helped on his journey through life. A father who had to go to work before he finished the sixth grade sacrificed everything he had so that his sons could go to college. A gentle Quaker mother with a passionate concern for peace, quietly wept when he went to war. . . . A courageous wife and loyal children stood by him in victory and also in defeat. . . . And tonight he stands before you, nominated for president of the United States.

To some it was mawkish, to others inspirational. But whatever the effect inside the convention, there was another reality in another part of the city, described in the reporting of Norman Mailer: ". . . out in Miami, six miles from Convention Hall . . . the Negroes were rioting, and three had been killed and five in critical condition as Miami policemen exchanged gunfire with snipers."

THIS, TOO, WAS AMERICA in the summer of 1968, and less than three weeks later when the Democrats met in Chicago, conditions outside the party's convention hall would be even worse.

There was drama, of course, inside the hall where three candidates were chasing the presidential nomination on the opening day of the Democratic National Convention. Eugene McCarthy had stepped out first against Lyndon Johnson, making the case against the war as a deeply felt matter of political principle. But McCarthy was a man of curious ambivalence. In *The Making of the President, 1968*, Theodore White recounted a conversation between McCarthy and several of his literary friends, including novelist William Styron and poet Robert Lowell, the day before the convention opened. Somebody asked if he thought he could win the nomination. "Who would want the job?" he replied.

Another candidate with more certitude had entered the race after the death of Robert Kennedy. George McGovern and Kennedy were friends, neither willing to run against the other. Kennedy had said early on that he would have felt no compulsion to run if McGovern had entered the race. Now, McGovern, a South Dakota liberal who called the bombing of North Vietnam "a policy of madness," offered himself as a heart-broken surrogate for his friend. McGovern had been a B-24 Liberator pilot in World War II, winner of the Distinguished Flying Cross for his conspicuous bravery on multiple occasions, and thus he understood the horrors of war. He had also seen in the ravaged Italian countryside of 1945, the starvation of civilians, and the issue of world hunger would become one of his political passions. His was a broader, more visceral liberalism than McCarthy's, but in McGovern's mind there was an even more basic difference between them: "Gene really doesn't want to be president, and I do."

And then there was Humphrey. As vice president of the United States, the one-time liberal Minnesota senator, a long-time champion of civil rights, had been compelled to defend Lyndon Johnson's war, and in the process his own reputation in the party was tarnished. So bitter, in fact, was the Democratic opposition to Johnson that close political friends had warned the president not even to come to the convention—he would certainly be booed, or worse. Johnson later recalled:

> I've never felt lower in my life. How do you think it feels to be completely rejected by the party you've spent your life with, knowing that your name cannot be mentioned without choruses of boos and obscenities? How would you feel? It makes me feel that nothing's been worth it. And I've tried. . . . God knows I've tried.

Such was the backdrop of tension inside the convention.

OUTSIDE WERE THE FORCES of protest. One of their organizers, David Dellinger, was in the words of the *New York Times*, "an avuncular figure among younger and more flamboyant mavericks." Dellinger was a Yale graduate and a lifetime pacifist who had, among other actions, helped negotiate the release of several American airmen held captive in North Vietnam. As coordinator of the National Mobilization Committee to End the War, Dellinger was one of the organizers of the 1967 march on the Pentagon. Now in Chicago, he was one of many determined to raise their voices. Tom Hayden was another cast, like Dellinger, into a leadership role during a time of emotional, philosophical turbulence. As the author of the Port Huron Statement, the founding document of SDS, Hayden believed in peaceful protest but was increasingly obsessed by the realities of violence. He had seen it in the South during the civil rights years and in the Newark ghetto where he worked as a community organizer—had seen, yes, the violence inflicted by the black citizens of Newark upon each other, but had seen also, and more disturbingly, the gratuitous violence of the Newark police. He was there in the riots of 1967 where twenty-six African Americans were killed, "two before his eyes," as his friend, Todd Gitlin, later wrote. Add the things he saw in North Vietnam, the carnage wrought by napalm and bombs, and Hayden could easily understand Gitlin's own description of the times.

> It was as if the assassinations, the riots, and the war distilled all the barely suppressed violence seething through American life. Palpably, just as Rap Brown said, violence was "as American as apple pie . . ."
>
> The enormity of what was happening in the world, even packaged in media images, swept us into a kind of voyeuristic complicity. Traces of Auschwitz and Hiroshima were still detonating like slow-motion time bombs. The fear of ultimate planet-death, to which Vietnam seemed an extended prologue, produced psychic defenses: an inner bravado, a fascination with precisely what we feared. . . .
>
> Rage was becoming the common coin of American culture."

And so they gathered in the streets of Chicago, caught in a cycle they feared and loathed, and faced off against Mayor Daley's police. Politically speaking, the mayor himself was a force of nature. Theodore White called him "the best old-fashioned mayor of the country." Oddly, in view of events that would soon transpire, Daley had serious misgivings about the war and had signaled the Robert Kennedy campaign that he would support their man at the Democratic Convention. Daley was fiercely proud of the city of Chicago. He was proud of its diversity, proud that African Americans had been included in the political process in ways that went far beyond tokenism. Chicago, he knew, was a place of opportunity for people with the grit to take advantage of it; he was proof of that point—the sixty-six-year-old son of a sheet-metal worker who had risen to a position of extraordinary power. But now Chicago was under siege, descended upon by thousands of demonstrators, and who knew what mischief was on their minds?

From the start he took a hard line. During the riots that followed the death of Dr. King, Daley ordered his police to "shoot to kill," and on two occasions later in the month police attacked peaceful demonstrators with clubs and mace. "I couldn't believe it," one officer remembered. "There was nobody bad there." In view of Daley's chilling, deliberate message, the planners of the convention protests simply assumed the police would attack. The question was what to do about it. In a curious cycle of mutual alarm, police infiltrators regarded movement debates about "self-defense" as a euphemism for violent intent. Each side hated and feared the other.

As the convention approached, the already disparate leadership of the protest splintered. Dellinger, the pacifist, wanted badly to keep the peace. Hayden and Rennie Davis talked tough in negotiations with the city, demanding permits for demonstrations in the parks. A faction known as the Yippies, directed loosely by Abbie Hoffman and Jerry Rubin, began to offer outrageous proclamations, nihilistic fantasies intended partly for their own amusement. There would be nude swim-ins on the beaches of Lake Michigan. Yippie girls would pose as prostitutes in order to compromise the delegates. The guys would build a bonfire of draft cards with the flames spelling out BEAT ARMY, and, oh yes, they would pour LSD into the city's water supply.

In the mounting absurdity, Hayden began to wear a wig, fake beard, pink sunglasses, to avoid police surveillance, and Gitlin, who expected the worst, wrote with dread in a radical newspaper: "If you're going to Chicago, be sure to wear some armor in your hair." His ironic paraphrase of Scott McKenzie's idyllic anthem from the Summer of Love was based on the certainty of Gitlin's foreboding: "I knew the Chicago cops. . . ."

Sure enough, all hell broke loose. For nearly a week beginning August 25, events unfolded like a national train wreck. "As I stood outside the Hilton Hotel across from Grant Park," remembered McCarthy speechwriter Richard Goodwin, "I saw the student encampment transformed into a battleground, as members of the Chicago police, unleashed by Mayor Daley without opposition from the White House, mounted attack after attack, clubbing unarmed youths to the ground, dragging them brutally across the trodden grass, shoving them into police wagons." Todd Gitlin, who had come to Chicago reluctantly, drawn "moth-like" to the looming confrontation, thought of Russian tanks rumbling through Prague only four days earlier. He asked rhetorically:

> Who beat whom?
>
> In brief, again and again, the police came down like avenging thugs. They charged, clubbed, gassed, and mauled—demonstrators, bystanders, and reporters. They did it when there were minor violations of the law, like the curfew; they did it when there were symbolic provocations, like the lowering of an American flag; they did it when provoked (with taunts, with rocks, and, at times, they claimed, with bags of shit); in crucial instances, like the assault outside the Hilton Hotel Wednesday evening, they did it when unprovoked. Sometimes in the heat of their fury, the police took little or no trouble to distinguish between provocateurs and bystanders. Sometimes they singled out longhairs. Monday night in Lincoln Park, they slashed the tires of some thirty cars bearing McCarthy stickers.

Just as I had friends who fought in Vietnam, I had friends in Chicago, too. Don Sawyer, an SDS member from Michigan State University, would later recall his own arrest—how a policemen yanked open the door of his car, pointed a gun at his head, and charged him with a felony. The police found camping gear in the car, and a machete packed away with the sleeping bags. Later, the machete was displayed in a cache of weapons seized, police said, from violent demonstrators in Chicago.

Even security forces inside the hall were caught in the lunacy. In what became a famous moment in American journalism, Dan Rather, a young correspondent for CBS, tried to interview a Georgia delegate who was being ejected from the convention. When the security men tried to shove him aside, on camera, Rather demanded with remarkable calm: "Don't push me, please! Take your hands off me unless you intend to arrest me." When one of the officers hit him in the stomach, doubling him over, Rather managed to right himself and explain: "This is the kind of thing that's been going on outside the hall. This is the first time we've had it inside the hall . . . Somebody belted me in the stomach during that . . ."

"I think we've got a bunch of thugs here," said Walter Cronkite from the CBS booth.

"It's all in a day's work," said Rather.

Other members of the press, including Mike Wallace, were also manhandled, as was activist Gloria Steinem, who was passing out leaflets in support of Cesar Chavez and his farmworkers union when Daley's personal security guards shoved her roughly enough to break her glasses. Senator Abraham Ribicoff, a Connecticut liberal, protested against such tactics from the podium, prompting a vulgar outburst from Daley: "Fuck you, you Jew son of a bitch, you lousy motherfucker, go home."

I ABSORBED THIS FROM a distance. Perhaps I lacked the commitment or the bravery to go to Chicago, or perhaps I simply thought it was futile. But like millions of Americans, I watched the spectacle unfold on television, and later, as if to confirm what I had seen with my own eyes, I read the extended accounts in sources such as *Newsweek*:

> Amid tumult and tears, amid wrenching emotion and skull-cracking violence, the Democratic Party, in convention assembled, held up a mirror to America last week—and the reflected image, distorted though it might be, would not be forgotten. . . .

Inside the convention, a bitterly divided Democratic Party nominated Hubert Humphrey. To many of us, it seemed the dreariest possible ending to a primary season that began with such promise, then was jarred by a moment of unspeakable tragedy. Now in the ravaged city of Chicago—synonymous with officially sanctioned violence—a candidate tainted by the blood of war would try to lead his party forward. It was hard to find adequate words for the gloom.

60

A Southern Strategy

In the interim, George Wallace had been a busy man. The old ambition burned inside him, and on May 27 he announced his return to presidential politics. Some people thought he was seeking to escape from a moment of devastating grief. Less than three weeks before his announcement, his wife Lurleen died of cancer, and the state of Alabama mourned her passing. Since the beginning of 1967 she had served as governor, a surrogate for her husband who nevertheless earned her own reputation as a woman of compassion. But her brief time in office was hampered by her fatal illness. Even so, she became, for a state in need of people to admire, a symbol of simple decency and goodness.

She visited her state's overcrowded mental institutions, and journalists reported her shock and sorrow for the warehoused patients in long rows of beds, the stench of urine, the little girl clutching at her waist, crying "Mama, Mama," while attendants tried to pull her away. Mrs. Wallace pushed for increased appropriations.

For a time George Wallace was devastated by her death. He made daily visits to her grave, and his occasional visitors found him red-eyed, nearly immobilized in his mourning. But campaigning quickly restored his spirits to a degree that some found unseemly. He admitted to reporters that wished he "could have waited a little longer," but the simple truth was he couldn't help himself. There was nothing he loved more than a crowd. In Chattanooga, Memphis, or Milwaukee, he knew exactly what they wanted to hear, perhaps more surely than they knew it themselves, and he served it up with a pugnacity that set him apart from every other politician of his time.

"You don't have to worry about figuring out where he stands," said a steelworker in Youngstown, Ohio. "He tells it like it really is."

Of all the reporters, historians, and biographers who have sought to understand the Wallace appeal, few have probed more thoroughly than Dan Carter, author of *The Politics of Rage.* Part of it was simply a matter of description, a portrait of defiance, Wallace lashing at those he disdained:

> hippies, civil rights agitators, welfare recipients, atheists, beatniks, antiwar protesters, Communists, street toughs who had "turned to rape and murder 'cause they didn't get enough broccoli when they were little boys."

Only a few months earlier, Robert Kennedy had reached some of those same people with a very different pitch, winning votes in Indiana, and cheers from an overflow crowd in Alabama, when he told them:

> Some have said there are many issues on which we disagree. For my part, I do not believe these disagreements are as great as the principles that unite us. . . . For history has placed us all, Northerner and Southerner, black and white, within a common border and under a common law. All of us, from the wealthiest and most powerful of men, to the weakest and hungriest of children, share one precious possession: The name American.

There was something raw and visceral in Kennedy's message and style that could engage, however tenuously, both the white South and the blue-collar North. But when his voice was silenced, a distorted echo of that passion was there in Wallace's voice as well. The message, of course was turned on its head—not a plea for common ground, but a rather a snarling, contemptuous dismissal, a reduction to mockery of anybody who disagreed with the governor: "liberal sob sisters" . . . "bleeding heart sociologists" . . . "some bearded Washington bureaucrat who can't even park a bicycle straight." He spoke of law and order and disparaged the liberals who worried about police brutality. And about the war in Vietnam, he declared that he would leave it to the Joint Chiefs of Staff—no political or diplomatic restraints, just whatever firepower they thought was required.

For his third-party running mate he chose former Air Force General Curtis LeMay, who presided during World War II over the firebombing of Japanese cities and who had developed since then a fascination with atomic bombs. At LeMay's first press conference, Jack Nelson of the *Los Angeles Times* asked if the general thought it was necessary to use nuclear weapons in Vietnam.

"We can win the war without nuclear weapons," LeMay said, but he went on to wax poetic about the possibilities. "I have to say we have a phobia about nuclear weapons. I think there may be times when it would be more efficient to use nuclear weapons. . . . I've seen a film of Bikini Atoll after twenty nuclear tests, and the fish are all back in the lagoons, the coconut trees are growing coconuts, the guava bushes have fruit on them, the birds are back." As George Wallace, standing nearby, tried desperately to change the subject, the general plunged ahead, admitting that the Bikini land crabs "are a little bit hot," but adding that "the rats are bigger, fatter, and healthier than they ever were before."

"General," said Wallace, "we got to go!"

To mainstream journalists the campaign was horrifying—not just LeMay, but Wallace himself, with all his snarling hostility and contempt, which set loose the same feelings among his followers. Theodore White, a summa cum laude graduate of Harvard, tried to follow the campaign for a while, tried to endure its homespun demagoguery, knowing the Alabamian would be a key figure in *The Making of the President, 1968*. Soon, however, White couldn't stand it. He could not bear another speech, another rally for Wallace's American Independent Party. Nor was he alone. Garry Wills wrote of the people in the Wallace crowds: "They vomit laughter. Trying to eject the vacuum inside them." And *Time* magazine concluded that the candidate failed to offer "one constructive proposal" to a nation in crisis.

What, then, was the source of his appeal?

To Douglas Kiker, an NBC political correspondent, the answer was simple. Wallace was a man with a vision, an epiphany about the state of white America. Kiker paraphrased it: "They all hate black people, all of them. They're all afraid, all of them. Great God! That's it! They're all Southern! The whole United States is Southern!"

To scholars like Dan Carter or Timothy Lombardo, the explanation was more nuanced. But there was truth in what Kiker said. As the civil rights movement changed the country, blacks were making economic progress, their upward mobility more conspicuous than that of some of their white neighbors. As Carter pointed out, between 1961–1968, the aggregate income for nonwhites in America went up 110 percent, nearly twice the rate for whites, and 30 percent of antipoverty money went to African American communities.

In addition to economic competition, Northern whites were uneasy about open housing and desegregated schools—advances that they were willing to support when the region in question was the backward South. If racism lurked at the heart of these surging resentments, Lombardo argued that there was more to it. There was also anxiety about urban crime, so easily conflated with the inner-city riots which now seemed to rage every summer. These things offended a deep sense of decency, and the feelings were compounded by the campus uprisings—privileged kids who let their hair grow long and chanted slogans about America's enemies, making themselves sound unpatriotic, and making their cause seem ethically absurd: a violent peace movement. In the minds of hard-working whites, nobody was addressing such frustrating spectacles as effectively as Wallace. And the great sin and failure of liberalism had been to unleash these forces on the country.

As the third-party candidate plowed this fertile ground, sowing the seeds of division, Richard Nixon was paying close attention. For his own running mate, he had chosen Maryland Governor Spiro Agnew, a man regarded as a racial moderate until the riots that followed the death of Dr. King. On that occasion, when the violence subsided in Baltimore, Agnew demanded a meeting with the city's black leaders, people described by Dan Carter as "respected community organizers, middle-class preachers, lawyers, businessmen, and politicians":

> Instead of holding a joint discussion, the governor lashed out at his audience's failure to condemn the "circuit-riding Hanoi-visiting . . . caterwauling, riot-inciting, burn-America-down type of leader" who, he said, had caused the rioting in the city. Pointing his finger for emphasis, he accused the moderates of "breaking and running" when faced with the taunts of "Uncle Tom" from black radicals like Stokely Carmichael and H. Rap Brown. Three fourths of his audience—many still exhausted from long days and nights on the street trying to calm the rioters—angrily walked out of the meeting. These were the "very people who were trying to end the riots," pointed out the executive director of the city's Community Relations Commission, but Baltimore's television stations reported a flood of telephone calls supporting the governor.

Nixon was one of those impressed with Agnew's performance. He would cite it twenty months later to defend his choice of a man who ultimately would be forced to resign the vice presidency.

In retrospect, the Agnew selection was an early indicator of sinister, lasting cynicism that Nixon brought to the DNA of his party—a moral dysfunction that was perhaps reminiscent of Democrats, who at various times in their history had supported segregation and slavery, given us the war in Vietnam, and in the closing years of the nineteenth century colluded with the Ku Klux Klan to restore white supremacy in the South. But in many ways Nixon changed the game. According to notes (discovered by historian John Farrell in the Nixon Presidential Library) from H. R. Haldeman, his closest aide, the Republican presidential candidate assured Southern members of his party that he would "lay off pro-Negro crap," if he became president. In those same notes is a Nixon directive, delivered October 22, 1968, for Haldeman to "monkey wrench" peace talks in Vietnam, lest those talks help the Democrats.

Writing in the *New York Times* on December 31, 2016, Farrell explained that the Nixon order came at the height of the presidential campaign, when the race was growing tighter. Hubert Humphrey, who had been running a dismal second, was showing signs of new life. His low point had come in Portland, Oregon, when demonstrators descended on a Humphrey speech, shouting "murderer," "racist," and "stop the war." For an old civil rights warrior like the vice president, the "racist" epithet had to sting, but the salt in the wound came later that night in the latest polls. Nixon stood at 42 percent, Humphrey at only 27, while Wallace had risen to 20.

Three days later, Humphrey delivered a half-hour speech on national television, seeking to define his own ground on Vietnam, to separate himself from Lyndon Johnson. "As president," he announced, "I would be willing to stop the bombing of the North as an acceptable risk for peace." Nixon had rejected such a policy as weak, and Johnson bitterly complained in private, "Nixon is following my policies more closely than Humphrey." But things began to turn.

"The heckling subsided," wrote Dan Carter, "and almost overnight Humphrey seemed revitalized."

In other times he had been known as the Happy Warrior, a politician whose exuberance was so undaunted you wondered how he sustained it. He was not classically charismatic—not handsome or glamorous like the Kennedys, not urbane like Eugene McCarthy—but he could be a powerful speaker. As early as 1948 he had made that known at the Democratic National Convention, where his speech in favor of a civil rights plank helped trigger a walkout by Southern Democrats. Humphrey had thundered:

> To those who say that this civil rights program is an infringement on states' rights, I say this: The time has arrived in America for the Democratic Party to get out of the shadow of states' rights and to walk forthrightly into the bright sunshine of human rights.

It was a metaphor that would have been worthy of Martin Luther King. In fact, Humphrey's political instincts may have come as close to King's economic views as those of any white politician. In 1976, Humphrey and California Representative Augustus Hawkins, an African American Democrat, introduced legislation that would have made the federal government the employer of last resort when unemployment rose above three percent.

In 1968, as Humphrey rediscovered his voice, Nixon grew increasingly concerned. Once he had worried about Wallace on his right, but that problem had taken care of itself. The Alabamian was careening out of the mainstream, his speeches brimming with allusions to violence. At Madison Square Garden, as Nazis and Klansmen outside the auditorium clashed with radicals from SDS, Wallace became enraged at three black demonstrators inside.

> Why do the leaders of the two national parties kowtow to these anarchists? One of them laid down in front of President Johnson's limousine last year. I tell you when November comes, the first time they lie down in front of my limousine, it'll be the last one they ever lay down in front of . . ."

As the frenzied audience screamed its approval, Wallace escalated his fantasies of violence:

> We don't have riots down in Alabama. They start a riot down there, first one of 'em to pick up a brick gets a bullet in the brain, that's all. And then you walk over to the next one and say, "All right, pick up a brick. We just want to see you pick up one of them bricks, now!"

Less than fifty years later, such rhetoric would carry a candidate to his party's nomination and all the way to the White House. But in 1968 it did not. Most Americans seemed to agree with the *New Republic's* Richard Strout, who wrote that the governor was the "bugle voice of venom." As the

Wallace poll numbers continued to shrink, Nixon had only to worry about Humphrey, for the hand of history had come into play. There were rumors of peace in Vietnam.

At negotiations in Paris, which had begun in May, U.S. representatives Averell Harriman and Cyrus Vance now focused their efforts on a critical objective: getting the South Vietnamese government to the talks. Amid a flurry of international diplomacy, reports of a breakthrough leaked to the press. The United States would cease its bombing of North Vietnam, the North Vietnamese would suspend attacks on South Vietnamese cities, and both the Saigon government and the National Liberation Front would send negotiators to Paris. With all the relevant parties at the table, the possibility of peace seemed real.

But as suddenly as these hopes appeared, the optimism collapsed. On Saturday, November 2, just three days before the election, a devastating headline appeared in the *New York Times*: SAIGON OPPOSES PARIS TALK PLANS. At the time nobody knew precisely what had happened. There were rumors, but nobody was sure. Later it became clear. Richard Nixon sabotaged the talks. He was afraid that peace on the eve of the election, negotiated on behalf of the sitting Democratic president, would help the Democratic nominee.

Fifty years later it is still difficult to believe, though even in 1968 that was where the evidence pointed. Anna Chennault, a Nixon fund-raiser with close ties to South Vietnam, urged South Vietnamese President Nguyen Van Thieu to undermine the talks. "Hold firm," she told him through an ambassador. Nixon was going to win the election, and Thieu's government would get a better deal from the Republicans. On the Friday before the U.S. election, Thieu announced that his government would not go to Paris.

Lyndon Johnson was livid. He called his old friend, Everett Dirksen, the Republican leader in the Senate. "I'm reading their hand, Everett," he said. "This is treason."

"I know," said Dirksen.

When Johnson confronted Nixon directly, the Republican candidate denied prior knowledge of Chennault's activities. "My God," he said. "I would never do anything to encourage [South Vietnam] not to come to the table." Nixon maintained that denial for the rest of his life, lying resolutely to the end.

In the crucible of the moment, during the final hours of the '68 campaign, the Democrats were forced to decide what to do. They knew they could poison the well for Nixon, casting such a shadow on his candidacy that voters might recoil. But they decided not to. As John Farrell would write, they lacked the definitive nugget of proof to accuse their opponent of being a traitor. Maybe one of his supporters had simply gone rogue. Thus, Johnson and Humphrey made a quiet and deliberate decision. They would spare the country an election-eve scandal. Theodore White wrote:

> Humphrey might have won the Presidency of the United States by making it [the peace talk scandal] the prime story of the last four days of the campaign. He was urged by several members of his staff to do so. And I know of no more essentially decent story in American politics than Humphrey's refusal to do so; his instinct was that Richard Nixon, personally, had no knowledge of Mrs. Chennault's activities; had no hand in them; and would have forbidden them had he known. Humphrey would not air the story.

Over the years, journalists from George Will to Seymour Hersh and Evan Thomas would write darkly about where the evidence pointed. But the definitive proof lay hidden until 2007 and the unsealing of a file at the Nixon Library. Even then the needle in the haystack remained to be discovered until Farrell came upon it in Haldeman's notes, a cryptic record of his orders from Nixon:

> Keep Anna Chenault working . . . Any other way to monkey wrench it? Anything RN can do.

When Nixon won a close election on November 5, 1968, defeating a principled, patriotic opponent, a new level of toxin was released. Nixon would do some good things as president; the Environmental Protection Agency and the opening of diplomatic relations with China would forever remain a part of his legacy. But when his presidency ended in the Watergate scandal, it confirmed what many of us feared in the sixties. The actual cynicism of people in power would sometimes exceed our ability to imagine it.

Writing of his feelings on Election Day, Richard Goodwin, who had worked for both Robert Kennedy and Eugene McCarthy, provided us with a gloomy epitaph: "Richard Nixon was elected President of the United States. The sixties were over."

A few days later, I was in Nashville and paid a visit to an old friend. I had worked with John Seigenthaler to invite Senator Robert Kennedy to the Vanderbilt campus. I knew the depths of their friendship—knew Seigenthaler had worked for Kennedy in the Justice Department and had been the attorney general's troubleshooter in the South. Later, when the presidential campaign floundered in California, Kennedy dispatched Seigenthaler to clean up the mess. At Kennedy's funeral, Seigenthaler was one of the pallbearers. I had written him a letter at that time, telling him of my own grief and that I could barely imagine what his must be. Within days I received a hand-written reply, a simple "Thanks."

Now in November 1968, Seigenthaler was editor of the Nashville *Tennessean* and I went to see him at his office. We talked of all that had happened that year, and for a while he sounded as he always did, blunt but measured. But when the conversation turned to Richard Nixon and I began to speak of my own loathing, Seigenthaler answered with an icy bitterness that I had never heard from him before.

"The country deserves Nixon," he said. "It really deserves Wallace. But it got Nixon."

61

The Global Sixties

In the United States and much of the world, the number one song in 1968 was the Beatles' "Hey Jude." It soared quickly to the top of the charts and stayed there for most of the fall, even though it violated the conventions of radio airplay. The song was seven minutes long, part ballad, part anthem, with overdubs from a thirty-six-piece orchestra.

It was written by Paul McCartney for reasons that were personal and private. He originally called it "Hey Jules," in honor of Julian Lennon, the five-year-old son of McCartney's fellow Beatle, John Lennon. Julian and Paul were always close, and in May 1968, knowing the boy was struggling with his parents' divorce, McCartney went to see Julian and his mother Cynthia. On the drive to their house he could hear a song taking shape in his mind. "I started with the idea 'Hey Jules,'" McCartney remembered, "which was Julian, don't make it bad, take a sad song and make it better. Hey try to deal with this terrible thing. I knew it was not going to be easy for him. I always feel sorry for kids in divorces."

The B-side of the record, written by Lennon, never received the airplay of "Hey Jude," but "Revolution" became part of a generational soundtrack—a cautionary embrace of the spirit of rebellion that was sweeping through multiple countries in the sixties. In his book *1968: The Year That Rocked the World*, author Mark Kurlansky described a convergence of forces that began in the middle of the decade and crescendoed in 1968. Two of those forces were American exports—inspiration from the civil rights movement and revulsion against the war in Vietnam—magnified by the power of television.

Earlier in the decade, Canadian philosopher Marshall McLuhan had written about a "global village," a brave new world of electronic connection in which nothing seemed as isolated as before. In a new way, we found ourselves sharing distant events—a moment of triumph in South Africa perhaps, in which surgeon Christiaan Barnard successfully transplanted a human heart. The beneficiary of the doctor's skill was a white man, while the donor was black. The achievement immediately prompted a debate: Was it the ultimate repudiation of apartheid, or the final exploitation of black by white?

Whatever it was, the medical miracle touched the consciousness of people all over the world. This was a time when almost everything felt political. Music, literature, even visual art were measured more and more by their social conscience and the power of their political impact. Increasingly, the audience was global. In Havana at the start of the year, Fidel Castro unveiled a sixty-three-foot mural of Che Guevara, his friend and fellow revolutionary, frozen in time at age thirty-two—handsome and dashing with his beard and beret, his long, flowing hair, and enigmatic eyes. The image went viral all across the planet, inspiring young radicals with its intimations of sensitivity and danger. Che was, in fact, a romantic figure, an Argentine-born guerilla in the Cuban revolution, and also a doctor and a poet; a man who saw suffering in Latin America and set out to end it, hating U.S. imperialism even more than the stultifying Communism of Russia.

In 1967 he was killed while seeking to export the Cuban revolution to Bolivia. In death he became a symbol of restless radicalism in the world, and by the spring of 1968 the spirit seemed everywhere—not only in the United States but from Czechoslovakia to China. In the fall of 1967, amid rumblings of discontent in Soviet-bloc countries, writers and students in Czechoslovakia were demonstrating in support of greater freedom—an echo, partly deliberate, of the Free Speech Movement at Berkeley and other places. The country's pro-Soviet leader, Antonin Novotny, promised a crackdown against dissent and ordered the arrest of Alexander Dubcek, a Communist politician who was part of the Slovak minority and was said to favor a more liberal government.

Early in the new year, the tables quickly turned. The Czech party leadership, disillusioned with Novotny, ordered him to step down and replaced him with Dubcek, who was introduced to the nation on January 5 as the Secretary General of the Czech Communist Party. In effect, he was the new leader of the country. Reforms soon followed that loosened restraints on individual freedom, and almost immediately young Czechs were listening to jazz and rock 'n' roll (including "Hey Jude," which reached number one in the eastern bloc country of Yugoslavia and number two in neighboring Poland; John

Lennon's "Revolution," the more topical B-side of the record, was also a part of this youthful awareness).

There was, in addition, a rapid renaissance of poetry and theater, including the works of Vaclav Havel, then thirty-one. Prague was ground zero, and soon in many parts of the world people were talking about a Prague Spring. Havel, a native of the city, wrote plays like *The Memorandum*, which mocked communism for its didacticism and intellectual sterility. Over the years, Havel became a national hero and later served as president. But in 1968 the unlikely champion of Czech liberalism was Alexander Dubcek.

In 1921, as Mark Kurlansky has pointed out, Dubcek came within a few months of being born in America. His mother, Pavlina, was pregnant when the family left Chicago, where his father, Stefan Dubcek, had come seeking economic opportunity and freedom. He found neither. Stefan was a socialist, pacifist factory worker who married a Slovakian communist in the United States. Disillusioned with American hostility to their political views, he and Pavlina moved back to Czechoslovakia, where Alexander was born.

As the boy grew into manhood, he journeyed through the ranks of the Communist Party, seldom making waves. By 1968, however, he had begun to seem like some kind of international Kennedy. He was not charismatic, not glamorous, for there was something about him that was, as one writer put it, "gray," as colorless as the communism he represented. But in a burst of political courage, he presided for a brief, meteoric time over surging optimism and creativity.

The Prague Spring, you could argue, began with the sudden discovery of freedom of the press. On January 27, a combination newsstand and coffeehouse opened in the center of the city, and the people of Prague found newspapers there from all over the world. Emboldened by the hungry response to such publications, Czechoslovakian newspapers grew more ambitious, more aggressive in their reporting, exposing official corruption in a way that never happened in the Soviet bloc. Dubcek was caught in the middle, eager to increase individual freedom and improve the economy of his country, while trying to appease the leaders in Moscow. He offered words of reassurance, proclamations of his friendship with Russia, but he also pushed ahead with reforms. By April these had become more specific. He proposed even greater freedom of speech, fewer restrictions on international travel, a more decentralized economy, and the division of the country into three federated republics.

By August the Soviets had had enough of the kind of liberalization that could cause an empire to come unraveled. On August 20 they sent in troops. The invasion occurred a week before the Democratic National Convention in Chicago, and soon the world saw images of demonstrators on two different continents, many of them students, battling against the governments that sought to control them.

Much of the Soviet bloc assumed the resistance in Prague would crumble quickly. The official newspaper in East Germany reported on August 20 that a new Czech government had been established, and had asked for Soviet military support. The paper was getting ahead of itself. Dubcek and his cabinet refused to resign, while at the same time, in an effort to prevent a bloodbath, ordering the Czech army not to resist this massive invasion: more than 4,000 tanks and 165,000 soldiers from the Soviet Union and four of its allies.

What the whole world saw in the weeks that followed was a wholly different kind of resistance, young Czechoslovakians pouring into the streets, blocking the path of tanks, shouting obscenities at the invaders, sometimes throwing Molotov cocktails. Some of the resisters were killed, but many of the others—like their counterparts in Chicago shouting "join us!" to young National Guardsmen—could be seen in earnest dialogue with Soviet soldiers, asking them why they were there. Graffiti soon appeared on walls: "Socialism, Yes; Occupation No," or "This is not Vietnam"; or more colorfully, "The Russian National Circus has arrived, complete with performing gorillas."

CBS News, prodded by the venerable Walter Cronkite, temporarily expanded its evening newscast to an hour and launched a new Sunday show called *60 Minutes*, the better to cover this avalanche of news. In Czechoslovakia, underground radio stations began reporting, from secret locations, everything from Soviet troop movements to the names of those arrested. In Yugoslavia and Romania, parts of the Soviet bloc, the heads of state denounced the invasion, and young demonstrators filled the streets of Belgrade and Bucharest, supporting their counterparts in Prague. The protests even spread to Japan.

This was the world of 1968, where the spirit of rebellion seemed to be everywhere. Eventually, in Czechoslovakia, Alexander Dubcek was removed from power, and the drabness of Soviet-style communism returned. But aspirations simmered just beneath the surface and rose again in 1989 when a new Soviet leader, Mikhail Gorbachev, sought to establish "socialism with a human face," citing Dubcek as one of his examples.

IN THE UNITED STATES, as we battled through the tragedies of 1968, our anger against the police in Chicago, and our disillusionment with electoral politics, we cheered for our peers in other places. There were demonstrations in Paris and a cultural revolution in China, and even in Mexico a wave of protests erupted in the summer. On the eve of the Olympic games, which Mexico had been chosen to host, the last thing the government wanted was unrest. This was a chance for the country to shine, to take its place among the most respected nations in the world. But storm clouds were on the horizon, including in the U.S., where San Jose State College sociologist Harry Edwards was seeking to organize an Olympic boycott by black athletes. One supporter of that effort was a young man who later won an Olympic gold medal. Tommie Smith already held several world records; he was a splendid athlete and a thoughtful student at San Jose State, one of the young Americans caught in a rising tide of black awareness. This was the year that "Negro" fell out of favor and was replaced with "Black," uttered most often with defiance and pride. Julius Lester, a gifted African American author, had recently published a book with the taunting title, *Look out, Whitey! Black Power's Gon' Get Your Mama!*, and the poet Leroi Jones, who would change his name to Amiri Baraka (and later become poet laureate of New Jersey), had been sentenced to prison for possessing a gun during the Newark riots. To many black athletes, the Olympic games seemed like a perfect occasion to stand against the racism of their country.

But unrest in Mexico, the kind that terrified the government, also had indigenous roots. In the summer, students from Mexico's major universities were becoming restless. They admired their counterparts in other places—Germany, France, Czechoslovakia, Poland, but most of all the United States. In their growing concern about justice, their martyred heroes ranged from Martin Luther King to Che Guevara, and among the living they admired Pete Seeger and Joan Baez and the Black Power icons of California, Eldridge Cleaver and Angela Davis, who would soon begin teaching at UCLA. But the spark for the local protests was wholly unexpected. There was a fight between students at two Mexico City high schools, and on July 22 and 23, police and soldiers summoned to the scene began beating students and some of their teachers. A wave of demonstrations followed, and Mexico's president Gustavo Diaz Ordaz promised to crack down.

"We will do what we have to," he said.

On October 2, Mexican troops and police surrounded demonstrators at Thatelolco Square, an ancient area in Mexico City bordered by Aztec ruins. The police opened fire, and estimates of the death toll ranged from twenty to more than three hundred. As the president hoped, the student movement was temporarily cowed, and there were no demonstrations to mar the Olympics—none at least in the streets of the city. But inside the arena, black athletes from the United States seized the moment.

Sprinters Tommie Smith and John Carlos, winners of gold and bronze respectively in the two-hundred-meter dash, offered their own dramatic protest against American racism. On the medal stand as the national anthem played, each raised his black-gloved fist in a black power salute. It was a gesture both somber and grave, dignified in its defiance, but at the Olympic Village and beyond, it produced shockwaves of indignation. Both Smith and Carlos were banned from the games and ordered to leave.

"They said we had to get out of Mexico City in forty-eight hours," Carlos told the Associated Press.

In the United States, politicians and pundits condemned the pair's lack of respect for the flag and for the spirit of the Olympic Games, but the athletes stood firm. They refused to apologize for what Smith called their "human rights salute."

"Black America will understand what we did tonight," he said.

Jesse Owens, the African American hero of the 1936 games that were held in Adolph Hitler's Berlin, was on friendly terms with Smith and Carlos, but he worried about the swirl of Olympic politics. A generation earlier, to the consternation of Hitler, he had simply let his skills do the talking. Now, in Mexico where he was working as a broadcaster, he saw the controversy, perhaps inevitably, through the lens of his own experience.

"We don't need all this," he said. "We should just let the boys go out and compete."

But the sixties athletes had a different view. Silver medal winner Peter Norman of Australia, a young man born to working-class parents, wore a human rights badge on his jacket, and on the medals platform, he stood in solidarity with Smith and Carlos. Norman was white. (When he died in 2006, Smith and Carlos served as pallbearers at his funeral.)

Over the years, the Mexico moment became a legend in the history of sports—an affirmation in a shrinking world, often misunderstood at the time, of values that helped define a generation.

62

Earthrise

Christmas Eve found three Americans reading aloud from the Book of Genesis. They had given careful thought to their text, choosing poetry as majestic as any ever written—the voice of Man trying to find words for the moment of creation.

In the beginning God created the heaven and earth.

And the earth was without form and void; and darkness was upon the face of the deep.

And the spirit of God moved upon the face of the waters.

And God said, Let there be light: And there was light.

And God saw the light, that it was good: And God divided the light from the darkness.

These were not sentimental men reading these words. Frank Borman, Jim Lovell, and Bill Anders were astronauts, and at that moment they were farther from home than any human beings had ever been. They were circling the Moon.

Theirs was a mission of breathtaking risk. Even if everything worked as it should, the astronauts would be sitting atop a Saturn V rocket that looked more like a skyscraper than a spaceship. "It was a monument to human audacity," wrote Andrew Chaikin, author of *A Man on the Moon.* "By morning its enormous rocket fuel tanks would be filled with super-cold propellants, until the rocket would contain the explosive energy of an atomic bomb." Its horsepower, a measurement that now seemed quaint, having originated during the transition from horse and buggy to combustion engine, was estimated at 160 million.

The mastermind of this mighty ship was none other than the famous Wernher von Braun, who, as a young scientist in Germany, had designed the V-2 rocket for Adolph Hitler—a mission accomplished with the use of slave labor. Historians have debated the degree of von Braun's complicity in the Holocaust crimes, but it seems clear that even during the war, the scientist saw rocketry primarily as a pathway to space. After surrendering to Americans in 1945, von Braun got his chance to pursue that dream. Deemed by the U.S. government never to have been an "ardent" Nazi, he went to work in Huntsville, Alabama, becoming, in 1960, director of the Marshall Space Flight Center. When President Kennedy pointed America toward the Moon, von Braun and his team set out to build the rocket.

The Saturn V was their crowning achievement, but the rocket was only one part of the mission. On January 27, 1967, design flaws in the command module where the astronauts rode had caused a deadly fire that killed Gus Grissom, Roger Chaffee, and Ed White. Manned Apollo flights were put on hold until the summer of 1968 when the decision was made to send Apollo 8 around the Moon.

NASA was behind schedule. More and more, the Kennedy target of an American on the Moon by the end of the decade seemed unrealistic, and now it was feared the Soviets might get there first. Plans called for flight tests of the redesigned command module and a lunar lander that would eventually take astronauts to the surface. Problems with the lander, however, were causing delays, until in August, with morale sinking, NASA engineer George Low proposed a resumption of flights without the lander. He included in that audacious plan a December orbit of the Moon. It was a bold idea, a departure from script which sent waves of nervousness even through those most fearless of Americans, the astronauts themselves.

But NASA decided to attempt it. On October 11, as an intermediate step, Wally Schirra, Donn Eisele, and Walt Cunningham entered the new command module—a redesigned version of the one that had burned three of their brothers to death. Throughout their Apollo 7 flight, a ten-day earth-orbit test, the members of the crew were snappish and so grumpy, wrote Chaikin, that one of the engineers in Houston "offered, only half-jokingly, to bring Apollo 7 down into a typhoon." But if the crew was tense, the machinery was almost flawless. A launch date was set for Apollo 8: December 21, 1968.

On December 20, Borman, Lovell and Anders met with another aviation pioneer, Charles Lindbergh, who, in 1927, had made the first solo flight across the Atlantic. They talked about the limits of human achievement, and Lindbergh, one of Borman's boyhood heroes, still tall and tanned at sixty-six, spoke with a smile about the upcoming mission: "In the first second of your flight tomorrow, you'll burn ten times more fuel than I did all the way to Paris."

When the morning came, the liftoff was loud and perfect.

NASA's own account of the mission was written by Apollo director Samuel Phillips:

> In the pink dawn of December 21, a quarter million persons lined the approaches to Cape Kennedy, many of them having camped overnight. At 7:51, amid a noise that sounded from three miles away like a million-ton truck rumbling over a corrugated road, the first manned Saturn V, an alabaster column as big as a naval destroyer, lifted slowly, ever so slowly, from the sea of flame . . .

It took three days to get to the Moon, where the spacecraft immediately went into orbit, circling the dark side—from which no communication was possible. The silence lasted thirty-four minutes. When the module finally emerged, to cheers from the NASA ground crew, the three astronauts witnessed a sight no human had ever beheld: an Earthrise. There was their planet, some 40 percent of it still in shadow, the rest nearly heartbreaking in its beauty: blue and fragile and covered with clouds, floating alone against the darkness of space. It was then that the Apollo crew began to read.

"For all the people on Earth," said Anders, "the crew of Apollo 8 has a message we would like to send you." When he finished the first four verses of Genesis, Jim Lovell continued:

> *And God called the light Day, and the darkness he called Night. And the evening and the morning were the first day.*

Back on Earth we listened spellbound, for it was Christmas Eve and nobody had ever told the story this way—from 250,000 miles away, with a black and white image of our planet on the screen. When Lovell paused, Frank Borman, the stocky, crew-cut commander of the mission, brought the reading to a close:

> *And God said, Let the waters under the heaven be gathered together unto one place, and let the dry land appear: and it was so.*

When the mission ended after ten lunar orbits, and Apollo 8 returned safely to Earth, Madalyn Murray O'Hair, founder of a group called American Atheists, sued the U.S. government for violating her First Amendment rights. In effect, she said, these Bible-reading astronauts, as representatives of the state, had established an official religion for the country. The Supreme Court dismissed her suit. Most of us could not have cared less, for we were still in awe, transfixed now by a color photograph taken by Anders, far more dramatic than the black and white image on TV. Galen Rowell, a young Californian who soon became an award-winning *National Geographic* photographer, called *Earthrise* "the most influential environmental photograph ever taken."

What Rowell understood was that the photo became the ultimate illustration of a new force in America, a rising environmental consciousness that was on its way to becoming a movement. In 1968 much of it was cultural, reflected, for example, in the writings of poets like Wendell Berry, a Kentuckian who worked a family farm while publishing novels, essays and poetry. In February, at a conference in his home state, he delivered a statement about the war in Vietnam—about the human and environmental devastations, and how in the end they were the same. Speaking collectively of his country, he said:

> We seek to preserve peace by fighting a war, or to advance freedom by subsidizing dictatorships, or to "win the hearts and minds of the people" by poisoning their crops and burning their villages and confining them in concentration camps; we seek to uphold the "truth" of our cause with lies, or to answer conscientious dissent with threats and slurs and intimidations.

That same year in *Openings*, his latest book of verse, Berry published a poem titled "The Peace of Wild Things," reflecting on the lessons to be learned from nature: the inevitable interdependence of humankind and the natural world, which we seemed to regard as a lesser creation.

When despair for the world grows in me
and I wake in the night at the least sound
in fear of what my life and my children's lives may be,
I go and lie down where the wood drake
rests in his beauty on the water, and the great heron feeds.
I come into the peace of wild things
who do not tax their lives with forethought
of grief. I come into the presence of still water.
And I feel above me the day-blind stars
waiting with their light. For a time
I rest in the grace of the world, and am free.

Now on Christmas Eve of 1968, a year overflowing with the kind of despair that Berry wrote about, three space cowboys orbiting another celestial body had turned to poetry to describe what they saw, then gave us a history-changing image. Inevitably, their photograph began to call forth a greater understanding, a sense of the Earth now seen as a whole, vulnerable, in need of stewardship. It was a notion at the heart of the environmental movement that would gain new strength in 1969.

At the very least, as the current year came mercifully to an end, *Earthrise* felt like a heart-wrenching flicker of hope, a touch of beauty in an ugly time. A friend of Frank Borman's may not have overstated the case when he telegraphed the mission commander, "You have bailed out 1968."

PART III

The Unfinished Story

1969—"Bad Moon Rising": *Nixon's War, Black Panthers, Women's Liberation; A burning river, busing to desegregate; Men on the Moon, Chappaquiddick; Johnny Cash, Merle Haggard, Bob Dylan, Woodstock; The Stonewall riots, Charles Manson; Days of Rage, the Moratorium, revelations of My Lai; Death of a Panther, Hells Angels and the Rolling Stones; Alcatraz, an Indian Manifesto*

63

President Nixon

Another year and the war went on, and we wondered what Richard Nixon would do. On Inauguration Day, January 20, we were reminded that he was a polarizing figure. In his inaugural address he spoke of peace:

> For the first time, because the people of the world want peace, and the leaders of the world are afraid of war, the times are on the side of peace . . . The greatest honor history can bestow is the title of peacemaker. This honor now beckons America—the chance to help lead the world at last out of the valley of turmoil and onto that high ground of peace that man has dreamed of since the dawn of civilization.

The streets of the capital were full of people who didn't believe him. Not since the 1853 inauguration of Franklin Pierce had there been street demonstrations on the first day of a presidency, but David Dellinger, chairman of the Mobilization Committee to End the War in Vietnam, had put out the call. Along with the leaders of SANE and other pacifist groups, he promised a "political, not a physical confrontation." But Dellinger was not the only one making plans. Jerry Rubin and Abbie Hoffman, Yippie leaders whose organization, if it could be called that, had cheerfully pledged to pour LSD into the drinking water of Chicago, now declared their intention to inaugurate a pig. "The only honest candidate," they said.

Nobody knew what combination of street theater and serious protest the city of Washington should expect. The antiwar paper *The Free Press* urged demonstrators to "bring a lot of eggs, tomatoes, and rotten fruit." More ominously, on the night of January 18, a firebomb was hurled through a window at the national Selective Service headquarters, causing what police officials called "extensive damage." The Yippies did arrive with their pig—two pigs, in fact, and the female, Mrs. Pigasus, promptly escaped, leading to a thoroughly undignified chase through the capital. A group of women marchers tried to break through police lines guarding a reception for Distinguished Ladies, and at one antiwar rally, feminist leaders Shulamith Firestone and Marilyn Salzman Webb spoke about the women's movement in the country: "There are millions of women out there desperate enough to rise . . ." They were greeted with boos and hecklers (nobody was sure who the hecklers were, except of course that they were male) shouting "take it off," and "take her off the stage and fuck her."

It was an ugly time in America, and the ugliest part was the war that felt like a nightmare with no end. In 1968, even as Lyndon Johnson retreated from the bombing of North Vietnam in pursuit of peace talks, he had intensified U.S. bombing of Laos, where communist forces known as the Pathet Lao controlled a region called the Plain of Jars. It was a prosperous area before the bombing, home to roughly fifty thousand people in the northeast corner of the country. But as B-52s began to darken the skies, all the more so after Nixon was president, everything changed in that part of Laos. Georges Chapelier, a Belgian working for the United Nations, reported:

> By 1968, the intensity of the bombing was such that no organized life was possible in the villages. . . . Villagers moved to the outskirts and then deeper and deeper into the forests as the bombing climax reached its peak in 1969 when jet planes came daily and destroyed all stationary structures. Nothing was left standing. . . . In the last phase, bombings were aimed at the systematic destruction of the material basis of the civilian society.

Historian Marilyn Young estimated that "between 74,000 and 150,000 tons of bombs were dropped on the Plain of Jars from 1964 to 1969." Giving that reality a face, she quoted a teenaged refugee who described the way it looked from the ground:

> There were rice fields next to the road. At first, the airplanes bombed the road, but not my village. At that time my life was filled with great happiness, for the mountains and forests were beautiful; land, water, and climate were suitable for us. And there were many homes in our little village. But that did

> not last long, because the airplanes came bombing my rice field until the bomb craters made farming impossible. And the village was hit and burned. And some relatives working in the fields came running out to the road to return to the village but the airplanes saw them and shot them . . .

From there, the war moved into Cambodia. That nation's leader, Prince Norodom Sihanouk, had sought to walk a tightrope of neutrality, permitting Viet Cong sanctuaries on the border between his country and Vietnam that sometimes crossed the invisible line. In March, less than two months after his inaugural promises of peace, and shortly after a wave of rocket attacks on Saigon, Nixon ordered the bombing of those sanctuaries. When the Vietnamese retreated deeper into the forests of Cambodia, the American warplanes followed, dropping 110,000 tons of bombs in thirteen months. The bombing had little effect on the fighting in Vietnam, but its devastation strengthened the communist hand in Cambodia. About all of this, Richard Nixon said nothing—refusing even to inform Congress that the war had spread to another country.

At the same time, Henry Kissinger, his chief foreign policy adviser, ordered the National Security Council to study new ways of inflicting pain—what he called "a savage, decisive blow against North Vietnam . . .

"You are not to exclude the possibility," Kissinger said, "of a nuclear device being used for purposes of a blockade in the pass to China." He told his team that he refused to believe "a little fourth-rate power like North Vietnam does not have a breaking point."

On September 2, Ho Chi Minh, the architect of Vietnamese independence, died in Hanoi. The previous May he had published a poem, a testament to his abiding faith that there was, in fact, no breaking point.

Our rivers, our mountains, our
people will always be;
The American aggressors defeated,
we will build a country
ten times more beautiful

As the war raged on, Nixon explained to his aide Bob Haldeman how he thought it might finally end:

> I call it the madman theory, Bob. . . . I want the North Vietnamese to believe

> I've reached the point where I might do anything. . . . We'll just slip word to them that, "for God's sake . . . he has his hand on the nuclear button."

It seemed, in the end, to be the core of Nixon's character that cynicism defined his calculations; if that was true with regard to Vietnam, it was even more so in domestic politics. Shortly after his inauguration, as his attention turned to his own reelection, he came to believe—more than he had in 1968—that the key to his political future lay in exploiting the issue of race. Nixon's top domestic adviser was Daniel Patrick Moynihan, a brilliant and controversial figure who, in 1965, had angered many civil rights leaders with his views on the breakdown of the black family. While working for the Johnson administration, Moynihan, who had grown up as an Irish Catholic in the tough Hell's Kitchen neighborhood in New York before earning a doctorate in sociology from Tufts University, had written a report called *The Negro Family: The Case for National Action.* In it, he noted the rise of out-of-wedlock births—25 percent among African Americans at the time, as compared to 3 percent among whites. The result, he argued, was the emergence of a permanent black underclass, of households headed by Negro women who were addicted to welfare. The system was generous enough (although just barely) to create dependence, but stingy enough to keep people poor, and it formed the heart of dysfunction in the black inner city. There was too much crime, not enough work, and social instability was erupting every summer in the form of riots.

In Moynihan's view, racism was only one component of the problem; there were also self-inflicted wounds that the black community itself must solve, but the welfare system was making things worse. "Men must have jobs," he wrote. They must be able to support their families, and the system was undermining that goal.

Black leaders were incensed at Moynihan's presumption, a paternalism they thought was inherent in his emphasis on the black family. Who was he to lecture women about having babies without being married, or black men for not supporting their children? He was "blaming the victim" (a phrase coined specifically in response to his work). In 1967, Moynihan doubled-down and told a group of Democratic liberals that they must stop "explaining away" the problems of black America as nothing but the product of racism. Crime, disorder, and instability, he said, were a threat to the country—perhaps most especially to the black community—and liberalism did not have all the answers.

Not surprisingly, civil rights leaders found this disturbing. Here was a white man de-emphasizing the centrality of racism and giving academic cover to the cry for law and order—which had been, of course, code words for police brutality and repression.

Nixon's response to Moynihan was complex. The two hit it off well, and together they set out to craft a new policy on poverty and race. It was part of Nixon's makeup that he wanted to be known as a president who confronted tough problems. Sometimes in the privacy of his office he would write out lists of the adjectives he hoped would describe him. "Strong—in charge President," he wrote on one occasion, and on another: "Bold—gutsy initiatives."

In forging a policy toward black America, part of his focus was what he called "black capitalism," incentives and support from the federal government in support of minority entrepreneurs. He created the Office of Minority Enterprises, called for the government to set aside a fixed percentage of its contracts for minority-owned business, and instituted a plan for any business doing work for the government to establish goals for the hiring and promotion of minorities.

But, as Dan Carter has written, "the centerpiece of the Nixon program remained the Family Assistance Plan—a bold measure by any standard." What the president proposed, at Moynihan's urging, was a system of direct payments, like Social Security checks, to low-income families in which the parent or parents were willing to work, in order to insure a decent standard of living. The dual goal was to break the cycle of welfare dependence, while lifting such families out of poverty. For their own separate reasons, organizations as diverse as the U.S. Chamber of Commerce and the National Welfare Rights Organization opposed the plan, which never made it out of Congress. Nevertheless, it was, as historians have noted, an effort that deserved to be taken seriously. Whatever the flaws or strength of the plan, it was part of the reality of Richard Nixon that he did put forward serious proposals to address the problems of poverty and race.

There was, unfortunately, a different Nixon side, one that had more lasting effects. Some of Nixon's aides, including senior staffer John Ehrlichman, believed the president in his heart was a racist, a man who believed that blacks were "genetically inferior." (Some historians, sifting through the evidence, have wondered if that was Ehrlichman's projection of his own prejudice.) What *is* clear is that Nixon sympathized with the growing alienation of whites toward blacks—and with the disdain of working-class whites in particular toward the various forces of social protest.

There had been too many riots, and too much crime in the inner city, and too many young people disrespecting the country as they demonstrated against the war in Vietnam. In 1968 and '69, some of the nation's finest journalists—Marshall Frady, Pete Hamill, and Peter Schrag—were writing about the explosive disaffections of white America. Even at their most just, said Schrag, the racial changes being asked of the country were not easy, and the white working man in the nation's cities could not escape the growing implications. "And yet for a decade," Schrag wrote, "he is the one who has been asked to carry the burden of social reform, to integrate his schools and his neighborhood, has been asked by comfortable people to pay the social debts due to the poor and the black."

For Schrag and other liberal journalists, the point of their stories was to explore a serious problem in the country, a division that was badly in need of healing. In his presidential campaign, Robert Kennedy had sought to reach across the great divide, affirming the values all Americans shared. But Nixon was beginning to see a different possibility. One of his advisers in the 1968 campaign was a young conservative named Kevin Phillips, a graduate of Colgate University and the Harvard School of Law. Nearly everybody agreed that Phillips was brilliant, but some observers were otherwise unimpressed. In his generally scathing *The Selling of the President 1968* (which I remember reading gleefully in 1969), journalist Joe McGinniss offered an unflattering description of Phillips and the way he was viewed by other Nixon staffers.

> Kevin Phillips, the "ethnic specialist," was twenty-seven years old, pale and dour. He worked at a desk in the hallway because by the time he had been hired all the offices at headquarters had been filled.
>
> "It took awhile to get programmed," he said, "but I've been effectively plugged in since late August."
>
> This was how he always talked. Len Garment called him "The Computer." Roger Ailes swore he was stuffed with sawdust.
>
> "Essentially what I do is determine what blocs can be moved in what states by what approach," he said. "'Group susceptibility' I call it."

In *The Politics of Rage*, Dan Carter described Phillips "hurrying through the halls of Nixon headquarters, trailing reams of computer printouts and breathing a kind of clarified cynicism." Phillips was, said Carter, a darkly brilliant political strategist who once told author Garry Wills that the "secret" to politics was who hates whom. But perhaps it was even more basic than that. Perhaps the heart of the matter was fear, which by the end of the 1960s was the fertile soil in which hate took root.

"Phillips," wrote Carter, "bluntly recognized the critical role fear in general, and white fear of blacks in particular, would play in guaranteeing the emerging Republican majority."

Phillips's book on the subject (which he called, appropriately, *The Emerging Republican Majority*) was treated like scripture by the cynical men who surrounded Richard Nixon. Attorney General John Mitchell, a sour, unsmiling lawyer, spoke approvingly of "positive polarization" in the country. And Nixon himself, after reading Phillips's book, sent a memo to his inner circle:

> Use Phillips as an analyst—study his strategy—don't think in terms of old-time ethnics, go for Poles, Italians, Irish, must learn to understand Silent Majority . . . don't go for Jews & Blacks.

For the Republican Party, this became a turning point, a mutation in its ancient DNA. The party of Lincoln—that most idealistic of American pragmatists—became overnight a party of the coldest kind of cynicism. If Democrats like Kennedy, who saw the same divisions, labored valiantly, perhaps quixotically, to find common ground, the Republicans set out to do the opposite. The politics of fear became their key to the future, to energizing their political base. George Wallace had already shown them the way—too crudely, perhaps, to win a majority, but he had a gift for turning anger into votes—and the Republicans knew they could do it better. They could stir the fears of white Americans, embrace a simmering sense of grievance, and turn former Democrats into Republicans.

Thus the great, enduring division in America became what to do about division itself. Should we try to heal it, or should we exploit it? That was the new American dilemma, the new fault line in our politics, which served to make other divisions worse. For the next fifty years, it would be a problem that we did not know how to solve.

64

After Black Power, Women's Liberation

In February, Ronald Reagan found the perfect foil. Radical feminist Angela Davis took a teaching job as an assistant professor of philosophy at the University of California, Los Angeles. Davis was African American, born and raised in Birmingham in a part of town known as Dynamite Hill. The nickname was a darkly ironic reference by the area's black residents to the well-developed habit of the Ku Klux Klan of setting off bombs in the community where several black leaders lived. Angela heard the first of those explosions when she was only five years old. The year was 1949, and her family had recently moved from the housing projects in another part of town. They were excited about this new opportunity, this rambling wood house, not fancy but spacious, flanked by woods where children could play, full of blackberry bushes and wild cherry trees.

The neighborhood, with its sloping hillsides and red clay streets, had been all-white, and as black families began to move in, they were sometimes greeted with violence. "I was in the bathroom," Davis remembered, "washing my white shoelaces for Sunday School the next morning when an explosion a hundred times louder than the loudest, most frightening thunderclap I had ever heard shook our house. Medicine bottles fell off the shelves, shattering all around me. The floor seemed to slip away from my feet as I raced into the kitchen and my frightened mother's arms."

Her mother, Sallye Davis, was an elementary schoolteacher and a member of the NAACP, a woman who was willing to take her stand. But she was worried about her daughter—and not just her fear on the night of that first bombing. As the years went by, she could see the anger in Angela's eyes, which seemed to be her defining response to the unrelenting hostility of the white world around her. Sallye Davies believed that it didn't have to be.

Angela wrote in her autobiography:

> The more steeped in violence our environment became, the more determined my father and mother were that I, the first-born, learn that the battle of white against Black was not written into the nature of things. On the contrary, my mother always said, love had been ordained by God. White people's hatred of us was neither natural nor eternal.

During Angela's high school years, she won a scholarship from the American Friends Service Committee, the activist arm of the Quakers, to enroll in an integrated school in New York. There, living with the family of a white Episcopal priest and attending classes at the progressive Elizabeth Irwin High School, she read a library copy of *The Communist Manifesto* by Karl Marx. After she read it the first time, she read it again. Then again. Later she wrote about her reaction.

> Images surged up in my mind of Black workers in Birmingham trekking every morning to the steel mills or descending into the mines. Like an expert surgeon, this document cut away cataracts from my eyes. The eyes heavy with hatred on Dynamite Hill; the roar of explosives, the fear, the hidden guns, the weeping Black woman at our door, the children without lunches, the schoolyard bloodshed, the social games of the Black middle class, . . . the back of the bus, police searches—it all fell into place. What had seemed like a personal hatred of me, an inexplicable refusal of Southern whites to confront their own emotions, and a stubborn willingness of Blacks to acquiesce, became the inevitable consequences of a ruthless system which kept itself alive and well by encouraging spite, competition and the oppression of one group by another. Profit was the word: the cold and constant motive for the behavior, the contempt and the despair I had seen.

Her understanding grew deeper in the course of her studies, perhaps, in a sense, more doctrinaire, on her journey through Brandeis University, to a master's degree from the University of California-San Diego and a doctorate from Humboldt University in East Berlin. Both at Brandeis and UC-San Diego, Davis knew and studied under Herbert Marcuse, a German-American philosopher whose *One-Dimensional Man: Studies in the Ideology of Advanced*

Industrial Society was one of the seminal works of the 1960s. Davis saw him first in 1962 at a campus rally protesting the Cuban Missile Crisis. Marcuse shared the stage with the author James Baldwin, calling upon the United States to retreat from the shadow of nuclear holocaust that its policies were imposing upon the world. That was the view of Marcuse and Baldwin, and Davis agreed. She regarded with disdain the self-centered fright of her fellow Brandeis students. As one of only three black students in her class, she had nurtured, by her own admission, a petulant sense of alienation, and now she listened with cold contempt as her classmates romanticized about being young lovers slipping away to their rooms for a final moment of hedonistic pleasure before the bombs began to fall, or perhaps fleeing to Canada, further from ground zero.

Davis thought instead of the people of Cuba and their extraordinary vulnerability in that moment. Always, it seemed, she absorbed the tumultuous events of the sixties as the flesh-and-blood truth of her academic studies. She was abroad in France, reading the works of Jean Paul Sartre in the original French, when she learned of the 1963 Birmingham church bombing. Three of the murdered girls were friends of her family, and she personally knew one, Cynthia Wesley, a child of rare potential who had an air of sweet wisdom that was unexpected in a girl her age. All that was snuffed out in a moment of hate—violent lunacy, some said, probably by the Ku Klux Klan. But through the lens of Marx and the existential philosophers, it was more than that. This was a predictable, systemic act—the product of the greed and exploitation of white racism.

Davis was determined to understand such things. During her senior year at Brandeis, having attended one of Marcuse's classes, she summoned her courage and made an appointment to see him in his office. She asked him for a list of readings that might give shape to her philosophical studies, and thus began a relationship that deepened the roots of her radicalism. In his own works, Marcuse wrote of totalitarian structures in U.S. society, arguing, in effect, that America was not as free as it seemed. The capitalism that shaped our lives was fundamentally undemocratic, and our racism aggravated the problem. Davis fiercely believed this was true, and when she began her studies in California she became more deeply involved in radical organizing. She saw the foolishness of its fratricidal struggles—two Black Panther parties, for example, the Black Panther Party for Self-Defense and the Black Panther

Political Party, ready almost to go to war over which should hold title to the Panther name. Nor was that all. The sexism of some movement leaders, who told her that as a woman she should be content with supporting her man, stirred her emerging feminist awareness. But through it all, she was drawn to the promise of black liberation.

In July 1968, she joined the Communist Party. She paid her inaugural dues of fifty cents to the Che-Lumumba Club, an all-black cell of the Communist Party USA, based in Los Angeles. (The club was named for revolutionary martyrs Che Guevara and Patrice Lumumba, the latter the independence leader in the Congo who was assassinated in 1961.) Simultaneously, Davis was also a member of the Black Panther Party, and that particular resume caught the attention of Ronald Reagan when in 1969 Davis was hired to teach philosophy at UCLA. The governor understood the symbolism of doing battle with radicals; he had already taken on the antiwar and free speech forces at Berkeley, and now he discovered a target even more enticing—an unapologetic member of the Communist Party who was also an outspoken feminist and a leader in the struggle for black liberation. Almost everything about Angela Davis, even her appearance, spoke to the fears of white America. She was attractive, light-skinned, with smoldering anger in her large brown eyes and an Afro hairstyle (she called it a "natural") that made her look even taller than she was.

Citing a 1949 law barring communists from teaching in the state's universities, the California Board of Regents, at Reagan's urging, demanded to know in writing if Davis was a communist. She replied that she was, and the Regents fired her. The courts quickly overturned that dismissal, first with an injunction to reinstate her to her teaching job until the case could be heard on its merits—then a ruling that the California law was unconstitutional.

For Reagan, despite the setback, the episode was good politics, for here was a conservative governor standing firm against radicalism. For Davis, it was a nightmare. She worried about her family back in Alabama, for she was now a national figure, a symbol of liberation to some, an object of fear and hatred to others. Death threats became so common that after a while the campus police stopped checking for bombs beneath the hood of her car; Davis learned to do it herself. The chair of her department was assaulted by a man who burst into his office, and her sister Fania and brother-in-law Sam Jordan were charged with attempted murder when police stormed their apartment in San Diego and shot Jordan in the shoulder. Jordan fired back, and the police retreated, before moving back in and making the arrests.

After a flurry of headlines the charges were dropped.

As the tension mounted in California, a young man was working to build a Black Panther Party in Illinois. At twenty-one, Fred Hampton was already proving himself one of the gifted organizers in the Black Power movement—or as Davis and others preferred to call it, the struggle for black liberation. Even in his suburban Chicago high school Hampton had been an activist, leading a successful push for more black teachers at his racially integrated school. As a freshman at Triton Junior College, Hampton joined the NAACP and soon became president of a local youth branch. He worked to develop recreational facilities in black neighborhoods, coordinated an effort to send food and clothing to civil rights organizers in Mississippi, and in 1968, played the role of peacemaker when a riot erupted at his former high school.

"Fred Hampton," wrote Jakobi Williams in *From the Bullet to the Ballot*, "seemed to have an effect on all who came in contact with him."

By most accounts, Hampton was always persuasive one-on-one, possessing a personality that one friend described as "fearless, arrogant, and selfless." But his abilities as an orator were even more impressive, especially in a person so young. He studied the speeches of Martin Luther King and Malcolm X, while imitating neither, and in November 1968, when he moved from the NAACP to the Black Panther Party, he was chosen as its spokesman in Chicago.

Hampton was drawn to the Panthers' ideology of anger. As James Baldwin had written, "To be black and conscious in America is to be in a constant state of rage." In Oakland where the Party began, much of that rage was directed at police, who were regarded essentially as an occupying army. But the anger was not freestanding. There was in both California and Chicago an overlay of socialist theory, a belief that racism was essentially an ally of economic exploitation. The Chicago Panthers, therefore, named three targets for their organizing efforts, phrasing their intentions with the pedantic certainty of late sixties radicals. They would oppose the "greedy, exploiting, avaricious businessman," the "misleading, lying, tricky, demagogic politician," and the "atrocious, murdering, brutalizing, intimidating, fascist, pig cops."

Young people were their core constituency, as Hampton became a sought-after speaker on Illinois campuses. In appearances at Roosevelt University, wrote Jakobi Williams:

> Hampton explained to the audience that to join the Party, one had to endure a six-week process of mastering certain political ideological literature (*The Autobiography of Malcolm X*, *Quotations of Chairman Mao Tse-Tung* . . . and *Guerilla Warfare* by Che Guevara) . . . He concluded that the Panthers did believe in the teachings of Martin Luther King but did not believe in "preaching nonviolence to the Ku Klux Klan."

Much of the Panthers' actual work, including free food programs for hungry and malnourished children, seemed more humanitarian than radical. But the rhetorical package made it frightening, especially to authorities in Chicago. As Hampton and his comrades gained momentum, the Chicago Police and the FBI were paying close attention. They decided that Hampton had to be stopped.

Police officials in California reached the same conclusion, both in Oakland and Los Angeles. By the end of 1969, the hostility would escalate into cold-blooded murder.

ON MARCH 21, 1969, Gloria Steinem had what she calls an "aha moment," an epiphany about her own life as an activist. She had demonstrated against the war in Vietnam and in favor of the rights of African Americans and of Mexican farmworkers in California. But on this particular night she found herself part of a crowd in Greenwich Village, listening to women talk about abortion. She herself had undergone the procedure in 1957 when she was twenty-two years old and pregnant by a man with whom she had recently broken off an engagement. She was in England when she discovered her pregnancy and went to Dr. John Sharpe (to whom she later dedicated one of her books). She asked him to help her arrange an abortion, and Sharpe agreed on two conditions: first, that she not tell anyone about his involvement, and second, that once freed from a pregnancy she did not choose, she would make the most of her life.

"Without question," wrote Steinem biographer Carolyn Heilbrun, "the abortion, and the decision to take charge of her own life and to speak of the matter to no one, indicated a newfound self-sufficiency, a sense that her destiny could be in her own hands."

At the time, Steinem did not think of it that way. "I did my best to just forget," she said. But on the night twelve years later, as she listened to other women talk about their abortion experiences, she could not help reflecting on her own. She had attended the "Abortion Speak-Out" as part of her job. She was a regular contributor to *New York* magazine, where the editor, Clay Felker, routinely and remarkably gave assignments to women that were not yet available to them in other publications. In 1968, for example, Steinem had covered the Nixon presidential campaign, writing astutely about its meaning for the future:

> A banner read REGISTER COMMIES NOT GUNS. It suddenly seemed that we were surrounded by anti-life, conserving, neighbor-fearing people . . . and that the enemy was going to win. . . . It was the death of our future, and of our youth, because we might be rather old before . . . compassionate men came back.

All of this was important work, but now came the moment that transformed Steinem's life and the feminist movement as well. Steinem had decided to cover the Speak-Out partly out of fascination with its sponsors. In mid-February, a group of radical feminists called the Redstockings had disrupted a New York legislative hearing on the subject of the state's abortion laws. Called to testify were fourteen men and a nun, which the Redstocking leaders found absurd. Steinem had written about that protest in her *New York* column called "City Politic."

> Policemen resorted to the rather feminine tactic of hair-pulling today in order to get a group of very vocal women out of the meeting on Abortion Law Reform. The women, mostly under thirty, disrupted the meeting in fine style, wanting to know why there was only one woman called to testify ("and she's a nun"), and why the abortion laws weren't just repealed, instead of compromising on reforms.
>
> Florynce Kennedy, a lawyer and black militant at whose name strong white men shake, went into her specialty—creating a newsworthy side show to call attention to a good cause. "Listen," she said cheerfully. "Why don't we shoot a New York State legislator for every woman who dies from an abortion?"

Those were the days when abortion was illegal and therefore dangerous, often accomplished in questionable "back-alley" circumstances that put desperate women at risk. At the Speak-Out, held in the basement of Washington Square Methodist Church, Steinem listened raptly as women described their experiences. She was not the only journalist in the room. Susan Brownmiller, who would soon write the groundbreaking book on rape, *Against Our Will*, was there on assignment for *The Village Voice.* Brownmiller, too, thought of her own experience and later wrote about her own wave of emotion:

> My abortions, numbering three, were in the pre-*Roe* '60s; that is, they were secret criminal acts driven by desperation and reckless trust in the unknown.
>
> One image will suffice: a solitary young woman with not enough money in her pocket clutches a scrap of paper. She is in a Spanish-speaking city, in an unfamiliar neighborhood, and she does not know the language. When the gringa finds the shuttered house she is looking for she pounds on the door and cries, for this address is her last hope. A window opens and slams shut. Somebody opens the door. Ten minutes later she breathes deeply into the anesthetic, her life becomes her own again, and she will never learn her savior's name.

In "After Black Power, Women's Liberation," Steinem's provocatively titled essay in *New York*, published on April 4, she wrote analytically, more dispassionately, than Brownmiller, seeking first of all to put the Speak-Out into historical context:

> Redstockings, an action group in the Women's Liberation Movement, sponsors a one-act play about abortion by the New Feminist Theater . . . plus two hours of personal and detailed testimony—in public—by girls who have had abortions and Tell It Like It Is, from humor through sadism. Nobody wants to reform the abortion laws. They want to repeal them. Completely.

This, Steinem argued, was part of a new and radical awareness:

> The women behind it, and influenced by it, usually turn out to be white, serious, well-educated girls; the same sort who have labored hard in what is loosely known as the Movement, from the Southern sit-ins of nine years ago to the current attacks on the military-industrial-educational complex. They

> have been jailed, beaten and Maced side-by-side with their social-activist male counterparts. (It's wonderful to see how quickly police from Selma to Chicago get over a reluctance to hit women.) They have marched on Senate committees, Pentagon hawks, their own college presidents and the Chase Manhattan Bank. But once back in the bosom of SDS, they found themselves typing and making coffee.
>
> "When it comes to decision-making or being taken seriously in meetings," said one revolutionary theorist from Berkeley, "we might as well join the Young Republicans."

Steinem welcomed the changing state of mind, and argued that the common ground which united all women cut across divisions of race and class. The notion that they should control their own bodies—the most basic idea at the heart of the cry for legalized abortion—was something every woman, regardless of circumstance, knew and understood in her heart.

Norma McCorvey was proof of that point. She was, in 1969, a young woman of twenty-two, pregnant and living in Texas. In many ways, her life resembled those of the women who fifty years earlier had inspired Margaret Sanger's birth control movement. Working as a nurse in the slums of New York at a time when birth control was illegal, Sanger saw dozens of lives destroyed by pregnancies that women didn't want.

In the autumn of 1969, when she discovered her third and latest pregnancy, Norma McCorvey clearly fell into that category. She had had a summertime affair with an older man before taking a job with a carnival troupe. She was in Florida when she began missing periods, and she immediately rushed back to Texas, searching desperately for help. She did not want to have this baby.

Like the unnamed women who inspired a half-century search for the Pill, McCorvey, too, would remain mostly anonymous. Until later in her life, the world knew her only as Jane Roe, the unnamed plaintiff in the landmark case of *Roe v. Wade*. In 2017, when McCorvey died at the age of sixty-nine, newspapers like the *New York Times* and the *Washington Post* treated her passing as historic. But perhaps the most eloquent of the obituaries, the one that captured the tragedy at the heart of her story, appeared in the British magazine, *The Economist.*

> At ten she ran away from home to stay with a girlfriend in a motel. At 16 she married a man who took her for a ride in his black Ford car, but she left after two

> months because he beat her. She lived on the streets, slept with women and men, got pregnant by the men. Pot, acid, mescaline, she did it all. Work was whatever came along: barhop, carnival barker, house-painter, cleaner. She got involved in the whole abortion debate first on one side and then, when she took Jesus Christ for her personal saviour, on the other. That made her famous, though nobody knew who the regular Norma McCorvey was. And maybe they didn't care.

In her own account of her life, McCorvey recalled rapes by a relative when she was young, and babies given away through adoption, and lesbian relationships that were sometimes more stable than those with men. She was, she knew, an unlikely heroine in feminist lore, and seeing herself through the lens of a victim—the circumstance in which she so often lived—she felt used and discarded in the years to come by people on both sides of the debate.

This included her attorneys, Linda Coffee and Sarah Weddington, who she hoped could help her obtain an abortion. What the lawyers needed instead was a plaintiff who could not find one. McCorvey ultimately agreed to be that person, but she was driven to suicidal despair (she tried to kill herself, but failed) when she gave birth for a third time out of wedlock—and for a third time, gave away the baby to be raised by others.

Long after *Roe v. Wade* was decided, affirming in 1973 that a woman had the right to an abortion, McCorvey decided to embrace her hidden role in history. She would occasionally join Gloria Steinem and other leaders as a speaker for women's reproductive rights. She felt, however, that her lack of education and hard-scrabble background—and perhaps also the lesbian life that she had adopted—stood as a barrier.

Later still, she converted to evangelical Christianity, and then to Catholicism, and embraced the other side of the clashing imperatives. Unborn babies, she came to believe, were the most helpless of all human beings, possessing a beating heart, the ability to feel pain, and perhaps most importantly, a soul, a self, an elemental humanity that was being destroyed in the most brutal way.

Abortion would become, in American life, the ultimate unresolvable issue—the rights of the unborn versus the rights of the mother. Indeed in 1969, when the Redstockings gathered in the basement of a New York church, when Gloria Steinem and Susan Brownmiller wrote their articles about it, and when Norma McCorvey found herself pregnant, abortion was affirmed by its feminist defenders—as birth control had been a half century earlier—as one of the keys, not just to liberation, but to a woman's humanity. In May of that year, twelve women in Massachusetts met and formed the Boston Women's Health Book Collective. They began work on a series of essays and writings that were later published in a watershed book, *Our Bodies, Ourselves*—its title making a clear philosophical point. For every human being, body and self were inseparable, but this was especially true for women. The Boston writers spoke of "reproductive justice," by which they meant that a woman's ability to choose and manage the circumstances of pregnancy was inseparable from her ability to live her own life.

To the radicalized women of 1969, it didn't get any more basic than that.

If it was true that in that year, the women's movement found a new, more passionate footing, going beyond the writings of Betty Friedan, or the efforts of NOW to break down barriers to women in the workplace, it was also true that feminism discovered a star. At the very least, it found its most engaging spokesperson. Gloria Steinem was not only a gifted writer and committed activist, she was also a beautiful woman, and the national media couldn't help but notice. Fortunately for feminism, Steinem was skillful in framing the issues and indefatigable in pushing the case. Nor was she alone in those skills. On January 3, 1969, another charismatic woman stepped into history, and as dramatically as any of the others. Shirley Chisholm became the first black woman to take a seat in Congress.

The daughter of Caribbean immigrants, Chisholm was elected from a district in New York City. She was disappointed at first when she was assigned by the House leadership to a seat on the Agricultural Committee. What did a woman from Brooklyn know about farms? Actually, she had spent five years as a child on her grandmother's farm in Barbados, but the assignment had little relevance for her urban constituents. It felt like a back-handed slap. But when Chisholm shared her complains with Rabbi Menachem Schneerson, whom she had known since her days as an educator in Brooklyn, the Rabbi suggested that she use the assignment in support of food programs for the hungry. Chisholm immediately went to work, sometimes across the aisle with Republican Senator Bob Dole of Kansas, first to expand food stamps and then to create the Special Supplemental Nutrition Program for Women, Infants, and Children (WIC). Because of the Rabbi, she later said, "poor babies have milk and poor children have food."

In her work in Congress, Chisholm embodied two movements in one—civil rights and feminism—in the push for equality in the United States. Two years later she was a founding member of the Congressional Black Political Caucus and the Women's Political Caucus. In 1972 she entered the Democratic presidential primaries—the first woman to seek the nomination of a major party.

In her restless ambition, Chisholm became one of those women—with Angela Davis, Gloria Steinem, Norma McCorvey, the Redstockings, and others—who reminded the nation of its unfinished business. If there was truth in the analysis of Ronald Reagan and Richard Nixon that the great white majority was tired of change and suspicious of the unrest that produced it, the evidence mounted in 1969 that the movement was not over yet.

65

The Specter of Busing

It had been a while since the South was been on the cutting edge, and even now not everybody noticed. But in a federal courtroom in North Carolina, soft-spoken Judge James McMillan was considering a case with landmark implications. McMillan had not asked to be in this position. He was new to the bench, having spent most of his adult life, after graduation from Harvard Law School, as a respected lawyer in Charlotte. It was true that in his own quiet way he had been a racial liberal. His first encounter with integration, he explained, came at a swimming hole in Robeson County, farming country in eastern North Carolina where the population was equally divided among black, white, and Lumbee Indian. He and the other boys growing up there swam together at a place in the swamp they laughingly called "Naked Tail Beach."

"I didn't see any ill effects," said McMillan.

But if that had been his natural introduction to what he thought America must be—a place where people really knew each other, where they interacted daily in ordinary ways—the issue, he could see, was about to get a lot more serious. At lunchtime one day in March, he and his law clerk were sitting in a diner not far from the courthouse, and the judge was making notes on a napkin. He was listing some of the major points in a recently concluded hearing—a case called *Swann v. Charlotte-Mecklenburg*. It was a school desegregation lawsuit, and the attorney for the plaintiff, Julius Chambers, was emerging at age thirty-two as one of the boldest, most imaginative civil rights lawyers in the country.

In *Swann*, Chambers was seeking to expand the precedent of *Green v. New Kent County* in which the Supreme Court had ruled that it was not enough for school officials to end the active practice of segregation. They must take affirmative steps to *integrate*—to undo the measurable effects of dual schools.

The 1968 ruling in *Green* applied most directly to rural school systems that had only minimally desegregated. Charlotte, on the other hand, had done more than most Southern districts, and the affirmative remedy that Chambers had in mind might involve busing students across neighborhoods to increase the level of integration. That was how it appeared to McMillan, and he was reluctant to reach that conclusion; he knew that it could have major implications, not only for Charlotte, but for the whole country. Nevertheless, on this particular day in March, after making his scribbles on a restaurant napkin, he turned to his clerk, Fred Hicks, and said: "I don't see that there is any choice."

Some years later he told a reporter, "It took me a while to work up the courage." But McMillan did, and on April 23 he issued his ruling, He concluded, essentially, that assigning students to schools by geography instead of race, as Charlotte-Mecklenburg had been doing it, was not as color-blind as it seemed. The racial identity of the city's neighborhoods was a product not only of private discrimination or individual choice, but of a whole range of public policies from zoning codes and urban renewal to decisions over where to place public housing. All of this, said McMillan, though common in cities across the country, amounted to officially contrived segregation that now, according to the Supreme Court, had to be removed "root and branch." Addressing himself to the Charlotte school board, McMillan wrote:

> The Board accurately predicted that black pupils would be moved out of their midtown shotgun houses (through urban renewal) and that white students would continue to move generally south and east. Schools were built to meet both groups. Black or nearly black schools resulted in the northwest and white or nearly all white schools resulted in the east and southeast. . . .
>
> School boards are now clearly charged with the affirmative duty to desegregate "now" by positive measures. The Board is directed to submit by May 15, 1969, a positive plan . . . for effective desegregation of pupil population, to be predominantly effective in the fall of 1969 and to be completed by the fall of 1970. . . . The Board is free to consider all known ways of desegregation, including busing . . .

The latter sentence sent a chill through the country, at least among people who were paying attention. When the case made its way to the U.S. Supreme Court, as surely it would, what if the justices agreed with McMillan? Already, outside the South, hearts and minds were beginning to change. Writing in the otherwise liberal *New Republic* magazine, Alexander Bickel, a Yale law professor, concluded that most whites simply would not accept desegregation. Nor, said Bickel, was it even "fruitful to ask whether the whites behave as they do because they are racists, or because everybody seeks in the schools some sense of social, economic, cultural group identity."

Already, in the election of 1968, both George Wallace and Richard Nixon had done well in certain Northern areas because of a rising fear of integration—both in housing and in the public schools. Now a respected legal scholar was deliberately adding legitimacy to those fears. Nixon, no doubt, was happy for the cover, for he was firmly on record in his opposition to busing and all the possibilities it unleashed. He knew the latest order from a Southern judge could affect the level of integration nationwide.

Nevertheless, in 1969 and early the next year, as the *Swann* case made its way through the courts on appeal, Nixon resisted the urging of his most conservative speechwriter, Pat Buchanan, to deliver an address that would "tear the scab off the issue of race in this country." As always, Nixon was, in the words of biographer Evan Thomas, "a man divided." He was torn between his street-fighting, mud-wrestling political instincts and a lingering inclination to statesmanship that sometimes prevailed in public policy.

With regard to school desegregation, Nixon told his aides that it was essential to push forward in a measured way, despite the rhetoric of his own Southern strategy. It was about this time, on July 1, 1969, that Attorney General John Mitchell, puffing thoughtfully on his omnipresent pipe, famously sought to reassure a delegation of African Americans who were complaining about the administration's civil rights policies. He told them, with a cynicism they found chilling: "You would be better advised to watch what we do, instead of what we say." By Mitchell's watch-what-we-do measurement, there was some reason for reassurance. In a fair-minded summary of Nixon's accomplishments, Evan Thomas concluded:

> In 1968, 68 percent of black children in the South attended all-black schools. By 1972, only 8 percent did. There were fierce battles ahead over court-ordered busing, but Nixon had achieved a milestone in race relations. In August 1970, reflecting on what they had accomplished . . . and what still lay ahead, Nixon was philosophical. "There are no votes in the desegregation of Southern schools,"

he said, "and the NAACP would say my rhetoric was poor if I gave the Sermon on the Mount. But I'm a firm believer that the law must be carried out."

Nixon, however, strongly disapproved of how the Supreme Court as led by Chief Justice Earl Warren understood the law and applied the tenets of the U.S. Constitution. When Warren announced his intention to retire, and when it fell to Nixon to choose his replacement, he turned to a man he regarded as more conservative, a "strict constructionist." Warren Burger was a U.S. Appeals Court Judge in the District of Columbia, a solid, Midwestern Republican, sixty-one years old, who had been, like Earl Warren, appointed to his post by President Eisenhower. Burger sailed through his Senate confirmation, and on June 23, 1969, he took the oath to become Chief Justice.

Nixon expected an immediate, dramatic shift to the right on the Supreme Court. In this, he was disappointed. Most significantly, as Charlotte, North Carolina, wrestled with Judge McMillan's busing order, Burger prepared to hear the case and would write in 1971 a landmark opinion affirming the district judge. It was, in many ways, the high-water mark in the legal push for civil rights, and it launched the country on an epic struggle with the issue of integrating its schools.

In Charlotte, where the stakes increased exponentially in 1969, the struggle was filled with redemption and hope, as a Southern community sought to come to terms with its segregated past. There was trouble at first—threats on the life of Judge McMillan, racial fighting in the local high schools, but within a remarkably short amount of time the community was able to make its peace. For the next twenty years, it would operate one of the most integrated school systems in the country, bearing witness to mountains of educational research that proved, as one scholar put it: "Avoiding socio-economic and racial isolation benefits all students."

Not every city was able to embrace that news. Some, including Boston and Louisville, were simply overwhelmed by resistance and conflict, and almost everywhere, as the decade moved toward a turbulent end, everybody knew it was going to be hard.

The bedrock issue of public education became, in 1969, one more uncertainty in an uncertain time.

66

The Burning River

At the midpoint in a year of unresolved issues, something truly extraordinary happened. On June 22, the Cuyahoga River caught fire. This occurred as the river flowed through Cleveland, and a spark from a passing train landed on a piece of oil-soaked debris. It was not the first industrial fire on the Cuyahoga's polluted surface. In 1952, the Associated Press published dramatic photos of billowing smoke, and flames dancing ominously on the surface of the water while a fireboat worked to put them out. In the torrent of national coverage, *Time* actually ran one of those archival images in its report on the blaze of 1969.

Many Clevelanders were puzzled. Why such fascination by editors? There had been at least a dozen Cuyahoga conflagrations through the years, and this one, explained Fire Chief William Barry, was "a run of the mill fire." But the context had changed, for the nation in the 1960s had become increasingly aware of environmental issues. Since the watershed writings of Rachel Carson, especially *Silent Spring*, there had been a slowly emerging movement, an increasingly politicized concern about what was happening to the natural world.

On August 23, 1968, *Life* had published a disturbing portrait of pollution in the Great Lakes, particularly Lake Erie, the destination toward which, in the words of *Life*'s sister periodical, *Time*, the Cuyahoga "oozes rather than flows." The *Life* spread featured full-color images of algae and slicks of oil and beach signs warning of polluted water. In the accompanying article, journalist Richard Woodbury warned about what was ultimately at stake.

> The photos on these pages point to the appalling conclusion that water pollution has brought the U.S. to a point of no return: either we curb the slatternly despoiling of our environment, or we accept the death of lakes and rivers and the denigration of the quality in our life. The choice is obvious, but expensive

> to implement; the $15 billion price tag on a Great Lakes cleanup comes from Secretary of the Interior Stewart Udall. At the present rate of weed growth, Lake Erie will become a Sargasso Sea within the lives of our children; already a foot-deep mat of algae covers several hundred square miles of Erie. But it is within man's competence to restore Erie, avert biological disaster in Michigan and Ontario and preserve Huron and Superior.

Philosophically, this was a message that the country was ready to hear. In addition to the warnings of Rachel Carson, which helped launch a nascent environmental movement, the consciousness had moved to the realm of aesthetics. In the poetry of Kentuckian Wendell Berry, the musings of California Buddhist Alan Watts, and the photographs of Earth sent back from Apollo 8, it seemed clear enough that a collective imagination had been tapped. The images of a burning river stirred not so much a feeling of revulsion as a feeling of purpose. Partly because of the work of Secretary of the Interior Udall, appointed by Kennedy and serving until the beginning of the Nixon administration, many were coming to believe that changes in policy could make a difference. In addition to his efforts to expand public lands (ten new national parks and monuments, eight national seashores and lakeshores, and fifty-six new national wildlife refuges), Udall worked hard for new environmental legislation. He supported the passage of the Clean Air Act, the Water Quality and Clean Water Restoration Acts, the Land and Water Conservation Fund, and the Wild and Scenic Rivers Act, among others.

In a retrospective on the Cuyahoga fire of 1969 and the changing times in which it occurred, *Time* later wrote, "It was the disaster that ignited an environmental revolution." But the magazine tempered that conclusion, quoting the *Washington Post* on the progress that had already occurred:

> The reality is that the 1969 Cuyahoga fire was not a symbol of how bad conditions on the nation's rivers could become, but how bad they had once been. The 1969 fire was not the first time an industrial river in the United States had caught on fire, but the last.

By 1969, no one was more heartened by the burgeoning awareness than Senator Gaylord Nelson of Wisconsin. Nelson was a progressive Democrat, raised in the North Woods of his state, and imbued with a love of the great outdoors.

He was still a young man when the sixties began, one year older than President John Kennedy, sharing with the new president a sense of boundless promise for the country. It was a legacy in part of World War II, when Kennedy, Nelson, and other men in their twenties had gone to war for the noblest of reasons. They had come home fully aware of the horrors, eager for peace, but filled with optimism about the future. For four years ending in 1963, Nelson had served as governor of his state—"the conservation governor," in popular lore, working to expand public lands and put an end to environmental degradation. When he came to Washington as a U.S. senator immediately after stepping down as governor, he supported the liberal legislation of Kennedy and his successor, Lyndon Johnson, including civil rights bills and the War on Poverty. But Nelson, it seemed, always saw things through the lens of the environment.

"Environment is all of America *and* its problems," he said. "It is rats in the ghetto. It is a hungry child in a land of affluence. It is housing not worthy of the name; neighborhoods not fit to inhabit."

It frustrated Nelson that other politicians did not see it that way. He did his best to persuade his colleagues in the Senate that they were lagging behind their constituents on environmental concerns. In his last year as governor, he had traveled to Washington to talk to John and Robert Kennedy about a national conservation tour by the president. Both brothers were receptive. John Kennedy was already worried about such environmental issues as nuclear fallout, and he had read and put his stamp of approval on Carson's *Silent Spring*. But Kennedy's five-day, multi-state tour did not have the galvanizing effect that Nelson had hoped. Thus, the senator continued his lonesome crusade. He could see bits and pieces of progress, the beginnings of environmental legislation and the sympathetic leadership of Stewart Udall, and he could sense rising concern in the country. But the environmental devastations continued.

On January 28, 1969, a blowout at Union Oil Company's Platform 5 off the coast of Santa Barbara, California dumped three million gallons of crude oil into the Pacific. It was the largest oil spill in the country's history (later to be surpassed by the *Exxon Valdez* in Alaska and *Deep Water Horizon* in the Gulf of Mexico). Beginning six miles off the coast, a massive oil slick began drifting toward the California beaches, killing thousands of birds and sea mammals and confronting the nation with the dangers of offshore drilling. As the story unfolded, it became clear that Union Oil had taken a shortcut. Having acquired an exemption from the U.S. government, the company used less steel casing than normally required on the sides of the well, which reached a depth of more than 3,000 feet beneath the ocean floor. When the well blew, attempts to plug the leak from the top increased the pressure further down, and a massive subterranean flood of oil soon made its way to the waters above. The story of malfeasance combined with the optics—images of floating seal carcasses and oil-covered birds and tarlike mats of oil on the beaches—prompted outrage, especially in California, where among other measures of public concern, membership in the Sierra Club doubled.

Not surprisingly, Gaylord Nelson shared that dismay. In the summer after the Cuyahoga River fire, he visited Santa Barbara, where the oil cleanup was still underway. It was the starting point of an environmental speaking tour that stretched from southern California to Seattle, and on his cross-country flight, Nelson began musing about how to galvanize public support for new environmental legislation. He recalled the antiwar teach-ins that had helped raise awareness a few years earlier. He, too, had opposed the war in Vietnam, and he thought the teach-ins had been effective. Already, several colleges, including the University of Michigan, a pioneer in those early antiwar protests, were planning similar events regarding the environment.

On September 20, at a speech in Seattle, Nelson proposed what he called Earth Day, a national time of discussion, protest and celebration, building on ideas that college students had already announced. Nelson, balding, earnest, ordinarily a quieter presence than some of his Senate colleagues, would later describe his excitement in the moment: "The wire services carried the story from coast to coast. The response was electric. Telegrams, letters, and telephone inquiries poured in from all across the country. The American people finally had a forum to express concern about what was happening to the land, rivers, lakes, and air—and they did so with spectacular exuberance."

On November 30, five months before the event, the *New York Times* reported on the grassroots momentum:

> Rising concern about the environmental crisis is sweeping the nation's campuses with an intensity that may be on its way to eclipsing student discontent over the war in Vietnam . . . a national day of observance of environmental problems . . . is being planned for next spring . . . when a nationwide environmental 'teach-in'. . . coordinated from the office of Senator Gaylord Nelson is planned. . . .

There were few dissenting voices. (The John Birch Society did worry that the date for Earth Day, April 22, 1970, was a covert celebration, communist-inspired, of the hundredth birthday of Vladimir Lenin.) With bipartisan support—Nelson's co-chair was Republican Congressman Pete McCloskey of California—the first Earth Day drew twenty million participants and led directly to the creation of the Environmental Protection Agency as well as new clean air and water legislation. Part of the credit lay in the organizing skills of Denis Hayes, a twenty-five-year-old former antiwar activist from Stanford, who had gone from there to Harvard's Kennedy School of Government. Nelson chose Hayes as staff coordinator for Earth Day, and under his leadership through the years the concept spread to more than 180 countries. But in many ways, the coordination that first year was easy. As the Earth Day Network later explained, in its official history of the event, there was in 1969 a spontaneous recognition of common ground: "Groups that had been fighting against oil spills, polluting factories and power plants, raw sewage, toxic dumps, pesticides, freeways, the loss of wilderness, and the extinction of wildlife suddenly realized they shared common values."

Earth Day, concluded Gaylord Nelson, "organized itself."

I remember the excitement of that time—and remember also that my own emerging environmental awareness had a personal source. In Mobile, Alabama, my uncle Wilson Gaillard was an old-line conservationist, a bespectacled nature lover who lived on a wooded, five-acre tract that he let grow wild, a tangle of underbrush and trees where birds and small mammals could thrive on the outskirts of the city. As an avid bird-watcher, he had spent a lot of his time on Dauphin Island, a spit of sand near the mouth of Mobile Bay that was part of a string of barrier islands stretching from Florida to Texas. The whole chain played a critical role in the ecology of the northern Gulf of Mexico, and none more so than Dauphin Island when it came to bird life. It lay, as Uncle Wilson knew, precisely in the center of the great flyway for virtually every species of bird in the eastern United States. Even hummingbirds came to the island to gorge for several days before setting off on an uninterrupted, four-day flight across the Gulf to Central and South America. The problem in the early 1960s was that rapid development on Dauphin Island threatened to eradicate the dune-protected forest of oak and pine from which the birds began their flight.

Patiently, my uncle, one of the most kind-hearted men I ever knew, began an effort to preserve these marshy woodlands. By 1967 he and a group of conservationist friends reached an agreement with the National Audubon Society, one of the country's oldest environmental organizations, to operate a bird sanctuary. "Imagine a world without the song of a bird," he said. The following year, he wrote a short book, *Moving the Earth for a Song,* about his efforts and about the urgency of conservation.

"It is late, yet not too late," he declared, "to make this land a better and more fruitful place in which we and future generations may live in harmony with nature." His views were rooted in his Presbyterian theology, a traditional understanding of the Genesis story, giving human beings dominion over other forms of life. He regarded this Biblical narrative not as a license for exploitation, but as a call for stewardship—proof of a gift to be diligently preserved. All of this fit with his natural conservatism, an instinct for maintaining things as they were, which had often run counter to the spirit of the sixties. My uncle and I had argued about this on other occasions, gently, respectfully, with regard to other issues, including poverty and civil rights. But now we found ourselves in agreement. The environment was the issue that crossed old divides.

Yet it was also more complicated, for it was the place, philosophically, where the ground began to shift beneath our feet. The *Earthrise* photo from Apollo 8 may have let us see the world as one, something that had never happened before, thus revealing its beauty in a way that was new. We could feel what the astronauts felt in that moment, that this was a planet in need of our care, for there it was, hanging fragile and alone, a flyspeck against the vastness of space. The stark emotional truth of that reality—of how *small* we were in the great scheme of things—was as unsettling as it was unifying. We had never had occasion to *see* it.

EVEN AS WE WERE absorbing all of this, forced to reflect on our place in the cosmos, other research raised new questions about our place in the order of things. Were we as different as we thought from other forms of life? Were we really, as our Sunday school teachers had always taught us, set apart as the ultimate act of creation? One unexpected source of these troubling questions that lingered vaguely in the back of our minds was the National Geographic Society. Founded in 1888 in Washington, D.C., the society was led at the turn of the twentieth century by Alexander Graham Bell, inventor of the telephone. Its signature publication, *National Geographic*, released its first issue in 1888 and soon became one of the most popular periodicals in the world, with dramatic photography and stories and a broad array of interlocking interests—geography, archaeology, natural science, conservation, world history, and culture—amounting to this: the interwoven story of humanity and nature.

The Geographic Society also sponsored various scientific research, including the remarkable work of Jane Goodall. In 1960, at age twenty-five, she began her legendary study of wild chimpanzees in Tanzania. Three years earlier, she had made her first trip to the African continent, having dreamed of such adventures since her mother had given her a stuffed toy chimpanzee when she was a year old; as an adult, she still kept it with her. On her initial visit to Africa, she met Louis Leakey, the famous anthropologist, who seemed quite taken with this shy and slender young woman and hired her to be his secretary. He took her to the Olduvai Gorge, where ancestors of modern human beings had found a final resting place, and he began to talk to Goodall about his plans to study chimpanzees. He wanted somebody who would try to live in close proximity with them, quietly, winning their trust, the better to observe their natural behaviors. Because of Goodall's self-sufficient demeanor, it did not matter to Leakey that she did not yet have a college degree. (Later, she would earn her doctorate from Oxford University, but only after she began her groundbreaking study.)

Goodall set up camp at Lake Tanganyika in the Gombe Stream Reserve, accompanied first by her mother, and later by *National Geographic* photographer Hugo van Lawick, with whom she fell in love and then married. Mostly alone, in a monumental display of patience, Goodall ventured into the forest and began the observations that would change our understandings of an animal species, of the nature of science itself, and for some, of what it means to be human. Perhaps the most remarkable thing was that in her first few months in the mountainous outback of Tanzania, Goodall did not simply give up.

Writing first in a doctoral dissertation in 1965, and later, more elegantly in a book, *In the Shadow of Man*, she described the fear her presence evoked when she first tried to contact the chimps. Week after week for more than six months, she made lonely treks through the woods, sometimes catching sight of the apes, who would, invariably, bound away in terror. Finally, one day around dusk, she came upon two male chimps whom she had seen before. She had given them names. David Graybeard had always been the boldest of the group, more curious about this female intruder and her daily wanderings into their domain. On this particular afternoon, David was sitting with another male that Goodall had named Goliath. Now, barely twenty yards away, they stared at her intently and then began to groom each other. She wrote:

> Their coats gleamed vivid black in the softening light of the evening.
>
> For more than ten minutes David Graybeard and Goliath sat grooming each other, and then, just before the sun vanished over the horizon behind me, David got up and stood staring at me. And it so happened that my elongated evening shadow fell across him. The moment is etched deep into my memory: the excitement of that first close contact with a wild chimpanzee and the freakish chance that cast my shadow over David even as he seemed to gaze into my eyes. Later it acquired an almost allegorical significance, for of all living creatures today only man, with his superior brain, his superior intellect, overshadows the chimpanzee. Only man casts his shadow of doom over the freedom of the chimpanzee in the forests with his guns and his spreading settlements and cultivation. At that moment, however, I did not think of this. I only marveled in David and Goliath themselves.

Some scientists questioned Goodall's methods. The very act of giving names to her subjects was, more traditional researchers believed, a lapse in her clinical objectivity. Better simply to give them numbers, for wasn't the whole purpose of her undertaking to observe chimpanzee behavior in the wild? Names implied something akin to humanity, which could bias her observations, causing her to project human qualities that were not there. Goodall confidently disagreed. The greater bias, she thought, lay in objectifying living things. As almost any pet owner could attest, animals had traits of personality and the ability to bond and display affection, and it would defy common sense to expect that wild chimpanzees would not. As time went by and her observations became more intimate, she was sure her initial assumptions were correct. These, quite clearly, were sentient beings. They formed deep attachments to one another and the social hierarchies in which they lived rewarded intelligence and problem-solving skills just as surely as brute strength. In addition to their diet of plants, they were also hunters and ate meat, which regularly ranged from termites to monkeys. They hunted cooperatively, sometimes finding a lone monkey in a tree, blocking all possible paths of escape and then moving in for the kill. And they used tools, something behavioral scientists had assumed was a skill only of man. But Goodall observed her subjects carefully inserting a blade of grass or a folded leaf into a termite habitat and withdrawing it slowly, eating the termites from the leaf as if it were a spoon. They threw rocks as weapons, and later—much later—in her studies, she watched with horror as disputes within a troop of chimpanzees caused them to wage a kind of civil war. It was again, more darkly, a pattern of behavior previously thought to be exclusively human.

Other researchers followed with studies of other species—gorillas, dolphins, parrots, elephants, even that most clever of mollusks, the octopus—and researchers again and again were struck by the level of intelligence and the depth of feeling possessed by their subjects. By the 1970s, an animal rights movement was spreading from England to the United States, both as a branch of ethical philosophy and as a focus of political activism. Jane Goodall expanded her work from the study of chimpanzees to a broad agenda of conservation based on a simple and fundamental premise: "Everything is connected. Everyone can make a difference."

Even amid a flood of global accolades, there was controversy about Goodall's work. Christian fundamentalists were offended by her observation that behavioral similarities between humans and chimpanzees provided further evidence of a common ancestor. Scientific theories of evolution reemerged as a focus of religious scorn, and within a few years political conservatives in the United States began to push back against environmental regulation—the legacies of Goodall, Gaylord Nelson, and all the other environmental pioneers. But for a time at the end of the 1960s, we were forced to contend with a basic idea that had profound implications for the future. We really are our planet's keeper.

67

Stonewall

From April until November of 1968, there was a sense of time having stopped, of treading water and wondering if we might slip beneath the surface of our rising grief and disillusionment and rage—and if it might be better that way. But 1969 was not like that. Rather, there was a feeling of everything moving quickly, though in which direction we could not be sure. So many things were happening at once. The radicalization of the women's movement, the specter of busing, the cry for Black Liberation, environmentalism, Nixon and the war, the protests against it—and now in June, there came a protest as wholly unexpected as any the country had ever seen. Unexpected, that is, among those of us who were not gay.

In New York City, during the early morning hours of June 28, police raided a homosexual bar in Greenwich Village, a place known as the Stonewall Inn, which would literally become a national monument to gay rights. In 1969, it was merely a place where gays could go in an era when being gay was a crime—and when police in New York and other places took delight in random acts of brutality. On June 28, the Stonewall clientele fought back, and the "rioting," as it was described at the time, erupted off and on for several more days. This came at a time of increasing militancy and discontent, a rising identity among many different groups who felt themselves pushed to the margins in America. Blacks and women were the most obvious, but in California Cesar Chavez's farmworker strike had become a national symbol for Mexican-Americans and other minorities. Filipinos and blacks were also part of the farmworkers' movement, which, in 1969, became linked to other causes, including the environment and the war in Vietnam.

Chavez and his union went to court to challenge the use of pesticides by California's grape growers, especially the dangerous, long-lasting DDT, which would later be banned. At the time, a California judge ruled against the union, concluding that while such chemicals might indeed be "highly toxic," the motive of Chavez and his followers was primarily to "keep alive controversy. . . ."

Meanwhile, the Nixon administration intervened on behalf of the growers by seeking to break the union's consumer boycott of grapes. Specifically, the administration detected a surge in the appetite for grapes among U.S. troops in Vietnam. The Defense Department increased its order from 6.9 million pounds in 1968 to 11 million pounds in 1969, quadrupling its shipments to Vietnam.

For those involved in radical protests, all of this added to a mounting sense of rage, an intensified feeling among Americans on the margins that the game was rigged; the courts, the corporations, the president himself were collaborators in the cynical pursuit of wealth. Despite its protestations to the contrary—its lip service, for example, to a war on poverty or the quest for civil rights—America was where the rich got richer, and everything else was just noise.

Some people thought the cynicism cut both ways. In the summer of 1969, journalist Tom Wolfe was at work on an article he called "Mau-Mauing the Flak Catchers," in which he argued that radical activists in California also regarded their protests as a game—a contest where militancy became an end in itself. As Wolfe saw it, the game had multiple players—blacks, Mexicans, Filipinos, Samoans, all of whom were engaged in a cheerful attempt to terrorize federal bureaucrats. Their staging ground was a summer jobs program, with radicals competing to see who could win the most jobs for their own group. Not that anybody cared about the jobs, for they didn't pay much, and the people who got them were seldom conscientious about the work. As far as Wolfe could see it was all about the status, the thrill of bullying bureaucrats into submission. He called it "mau-mauing," a description with its share of racial overtones in which Wolfe clearly took some delight.

> . . . there was some fierce mau-mauing that went on over summer jobs, especially in 1969, when the O.E.O. started cutting back funds and the squeeze was on. Half of it was sheer status. There were supposed to be strict guidelines determining who got the summer jobs—but the plain fact was half the jobs were handed out organization by organization, according to how heavy your organization was. If you could get twenty summer jobs for your organization,

> when the next organization got only five, then you were four times the aces they were . . . no lie . . . but there were so many groups out mau-mauing, it was hard to make yourself heard over the uproar. You practically had to stand in line. It was a situation that called for a show of class. You had to show some style, some imagination, some ingenuity.

As a generalization, the American left didn't care for Tom Wolfe, finding him too smug to be taken seriously. *Ramparts*, the voice of radicalism, soon published an article called "Reactionary Chic," in which it mocked Wolfe's preoccupation with style (including his habit of wearing white suits: "his patented Tom Wolfe vanilla ice cream suit . . .") What Wolfe lacked, in the view of his critics, was the final grounding of empathy and heart, the preoccupation with justice, that defined the work of such great journalists as Pete Hamill, Willie Morris, and David Halberstam. The problems of the country were too serious, the alienations too real, for Wolfe's sarcasms to be anything more than a sideshow for people who needed to be entertained. Even if it was true that the anger among American minorities, ethnic or otherwise, was hardening into a cynicism vastly different from the idealism with which it began, Wolfe's inclination to trivialize struck many radicals as callous. Their sense of grievance ran too deep.

Nowhere was that grievance more profound than in the homosexual community. These were Americans who faced discrimination and scorn, but more than that, the criminalization of their very existence whenever they came together in public. In most of the country, homosexual sex was still a crime. Even *agreeing* to such an act could lead to arrest, and police brutality was an everyday threat. In such a climate, thousands of gay men and women tried to live a double life, hiding their identities from the rest of the world. By the sixties, however, some resisted that crippling decision. In San Francisco, which *Life* in 1964 dubbed "the gay capital of America," a civil rights organization called the Society for Individual Rights (SIR) published the magazine *Vector* and argued against the idea that homosexuality should be kept secret. In 1966, three years before Stonewall, a group of transgender women and gay men fought with police and staged demonstrations in what became known as the Compton Cafeteria Riot. Increasingly, by the mid-sixties gay San Franciscans found the courage—some might say, the audacity—to be who they were.

Artists often led the way. In California, poets like Allen Ginsberg or the lesbian writer Elsa Gidlow, who lived in Muir Woods, made no apology for their sexuality. Back east, such Harlem artists as Bessie Smith and Jackie "Moms" Mabley had publicly acknowledged same-sex relationships, and novelist Truman Capote was not only gay, but also effeminate and boastful about his sexual prowess. "Truman says he can get anyone he wants," remembered artist Andy Warhol, who added wistfully, "I don't want anyone I can get."

Warhol was born in 1928 of immigrant parents in Pittsburgh. In the 1950s he painted male nudes, and in 1955 his first exhibition of overtly homosexual drawings received mixed reviews in New York. Warhol was living in Greenwich Village where he soon became a part of what one biographer called "New York's gay elite, a very discreet, not to say clandestine, scene." In those days Warhol mostly labored in obscurity, a condition that changed abruptly in 1962 with a show at the Ferus Gallery in Los Angeles—thirty-two portraits of Campbell's soup cans. The outrageousness of it made Warhol a pop icon, but also a controversial figure. It was as if he were jeering, some people said, belittling the very idea of art. It was a curious fact that in Warhol's sudden explosion of fame (everybody, he said, deserved their fifteen minutes), many who debated his art had never actually seen it. As critic G. J. Nicholson noted, you didn't really have to.

Warhol added to the mystery of his persona by claiming that there was none, no particular passion, not even any sense of artistic mission. "Paintings are too hard," he told *Time*. "The things I want to show are mechanical. Machines have less problems. I'd like to be a machine. Wouldn't you?"

At times he seemed content to skim the surface of popular culture, with paintings of dollar bills, cartoon characters, and Coke bottles—and portraits of Elvis and Marilyn Monroe. But there were also reminders of another sensibility: his portrait of a grieving Jacqueline Kennedy, his images of the electric chair, race riots, the atom bomb—an iconography of American violence.

On June 3, 1968, he became a victim of that violence himself. An angry feminist, Valerie Solanas, who had founded SCUM, the Society for Cutting Up Men, came to him with a movie script she wanted him to produce. She called it *Up Your Ass.* Warhol was intrigued, but when he lost the script and balked when she asked him to pay for it, Solanas pulled out a pistol and shot him. The wounds were serious, resulting in the removal of Warhol's spleen, and as Nicholson wrote, "The story would no doubt have run longer in the media had it not been rapidly replaced by another shooting, the assassination of Robert Kennedy."

Throughout Warhol's eventful life (in 1987, he died at the age of fifty-eight), there was always the fact that he was gay. His legacy lay in being an artist, but his life was set in a pivotal time. It was still the case in the 1960s that even people who should have known better refused to embrace the dignity of homosexuals. Betty Friedan, president of the National Organization for Women, warned darkly in 1969 of the "lavender menace," by which she meant the presence of lesbians in the feminist movement. Earlier, she had written of "homosexuality that is spreading like a murky smog over the American scene." By 1977, Friedan had repudiated her own homophobia and pledged her support for lesbian feminists. But her views in 1969 caused bitter divisions. Rita Mae Brown, a popular author who was also a lesbian, resigned in protest from her administrative job at NOW.

It is not surprising, in retrospect, that feelings of alienation would one day explode, or that the explosion might come at the Stonewall Inn. There were few cities more oppressive than New York when it came to citizens who were gay. Mayor John Lindsay had ordered an end to police entrapment procedures—undercover officers engaging a man in conversation, trying to steer the verbal exchange toward a homosexual encounter, then making an arrest. Even with the scaling back of that practice, police raids on gay bars, including the Mafia-run Stonewall, were routine. Stonewall had its own protocol—lights turned up at the sign of a cop and an immediate end to the dancing for which the bar was famous, at least in some circles. Its clientele was not only gay, but consisted of the people living closest to the margins—drag queens, effeminate men, butch lesbians; people with no other place to go.

The police raid in the early morning hours of June 28 felt rougher than most to some who were caught up in it, and a crowd began to gather outside the bar. When a lesbian woman, complaining that her handcuffs were too tight, began to fight back, the resistance became contagious. Stonewall patrons and their supporters began to shout and throw things at police, as the confrontation spread to nearby Christopher Park. Six days of demonstrations followed, with intermittent standoffs and fights, and Stonewall became a symbol for gay America.

It was "the shot heard round the world," wrote historian Lillian Faderman, "crucial because it sounded the rally for the movement." Nance Lomax, a transgender teenager who went often to Stonewall in search of community, told the *New York Times*: "Stonewall meant the world to me. It taught me that I could be or do anything." By the following summer, on the anniversary of the riot, New York joined at least three other cities—Chicago, San Francisco, and Los Angeles—in holding gay pride parades that became an annual rite of summer.

As the 1960s moved toward an end, gay rights took its place among the other movements—the quest for dignity and simple justice that had gained momentum with the sit-ins of 1960, and ended the decade still unresolved. Whatever the cause that stirred us most, those of us then coming of age were moved to reflect more deeply on our country's founding:

We hold these truths to be self-evident . . .

68

Dylan, Woodstock, and Cash

In the spring, a song came on the radio that sounded as fresh and different as anything we had heard in a while. "Bad Moon Rising" was not the first hit by Creedence Clearwater Revival, but it confirmed an unexpected talent. The band's lead singer, John Fogerty, was barely twenty-four when the record began its rapid climb up the charts. The critics were calling it "swamp rock," and as we listened to the voice, which was simultaneously raw and melodic, we understood exactly what the critics meant. We assumed that Fogerty must have come from Louisiana.

In fact, he and the other members of the band were from El Cerrito, California. They were part of the San Francisco music scene at a time when drugs and rock 'n' roll often went together. But Fogerty rejected that connection. He said he had dabbled with marijuana but didn't like the feeling of paranoia it gave him, which may have been mainly the fear of getting caught. As the writer for most of the Creedence songs, Fogerty also rejected the easy lure of leftist politics, and his records were a favorite among the troops in Vietnam. But they had nevertheless the unmistakable presence of social commentary. "Bad Moon Rising" might have been a metaphorical description of the times, and the lyrics sustained the promise of the title.

I hear hurricanes a-blowing
I know the end is coming soon
I fear rivers over flowing
I hear the voice of rage and ruin

One of the other cuts on the album *Green River*, which contained "Bad Moon Rising" and its flip side, "Lodi," was the Fogerty composition, "Wrote a Song for Everyone," where the commentary went even deeper.

Saw the people standin' thousand years in chains.

Somebody said it's different now, look, it's just the same.
Pharoahs spin the message, 'round and 'round the truth.
They could have saved a million people, how can I tell you?

The Creedence sound was often up-tempo and made us smile, a counterpoint to the reflective lyrics. But the somber message was hard to miss, as it so often was in the music of 1969. This was the year of Elvis Presley's "In the Ghetto," a ballad written by country singer Mac Davis, recounting the cycle of poverty and violence in urban Chicago. Smokey Robinson and the Miracles, generally best-known for their Motown sweetness, covered Dion's hit from the year before, an elegy for martyrs called "Abraham, Martin and John." Even country music provided its share of commentary, though often from a different political perspective.

In September, Merle Haggard released his signature song, "Okie from Muskogee," a patriotic anthem for middle America, giving voice to a wave of national disgust toward the leftist counterculture. As the title suggested, Haggard did trace his roots to Oklahoma. His family was part of the Dust Bowl migration of the 1930s, when the economy and environment in the southern plains collapsed at the same time. Topsoil depleted by too much farming and too little rain began to blow away in large dark clouds that sometimes blotted out the sun, even as the Great Depression fell hard. Woody Guthrie, the greatest of the Dust Bowl balladeers, wrote often of those times—the exploitation endured by the Okies when they came to California and tried to find work on farms often run by large corporations. Their struggles inspired Guthrie's most famous song, "This Land Is Your Land (This Land Is My Land)" with its message of patriotic defiance: *I may be poor but it's my country, too.*

Haggard also wrote about such things. Early in 1969, his iconic ballad "Hungry Eyes" reached the top of the country music charts, paying tribute to the tattered determination of his itinerant family.

I remember Daddy prayin' for a better way of life
But I don't recall a change of any size
Just a little loss of courage as their age began to show
And more sadness in my Mama's hungry eyes

I had friends who were radical organizers, and they were ecstatic when the song came out. Here was a country music star singing about life in the migrant labor camps at a time when Cesar Chavez and his followers were engaged in a life-and-death organizing struggle. It was true that Haggard was writing about an earlier generation, but that was precisely the point: Over the years, economic exploitation in America knew no color; its victims were as likely to be white as black or brown, which was a message that Haggard had delivered before. He had already written "Working Man's Blues," which was about exactly what its title suggested, and "Branded," which recounted the struggles of an ex-convict—a canon of songs about people on the margins. But it was also true that in the expanding economy of the 1960s, the white middle class now included some of those survivors of hardship, and with the pride and satisfaction of their prosperity came an impatience with the counterculture critics of America. As Haggard wrote in "Okie from Muskogee":

We don't smoke marijuana in Muskogee
We don't take our trips on LSD
We don't burn our draft cards down on Main Street
We like livin' right, and bein' free

To most of his fans, Haggard was speaking the gospel truth, giving a rhyme and a tune to what they knew in their hearts. But to others his message was offensive, belittling not only youthful hedonism but also resistance to a bloody and unjust war.

IN NASHVILLE, JOHNNY CASH worried about these things. Although he appealed to the same country audience, he saw the purpose of music differently. In his experience, the power that it held was to cross old barriers—to bridge the chasms of race and class and bring people together. In the 1950s, Cash was a part of the Sun Records scene in Memphis, casting his lot with producer Sam Phillips about the same time that Elvis Presley did. Cash, like Presley, understood the connection between the blues and country music, and how a fusion of the two produced rock 'n' roll—and how the artists who made their way to Sun Records included great black performers like B. B. King or Bobby Blue Bland, as well as Elvis, Roy Orbison, and Jerry Lee Lewis. Phillips wanted it that way. An Alabamian by birth, he always had a conviction he couldn't explain—a feeling that was simply there—that the things people had in common ran deeper than the things that kept them apart.

Cash, for sure, believed that was true, and in the summer of 1969 he set out to put his intuition to the test. On June 7, he launched his own national television show, a network deal with ABC that allowed him to present a wide array of performers. His guests were country music legends like Haggard, the

Carter Family, Roger Miller, and Tom T. Hall, and folk music stalwarts like Gordon Lightfoot, Pete Seeger, Judy Collins, and Buffy Saint-Marie. There were country rockers like Linda Ronstadt and Creedence Clearwater, rockabilly icons Carl Perkins and the Everly Brothers, and there were black singers, too: Odetta, Joe Tex, O. C. Smith, Charley Pride, and Ray Charles.

In his choice of guests, Cash was trying to make a fundamental point, using music as a tool of reconciliation. If the fans of Pete Seeger, folk music's apostle of peace and civil rights, and the fans of Merle Haggard, the voice of middle-class alienation, might not have expected to like each other, or to appreciate each other's music, Johnny Cash was determined to make them at least listen.

"A lot of people," he told me once in an interview, "got their first look at American folk on my country show. I thought at first we might get some flak for it, but we didn't really. Only Pete Seeger was a problem because of his politics. But I just told the network he was a fine performer and writer, and a legend in folk music. His stand on ecology I appreciated. I just said I wanted him on the show. It wasn't a big deal, really. I saw that country and folk had a lot in common."

One of Cash's most memorable shows was the first one. It featured Joni Mitchell, Cajun fiddler Doug Kershaw, and most remarkably, Bob Dylan, who had shown little interest in television. But Cash and Dylan were friends going back to 1963 and the release of the album, *The Freewheelin' Bob Dylan*.

"I didn't know him back then," said Cash, "but I liked the album so much I wrote him a letter—got his address from Columbia Records [which was also Cash's label at the time] and I congratulated him on a fine country record. I could hear Jimmie Rodgers in his record and Vernon Dalhart from back in the twenties, the whole talking blues genre. I said, 'You're about the best country singer I've heard in years.' He wrote back and seemed kind of flabbergasted. He said, 'I remember one time back in Hibbing, Minnesota, in 1957, you were there and I was one of the people out there listening.' He said, 'All during the fifties, it was you and Hank Williams.'"

Dylan's appearance on *The Johnny Cash Show* came at a significant time. He had just recorded his third album in Nashville, and *Nashville Skyline*, even more than the others, was part of a pattern of unpredictability going back to 1965. That was the year that Dylan played an electric guitar at the Newport Folk Festival, a Mecca for lovers of acoustic music. He was booed on that occasion, and folk music purists were roundly offended. Writing in the folk journal *Sing Out!*, English songwriter Ewan MacColl, best known for his composition, "The First Time Ever I Saw Your Face," called Dylan's Newport performance "tenth-rate drivel." Dylan was undeterred. He soon released a definitive rock 'n' roll single called "Like a Rollng Stone," about which Bruce Springsteen later raved: "It sounded like someone had kicked open the door of your mind."

In 1969, music critics—once again to their collective surprise—regarded *Nashville Skyline* as something close to a pure country record. It featured a duet between Dylan and Cash on the Dylan original, "Girl from the North Country," and a mellow, country-rock single of romantic love, "Lay Lady Lay," which climbed to number seven on the *Billboard* charts. The studio band consisted of some of Nashville's most accomplished session men: Pete Drake on steel guitar, Kenny Buttrey on drums, and Charlie McCoy on harmonica and guitar. McCoy, who also played on Dylan's first Nashville album, *Blonde on Blonde*, would later remember how Dylan was in the middle of writing "Sad-Eyed Lady of the Lowlands" when the first recording session was about to begin. With the musicians being paid by the hour, Dylan kept writing—and then writing some more—while McCoy and the others simply waited.

"About 4 a.m.," remembered McCoy, "he was ready to record."

"Sad-Eyed Lady of the Lowlands," an enigmatic tribute to Dylan's wife Sara (later recorded by his former lover, Joan Baez), lasted eleven minutes and twenty-two seconds, and some of the musicians in the Nashville sessions were astonished by the experience. "Really," said Wayne Moss, who played guitar, "we used to think of Nashville sessions as being relaxed, but Dylan changed our whole approach. He was so relaxed and laid-back that your creative juices took on an entirely different aspect. He took the time to think the session out. Anything we wanted to try, it was 'have at it.' He was very critical of himself, not so much the musicians around him."

On the *Johnny Cash Show*, Dylan and the host sang their duet of "Girl from the North Country," and Dylan left behind a signed copy of the album cover, which Cash later framed and hung in his office. The inscription read: "To John and June, Love, Bob Dylan."

The affinity between Dylan and Cash, and Cash's wife, June Carter, lay in their similar understanding of music. If Dylan refused to be pigeon-holed by his fans, moving resolutely wherever his artistry might take him—from folk-protest to rock 'n' roll and country—Cash saw the same musical continuum and set out to show it on national TV. He wanted to make a personal declaration, to remind people through the metaphor of music that America was a land of many tastes and opinions, all springing from a common humanity.

A few years later, I had a chance to ask him if these were really the things on his mind. "Yeah," he said, "I guess that's right. That is what I'm trying to do."

THE MIDDLE OF AUGUST was an important time for New York folk singer Melanie Safka, who performed under her first name. Not only did she appear on the tenth episode of *The Johnny Cash Show*, which aired August 16, she also performed at a musical event that dwarfed anything on television. Woodstock took its name from a town in upstate New York, but the meaning of the word would be forever linked to 400,000 music fans who gathered from August 15–18, 1969. Some put the number closer to half a million. The images in *Life* magazine and other publications showed a seemingly endless sea of young faces, drawn in part by the all-star lineup of talent. Creedence Clearwater Revival was the first major group to accept the promoters' invitation, but others quickly followed: Richie Havens, Arlo Guthrie, Joan Baez, The Who, John Sebastian, Country Joe McDonald, the Grateful Dead, Janis Joplin, Jefferson Airplane, Santana, Sly and the Family Stone, The Band, Ravi Shankar, Jimi Hendrix. The list went on, and the organizers were not prepared for the result. They were expecting—hoping—for as many as 50,000 people a day, but when the number soared by a factor of ten, many of their best-laid plans collapsed.

The original site was in Wallkill, just outside of Woodstock, but after residents there threatened a lawsuit the promoters found Max Yasgur's dairy farm in the Catskill Mountains near the town of White Lake. One of the farmer's alfalfa fields created a kind of natural bowl, and for three days, spilling over to a fourth, young people were crammed together in weather that was sometimes rainy and miserable. In *Life*'s August 1969 special issue about the event, the magazine offered this description:

> For three days nearly a half million people lived elbow to elbow in the most exposed, crowded, rain-drenched, uncomfortable kind of community, and there wasn't so much as a fistfight. The whole world was watching, and never before had a hippie gathering been so large or so successful; so impressive.

Life estimated the event would lose as much as $2 million because, ironically, the attendance overwhelmed organizers' ability to sell tickets. By the tens of thousands, fans streamed in for free. Janis Joplin, awestruck by the size of the throng, told the helicopter pilot who was flying her in, "Even Billy Graham doesn't draw *that* many people."

Richie Havens was the first performer to take the stage, his deep, soothing voice amplified by the powerful sound system the festival engineers had created. Three days later Jimi Hendrix was the closing act. In between, two babies were born and a young man was killed when a tractor ran over him in the alfalfa field where he was sleeping. People swam naked in Max Yasgur's pond, and some, their clothes soaked by rain and mud, simply stripped them away in the field. Who needed them anyway, bathed as all were in a feeling of freedom and the joy of rock 'n' roll?

Musically, the high point was Hendrix. He didn't begin his performance until 8 a.m. Monday. Most people saw him as the pinnacle of an all-star cast, the biggest name in psychedelic rock 'n' roll, and while the promoters offered him a chance to play earlier, he said he wanted to listen to the other musicians. He was a part of this community, too. When he finally took the stage, he seemed undismayed by the thinning crowd. "You can leave if you want to," he said. "We're just jammin'." He played a few of his standards—"Red House," "Foxy Lady," "Voodoo Child"—then glanced at cameraman Michael Wadleigh who was filming what would become *Woodstock*, an Academy Award-winning documentary.

"If you look at the footage closely," said Wadleigh, "he looked right over at me as if to say, 'Listen to this. You're gonna love it.'"

Hendrix began to play "The Star Spangled Banner," slow and haunting, solo on his electric guitar. Some of the best music critics in the country have tried to put the moment into words, and a few of them have come pretty close. Writing for MSNBC, Michael Ventre remembered:

> The jarring, uplifting, haunting, energizing anthem was done at times in straight single notes, but the entire song is spiced with trademark Hendrix innovations, especially the use of amplifier feedback, sometimes to convey the sounds of war—bombs falling, jets overhead, perhaps even the cries of human anguish. At one point, Hendrix interrupts the anthem to play "Taps," then resumes.

Greil Marcus added:

> It is significant in American discourse, whether cultural or political. I've listened to the performance many times. It's so complex, with so many different layers of disgust and celebration and alienation and engagement. There's really no way to just characterize it as a protest against the war. It's certainly that. But he's also saying, "I'm a citizen of this country, too."

Late night talk show host Dick Cavett, who, along with *The Smothers Brothers Comedy Hour*, brought a combination of intelligence and humor to the political issues of 1969, interviewed Hendrix about the controversy from his playing the anthem in an unexpected way. The previous year in Detroit, before Game 5 of the World Series, Jose Feliciano faced storms of outrage and felt his career skidding to a halt after he played what one critic called "a rousing, soulful version . . . on acoustic guitar." Cavett asked Hendrix why he decided to take the same chance. "I don't know, man," Hendrix replied. "All I did was play it. I'm an American, so I played it."

Noting the controversies of "unorthodox" renditions, Cavett told the TV audience, "This man was in the 101st Airborne, so when you send your nasty letters in . . ."

"I didn't think it was unorthodox," Hendrix insisted. "I thought it was beautiful."

To the counterculture fans of rock 'n' roll, it was. Hendrix was a virtuoso, an African American artist twenty-six years old, troubled, funny, charismatic and charming; a devotee of blues greats Muddy Waters and Albert King. In his early career he had backed such stars as the Isley Brothers and Little Richard, but in the last three years of his life he was an icon in his own right. Many said he was the best rock guitarist ever to play.

It is safe to say that nobody who heard him ever forgot it, and certainly not if they heard him at Woodstock. But there was also this. By September 18, 1970, thirteen months after his festival triumph, Jimi Hendrix was dead, the victim of a drug overdose. One month later Janis Joplin followed, and the youth culture reeled in shock and grief. These were two of their heroes and stars, reminders at the end of the 1960s of something they did not want to face: the dangers of a culture of sex and drugs, wrapped in the passionate beauty of rock.

69

'One Small Step'

In the summer of Woodstock, on July 20, the gray and definitive front page of the *New York Times* was dominated by only two stories. One in other circumstances might have been a cause for unrestrained celebration. Three Americans were on their way to the Moon, and this time they were planning to land. Command module pilot Michael Collins was assigned to stay with the mother ship, but Buzz Aldrin and Neil Armstrong would descend to the surface, piloting a lunar module that had worked imperfectly on one of its test flights.

Two months earlier, on Apollo 10, the final trip to the Moon without actually landing, astronauts Eugene Cernan and Thomas Stafford had climbed into the landing craft and flown it to within ten miles of the surface. They drifted across the Sea of Tranquility, the site where Apollo 11 would touch down, marveling at geologic features they had seen on maps. But when they fired the ascent engine to return the lander to the command module, they suddenly began to pitch and roll.

"Son of a bitch!" blurted Cernan. "What the hell happened?"

This was not standard astronaut-speak. Described by Apollo historian Andrew Chaikin as "gregarious, easy-going, and well liked," Cernan carried himself with a genial swagger—a touch of macho not at all surprising for somebody willing to brave outer space. On the way to the Moon he had been as mesmerized as the earlier crew of Apollo 8 by the Earth receding into the vastness—"a blackness beyond your comprehension that envelops the Earth, the infinity of time, the infinity of space, the endlessness of it all." But now, after he and Stafford inadvertently flipped the same control switch in opposite directions, the horizon of the Moon was spinning wildly outside, and his sacred ruminations gave way to the profane. Under these conditions, "son of a bitch" would have seemed a mild epithet. But Cernan's microphone was live, and his words went beaming back to the planet, bringing a touch of reality to the Boy Scout-image of astronauts carefully cultivated by NASA. In the teapot tempest that followed, one salient fact was largely overlooked. Cernan and Stafford were almost killed. Another two or three rolls and they would have crashed into the surface of the Moon.

For the astronauts of Apollo 11, who would take the lander all the way to the Sea of Tranquility, it was comforting to know that the problem was not in the craft itself. It was, as NASA euphemistically put it, "an error in a flight plan checklist."

On July 16 at 9:32 a.m., Apollo 11 began its journey from Cape Canaveral. As the Saturn V rocket began its slow and mighty ascent, it was easy to make the case, and many did, that it was the most historic voyage ever attempted. Some observers thought of President Kennedy, who had sent us on this path. We thought of his young and handsome face, his certainty and earnestness, and his capacity to make us believe. We had believed in other things, too, of course, besides space flight. Not all of these things were of Kennedy's creation, but somehow he had embodied our hopes, and so we thought of the moment he died, all of the crushing, unforgettable sadness—and yet also the survival of hope. Now it was battered beyond recognition, torn apart by the war and national division, and the certainty that nothing would be the same. Yet here was a flicker of something we remembered, something beyond this history-making feat of engineering. We could feel again, perhaps, an intimation of grand possibility for the country. But the feeling was brief—ended, tainted, by a reckless act from the last surviving brother of the president.

On the night of July 18, with Apollo 11 halfway to the Moon, Senator Edward Kennedy drove his car off a bridge on Chappaquiddick Island in Massachusetts. Mary Jo Kopechne, who was riding with him, was eight days short of her twenty-eighth birthday; pretty, if not classically beautiful, in her college yearbook, with confident eyes, high cheekbones, and a smile that revealed a trace of shyness. The newspaper stories called her a secretary, but in her ambition and her level of engagement with the political process, she was more than that. In 1962, after graduation from Caldwell College, a Catholic school in New Jersey, she took a teaching job at the Mission of St. Jude in Montgomery, Alabama, and worked in support of the civil rights movement. In 1964, she joined the secretarial staff of Senator Robert Kennedy and became one of his most trusted assistants. She was one of the "boiler room girls" who worked during the 1968 presidential campaign in a small, hot, windowless office. These were extraordinary young women, assigned the delicate task of tracking the allegiance of convention delegates and trying to persuade them to support Robert Kennedy. Kopechne was devastated by his death, and considered leaving Washington altogether.

"I just feel Bobby's presence everywhere," she said. "I can't go back because it will never be the same again."

But she did go back and took a job with a political consulting firm. "It was a good career, working with the politicians," her mother, Gwen Kopechne, told the *New York Times*. "It was what she wanted to do."

Mary Jo had come to Chappaquiddick, just east of Martha's Vineyard, for a reunion of campaign workers. There were six young women, including herself, and six men, including Ted Kennedy, who had gathered for a cookout. Kopechne seldom drank, but she did that night. Blood tests would reveal that she was not legally drunk but probably had had several drinks over the course of the evening, as people do on such an occasion, with steaks on the grill and conversations filled with memories and warmth.

At 11:15 p.m. she got into a car with Ted Kennedy, whom she did not know well, and when Kennedy drove off a narrow, unlit bridge, into a darkened saltwater inlet, Kennedy escaped but Kopechne did not. He told authorities—and later the public—that he dove multiple times to try to save her, but failed. Kopechne drowned. That was the coroner's ruling, but there was no autopsy and a rescue diver speculated that she may have survived for a long time in the terrifying blackness of the water, trapped in the car, breathing desperately from a pocket of air until it was gone. Might she have survived if Kennedy had called immediately for help? All we know is that Kennedy didn't. Believing that Kopechne must surely be dead, he left the scene and in an extended moment of moral failure began to calculate how to save his career.

In many ways, this was starkly out of character. Following the second assassination of a brother, Ted, though personally devastated, had assumed the mantle of family leadership, summoning the strength to be there in support of nephews, nieces and two widows, and to carry on the legacy of two fallen brothers. Democratic leaders, including Chicago Mayor Richard Daley, pushed him to accept the presidential nomination in 1968, and thus to heal their devastated party. In their book, *Last Lion: The Fall and Rise of Ted Kennedy,* staff members of the *Boston Globe*, the newspaper that knew him best, wrote of Kennedy's reluctance. Mentally, he was in no shape to do it. He spent much of his time that summer at the Kennedy compound in Hyannis Port, finding solace and refuge with the sea. Nevertheless, he wrestled with the notion that he ought to step forward for the sake of his brothers, for the sake of the country. But in the end he did not.

By 1969, he was content with that decision. He knew his time would come again, probably in 1972, for he carried the magic of the Kennedy name and could feel the yearning out there in the country for a dream and a promise not yet fulfilled. At the same time, he had carved out a place for himself in the Senate. He was popular and respected among colleagues on both sides of the aisle and had a knack for getting things done. Whatever direction his ambitions might take him, he was, without question, an ambitious man—handsome, gregarious, more naturally outgoing than either of his brothers, and increasingly serious about his Senate duties. But at the age of thirty-seven Kennedy also loved a good party, sometimes drank too much, and like his older brother John, had a wandering eye for young women.

These back stories converged on the tragic night of July 18. Kennedy testified later that he dove seven or eight times trying to reach Mary Jo, becoming more exhausted with each attempt, until finally he let himself be pulled away by the current. He climbed weakly onto the shore, where he lay in the grass and coughed up water. Finally he pulled himself together and set out for the cottage, "walking, trotting, jogging, stumbling, as fast as I possibly could." Piecing together the scene from Kennedy's testimony and others, the *Boston Globe* authors wrote in *Last Lion*:

> It would have been a dark walk, dogged by panic and mosquitoes and slowed by powdery sand. There was a crescent moon that night, but trees cocooned the road. He passed houses but did not stop for help, later saying he saw no lights. Back at the cottage, spent and soaking wet, Ted collapsed in the backseat of the rental car outside.

He told his friend Paul Markham, a former U.S. Attorney who was at the party, and his cousin Joey Gargan, who had rented the house, that Mary Jo was trapped in his car and the three of them rushed back to the scene. Again they dove to try to save her, battling the swiftness of the current, and again they failed. Kennedy, who was later diagnosed with a concussion, broke down and wept, and according to Markham he kept repeating, "This couldn't have happened, I don't know how it happened." More than two hours had passed by now, and still they had not reported the accident. Kennedy said later he felt a powerful sense of denial: maybe it was just a dream, maybe Mary Jo had escaped from the car and now was waiting for them back at the cottage. Maybe, maybe . . .

More time passed. The men agreed the accident had to be reported, but still they delayed. Finally, Kennedy told his friends, "You take care of the girls; I will take care of the accident." With that he dove into the channel that separated Chappaquiddick from the village of Edgartown, and began to swim across. Again, wrote the authors of *Last Lion*,

> Ted felt, for the second time that night, like he might drown . . .
>
> When he finally struggled onto land in Edgartown, he leaned against a tree to rest. Then he continued up the street to his hotel, the Shiretown Inn, a pair of shingled houses a few steps from the harbor, connected by two outdoor walkways like a spider's web.
>
> Shaking with the chill, he went to his room, took off his clothes and collapsed on the bed, conscious of throbbing pain in his head, back, and neck. Confused, after a while, about how much time had passed, Ted said he dressed and went out to the walkway, spotted a man standing below, and asked him the time. It was 2:25 a.m. The senator went back to his room. He did not go to the police, as he had told his friends he would.

In the morning, when Kennedy finally called the authorities, the accident had already been discovered, and the unanswered questions about his behavior triggered conspiracy theories that dogged him for the rest of his life. The accident itself was not hard to understand. The road was dark and the bridge was narrow with no guardrails, and it veered at an angle from the sandy lane. It was a tragedy waiting to happen. But why did Kennedy make that turn, and why was Mary Jo Kopechne in his car? Those were the questions he did not want to answer, and in the course of his delays and hedgings—and almost certainly, his lies—he only made himself look worse. Much worse. He pled guilty to leaving the scene of an accident, and even if his version of events was true, his lapse of judgment and ethical myopia cast a pall across his career.

Ironically, he may have been driven by those very failings to become one of the finest senators in U.S. history, a liberal lion who not only continued but expanded the commitment of his brothers—sons of one of the richest families in America—to the health and well-being of people on the margins. In the process, he was known in the Senate as perhaps the hardest worker in the chamber and maybe the most popular with Republicans and Democrats alike.

But on the night of July 18, a young woman was dead—and not just any young woman, but one of great talent who had committed herself to the career of his brother. In the immediate aftermath of her death, the man who had been with her in the sunken Oldsmobile had thought primarily about himself. Even at the time, as we tried to fathom this terrible news, we knew there would never be another President Kennedy. At least not in our generation.

It was nearly surreal that this Chappaquiddick drama could be overshadowed, and it wasn't entirely. But on July 21 the lead headline in the *New York Times* was not about Edward Kennedy. It was about three Americans 250,000 miles from home and an accomplishment so remarkable that it was a hard to take it in: MEN WALK ON MOON.

On their four-day journey from Earth, Michael Collins, Buzz Aldrin, and Neil Armstrong played a mental game with themselves. The mission, they decided, had not even begun as they coasted from their planet to the Moon; this was the time for getting their rest, getting as much sleep as they could, so they would be ready for July 20. That was when Aldrin and Armstrong, floating weightless in the main cabin, would propel themselves to the lunar module and wriggle inside.

Then things would get serious.

As Andrew Chaikin wrote in *A Man on the Moon*, Armstrong—the man designated to take the first step—was cautiously optimistic. He said privately he was sure they could make it safely back to earth, but the landing itself? No more than fifty-fifty, he figured. All three were feeling the pressure, building steadily as they entered the darkened shadow of the Moon, tempered—heightened?—by the moment of wonder when they first saw it: "a huge magnificent sphere bathed in the eerie blue light of earthshine, each crater rendered in ghostly detail, all except for a third of the globe, which was a crescent of blackness."

At 12:18 p.m., Houston time, Collins pushed the button to separate the lander from the main spacecraft. Speaking quietly on the radio, he wished his comrades a safe flight. He, too, rated their chances at about fifty-fifty.

"You guys take care."

"See you later," Armstrong answered.

Soon after the lander disengaged from the command module, both spacecraft began their loop around the dark side of the Moon, losing all communication with the Earth. When they emerged, the problems began. Radio communication cut in and out, and the lander's computer and its radar disagreed about the altitude as the craft began its descent. Trusting the radar more than the computer, Aldrin prepared to issue an override, when he heard an alarm—a high buzzing sound—that he had never heard before in simulation practice. A warning number, 1202, flashed on the screen and even Mission Control in Houston was not sure what it meant. But the descent was actually going as it should. They were 5,000 feet above the surface and traveling at 100 feet per second when Armstrong first took over manual control. They drifted across the dusty plain, skirting a cratered field of boulders close to where they expected to land. They were running low on fuel, only ninety seconds left, and stirring so much lunar dust that it was hard for Armstrong to gauge their descent. Finally, gently, with their fuel level reaching a danger point, they settled on the surface and the two men looked at each other and smiled. Armstrong reached for the mike, and he and the flight controllers in Houston began their historic exchange, so deliberately, improbably casual it was as if they were saying to the world, "we do this kind of thing all the time." With millions listening to his words in real time, Armstrong announced:

"Houston, Tranquility Base here. The Eagle has landed."

"Roger, Tranquility, we copy you on the ground. You've got a bunch of guys about to turn blue. We're breathing again. Thanks a lot."

"Thank you."

"You're looking good here."

"A very smooth touchdown."

Andrew Chaikin compared the landing to the closest analogy he could think of, the arrival of Edmund Hillary and Tenzing Norgay on the pinnacle of Mount Everest. Hillary's actions, wrote Chaikin, "were those of the conqueror," as he began to photograph every craggy, ice-covered angle below, proving beyond doubt that he had made it to the top. Norgay prayed. "For him," wrote Chaikin, "the climb was not a conquest but a pilgrimage."

On the Moon, after completing a checklist of chores and before stepping from the capsule onto the surface, Buzz Aldrin took communion. He did not announce this to the world, for his point was not to impose his own faith, but to seek a context for their achievement.

"This is the LM pilot," he said on the radio. "I'd like to take this opportunity to ask every person listening in, whoever and wherever they may be, to pause for a moment and contemplate the events of the past few hours, and to give thanks in his or her own way."

When it was time to step from the capsule, creating the first human footprint on another celestial body, Armstrong, by prearrangement, went first. He was not a man of words, but he had thought about the irony of such a small and ordinary step being tied to this staggering human accomplishment.

"That's one small step for man," he said, "one giant leap for mankind."

He had meant to say, "That's one small step for *a* man," and there would be historical nitpickers who wondered if he had blown the line or if the smallest word in the English language was simply lost in transmission.

It really didn't matter. Armstrong was standing on the surface of the Moon, marveling at what he could see all around him—the fine, powdered dust, a ridge in the distance, all the small craters and boulders and rocks that were somehow both awe-inspiring and familiar, creating the sense that this was, in fact, a real *place.*

Back on earth, the marveling for many of us was multilayered. Not only were two men in bulky space suits bouncing in the one-sixth gravity of the Moon, but we were watching it on TV—in real time, fearful perhaps when we thought about exactly what they were doing, but amazed at what human beings could achieve.

We had seen the other side in recent years, our capacity for bloodshed and suffering and death; we had seen it even in that same week with the stunning tragedy coming out of Chappaquiddick. But this moment was a testament to things we could do, and places we could go, if we only had the will. I remember wondering if President Kennedy, when he pointed us in this direction—and did it in the context of all the other hopes of his young and vibrant presidency—really believed we would get there. There were so many ways that we had fallen short.

But not this time; not on July 20, 1969.

Houston, Tranquility Base here. The Eagle has landed.

70

Toward a Bloody Ending

If the Moon landing, in all its magnificence, was nevertheless stalked by Chappaquiddick, there were other, more disturbing events that began that summer and continued until the end of the year. In the suburban hills outside Los Angeles, home to Hollywood stars and other rich and famous Californians, five people were murdered in the early morning hours of August 9. The crime at 10050 Cielo Drive was so hideously savage as to attract immediate international attention—the victims shot or beaten or stabbed, some of them bound, some not, and the letters PIG smeared in blood on the front door. The blood belonged to Sharon Tate, a twenty-six-year-old actress of extraordinary beauty and modest success, perhaps best-known for her marriage to film director Roman Polanski. The previous year, Polanski had won acclaim for *Rosemary's Baby*, in which actress Mia Farrow—a friend of Tate's—played a woman whose child is fathered by Satan. Two years earlier, in Tate's first starring role, she had played a beautiful witch in the film *Eye of the Devil*, and speculation followed that Tate and her guests were part of some kind of hideous cult.

They were not, but the nature of the crime—"the brutality of the killings shocked even homicide-squad detectives," reported *Time*—led to a wave of magnifying rumors. Tate was eight months pregnant, and according to one report her baby had been cut from her abdomen and one of her breasts had been slashed away. Neither of those gruesome details was true (though the baby did not survive). There was also the fact that Tate was bound by a rope to another of the victims, Hollywood hairdresser Jay Sebring, who was a former lover she had left to marry Polanski. Was this some kind of orgy gone wrong? In *Helter Skelter*, the bestselling true-crime book of all time, prosecutor Vincent Bugliosi and co-author Curt Gentry noted that while

"Sharon Tate looked the part of a starlet, she didn't live up to at least one portion of that image. She was not promiscuous. Her relationships were few, and rarely casual, at least on her part." She and Sebring had remained friends after their affair, though he may have harbored the hope, in the midst of his one-night stands with other women, that he and Sharon would reunite if her marriage to Polanski did not work. In the meantime he was a friend of both.

Recreational drugs— marijuana, cocaine— were found at the scene, and for a while police followed that lead. But soon there were copycat crimes— more bodies, more blood-smeared words, including the enigmatic phrase, "helter skelter," oddly misspelled as HEALTER SKELTER on a refrigerator door. Slowly it began to occur to the homicide detectives that the killings were related and that they were dealing with something more chilling and bizarre than drug-related executions.

By the fall they caught a break. A woman named Susan Atkins, a twenty-one-year-old brunette, surprisingly pretty, who looked even younger in her photographs, was awaiting trial on a murder charge when she began talking to two fellow inmates about the Sharon Tate killings. She described them in such detail—Sharon's desperate pleas for her life, while Atkins stabbed her again and again, a feeling she described as orgasmic—that the inmates gradually came to believe her. Atkins said she was part of a family led by a man named Charles Manson, who was both Jesus Christ and the devil. Later, she said they were trying to start a race war. That was what the words Helter Skelter meant, she explained—a phrase Manson borrowed from the Beatles—and when the race war came the family would burrow deep into the desert, hiding in a secret place that only Charlie knew, and when the war was over and the blacks had won, the family would emerge and take control because the blacks would not be able to govern.

The other prisoners thought Atkins was crazy—and a cold-blooded, psychopathic killer.

At about the same time, other leads began to converge, interrogations of biker gang members who had spent time with the Manson family and heard loose talk about multiple murders. In November, Deputy District Attorney Bugliosi began to put the pieces together, and on December 8, Manson, Atkins and three others were indicted for the Sharon Tate murders.

IT HAD BEEN A very bloody year in many aspects.

With only a few cosmetic changes, the war in Vietnam continued. Richard Nixon and Henry Kissinger announced a new strategy, a policy they called Vietnamization. By this they meant a reduction in the number of U.S. ground forces, with more resources going to the South Vietnamese army. Politically in the United States, the policy met with cautious approval. After years of escalation, the number of U.S. troops was slowly declining. Two of the national news networks, ABC and NBC, had already made an editorial decision to show less combat footage each night, so the impression began to grow that the level of hostility was decreasing. It was not. As historian Marilyn Young has written, the gradual reduction in U.S. ground forces was accompanied by an escalation of American bombing. This included not only Vietnam, but deeper—and secret—incursions into Cambodia where the leader Norodom Sihanouk struggled to maintain his stance of neutrality, to save his country from total immersion into the war The following year, Sihanouk would be overthrown, and Cambodia veered first to the right and then to the left, with disastrous results for the Cambodian people. In the "killing fields" of that country, millions would die in the next several years—one more casualty of U.S. intervention.

In Vietnam itself, intensified bombing accompanied more urgent efforts at often-brutal "pacification" attempts by U.S. and South Vietnamese forces to install sympathetic leadership in the countryside. Traveling with the troops on one of these missions, *Wall Street Journal* reporter Peter Kann described a

> largely fruitless interrogation of fearful, tight-lipped villagers, calculated brutality applied to suspected Viet Cong, the execution of one suspect, looting of homes by Vietnamese troops, systematic destruction of village installations and a largely unproductive hunt for Viet Cong officials who apparently had fled by sampan long before. . . .

Many war-weary Americans no longer even read such stories, but they did pay attention in November when Seymour Hersh began his revelations about My Lai, a massacre by U.S. forces that had occurred in 1968. Among those he quoted in a series of dispatches beginning November 12 was Sergeant Michael Bernhardt of Franklin Square, New York, who was there when the massacre took place. With an obvious mixture of outrage and dismay,

Bernhardt described the actions of Lieutenant William Calley and the men of his platoon in a village where they met no resistance:

> The whole thing was so deliberate. It was point-blank murder and I was standing there watching it. . . . They were doing it three ways. One: They were setting fire to the hootches and huts and waiting for people to come out and then shooting them up. Two: They were going into the hootches and shooting them up. Three: They were gathering people in groups and shooting them. As I walked in, you could see piles of people all through the village. . . . all over. They were gathered up into large groups. I saw them shoot an M-79 (grenade launcher) into a group of people who were still alive. But it (the shooting) was mostly done with a machine gun. They were shooting women and children just like anybody else.

The details from there only got worse, as we learned about the rapes of women before they were murdered, and I remember juxtaposing in my mind the scenes from My Lai with media descriptions of the Manson murders—the screams of a man in the last seconds of life: *Oh God, no, please don't! Oh, God, no, don't, don't* . . . I wondered about the words in Vietnamese, and how in the wanton butchery of the moment mothers must have begged for the lives of their children. I also knew—all of us knew—that there was a difference in these terrible scenes. The American killers at My Lai were not psychopaths, as Manson and his followers had been. They were not *crazy*. They were driven, perhaps, by the lunacy of war—in particular *this* war where the enemy began to feel like the whole population, and a U.S. soldier could never be sure who was hostile and who was not, and where the next deadly threat might appear. That was part of the problem, of course, part of the policy miscalculation, perpetuated by the pride of men in charge who lacked the humanity to admit their mistakes.

Under these circumstances there were venomous men like George Wallace who sprang preposterously to the defense of William Calley: "Every time a soldier seeks out the enemy, he will be charged with murder." But there were many more who reeled from the loss of a fundamental truth, an article of faith, summed up in the words of Marilyn Young.

> My Lai was an event the more terrifying because it seemed inexplicable. Indeed, the comfortable paradigm of the nation's history—as taught in school,

> celebrated on holidays, so fully embraced it felt natural rather than learned—had no more room for My Lai than it had for the genocide of American Indians, for slavery, for the conquest of the Philippines, or the persistence of poverty and inequality. Used to thinking of their country as America the Good, Americans were shocked to see the streets filled with angry young people who insisted it was America the Bad. The massacre at My Lai, they accused, was neither impossible nor aberrational.

The My Lai revelations came at a time of continuing massive antiwar demonstrations; on October 15, millions of people around the world had participated in a Moratorium to End the War in Vietnam. In the United States, the largest gathering occurred in Boston where Senator George McGovern addressed a crowd of 100,000. It was, according to the *Boston Globe*, the largest demonstration in the history of the city.

In Washington, on that same night, Coretta Scott King led a candlelight march of 30,000 past the White House, picking up her fallen husband's mantle—though it was, even more than most people knew, Coretta's personal crusade as well. She was a pacifist who in 1962 had traveled to Switzerland as part of Women Strike for Peace, a protest movement against the nuclear arms race. In 1967, she was among those who pushed Dr. King to speak out against the War in Vietnam. She saw the great causes of the 1960s as being essentially of one piece; she had once called for "a solid block of women power to fight the three great evils of racism, poverty, and war."

The world remembered her dignity at Dr. King's funeral as it remembered the same inner strength of Jacqueline Kennedy. Indeed, the similarities went even deeper than either woman would have preferred: they were widows of husbands great and flawed, who inspired a generation, but who were serially unfaithful to their wives. Personally, of course, these were complicated histories to absorb, but Jackie and Coretta both threw themselves into shaping the legacies of their men, celebrating the greatness, glossing over the feet of clay.

Mrs. King, more than Mrs. Kennedy, also became a human rights icon. Even before Dr. King's funeral, she traveled to Memphis to march with the garbage workers whose cause he was championing on the eve of his death. Later in 1968, she spoke at the Poor People's Campaign in Washington, and always, in the coming years, her definition of the movement was broad. She supported gay rights, worked with the National Organization for Women to campaign for an Equal Rights Amendment, and of course she marched against the War in Vietnam. Somehow in October 1969, on this candlelit moment in a protest for peace, Mrs. King offered a reminder of many things: the role of women for one; people as diverse as Gloria Steinem, Bella Abzug, or Joan Baez, who came to their feminism through work for other causes. Despite the palpable sadness of Mrs. King's life, there was a flickering reminder of the optimism, the strong sense of purpose, that went with those causes—civil rights, peace, justice for the farmworkers of California. As an activist friend later put it, "there was joy in those communal projects," and Mrs. King helped us remember.

On November 15, she returned to Washington as part of a second Moratorium march—ironically, the largest demonstration in the nation's capital since her husband's 1963 "I Have a Dream" speech. Crowd estimates ran as high as 500,000, and the protest lasted three days. In the White House, presidential adviser Daniel Patrick Moynihan urged Nixon to "show the little bastards"—he knew Nixon liked that kind of talk—by delivering a statesmanlike address on the subject of peace. Nixon, instead, dismissed the march as irrelevant, saying that he would be watching football. The protests began on the bitterly cold evening of November 13, as 45,000 marchers gathered at Arlington National Cemetery and walked single file across the Arlington Memorial Bridge to the White House nearly four miles away. Bearing candles and each carrying the name of a fallen soldier or a village destroyed by American bombs, they marched, as historians Nancy Zaroulis and Gerald Sullivan would record, "through two nights and into Saturday morning, through rain and thunderstorms, wind and biting cold, in what may have been the longest 'parade' in American history."

By Saturday, the crowd had swollen to a half million, the massive numbers making clear, in the words of *Time*, that the antiwar movement "comprised more than just politicized youth." Senators McGovern and McCarthy addressed the marchers, and folk singers Pete Seeger, Arlo Guthrie, and Peter, Paul and Mary led them in the anthems of peace. Some people said the high point came with Seeger's ten-minute rendition—amplified by the soaring voices of the crowd—of John Lennon's "Give Peace a Chance."

For the most part, the event was dignified and somber, a peacefulness consistent with its purpose. But there was sporadic violence on Friday, including a confrontation at Dupont Circle in which police sprayed the crowd with tear gas. For the New Left, the angriest, most passionate opponents of the war, this was a time of complicated emotion. During much of 1969, after the Nixon inauguration, some were drawn to a moral absolutism even more consuming than in the past. "We were hell-bent for the promised, not the compromised, land," remembered Todd Gitlin.

In his heralded memoir, *The Sixties: Years of Hope, Days of Rage,* Gitlin was candid about the mood of those final days—the mixture of passion and disillusionment, of commitment, foolishness, and confusion:

> Everything was at stake, anything seemed possible, there was the promise of universal liberation, there was the profaning of everything holy, the end of time was approaching, nothing was changing, there was a leap toward equality, there was a degradation of standards, there was disgust with the Pentagon's perversion of reason, there was a flight from the rigors of intellect, there was the revelation that America benefited from the misery of the poor countries, there was the glorification of Third World tyrannies, there was the unmasking of capitalism, there was the reflex that capitalism was the root of all evil, there was a revulsion against vast and impersonal violence, there was violence that was going to end all violence, there was an opening of doors, there was a closing of minds, there was psychedelic rapture, there was the scrambling of brains by bad drugs and too many drugs and the siren song of madness, there was a search for fresh language, there was an epidemic of cant, there was universal love, there was the right to say "fuck" on the movie screen. For every face of authority, there was someone to slap it.

In the spring of 1969, strikes, disruptions of classes, student occupations of buildings, or other demonstrations erupted on more than three hundred college campuses. At Harvard, students took over University Hall, one of the oldest buildings on the nation's oldest campus, demanding an end to Harvard's Reserve Officer Training Corps program. The *Harvard Crimson,* the university's student newspaper, charged that the presence of ROTC was "based on the notion that country's universities should serve the needs of the warfare state." Several hundred students, led by SDS, marched to the home of Harvard President Nathan Pusey and—Martin Luther-like—taped a list of demands to his door. On April 10, Harvard administrators called in the police to remove the occupiers of University Hall. The police used billy clubs and mace, adding to a mood of campus outrage.

At Cornell, another Ivy League institution, somebody burned a cross outside a cooperative for black women students, prompting the Afro-American Students (AAS) to take over Willard Straight Hall. When white fraternity students fought with the African American occupiers, black students armed themselves with rifles. Outside the building, now ringed by competing forces of state and local police and SDS allies of the blacks, a young campus policeman named George Tabor hoped against hope for a peaceful solution.

"I was a raw rookie. I had no idea what was going on," he told the *Cornell Chronicle*, adding that if police had gotten the order, "they would have gone and taken the Straight back and arrested people, or who knows what would have happened. . . . It would have been just absolutely terrible."

Fortunately, the standoff was settled by negotiation, and on Sunday April 20, the black students, still bearing their rifles, filed out of the building. Associated Press photographer Steve Starr snapped a Pulitzer Prize-winning photo that ran on the cover of *Newsweek*. The headline read: "Universities Under the Gun."

Tensions continued through the summer with student protests against Dow Chemical (the maker of napalm) and other war profiteers, and into the fall with the massive Moratorium marches. In June, a radical faction calling itself Weatherman, and later the Weather Underground, broke away from SDS and in October staged a three-day rampage of window-smashing demonstrations in Chicago. Two of the most visible leaders were John Jacobs, who had coined the slogan, "bring the war home," and Bernadine Dohrn, who would soon make the FBI's Most Wanted List. Even the Black Panthers kept their distance from Weatherman. "We do not support people," said Chicago leader Fred Hampton, "who are anarchistic, opportunistic, adventuristic, and Custeristic."

The following year, as Weatherman began an escalation from militant vandalism to bombs, four antiwar students would die at Kent State at the hands of frightened National Guardsmen. Eleven days later at Jackson State University, two more students would be killed by police following a racial confrontation. Despite the efforts of Coretta Scott King and others to uphold the nonviolent ideals of her husband (was her struggle prophetic, or merely quixotic?) it was easy to believe in those awful days that America was losing its mind.

In Chicago, despite his caution about the Weatherman people, Fred Hampton felt like a man with a target on his back. Still only twenty-one years old, the Black Panther leader was a driving force behind Chicago's Rainbow Coalition, an interracial alliance established in 1968, which grew even stronger the following year. Many of its members were young, and most were poor and angry. They shared an outrage over such issues as police brutality, exploitation by slumlords, evictions caused by urban renewal, and other indignities of big-city poverty. Perhaps the most unexpected link in this multiracial chain was a partnership between the Black Panthers and the Young Patriots, an organization of Appalachian whites whose symbol was the Confederate flag.

Their alliance was forged through the organizational skill of a Black Panther activist, a Southern black man with the unlikely name of Robert E. Lee III. Bob Lee formed an easy rapport with Young Patriots leaders like William Fesperman, known to his friends as "Preacherman." To Fesperman, the Confederate emblem he wore on his cap was a double-edged symbol—a reminder of Southern heritage, yes, but a reminder also of how it felt to be "beat down." Historically, he said, that was a part of the Southern experience, but it was also the Appalachian reality in Chicago. Fesperman, like the Black Panthers, regarded Mayor Daley's political machine as a "monster," indifferent to grass-roots people of every race.

"The jaws of the monster in Chicago are grinding up the flesh, and spitting out the blood of the poor and oppressed people," Fesperman declared, "blacks . . . the browns . . . the reds . . . the yellow . . . and yes, the whites. . . ."

The Black Panthers-Young Patriots alliance was not the only example of interracial cooperation among the working class and poor. In Baltimore, Barbara Mikulski, a Polish-American social worker and future U.S. Senator, was building a multiethnic coalition against an interstate highway that threatened to destroy inner-city neighborhoods. The Black-Polish Conference of Greater Detroit, established in 1968, was working successfully on a range of issues affecting those communities. But nowhere was the alliance broader—or more militant—than in Chicago.

As Jakobi Williams wrote in *From the Bullet to the Ballot*, Hampton and friends were preaching their rainbow gospel to blacks, whites, Puerto Ricans, Asians, and American Indians. Their converts came not only from Illinois colleges, but also from such unexpected sources as youth gangs. For local police officials in Chicago, and for J. Edgar Hoover's FBI, this was a disturbing turn of events. The Panthers, after all, were fond of slogans like "Black power comes from the barrel of a gun." Never mind that much of what they did was provide free breakfasts to hungry children. These were seen by the establishment as people with a dangerous ideology, who rallied in support of California Black Panther Huey Newton, an accused cop killer; the Chicago 8 who were on trial for their role in the riots at the Democratic Convention; and even Ho Chi Minh. In September 1969, the Chicago Panthers joined with a former Puerto Rican gang called the Young Lords to hold a memorial service for Ho and Panther Larry Roberson, who had died in a shoot-out with police. The Puerto Rican group, meanwhile, became a crucial part of the Rainbow Coalition. They ran community service projects, including a day-care center, marched for the independence of Puerto Rico, and made a citizen's arrest of an off-duty policeman who had killed a member of their group.

By the end of 1969, these interrelated developments were becoming intolerable to law enforcement, and they blamed Fred Hampton. He, more than anyone else, had envisioned this broad and radical multi-ethnic coalition, with its simultaneous pursuit of community building and confrontation, that made it, the police and the FBI believed, one of the most dangerous forces in the country. Already, the Rainbow philosophy was spreading to other cities, and Hampton, as the Party's rising star, felt like a marked man. Based on the word of a confidential informant, a Chicago police memo reported: "Fred Hampton stated that he is scared that he will be killed."

Around 4 a.m. on December 4, fourteen Chicago police burst through the door of Hampton's apartment and fired a hundred rounds. They had studied a floor plan of the apartment supplied by FBI informant William O'Neal—a detailed sketch that included an X to mark Hampton's bed. Forensic evidence indicated that Black Panther members in the apartment, which also served as a de facto Party headquarters, fired one shot. It came from Mark Clark, a Panther official from Peoria, who discharged his shotgun involuntarily when he was fatally struck by a bullet.

Hampton sustained multiple wounds while he lay in his bed. He died from two bullets to the head, fired from point-blank range. Four other Black Panthers were seriously wounded.

Police insisted they fired in self-defense, but their claims unraveled during multiple investigations by a federal grand jury, committees of Congress, and a civil lawsuit that resulted in a $1.85 million settlement.

"If the Panthers fired at all," wrote Jeff Cohen and Jeff Gottlieb, summarizing the evidence for *The Nation*, "it was one shot that Mark Clark fired—apparently after he had been shot in the heart. If the cops had, in fact, demanded a ceasefire on three occasions, they were talking only to themselves. The official explanation amounted to a cover-up, and a massive one."

The raid, nevertheless, accomplished the goal set forth by J. Edgar Hoover, who had ordered his agents to "neutralize" the Panthers. Without Fred Hampton's charisma and vision, the Illinois chapter began to fall apart.

Two days after the Hampton murder, as if to punctuate the year, the Rolling Stones staged a free concert in Altamont, California. The Stones had been recording in Muscle Shoals, Alabama, in studios made famous earlier in the decade by such black artists as Wilson Pickett, Percy Sledge, and Arthur Alexander. The British band recorded three tracks, "Brown Sugar," "Wild Horses," and the old-fashioned blues of "You Got to Move," before heading off to California. In Altamont, remarkably, the Stones' management hired the Hell's Angels to protect the stage and paid them in beer. The Angels killed an armed, drug-crazed fan a few feet from where Mick Jagger was singing. It was the anti-Woodstock. No peace and love this time. Just more violence, madness and blood.

71

Homecoming

Late in the year, at a time when the war seemed to have no end, John Kerry, a naval officer who had served as a Swift Boat commander in Vietnam, was reassigned to the United States. Kerry had recently received his third shrapnel wound, resulting in his third Purple Heart, and had been awarded a Bronze Star and a Silver Star for heroism.

But Kerry had misgivings about the war. He could see what the violence and the moral ambiguities were doing to the men who were assigned to fight it, and after his discharge from active duty he joined a group called Vietnam Veterans Against the War. The group began spontaneously in 1967 when some twenty veterans participated in a peace march and carried a banner that soon became the name of their organization. By the early 1970s, as Kerry emerged as a leading spokesman, VVAW would have twenty thousand members. Like many of them, Kerry saw the horrors of conflict through the lens of a veteran—concerned, yes, about what the war was doing to the people of Vietnam, but more immediately with what it was doing to U.S. troops. Even those who had committed atrocities, like the men at My Lai, were, Kerry thought, caught up in a policy insanity that was ultimately not of their creation. In testimony before the Senate Foreign Relations Committee, he spoke of his conversations with other veterans:

> I would like to talk on behalf of all those veterans and say that several months ago in Detroit we had an investigation at which over 150 honorably discharged, and many very highly decorated, veterans testified to war crimes committed in Southeast Asia. These were not isolated incidents but crimes committed on a day-to-day basis with the full awareness of officers at all levels of command. It is impossible to describe to you exactly what did happen in Detroit—the

> emotions in the room and the feelings of the men who were reliving their experiences in Vietnam. They relived the absolute horror of what this country, in a sense, made them do.
>
> They told stories that at times they had personally raped, cut off ears, cut off heads, taped wires from portable telephones to human genitals and turned up the power, cut off limbs, blown up bodies, randomly shot at civilians, razed villages in fashion reminiscent of Genghis Khan, shot cattle and dogs for fun, poisoned food stocks, and generally ravaged the countryside of South Vietnam in addition to the normal ravage of war and the normal and very particular ravaging which is done by the applied bombing power of this country.

My friend Graham Timbes was part of the fighting in 1969. He was a private first class in the 101st Airborne Division, and the casualty rate in his particular unit was among the highest of any U.S. military units. He remembered thinking, when he heard about My Lai, or similar crimes, that the men who committed these terrible acts—things he could not imagine doing himself—must have been obeying orders from above, and the orders must have gone higher than Lieutenant Calley. Timbes had seen men do awful things. Once a sergeant he knew fairly well, a man he and others called Scotty, shot an enemy soldier and dragged the body back to his own lines. At that point, said Timbes, "he shot him about 150 times, then started jumping on him." When Timbes asked Scotty why, the sergeant said he wanted to see how much blood he could get out of one body. Most soldiers were not like Scotty; most, said Timbes, were people like himself, "a scared kid" just trying to stay alive and help his comrades do the same.

Once he came within an inch or two of a trip wire on a booby trap which would have blown him into unrecognizable pieces. Later that day he developed a migraine and began to see spots in one of his eyes. It was a problem he had battled periodically since he was twelve, and the medic in his unit—a black man everybody called "Dixie"—examined the eye in which his vision was blurred and ordered him evacuated from the front. Timbes spent the rest of the war in a communications unit, maintaining radio contact with men in the field, but he never forgot those feelings on patrol—the conviction that on any given day he had about a fifty-fifty chance of survival.

"That *is* traumatic stress," he said, and he knew that many men never recovered. He wrote poems about this strange brotherhood, about bonds that were forged in the middle of terror, and some of the poems were later published.

The motion was unnoticed
as the hardcore sarge bent at Ponder's side;
grasped the wet poncho and covered the legs
and settled back in his position
eyes unchanged, staring at the night

If Timbes saw humanity in the midst of the fighting, he also understood the wounds and knew that not all were physical. He thought they would take a long time to heal.

ANOTHER FRIEND, LYNN BRANDON, also saw the lasting effects of the war. It hurt her in those last days of the sixties to see soldiers abused when they came home—taunted, ostracized, accused of being criminals, even though she too had deep misgivings about the conflict. Her father, Colonel William Douglas Brandon, was one of the first Americans sent to Vietnam, back when John F. Kennedy was president and U.S. troops were known as "advisers." Although Colonel Brandon believed, almost from the start, that the war was unwinnable, he and his fellow troops did more than advise. They also began the decade-long dumping of Agent Orange and other chemicals to defoliate the Vietnamese countryside—to kill the jungle and thus, theoretically, destroy the hiding places of the enemy.

When he returned from the war, Colonel Brandon wanted to do something life-affirming. He had two children already, but he and his wife decided to have a third, and almost immediately they saw that something was terribly wrong with the newborn. Catherine Ann Brandon had suffered genetic damage. She was missing, they later discovered, chromosome 22; the symptoms included hyperthyroidism, learning disabilities, difficulty speaking clearly enough to be understood, and other problems that would haunt her life. Nor did the problems end with her generation. Catherine's daughter, according to documents filed by the family, suffered from "rheumatoid arthritis; scoliosis; seizure disorder; periodic delusional hallucinations . . ." Her toes grew out of the top of her foot. Another child required two surgeries to correct a deformity of the heart, and another operation on her spine, and Colonel Brandon himself developed prostate cancer. All of these became recognized symptoms of Agent Orange, a chemical the military had insisted was safe.

The Brandons were one of nearly forty thousand families to file claims with the Department of Veterans Affairs, beginning a long and frustrating struggle with a government that had sent them to Vietnam in the first place. Estimates of the number of Vietnamese battling the effects of this chemical warfare vary widely but run into the millions.

In his Congressional testimony on the multiple tragedies of the war, John Kerry wondered rhetorically—as the killing continued in Vietnam—who would be "the last man to die for a mistake?"

In addition to that unsettling question, others would haunt us for the next fifty years. Would we—the people who fought and the people who did not—find a way to *live* with this mistake? Would we learn something from it? Or would we repeat it again and again?

72

Redemption

At the end of another disheartening year, I found myself, as a young reporter, getting ready to cover a new story. I had read a book published earlier in 1969 with an ironic and grimly humorous title: *Custer Died for Your Sins: An Indian Manifesto.* It was the seminal work of Vine Deloria Jr., a Standing Rock Sioux from North Dakota. For three years beginning in 1965, Deloria served as executive director of the National Congress of American Indians, which some have called the native answer to the NAACP. Whatever the organizational comparison, Deloria brought a philosopher's eye to his work—really a theologian's, for he came from a line of Episcopal priests and had earned his master's degree from a Lutheran seminary. Another of his books, *God Is Red,* was widely praised as an important work of twentieth-century theology. In it, Deloria offered comparative reflections on Christianity and Native American spirituality, making a scholar's case for the wisdom of his Indian ancestors.

Custer Died for Your Sins was not without its spiritual dimension. But its fundamental purpose was secular. In a manifesto addressed to white America, Deloria pointed out that despite the country's genocidal past—the Indian wars and the theft of land and efforts by the Bureau of Indian Affairs to snuff out the remnants of Indian culture, the native people had not gone away. Nor would they. On the contrary, they were reasserting their rights, but more than that, their Indian identity, which was more complex and multilayered than the stereotypes. Deloria made his case with a passion shaped, if not exactly softened, by a wicked sense of humor. Writing, for example, about white nonprofit organizations, he concluded:

> In the private sector . . . paternalism is a fact of life. Nay it is standard operating procedure. Churches, white interest organizations, universities, and

> private firms come out to the reservations asking only to be of service IN THEIR OWN INIMITABLE WAY. No one asks them to come out. It is very difficult, therefore, to get them to leave.

In the defiant first chapter of *Custer*, Deloria told the story of Alex Chasing Hawk, a member of the tribal council at the Cheyenne River Sioux Reservation, a part of South Dakota where the high plains break and the buffalo roam—a place later famous as the cinematic backdrop for *Dances With Wolves*. At a Congressional hearing in Washington, Chasing Hawk was asked by a member of the U.S. House of Representatives, "Just what do you Indians want?"

"A leave-us-alone law!" Chasing Hawk responded. To which Deloria added:

> The primary goal and need of Indians today is not for someone to feel sorry for us and claim descent from Pocahontas to make us feel better. Nor do we need to be classified as semi-white and have programs and policies to bleach us further. Nor do we need further studies to see if we are feasible. We need a new policy by Congress acknowledging our right to live in peace, free from arbitrary harassment. We need the public at large to drop the myths in which it has clothed us for so long. We need fewer and fewer "experts" on Indians.
>
> What we need is a cultural leave-us-alone agreement, in spirit and in fact.

At the moment I came upon Deloria's book, I was preparing to take a job in Nashville with the Race Relations Information Center (RRIC), a Ford Foundation-sponsored project aimed at chronicling the ethnic uprisings then taking place in America. Though small, the RRIC had amassed a remarkable staff of writers. Jim Leeson would later teach journalism at Vanderbilt University. John Egerton would soon emerge as one of the South's finest authors with his books, *The Americanization of Dixie* and *Speak Now Against the Day*. Jack White and Bernard Garnett would go on to distinguished careers at *Time* and the *Wall Street Journal*, respectively. I was the rookie member of the group, twenty-two years old, and to secure a place for myself, I volunteered to cover the Indian beat. I had no idea what I was doing, but with some trepidation and full awareness of my own presumption, I tracked down a phone number and called Vine Deloria.

Indian protests had been in the news, and we talked about that, specifically about the seventy-eight, mostly college-educated young Native Americans who had occupied Alcatraz Island since the night of November 20. Shielded by the foggy mists of San Francisco Bay, they had arrived in small groups on multiple boats and scaled the rugged slopes of the Rock, as the abandoned prison was called. Some of them were surprised by the cold, and when they gathered in what had been the warden's office, they broke wooden furniture into kindling for a fire. Their spokesman was Richard Oakes, a Mohawk from New York State, who had, like other members of his tribe, dropped out of school to find a job as an high-beam ironworker. He made good money off and on, walking the steel girders of Manhattan skyscrapers, a job that was not for the faint of heart. People said Oakes was both friendly and fearless—and gravely concerned about the realities of life among Native Americans.

He had worked for a while in San Francisco as a bartender in an establishment where Indians made up much of the clientele. Bar fights were common, as if these Native American men were aiming a larger frustration at each other. Moved in part to understand such things, Oakes enrolled in San Francisco State College and became a student in its new Native American studies program. Similar programs for black students were becoming popular across the country. In many ways the student occupiers at Alcatraz were strongly influenced by the Black Power movement. They proudly embraced the idea of Red Power, a bold assertion of anger and strength by Indian people who were battling against a long history of oppression.

Many Native Americans in the San Francisco Bay area were there as a direct result of the most unpopular Indian policy since the nineteenth century. In 1950, President Harry Truman appointed Dillon Myer as Commissioner of Indian Affairs. During World War II, Myer had directed the U.S. War Relocation Authority, which performed the historically repugnant task of removing more than 120,000 Japanese Americans to internment camps. What better person to direct the removal of Indians from their reservations under a policy known as termination? The stated goal was to end the treaty relationships between the government and the Indian tribes and to assimilate Native Americans into the national mainstream. One-way bus tickets from reservations to cities like San Francisco, and unfulfilled promises of good jobs, accompanied a far-reaching plan to send Indian children to boarding schools where they were forbidden to speak their native languages.

In their book *Like a Hurricane*, recounting the story of the modern Indian movement, Paul Chaat Smith and Robert Allen Warrior quoted the summation of Earl Old Person, a leader in the National Congress of American Indians, regarding the policy of termination:

> It is important to note that in our . . . language the only translation for termination is to 'wipe out' or 'kill off'. . . . Why is it so important that Indians be brought into the "mainstream of American life"? . . . The closest I would be able to come to "mainstream" would be so say . . . "a big, wide river." Am I to tell my people that they will be "thrown into the Big, Wide River of the United States?"

By the 1960s, many of the urban Indians in San Francisco found themselves drowning in alcohol and poverty, invisible almost in their low-paying jobs. Against that backdrop the idea of the Alcatraz occupation caught on quickly. In 1962, the U.S. government had decided to close this most forbidding of federal prisons, due in part to maintenance costs, and the Indians came upon the language of a treaty, signed in 1868 by the Sioux at Fort Laramie, promising surplus federal land to the tribe. Citing that somewhat shaky legal ground, the native demonstrators seized the island to a wave of favorable national publicity. With its menacing deployment of Coast Guard cutters, the government, for a time, played the role of villain, and for the whole country the Alcatraz story proved a welcome respite to media accounts of My Lai and Vietnam.

Vine Deloria and I talked about these things, and while he welcomed the new wave of militancy, he pointed to other protests—more substantial, in his view—involving the rights and identity of reservation people. I asked him in that first conversation if he found it presumptuous for a white reporter, starting from scratch, to undertake coverage of the "Indian beat." His answer—delivered, I thought, with extraordinary kindness—represented a solid piece of advice for a journalist writing about anything.

"No, it's not presumptuous," he said, "as long as you listen."

With that cautionary encouragement, I embarked immediately on a series of stories, ranging geographically from the Pacific Northwest, to Navajo country in New Mexico, to the coastal plains of North Carolina. In the state of Washington, a veteran activist named Hank Adams was leading a "fish-in" movement to reassert the treaty rights of the Northwestern tribes. Adams, an Assiniboine-Sioux, had grown up on the Quinalt Reservation in Washington and had been part of an effort since 1964 to reclaim the unfettered right to fish the waters that had sustained the Quinalts since long before the coming of the white man. As Adams and other activists understood it, the state's attempts to impose its fishing regulations upon the Indians represented a multilayered threat—to the economic well-being of the tribes, to the legal rights enshrined in the treaties they had signed, and perhaps most importantly to the heart of their identity as a people: their connection to their history, to the land and the water, and to each other.

Further south in Washington, the Yakima Indians were fighting for the return of their sacred mountain, a glacier-capped volcano known as Mt. Adams, which rose high above the surrounding valley, appropriated now by the National Forest Service for the valuable timber that grew on its slopes. Remarkably, the stories I wrote for our small publication seemed to embarrass the Nixon administration, and the Yakimas got their mountain back. I wrote also of Navajo children taken from their homes and sent away to boarding school in an unfamiliar place—physically abused and forbidden to speak the Navajo language, while their teachers tried to turn them into somebody else. In North Carolina, the Lumbees feared the same fate for their children, less dramatically, as their Indian schools were lost to desegregation.

I wrote about these and other stories, talking with Deloria periodically until I felt more comfortable with my own understandings. In the course of those conversations we spoke not only about Indian protests, but about artists and writers and the understanding of the world contained in their work. In particular, we talked about a novel that in 1969 won the Pulitzer Prize for fiction. *House Made of Dawn* was then, and remains, the most heralded work by N. Scott Momaday, a Kiowa from the southern plains, who spent time growing up among the Pueblo people in the desert Southwest. I thought his novel read like a painting.

> The old man Francisco drove a team of roam mares near the place where the river bends around a cottonwood. The sun shone on the sand and the river and the leaves of the tree, and waves of heat shimmered from the stones. The colored stones on the bank of the river were small and smooth, and they rubbed together and cracked under the wagon wheels. Once in a while one of the roan mares tossed its head, and the commotion of its dark mane sent a swarm of flies into the air. Downstream the brush grew thick on a bar in the

> river, and there the old man saw the reed. He turned the mares into the water and stepped down on the sand. A sparrow hung from the reed.

And this:

> *They were* golden eagles, a male and a female, in their mating flight. They were cavorting, spinning and spiraling on the cold, clean columns of air, and they were beautiful. They swooped and hovered, leaning on the air, and swung close together, feinting and screaming with delight. The female was full-grown, and the span of her broad wings was greater than any man's height. There was a fine flourish to her motion; she was deceptively, incredibly fast and her pivots and wheels were wide and full-blown. But her great weight was streamlined and perfectly controlled. She carried a rattlesnake; it hung shining from her feet, limp and curving out in the trail of her flight. Suddenly her wings and tail fanned, catching full on the wind, and for an instant she was still, widespread and spectral in the blue, while her mate flared past and away, turning around in the distance to look at her. Then she began to beat upward at an angle from the rim until she was small in the sky, and she let go of the snake. It fell slowly, writhing and rolling, floating like a bit of silver thread against the wide backdrop of the land.

And finally this about the native people of New Mexico:

> They do not hanker after progress and have never changed their essential way of life. Their invaders were a long time in conquering them; and now, after four centuries of Christianity, they still pray in Tanoan to the old deities of the earth and sky and make their living from the things that are and have always been within their reach; while in the discrimination of pride they acquire from their conquerors only the luxury of example. They have assumed the names and gestures of their enemies, but have held on to their own, secret souls; and in this there is a resistance and an overcoming, a long outwaiting.

Against this backdrop of tradition, and an awareness of the land—of a *place*—as a living entity of many parts, the flawed protagonist in Momaday's novel is an Indian veteran of World War II. Damaged emotionally by his experience, Abel becomes an alcoholic drifter whose nihilism drives him to an affair with a white woman, then to murder and a six-year prison term. After his release, he finds himself in Los Angeles living in an urban Indian community and still on an aimless downward spiral. In the midst of a flailing, drunken rage he is badly beaten by a policeman and almost dies. His friends put him on a train to New Mexico, where he reunites with the grandfather who raised him, but who is now on his deathbed. Abel waits at the old man's side, lost in bits and pieces of memory, the lessons his grandfather taught him, and when death finally comes, he prepares the body for burial in the Indian way. Then in the frigid light of dawn he begins to run.

> Pure exhaustion took hold of his mind, and he could see at last without having to think. He could see the canyon and the mountains and the sky. He could see the rain and the river and the fields beyond. He could see the dark hills at dawn. He was running, and under his breath he began to sing.

The reader does not know what happens next, but we are left to assume that Abel now has found his way home, back to his people and a place inseparable from who he is, who he always was. In that way he becomes a metaphor for his generation, Native Americans born in the twentieth century, who struggled with a feeling of dual identity. This character from Momaday's novel has dealt, perhaps, with some of the demons that afflicted Ira Hayes, the Indian hero of World War II about whom Johnny Cash once sang—a young man who never found his way back and finally, in an alcoholic stupor, passed out and died in a drainage ditch.

NOW IN THE CLOSING years of the sixties, the story at last was beginning to change. That was Momaday's leap of faith, and Deloria's too, though they acknowledged the struggle was difficult, involving a cosmic dislocation amid competing views of the world. In an essay called "Thinking in Time and Space," Deloria argued that white America has thought of itself as moving through time, its history unfolding in a linear way—with inevitability and purpose, as when Europeans conquered the North American continent. Indians, on the other hand, have thought less about time and more about space—"a sacred center at a particular place," in Deloria's words, which may be a mountain, a river, or valley, or some other feature on the face of the land. And though the winds of history may blow, the sense of place is meant to endure, and to nurture the truth of what it means to be alive. Thus, Hank Adams's fish-ins in the state of Washington, or the Yakimas' quest to get their mountain back, had a meaning that was more than economic or political. These were acts of renewal—of renaissance and redemption, the present reconnecting with the past, as if history moved in a whole different way.

In these final days of the 1960s, our decade of hope and tragedy and blood, I was gratified to have discovered this story, grateful to blind, inscrutable luck for the chance to be writing about redemption. In the coming years, I would search subconsciously for that theme in other places and would sometimes find it. In Charlotte, North Carolina, I covered the landmark school busing case, which began in 1969 and compelled a Southern community to come to terms with its segregated past. I wrote about the music of Johnny Cash and other artists who reminded us of the things we held in common, and about the Presidency of Jimmy Carter, which failed in the end but began with such promise.

Carter was one of those New South governors who emerged at the close of the 1960s. He joined Democrat Reubin Askew of Florida and Republican Linwood Holton of Virginia on what seemed to be the cutting edge of history. Carter especially made his mark when he declared in his inaugural address, "I say to you . . . that the time for racial discrimination is over." In a sense, Carter rode that moment to the presidency, and once in office he would make it clear that the civil rights lessons of the 1960s informed the human rights policies of his administration. He said:

> I'm the product of an emerging South. I see the clear advantages of our throwing off the millstone of racial prejudice. I think it's a process that's compatible with the moral and ethical standards of our nation—the heritage of our country, as envisioned by our forefathers. I also see that we have a special responsibility here. When we are meek, or quiescent, or silent on the subject of civil rights at home or human rights abroad, there is no other voice on Earth that can replace the lost voice, the absent voice, of the United States.

If Carter as president echoed the idealism of civil rights, one of the most powerful movements of the sixties, he also believed that there were other echoes. The conservatism represented by his successor Ronald Reagan had its roots in that pivotal decade, as did Reagan's political career. At its best this was a movement that emphasized fiscal restraint and personal responsibility, and gave voice to a populist rejection of left-wing excess—the burning of ghettos, draft cards, and flags that offended the sensibilities of mainstream Americans. But it was also a movement with its own share of baggage. George Wallace, master of the "politics of rage," had a gift for symbolic gestures of division—standing in the schoolhouse door or outside the prison stockade at Fort Benning, Georgia, expressing his support for Lieutenant William Calley. As a presidential nominee, Ronald Reagan, viewed by some as more benign, chose to make his campaign's opening stop in Philadelphia, Mississippi, site of the infamous murders of the civil rights workers Chaney, Goodman, and Schwerner during Freedom Summer in 1964. There in 1980, Reagan chose to speak about states' rights, still in that part of the world a code word for segregation and for the racism that had given it life. A strategy of division—of appealing directly to our national mean streak—continued as a staple of the political right.

History did not stop as the 1960s came to an end, nor did the great American schizophrenia, that cleavage in our national heart and soul that had come so painfully into sharper focus. I would find myself thinking periodically as the years went by of that moment in 1968, described earlier, that embodied so clearly both sides of that divide—the image of Robert Kennedy standing on a flatbed truck in Indianapolis, telling an all-black crowd, who didn't yet know, about the murder of Martin Luther King. He looked so small and frail in that instant, hunched against the cold, delivering an appeal for peace and justice that seemed to tear from his heart. He spoke without notes.

> My favorite poet was Aeschylus and he once wrote, "Even in our sleep, pain which cannot forget falls drop by drop upon the heart, until, in our own despair, against our will, comes wisdom through the awful grace of God."

I have often wondered in the years since if Kennedy and Aeschylus were right about that, if their affirmation of wounded hope was a match for the realities of history. Or does hurt, if it's massive enough, only beget more of the same?

Even now, I do not know the answer.

Notes and Acknowledgments

Because this is a work of synthesis, the contributions of other authors, journalists, historians and interview subjects are crucially important, and I seek, in the pages that follow, to acknowledge my debt in some detail. Reading David Halberstam's book, *The Fifties*, more than a decade ago helped stir my first thoughts of a book on the sixties. Todd Gitlin's much-praised historical memoir, *The Sixties: Years of Hope, Days of Rage*, offers a thorough and insightful overview of the radical political currents of that decade, and I read and benefited from Heather Ann Thompson's *Speaking Out: Activism and Protest in the 1960s and 1970s*. Taylor Branch's civil rights trilogy, *America in the King Years*, provides something close to a definitive civil rights history of the time, as does David Garrow's King biography, *Bearing the Cross*. For me, the most compelling Vietnam War history was Marilyn Young's, *The Vietnam Wars: 1945–1990*.

Scholars with particular realms of expertise who shared important thoughts with me include Jonathan Kauffman and Drs. Lewis Baldwin, Paige Vitulli, Timothy Lombardo, Stephanie Gray, Steven Trout, and Shane Dillingham. I'm also grateful for the feedback, insights and support I received from Stephen Dill, Becky McLaughlin, Marti Rosner, John T. Edge, Charisse Coleman, Erin Shim, Miller McPherson, Lynn Smith-Loving, Wendy Reed, Anne E. DeChant, Kathryn Scheldt, Claire Cage, Jamie Poole, Barbara Filion, Emily Blejwas, Doug Tanner, Ted Fillette, Paul Kurtz, Roy Hoffman, and Tom Lawrence. Special thanks to family members and friends who read and critiqued the whole manuscript: Kent Rush, Tom Peacock, and my wife Nancy Gaillard. My research assistant, Justine Burbank, was tireless and thorough and worked closely with me for more than two years. Thanks to two of my students, Megan McDowell and Taylor Kingrea, who also helped with research, and to Joel Sanders and Bob and Marilyn Bickel, who read the final page proofs and caught typos and errors that I and my editor had missed.

And, finally, thanks to the staff at the University of South Alabama's Marx Library. Here, chapter by chapter, are the sources for my reconstruction of this hope-filled, heartbreaking decade:

PREFACE: In his book, *Ask Not: The Inauguration of John F. Kennedy and the Speech That Changed America*, Thurston Clarke takes note of the words from President Kennedy's inaugural that are enshrined on his grave. The quote from Martin Luther King is taken from his August 28, 1963, "I Have a Dream" speech. My description of Robert Kennedy's speech at Vanderbilt is based on my own memory as well as an interview with Kennedy's friend, John Jay Hooker, who was with him on that occasion. The quote is taken from *RFK: Collected Speeches*, edited by Edwin O. Guthman. CBS anchor Walter Cronkite's famous announcement of President Kennedy's death is as heartbreaking today as when he delivered it. Robert Kennedy's quote, shrugging off the possibility of his own assassination, was taken from my interview with John Jay Hooker. I read again President Eisenhower's January 17, 1961, speech which contained his prophetic warning about a "military-industrial complex." Halberstam's description of the American Dream is taken from his book, *The Fifties*. Jack Newfield's similar description comes from his book, *A Prophetic Minority*.

CHAPTER 1: The description of the first sit-in of the 1960s is constructed primarily from my interviews with participants Franklin McCain, Joe McNeill, and Ezell Blair. I have written about that event and the movement it sparked in articles for the *Charlotte Observer* and the alternative newspaper, *Creative Loafing*, as well as in a monograph, *The Greensboro Four*, and in my earlier books, *Cradle of Freedom* and *With Music and Justice for All*. Historian William Chafe has also written extensively about the Greensboro movement, particularly in his award-winning book, *Civilities and Civil Rights: Greensboro, North Carolina, and the Black Struggle for Freedom*.

The account of the Charlotte sit-ins was based on interviews I did with Charles Jones and B. B. DeLaine for an article in *Creative Loafing* and later, in slightly different form, a chapter in *With Music and Justice for All*. For my account of the Nashville sit-ins, I relied on interviews with John Lewis, Diane Nash, Bernard Lafayette, and C. T. Vivian, and with the Reverend Will Campbell. Campbell recounted the story of Kelly Miller Smith and his daughter, Joy, desegregating Nashville's public schools, and their response to the bombing of one of those schools. The portrait of James Lawson is based on interviews with those same participants, as well as on Halberstam's *The Children* and John Lewis's memoir, *Walking with the Wind*. I also wrote about those sit-ins in *Cradle of Freedom*. Halberstam, Lewis, and Taylor Branch in his book, *Parting the Waters*, provided thorough accounts of the basic sequence of events in Nashville. Halberstam wrote about folk singer Guy Carawan, and I also interviewed Carawan's fellow folk artist Si Kahn about Carawan's influence.

James Lawson's pronouncements about radical love and nonviolence were delivered at the founding conference of SNCC and became part of the organization's statement of principle, which can be found online at the National Humanities Center Resources Toolbox—The Making of African American Identity: Vol. III, 1917–1968. In *Ella Baker and the Black Freedom Movement*, Barbara Ransby documents Baker's crucial role in the quest for civil rights. James J. Kilpatrick's quote on Negro inferiority originally appeared in *The Saturday Evening Post* and was quoted again by Garrett Epps in *The Atlantic* on August 18, 2010. Kilpatrick's description of the dignity of black protesters as compared to their white tormentors appeared in *Freedom*

Road: A History of America's Civil Rights Movement by Robert Weisbrot.

CHAPTER 2: Much of the description of Sam Cooke and Elvis Presley is based on Peter Guralnick's excellent biographies, *Dream Boogie: The Triumph of Sam Cooke* and *Last Train to Memphis: The Rise of Elvis Presley*. George Hamilton IV described to me the scenes of Cooke and the Everly Brothers trading songs on a tour bus. The Alabama Music Hall of Fame in Tuscumbia, Alabama, offers a good account of the life of Sam Phillips, as does Guralnick. The White Citizens Councils' racist condemnation of rock 'n' roll appeared in Craig Hansen Werner's book, *A Change is Gonna Come: Music, Race & the Soul of America*.

In describing the early life and career of Joan Baez, I relied on her autobiography, *And a Voice to Sing With*, and David Hajdu's *Positively Fourth Street: The Lives and Times of Joan Baez, Bob Dylan, Mimi Baez Farina, and Richard Farina*. The Baez quote about MLK comes from her autobiography. The quote from folksinger Odetta appeared in a 2007 interview with the *New York Times* and in several obituaries when she died the following year, including one in the *Times* and another in *Worker's World*. Writing about John Howard Griffin, I read his book, *Black Like Me*, and his earlier six-part series in *Sepia*. His reflections on blindness appeared in his book, *Scattered Shadows: A Memoir of Blindness and Vision*. The quotes about his disheartening experiences after assuming the identity of a Negro came from *Black Like Me*. The description of Harper Lee's frustrations while writing *To Kill a Mockingbird* is based on an account in the biography, *Mockingbird: A Portrait of Harper Lee*, by Charles J. Shields.

CHAPTER 3: Reflections on the issues of segregation and race by Lillian Smith are taken from her book, *Killers of the Dream*. The story of MLK's arrest while driving Smith to an Atlanta hospital is told in multiple places, including Branch's *Parting the Waters*, Garrow's *Bearing the Cross*, and my own *The Books That Mattered*. The account of JFK's presidential campaign is synthesized from Theodore White's *The Making of the President: 1960*, Ted Sorensen's *Kennedy*, Arthur Schlesinger's *A Thousand Days*, and Larry Sabato's *The Kennedy Half Century*. The account of Richard Nixon's 1960 run is based primarily on White's *The Making of the President*, Evan Thomas's *Being Nixon: A Man Divided*, and Jeffrey Frank's *Ike and Dick: Portrait of a Strange Political Marriage*. Frank, especially, offers a poignant portrait of the relationship between Eisenhower and Nixon and the condescension Nixon sometimes endured. White and Sabato offer compelling descriptions of the differing preparations by Nixon and Kennedy for their fateful presidential debate, and of the aftermath of that watershed moment—not only for politics, but also for the future of television. Rose Kennedy's ironic comment, "Nixon was smoother," is taken from Sabato's account.

Branch, Garrow, Schlesinger, White, and Sabato recount the spontaneous intervention of John Kennedy on behalf of an imprisoned MLK during the 1960 campaign. The Kennedy quotes are taken from Branch's *Parting the Waters*, as is the statement by Martin Luther King Sr., about why he would be voting for Kennedy, despite the candidate's Catholicism. Branch also quoted Kennedy's ironic response about fathers.

CHAPTER 4: The remarkable story of Margaret Sanger and Katharine McCormick's birth control movement is recounted in the following books, which served as the basis for my version: *Margaret Sanger: A Life of Passion* by Jean H. Baker; *Woman of Valor: Margaret Sanger and the Birth Control Movement in America* by Ellen Chesler; *Birth Control in America: The Career of Margaret Sanger* by David M. Kennedy; *Margaret Sanger: Pioneer of the Future* by Emily Douglas; *My Fight for Birth Control* by Margaret Sanger; *Selected Papers of Margaret Sanger, The*

Woman Rebel, 1900–1928, edited by Esther Katz; and *Katharine Dexter McCormick: Pioneer for Women's Rights* by Armond Fields. The story of John Rock and Irwin Winter meeting with the Food and Drug Administration was told in PBS's *American Experience* segment about the Pill, which can be found online at www.pbs.org. Natalie Angier's historical assessment of the Pill appeared in the November 2013 *Smithsonian.*

Two of the most useful accounts of Timothy Leary's life were *The Harvard Psychedelic Club: How Timothy Leary, Ram Dass, Huston Smith, and Andrew Weil Killed the Fifties and Ushered in a New Age for America* by Don Lattin; and more briefly, Leary's obituary by Laura Mansnerus in the *New York Times*, June 1, 1996. I also read *The Psychedelic Experience: A Manual Based on the Tibetan Book of the Dead* by Ram Das, with Leary and Ralph Metzner. My summary of the early life and career of Barry Goldwater was based on Rick Perlstein's *Before the Storm: Barry Goldwater and the Unmaking of the American Consensus* and White's *The Making of the President: 1964.* White's quote, "The Goldwaters helped build the State of Arizona," comes from *The Making of the President.* Goldwater's quote about the Supreme Court's landmark *Brown* decision appears in his book, *Conscience of a Conservative.*

I told the story of the Supreme Court's *Boynton v. Virginia* decision in my book, *Cradle of Freedom.* The quotes from Bruce Boynton came from his interviews with me. The quote from Reconstruction Congressman Robert Smalls came from an essay, "Election Methods in the South," written by Smalls in the *North American Review*, December 1890.

CHAPTER 5: There have been abundant and thoughtful works on the Eisenhower presidency, including Halberstam's reflections in *The Fifties.* The interpretation in this chapter is essentially my own, buttressed by *The Huffington Post*'s January 18, 2011, retrospective on Eisenhower's "military-industrial complex" speech. In their books *Ask Not, A Thousand Days, Kennedy,* and *The Kennedy Half Century*, authors Clarke, Schlesinger, Sorensen, and Sabato capture different dimensions of the John Kennedy inaugural. All agree on the power of Kennedy's address, but Sabato also reminds of Kennedy's "darker" side, including his sexual dalliance with actress Angie Dickinson during a break in the inaugural celebration. Sabato is also the source for future House Speaker Nancy Pelosi's reaction to Kennedy's address. Clarke quoted Barry Goldwater's response to the speech in a *New York Times* op-ed piece, January 15, 2005.

I reread *The Ugly American* by William Lederer and Eugene Burdick, an indictment of the arrogance of U.S. diplomats. The book was one of Kennedy's favorites and indirectly was one of the inspirations for the Peace Corps. The Peace Corps website tells the story of Kennedy's speech at the University of Michigan on October 14, 1960, in which he proposed such a venture. Nixon's worry that the Peace Corps would become "a haven for draft dodgers" has been cited in multiple sources, including the National Archives Educator Resources (see Archives.gov) and a *Time* retrospective published September 2, 2011.

Tom Wolfe's *The Right Stuff* offers a colorful history of the Mercury astronaut program, supplemented in my research by NASA's own records. Wolfe best captures Alan Shepard's impatience with NASA's delay of his flight. My account of the pioneering flight of Ham, the space chimpanzee, is taken primarily from earlier research with co-author Melinda Farbman for *Spacechimp: NASA's Ape in Space*, a children's book. Farbman and I condensed the details made available by NASA historians into a detailed account of Ham's flight. The quote from a Soviet doctor about the character of cosmonaut Yuri Gagarin, the first man in space, can be found in the European Space Agency's online history, "50 Years of Humans in Space."

CHAPTER 6: Stokely Carmichael's "simplicity" quote about the freedom rides appears in Raymond Arsenault's book, *The Freedom Riders: 1961 and the Struggle for Racial Justice*. The dramatic story of these rides has also been told well in Diane McWhorter's *Carry Me Home*, Halberstam's *The Children*, Lewis's *Walking With the Wind*, Branch's *Parting the Waters*, B. J. Hollars's *The Ride Rolls On*, Fred Powledge's *The Civil Rights Movement and the People Who Made It*, Howell Raines's *My Soul Is Rested*, Andrew Manis's *A Fire You Can't Put Out*, Garrow's *Bearing the Cross*, and in the documentary film series, *Eyes on the Prize*. I wrote about the subject extensively in my own *Cradle of Freedom*, basing my account, then as now, partially on the insights of other writers, but even more on my interviews with participants, in various ways, John Lewis, Bernard Lafayette, Diane Nash, C. T. Vivian, Fred Shuttlesworth, Colonel Stone Johnson, John Patterson, and John Seigenthaler. The quote from journalist Howard K. Smith appeared in his memoir, *Events Leading Up to My Death*. The "Burn them alive" cry by Klansmen appears in Arsenault's book, as does the story of Janie Miller, a twelve-year-old girl who brought water to the wounded riders. The quotes from Johnson and Seigenthaler are taken from my own interviews with them. The account of the negotiations between Seigenthaler and Patterson is based primarily on the compatible memories of both men. Floyd Mann's heroism has been detailed in multiple places; his "no killing here today" quote is in Arsenault's book and in David Niven's *The Politics of Injustice: The Kennedys, the Freedom Rides, and the Electoral Consequences of a Moral Compromise*. Though others have written about the mob siege at Ralph Abernathy's First Baptist Church in Montgomery, and footage from *Eyes on the Prize* helped bring it to life, my account is informed primarily by my interviews with Lafayette, Lewis, Shuttlesworth, and the reporter Bob Ingram. King's calming quote appears in *Eyes on the Prize*, as does Fred Leonard's account of Parchman prison.

As I say in the text, my description of the Bay of Pigs disaster was based substantially on Schlesinger's account in *A Thousand Days*. Schlesinger's perspective was unique. As an adviser to President Kennedy, he opposed the Bay of Pigs mission and writes informatively and with firsthand knowledge about the inner workings of presidential decision-making. I also read the accounts from Sabato and Sorensen, but quoted most extensively from Schlesinger's.

CHAPTER 7: My account of the 1961 Berlin crisis is synthesized from contemporary news reports, particularly from the *New York Times*, and the analyses of Schlesinger and Sabato, which differ primarily in tone. Schlesinger admired Kennedy much as the rest of us did at a distance—as a gifted politician and a leader with a remarkable capacity to inspire. Sabato, whose work about Kennedy and other subjects I have long respected, is colder, more objective, less sentimental about Kennedy's legacy. I benefited from both perspectives, applied essentially to the same set of facts, and the emphases here are my own. The Kennedy quotes in this chapter came from Schlesinger's *A Thousand Days* and Sabato's *The Kennedy Half Century*. John Seigenthaler, an avid reader, once told me of Kennedy's respect for John Hersey's book, *Hiroshima*.

Sabato reports Henry Kissinger's odd analysis regarding a "limited" nuclear war. Schlesinger quotes Kennedy's bland and somewhat misleading summary of the Vienna summit, which he initially offered to the American public, and Sabato quotes at length from the more sobering and bellicose speech that followed. Sabato describes East German leader Walter Ulbricht's suggestion that the Berlin crisis might be solved by the building of a wall. Sabato also describes a relieved and smiling Kennedy photographed at Nantucket Sound.

Kennedy's September 7, 1961, meeting with the first group of Peace Corps volunteers was described in a September 15, 2011, *Peace Corps Online* article by one of those young men, Ronald Schwarz, who also recounted the deaths of two of his fellow volunteers and quoted from the letter of David Crozier to his parents. Schwarz recalled how the people of Colombia referred to the first volunteers as "Kennedy's children." The quote from Colombia's President Alberto Lleras to Kennedy, explaining the massive crowds that turned out to greet him on December 17, 1961, is online at *Daily JFK: The Life of John F. Kennedy*.

Kennedy's quote to Adlai Stevenson regarding the resumption of nuclear testing appears in Schlesinger's *A Thousand Days*. The story of Women Strike for Peace is in Amy Swerdlow's book, *Women Strike for Peace: Traditional Motherhood and Racial Politics in the 1960s*. The records of the Women Strike for Peace organization are part of the Swarthmore College Peace Collection.

CHAPTER 8: With only minor errors of fact, Billy Crystal's 2001 HBO film *61* offers a touching overview of the drama, civility, and friendship surrounding the Maris/Mantle attempts to break Ruth's home run record set thirty-four years earlier. Historian Michael Beschloss wrote respectfully of the Mantle-Maris relationship in a *New York Times* article, "The M&M Boys: A Profile in Civility," published May 22, 2015. That article was my source for the Mantle quote, "Maris, I hate your guts," delivered as a joke within the hearing of several sportswriters who had written about a rivalry between the two. To me, the best profile of Maris during that time was by Roger Kahn in the October 2, 1961, *Sports Illustrated*. All Maris quotes in this chapter were taken from that article, "Pursuit of No. 60: The Ordeal of Roger Maris." So were the quotes from Rogers Hornsby and Whitey Ford. The description of Maris breaking the record on the final day of the season is based on stories in the October 2 *New York Times* and the October 9 *Sports Illustrated*. The radio call of that home run by Red Barber and Mel Allen can still be heard on Youtube.com.

CHAPTER 9: My thoughts on Walker Percy were shaped by rereading *The Moviegoer* and *Love in the Ruins* and by the depictions of Percy in Paul Elie's *The Life You Save May Be Your Own: An American Pilgrimage* and Albert Murray's *South to a Very Old Place*. Elie wrote about Percy through the lens of Catholicism and existentialist philosophy, Murray through the lens of race. Writing in *Slate* on November 2, 2012, critic Benjamin Hedin recounted the controversial selection of *The Moviegoer* as a National Book Award winner in 1962, calling it "one of the great upsets in the history of the National Book Awards."

Critic Neil Baldwin's description of *The Sea Around Us* appeared in an essay in the March 2003 issue of Ingram's *Advance* e-letter, as part of National Book Award Classics, a monthly series highlighting past winners. Baldwin was also the source for Carson's quote about the "winds, the sea, and the moving tides." Carson's quotes about the dangers of pesticides come from *Silent Spring*. Harvard environmentalist E. O. Wilson's commentary on *Silent Spring* came in an Afterword to a 2002 edition of Carson's book. The quote from Carson biographer Linda Lear came from her introduction to that same edition of *Silent Spring*. My summary of Carson's life was based on that introduction and on Lear's book, *Rachael Carson: Witness for Nature*. The fact that Carson's books sat on John Kennedy's bookshelf next to the writings of Henry David Thoreau appeared in an article by historian Douglas Brinkley in the May-June 2012 edition of *Audubon*. Brinkley described Kennedy's cautious, but important political embrace of Carson's work. The quote from William O. Douglas comparing *Silent Spring* to *Uncle Tom's Cabin* came from Brinkley's article.

In the *Huffington Post* on February 11, 2015, Peter Drier wrote incisively about Tom Hayden's emergence as a student radical. Hayden's quote about his encounter with MLK comes from Drier's article, and Drier writes as well about the political affinity between Hayden and Michael Harrington.

CHAPTER 10: The story of Illinois becoming the first U.S. state to decriminalize homosexuality is based on a December 21, 1961, *Chicago Sun-Times* article, the 1961 *Police Officer's Guide to Illinois Criminal Conduct*, and *Chicago Whispers: A History of LGBT Chicago Before Stonewall* by St. Sukie de la Croix. The quote from lesbian lawyer and activist Pearl Hart appeared in *Chicago Whispers. The Ladder*, a San Francisco publication that offered a fatalistic assessment of the Illinois law, is the oldest nationally distributed lesbian periodical in the country, going back to 1956. Its importance in the 1960s is documented in Lillian Faderman's *The Gay Revolution: The Story of Struggle.*

Ray Charles's quote about his love of country music came from my interview with him for *Watermelon Wine*. Permanent exhibits in the Alabama Music Hall of Fame tell of recording artist Arthur Alexander, as did a later exhibition in the Country Music Hall of Fame in Nashville. The documentary film *Muscle Shoals* offers one of the best depictions of the importance of the music scene in that remarkable town in north Alabama. One of the most intriguing accounts of the tragic lonely death in 1962 of Marilyn Monroe is in Susan B. Cloninger's *Theories of Personality*. Cloninger reflected on Monroe's life through the psychological theories of Karen Horney. I also benefited from Robert Gore-Langton's "The sad story of how beauty Marilyn Monroe was let down by her brains," published October 23, 2015, in the *Express.*

In his book, *Monologue: What Makes Americans Laugh Before Bed*, comedian Jon Mack wrote about the gold standard set by Johnny Carson for late-night talk show hosts. Billy Wilder's quote comes from *Monologue*. I reread James Baldwin's 1962 articles in *The New Yorker* and *The Progressive*, which became his prophetic book, *The Fire Next Time*.

CHAPTER 11: Some of the best accounts of the 1962 Albany, Georgia, civil rights standoff can be found in Branch's *Parting the Waters*, Garrow's *Bearing the Cross*, and Lewis's *Walking with the Wind*. I also wrote about the Albany Movement in *Cradle of Freedom* and *With Music and Justice for All* and interviewed SNCC participant Charles Jones. In *An American Insurrection: The Battle for Oxford, Mississippi, 1962*, historian William Doyle correctly frames the resistance to the admission of James Meredith to the University of Mississippi. I also read the accounts of Branch, Garrow, and Lewis, as well as James Silver's *Mississippi: The Closed Society*, and Schlesinger's recounting in *A Thousand Days* of the Kennedy brothers' role in the crisis. But two of the most vivid portraits of those extraordinary events were offered in *Son of the Rough South*, a memoir by *Newsweek* journalist Karl Fleming, who covered the crisis, and Will Campbell's *And Also With You*, a biography of the brave Episcopal priest Duncan Gray, who tried to calm the angry crowd. Claude Sitton's daily coverage in the *New York Times* was also extraordinary.

Fleming quoted Meredith's letter to university officials and the defiant assessment of Meredith's father. Lewis's assessment that Meredith was "a strange bird" appeared in *Walking with the Wind*. Fleming is the source for Meredith's "not a happy occasion" quote and of Ross Barnett's avowal that no Mississippi schools would be integrated along with Barnett's racist statement about blacks being evil. Barnett's "the Good Lord is the original segregationist" can be found in Doyle's *An American Insurrection*, as well as *The Ku Klux Klan in Mississippi: A History* by Michael Newton, and in Michael J. Klarman's *From Jim Crow to Civil Rights: The*

Supreme Court and the Struggle for Racial Equality. Karl Fleming documented Barnett's other buffooneries and his halftime speech at an Ole Miss football game. Will Campbell relates the story of the University Grays in the Civil War and Duncan Gray's bravery in opposing segregation, including his sermon during that time of crisis.

Schlesinger was the source for the Kennedy brothers' interactions with Barnett and the private banter that preceded that phone call. General Edwin Walker's cry of resistance is in Curtis Wilkie's *Dixie: A Personal Odyssey Through Historic Events That Shaped the Modern South*, and Walker's exhortations on the Ole Miss campus were quoted by Fleming. The description of the insurrection is based primarily on Fleming's vivid account, including the racist epithets from the mob. The reference to the "execution-style" killing of a French journalist can be found in Nick Bryant's article, "Black Man Crazy Enough to Apply to Ole Miss," which appeared in the Autumn 2006 *Journal of Blacks in Higher Education*.

Branch's quote of MLK's assessment of Kennedy and Barnett is from *Parting the Waters*. Garrow offers a powerful description of King's response to a physical assault by Nazi sympathizer Roy James in Birmingham, but my portrayal is based primarily on the eyewitness memory of Birmingham activist Lola Hendricks.

CHAPTER 12: This interpretation of the Cuban Missile Crisis is a synthesis of accounts in these sources: Graham Allison's *The Cuban Missile Crisis at 50* and Sabato's *The Kennedy Half Century*, two books with the advantage of historical perspective; and versions with the advantage of greater immediacy, including Schlesinger's *A Thousand Days* and *Robert F. Kennedy and His Times*, Sorensen's *Kennedy*, Robert Kennedy's *Thirteen Days: A Memoir of the Cuban Missile Crisis*, Defense Secretary Robert McNamara's introduction to *Thirteen Days* in which he offers his own recollection as a participant in those events, McNamara's additional reflections in the film, *The Fog of War*; an interview with John Jay Hooker; and accounts by PBS, *The Guardian*, and *National Geographic* about the spontaneous heroism of Soviet naval officer Vasil Arkhipov. I was also fortunate, years ago, to have a conversation with my cousin, Admiral Alfred Ward, who commanded the U.S. naval blockade. Quotes and specific episodes in the crisis that require attribution beyond those that are outlined here, or appear in the text, include the following:

Schlesinger quoted Khrushchev's boasts about the power of Soviet weapons in *A Thousand Days*. In his introduction to RFK's *Thirteen Days*, McNamara described the attorney general's role in the decision-making process as "far more than administrative." Sabato described the verbal confrontation between President Kennedy and General Curtis Lemay, as well as Kennedy's decision to stop at St. Matthew's Cathedral, and the measured advice offered by Roswell Gilpatric. Sorensen quoted Kennedy's "If they want this job . . ." response after meeting with members of Congress. Jacqueline Kennedy's conversation with her husband is based on more than eight hours of interviews she conducted with Schlesinger in 1964, published forty-seven years later in *Jacqueline Kennedy: Historic Conversations on Life With John Kennedy*, edited with annotations by Michael Beschloss. The quote also appeared in the *New York Times* on September 11, 2011. In *A Thousand Days*, Schlesinger quoted Bertrand Russell's criticism of Kennedy and praise for Khrushchev. Hooker described his late-night advice to RFK to get some sleep.

Many accounts have cited RFK's wise suggestion that his brother ignore a bellicose letter from Khrushchev and respond to a more conciliatory one, and most also credit JFK for rejecting the advice for a military attack on Cuba. Sabato called it Kennedy's "finest hour." Allison makes clear the probability of war if such a U.S. attack had occurred.

CHAPTER 13: The commentary on George Wallace is guided by two sources in addition to my own memory, shaped by a brief encounter with Wallace and having grown up in his state: Dan Carter's biography, *The Politics of Rage*, and the PBS documentary, *George Wallace: Settin' the Woods on Fire*, which aired as part of *The American Experience*. The quotes about Wallace from J. L. Chestnut and Seymore Trammell came from that documentary. All quotes from Eleanor Roosevelt are in the Eleanor Roosevelt Papers Project, associated with the History Department in the Columbian College of Arts and Sciences, George Washington University. The FDR quote about his affection for his Hudson River home comes from the National Park Service website, Home of Franklin Roosevelt National Historic Site.

CHAPTER 14: In *The Politics of Rage* Carter tells of a young Wallace standing where Jefferson Davis took the oath of office and knowing that he would one day return as governor. Carter, I, and others, including Marshall Frady in *Wallace*, have written about Wallace's ability to summon a shared memory of the Southern past. Wayne Greenhaw wrote about Asa Carter and his reinvention of himself as author Forrest Carter. Historians Garrow, Branch, and Dianne McWhorter have written well and extensively about the Birmingham movement. For my own account in *Cradle of Freedom* I interviewed many of the key leaders in Birmingham, including Fred Shuttlesworth. My friend Will Campbell described the fire hoses knocking demonstrators down. Many of us have quoted Klan leader Robert Shelton and his lieutenants at the time of the Birmingham movement. My account appears in *Cradle of Freedom*. I interviewed reporter Bob Ingram about Wallace on *Meet the Press* just before the stand in the schoolhouse door.

CHAPTER 15: The description of the murder of Medgar Evers was based primarily on the account in Branch's *Parting the Waters* and on the documentary, *Eyes on the Prize*. Mississippian Eudora Welty's short story, "Where Is the Voice Coming From?" was in *The New Yorker* on July 6, 1963.

In the June 11, 1963, *New York Times*, David Halberstam described the self-immolation of Buddhist monk Thich Quang Duc, and a photo by Malcolm Browne of the AP appeared in multiple newspapers. President Kennedy's quote about that photo appeared in numerous places, including the website of the Council on Foreign Relations. Kennedy's off-the-record "Jesus Christ!" was quoted in a retrospective by the British magazine *New Statesman* on April 1, 2010. Halberstam's haunting description appeared in his 1965 book, *The Making of a Quagmire*.

Schlesinger's reflections on the emotional truth of the Cuban Missile Crisis experienced by Kennedy and Khrushchev appeared in *A Thousand Days*. I quoted at length from Kennedy's American University speech because of the insight it offers into Kennedy's thinking about war and peace and the need for a nuclear test ban treaty. The statistic on nuclear material "ventings" from underground U.S. testing comes from *A Thousand Days*. Schlesinger offers perhaps the most detailed account of the negotiation of the 1963 test ban treaty.

In *Walking with the Wind*, John Lewis recounted A. Philip Randolph's role in persuading FDR to ban racial discrimination in defense industries. Lewis also recalled Randolph's response to Kennedy's argument against the 1963 March on Washington. The description of Dylan and Baez singing together at the March is based on David Hajdu's account in *Positively 4th Street*. King biographer Lewis Baldwin told me of King's affection for Mahalia Jackson's version of "A Balm in Gilead." Her quote, "Tell them about the dream," is in *Parting the Waters*, as is Kennedy's "damn good" assessment of King's speech.

CHAPTER 16: In writing about Betty Friedan, I reread *The Feminine Mystique* as well as some of her other writings. I also read *Betty Friedan and the Making of "The Feminine Mystique"* by

Daniel Horowitz. *Redbook's* editor's "off her rocker" comment is in a March 4, 1973, *New York Times* essay by Friedan, as is the quote about every woman "living a lie." Country singer George Hamilton IV's reflections on Patsy Cline were offered in interviews with me. The story of Loretta Lynn's relationship with Cline is based on a January 22, 2015, article by Juli Thanki in the *Nashville Tennessean*. Gloria Steinem's two-part expose of Hugh Hefner's Playboy Clubs appeared in the May 1 and June 1, 1963, issues of *Show* magazine. Her essay on her mother, "Ruth's Song," appeared in her book, *Outrageous Acts and Everyday Rebellions*, as did her comments on her suffragist grandmother.

CHAPTER 17: I first wrote about the Birmingham church bombing in a pair of retrospective articles in 1977 in the *Charlotte Observer* and *New West* magazine, and later in slightly different form in my books, *Race, Rock & Religion, Cradle of Freedom,* and *The Books That Mattered.* I interviewed many of those caught in the events of that day, including the Reverend John Cross, minister of the church that was bombed; his daughter, Barbara Cross, who had just left the four girls who were killed; the Reverend John Porter, who offered his church for the funeral; and Claude Wesley, whose daughter Cynthia was one of the victims. The extended excerpt comes from my own *The Books That Mattered.* I have also read other powerful accounts, including those in *Carry Me Home, Parting the Waters, Bearing the Cross, Walking with the Wind, The Politics of Rage*, and *Angela Davis: An Autobiography.* In *Cradle of Freedom* I quoted the statements of MLK and Alabama Attorney General Richmond Flowers, pointing the finger of blame at George Wallace.

In the *Washington Post* on October 24, 2013, Steven Levingston quoted Pierre Salinger and Secret Service agent Clint Hill on a new closeness between John and Jacqueline Kennedy after the death of their infant son, Patrick. In *A Thousand Days*, Schlesinger noted Kennedy's 59 percent approval rating in the polls in November 1963. Schlesinger also acknowledged that Kennedy "realized that Vietnam was his great failure." Sabato in *The Kennedy Half Century* also wrote about the president's indecision and ambivalence about Vietnam. For an understanding of the history of the war, I relied on multiple sources, the most succinct and accessible of which was Marilyn Young's *The Vietnam Wars.* Schlesinger wrote of Kennedy's growing preoccupation with poverty and the influence of John Kenneth Galbraith's *The Affluent Society* and Michael Harrington's *The Other America* on the president's thinking. Schlesinger also described Kennedy doodling "poverty . . . poverty" during a cabinet meeting on October 29.

In *A Thousand Days*, Schlesinger recounted Adlai Stevenson's concern about Kennedy's upcoming trip to Dallas. Sabato quotes Kennedy's philosophical "headed into nut country" comment, but the anecdote appeared first in *Johnny, We Hardly Knew Ye* by Kennedy advisers Kenneth O'Donnell and David Powers, with journalist Joe McCarthy. Sabato quotes a Secret Service agent's gentle words to Mrs. Kennedy after Kennedy was shot. I rewatched on YouTube.com Walter Cronkite's heart-breaking announcement of Kennedy's death, and NPR offered an excellent segment about Cronkite on November 22, 2013, the 50th anniversary. In *The Fog of War*, McNamara tearfully described selecting Kennedy's gravesite in consultation with Mrs. Kennedy. Sabato describes Mrs. Kennedy's careful planning of her husband's funeral, including her deliberate evocation of the memory of Abraham Lincoln under the guidance of historian James Robertson. Sabato also referenced Kennedy's "darker side," including his sexual appetites.

CHAPTER 18: Sabato, in *The Kennedy Half Century*, offers a detailed analysis of the Warren Commission. In seeking to understand the new and almost instant sense of national community forged by tragedy and grief and television, I read Benedict Anderson's *The Imagined Community* and discussed it with Dr. Stephanie Gray, who had written about it at the University of Georgia. Seigenthaler's remembrance of Robert Kennedy's bitter quip after the assassination of his brother is quoted in *Bobby Kennedy: The Making of a Liberal Icon* by Larry Tye and *Robert Kennedy and His Times* by Schlesinger. Schlesinger also quoted Salinger's assessment of the younger Kennedy as "shattered." In *Lyndon Johnson and the American Dream*, historian Doris Kearns (now known as Doris Kearns Goodwin) describes LBJ's assumption of presidential power with an authority and grace that surprised his critics. *Time,* Robert Caro in *The Passage of Power: The Years of Lyndon Johnson*, and Kearns all described Johnson as "sounding like a president" in his first major speech to Congress on November 27, 1963. In *The Death of a President,* William Manchester quoted Earl Warren's account of Johnson asking him to chair the commission investigating Kennedy's death. Sabato called that commission "the first damaging government whitewash in the 1960s."

CHAPTER 19: This description of LBJ's state of mind and governing style is synthesized from the accounts in *Lyndon Johnson and the American Dream*, *The Making of the President 1964*, and Taylor Branch's *Pillar of Fire*. Kearns, especially, described Johnson's meticulous preparations for each meeting he held with a national leader. Louis Lomax, one of the country's great African American journalists, wrote about Johnson in *Look* on March 10, 1964. Branch, Kearns, and Nick Kotz in his book, *Judgment Days: Lyndon Baines Johnson, Martin Luther King Jr., and the Laws That Changed America*, all described Johnson's initially promising conversations with King, and Branch and Kearns recount Johnson's advice to NAACP leader Roy Wilkins to court the support of Republican Senator Everett Dirksen. Kearns wrote with sympathy and insight of Johnson's instinctive understanding of poverty, even as he exaggerated his own experience of it. Kearns also wrote of Johnson's intention to build his own legacy as a president who got things done, by embracing John Kennedy's legacy of inspiration. Much of this is also revealed in Johnson's own State of the Union Address in 1964, which I have quoted at length.

On the website of the American Psychological Association, Executive Director Gwendolyn Puryear Keita quoted U.S. Surgeon General Luther Terry's assessment that his advisory commission's findings on the harmful effects of smoking "hit the country like a bombshell." Marcos Sueiro Bal cited the quote in a January 30, 2014, retrospective on WNYC Public Radio.

Figures on the national unemployment rate during Johnson's presidency were taken from the Bureau of Labor Statistics. Michael Hiltzik in the June 29, 2015, *Los Angeles Times* and the HBO film, *All the Way,* reference in slightly different words LBJ's threat to segregationist Senator Richard Russell of Georgia. Kearns described the affectionate and respectful dynamic that ordinarily prevailed in the relationship between Johnson and Russell. So did historian William Leuchtenburg in his book, *The White House Looks South: Franklin D. Roosevelt, Harry S. Truman, Lyndon B. Johnson*. Russell's pledge to "resist to the bitter end" was made to the U.S. Senate as he organized a filibuster against Johnson's civil rights bill. I relied primarily on Frady's *Wallace* and Carter's *The Politics of Rage* for my description of Wallace's 1964 presidential campaign. Carter wrote about Eliot Janeway coining the term "backlash" in 1963, and about the demonstrators who greeted Wallace at the University of Wisconsin. Carter also quoted the dismayed student who said of Wallace, "Southern charm oozed out." Wallace's quote, "'Dixie' sounds mighty good in Polish," is taken from the documentary, *George Wallace: Settin' the Woods on Fire*. Carter vividly describes the racial tension during a Wallace rally at the Serb Memorial Hall in Milwaukee.

In *Pillar of Fire*, Branch writes about Representative Howard Smith's introduction of provisions banning discrimination against women into the Civil Rights Act of 1964. Representative Carl Elliott's assessment of Smith's motives was quoted by Bruce Dierenfield in the *Virginia Magazine of History and Biography*. In *Bearing the Cross*, Garrow describes Johnson's attempt at the signing of the Civil Rights Act to persuade black leaders to forgo future demonstrations.

White's description of Johnson's "superb" performance in the early days of his presidency appears in *The Making of the President: 1964*. Kearns quotes *Fortune* and *New York Times* columnist James Reston offering similar assessments.

CHAPTER 20: *Time*'s description of Ed Sullivan was published October 17, 1955. The testy exchange between Sullivan and Harriet Van Horne is quoted on the Official Ed Sullivan Website. My summary of the Beatles' first U.S. trip is based primarily on Jonathan Gould's biography, *Can't Buy Me Love: The Beatles, Britain and America*; Mikal Gilmore's article, "How the Beatles Took America," in the January 16, 2014 *Rolling Stone*; and Ben Wener's fiftieth anniversary retrospective in the *Orange County Register*, January 14, 2014. John Lennon's quote about the influence of "Heartbreak Hotel" appears in Gould's biography. The dismissive estimate of the Beatles' talent by Dave Dexter was quoted in *Rolling Stone*. On November 15, 1963, *Time* described the band as "shaggy Peter Pans," and on November 22 *CBS Morning News* critic Alexander Kendrick declared that the Beatles "make non-music."

Paul McCartney offered his assessment of Kennedy in an interview with Larry Kane when the Beatles played at Comiskey Park in Chicago on August 20, 1965; a transcript is at www.beatlesinterviews.org. *Rolling Stone* recounted the Beatles clowning with reporters about baldness. Author Robert Lipsyte had reported Sonny Liston saying he wouldn't pose with "sissies" and on March 31, 2011, at a Manhattan Barnes & Noble, he described the scene in which the Beatles met then-Cassius Clay.

Four Tops lead singer Levi Stubbs's quote about Motown and the merger of black and white music appears in Kevin Phinney's *Souled American: How Black Music Transformed White America*, as did rock 'n' roller Mitch Ryder's comment about Motown sophistication. In *Sweet Soul Music*, Peter Guralnick describes Sam Cooke's decision to write "A Change Is Gonna Come." On NPR's *All Things Considered* on February 1, 2014, Guralnick spoke of how easily the song had come to Cooke. In an interview with me (and elsewhere), SNCC leader John Lewis described the inspiration he drew from the song. I interviewed Johnny Cash about his album of American Indian protest songs and his affiliation with Native American folksinger Peter LaFarge. Ira Hayes's story has been told in many places, including *Indian Country Today*, which called him a "reluctant hero."

CHAPTER 21: For this account of Freedom Summer and the events leading up to it, I relied on the following: Lewis's *Walking with the Wind*; Jack Newfield's *A Prophetic Minority*; Branch's *Pillar of Fire* and *Parting the Waters*; Garrow's *Bearing the Cross*; Pete Daniel's *Lost Revolutions: The South in the 1950s*; the photographic record, *Faces of Freedom Summer*, by Herbert Randall and Bobs M. Tusa; *The Speeches of Fannie Lou Hamer: To Tell It Like It Is*, edited by Maegan Parker Brooks and Davis W. Houck; *Student Activism and Civil Rights in Mississippi: Protest Politics and the Struggle for Racial Justice, 1960–65* by James P. Marshall; *Freedom's Orator: Mario Savio and the Radical Legacy of the 1960s* by Robert Cohen; the PBS documentary film series, *Eyes on the Prize*; the 2014 *American Experience* segment on PBS, "Fannie Lou Hamer's Powerful Testimony"; Debbie Elliot's 2014 *All Things Considered* report on NPR, "Freedom Strategy

Put to the Test"; and Sue Sturgis's article, "I Question America," in *Facing South*, published by the Institute for Southern Studies in Durham, North Carolina. Sources for specific quotes include the following:

Will Campbell's description of Bob Moses came from an interview I did with Campbell, though I heard him use similar words in other conversations. E. W. Steptoe's quote about a bloody Bob Moses came from *A Prophetic Minority*. Fannie Lou Hamer's quotes were part of her testimony before the Credentials Committee at the 1964 Democratic National Convention, reprinted in *Facing South*. In *Walking with the Wind*, Lewis wrote with admiration for Mrs. Hamer; described Moses's guilt over the death of Louis Allen; told of SNCC leaders' calculation that if harm came to young white activists the public would pay attention; and quoted John Doar's warning to the Freedom Summer volunteers and the Klan's description of CORE organizer Mickey Schwerner. Stephen Bingham's account of being warned in advance of civil rights murders in Mississippi appeared in a mimeographed letter he wrote in February 1964, and was quoted in Marshall's *Student Activism and Civil Rights in Mississippi*. In *Pillar of Fire*, Branch quotes Lawrence Rainey's suggestion that the three missing civil rights workers were part of a publicity stunt. In my book *As Long As the Waters Flow*, I wrote about the irony of the murdered workers' car being found near one of the holiest sites of the Choctaw Nation and an Indian mission being bombed, apparently by the Ku Klux Klan.

Jane Stembridge's letters to Lillian Smith were quoted in *Lost Revolutions*. In *Pillar of Fire*, Branch quoted Theodore White's dismayed response to the Harlem riots of 1964. In *Lyndon Johnson and the American* Dream, Kearns wrote about the president's meeting with civil rights leaders regarding the riots, and Branch recounted the FBI's investigation of the unrest. Charles Silberman's *Crisis in Black and White* provided for me and many others in the 1960s one of the best overviews of America's racial problems and my first introduction to Malcolm X. The quotes by and about Malcolm appeared in Silberman's book. The dialogue between Schwerner and the Klansmen who killed him is based on FBI interviews with informants and appeared in the July 23, 1989, *New York Times Magazine* article by Jesse Kornbluth. Lewis quoted the remarks of David Dennis and Arthur Lelyveld at the funeral of James Chaney. The depth of Dennis's rage comes through even more clearly in *Eyes on the Prize*.

CHAPTER 22: Most of the sources from the previous chapter were also the basis for my account of the Mississippi Freedom Democratic Party and its attempt to win seats at the Democratic National Convention. Hamer's quotes appear in *The Speeches of Fannie Lou Hamer*, *Walking with the Wind*, and Sturgis's article, "I Question America." Lewis describes Joseph Rauh's attempt to represent the Freedom Democrats at the convention. The Southern governor's "black buggers" comment to LBJ is in John Dittmer's *Local People: The Struggle for Civil Rights in Mississippi* and Bruce Watson's *Freedom Summer: The Savage Season of 1964 That Made Mississippi Burn and Made America a Democracy*. Both Lewis and Branch described LBJ's machinations to minimize publicity for the Freedom Democrats. The exchange between Hubert Humphrey and Hamer was described by Freedom Democrat leader Ed King and is quoted in *This Little Light of Mine: The Life of Fannie Lou Hamer* by Kay Mills. Lewis's desultory assessment of the convention and its impact on the civil rights movement appeared in *Walking with the Wind*.

In researching Mario Savio and the Free Speech movement at the University of California at Berkeley, I visited the UCB library and its extensive collection on the history of the movement. I also visited the Free Speech Movement Café, with quotes from Savio and other students posted on the walls, along with enlarged photographs and excerpts from Berkeley's student newspaper, the *Daily Californian.* I also relied on the excellent and very readable biography, *Freedom's Orator: Mario Savio and the Radical Legacy of the 1960s* by Robert Cohen. Most of the quotes from and about Savio come from Cohen's book, which, though sympathetic to Savio, offers a warts-and-all depiction of one of the most eloquent orators of the decade and a thorough account of the Free Speech crisis of 1964.

CHAPTER 23: Johnson's telephone conversation with Richard Russell was taped by the president on May 27, 1964, and quoted in part by Branch in *Pillar of Fire.* Robert Scheer also wrote about that conversation in the *Los Angeles Times* on March 25, 1997, following the release of tapes by the Johnson Library. My account of the Tonkin Gulf Resolution was synthesized from *Pillar of Fire*; *Lyndon Johnson and the American Dream*; the *Encyclopedia of the Vietnam War*, edited by Spencer C. Tucker; and Marilyn B. Young's *The Vietnam Wars, 1945–1990.* In addition, *Rolling Thunder in a Gentle Land: The Vietnam War Revisited* offers astute analysis of early military calculations in the war.

Rick Perlstein in *Before the Storm: Barry Goldwater and the Unmaking of the American Consensus* provided what was for me a breakthrough analysis of Goldwater's legacy and the birth of a powerful conservative movement in the wake his electoral defeat. In *The Making of the President—1964*, Theodore White also offers an astute analysis of Goldwater's campaign. One of White's obituaries noted that late in his life he regretted spending so much of his career caught in the daily rush of history, instead of stepping back and offering, over time, a broader analysis of the events he covered. But to me, the striking thing about *The Making of the President* series was how well it stood up to historical hindsight. He was a brilliant reporter. I also reread Phyllis Schlafly's *A Choice Not An Echo*, which became a grass-roots conservative manifesto and sounded the call for Goldwater's campaign.

White provided nuanced portraits of Goldwater's opponents for the Republican nomination, including two of the party's principled liberals, Nelson Rockefeller and William Scranton. Rockefeller's quote on corporate responsibility is in the 1974 edition of *CQ Almanac*, available through Princeton University Library. Perlstein wrote of Kennedy and Goldwater's mutual affection and respect and their idle conversations about sharing a campaign plane. Perlstein and White both wrote of Goldwater's depression and second thoughts about running for president after the Kennedy assassination, and Perlstein repeated Goldwater's candid "not even sure I've got the brains" quote in an interview with the *Chicago Tribune.* White reported that Goldwater told his wife he would not run. White also recounted a litany of Goldwater's most disturbing quotes, including "Let's lob one" and that poverty was tied to "low intelligence." Goldwater's more eloquent Memorial Day speech was quoted in, among other places, Michael W. Flamm's *In the Heat of the Summer: The New York Riots of 1964 and the War on Crime.* (The quote varies slightly in different accounts.)

Just as Perlstein understood the sweep of Goldwater's legacy, despite his presidential defeat, journalist E. J. Dionne, in *Why the Right Went Wrong*, understood the emergence of Ronald Reagan in that same 1964 campaign. If Goldwater had mobilized conservatives to political action, Reagan promised to give them a whole new voice.

CHAPTER 24: In *Robert Kennedy: His Life*, biographer Evan Thomas quotes the younger Kennedy's anguished cry when his brother, the president, was murdered: "Why God?" Both Thomas and Schlesinger, in *Robert Kennedy and His Times*, quote Kennedy's other existential question about God and the suffering of innocents. Schlesinger, whose affection for Robert Kennedy seemed to run as deep as for JFK, wrote of the depth of RFK's search for philosophical understanding after the most devastating event in his life. Newfield did the same in *RFK: A Memoir.* Newfield and RFK's friends Seigenthaler and Hooker each talked in conversations with me about Kennedy's spiritual search. Though I reread accounts in various biographies, I remember even now watching the Democratic National Convention on television in 1964 when Kennedy stood red-eyed through a twenty-two-minute ovation for his late brother. In *Bad Blood: Lyndon B. Johnson, Robert F. Kennedy and the Tumultuous 1960s*, Jeffrey K. Smith, among others, quotes Kennedy's joking comment about lowering the voting age to six.

Both Garrow in *Bearing the Cross* and Branch in *Pillar of Fire* describe the drama around Martin Luther King's acceptance of the Nobel Peace Prize, and the growing FBI campaign against him.

Chapter 25: For this chapter on Malcolm X, I read C. Eric Lincoln's *The Black Muslims in America*, the relevant chapters in Silberman's *Crisis in Black and White* and Baldwin's *The Fire Next Time*, and watched again Spike Lee's 1992 film, *Malcolm X.* But the most important source was *The Autobiography of Malcolm X*, especially Alex Haley's epilogue. I was also privileged to have a short, informative conversation with Haley about his project with Malcolm, and several conversations with Lincoln, who also knew Malcolm well. M. S. Handler's quote appears in his introduction to *The Autobiography of Malcolm X.* Elijah Muhammad's "hypocrites like Malcolm" quote appears in multiple places, including *The Savage Years: Tales From the 20th Century* by Rupert Colley, and *Days of Rage: America's Radial Underground, the FBI, and the Forgotten Age of Revolutionary Violence* by Bryan Burrough. I wrote about Malcolm's 1965 visit to Selma in *Cradle of Freedom.* Other accounts include those in *Walking with the Wind, Bearing the Cross,* and *Pillar of Fire.* Spike Lee used much of Ozzie Davis's powerful eulogy in *Malcolm X.* The eulogy can also be found on YouTube.

Chapter 26: For *Cradle of Freedom* I interviewed many of the participants in the tragic and triumphant events that took place in Selma, Marion, and other parts of the Alabama Black Belt. The quote from Dr. King, "You are as good as any white person," was delivered during a 1965 visit to Gees Bend, Alabama, and appears in my book, *Alabama's Civil Rights Trail,* co-authored with Jennifer Lindsay and Jane DeNeefe. John Herbers's description of the police attack on demonstrators in Marion was in the February 19, 1965, *New York Times.* Reverend L. L. Anderson's quote came in a 1977 interview with me for *New West* magazine. John Lewis told me about carrying a book by Thomas Merton in his backpack on Bloody Sunday. Merton's anguished response to the assassination of President Kennedy, written immediately after that event, appears in the November 3, 2015, *New Republic,* in an article by Michael Lindenburger. My description of the beatings on the Edmund Pettus Bridge was based on the Lewis's description in *Walking with the Wind,* documentary footage in *Eyes on the Prize,* and my own interviews with multiple participants, including Bob Mants, Amelia Boynton, and JoAnne Bland. I also read the accounts in *Bearing the Cross, Pillar of Fire,* and Nick Kotz's *Judgment Days.* In *Eyes on the Prize,* Andrew Young described his efforts to persuade angry African Americans not to abandon nonviolence in the immediate aftermath of the march. In an interview with me, quoted in *Cradle of Freedom,* F. D. Reese spoke of the importance of white volunteers answering the call of Dr. King. Abraham Heschel's quotes about King and the Selma march appear in multiple places, including Edward Kaplan's biography, *Spiritual*

Radical: Abraham Joshua Heschel in America, 1940–1972. In the January–February 2018 issue of the periodical *Moment,* Heschel's daughter, Susannah, recalled that her father wrote in his diary that he felt as if "my legs were praying." Lewis's quote, "SCLC is not the enemy," appears in *Walking with the Wind.* C. T. Vivian described to me the experience of watching President Johnson's speech about Selma and seeing Dr. King's tears. In an interview with me, quoted in *Cradle of Freedom,* Annie Cooper described her response to King's "The Arc Is Long" speech. In his testimony at the trial of Viola Liuzzo's killers, Leroy Moton described her singing "We Shall Overcome" during the final moments of her life.

CHAPTER 27: Billy Graham's "narrow gift" quote came from my interview with him for the *Charlotte Observer* in 1979. For three years as that paper's religion writer I covered Graham and his ministry extensively, and Graham spoke with me at length about his relationship with MLK. I later wrote about Graham's cautiously evolving social conscience for *The Progressive* and the *Washington Post.* Dorothy Counts showed me the postcard she received from Graham in 1957 after she was heckled and spat upon by a white mob in Charlotte. I wrote about that event, and Graham's words of encouragement to her, in my book, *The Dream Long Deferred.* For much of this chapter, I relied on Marshall Frady's *Billy Graham: A Parable of American Righteousness* and William Martin's *A Prophet with Honor: The Billy Graham Story.* Graham's quote about the ground at the foot of the cross appears in Martin's *With God on Our Side: The Rise of the Religious Right in America.* Graham's quote, "I haven't been to jail yet," appears in *The Preacher and the Presidents: Billy Graham in the White House* by Nancy Gibbs and Michael Duffy. I interviewed Stephen Dill at the time of Graham's visit to Montgomery, Alabama. Later, I had the privilege of writing the introduction to Dill's book, *The Poetry of Faith: Sermons Preached in a Southern Church.* Included among Dill's reflections were prophetic sermons on the issue of race. As a committed liberal, Dill said he felt encouraged and supported by Graham's Montgomery visit during the tension that followed the Selma to Montgomery march. In *A Prophet with Honor,* Martin wrote of Graham's caution about social pronouncements but his genuine commitment to racial understanding.

CHAPTER 28: Lyndon Johnson offered poignant insight into his decision to escalate the Vietnam War in his interviews with Doris Kearns for *Lyndon Johnson and the American Dream.* To me, the excerpt from Johnson quoted in this chapter went to the heart of his fateful choice.

The description of the antiwar teach-ins of 1965 is based on Marilyn Young's *The Vietnam Wars* and contemporary accounts in the University of Michigan student newspaper, the *Michigan Daily.* The reflections of sociology professor Thomas Mayer were published online March 22, 2015, in an article by Jeremy Allen in *MLive.* The description of police response to the teach-in appeared in the *Michigan Daily* on March 25, 1965. The pro-war opinions by professors at Yale and American University appeared in the *New York Times* on May 23, 1965. On April 18, 1965, the *Times* described the antiwar protests in Washington. Journalist and commentator I. F. Stone, a participant in the May 21, 1965, antiwar demonstrations at Berkeley, published his pointed observations on those and other events in his newspaper, *I. F. Stone's Weekly.* LBJ's early responses to the protests were described in *The Vietnam Wars* and in Merle Miller's *Lyndon: An Oral Biography.* The historical backdrop for the war, as I have written it here, was synthesized from numerous sources, but particularly from *The Vietnam Wars* and from Halberstam's *Ho,* a brief but incisive biography of Ho Chi Minh. The quotes from a Vietnam peasant about the cruelty of the South Vietnam regime and from a non-Communist supporter of the National

Liberation Front appeared in *The Vietnam Wars*, as did the rhetorical exhortations of Ho Chi Minh. As Marilyn Young makes clear, Ho for many years held to the hope that the American government would understand his cause. But Young, Kearns, and other historians make it equally clear that U.S. presidents, especially Johnson, saw Vietnam only through the lens of the Cold War, miscalculating the power of Vietnamese nationalism.

CHAPTER 29: Ronald Reagan offered his criticisms of Medicare soon after President Johnson proposed it. During the presidential campaign of 1980, after Medicare had become popular, Jimmy Carter was fond of quoting Reagan's words of opposition, as he did at a town hall meeting in Miami on October 21. Kearns and others wrote about Johnson's love of such programs, which fulfilled his ideal of government making life better for ordinary people. Senator Sam Ervin's quote about "Ethiopians" can be found in the transcript of an October 3, 2015, broadcast on NPR's *Weekend Edition.* I wrote in *Cradle of Freedom* about the trial of Viola Liuzzo's killer, which ended in a hung jury, relying on newspaper accounts in the *New York Times* and the *New York Herald Tribune* and on interviews I did with the prosecutor and witnesses in the courtroom. In *The Music Went Out of the Movement*, historian David Carter wrote about the importance of a speech by Johnson at Howard University on June 5, 1965, introducing the complexity of affirmative action into the national civil rights debate.

For this account of the Watts riots in 1965, I relied on contemporary reporting in the *New York Times, Newsweek,* and the *Los Angeles Times*, as well as historical accounts in *Bearing the Cross* and *Pillar of Fire.* One of the most vivid and personal descriptions of the violence is in Karl Fleming's memoir, *Son of the Rough South.* In the August 14, 2015, *Los Angeles Times,* writers Daina Beth Solomon and Dexter Thomas looked back on the courageous and effective reporting of Robert Richardson. Fleming quoted Police Chief William Parker's "monkeys in a zoo" remark and the rebuke of MLK by an angry black man in Watts. Garrow also wrote about King's visit to Los Angeles immediately after the riots and how it shaped King's new priority, economic justice. Bayard Rustin's comments about King's epiphany appeared in *Bearing the Cross.* King biographer Lewis Baldwin also talked with me at length about King's goals for the movement during the final three years of his life.

CHAPTER 30: In *The Books That Mattered: A Reader's Memoir*, I wrote about the interplay of John Steinbeck's novel, *The Grapes of Wrath*, and Carey McWilliams's work of journalism, *Factories in the Field*, in bringing alive the troubled agricultural history of California. In seeking to understand the attempt of Cesar Chavez to confront that history, I found two biographies to be particularly helpful: Miriam Pawel's *The Crusades of Cesar Chavez* and Peter Matthiessen's *Sal Si Puedes: Cesar Chavez and the New American Revolution.* I also read Schlesinger's *Robert Kennedy and His Times* and Thomas's *Robert Kennedy: His Life* for their depictions of the relationship between Chavez and Kennedy. To better understand the workings of Saul Alinski's Industrial Areas Foundation, which supported Chavez, I reread the chapters on Alinski in Silberman's *Crisis in Black and White.* Pawel describes Walter Reuther's crucial support for Chavez and the farmworkers and Reuther's "blot on American democracy" quote is in her book as is Chris Hartmire's "no relevant middle ground."

CHAPTER 31: Thomas Wolfe's praise for Ecclesiastes was quoted in Eric S. Christianson's *Ecclesiastes Through the Centuries.* Seeger's wry "I did write six words" appeared in the article "Pete Seeger's role in ending Israeli house demolitions" by Nir Hassan, published in the Jerusalem-based online journal *DesertPeace.* The article noted that Seeger gave 45 percent of the royalties for the song to the Israeli Committee Against House Demolition, which worked nonviolently against the Israeli government's demolition of Palestinian houses on the West Bank. In the September 2012 *San Diego Troubadour,* Frank Kocher wrote about Roger McGuinn's guitar, as did David Fricke in the August 23, 1990, *Rolling Stone.*

In *Because of Their Faith: CALCAV and the Religious Opposition to the Vietnam War,* Michael K. Hall quoted Nicholas Katzenbach's speculation about Communist influence in the antiwar movement. Hall also described the response of national religious leaders to what they saw as red-baiting by the Johnson Administration. The *New York Times* reported on the antiwar clergy on October 26, 1965, and on December 1, on the transfers of Catholic priests, including Daniel Berrigan. That same month, the Catholic publications *Commonweal* and the *National Catholic Reporter* condemned the transfers. The *Washington Post* on December 2, 1985, and November 1, 2015, and *The Guardian* on October 15, 2010, published retrospectives on the self-immolation of Quaker activist Norman Morrison.

On March 3 and 7, 1965, film critic Bosley Crowther of the *New York Times* devoted two columns to his distaste for *The Sound of Music.* I read Maria Von Trapp's memoir, *The Story of the Trapp Family Singers,* for the historical and biographical context for this iconic film.

Angela Livingstone's book, *Boris Pasternak, Doctor Zhivago,* provided excellent context for the film adaptation of Pasternak's novel. On December 3, 1965, Bosley Crowther reviewed the film critically. The scholar who described it as "sprawling" was Dr. Steven Trout, chair of the English Department at the University of South Alabama, in an interview with me. Pasternak's quote on the nature of life comes from the novel. Pasternak's wry "firing squad" comment is in, among other places, *The Sword and the Shield: The Mitrokhin Archive and the Secret History of the KGB* by Christopher Andrew and Vasili Mitrokhin.

CHAPTER 32: U Thant's rebuke is quoted in Young's *The Vietnam Wars,* as is George Ball's lonesome dissent. Kearns wrote about Johnson's fear of being known for "losing" Southeast Asia. I first read *The Other Side* by Staughton Lynd and Tom Hayden shortly after its publication in 1966. Rereading it for this book, I found more insight into the minds of two American radicals, who saw the horrors of U.S. policy and the link between the war and our reluctance to deal fully with the issue of race. Lynd and Hayden gave a human face to the people of North Vietnam, but they were less insightful about the brutality of our adversaries, especially their torture of American POWs. *The Other Side,* nevertheless, remains a gripping and heartfelt diary. In articles from December 28, 1965, to January 12, 1966, the *New York Times* provided extensive coverage of the activists' trip.

Lyndon Johnson's "going up her leg" analogy appears in several places, including Robert D. Dean's essay, "An Assertion of Manhood," in *Light at the End of the Tunnel: A Vietnam Anthology,* edited by Andrew Jon Rotter, and in *The Vietnam Wars.* Bill Moyers's Ho Chi Minh-George Meany quote was offered in an interview at Columbia University and appears in *Leadership in the Modern Presidency,* edited by Fred I. Greenstein. In *The Other Side,* Lynd and Hayden quote Pham Van Dong's reflections. Hayden wrote descriptively about the Vietnamese countryside and about the tributes paid by the Vietnamese to the memory of Norman Morrison.

The story of Julian Bond's expulsion from the Georgia legislature is based on contemporary accounts by Roy Reed in the *New York Times* January 10–12, 1966. The quote from a Georgia legislator accusing Bond of treason came from the *Times.* The *New Georgia Encyclopedia* offers a well-researched summary of Bond's life. Friends of Julian Bond recounted his irreverent quip about Ray Charles, but it should be said that Bond deeply admired Charles and his music. Bond, a gifted poet, wrote in "I, Too, Hear America Singing": "*I too, hear America singing / But from where I stand / I can only hear Little Richard / And Fats Domino. / But sometimes / I hear Ray Charles / Drowning in his own tears.*" Bond's poem was published in 1960 while he was still a student at Morehouse College.

The account of my conversations with Bond in 1967 and 1968 is based on memory. The story of my friend John Slattery's tour of duty in Vietnam, and its painful aftermath, comes from two taped interviews with Slattery conducted during the research for this book. I read other books about the on-the-ground experience of soldiers in Vietnam, including *The Boys of '67: Charlie Company's War in Vietnam* by Andrew Wiest. I wrote about the Vietnam experience of Major Jim Bowman, a Cherokee Indian from North Carolina, in my book, *As Long As the Waters Flow: Native Americans in the South and East.* The story of POW and future U.S. Senator Jeremiah Denton is in the *Encyclopedia of Alabama.* One soldier's letter to the *Akron Beacon-Journal* was published on March 27, 1967. Donald Duncan's February 1966 *Ramparts* article, "The Whole Thing Was a Lie," was one of many powerful indictments of the war, and the policy behind it, published in that magazine.

CHAPTER 33: My interest in Robert Kennedy began with the 1964 Democratic National Convention. I was a seventeen-year-old recent high school graduate and was moved and mesmerized by the DNC moment described earlier in the notes for Chapter 23. In 1968, I briefly met him at Vanderbilt, and later I had conversations with his friends John Seigenthaler and John Jay Hooker and his reporter friends David Halberstam and Jack Newfield.

The anecdote about Kennedy's mother's response to his climbing Mount Kennedy comes from Schlesinger's *Robert Kennedy and His Times*, as does Kennedy's quip about never thereafter venturing above the first floor. Schlesinger wrote about Kennedy's fear of heights, his qualities of courage, and his courtship of danger. Newfield in *RFK: A Memoir* detected in him an ambivalence toward risk, particularly political risk, as did Joseph Palermo in *Robert F. Kennedy and the Death of American Idealism.* The exchange about sending blood to war victims is quoted by Palermo, who also wrote about the scorn for Kennedy's proposal for giving the National Liberation Front "a share of power" in South Vietnam. Hubert Humphrey's "dose of arsenic" quote comes from *Robert Kennedy and His Times* and the *Chicago Tribune* reference to "Ho Chi Kennedy" was quoted by Palermo. The front-page editorial with that headline appeared on February 21, 1966. The cited headline in *I. F. Stone's Weekly* appeared on October 24, 1966. In *RFK: A Memoir*, Newfield wrote of the aura of pain that seemed always to follow Kennedy after the death of his brother. Evan Thomas, in *Robert Kennedy: His Life*, saw, at the same time, a lingering insensitivity that came with Kennedy's privilege and wealth.

I relied most on Newfield's account of Kennedy's attempts to take on the problems of urban poverty. Hooker's quote that RFK "was who he said he was" was offered in an interview with me. Kennedy's critique of welfare was quoted in Thomas's *Robert Kennedy: His Life.* Newfield wrote about the mutual affection between Kennedy and Chavez, as did Schlesinger and Thomas. Miriam Pawel also wrote about that relationship in her biography, *The Crusades of Cesar Chavez.* Evan Thomas quoted Kennedy's remark on "dragging my ass . . . out to California." But Thomas, more critical than some RFK biographers, also noted Chavez's worry that Kennedy was going too far, and it would "hurt him." Pawel cited Kennedy's exchange with local officials sympathetic to wealthy California growers.

Kennedy's trip to South Africa has been written about by many biographers. My description is synthesized primarily from the narratives of Schlesinger and Thomas. Three South Africa speeches are quoted at length in *RFK: Collected Speeches*, edited by Edwin O. Guthman and C. Richard Allen. Schlesinger recounted Kennedy's awkward response when thousands of Africans cried out to him, "Master, Master." He also wrote about Kennedy's visit with Albert Luthuli and quoted the description of Luthuli that RFK wrote in his diary. The article in the South African *Cape Times* ran on June 10, 1966, the *Rand Daily Mail* on June 9, and the *Cape Argus on* June 10. The grateful summation by anti-apartheid activist Margaret Marshall appeared in Thomas's *Robert Kennedy: His Life*.

In *The Politics of Rage*, Dan Carter wrote about George Wallace's decision to run his wife Lurleen for governor in 1966. Carter quoted political reporter Bob Ingram's commentary in the October 24, 1965, *Montgomery Advertiser-Journal* calling the idea "bizarre." Carter quoted Lurleen: "I did it for George." Later, I heard a speech by Wallace's daughter, Peggy Wallace Kennedy, in which she recalled her own response to her father's decision. Matthew Dalleck's summary of Ronald Reagan's run for governor of California appeared in *The Right Moment: Ronald Reagan's First Victory and the Decisive Turning Point in American Politics*.

CHAPTER 34: The Adolph Rupp quote about recruiting black players comes from *Strong Inside: Perry Wallace and the Collision of Race and Sports in the South* by Andrew Maraniss. Frank DeFord, one of the country's great sportswriters, wrote about the Kentucky-Texas Western matchup in the March 14, March 21, and March 28, 1966, issues of *Sports Illustrated*. Rupp's "No five blacks are going to beat Kentucky" appeared in an April 6, 1998, *Sports Illustrated* retrospective. Perry Wallace's description of David Lattin appeared in Maraniss's book, as did Lattin's taunt of Pat Riley after a dunk.

The story of Wallace's experience as the first black basketball player in the Southeastern Conference was based in part on my five-hour interview with him for "Perry Wallace, the Long Road Home," which appeared first in *Vanderbilt Magazine*, and later in my book, *With Music and Justice for All*. Wallace's "in denial" quote came from that interview. I also relied on Maraniss's excellent biography, especially his account of Rupp and the banning of the dunk. Roy Skinner's "NCAA crapped on Perry" quote came from Maraniss. Kareem Abdul-Jabbar's quote is from *Giant Steps: The Autobiography of Kareem Abdul-Jabbar*.

Karl Fleming's account of being beaten in Watts appeared in his autobiography, *Son of the Rough South: An Uncivil Memoir*. *Newsweek's* tribute to Fleming appeared in the May 23, 1966, issue. Both Fleming and Reagan biographer Dalleck wrote about the changing racial mood in California.

My account of the shooting of James Meredith was synthesized from *Walking with the Wind*, *Bearing the Cross*, and *Pillar of Fire*, as well as contemporary reports by the *New York Times* and the Associated Press. Bob Mants's description of Stokely Carmichael was offered in an interview with me. Julian Bond's "the crazies" observation is in *Walking with the Wind*, as is Carmichael's "ain't going to jail no more" and beginning to use the phrase "Black Power!" Both Lewis and Garrow described the crowd's call and response as Carmichael and Willie Ricks led the chant. Garrow quoted MLK's "reservations" about the slogan. The story of the emergence of the Black Panther Party in Lowndes County, Alabama, is based primarily on my own reporting and interviews for *Cradle of Freedom*. I also reread *Black Power* by Carmichael and Charles V. Hamilton, in which Carmichael explained the power of the vote in rural Alabama. Hulett's quote, "We won't give up," appears in *Cradle of Freedom*.

CHAPTER 35: The Alabama Music Hall of Fame in Tuscumbia offers an informative, compelling account of the musical history of a corner of northern Alabama that includes the towns of Florence, Muscle Shoals, and Sheffield, as well as Tuscumbia. Percy Sledge's quote about musical brotherhood is found in a Hall of Fame exhibit. Peter Guralnick in *Last Train to Memphis* tells the story of Sam Phillips. Tom Pinnock looked back on the making of the Beach Boys' "Good Vibrations" in the June 2007 issue of *Uncut* magazine. On its yearend chart for 1966, *Billboard* pronounced Staff Sergeant Barry Sadler's "The Ballad of the Green Berets" the biggest hit that year, coming in ahead of Nancy Sinatra's "These Boots Are Made for Walkin'." In a January 27, 1989, story on the ironies of Sadler's life, the *Los Angeles Times* wrote about his wound from a punji stick.

CHAPTER 36: I relied first of all on *In Cold Blood* itself. But I also read Gerald Clarke's *Capote: A Biography* and Charles J. Shields' *Mockingbird: A Portrait of Harper Lee*, which describes and quotes extensively from the research Lee did with Truman Capote for *In Cold Blood.* His quote about early success is in Anne Taylor Fleming's July 9, 1978, profile in the *New York Times*, "The Private World of Truman Capote." His quote about homosexuality and genius is in a self-interview for *Music for Chameleons*. His assessment of himself as "intelligent and sensitive and perceptive" was recounted in his August 2, 1984, *New York Times* obituary by Albin Krebs. Clarke and Krebs both wrote about the provocative jacket photo of Capote which became an ingredient in the success of *Other Voices, Other Rooms*. Capote's explanation of why he never took notes during interviews also appeared in Krebs's obituary. Mark Slonim's *New York Times* review of *The Muses Are Heard*, which I have quoted in this chapter, appeared on December 2, 1956. Clarke wrote about how the experience of writing that book, and the *New Yorker* articles that preceded it, suggested larger possibilities to Capote that came into focus when he read of the murder of a farm family in Kansas. My depiction of the crime and the attempts to solve it are based on *In Cold Blood.* Clarke's assessment of the book is found in his biography of Capote. Clarke also argued that Capote saw his own "dark side" in one of the murderers, Perry Smith.

Stanley Kauffmann reviewed *In Cold Blood* in the January 22, 1966, *The New Republic.* Tom Wolfe's analysis of the book's appeal appeared in Wolfe's own collection of essays, *Mauve Gloves & Madmen, Clutter & Vine*, published in 1976. Columnist Jimmy Breslin wrote about Capote in the *New York Herald Tribune* and his quote is found in the book, *Literary Brooklyn: The Writers of Brooklyn and the Story of City Life* by Evan Hughes.

The story of the Richard Speck murders is synthesized from contemporary news accounts, including Robert Weidrich's reconstruction of the crime in the July 23, 1966, *Chicago Tribune.* United Press International reporter Thomas Pledge described the lone survivor of the Speck attacks, Corazon Amurao, confronting Speck during her testimony at his trial on April 6, 1967. I also read several journalistic retrospectives and historical summaries of Speck's life, including one on the website, *Biography*.

CHAPTER 37: *Time* magazine's "Is God Dead?" cover appeared on the April 8, 1966, issue. Thomas J. J. Altizer was interviewed in the Autumn 2006 issue of *Emory Magazine* about his legacy with the story and the issues of academic freedom it raised for the university and its president, Sanford Atwood. Altizer's quotes come from that article, as do Atwood's. Altizer co-author William Hamilton's quote about God and the Holocaust appeared in Hamilton's *Los Angeles Times* obituary, March 3, 2012. The quote from the newspaper, "He discovered he no longer believed in an active God," appeared in that same obituary. I reread Harvey Cox's important book, *The Secular City*. The description of a Billy Graham crusade is based on my coverage of several Graham crusades and appears in my 1982 book, *Race, Rock & Religion*. Lewis Baldwin's quote about Martin Luther King's belief in a personal God came from an interview with me. The description of King's crisis of faith in Montgomery is synthesized from accounts in Garrow's *Bearing the Cross* and Stephen B. Oates's *Let the Trumpet Sound: The Life of Martin Luther King, Jr.*, as well as my own research for *Cradle of Freedom*, which included interviews with members of King's Montgomery congregation. King's prayer, "I'm weak now," appeared in *"Thou, Dear God" Prayers that Open Hearts and Spirits, The Reverend Dr. Martin Luther King, Jr.*, edited by Lewis Baldwin. Mother Pollard's quote appears in *The Papers of Martin Luther King, Jr., Vol. VI*. Baldwin's quote about King as a theologian was offered in an interview with me, as was the quote from Theoda Smith, which appears in *Race, Rock & Religion*.

For insight into Thomas Merton and Dorothy Day, I was guided by Paul Elie's *The Life You Save May Be Your Own: An American Pilgrimage*. I also read Jeff Kisseloff's *Generation on Fire*, which included an insightful interview with Daniel Berrigan and an essay on his radical Christian witness. Dorothy Day's comments on Roger LaPorte appeared in *The Catholic Worker*, November 1965. Reflections on the enduring influence of Mario Savio's Catholicism were shaped by the biography, *Freedom's Orator*. William Sloane Coffin's quote, "Jesus is my kind of guy," appeared in the April 8, 1966, issue of *Time*.

William Martin in *With God on Our Side* wrote insightfully about the rise of Jerry Falwell. So did Frances Fitzgerald in *The Evangelicals: The Struggle to Save America*. In 1987, I also profiled Falwell for the *Charlotte Observer*. The quotes from Falwell's sermons come from Martin's book.

CHAPTER 38: The federal judge who spoke philosophically about the role of the courts was U.S. District Judge James McMillan in Charlotte, who offered those comments in an interview with me. Judge Robert Mehrige of Richmond said almost exactly the same thing in another interview, and his quote appears in my book, *The Heart of Dixie*. In an article entitled "You Have the Right to Remain Silent," the August/September 2006 issue of *American Heritage* recounted the human and legal story of the landmark case, *Miranda v. Arizona*. The quotes from the rapist in that case are found in the *American Heritage* article. PBS.org offers a good summary of *Gideon v. Wainright*. Robert Kennedy's 1963 quote about the case is found in the essay, "*Clarence Earl Gideon v. Wainright*, U.S. Supreme Court 1963: A Landmark in the Law," Division of Public Defender Services, State of Connecticut. Ronald Reagan's complaint that the First Amendment was being "turned on its head," came in a radio address, February 25, 1984. Fred Shuttlesworth's observation that he saw the Supreme Court's *Brown* decision as evidence that "God was moving in the world," was offered in an interview with me and appears in *Cradle of Freedom*. Journalist-historian Jack Bass's book, *Unlikely Heroes*, offers a detailed history of the judicial courage of federal judges in the South, especially those on the U.S. Fifth Circuit Court of Appeals. Earl Warren's observation, "Everything I did in my life that was worthwhile, I caught hell for," is found on the website of the National Constitution Center. The conclusion that Warren shifted the Supreme Court's emphasis from property rights to personal rights is found in *The Reader's Companion to American History*, edited by Eric Foner and John A. Garrity, for the website, *History.com*. A differently phrased version of that observation appears in *The Supreme Court Justices: An Illustrated History. 1789–2012*, edited by Clare Cushman.

For this chapter, I reread Ralph Nader's *Unsafe at Any Speed*, a cornerstone of the emerging concept of consumer rights. On June 30, 2017, the *Writer's Almanac with Garrison Keillor* told of the founding of the National Organization for Women, including Betty Friedan's quote about her realization that the assembled women "had now indeed entered history." The story is also told at NOW.org. The observations in this chapter on the women's movement and changing sexual values were shaped by readings from Masters and Johnson's *Human Sexual Response*, Germaine Greer's *The Female Eunuch*, and *Jane Sexes It Up: True Confessions of Feminist Desire*, edited by Merri Lisa Johnson. I also interviewed Becky McLaughlin, author of "Sex Cuts," one of the essays in that book.

CHAPTER 39: In writing here about federal voting registrar Bill Meeks, I wanted to acknowledge the competence and bravery of those civil servants charged with actually implementing the Voting Rights Act of 1965. Meeks's story is based on an interview I did with him and on an undergraduate paper for one of my classes at the University of South Alabama, written by Meeks's daughter, Collen Clover, an educator in Mobile, Alabama. Meeks also shared files from his days as a registrar.

In writing the story of Martin Luther King in Chicago, I relied most heavily on *Bearing the Cross*. I also read *Jesse*, Marshall Frady's biography of Jesse Jackson, and Frady's *Martin Luther King, Jr.: A Life*. David Halberstam's quote is found in Frady's latter book. Halberstam's full essay containing that quote appears in *Martin Luther King, Jr.: A Profile*, edited by C. Eric Lincoln. *Pillar of* Fire, as always, offers useful insights into this period of King's life. *Eyes on the Prize* has vivid footage of King's marches in the Chicago area. The quotes from King in this chapter are found in *Bearing the Cross*. Some of the observations regarding Jesse Jackson, King's cocky young protégé in Chicago, were based on my own 1984 profile of Jackson in the *Charlotte Observer* and later in my book, *Southern Voices*.

In *Before the Storm*, Rick Perlstein noted the upsurge in conservative governors elected in 1966. Branch's quote about Chicago nationalizing the issue of race is found in *Pillar of Fire*. The *Saturday Evening Post*'s editorial comment in the summer of 1966, "We are all, let's face it, Mississippians," can be found on the website *AfricanAmerica.com*.

CHAPTER 40: This summary of the life of Edward Brooke is based primarily on his obituary in the January 3, 2015, *New York Times*; he was ninety-five. I have written on several occasions about Hiram Revels, the first black senator in U.S. history. This account is based primarily on the website of the Senate Historical Office. Chief Justice Earl Warren ordered the seating of Georgia Representative Julian Bond in *Bond v. Floyd*. The reflections on MLK's increasing concerns about the Vietnam War and poverty in America are based in part on conversations with Lewis Baldwin, author of *To Make the Wounded Whole: The Cultural Legacy of Martin Luther King, Jr.* Garrow, Branch, and others have also written about this period in King's life.

CHAPTER 41: The story of *New York Times* journalist Harrison Salisbury's reporting from North Vietnam is based on his dispatches between December 25, 1966, and January 7, 1967, a *Times* editorial on January 6, and on Marilyn Young's *The Vietnam Wars: 1945–1990*. The *Washington Post*'s criticism of Salisbury was published January 1, 1967. Neil Sheehan's praise of Salisbury appeared in Salisbury's *New York Times* obituary, July 7, 1993. Young's descriptions of U.S. bombing raids in South Vietnam are found in her book. Jonathan Schell's *New Yorker* article, "The Village of Ben Suc," was published July 15, 1967. Japanese journalist Katsuichi Honda's account of plunder by U.S. troops in South Vietnam was quoted in *The Vietnam Wars*. In *Lyndon Johnson and the American Dream*, Kearns wrote of the president's nightmares about the war. Ramsey Clark's statement to Merle Miller appeared in Miller's *Lyndon: An Oral Biography* and in *The Vietnam Wars*. Robert McNamara's astonished observation about the determination and fighting ability of the North Vietnamese and the Viet Cong is found in Halberstam's *The Best and the Brightest*. Ho Chi Minh's quote from a 1966 conversation with theologian Martin Niemoeller is in *The Vietnam Wars*.

The story of the ill-fated Apollo 1 mission is based on Andrew Chaikin's book, *A Man on the Moon*; John Barbour's *Footprints on the Moon*; the transcript, "Apollo Accident: Hearings Before the Committee on Aeronautical and Space Sciences, Nineteenth Congress, first session, 1967"; and on contemporary reporting in the *New York Times* from January 27–30. Astronaut Gus Grissom's complaints about communications malfunctions are in *A Man on the Moon*; Grissom's reflections on the possibility of astronaut deaths were offered at a press conference and quoted in *Footprints on the Moon*. Roger Chafee's first words of alarm about a fire are in an essay by Ben Evans for the website *AmericaSpace*. Chaikin quotes Chafee as simply shouting "Fire!"

CHAPTER 42: David Garrow writes of Martin Luther King's response to the *Ramparts* coverage on Vietnam in January 1967. I have quoted William F. Pepper and have described Pepper's photographs that accompanied his words and the Benjamin Spock essay. Garrow offers one of the best descriptions of the debate within King's organization about his decision to speak out on the war, as well as King's meeting with Muhammad Ali, and his public praise of Ali's personal stand against the war. The quotes from King's February 25 speech are in *Bearing the Cross*. I rewatched the *Eyes on the Prize* segment with portion's of King's April 2 sermon. I have quoted at length from King's April 4 address at Riverside Church because of its historical importance. The excerpts from editorials in the *Washington Post*, the *New York Times*, and *Life* magazine—each rebuking King's speech—are also in *Bearing the Cross*. Garrow describes the exchange between King and Roy Wilkins. Robert Kennedy's increasingly outspoken opposition to the war is documented in Schlesinger's *Robert Kennedy and His Times*, Thomas's *Robert Kennedy: His Life*, and Newfield's *RFK: A Memoir*. Charles De Gaulle's advice to Kennedy was quoted by Schlesinger, as was Pope Paul VI's suggestion that peace talks were possible with North Vietnam. Schlesinger also recounted the details of Kennedy's unpleasant meeting with Lyndon Johnson, after which Kennedy felt he had little to lose by speaking more forcefully about Vietnam. Newfield wrote about Kennedy's vow to columnist Mary McGrory that he would escalate his political war with Johnson. Newfield also told the story of Kennedy's gentle reassurance when Staughton Lynd's young son spilled Coke. Schlesinger quoted Kennedy's quip about his brother Ted's reservations about RFK's planned antiwar speech. Perhaps the best news coverage of Kennedy's trip to the Mississippi Delta in early April 1967 came from reporter Nick Kotz in the *Des Moines Register*, which Schlesinger quoted in describing Kennedy's trip. Kotz was so moved by the poverty in rural Mississippi that he later wrote a landmark book, *Let Them Eat Promises: The Politics of Hunger in America*. The quotes from Charles Evers and Marian Wright appeared in Schlesinger's biography, as did Vine Deloria's description of Kennedy: "Spiritually, he was an Indian." Schlesinger also wrote of Robert Coles's visit to the Delta and Kennedy's encouragement of his efforts to secure more money for Food Stamps. In *Let Them Eat Promises*, Kotz described Johnson's resistance to additional emergency aid for hungry children in Mississippi. Schlesinger quoted Hubert Humphrey's lament about Johnson's failure to do all he could to ease the suffering.

CHAPTER 43: In rereading the May 16, 1967, issue of *Look*, which contained Norman Rockwell's famous illustration, *New Kids in the Neighborhood*, I was stuck, as I had been so often in researching this book, by the quality of journalism that enriched our real-time understanding of the sixties. The story of Rockwell's powerful paintings about race, including those that appeared in *Look,* can be found in "Rockwell and Race, 1963–1968," on the website *The Pop History Dig.* Regarding the work of Jacob Lawrence, I interviewed Dr. Paige Vitulli, professor of art education at the University of South Alabama. Geetika Rao, a student at the University of Texas, described the "bright colors" of Lawrence's *Soldiers and Students,* after it was displayed at the Blanton Museum of Art in Austin. Lawrence's quote comparing the natural use of color in African American homes with the paintings of Matisse appears in *Challenge of the Modern: African-American Artists, 1925–1945,* by Lowery Stokes Sims. I have long been a fan of Romare Bearden and have viewed several exhibitions of his work. The references in this chapter were shaped by *Romare Bearden: His Life and Art* by Myron Schwartzman. In October 1964, a Bearden exhibition entitled "Projections" opened at the Cordier and Ekstrom gallery in New York, and the quote about Bearden's "pride in tradition" as an underpinning of the push for social change appeared in an essay by gallery owner Arne Ekstrom. The quote is found also in *Mercy, Mercy Me: African-American Culture and the American Sixties* by James C. Hall. This account of the famous quilters in Gees Bend, Alabama is based on interviews for my books, *Cradle of Freedom* and *Alabama's Civil Rights Trail,* the latter co-authored with Jane DeNeefe and Jennifer Lindsay; DeNeefe wrote the chapter on Gees Bend.

Chapter 44: In this chapter on free speech at Vanderbilt and a university's encounter with the Black Power movement, I have drawn on my own memories of working on the student-run Impact Symposium, an organization founded and ably run by a group of young men who became my friends: Dan Brasfield, Wayne Hyatt, Tom Lawrence, and Robert Eager. The recounting here of Stokely Carmichael's evolution as a radical activist is based on several sources, including Lewis's *Walking with the Wind,* Carmichael's own book, *Black Power: The Politics of Liberation,* co-authored with Charles V. Hamilton, and my interviews for *Cradle of Freedom.* Among the subjects of those interviews were Hamilton and civil rights activists Bob Mants, John Hulett, Thomas Gilmore, and Francis Walter, all of whom knew Carmichael. The quotes from Hamilton, Mants, and Hulett also appeared in *Cradle of Freedom.* Carmichael's quote, "To hell with the laws. . .," appeared in an AP dispatch in the Nashville *Tennessean* on April 5, 1968. The *Tennessean* and Vanderbilt's student newspaper, the *Vanderbilt Hustler,* provided the best coverage of Carmichael's appearance at Vanderbilt and the controversies before and after his visit. The story of my personal encounter with SNCC activists and black author Eldridge Cleaver is based on memory. I also reread Cleaver's memoir, *Soul on Ice.* The *Tennessean* provided a good account of Carmichael's speech at Vanderbilt, but I discovered there were passages I remembered almost by heart, such was the force of the moment. The story of the riots in Nashville's African American neighborhoods is based on reporting in the *Tennessean* and the *Nashville Banner.* The *Banner's* front-page editorial condemning Vanderbilt's invitation to Carmichael was published April 10, 1967. I quoted Alexander Heard's defense of academic freedom in the Fall 2009 issue of *Vanderbilt Magazine.* Excellent accounts of the Carmichael visit and its aftermath can also be found in Paul Keith Conklin's *Gone With the Ivy: A Biography of Vanderbilt University* and in Heard's *Speaking of the University.*

John Hulett, in an interview with me, described his encounters with Huey Newton in Lowndes County, Alabama. I also interviewed Bob Zellner about being the last white staffer in SNCC. Bobby Seale's call for blacks to arm themselves is in *Liberation, Imagination, and the*

Black Panther Party: A New Look at the Panthers and Their Legacy, edited by Kathleen Cleaver and George Katsiaficas. Rap Brown's quote about violence appeared in the *Washington Post*, July 28, 1967.

CHAPTER 45: In *The Vietnam Wars,* Marilyn Young noted the change in support for the war, as reflected in the Gallup and Harris polls. My reflections on the Six-Day War of 1967 were shaped by my trip to Israel in 1983 for the *Charlotte Observer*. Mattityahu Peled was among my interviewees.

My account of the Newark riots is based on contemporary coverage by the *New York Times*, as well as Branch's *At Canaan's Edge*, and Tom Hayden's *Rebellion in Newark*, which is a combination of his own observation and memories, as well as his sifting through the public record, including accounts in *Life*, the *New York Times*, the *Trentonian*, and the *Newark Star Ledger*. He also conducted personal interviews with victims of police brutality. At the time and later, I found his book to be a passionate, coherent analysis. Hayden quoted John Smith's description of being beaten. The *New York Times* on July 14 reported police officers pleading for the order to shoot. The *Times* also reported Mayor Addonizio giving the order and on July 15 quoted Governor Hughes on drawing a line "between the jungle and the law." On July 17, the *Times* editorial board argued that Hughes was being "simplistic." On July 22, *Times* writer Richard Reeves wrote of white fear and "open hatred," quoting one National Guardsman that "next time" he would shoot to kill. *Trentonian* reporter Bill Lowe described his beating by the Newark police in a thirty-minute film, *Birthmarks*.

The initial AP dispatch about the Detroit riots ran in newspapers across the country. I also relied on reporting by the *New York Times* and the *Detroit Free Press*. The website www.detroits-great-rebellion.com offers a detailed account of the violence and the conditions leading up to it in an essay entitled, "The Great Rebellion: A Socio-Economic Analysis of the 1967 Detroit Riot." That website also includes excerpts from the writings of Albert Cleage, including his searing description of desperation in America's urban ghettos, and the quote from H. Rap Brown. I read the summary of the riot in Branch's *At Canaan's Edge*, and reread the report of the Kerner Commission. My synopsis of the Algiers Motel killings is based on John Hersey's *The Algiers Motel Incident* and on "The Great Rebellion" website. The death of Jerome Olshove is told on that site and in the July 22, 1967, *Detroit Free Press*, which includes a description of all forty-three fatalities. The differing reflections by MLK and Ronald Reagan on the meaning of the riots appeared in Branch's book. The Detroit mayor's painful epitaph "amidst the ashes of our hopes," has been quoted in multiple places including Berl Falbaum's retrospective on the riots, published July 17, 2017, in the *Detroit Jewish News*.

CHAPTER 46: In researching the counterculture movement in San Francisco, I spoke with several friends who were participants, including Pamela Smith and Anne Kent Rush. I also corresponded with scholars Jonathan Kauffman and John T. Edge, both of whom have written about Stephen Gaskin, one of the Bay area gurus. The quote from Gaskin is in Edge's *The Potlikker Papers: A Food History of the Modern South*. I also read *The Haight Asbury: A History* by Charles Perry, *The Electric Kool-Aid Acid Test* by Tom Wolfe, *Hells Angels: The Strange and Terrible Saga of the Outlaw Motorcycle Gangs* by Hunter S. Thompson, and *The Harvard Psychedelic Club* by Don Lattin. Sheila Weller's July 2012 *Vanity Fair* article, "Suddenly That Summer," offers a readable retrospective on "the summer of love." I read the poetry of Lenore Kandel, including her controversial *The Love Book*, and quoted from her *Word Alchemy*. Charles

Perry wrote about Kandel's emergence as an important San Francisco poet. Jerry Rubin's quote came from Perry's book, as did the quote from the *Berkeley Barb* and much of the description of the Human Be-In. Perry also quoted the *San Francisco Oracle* regarding the limitations of political protest and wrote about Ken Kesey's psychedelic parties with the Hell Angels. Tom Wolfe also wrote about Kesey and the motorcycle gang. Wolfe's quote about Kesey's fake suicide appears in Wolfe's anthology, *The New Journalism*, co-edited with E. W. Johnson, as does Hunter Thompson's quote about Hells Angel leader Sonny Barger. Warren Hinkle's article, "Social History of the Hippies," was in the March 1967 issue of *Ramparts*. Journalist William Hedgepeth's remembrance appeared in Aaron Millar's retrospective "Golden Daze: 50 Years on from the Summer of Love," published in the May 21, 2017, *Guardian*. Nicholas von Hoffman's cautionary quote about the legacy of drug use appeared in Weller's *Vanity Fair* essay. Bob Weir's "exchange of ideas" quote came from his preface to Perry's book. My friend Anne Kent Rush introduced me to the writings of Alan Watts and the poetry of Elsa Gidlow, and first told me the story of Margo St. James. I read St. James's interview that appeared online in *SFGate*, May 20, 2007. Rush's "new world" summation was offered in an interview with me.

CHAPTER 47: The reflections on Janis Joplin are based primarily on Myra Friedman's *Buried Alive: A Biography of Janis Joplin*, and on interviews with Joplin on *The Dick Cavett Show*, which can be found on YouTube. The section on Linda Ronstadt is based on her autobiography, *Simple Dreams*, and on my 1974 interview with her for the *Charlotte Observer*, a part of which also appeared in *Watermelon Wine: The Spirit of Country Music*. Ronstadt's quote about Lola Beltran comes from *Simple Dreams*. Don Henley's expressions of admiration for Ronstadt and her music are part of his jacket blurb for her book. I wrote about country singer George Hamilton IV's interactions with songwriter Joni Mitchell in *Watermelon Wine*. Hamilton's quote about Mitchell appeared in that book. So did Charley Pride's quip about his "permanent tan."

CHAPTER 48: Two of the best accounts of Thurgood Marshall are in Richard Kluger's *Simple Justice* and Juan Williams's *Thurgood Marshall: American Revolutionary*. The advice given to Marshall by his father appears in Williams's book. The summary of Marshall's strategy in *Brown* is based primarily on *Simple Justice*, though I also interviewed several people involved in one of those cases for articles I wrote for the *Charlotte Observer*. Portions of those interviews, including the quote from Billie S. Fleming, also appear in my books, *Race, Rock & Religion* and *With Music and Justice for All*. Kenneth Clark's quote about the learning atmosphere of Howard University is found in *Simple Justice*, as is Kluger's eloquent summation of the effects of segregation on black children. Kluger also quoted Marshall's explanation of the way he approached *Brown*. Williams wrote about the backstage drama surrounding Marshall's appointment to the U.S. Supreme Court.

The story of *Loving v. Virginia* is drawn primarily from Arica Coleman's *That the Blood Stay Pure* and Peter Wallenstein's *Race, Sex, and the Freedom to Marry: Loving v. Virginia*. Additional perspective came from David Garrow's *Liberty and Sexuality: The Right to Privacy and the Making of Roe v. Wade*. Mildred Loving's memory of the police bursting into her bedroom appears, with slight variations, in multiple places, as does Richard Loving's famous comment to his lawyer to "tell the Court I love my wife."

CHAPTER 49: The section on Jonathan Kozol is based on his book *Death at an Early Age* and an excerpt from it in the September 1967 *Atlantic Monthly*. On June 15, 2015, NPR's *All Things Considered* broadcast an interview with Kozol and Thelma Burns, a parent at the school he had written about. The excerpts here from Kozol's writing are found in *The Atlantic Monthly*. Kozol told of riding the subway train with Fred Rogers in *Bates Magazine*, published by Bates College in Lewiston, Maine, copyright 2001. Tom Jurod's moving profile of Mister Rogers was published in the November 1998 *Esquire*.

CHAPTER 50: Norman Mailer's "The Steps of the Pentagon" was published in *Harper's* in March 1968. Willie Morris, former editor of *Harper's,* told the backstory of the article in his memoir, *New York Days*. William Westmoreland's November 1967 speech to the National Press Club is quoted in Marilyn Young's history of the Vietnam War, as were K. Barton Osborne's descriptions of torture. In *The Sixties: Years of Hope, Days of Rage,* Todd Gitlin described the growing militancy of the antiwar movement, recounted the "Bloody Tuesday" clash between Oakland police and anti-draft protesters, and quoted from the October 17, 1967, *San Francisco Chronicle* descriptions of the police attack. On October 22, the *Washington Post* reported on similar clashes in the nation's capitol. Gitlin quoted at length from Christopher Jencks's *New Republic* article on the infatuation of New Left radicals toward the Viet Cong. John McCain's recollections were in the March 14, 1973, *U.S. News and World Report*.

In "The Man Who Ran Against Lyndon Johnson," a profile of Allard Lowenstein in the December 1968 *Harper's*, David Halberstam described Lowenstein's attempts to persuade Robert Kennedy to run. So did Jack Newfield in *RFK; A Memoir*. Arthur Schlesinger also wrote of Kennedy's agonizing path toward a decision, as well as Kennedy's astonishment at the pro-war sentiments of students at a women's college. In his memoir, Newfield told of Kennedy's response to a December 1967 *Village Voice* article in which Newfield had urged Kennedy to run.

CHAPTER 51: Doris Kearns and Nick Kotz both wrote of Lyndon Johnson's attempt to shift the national conversation after the difficult summer of 1967. Johnson's speech about the Clean Air Act was delivered on November 21. Newfield wrote of the growing national disillusionment with Johnson in his book on RFK. Historian Timothy Lombardo spoke with me about the disaffection that many white working class Americans felt toward Johnson's brand of liberalism, a subject Lombardo explored in *Blue-Collar Conservatism: Frank Rizzo's Philadelphia and Populist Politics*. In *Up South: Civil Rights and Black Power in Philadelphia*, Matthew Countryman offered a thorough account of the events in Philadelphia in November 1967. Rizzo's incendiary language, as reported by eyewitnesses, has been recounted in multiple places, including *Prison Power: How Prison Influenced the Movement for Black Liberation* by Lisa M. Corrigan.

CHAPTER 52: My thoughts on *The Graduate*, based partly on memory, were informed and deepened by Sam Kashner's "Here's to You, Mr. Nichols: The Making of *The Graduate*," published in the March 2008 *Vanity Fair*. The quotes from Dustin Hoffman and Robert Redford come from that article. I also read Roger Ebert's review, published December 26, 1967, in the *Chicago Sun-Times*. Although Ebert liked the movie, he dismissed director Mike Nichols's memorable use of music by Simon and Garfunkel. The reflections on other movies in this chapter are based primarily on my own memories. I have viewed *In the Heat of the Night* on multiple occasions, partly out of admiration for the dramatic performance by Rod Steiger. It was also, as the chapter affirms, a groundbreaking year for Sidney Poitier.

CHAPTER 53: In *The Vietnam Wars: 1945–1990*, Marilyn Young described the 1968 Tet offensive and its ironies, including U.S. Ambassador Ellsworth Bunker's "light at the end of the tunnel" party just before the attacks. Young described the fighting in Saigon, Hue, and Khe Sanh, where, as she wrote, American napalm "denuded the mountainside." The journalist who described "the most hysterical use of American firepower" in Hue was Philip John Griffiths. Young recounted the Viet Cong war crimes in Hue, and although she argued that the carnage was overstated by American propaganda, there can be little doubt that the execution of civilians sent waves of fear through the South Vietnamese countryside. In the United States, that revulsion was overshadowed by AP photographer Eddie Adams's photograph of the execution of a Viet Cong suspect by a South Vietnam commander. The killing, accomplished with such apparent indifference, was also shown on NBC News, edited so that most of us did not see until later the arc of blood spurting from the victim's temple. Young quoted the U.S. officer who said of Ben Tre, "We had to destroy the town to save it." I rewatched Walter Cronkite's influential and desultory assessment of U.S. credibility after Tet. Young quoted Senator Eugene McCarthy's campaign critique of his own party for breaking its promise of "no wider war."

My account of Robert Kennedy's indecision about running for president in 1968 is based on those of Newfield, Schlesinger, Halberstam in his book *The Unfinished Odyssey of Robert Kennedy*, and on conversations with Kennedy's friend, John Seigenthaler. Newfield quoted from journalist Pete Hamill's moving letter to Kennedy, urging him to run. This synopsis of the My Lai massacre is based in part on Marilyn Young's account, but primarily on the reporting of Seymour Hersh. I read Hersh's initial dispatches that appeared in the *St. Louis Post-Dispatch* and other papers, as well as Hersh's longer, more comprehensive article in the January 22, 1972, issue of the *New Yorker.*

Chapter 54: This description of Kennedy's presidential campaign is based on the previously cited books by Newfield, Schlesinger, Halberstam, Palermo, and Thomas, and on Jules Witcover's *85 Days: The Last Campaign of Robert Kennedy* and Thurston Clarke's *The Last Campaign: Robert F. Kennedy and 82 Days That inspired America.* My account of Martin Luther King's final days is based on *Bearing the Cross*, *At Canaan's Edge*, Ralph Abernathy's *And the Walls Came Tumbling Down*, Frady's *Martin Luther King Jr: A Life*, the essay "The Radicalization of Martin Luther King Jr.: The Last Three Years" by Kenneth L. Smith in the Spring 1989 *Journal of Ecumenical Studies*, and conversations with King biographer Lewis Baldwin.

My description of RFK's trip to California in support of Cesar Chavez is based on the accounts in Miriam Pawel's biography of Chavez and Newfield's memoir about Kennedy. I also spoke with Seigenthaler, who traveled with Kennedy on that occasion, about the relationship between Kennedy and Chavez. Newfield makes the case that Kennedy had already decided by then to run for president—*before* the New Hampshire primary and Eugene McCarthy's strong showing. Newfield also described Kennedy's first encounters with the crowds in Kansas, punctuated by self-deprecating humor, as he began his presidential campaign. Most of Kennedy's biographers, including Newfield, Schlesinger, and Thomas, wrote about his eloquent speeches at Kansas State University and the University of Kansas. Those speeches are in *RFK: Collected Speeches*, edited by Edwin O. Guthman and C. G. Allen. The description of Kennedy's visit to Vanderbilt, where I served as his student host, is based on my memory of that event, as well as coverage in the Nashville *Tennessean.* That speech was also included in the Guthman collection. Kennedy's quote about the dangers of assassination—"What happens, happens"—came from my interview with John Jay Hooker.

My account of Johnson's decision not to seek reelection relies on those in *Judgment Days*, *Lyndon Johnson and the American Dream*, and Merle Miller's *Lyndon: An Oral Biography*. Johnson's quote, "I don't give a damn about the election," appears in multiple places, including

Judgment Days. Miller quoted Lady Bird Johnson's description of her husband final hours before announcing that he would not run. Clark Clifford's stunned reaction to Johnson's decision—"You've made up your mind?"—comes from an oral history interview with Clifford conducted by Joe B. Frantz on August 7, 1969. The transcript of that interview can be found at the Lyndon Baines Johnson Library and is available online. Nick Kotz and Willie Morris have offered moving reflections on the flawed greatness of LBJ. The quote from Morris comes from his memoir, *New York Days*.

Kotz related the admiring conversation between MLK and Johnson after the passage of major civil rights legislation, and wrote, as others have (including historians Branch, Garrow, and David Carter), of the decline of that relationship. The force of King's address at the National Cathedral on March 31, 1968—the same day Johnson announced he would not seek reelection—comes through clearly in *Eyes on the Prize*. Kenneth L. Smith wrote about the radical sweep of that address in his essay, "The Radicalization of Martin Luther King, Jr." Smith and Lewis Baldwin have both reflected on King's growing disillusionment with white America. His quote "the vast majority of white Americans are racists" has appeared in multiple places, including a January 23, 2000, *New York Times* review of Michael Eric Dyson's book, *I May Not Get There With You: The True Martin Luther King Jr.* King's discouraged musing about letting "violence take its course" can be found in *Bearing the Cross*. The jeering editorial cartoon "Chicken a la King" appeared in the *Memphis Commercial Appeal* on March 29, 1968. In *Eyes on the Prize* and in *Bearing the Cross*, Andrew Young described the pillow fight just before King was shot on April 4. Young's agonized response to the shooting has appeared in several accounts, including David Goldfield's excellent *Black, White, and Southern: Race Relations and Southern Culture, 1940 to the Present*. Ralph Abernathy's final words to King can be found in *And the Walls Came Tumbling Down* and in *Eyes on the Prize*.

CHAPTER 55: Jack Newfield's description of Robert Kennedy's extemporaneous speech announcing the death of Dr. King to a ghetto crowd in Indianapolis reveals the evolution of Newfield's views about Kennedy—from deep skepticism to feelings of admiration and friendship. The same tone was present in Thurston Clarke's *The Last Campaign*. Evan Thomas was much more measured and detached in his writings about Kennedy, but his description of the speech is, to me, as moving as Clarke's and Newfield's. Extended excerpts are found in *RFK: Collected Speeches* and Newfield's *RFK: A Memoir*. In addition, I watched a five-minute excerpt on YouTube. Kennedy's more formal speech from the following day is also found in *RFK: Collected Speeches*, in Newfield's memoir, and can be heard online.

The role of the great educator Benjamin Mays at the funeral of Martin Luther King Jr. is detailed on the website of Bates College in Lewiston, Maine, an institution Mays attended as a young man. In his memoir, Ralph Abernathy offers a moving account of the funeral, including his own central role. Nick Kotz in *Judgment Days* wrote about Lyndon Johnson's legislative response to the tragedy—pushing an open housing bill through Congress after wrangling bipartisan support.

In writing about the student protests at Columbia University, I relied on the *New York Times* coverage between April 23 and April 30, 1968, and on *The Strawberry Statement*, a witty and caustic memoir of the crisis by participant James Simon Kunen. My account of the protests at South Carolina State University and Claflin College and the killing of three students by police is based on *The Orangeburg Massacre* by Jack Nelson and Jack Bass, two reporters who covered the tragedy for the *Los Angeles Times* and the *Charlotte Observer*. Edward Hoagland's critique of press coverage of those events appeared in the Spring 1968 *Columbia Journalism Review*. Will Campbell's criticisms of that coverage, and the words he offered at a memorial service for the fallen students, are found in his introduction to Nelson and Bass's book.

Chapter 56: Evan Thomas wrote about Kennedy's teasing interaction with a crowd in the town of Crete, Nebraska—and the crowd's delighted response—during the 1968 presidential primary. My account of the critically important Indiana primary is based on those by Thomas, Newfield, Schlesinger, Clarke, and Palermo. Thomas and Schlesinger both described the role of journalist and Indiana native John Bartlow Martin in Kennedy's Indiana campaign. Thomas quoted Martin's amazed response to Kennedy's ability to reach white Indiana audiences with his deep concern about people of color. Schlesinger and Newfield quoted from Kennedy's testy exchange with students at the University of Indiana Medical School. Clarke described Kennedy's ride through black and white neighborhoods in northern Indiana with Tony Zale, a Polish-American former middleweight champion, and Richard Hatcher, the newly elected black mayor of Gary. Palermo concluded that Kennedy, in those moments, "pointed the way toward bridging the racial divide."

Newfield told of Kennedy's encounter with two disheartened student volunteers (one of whom was the future award-winning historian, Taylor Branch) for McCarthy in a near-empty Indiana airport.

Chapter 57: George Mische's *National Catholic Reporter* article about the draft protest in Catonsville was published in May 2013. Daniel Berrigan's poem was included in his play, *The Trial of the Catonsville Nine*, and the poem was quoted by Maureen Fiedler in the May 3, 2016, online edition of the *National Catholic Reporter*. The excerpt from John Neary's June 28, 1968, article in *Life* telling the story of the Poor People's March also appeared in Jane Sloane's series of letters, *Jane in the World*.

I relied on the same group of RFK biographers—Newfield, Schlesinger, Thomas, Clarke, Palermo, Halberstam, as well as Theodore White's *The Making of the President, 1968*—for the synopsis of the Kennedy loss to McCarthy in the Oregon primary, and for my account of the Kennedy campaign in California. For the California part of the story, I also interviewed John Seigenthaler and A. J. Cooper.

Newfield wrote about Kennedy's candid exchange on the issue of gun control with a crowd of hunters in Roseburg, Oregon. Thomas offered a nuanced account of the Drew Pearson column about wiretapping. Newfield quoted Kennedy's quip after his loss in Oregon, comparing the experience to being ridden out of town on a rail. White wrote of the furious pace of the Kennedy campaign in California and the sometimes frightening delirium of the crowds. Clarke offered a full account of Kennedy's meeting with a group of black militants in Oakland. Clarke, Palermo, and Thomas each wrote about Kennedy's twelve-year-old son being caught in the undertow on Malibu Beach. Schlesinger, Palermo, and Clarke each reported Kennedy's promise to "chase Hubert's ass all over the country." The story of busboy Juan Romero is based on an August 29, 2015, column by Steve Lopez in the *Los Angeles Times*. The story of my encounter with Kennedy at Vanderbilt is based on memory. Willie Morris's reflections on Kennedy's death, and his quoting of Schlesinger, appeared in *New York Days*.

Chapter 58: The story of Helen Keller was based on the following articles and essays: "The Radical Dissent of Helen Keller" by Peter Dreier in *Yes! Magazine*, July 12, 2012; "The Politics of Helen Keller" by Keith Rosenthal in the *International Socialist Review*, Spring 2015; Sascha Cohen's *Time* story about Keller, posted online July 26, 2015; and her obituary by Alden Whitmore in the *New York Times*, June 2, 1968.

Perhaps the most powerful depiction of the final days of Resurrection City is in *Eyes on the Prize*. Frady also wrote about it vividly in *Jesse*, his biography of Jesse Jackson. The story behind the first African American character in *Peanuts* is found in Maria Popova's online newsletter, *Brain Pickings*, and in Chip Kidd's *Only What's Necessary: Charles M. Schultz and the Art of Peanuts*.

CHAPTER 59: This synopsis of the Republican nominating process relies on *The Making of the President, 1968*, Evan Thomas's *Being Nixon: A Man Divided*, Lou Cannon's *Reagan* and Norman Mailer's *Miami and the Siege of Chicago: An Informal History of the Republican and Democratic Conventions of 1968*. White's story of Goldwater speechwriter Karl Hess appeared in *The Making of the President, 1968*, and my summary of the Republican field is based primarily upon White's. Cannon wrote about Reagan's ambitions and the Drew Pearson "homosexual ring" column. George Romney's affirmation that blacks and whites in America needed to know each other was central to White's sketch of him. White also reported on Romney's statement about "brainwashing."

Thomas wrote about Nixon's readings in political philosophy, Nixon's favorite quote from Charles de Gaulle, and de Gaulle's influence on Nixon, including the idea of a grand overture to Communist China. Germany's Konrad Adenauer offered similar advice, and Nixon took it all to heart. Nixon's vague statement on Vietnam after he announced his candidacy for president in 1968 was reported by Thomas, as was Nixon's handling of the death of Martin Luther King and his attempt to win the endorsement of Strom Thurmond. White also wrote about Nixon's pursuit of Thurmond and John Tower. White wrote, with hyperbolic eloquence, about Nelson Rockefeller's decision to seek the Republican nomination. Mailer wrote about the race riots six miles from the convention center in Miami, as Nixon won his party's nomination.

My account of the Democratic Convention in Chicago, aside from my own vivid memory of watching the drama on TV, owes a debt to White; Mailer; Todd Gitlin and his powerful work of memoir/history, *The Sixties: Years of Hope, Days of Rage*; Richard Goodwin's *Remembering America: A Voice from the Sixties;* the contemporary coverage of *Newsweek*, the *New York Times*, and *CBS News* (especially the remarkable reporting by Dan Rather and the steady, but sometimes impassioned voice of Walter Cronkite); and an interview with my friend Don Sawyer, an SDS protester who became a teacher and author, and shared his contemporaneous writings with me.

White wrote about Eugene McCarthy's curious ambivalence about actually winning the presidency. George McGovern's observation, "Gene, doesn't really want to be President, and I do," appeared in, among other places, Rick Perlstein's obituary of McGovern in the *New Republic*, October 20, 2012. Lyndon Johnson's lament about not being able to attend the convention is in Goodwin's *Remembering America*. The description of "an avuncular" David Dellinger was in his May 27, 2004, *New York Tines* obituary by Michael Kaufman. The story of Tom Hayden's disguise was in the *New York Times* on August 30, 1968. Todd Gitlin's insightful descriptions of the characters leading the Chicago demonstrations come from his book, *The Sixties*. His pre-convention warning about "armor in your hair" appeared in the *San Francisco Express Times* and was later quoted in *The Sixties*. Theodore White offered a differing view of Chicago Mayor Richard Daley from those of Gitlin or Goodwin. A Chicago policeman's astonished response to police attacks on peaceful demonstrators—"I couldn't believe it. There was nobody bad there"—has been quoted in several places, including *The Hippies: A 1960s History* by John Anthony Moretta and *American Pharoah: Mayor Richard Daley—His Battle for Chicago and the Nation* by Adam Cohen and Elizabeth Taylor. Goodwin's eyewitness recollection of police attacks appeared in *Remembering America.*

The assault on Dan Rather inside the convention hall, and Cronkite's commentary, can be viewed on YouTube. In *The Sixties,* Gitlin reported Daley's verbal assault on Senator Abraham Ribicoff. In *Gloria Steinem: Women's Liberation Leader,* biographer Erika Wittekind wrote about Steinem being shoved and her glasses broken. *Newsweek's* cover story on Chicago appeared September 9, 1968.

CHAPTER 60: In speeches and in private conversation, I have heard Peggy Wallace Kennedy, daughter of George and Lurleen Wallace, speak with deep affection about the decency of her mother. Historian Dan Carter, in *The Politics of Rage,* described Mrs. Wallace's visit to state mental institutions and her compassion for the patients. Carter also wrote about her illness and death, the tearful grief of her husband, and the relief Wallace found on the campaign trail.

Carter recounted Wallace's stock epithets about "liberal sob sisters" and Washington bureaucrats, and quoted the horrified responses of Garry Wills and Douglas Kiker. In *The Making of the President, 1968* White made plain his own distaste. Robert Kennedy's campaign speech in Alabama is in *RFK: Collected Speeches.* In a September 27, 2015, article in *Slate* comparing the appeal of Wallace and Donald Trump, political writer Jamele Bouie quoted Carter and another Wallace biographer, Jody Carlson, author of *George C. Wallace and the Politics of Powerlessness,* about the combination of psychological forces that Wallace was able to tap. Bouie also quoted the Youngstown steel worker about how Wallace "tells it like it really is." Carter described Wallace's frustration with running mate Curtis LeMay.

In interviews with me and in *Blue-Collar Conservatism,* Timothy Lombardo talked about the intricate web of anger, fear, racism and a genuine sense of traditional values that threaded through populist conservatism in the 1960s. It was easy for some in that milieu to conflate street crime with ghetto rebellion, as politicians like Wallace and Spiro Agnew did. Dan Carter quoted at length from the racially charged Agnew speech that was instrumental in Nixon's choice of a running mate. In the December 31, 2016, *New York Times,* historian John Farrell wrote about Nixon's promise to "lay off pro-Negro crap," a revelation discovered in his presidential papers. In those same papers, Farrell also uncovered Nixon's sabotaging the 1968 Vietnam peace talks because he feared that peace would damage his chances to win the election. Carter and Theodore White recounted the resurgence of Humphrey's campaign as the election approached, and Carter wrote about Wallace's fading appeal, quoting some of his most incendiary statements. Richard Strout's *New Republic* column appeared November 9, 1968.

White and Thomas wrote about the circumstantial evidence pointing toward Nixon's involvement in undermining the Paris peace talks, as did columnist George Will. Johnson's telephone conversation with Everett Dirksen accusing Nixon of "treason" occurred and was recorded on November 4, 1968, and was quoted in part by Thomas. White wrote with admiration about Hubert Humphrey's principled decision—based on the absence of "smoking gun" evidence, and Humphrey's belief that Nixon, personally, would not stoop so low—not to make a last-minute issue of the Nixon campaign's interference. In his groundbreaking *New York Times* article, Farrell unearthed Haldeman's notes confirming the depth of Nixon's cynicism. Thus, I have argued in these pages, a new era in American politics began.

Richard Goodwin's epitaph on the sixties appeared in *Remembering America.* My account of a conversation with John Seigenthaler is based on memory.

CHAPTER 61: The story of "Hey Jude" is told in Barry Miles's *Paul McCartney: Many Years from Now*, Craig Cross's *The Beatles: Day-by-Day, Song-by Song*, and Mark Langsohn's *The Beatles Recording Sessions.* Cynthia Lennon told Cross how McCartney wrote the song after her divorce from John Lennon. McCartney's quote about his concern for Julian Lennon appeared in Miles's book.

For an overview of the global sixties I relied most heavily on Mark Kurlansky's *1968: The Year That Rocked the World.* I also interviewed Spring Hill College historian Shane Dillingham, who teaches a course on the worldwide implications of the sixties. The quote about "the Russian National Circus" appeared in Kurlansky's book. Kurlansky and Dillingham provided the backstory for the 1968 Olympic protests. The sources for the Olympic protest itself, in addition to Kurlansky, included *Silent Gesture: Autobiography of Tommie Smith*, and *Sports Matters: Race, Recreation, and Culture*, edited by John Bloom and Michael Willard, as well as contemporary accounts from the *New York Times*, October 17–19, 1968; the BBC, October 17; the Associated Press, October 18; *Time*, October 25; and retrospectives in *The Guardian*, published October 5, 2006, and in the *Sunday Times*, London, October 8, 2006. Smith's quote, "Black America will understand what we did tonight," was aired on the BBC. *Time* was part of the chorus of disdain, calling the protests "angrier, nastier, uglier" than anything that should happen at the Olympic games. Jesse Owens's quote on an Olympic boycott is found in *Sports Matters.*

The remarkable story of Australian silver medalist Peter Norman has been told in many places. One of the moving accounts was James Montague's CNN story, posted online April 25, 2012.

CHAPTER 62: Andrew Chaikin, in *A Man on the Moon: The Voyages of the Apollo Astronauts*, wrote about the Apollo 8 crew reading from *Genesis.* Chaikin also wrote about the power of the Saturn rocket and the proposal by NASA engineer George Low to speed up the pace of the Apollo missions. The NASA website acknowledges Wernher von Braun's background during World War II; the degree of his complicity with Nazi atrocities has been a matter of historical debate, which, in this context, I chose not to engage.

NASA's official histories were, of course, highly useful, including the *Apollo 8 Mission Report*, published in February 1969, Richard Orloff's *Apollo by the Numbers: A Statistical Reference*, and *Apollo Expeditions to the Moon*, which was the source for Samuel Phillips's description of liftoff. Andrew Chaikin recounted aviation pioneer Charles Lindbergh's pre-flight visit with the Apollo 8 astronauts and his comment about the amount of fuel they would burn.

Galen Rowell's assessment of the *Earthrise* photograph appeared in *Life* magazine's special edition, "100 Photographs that Changed the World." It can also be found on NASA's website where Anders recounts the story of the photo. A friend's telegram to Frank Borman, "You have bailed out 1968," was quoted in Howard Benedict's Associated Press retrospective, published December 25, 1988, in the *Los Angeles Times* and other newspapers.

CHAPTER 63: This account of Nixon's inauguration and accompanying street demonstrations is based in part on *Being Nixon*, but primarily on Craig Simpson's retrospective in *Washington Area Spark*, January 9, 2017. Simpson quoted David Dellinger, described the Yippies' attempt to inaugurate a pig, and quoted the *The Free Press* urging demonstrators to arm themselves with eggs and rotten fruit.

The essay also described the ugly scene when Shulamith Firestone and Marilyn Salzman Webb spoke at an antiwar rally. Alice Echols in her book, *Daring to be Bad: Radical Feminism in America, 1967–1975*, recounted that moment in vivid detail.

Marilyn Young described the expansion of the war into Laos and Cambodia. She quoted UN worker Georges Chapelier about the bombing in Laos. Young, Evan Thomas, and James Wright in *Enduring Vietnam: An American Generation and Its War*, all noted Henry Kissinger's disdain for North Vietnam. The National Security Archives Briefing Book No. 195, posted online July 31, 2006, reported that the Nixon Administration, at least in part at Kissinger's urging, contemplated the use of a "nuclear device," against the North. Young and Thomas both wrote about Nixon's "madman" theory of war and diplomacy. Young quoted Ho Chi Minh's poem extolling the beauty of his country.

In *The Politics of Rage*, Dan Carter wrote about Daniel Patrick Moynihan's *The Negro Family: The Case for National Action*. Carter noted Moynihan's conclusion that "Men must have jobs." Carter also reported the charge by civil rights leaders that Moynihan was "blaming the victim." (That phrase entered the American lexicon after psychologist William Ryan chose it as the title of a best-selling book that took issue with Moynihan's theories.) As Carter noted, Moynihan also lectured white liberals about "explaining away" the problems of black America. Carter and Thomas both wrote about the relationship between Nixon and Moynihan, and Carter wrote in detail about Nixon's black capitalism initiative and his proposal for a Family Assistance Plan. Richard Reeves, in *President Nixon: Alone in the White House*, wrote of Nixon's scribbled admonition to himself: "Strong—in charge President," and Thomas added another Nixon scribble: "Bold—gutsy initiatives."

Carter wrote about John Ehrlichman's assessment that Nixon saw blacks as "genetically inferior" to whites. Thomas reported that Nixon told Ehrlichman blacks were "just down out of the trees." As Nixon struggled with his own innate racism, political cynicism, and policy advice from Moynihan about a new approach to the issues of poverty and race, liberal journalists were writing with a mixture of sympathy and alarm about a mounting sense of grievance among working-class whites. I have quoted here from one of those articles, Peter Schrag's "The Forgotten American," which appeared in the August 1969 *Harper's*. Dan Carter, Joe McGinniss in *The Selling of the President 1968*, columnist Garry Wills, and Evan Thomas all wrote about the influence of Republican strategist Kevin Phillips who advocated a policy of division. Phillips own writing on the subject appeared in *The Emerging Republican Majority*. Nixon's response to the book appeared in Carter's *The Politics of Rage*.

Chapter 64: The opening section is based on *Angela Davis: An Autobiography*. I also read Lou Cannon's *Reagan*, regarding Ronald Reagan's period as governor of California, and his stance toward radical movements. One of the most thorough accounts of the Black Panther movement is Jakobi Williams's *From the Bullet to the Ballot: The Illinois Chapter of the Black Panther Party and Racial Coalition Politics in Chicago*. For the part on Gloria Steinem and the abortion issue in the women's movement, I relied on Carolyn Heilbrun's *The Education of a Woman: The Life of Gloria Steinem*, Steinem's own writings in *New York* magazine, Susan Brownmiller's writings in *The Village Voice*, David Garrow's *Liberty and Sexuality: The Right to Privacy and the Making of Roe v. Wade*, and *The Economist's* obituary of Norma McCorvey,. Steinem's influential *New York* article, "After Black Power, Women's Liberation," was published April 4, 1969. Steinem's October 28, 1968 *New York* article on Nixon's presidential campaign helped establish her as a political reporter who wrote with uncommon depth and insight, and was one more way Steinem pushed gender boundaries in the 1960s. Heilbrun, in her biography of Steinem, quoted her *New York* article about "hair-pulling" policemen. Susan Brownmiller's *Village Voice* article on the Redstocking abortion event in New York appeared on March 27, 1969. The longer quote about Brownmiller's own experiences with abortion appeared in the *Village Voice* on January 27, 1998. Norma McCorvey's story has been told in Garrow's *Liberty and Sexuality*, McCorvey's autobiography *I Am Roe: My Life, Roe v. Wade, and Freedom of Choice,* co-authored by Andy Meisler, and her February 29, 2017, obituary. The twelve women who created the Boston Women's Health Book Collective in 1969 were Ruth Davidson, Bell Alexander, Pamela Berger, Vilunya Diskin, Joan Ditzion, Paula Doress-Worters, Nancy Miriam Hawley, Elizabeth MacMahon-Herrera, Pamela Morgan, Judy Norsigian, Jane Kates Pincus, Esther Rome, Wendy Sanford, Norma Swenson, and Sally Whelan.

Joseph Telushkin told the story of Congresswoman Shirley Chisholm and Rabbi Menachem Schneerson in *Rebbe: The Life and Teachings of Menachem M. Schneersoon, The Most Influential Rabbi in Modern History*. Chisholm's "poor babies" quote appears in an article by David Zaklikowski at *TheRebbe.org.*

CHAPTER 65: The section on the Charlotte-Mecklenburg school desegregation case is based on research I did for my book, *The Dream Long Deferred: The Landmark Struggle for Desegregation in Charlotte, North Carolina*. In addition to reading the court files and interviewing many of the participants, I covered the case for the *Charlotte Observer* as events unfolded in that city. The quotes from Judge McMillan and others come from that work.

Dan Carter in *The Politics of Rage* and Evan Thomas in *Being Nixon* each wrote about the Nixon Administration's ambivalence regarding school desegregation at a time of changing attitudes nationally. Carter wrote about Alexander Bickel's article questioning the efficacy of integration, and Thomas offered a fair-minded summary of the administration's record. Pat Buchanan's "tear the scab off" and John Mitchell's "watch what we do" quotes are found in Thomas's book.

The scholar who cited national research showing that "avoiding socio-economic and racial isolation benefits all students" was Amy Hawn Nelson of the University of North Carolina-Charlotte.

CHAPTER 66: On June 22, 2015, the forty-sixth anniversary of the Cuyahoga River fire in Cleveland, *Time* magazine published an informative retrospective, including the AP photo that had run in the magazine shortly after the 1969 fire. *Time* acknowledged that the photo was actually taken during a much worse fire in 1952. According to multiple sources, there was no photo of the 1969 fire. The quote from *Time* declaring that the river "oozes" was repeated in a *Washington Post* essay by Jonathan Adler on June 22, 2014. I read other historical reflections on the fire, including Justin Glanville's "A River Burns Through It" in the Spring 2015 *Kent State Magazine*, and a June 22, 2007, article on *Wired.com* in which Cleveland's fire chief characterized the 1969 blaze as "a run of the mill fire." *Life* magazine's spread on pollution in the Great Lakes appeared August 23, 1968.

The website, *Gaylord Nelson and Earth Day: The Making of a Modern Environmental Movement*, offers a fact-laden account of Nelson's career, including the conflation in his mind of environmentalism and social justice. Nelson's quote, "Environment is all of America and it's problems," is on that website, as is his assessment that Earth Day "organized itself." His description of the "electric" news media response to the Earth Day idea can be found at *History.com*. The story of Denis Hayes's organizational role is told in several places, including the website of the Earth Day Network. Important contemporary coverage of the Earth Day plans included an article in *Time* on October 10, 1969, and in the *New York Times* on November 30. *Time* and its sister publication, *Life*, each did aggressive reporting about environmental issues as the 1960s moved toward an end.

I reread *Moving the Earth for a Song*, written by my uncle, Wilson Gaillard, and published in 1968. The book prompted reflections on the interplay of conservation and conservative idealism—a respect for tradition and stewardship—that was evident in Wilson Gaillard's writing and may have been part of the broad support for environmentalism in those days. But I juxtaposed that with the introduction of *new* ideas under the same environmental banner, including those of Jane Goodall. In writing about Goodall, I read her first cover story in *National Geographic* in August 1963 and her book, *In the Shadow of Man*. In October 2017, *National Geographic* published a cover story entitled "Becoming Jane Goodall," a helpful summary of her life's work. The extended quote from her writing comes from *In the Shadow of Man*.

Chapter 67: The National Park Service website for the Stonewall National Monument provides a history of the riots and the movement they spawned, as well as an overview of homosexual life in America. On July 4, 1969, in a major article about Cesar Chavez and the grape boycott, *Time quoted* Ronald Reagan calling the movement "immoral." The magazine also noted the Nixon Administration's increase in its purchase of grapes for U.S. soldiers.

The Tom Wolfe quote came from *Radical Chic and Mau-Mauing the Flak Catchers*. The *Ramparts* article, "Tom: Wolfe: Reactionary Chic" by John Gordon, appeared in the January 1972 issue of the magazine.

The *Life* article and photo essay, "Homosexuality in America," which focused on gay life in San Francisco, appeared June 26, 1964. That issue of the magazine, it should be noted, has become an infamous touchstone for many gay activists because of its condescending tone, including references to men "openly admitting, even flaunting, their deviation." On June 10, 2015, *Time* wrote about the article and its place in the history of gay rights, noting that despite being a product of its time, the article did expose some of the cruel pressures gay men were forced to endure.

My summary of the role of artists and writers, from Moms Mabley to Andy Warhol, in displaying the courage to be who they were, is based in part on the Stonewall National Monument website. My take on the life of Andy Warhol is based on several sources, including an interview with Dr. Paige Vitulli, a professor of art education at the University of South Alabama, and three highly accessible books, *The Philosophy of Andy Warhol*; *Andy Warhol: Everyone Will Be Famous for 15 Minutes* by Edward Willett, and *Andy Warhol: A Beginner's Guide* by Geoff Nicholson. Warhol's self-deprecating assessment of his own sexual prowess as compared to Truman Capote's is found in Nicholson's book, as is the story of Warhol and violent feminist Valerie Solanas. Warhol's comment about machines appears in Willett's biography.

In an expansive *New York Times* essay on radical feminism published March 15, 1970, Susan Brownmiller wrote of Betty Friedan's concerns about a "lavender menace," the influence of lesbians within the women's movement. In a 2013 article for *The Atlantic*, "4 Big Problems with the Feminine Mystique," Ashley Fetters wrote about Friedan comparing homosexuality to "a murky smog." The National Park Service website on Stonewall quoted Lillian Federman about the protests being "the shot heard round the world." On June 10, 2017, Tom Gilson noted in *The Stream* that Federman's full quote began, "To many homosexuals, male and female alike, the Stonewall Rebellion was the shot heard round the world." Transgender teenager Nance Lomax's observation, "Stonewall meant the world to me," appeared in the *New York Times,* June 24, 2016.

CHAPTER 68: The biographical background on John Fogerty and Creedence Clearwater Revival comes from *The Penguin Encyclopedia of Popular Music* and *Off the Record: An Oral History of Popular Music*. The observations on Woody Guthrie and Merle Haggard are based in part on research for my reader's memoir, *The Books That Mattered*, in which I wrote about four American songwriters—Guthrie, Haggard, Kris Kristofferson and Bruce Springsteen—drawing inspiration from *The Grapes of Wrath*. The story of Johnny Cash is based on research I did from my book, *Watermelon Wine: The Spirit of Country Music*, including a lengthy interview with Cash. During that interview, Cash spoke warmly of his friendship with Bob Dylan. Nashville session player Charlie McCoy's memories of recording with Dylan were offered in an interview with me. Ewan McColl's critical comments about Dylan in *Sing Out* appeared in September 1965. They were also quoted in George Frangoulis *Bob Dylan: The 1960s*, a book that puts the evolution of Dylan's music into the context of the times, as does David Hajdu's *Positively Fourth Street*. Bruce Springsteen's praise for Dylan's "Like a Rolling Stone" appeared in a November 29, 2009, article that Springsteen wrote in *Rolling Stone* magazine.

Life magazine's August 1969 special issue on Woodstock was my primary source for writing about that event, along with the documentary, *Woodstock*. In its special issue, "The 60s," published December 26, 1969, *Life* quoted Janis Joplin's observation: "Even Billy Graham doesn't draw *that* many people." In an article on the *Today* website, posted August 10, 2009, MSNBC contributor Michael Ventre quoted Michael Wadleigh's account of Jimi Hendrix getting ready to play "The Star Spangled Banner." The quote from Ventre describing Hendrix's iconic rendition comes from that same article. Greil Marcus's quote about Hendrix and the anthem also came from Ventre's article, as did the description of Hendrix on *The Dick Cavett Show*. Ventre also described Jose Feliciano's version at the 1968 World Series.

Cavett's interview with Hendrix about the anthem aired September 9, 1969.

CHAPTER 69: The *New York Times* front page on July 20, 1969, offered a striking juxtaposition of the two main stories dominating the news: the Apollo 11 moonshot and Sen. Edward Kennedy's auto accident on Chappaquiddick Island. In addition to coverage in the *Times*, I relied on Andrew Chaikin's *A Man on the Moon* for details of that Apollo flight. The story of astronaut Eugene Cernan's reaction to a problem on the lunar lander during the Apollo 10 mission is based on Chaikin's account.

Much has been written about Kennedy and Chappaquiddick, including Robert Sherrill's *The Last Kennedy: Edward M. Kennedy of Massachusetts, Before and After Chappaquiddick* and Garry Wills's April 29, 1976, article in the *New York Review of Books*, "The Real Reason Chappaquiddick Disqualifies Kennedy." These and other analyses are both critical and insightful. But I chose to rely most heavily on *The Last Lion: The Fall and Rise of Ted Kennedy* by a team of reporters from the *Boston Globe*, led and edited by Peter S. Canellos. This was, after all, the newspaper that knew Kennedy best, and I found the book to be balanced and persuasive.

Gwen Kopechne's *New York Times* quote about her daughter's career appeared in newspapers all over the country, including the *Cincinnati Inquirer*, on July 20, 1969. Mary Jo Kopechne's quote, "I just feel Bobby's presence everywhere," appeared in *The Last Lion*, as did Edward Kennedy's quotes "This couldn't have happened . . ." and "You take care of the girls . . ."

The July 21, 1969, edition of the *Times* has one of the most dramatic front pages in U.S. history. For the details of the lunar landing, I relied on the account in *A Man on the Moon*. I was particularly struck by Chaikin's comparison of the moon landing with the ascent of Mount Everest and the similar spiritual responses of Tenzing Norgay and Buzz Aldrin. My reflections on President Kennedy in the context of the landing are based on my memory of how I felt as I watched the event on television.

Chapter 70: For the story of the Charles Manson murders, I read *Helter Skelter*. The *Time* quote about the brutality of the killings is in an August 9, 2015, online story looking back on the crimes.

Marilyn Young wrote about the expansion of the Vietnam War into Cambodia and quoted reporter Peter Kann. In writing about My Lai, Seymour Hersh first quoted Sergeant Michael Bernhardt in a Dispatch News Service article on November 20, 1969, that appeared in multiple newspapers. In *The Politics of Rage*, Dan Carter wrote about George Wallace's support for Lieutenant William Calley. A photo of Coretta Scott King leading a peace march on October 15, 1969, is on the Library of Congress website. The *New York Times* January 31, 2006, obituary of Mrs. King quoted her call for "women power." In their book *Who Spoke Up: American Protest Against the War in Vietnam, 1963–1975*, Nancy Zaroulis and Gerald Sullivan also wrote about Mrs. King's graceful leadership in the peace movement. Writing in *The Nation* on January 12, 2010, Jon Wiener repeated Moynihan's advice to Nixon that he "show the little bastards" by speaking out for peace. The website Massmoments.org offers an account of the Harvard ROTC protests in April 1969 and quotes a *Harvard Crimson* editorial charging that the ROTC program served the "warfare state." The *Newsweek* cover story, "Universities Under the Gun," appeared May 5, 1969. Campus policeman George Taber's memory of the Cornell University protests in April 1969 is in a *Cornell Chronicle* online post by George Lowery published April 16, 2009.

In *From the Bullet to the Ballot*, Jakobi Williams wrote about Fred Hampton's skepticism toward the Weathermen's Days of Rage protests in Chicago. Todd Gitlin noted that Hampton called the protests "Custeristic"; a fuller version of that quote can be found at studentactivism.net and onthisday.com. The synopsis here of the Black Panthers in Chicago under the leadership of Fred Hampton and the killing of Hampton by Chicago police is based on Williams's book. The quote from Young Patriots leader William Fesperman comes from that book. In *The Nation* on December 25, 1976, Jeff Cohen and Jeff Gottlieb also wrote about Hampton's death in "Was Fred Hampton Executed?"

Chapter 71: John Kerry's testimony before the Senate Foreign Relations Committee on April 22, 1971, was reposted by National Public Radio on April 25, 2006. In the July 1971 *Ramparts*, Art Goldberg wrote about the origins of Vietnam Veterans Against the War. I interviewed Graham Timbes and quoted from his book of poetry, *Scribblings of a Godless Anarchist: Part One*. Lynn Brandon shared with me a part of her family's files regarding their dealings with the U.S. government about the ravages of Agent Orange.

Chapter 72: For this chapter, I read or reread the works of several important American Indian authors: Vine Deloria Jr.'s *Custer Died for Your Sins: An Indian Manifesto* and *God Is Red: A Native View of Religion*; Paul Chatt Smith and Robert Allen Warrior's *Like a Hurricane: The Indian Movement from Alcatraz to Wounded Knee*; and N. Scott Momaday's *House Made* *of Dawn* and *The Names*. Deloria provided historical and philosophical context for the 1960s Indian movement, Smith and Warrior provided many details, and Momaday provided poetry and literary depth. I reread my own articles for the *Race Relations Reporter* on activist Hank Adams and the struggle for fishing rights in the Pacific Northwest in the 1960s and '70s, and on the Yakima Indians' successful efforts in the state of Washington to reassert their claim to Mount Adams. Smith and Warrior wrote about Adams as well. I am grateful to Vine Deloria for his friendship and guidance in the early days of my career as a writer. Thanks also to Dr. Stephanie Gray, who has taught the writings of Momaday and Deloria at several universities, for insights offered in conversations with me, especially her recommendation of Deloria's essay, "Thinking in Time and Space," which appeared in *God Is Red*.

Jimmy Carter's quote about "throwing off the millstone of racial prejudice" is from a 1985 interview I did with him for the *Charlotte Observer*. The quote also appears in my book, *Prophet from Plains: Jimmy Carter and His Legacy*. As mentioned in the notes for chapter 70, Dan Carter wrote about George Wallace's support of William Calley. On her nightly program on MSNBC, Rachel Maddow first called my attention to Ronald Reagan's 1980 campaign visit to Philadelphia, Mississippi. I have argued here that Reagan, who began his political career in the sixties, continued the ethical devolution of the Republican Party begun by the Southern strategy of Richard Nixon.

Index

C

H

L

M

S

T